COMMUNICATION POWER

Manuel Castells is University Professor and the Wallis Annenberg Chair of Communication Technology and Society at the University of Southern California, Los Angeles, as well as Professor of Sociology at the Open University of Catalonia, Barcelona. He is Distinguished Visiting Professor of Technology and Society at MIT, and Distinguished Visiting Professor of Internet Studies at Oxford University.

He was Professor of Planning and of Sociology at the University of California, Berkeley from 1979 to 2003. He has published 24 books including the trilogy *The Information Age: Economy, Society, and Culture* (Blackwell, 1996–2000), translated into 22 languages, and *The Internet Galaxy* (OUP, 2001), translated into 17 languages. He is a fellow of the American Academy of Political and Social Science, of the Academia Europea, of the British Academy, of the Mexican Academy, and of the Spanish Royal Academy of Economics. He has received 14 honorary doctorates. He was a founding member of the European Research Council. He is a member of the Board of the European Institute of Innovation and Technology (EIT) and a member of the Scholars' Council of the U.S. Library of Congress.

COMMUNICATION POWER

MANUEL CASTELLS

OXFORD
UNIVERSITY PRESS

OXFORD
UNIVERSITY PRESS

Great Clarendon Street, Oxford OX2 6DP

Oxford University Press is a department of the University of Oxford.
It furthers the University's objective of excellence in research, scholarship,
and education by publishing worldwide in

Oxford New York

Auckland Cape Town Dar es Salaam Hong Kong Karachi
Kuala Lumpur Madrid Melbourne Mexico City Nairobi
New Delhi Shanghai Taipei Toronto

With offices in

Argentina Austria Brazil Chile Czech Republic France Greece
Guatemala Hungary Italy Japan Poland Portugal Singapore
South Korea Switzerland Thailand Turkey Ukraine Vietnam

Oxford is a registered trade mark of Oxford University Press
in the UK and in certain other countries

Published in the United States
by Oxford University Press Inc., New York

British Library Cataloguing in Publication Data

Data available

Library of Congress Cataloging in Publication Data

Data available

Typeset by SPI Publisher Services, Pondicherry, India
Printed in Great Britain
on acid free paper by
Clays Ltd. St Ives Plc

ISBN 978-0-19-956704-1
ISBN 978-0-19-959569-3 (pbk.)

1 3 5 7 9 10 8 6 4 2

To the memory of Nicos Poulantzas,
my brother,
theorist of power

Contents

Contents

Acknowledgments

Books are usually a collective endeavor under the author's sole responsibility. This one is no exception. It was born in my mind a long time ago, but it has evolved in interaction with colleagues and students from around the world, and has been shaped by the academic and social environments in which I have lived and worked since the beginning of this millennium. And so, to name the people and institutions who are the co-producers of this work is not a matter of courtesy, but of accuracy in signing the book.

My first acknowledgment goes to Amelia Arsenault, my doctoral student, an outstanding research assistant, and the Wallis Annenberg Graduate Research Fellow at the Annenberg School for Communication, University of Southern California. Simply put, without the intellectual quality and personal dedication of her work over the years, this book would not exist in its current form. She will go on in her academic career to become a great scholar with wonderful values as she engages in understanding the world to make it a better place.

Additional support for the research on which this book is based came from the excellent research assistance of Lauren Movius, Sasha Costanza-Chock, and Sharon Fain, graduate students at the Annenberg School for Communication, and from Dr. Meritxell Roca, my collaborator at the Internet Interdisciplinary Institute of the Universitat Oberta de Catalunya in Barcelona. Earlier versions of the analyses presented in this volume have been discussed and modified through interaction with my students at the Annenberg School for Communication. I wish to convey special thanks to the students of my research seminar Comm620: "Communication, Technology, and Power" in the spring of 2008. Specific acknowledgment of the work of several students in this and other seminars can be found in the book's notes and references.

My current research, in this book and in other works, has benefited considerably from the intellectual stimulation of my two academic homes: the Annenberg School for Communication at the University of Southern

Acknowledgments

California (USC) in Los Angeles, and the Internet Interdisciplinary Institute of the Universitat Oberta de Catalunya (UOC) in Barcelona. I feel deeply indebted to my colleagues in both institutions for the support and collegiality they have provided over the years. I particularly thank Dean Geoffrey Cowan, Dean Ernest Wilson, Director Larry Gross, and Director Patricia Riley at USC, and Rector Imma Tubella at UOC, for the wonderful personal and institutional support they have given my research since joining the Annenberg School for Communication at USC and the Internet Interdisciplinary Institute at UOC. These academic institutions are at the cutting edge of research and teaching on the global network society, and I feel proud to share their meaningful project of situating the university within the technological and intellectual conditions of the Information Age.

I am also grateful to my colleagues and students at the Massachusetts Institute of Technology (MIT Science, Technology, and Society Program; Department of Urban Studies and Planning; and Media Lab) for their meaningful interaction during my regular teaching periods as a visiting professor in one of the leading scientific institutions of the world. My special thanks go to William Mitchell, Rosalind Williams, David Mindell, Larry Vale, and Malo Hutson.

When I say that this book is a collective work, I mean it. It has received the most generous intellectual contribution from a number of colleagues who have read all or parts of various drafts of the manuscript, and commented extensively on it. I have gone through several rounds of revisions for each chapter, since each time I thought I had reached the point at which my research could be communicated, new comments and suggestions would come from colleagues willing to engage in a dialogue with me during the process of elaborating this book. I have modified my argument, updated my data, and tightened my writing as a result of these multiple interactions with colleagues from different academic institutions. I have not been able to integrate every comment, as many of them came from different perspectives, but I have seriously considered every single comment I received, and this has led to substantial changes in the theory and analyses presented in the book. Of course, misunderstandings and mistakes during this lengthy revision process are my exclusive responsibility. And so, I want to publicly express my deepest gratitude to Antonio Damasio, Hanna Damasio, Jerry Feldman, George Lakoff, Jonathan Aronson, Tom Hollihan, Peter Monge, Sarah Banet-Weiser, Ernest Wilson, Jeffrey Cole, Jonathan Taplin, Marty Kaplan, Elizabeth Garrett, Robert Entman, Lance Bennett, Frank Webster, Robin Mansell, William Dutton, Rosalind Williams, Imma Tubella,

Acknowledgments

Michael Dear, Ingrid Volkmer, Geoffrey Bowker, John Thompson, Ronald Rice, James Katz, W. Russell Neuman, George Marcus, Giancarlo Bosetti, Svetlana Balmaeva, Eric Klinenberg, Emma Kiselyova, Howard Tumber, Yuezhi Zhao, René Weber, Jeffrey Juris, Jack Linchuan Qiu, Irene Castells, Robert McChesney, and Henry Jenkins. Their collegiality demonstrates that open-source co-production is actually a medieval invention that began in the university environment, and continues today as an essential practice in scientific inquiry.

I am also grateful to the colleagues, students, and citizens at large who commented on my public presentations of the ideas and analyses on communication and power that ultimately led to the elaboration of this book. This interaction at different venues between 2003 and 2008 considerably sharpened the tentative argument I had in my mind years ago when I first engaged in this research project. In particular, I would like to acknowledge the Board of the International Communication Association (ICA), with special thanks to Ingrid Volkmer and Ronald Rice, and the attendees of my lecture at the 2006 meeting of the ICA in Dresden; the American Political Science Association, and the attendees of my 2004 Ithiel de Sola Pool Lecture in Chicago; the London School of Economics and Political Science; the Program in Science, Technology, and Society at MIT; the Milano Graduate School of Management at the New School University in New York; the De Balie Cultural Center in Amsterdam; the Spanish Academy of Cinema and Television in Madrid; the Catalan Parliament in Barcelona; the Institute Fernando Henrique Cardoso in São Paulo; the World Political Forum in Venice; the Gulbenkian Foundation in Lisbon; the School of Information Science at the University of California, Berkeley; my colleagues at the Center for Science, Technology, and Society at Santa Clara University; and my fellows at the Los Angeles Institute of the Humanities.

The elaboration and production of this book have been made possible by the professionalism and dedication of Melody Lutz, my personal assistant at the Annenberg School for Communication, and Anna Sanchez-Juarez, my personal assistant at the Universitat Oberta de Catalunya. Without their careful coordination, planning, and execution, this complex project could not have been managed toward its completion. My heartfelt gratitude goes to both of them.

The writing of this book has benefited from outstanding editorial work. My assistant Melody Lutz, a professional writer herself, guided my writing while respecting my style, a style resulting, for good or ill, from the remix culture that characterizes my life. I am sure that her effort will be rewarded

Acknowledgments

by the gratitude of many readers, particularly those students who usually have to struggle through the pages of my books to satisfy their assignments.

As with all my books in the past decade, the final link between you, the reader, and me, the author, has been my copy-editor, Sue Ashton. I am grateful for her help over the years.

I also want to sincerely thank my editor at Oxford University Press, David Musson, with whom I engaged in an open-ended intellectual conversation a decade ago, a conversation from which a number of projects have resulted, including this book. I also wish to acknowledge the fine editorial work of Matthew Derbyshire and Kate Walker during the production of this book at Oxford University Press.

I feel greatly obliged to the physicians who have kept me afloat during all these years, bringing me back from a serious illness to a normal and productive life. I wish my experience can provide hope for people who need it. For this, I am deeply indebted to Dr. Peter Carroll and Dr. James Davis of the University of California, San Francisco Medical Center; to Dr. Benet Nomdedeu of the Hospital Clinic, University of Barcelona; and to Dr. John Brodhead of the Keck School of Medicine, University of Southern California.

Last, but certainly not least, my family has continued to provide the affective environment that makes me a person, and in fact a happy person. For this, I want to express my gratitude to, and my love for, my wife Emma Kiselyova, my daughter Nuria, my step-daughter Lena, my grandchildren Clara, Gabriel, and Sasha, my sister Irene, and my brother-in-law José Bailo. Special thanks go to Sasha Konovalova, with whom I have shared a room for a whole year during the final period of writing this book, while she was writing her college assignments. Not only did she not disturb my concentration, but she also became an insightful commentator and a point of reference in my exploration of youth culture in the new communication environment.

And so, this is another book, but a special one for me because it brings together my research and my desire for a world made better by people communicating freely. Unfortunately, as you will see if you go beyond this page, matters are not that simple. I invite you now to share my intellectual journey.

Manuel Castells

Santa Monica, California, August 2008

List of Figures

Acknowledgments

List of Tables

Acknowledgments

Opening

I was eighteen years old. My urge for freedom was bumping against the walls that the dictator had erected around life. My life and everybody else's life. I wrote an article in the Law School's journal, and the journal was shut down. I acted in Camus' *Caligula*, and our theater group was indicted for promoting homosexuality. When I turned on the BBC world news to find a different tune, I could not hear a thing through the stridency of radio interference. When I wanted to read Freud, I had to go to the only library in Barcelona with access to his work and fill out a form explaining why. As for Marx or Sartre or Bakunin, forget it – unless I would travel by bus to Toulouse and conceal the books at the border crossing, risking the unknown if caught transporting subversive propaganda. And so, I decided to take on this suffocating, idiotic, Franquist regime, and joined the underground resistance. At that time, the resistance at the University of Barcelona consisted of only a few dozen students, since police repression had decimated the old democratic opposition, and the new generation born after the Civil War was barely entering adulthood. Yet, the depth of our revolt, and the promise of our hope, gave us strength to engage in a most unequal combat.

And there I was, in the darkness of a movie theater in a working-class neighborhood, ready to awaken the consciousness of the masses by breaking through the communication firewalls within which they were confined – or so I believed. I had a bunch of leaflets in my hand. They were hardly legible as they were printed on a primitive, manual copying device, soaked with purple ink that was the only communication medium available to us in a country blanketed by censorship. (My uncle, a military colonel, had a cozy job as censor, reading every possible book – he was a writer himself – and, moreover, previewing all the sexy films to decide what to cut for the audience and what to keep for himself and his colleagues in the church and the army.) So I decided to make up for my family's collaboration with the forces of darkness by distributing a few sheets of paper to workers, to reveal how bad their lives really were (as if they would not know it), and call them to action against the dictatorship, all the while keeping an eye on the future overthrow of capitalism, the root of all evil. The idea was to leave the leaflets in the empty seats on my way out of the theater, so that at the end of the session, when the lights came on, the moviegoers would pick up the message – a daring message from the resistance intended to give them enough hope to engage in the struggle for democracy.

I did seven theaters that evening, moving each time to a distant location in another workers' lair to avoid detection. As naïve as the communication strategy was, it was no child's game, as being caught meant being beaten up by the police and most likely going to jail, which is what happened to several of my friends. But, of course, we were getting a kick out of our prowess, while hoping to avoid other kinds of kicks. As I finished that revolutionary action for the day (one of many until I ended up in exile in Paris two years later), I called my girlfriend, proud of myself, feeling that the words I had conveyed could change a few minds which could ultimately change the world. I did not know many things at that time. Not that I know substantially more now. But I did not know then that the message is effective only if the receiver is ready for it (most people were not) and if the messenger is identifiable and reliable. And the Workers Front of Catalonia (of whom 95 percent were students) was not as serious a brand as the communists, the socialists, the Catalan nationalists, or any of the established parties, precisely because we wanted to be different – we were searching for identity as the post-Civil War generation.

Thus, I doubt that my actual contribution to Spanish democracy was equal to my expectations. And yet, social and political change has always been enacted, everywhere and at all times, from a myriad of gratuitous actions, sometimes uselessly heroic (mine was certainly not that) to the point of being out of proportion to their effectiveness: drops of a steady rain of struggle and sacrifice that ultimately floods the ramparts of oppression when, and if, the walls of incommunication between parallel solitudes start cracking down, and the audience becomes "we the people." After all, as naïve as my revolutionary hopes were, I did have a point. Why would the regime close down every possible channel of communication outside its control if censorship were not of the essence for the perpetuation of its power? Why would Ministries of Education, then and now, want to make sure that they commissioned history books and, in some countries, ensure that the gods (only the authentic ones) descended on the classroom? Why did students have to fight for the right to free speech; unions to fight for the right to post information about their company (then on the billboard, now on the website); women to create women's bookstores; subdued nations to communicate in their own language; Soviet dissidents to distribute samiz-dat literature; African Americans in the US, and colonized people around the world, to be allowed to read? What I sensed then, and believe now, is that power is based on the control of communication and information, be it the macro-power of the state and media corporations or the micro-power of organizations of all sorts. And so, my struggle for free communication, my primitive, purple-ink blog of the time, was indeed an act of defiance, and the fascists, from their perspective, were right to try to catch us and shut us off, so closing the channels connecting individual minds to the public mind. Power is more than communication, and communication is more than power. But power relies on the control of communication, as counterpower depends on breaking through such control. And mass communication, the communication that potentially reaches society at large, is shaped and managed by power relationships, rooted in the business of media and the politics of the state. Communication power is at the heart of the structure and dynamics of society.

This is the subject matter of this book. Why, how, and by whom power relationships are constructed and exercised through the management of communication processes, and how these power relationships can be altered by social actors aiming for social change by influencing the public mind. My working hypothesis is that the most fundamental form of power lies in the ability to shape the human mind. The way we feel and think determines the way we act, both individually and collectively. Yes, coercion, and the capacity to exercise it, legitimate or not, is an essential source of power. But coercion alone cannot stabilize domination. The ability to build consent, or at least to instill fear and resignation vis-à-vis the existing order, is essential to enforce the rules that govern the institutions and organizations of society. And these rules, in all societies, manifest power relationships embedded in the institutions as a result of processes of struggle and compromise between conflicting social actors who mobilize for their interests under the banner of their values. Furthermore, the process of institutionalizing norms and rules and the challenge to these norms and rules by actors who do not feel adequately represented in the workings of the system go on simultaneously, in a relentless movement of reproduction of society and production of social change. If the fundamental battle about the definition of the norms of society, and the application of these norms in everyday life, revolves around the shaping of the human mind, communication is central to this battle. Because it is through communication that the human mind interacts with its social and natural environment. This process of communication operates according to the structure, culture, organization, and technology of communication in a given society. The communication process decisively mediates the way in which power relationships are constructed and challenged in every domain of social practice, including political practice.

The analysis presented in this book refers to one specific social structure: the network society, the social structure that characterizes society in the early twenty-first century, a social structure constructed around (but not determined by) digital networks of communication. I contend that the process of formation and exercise of power relationships is decisively transformed in the new organizational and technological context derived from the rise of global digital networks of communication as the fundamental symbol-processing system of our time. Therefore, the analysis of power relationships requires an understanding of the specificity of the forms and processes of socialized communication, which in the network society means both the multimodal mass media and the interactive, horizontal networks of communication built around the Internet and wireless communication. Indeed, these horizontal networks make possible the rise of what I call mass self-communication, decisively increasing the autonomy of communicating subjects vis-à-vis communication corporations, as the users become both senders and receivers of messages.

However, to explain how power is constructed in our minds through communication processes, we need to go beyond how and by whom messages are originated in the process of power-making and transmitted/formatted in the electronic networks of communication. We must also understand how they are processed in the networks of the brain. It is in the specific forms of connection between networks of communication and meaning in our world and networks of communication and meaning in our brains that the mechanisms of power-making can ultimately be identified.

4

This research agenda is a tall order. Thus, in spite of the many years dedicated to the intellectual project communicated in this book, I certainly do not pretend to provide definitive answers to the questions I raise. My purpose, ambitious enough, is to propose a new approach to understanding power in the network society. And, as a necessary step toward this goal, to specify the structure and dynamics of communication in our historical context. To advance the construction of a grounded theory of power in the network society (which, for me, is tantamount to a theory of communication power), I will focus my effort on studying the current processes of asserting political power and counterpower, by using available scholarly research on the matter, and conducting a number of case studies in a diversity of social and cultural contexts. However, we know that political power is only one dimension of power, as power relationships are constructed in a complex interaction between multiple spheres of social practice. And so, my empirical analysis will be necessarily incomplete, although I hope to stimulate a similar analytical perspective for the study of power in other dimensions, such as culture, technology, finance, production, or consumption.

I confess that the choice of political power as the main object of my investigation has been determined by the existence of a considerable scientific literature that has examined in recent years the connection between communication and political power at the frontier between cognitive science, communication research, political psychology, and political communication. In this book, I combine my own expertise on sociopolitical analysis and the study of communication technologies with the works of scholars investigating the interaction between the brain and political power in order to build a body of observation that may provide a measure of the relevance of this interdisciplinary approach. I have explored the sources of political power relationships in our world by trying to link the structural dynamics of the network society, the transformation of the communication system, the interaction between emotion, cognition, and political behavior, and the study of politics and social movements in a variety of contexts. This is the project behind this book, and it is up to the reader to evaluate its potential usefulness. I continue to believe that theories are just disposable tools in the production of knowledge, always destined to be superseded, either by being discarded as irrelevant or, hopefully in this case, folded into an improved analytical framework elaborated somewhere by someone in the scientific community to make sense of our experience of social power.

To help the communication process between you and me, I will outline the structure and sequence of this book which, in my view, follows the logic of what I have just presented. I start by defining what I understand to be power. Thus, Chapter 1 tries to clarify the meaning of power by proposing some elements of power theory. To do so, I make use of some classical contributions in social science that I find relevant and useful for the kind of questions I am asking. It is, of course, a selective reading of power theories, and in no way should it be understood as an attempt to place myself in the theoretical debate. I do not write books about books. I use theories, any theory, in the same way that I hope my theory will be used by anyone: as a toolbox to understand social reality. So I use what I find useful and I do not consider what is not directly related to the purpose of my investigation, which is the majority of contributions to power theory. Therefore, I do not intend to contribute to the deforestation of the planet by printing paper to criticize works that, in spite of their intellectual elegance or political interest, are not on the horizon of my research. Furthermore, I situate my understanding of power relationships in our type of society, which I conceptualize as the network society, which is to the Information Age what the industrial society was to the Industrial Age. I will not go into the detail of my network society analysis since I dedicated a full trilogy to this task a few years ago (Castells, 2000a, c, 2004c). I have, however, recast, in Chapter 1, the key elements of my conceptualization of the network society as they relate to the understanding of power relationships in our new historical context.

After establishing the conceptual foundations of the analysis of power, I proceed, in Chapter 2, with a similar analytical operation concerning communication. Yet, when it comes to communication, I go further by empirically investigating the structure and dynamics of mass communication under the conditions of globalization and digitalization. I analyze both the mass media and the horizontal networks of interactive communication, focusing on both their differences and their intersections. I study the transformation of the media audience from receptors of messages to senders/receivers of messages, and I explore the relationship between this transformation and the process of cultural change in our world. Finally, I identify the power relationships embedded in the mass-communication system and in the network infrastructure on which communication depends, and I explore the connections between business, media, and politics.

Having set up the structural determinants of the relationship between power and communication in the network society, I change the perspective of my analysis from the structure to the agency. If power works by acting on the human mind by the means of communicating messages, we need to understand how the human mind processes these messages, and how this processing translates into the political realm. This is the key analytical transition in this book, and perhaps the one element in the investigation that will require a greater effort on the part of the reader (as it did on my part) because political analysis is only beginning to integrate structural determination with cognitive processes. I did not embark on this complex enterprise to honor fashion. I did it because I found the large body of literature that, in the past decade, has conducted experimental research to unveil the processes of individual political decision-making revealing in terms of the relationship between mental processes, metaphorical thinking, and political image-making. Without accepting the reductionist premises of some of these experiments, I think that the research of the school of affective intelligence, and other works of political communication, provide a most-needed bridge between social structuration and the individual processing of power relationships. The scientific foundations of much of this research are to be found in the new discoveries of neuroscience and cognitive science, as represented, for instance, in the works of Antonio Damasio, Hanna Damasio, George Lakoff, and Jerry Feldman. Thus, I anchored my analysis of the relationship between communication and political practice in these theories, and in the empirical evidence in the field of political psychology that can be better understood from a neuroscientific perspective, such as the work of Drew Westen.

While I do not have any particular expertise in this field, with the help of my colleagues I have tried to present in Chapter 3 an analysis of the specific relationships between emotion, cognition, and politics. I then relate the results of this analysis to what communication research knows about the conditioning of political communication by social and political actors deliberately intervening in the media and other communication networks to foster their interests, through mechanisms such as agenda-setting, framing, and priming of the news and other messages. To illustrate the potential explanatory value of this perspective, and to simplify its complexity, I proceed in Chapter 3 with an empirical analysis of the process of misinformation of the American public by the Bush administration concerning the Iraq War. So doing, I hope to be able to draw the practical political implications of a complicated analytical approach. Processes are complex but the outcomes of such processes are both simple and consequential, as communication processes have implanted the "war on terror" frame into the minds of millions of people, inducing a culture of fear in our lives.

Opening

Thus, the first three chapters of this book are inextricably linked because an understanding of the construction of power relationships through communication in the network society requires the integration of the three key components of the process explored separately in each one of the chapters:

- The structural determinants of social and political power in the global network society.
- The structural determinants of the process of mass communication under the organizational, cultural, and technological conditions of our time.
- The cognitive processing of the signals presented by the communication system to the human mind as it relates to politically relevant social practice.

I will then be in a position to undertake specific empirical analyses that will make use, at least to some extent, of the concepts and findings of the first three chapters which, together, constitute the theoretical framework proposed in this book. Chapter 4 will explain and document why, in the network society, politics is fundamentally media politics, focusing on its epitome, the politics of scandal, and relating the results of the analysis to the worldwide crisis of political legitimacy that challenges the meaning of democracy in much of the world. Chapter 5 explores how social movements and agents of political change proceed in our society through the reprogramming of communication networks, so becoming able to convey messages that introduce new values to the minds of people and inspire hope for political change. Both chapters will deal with the specific role of mass media and horizontal communication networks, as media politics and social movements use both sets of networks, and as media networks and Internet networks are inter-related. Yet, my assumption, which will be tested, is that the greater the autonomy provided to the users by the technologies of communication, the greater the chances that new values and new interests will enter the realm of socialized communication, so reaching the public mind. Thus, the rise of mass self-communication, as I call the new forms of networked communication, enhances the opportunities for social change, without however defining the content and purpose of such social change. People, meaning ourselves, are angels and demons at the same time, and so our increased capacity to act on society will simply project into the open who we really are in each time/space context.

In proceeding with a series of empirical analyses, I will rely on available evidence, as well as some case studies of my own, from a variety of social, cultural, and political contexts. A majority of the material, however, concerns the United States for the simple reason that there has been more scholarly research done there on the topics covered in this book. However, I am convinced that the analytical perspective put forward in this book is not context-dependent, and could be used to understand political processes in a diversity of countries, including the developing world. This is because the network society is global, and so are the global communication networks, while cognitive processes in the human mind universally share basic features, albeit with a range of variation in the cultural forms of their manifestation. After all, power relationships are the foundational relations of society throughout history, geography, and cultures. And if power relationships are constructed in the human mind through communication processes, as this book will try to demonstrate, these hidden connections may well be the source code of the human condition.

The lights are now on in the movie theater. The room empties slowly as viewers make the transition between images on the screen and images in their lives. You queue toward the exit, any exit to anywhere. Maybe some of the words from the film still resonate inside you. Words such as those ending Martin Ritt's *The Front* (1976), particularly Woody Allen's words to the McCarthyites: "Fellas ... I don't recognize the right of this committee to ask me these kinds of questions. And furthermore, you can all go f__ yourselves." Then, the images of Allen, handcuffed and on his way to prison. Power and challenge to power. And the girl's kiss. Handcuffed, but free and loved. A whirlwind of images, ideas, feelings.

Then, suddenly you see this book. I wrote it for you, and left it for you to find. You notice the nice cover. Communication. Power. You can relate to that. Whatever the connection with your mind, it worked because you are now reading these words. But I am not telling you what to do. This much I learned in my long journey. I fight my fights; I do not call upon others to do it for me, or even with me. Still, I say my words, words learned from and through my work and my job as a social science researcher. Words that, in this case, tell a story about power. In fact, the story of power in the world we live in. And this is my way, my only real way to challenge the powers that be by unveiling their presence in the workings of our minds.

Chapter 1

Power in the Network Society

What is Power?

Power is the most fundamental process in society, since society is defined around values and institutions, and what is valued and institutionalized is defined by power relationships.

Power is the relational capacity that enables a social actor to influence asymmetrically the decisions of other social actor(s) in ways that favor the empowered actor's will, interests, and values. Power is exercised by means of coercion (or the possibility of it) and/or by the construction of meaning on the basis of the discourses through which social actors guide their action. Power relationships are framed by domination, which is the power that is embedded in the institutions of society. The relational capacity of power is conditioned, but not determined, by the structural capacity of domination. Institutions may engage in power relationships that rely on the domination they exercise over their subjects.

This definition is broad enough to encompass most forms of social power, but requires some specifications. The concept of *actor* refers to a variety of subjects of action: individual actors, collective actors, organizations, institutions, and networks. Ultimately, however, all organizations, institutions, and networks express the action of human actors, even if this action has been institutionalized or organized by processes in the past. *Relational capacity* means that power is not an attribute but a relationship. It cannot be abstracted from the specific relationship between the subjects of power, those who are empowered and those who are subjected to such empowerment in a given context. *Asymmetrically* means that while influence in a relationship is always reciprocal, in power relationships there is always a greater degree of influence of one actor over the other. However, there is never absolute power, a zero degree of influence of those subjected to power vis-à-vis those in power positions. There is always the possibility of resistance that calls into question the power relationship. Furthermore, in any power relationship there is a certain degree of compliance and acceptance by those subjected to power. When resistance and rejection become significantly stronger than compliance and acceptance, power relationships are transformed: the terms of the relationship change, the powerful lose power, and ultimately there is a process of institutional change or structural change, depending on the extent of the transformation of power relationships. Or else power relationships become non-social relationships. This is because, if a power relationship can only be enacted by relying on structural domination backed by violence, those in power, in order to maintain their domination, must destroy the relational capacity of the resisting actor(s), thus canceling the relationship itself. I advance the notion that sheer imposition by force is not a social relationship because it leads to the obliteration of the dominated social actor, so that the relationship disappears with the extinction of one of its terms. It is, however, a social action with social meaning because the use of force constitutes an intimidating influence over the surviving subjects under similar domination, helping to reassert power relationships vis-à-vis these subjects. Furthermore, as soon as the power relationship is re-established in its plural components, the complexity of the multilayered mechanism of domination works again, making violence one factor among others in a broader set of determination. The more the construction of meaning on behalf of specific interests and values plays a role in asserting power in a relationship, the less the recourse to violence (legitimate or not) becomes necessary. However, the institutionalization of the recourse to violence in the state and its derivatives sets up the context of domination in which the cultural production of meaning can deploy its effectiveness.

There is complementarity and reciprocal support between the two main mechanisms of power formation identified by theories of power: violence and discourse. After all, Michel Foucault starts his *Surveiller et Punir* (1975) with the description of the torture of Damiens before going on to deploy his analysis of the construction of disciplinary discourses that constitute a society in which "factories, schools, military barracks, hospitals, all look like prisons" (1975: 264, my translation). This complementarity of the sources of power can also be perceived in Max Weber: He defines social power as "the probability that one actor within a social relationship will be in a position to carry out his own will despite resistance, regardless of the basis on which this probability rests" ([1922] 1978: 53), and he ultimately relates power to politics and politics to the state, "a relation of men dominating men, a relation supported by means of legitimate (i.e. considered to be legitimate) violence. If the state is to exist the dominated must obey the authority claimed by the powers that be . . . the decisive means for politics is violence" ([1919] 1946: 78, 121). But he also warns that an existing state "whose heroic age is not felt as such by the masses can nevertheless be decisive for a powerful sentiment of solidarity, in spite of the greatest internal antagonisms" ([1919] 1946: 177).

This is why the process of legitimation, the core of Habermas's political theory, is the key to enable the state to stabilize the exercise of its domination (Habermas, 1976). And legitimation can be effectuated by diverse procedures of which constitutional democracy, Habermas's preference, is only one. Because democracy is about a set of processes and procedures, it is not about policy. Indeed, if the state intervenes in the public sphere on behalf of the specific interests that prevail in the state, it induces a legitimation crisis because it reveals itself as an instrument of domination instead of being an institution of representation. Legitimation largely relies on consent elicited by the construction of shared meaning; for example, belief in representative democracy. Meaning is constructed in society through the process of communicative action. Cognitive rationalization provides the basis for the actions of the actors. So, the ability of civil society to provide the content of state action through the public sphere ("a network for communicating information and points of view" [Habermas, 1996: 360]) is what ensures democracy and ultimately creates the conditions for the legitimate exercise of power: power as representation of the values and interests of citizens expressed by means of their debate in the public sphere. Thus, institutional stability is predicated on the capacity to articulate different interests and values in the democratic process via communication networks (Habermas, 1989).

When there is separation between an interventionist state and a critical civil society, the public space collapses, thus suppressing the intermediate sphere between the administrative apparatus and the citizens. The democratic exercise of power is ultimately dependent on the institutional capacity to transfer meaning generated by communicative action into the functional coordination of action organized in the state under the principles of constitutional consensus. So, *constitutional access to coercive capacity and communicative resources that enable the co-production of meaning complement each other in establishing power relationships.*

Thus, in my view, some of the most influential theories of power, in spite of their theoretical and ideological differences, share a similar, multifaceted analysis of the construction of power in society:[1] *violence, the threat to resort to it, disciplinary discourses, the threat to enact discipline, the institutionalization of power relationships as reproducible domination, and the legitimation process by which values and rules are accepted by the subjects of reference, are all interacting elements in the process of producing and reproducing power relationships in social practices and in organizational forms.*

This eclectic perspective on power – useful, hopefully, as a research tool beyond its level of abstraction – articulates the two terms of the classical distinction between *power over* and *power to* proposed by Talcott Parsons (1963) and developed by several theorists (for example, Goehler's [2000] distinction between transitive power [power over] and intransitive power [power to]). Because, if we assume that all social structures are based on power relationships that are embedded in institutions and organizations (Lukes, 1974), for a social actor to engage in a strategy toward some goal, being empowered to act on social processes necessarily means intervening in the set of power relationships that frame any given social process and condition the attainment of a specific goal. The empowerment of social actors cannot be separated from their empowerment against other social actors, unless we accept the naïve image of a reconciled human community, a normative utopia that is belied by historical observation (Tilly, 1990, 1993; Fernández-Armesto, 2000). The power to do something, Hanna Arendt (1958) notwithstanding, is *always* the power to do something against someone, or against the values and interests of this "someone" that are enshrined in the apparatuses that rule and organize social life. As Michael Mann has written in the introduction to his historical study of the sources of social power, "in its most general sense, power is the ability to pursue and attain goals through the mastery of one's environment"

---

[1] Gramsci's analysis of the relationships between the state and civil society in terms of hegemony is close to this formulation, although conceptualized in a different theoretical perspective, rooted in class analysis (see Gramsci, 1975).

(1986: 6). And, after referring to Parsons's distinctions between distributive and collective power, he states that:

In most social relations both aspects of power, distributive and collective, exploitative and functional, operate simultaneously and are intertwined. Indeed, the relationship between the two is dialectical. In pursuit of their goals humans enter into cooperative, collective power relations with one another. But in implementing collective goals, social organization and a division of labor are set up...The few at the top can keep the masses at the bottom compliant, provided their control is *institutionalized* in the laws and norms of the social group in which both operate.

(1986: 6–7)

Thus societies are not communities, sharing values and interests. They are contradictory social structures enacted in conflicts and negotiations among diverse and often opposing social actors. Conflicts never end; they simply pause through temporary agreements and unstable contracts that are transformed into institutions of domination by those social actors who achieve an advantageous position in the power struggle, albeit at the cost of allowing some degree of institutional representation for the plurality of interests and values that remain subordinated. So, the institutions of the state and, beyond the state, the institutions, organizations, and discourses that frame and regulate social life are never the expression of "society," a black box of polysemic meaning whose interpretation depends on the perspectives of social actors. They are crystallized power relationships; that is, the "generalized means" (Parsons) that enable actors to exercise power *over* other social actors in order to have the power *to* accomplish their goals.

This is hardly a novel theoretical approach. It builds on Touraine's (1973) theory of the production of society and on Giddens's (1984) structuration theory. Actors produce the institutions of society under the conditions of the structural positions that they hold but with the capacity (ultimately mental) to engage in self-generated, purposive, meaningful, social action. This is how structure and agency are integrated in the understanding of social dynamics, without having to accept or reject the twin reductionisms of structuralism or subjectivism. This approach is not only a plausible point of convergence of relevant social theories, but also what the record of social research seems to indicate (Giddens, 1979; Mann, 1986, 1992; Melucci, 1989; Dalton and Kuechler, 1990; Bobbio, 1994; Calderon, 2003; Tilly, 2005; Sassen, 2006).

However, processes of structuration are multilayered and multiscalar. They operate on different forms and levels of social practice: economic (production, consumption, exchange), technological, environmental, cultural, political, and military. And they include gender relations that constitute transversal power relationships throughout the entire structure. These multilayered processes of structuration generate specific forms of time and space. Each one of these levels of practice, and each spatiotemporal form, (re)produce and/or challenge power relationships at the source of institutions and discourses. And these relationships involve complex arrangements between different levels of practice and institutions: global, national, local, and individual (Sassen, 2006). Therefore, if structuration is multiple, the analytical challenge is to understand the specificity of power relationships in each one of these levels, forms, and scales of social practice, and in their structured outcomes (Haugaard, 1997). Thus, *power is not located in one particular social sphere or institution, but it is distributed throughout the entire realm of human action. Yet, there are concentrated expressions of power relationships in certain social forms that condition and frame the practice of power in society at large by enforcing domination. Power is relational, domination is institutional.* A particularly relevant form of domination has been, throughout history, the state in its different manifestations (Poulantzas, 1978; Mulgan, 2007). But states are historical entities (Tilly, 1974). Therefore, the amount of power they hold depends on the overall social structure in which they operate. And this is the most decisive question in understanding the relationship between power and the state.

In the classical Weberian formulation, "ultimately one can define the modern state only in terms of the specific means peculiar to it, as to every political association, namely the use of political force. *Every state is founded on force*" ([1919] 1946: 77; emphasis added). As the state can be called upon to enforce power relationships in every domain of social practice, it is the ultimate guarantor of micro-powers; that is, of powers exercised away from the political sphere. When micro-power relationships enter into contradiction with the structures of domination embedded in the state, either the state changes or domination is reinstated by institutional means. Although the emphasis here is on force, the logic of domination can also be embedded in discourses as alternative or complementary forms of exercising power. Discourses are understood, in the Foucauldian tradition, as combinations of knowledge and language. But there is no contradiction between domination by the possibility of resorting to force and by disciplinary discourses. Indeed, Foucault's analysis of domination by the disciplinary discourses underlying the institutions of society refers mainly to state or para-state institutions: prisons, the military, asylums. The state-based logic is also extended to the disciplinary worlds of production (the factory) or of sexuality (the heterosexual, patriarchal family; Foucault, 1976, 1984a, b). In other words, disciplinary discourses are backed up by the potential use of violence, and state violence is rationalized, internalized, and ultimately legitimized by the discourses that frame/shape human action (Clegg, 2000). Indeed, the institutions and para-institutions of the state (for example, religious institutions, universities, the learned elites, the media to some extent) are the main sources of these discourses. To challenge existing power relationships, it is necessary to produce alternative discourses that have the potential to overwhelm the disciplinary discursive capacity of the state as a necessary step to neutralizing its use of violence. Therefore, while power relationships are distributed in the social structure, the state, from an historical perspective, remains a strategic instance of the exercise of power through different means. But the state itself is dependent on a diversity of power sources. Geoff Mulgan has theorized the capacity of the state to assume and exercise power through the articulation of three sources of power: violence, money, and trust.

The three sources of power together underpin political power, the sovereign power to impose laws, issue commands and hold together a people and a territory...It concentrates force through its armies, concentrates resources through exchequers, and concentrates the power to shape minds, most recently through big systems of education and communication that are the twin glues of modern nation states...Of the three sources of power the most important for sovereignty is the power over the thoughts that give rise to trust. Violence can only be used negatively; money can only be used in two dimensions, giving and taking away. But knowledge and thoughts can transform things, move mountains and make ephemeral power appear permanent.   (Mulgan, 2007: 27)

However, the modes of existence of the state and its capacity to act on power relationships depend on the specifics of the social structure in which the state operates. Indeed, the very notions of state and society depend on the boundaries that define their existence in a given historical context. And our historical context is marked by the contemporary processes of globalization and the rise of the network society, both relying on communication networks that process knowledge and thoughts to make and unmake trust, the decisive source of power.

State and Power in the Global Age

For Weber, the sphere of action of any given state is territorially bounded: "Today we have to say [in contrast to various force-based institutions in the past] that the state is a human community that (successfully) claims the monopoly of the legitimate use of physical force within a given territory. Note that territory is one of the characteristics of the state" ([1919] 1946: 78). This is not necessarily a nation-state, but it is usually so in its modern manifestation: "A nation is a community of sentiment which would adequately manifest itself in a state of its own; hence, a nation is a community which normally tends to produce a state of its own" ([1922] 1978: 176). So, nations (cultural communities) produce states, and they do so by claiming the monopoly of violence within a given territory. The articulation of state power, and of politics, takes place in a society that is defined as such by the state. This is the implicit assumption of most analyses of power, which observe the power relationships within a territorially constructed state or between states. Nation, state, and territory define the boundaries of society.

This "methodological nationalism" is rightly challenged by Ulrich Beck because globalization has redefined the territorial boundaries of the exercise of power:

Globalization, when taken to its logical conclusion, means that the social sciences must be grounded anew as a reality-based science of the transnational – conceptually, theoretically, methodologically, and organizationally as well. This includes the fact that there is a need for the basic concepts of "modern society" – household, family, class, democracy, domination, state, economy, the public sphere, politics and so on – to be released from the fixations of methodological nationalism and redefined and reconceptualized in the context of methodological cosmopolitanism.   (Beck, 2005: 50)

David Held, starting with his seminal article in 1991, and continuing with a series of political and economic analyses of globalization, has shown how the classical theory of power, focused on the nation-state or on subnational government structures, lacks a frame of reference from the moment that key components of the social structure are local and global at the same time rather than local or national (Held, 1991, 2004; Held et al., 1999; Held and McGrew, 2007). Habermas (1998) acknowledges the problems raised by the coming of what he calls "the postnational constellation" for the process of democratic legitimacy, as the Constitution (the defining institution) is national and the sources of power are increasingly constructed in the

17

supranational sphere. Bauman (1999) theorizes a new understanding of politics in a globalized world. And Saskia Sassen (2006) has shown the transformation of authority and rights, and thus power relationships, by the evolution of social structure toward "global assemblages."

In sum: if power relationships exist in specific social structures that are constituted on the basis of spatiotemporal formations, and these spatiotemporal formations are no longer primarily located at the national level, but are global and local at the same time, the boundary of society changes, and so does the frame of reference of power relationships that transcend the national (Fraser, 2007). This is not to say that the nation-state disappears. But it is to say that the national boundaries of power relationships are just one of the dimensions in which power and counterpower operate. Ultimately, this affects the nation-state itself. Even if it does not fade away as a specific form of social organization, it changes its role, its structure, and its functions, gradually evolving toward a new form of state: the network state that I analyze below.

How, in this new context, can we understand power relationships that are not primarily defined within the territorial boundaries established by the state? The theoretical construction proposed by Michael Mann for understanding the social sources of power provides some insights into the matter because, on the basis of his historical investigation, he conceptualizes societies as "constituted of multiple, overlapping and interacting sociospatial networks of power" (1986: 1). Therefore, rather than looking for territorial boundaries, we need to identify the sociospatial networks of power (local, national, global) that, in their intersection, configure societies. While a state-centered view of world political authority provided a clear indication of the boundaries of society and, therefore, of the sites of power in the context of the global age, to use Beck's characterization, we have to start from networks to understand institutions (see Beck, 2005). Or, in Sassen's (2006) terminology, the forms of assemblages, neither global nor local but both simultaneously, define the specific set of power relationships that provide the foundation for each society. Ultimately, the traditional notion of society may have to be called into question because each network (economic, cultural, political, technological, military, and the like) has its own spatiotemporal and organizational configurations, so that their points of intersection are subjected to relentless change. Societies as national societies become segmented and are constantly reshaped by the action of dynamic networks on their historically inherited social structures. In Michael Mann's terms, "a society is a network of social interaction at the boundaries of which is a certain level of interaction cleavage between it and its environment. A society is a unit with boundaries" (1986: 13).

Indeed, it is difficult to conceive of a society without boundaries. But networks do not have fixed boundaries; they are open-ended and multi-edged, and their expansion or contraction depends on the compatibility or competition between the interests and values programmed into each network and the interests and values programmed into the networks they come into contact with in their expansionary movement. In historical terms, the state (national or otherwise) may have been able to function as a gatekeeper of network interaction, providing some stability for a particular configuration of overlapping networks of power. Yet, under the conditions of multilayered globalization, the state becomes just a node (however important) of a particular network, the political, institutional, and military network that overlaps with other significant networks in the construction of social practice. Thus, the social dynamics constructed around networks appears to dissolve society as a stable social form of organization. However, a more constructive approach to the understanding of the process of historical change is to conceptualize a new form of society, the network society, made up of specific configurations of global, national, and local networks in a multidimensional space of social interaction. I hypothesize that relatively stable configurations built on the intersections of these networks may provide the boundaries that could redefine a new "society," with the understanding that these boundaries are highly volatile because of the relentless change in the geometry of the global networks that structure social practices and organizations. To probe this hypothesis, I need to make a detour through network theory, and then I must introduce the specificity of the network society as a particular type of social structure. Only then can we redefine power relationships under the conditions of a global network society.

Networks

A network is a set of interconnected nodes. Nodes may be of varying relevance to the network, and so particularly important nodes are called "centers" in some versions of network theory. Still, any component of a network (including "centers") is a node and its function and meaning depend on the programs of the network and on its interaction with other nodes in the network. Nodes increase their importance for the network by absorbing more relevant information, and processing it more efficiently. The relative importance of a node does not stem from its specific features but from its ability to contribute to the network's effectiveness in achieving its goals, as defined by the values and interests programmed into the networks. However, all nodes of a network are necessary for the network's performance, although networks allow for some redundancy as a safeguard for their proper functioning. When nodes become unnecessary for the fulfillment of the networks' goals, networks *tend* to reconfigure themselves, deleting some nodes, and adding new ones. Nodes only exist and function as components of networks. The network is the unit, not the node.

In social life, networks are communicative structures. "Communication networks are the patterns of contact that are created by the flow of messages among communicators through time and space" (Monge and Contractor, 2003: 3). So, networks process flows. Flows are streams of information between nodes, circulating through the channels of connection between nodes. A network is defined by the program that assigns the network its goals and its rules of performance. This program is made of codes that include valuation of performance and criteria for success or failure. In social and organizational networks, social actors, fostering their values and interests, and in interaction with other social actors, are at the origin of the creation and programming of networks. Yet, once set and programmed, networks follow the instructions inscribed in their operating system, and become capable of self-configuration within the parameters of their assigned goals and procedures. To alter the outcomes of the network, a new program (a set of goal-oriented, compatible codes) needs to be installed in the network – from outside the network.

Networks (and the sets of interests and values they embody) cooperate or compete with each other. Cooperation is based on the ability to communicate between networks. This ability depends on the existence of codes of translation and inter-operability between the networks (protocols of communication) and on access to connecting points (switches). Competition depends on the ability to outperform other networks by superior efficiency in performance or in cooperation capacity. Competition may also take a destructive form by disrupting the switchers of competing networks and/or interfering with their communication protocols. Networks work on a binary logic: inclusion/exclusion. Within the network, distance between nodes tends toward zero when every node is directly connected to every other node. Between nodes in the network and outside the network, distance is infinite, since there is no access unless the program of the network is changed. When nodes in the network are clustered, networks follow the logic of small worlds' properties: nodes are able to connect with a limited number of steps to the entire network and related networks from any node in the network (Watts and Strogatz, 1998). In the case of communication networks, I would add the condition of sharing protocols of communication.

Thus, networks are complex structures of communication constructed around a set of goals that simultaneously ensure unity of purpose and flexibility of execution by their adaptability to the operating environment. They are programmed and self-configurable at the same time. Their goals and operating procedures are programmed, in social and organizational networks, by social actors. Their structure evolves according to the capacity of the network to self-configure in an endless search for more efficient networking arrangements.

Networks are not specific to twenty-first-century societies or, for that matter, to human organization (Buchanan, 2002). Networks constitute the fundamental pattern of life, of all kinds of life. As Fritjof Capra writes, "the network is a pattern that is common to all life. Wherever we see life, we see networks" (2002: 9). In social life, social network analysts have long investigated the dynamic of social networks at the heart of social interaction and the production of meaning (Burt, 1980), leading to the formulation of a systematic theory of communication networks (Monge and Contractor, 2003). Furthermore, in terms of social structure, archeologists and historians of antiquity have forcefully reminded us that the historical record shows the pervasiveness and relevance of networks as the backbone of societies, thousands of years ago, in the most advanced ancient civilizations in several regions of the planet. Indeed, if we transfer the notion of globalization into the geography of the ancient world, as determined by available transportation technologies, there was networked globalization of a sort in antiquity, as societies depended on the connectivity of their main activities to networks transcending the limits of their locality for their livelihood, resources, and power (LaBianca, 2006). Muslim culture has been historically based on global networks (Cooke and Lawrence, 2005). And McNeill and McNeill (2003) have demonstrated the critical role of networks in social organization throughout history.

This observation of the actual historical record runs counter to the predominant vision of the evolution of society that has focused on a different type of organization: hierarchical bureaucracies based on the vertical integration of resources and subjects as the expression of the organized power of a social elite, legitimized by mythology and religion. This is to some extent a distorted vision, as historical and social analysis, more often than not, was built on ethnocentrism and ideology rather than on the scholarly investigation of the complexity of a multicultural world. But this relative indifference of our historical representation to the importance of networks in the structure and dynamics of society may also be linked to the actual subordination of these networks to the logic of vertical organizations, whose power was inscribed in the institutions of society and distributed in one-directional flows of command and control (Braudel, 1949; Mann, 1986, 1992; Colas, 1992; Fernández-Armesto, 1995). My hypothesis to explain the historical superiority of vertical/hierarchical organizations over horizontal networks is that the non-centered networked form of social organization had material limits to overcome, limits that were fundamentally linked to available technologies. Indeed, networks have their strength in their flexibility, adaptability, and capacity to self-reconfigure. Yet, beyond a certain threshold of size, complexity, and volume of flows, they become less efficient than vertically organized command-and-control structures, *under the conditions of pre-electronic communication technology* (Mokyr, 1990). Yes, wind-powered vessels could build sea-crossing and even trans-oceanic networks of trade and conquest. And horse-riding emissaries or fast-running messengers could maintain communication from the center to the periphery of vast territorial empires. But the time-lag of the feedback loop in the communication process was such that the logic of the system amounted to a one-way flow of the transmission of information and instruction. Under such conditions, networks were an extension of power concentrated at the top of the vertical organizations that shaped the history of humankind: states, religious apparatuses, war lords, armies, bureaucracies, and their subordinates in charge of production, trade, and culture.

The ability of networks to introduce new actors and new contents in the process of social organization, with relative autonomy vis-à-vis the power centers, increased over time with technological change and, more precisely, with the evolution of communication technologies. This was particularly the case with the possibility of relying on a distributed energy network that characterized the advent of the industrial revolution (Hughes, 1983). Railways and the telegraph constituted the first infrastructure for a quasi-global network of communication with self-reconfiguring capacity (Beniger, 1986). However, the industrial society (both in its capitalist and its statist versions) was predominantly structured around large-scale, vertical production organizations and extremely hierarchical state institutions, in some instances evolving into totalitarian systems. This is to say that early, electrically based communication technologies were not powerful enough to equip networks with autonomy in all their nodes, as this autonomy would have required multidirectionality and a continuous flow of interactive information processing. But it also means that the availability of proper technology is a necessary, but not sufficient, condition for the transformation of the social structure. It was only under the conditions of a mature industrial society that autonomous projects of organizational networking could emerge. When they did, they could use the potential of microelectronics-based digital communication technologies (Benkler, 2006).

Thus, networks became the most efficient organizational forms as a result of three major features of networks which benefited from the new technological environment: flexibility, scalability, and survivability. *Flexibility* is the ability to reconfigure according to changing environments and retain their goals while changing their components, sometimes bypassing blocking points of communication channels to find new connections. *Scalability* is the ability to expand or shrink in size with little disruption. *Survivability* is the ability of networks, because they have no single center and can operate in a wide range of configurations, to withstand attacks to their nodes and codes because the codes of the network are contained in multiple nodes that can reproduce the instructions and find new ways to perform. So, only the material ability to destroy the connecting points can eliminate the network.

At the core of this technological change that unleashed the power of networks was the transformation of information and communication technologies, based on the microelectronics revolution that took shape in the 1950s and 1960s (Freeman, 1982; Perez, 1983). It constituted the foundation of a new technological paradigm, consolidated in the 1970s, first in the United States, and rapidly diffused around the world, ushering in what I have characterized as the Information Age (Castells, 2000a, c, 2004c). William Mitchell (2003) has conceptualized the evolving logic of information and communication technology throughout history as a process of expansion and augmentation of the human body and the human mind: a process that, in the early twenty-first century, is characterized by the explosion of portable devices that provide ubiquitous wireless communication and computing capacity. This enables social units (individuals or organizations) to interact anywhere, anytime, while relying on a support infrastructure that manages material resources in a distributed information power grid (Castells et al., 2006b). With the advent of nanotechnology and the convergence of microelectronics and biological processes and materials, the boundaries between human life and machine life are blurred, so that networks extend their interaction from our inner self to the whole realm of human activity, transcending barriers of time and space. Neither Mitchell nor I indulge in science fiction scenarios as a substitute for analyses of the technosocial transformation process. But it is essential, precisely for the sake of analysis, to emphasize the role of technology in the process of social transformation, particularly when we consider the central technology of our time – communication technology – that relates to the heart of the specificity of the human species: conscious, meaningful communication (Capra, 1996, 2002; Damasio, 2003). It was because of available electronic information and communication technologies that the network society could deploy itself fully, transcending the historical limits of networks as forms of social organization and interaction.

The Global Network Society[2]

A network society is a society whose social structure is made around networks activated by microelectronics-based, digitally processed information and communication technologies. I understand social structures to be the organizational arrangements of humans in relationships of production, consumption, reproduction, experience, and power expressed in meaningful communication coded by culture.

Digital networks are global, as they have the capacity to reconfigure themselves, as directed by their programmers, transcending territorial and institutional boundaries through telecommunicated computer networks. So, a social structure whose infrastructure is based on digital networks has the potential capacity to be global. However, network technology and networking organization are only means to enact the trends inscribed in the social structure. The contemporary process of globalization has its origin in economic, political, and cultural factors, as documented by scholarly analyses of globalization (Beck, 2000; Held and McGrew, 2000, 2007; Stiglitz, 2002). But, as a number of studies have indicated, the forces driving globalization could only be effectuated because they have at their

[2] This section elaborates and updates the analysis presented in my book *The Rise of the Network Society* (2000c). I take the liberty of referring the reader to that book for further elaboration and empirical support of the theorization presented here. Additional supporting material can be found in some of my writings in recent years (Castells, 2000b, 2001, 2004b, 2005a, b, 2008a, b; Castells and Himanen, 2002; Castells et al., 2006b, 2007).

disposal the global networking capacity provided by digital communication technologies and information systems, including computerized, long-haul, fast, transportation networks (Kiyoshi et al., 2006; Grewal, 2008). This is, in fact, what separates, in size, speed, and complexity, the current process of globalization from previous forms of globalization in earlier historical periods.

Thus, the network society is a global society. However, this does not mean that people everywhere are included in these networks. For the time being, most are not (Hammond et al., 2007). But everybody is affected by the processes that take place in the global networks that constitute the social structure. The core activities that shape and control human life in every corner of the planet are organized in global networks: financial markets; transnational production, management, and the distribution of goods and services; highly skilled labor; science and technology, including higher education; the mass media; the Internet networks of interactive, multi-purpose communication; culture; art; entertainment; sports; international institutions managing the global economy and intergovernmental relations; religion; the criminal economy; and the transnational NGOs and social movements that assert the rights and values of a new, global civil society (Held et al., 1999; Volkmer, 1999; Castells, 2000a; Jacquet et al., 2002; Stiglitz, 2002; Kaldor, 2003; Grewal, 2008; Juris, 2008). Globalization is better understood as the networking of these socially decisive global networks. Therefore, exclusion from these networks, often in a cumulative process of exclusion, is tantamount to structural marginalization in the global network society (Held and Kaya, 2006).

The network society diffuses selectively throughout the planet, working on the pre-existing sites, cultures, organizations, and institutions that still make up most of the material environment of people's lives. The social structure is global, but most of human experience is local, both in territorial and cultural terms (Borja and Castells, 1997; Norris, 2000). Specific societies, as defined by the current boundaries of nation-states, or by the cultural boundaries of their historical identities, are deeply fragmented by the double logic of inclusion and exclusion in the global networks that structure production, consumption, communication, and power. I propose the hypothesis that this fragmentation of societies between the included and the excluded is more than the expression of the time-lag required by the gradual incorporation of previous social forms into the new dominant logic. It is, in fact, a structural feature of the global network society. This is because the reconfiguring capacity inscribed in the process of networking allows the programs governing every network to search for valuable additions everywhere and to incorporate them, while bypassing and excluding those territories, activities, and people that have little or no value for the performance of the tasks assigned to the network. Indeed, as Geoff Mulgan observed, "networks are created not just to communicate, but also to gain position, to outcommunicate" (1991: 21). The network society works on the basis of a binary logic of inclusion/exclusion, whose boundaries change over time, both with the changes in the networks' programs and with the conditions of performance of these programs. It also depends on the ability of social actors, in various contexts, to act on these programs, modifying them in the direction of their interests. The global network society is a dynamic structure that is highly malleable to social forces, to culture, to politics, and to economic strategies. But what remains in all instances is its dominance over activities and people who are external to the networks. In this sense, the global overwhelms the local – unless the local becomes connected to the global as a node in alternative global networks constructed by social movements.

Thus, the uneven globalization of the network society is, in fact, a highly significant feature of its social structure. The coexistence of the network society, as a global structure, with industrial, rural, communal, or survival societies, characterizes the reality of all countries, albeit with different shares of population and territory on both sides of the divide, depending on the relevance of each segment for the dominant logic of each network. This is to say that various networks will have different geometries and geographies of inclusion and exclusion: the map of the global criminal economy is not the same as the map resulting from the international location patterns of high-technology industry.

In theoretical terms, the network society must be analyzed, first, as a global architecture of self-reconfiguring networks constantly programmed and reprogrammed by the powers that be in each dimension; second, as the result of the interaction between the various geometries and geographies of the networks that include the core activities – that is, the activities shaping life and work in society; and, third, as the result of a second-order interaction between these dominant networks and the geometry and geography of the disconnection of social formations left outside the global networking logic.

The understanding of power relationships in our world must be specific to this particular society. An informed discussion of this specificity requires a characterization of the network society in its main components: production and appropriation of value, work, communication, culture, and its mode of existence as a spatiotemporal formation. Only then can I meaningfully introduce a tentative hypothesis on the specificity of power relationships in the global network society – a hypothesis that will guide the analysis presented throughout this book.

What is Value in the Network Society?

Social structures, such as the network society, originate from the processes of the production and appropriation of value. But what constitutes value in the network society? What moves the production system? What motivates the appropriators of value and controllers of society? There is no change here in relation to earlier social structures in history: value is what the dominant institutions of society decide it is. So, if global capitalism shapes the world, and capital accumulation by the valuation of financial assets in the global financial markets is the supreme value, this will be value in every instance, as, under capitalism, profit-making and its materialization in monetary terms can ultimately acquire everything else. The critical matter is that, in a social structure organized in global networks, whatever the hierarchy is between the networks will become the rule in the entire grid of networks organizing/dominating the planet. If, for instance, we say that capital accumulation is what moves the system, and the return to capital is fundamentally realized in the global financial markets, the global financial markets will assign value to every transaction in every country, as no economy is independent of financial valuation decided in the global financial markets. But if, instead, we consider that the supreme value is military power, the technological and organizational capacity of military machines will structure power in their spheres of influence, and create the conditions for other forms of value – for example, capital accumulation or political domination – to proceed under their protection. However, if the transmission of technology, information, and knowledge to a particular armed organization is blocked, this organization becomes irrelevant in the world context. Thus, we may say that global networks of information and technology are the dominant ones because they condition military capacity which, in turn, provides security for the market to function. Another illustration of this diversity of value-making processes: we can assert that the most important source of influence in today's world is the transformation of people's minds. If it is so, then the media are the key networks, as the media, organized in global conglomerates and their distributive networks, are the primary sources of messages and images that reach people's minds. But if we now consider the media as primarily media business, then the logic of profit-making, both in the commercialization of media by the advertising industry and in the valuation of their stock, becomes paramount.

Thus, given the variety of the potential origins of network domination, the network society is a multidimensional social structure in which networks of different kinds have different logics of value-making. The definition of what constitutes value depends on the specificity of the network, and of its program. Any attempt to reduce all value to a common standard faces insurmountable methodological and practical difficulties. For instance, if profit-making is the supreme value under capitalism, military power ultimately grounds state power, and the state has a considerable capacity to decide and enforce new rules for business operations (ask the Russian oligarchs about Putin). At the same time, state power, even in non-democratic contexts, largely depends on the beliefs of people, on their capacity to accept the rules, or, alternatively, on their willingness to resist. Then, the media system, and other means of communication, such as the Internet, could precede state power, which, in turn, would condition the rules of profit-making, and thus would supersede the value of money as the supreme value.

Thus, *value is, in fact, an expression of power*: Whoever holds power (often different from whoever is in government) decides what is valuable. In this sense, the network society does not innovate. What is new, however, is its global reach, and its networked architecture. It means, on one hand, that relations of domination between networks are critical. They are characterized by constant, flexible interaction: for instance, between global financial markets, geopolitical processes, and media strategies. On the other hand, because the logic of value-making, as an expression of domination, is global, those instances that have a structural impediment to exist globally are at a disadvantage vis-à-vis others whose logic is inherently global. This has considerable practical importance because it is at the root of the crisis of the nation-state of the industrial era (not of the state as such, because every social structure generates its own form of state). Since the nation-state can only enforce its rules in its territory, except in the case of alliances or invasion, it has to become either imperial or networked to relate to other networks in the definition of value. This is why, for instance, the US state, in the early twenty-first century, made a point of defining security against terrorism as the overarching value for the entire world. It was a way of building a military-based network that would assure its hegemony by placing security over profit-making, or lesser goals (such as human rights or the environment), as the supreme value. However, the capitalist logic often becomes quickly overlaid on security projects, as the profitable business of American crony companies in Iraq strikingly illustrates (Klein, 2007).

Capital has always enjoyed the notion of a world without boundaries, as David Harvey has repeatedly reminded us, so that global financial networks have a head start as the defining instances of value in the global network society (Harvey, 1990). Yet, human thought is probably the most rapidly propagating and influential element of any social system, on the condition of relying on a global/local, interactive communication system in real time – which is exactly what has emerged now, for the first time in history (Dutton, 1999; Benkler, 2006). Thus, ideas, and specific sets of ideas, could assert themselves as the truly supreme value (such as preserving our planet, our species, or else serving God's design), as a prerequisite for everything else.

In sum: the old question of industrial society – indeed, the cornerstone of classical political economy – namely, "what is value?," has no definite answer in the global network society. Value is what is processed in every dominant network at every time in every space according to the hierarchy programmed in the network by the actors acting upon the network. Capitalism has not disappeared. Indeed, it is more pervasive than ever. But it is not, against a common ideological perception, the only game in the global town.

Work, Labor, Class, and Gender: The Network Enterprise and the New Social Division of Labor

The preceding analysis of the new political economy of value-making in the global networks paves the way to understanding the new division of labor, and thus work, productivity, and exploitation. People work; they always have. In fact, today people work more (in terms of total working hours in a given society) than they ever did, since most of women's work was previously not counted as socially recognized (paid) work. The crucial matter has always been how this work is organized and compensated. The division of labor was, and still is, a measure of what is valued and what is not in labor contribution. This value judgment organizes the process of production. It also defines the criteria according to which the product is shared, determining differential consumption and social stratification.

Power in the Network Society

The most fundamental divide in the network society, albeit not the only one, is between self-programmable labor and generic labor (Carnoy, 2000; Castells, 2000c; Benner, 2002). *Self-programmable labor* has the autonomous capacity to focus on the goal assigned to it in the process of production, find the relevant information, recombine it into knowledge, using the available knowledge stock, and apply it in the form of tasks oriented toward the goals of the process. The more our information systems are complex, and interactively connected to databases and information sources via computer networks, the more what is required from labor is the capacity to search and recombine information. This demands appropriate education and training, not in terms of skills, but in terms of creative capacity, as well as in terms of the ability to co-evolve with changes in organization, in technology, and in knowledge. By contrast, tasks that are little valued, yet necessary, are assigned to *generic labor*, eventually replaced by machines, or shifted to lower-cost production sites, depending on a dynamic, cost–benefit analysis. The overwhelming mass of working people on the planet, and the majority in advanced countries, are still generic labor. They are disposable, unless they assert their right to exist as humans and citizens through their collective action. But in terms of value-making (in finance, in manufacturing, in research, in sports, in entertainment, in military action, or in political capital), it is the self-programmable worker who counts for any organization in control of resources. Thus, the organization of the work process in the network society acts on a binary logic, dividing self-programmable labor from generic labor. Furthermore, the flexibility and adaptability of both kinds of labor to a constantly changing environment is a precondition for their use as labor.

This specific division of labor is gendered. The rise of flexible labor is directly related to the feminization of the paid labor force, a fundamental trend of the social structure in the past three decades (Carnoy, 2000). The patriarchal organization of the family induces women to value the flexible organization of their professional work as the only way to make family and job duties compatible. This is why the large majority of temporary workers and part-time workers in most countries are women. Furthermore, while most women are employed as generic labor, their educational level has improved considerably vis-à-vis men, while their wages and working conditions have not risen at the same pace. Thus, women have become the ideal workers of the networked, global, capitalist economy: on one hand, they are able to work efficiently, and adapt to the changing requirements of business; on the other hand, they receive less compensation for the same work, and have fewer chances for promotion because of the ideology and practice of the gendered division of labor under patriarchalism. However, reality is, to use an old word, dialectical. Although the mass incorporation of women into paid labor, partly because of their condition of patriarchal subordination, has been a decisive factor in the expansion of global, informational capitalism, the very transformation of women's condition as salaried women has ultimately undermined patriarchalism. The feminist ideas that emerged from the cultural social movements of the 1970s found fertile ground in the experience of working women exposed to discrimination. Even more importantly, the economic bargaining power earned by women in the family strengthened their power position vis-à-vis the male head of the family, while undermining the ideological justification of their subordination on the grounds of the respect due to the authority of the male breadwinner. Thus, the division of labor in the new work organization is gendered, but this is a dynamic process, in which women are reversing dominant structural trends and inducing business to bring men into the same patterns of flexibility, job insecurity, downsizing, and offshoring of their jobs that used to be the lot of women. Thus, rather than women rising to the level of male workers, most male workers are being downgraded to the level of most women workers, while professional women have reached a higher level of connectivity into what used to be the old boys networks. These trends have profound implications for both the class structure of society and the relationship between men and women at work and in the family (Castells and Subirats, 2007).

The creativity, autonomy, and self-programmable capacity of knowledge labor would not yield their productivity pay-off if they were not able to be combined with the networking of labor. Indeed, the fundamental reason for the structural need for flexibility and autonomy is the transformation of the organization of the production process. This transformation is represented by *the rise of the network enterprise*. This new organizational business form is the historical equivalent under informationalism of the so-called Fordist organization of industrialism (both capitalist and statist), which is the organization characterized by high-volume, standardized, mass production and vertical control of the labor process according to a top-down, rationalized scheme ("scientific management" and Taylorism, the methods that prompted Lenin's admiration, leading to their imitation in the Soviet Union). Although there are still millions of workers in similarly run factories, the value-producing activities in the commanding heights of the production process (R&D, innovation, design, marketing, management, and high-volume, customized, flexible production) depend on an entirely different type of firm and, therefore, a different type of work process and of labor: the network enterprise. This is not the equivalent of a network of enterprises. It is a network made from either firms or segments of firms, and/or from the internal segmentation of firms. Thus, large corporations are internally decentralized as networks. Small and medium businesses are connected in networks, thus ensuring the critical mass of their contribution as subcontractors, while keeping their main asset: flexibility. Small and medium business networks are often ancillary to large corporations; in most cases to several of them. Large corporations, and their subsidiary networks, usually form networks of cooperation, called, in business practice, strategic alliances or partnerships.

But these alliances are rarely permanent cooperative structures. This is not a process of oligopolistic cartelization. These complex networks link up on specific business projects, and reconfigure their cooperation in different networks with each new project. The usual business practice in this networked economy is one of alliances, partnerships, and collaborations that are specific to a given product, process, time, and space. These collaborations are based on sharing capital and labor, but most fundamentally information and knowledge, in order to win market share. So these are primarily information networks, which link suppliers and customers through the networked firm. The unit of the production process is not the firm but the business project, enacted by a network, the network enterprise. The firm continues to be the legal unit of capital accumulation. But, since the value of the firm ultimately depends on its financial valuation in the stock market, the unit of capital accumulation, the firm, becomes itself a node in a global network of financial flows. Thus, in the network economy, the dominant layer is the global financial market, the mother of all valuations. The global financial market works only partly according to market rules. It is also shaped and moved by information turbulences of various origins, processed and communicated by the computer networks that constitute the nerve system of the global, informational, capitalist economy (Hutton and Giddens, 2000; Obstfeld and Taylor, 2004; Zaloom, 2006).

Financial valuation determines the dynamics of the economy in the short term, but, in the long run, everything depends on productivity growth. This is why the source of productivity constitutes the cornerstone of economic growth, and therefore of profits, wages, accumulation, and investment (Castells, 2006). And the key factor for productivity growth in this knowledge-intensive, networked economy is innovation (Lucas, 1999;

Tuomi, 2002), or the capacity to recombine factors of production in a more efficient way, and/or produce higher value added in process or in product. Innovators depend on cultural creativity, on institutional openness to entrepreneurialism, on labor autonomy in the labor process, and on the appropriate kind of financing for this innovation-driven economy.

The new economy of our time is certainly capitalist, but of a new brand of capitalism: it depends on innovation as the source of productivity growth; on computer-networked global financial markets, whose criteria for valuation are influenced by information turbulences; on the networking of production and management, both internally and externally, locally and globally; and on labor that is flexible and adaptable. The creators of value have to be self-programmable and able to autonomously process information into specific knowledge. Generic workers, reduced to their role as executants, must be ready to adapt to the needs of the network enterprise, or else face displacement by machines or alternative labor forces.

In this system, besides the persistence of exploitation in the traditional sense, the key issue for labor is the segmentation between three categories: those who are the source of innovation and valuation; those who are mere executants of instructions; and those who are structurally irrelevant from the perspective of the profit-making programs of global capitalism, either as workers (inadequately educated and living in areas without the proper infrastructure and institutional environment for global production) or as consumers (too poor to be part of the market), or both. The primary concern for much of the world's population is to avoid irrelevance, and instead engage in a meaningful relationship, such as that which we call exploitation – because exploitation does have a meaning for the exploited. The greatest danger is for those who become invisible to the programs commanding the global networks of production, distribution, and valuation.

The Space of Flows and Timeless Time

As with all historical transformations, the emergence of a new social structure is linked to the redefinition of the material foundations of our existence, space and time, as Giddens (1984), Adam (1990), Harvey (1990), Lash and Urry (1994), Mitchell (1999, 2003), Dear (2000, 2002), Graham and Simon (2001), Hall and Pain (2006), and Tabboni (2006), among others, have argued. Power relationships are embedded in the social construction of space and time, while being conditioned by the time–space formations that characterize society.

Two emergent social forms of time and space characterize the network society, while coexisting with prior forms. These are the *space of flows* and *timeless time*. Space and time are related, in nature as in society. In social theory, space can be defined as the material support of time-sharing social practices; that is, the construction of simultaneity. The development of communication technologies can be understood as the gradual decoupling of contiguity and time-sharing. The *space of flows* refers to the technological and organizational possibility of practicing simultaneity without contiguity. It also refers to the possibility of asynchronous interaction in chosen time, at a distance. Most dominant functions in the network society (financial markets, transnational production networks, media networks, networked forms of global governance, global social movements) are organized around the space of flows. However, the space of flows is not placeless. It is made of nodes and networks; that is, of places connected by electronically powered communication networks through which flows of information that ensure the time-sharing of practices processed in such a space circulate and inter-act. While in the space of places, based on contiguity of practice, meaning, function, and locality are closely inter-related, in the space of flows places receive their meaning and function from their nodal role in the specific networks to which they belong. Thus, the space of flows is not the same for financial activities as for science, for media networks as for political power networks. In social theory, space cannot be conceived as separate from social practices. Therefore, every dimension of the network society that we have analyzed in this chapter has a spatial manifestation. Because practices are networked, so is their space. Since networked practices are based on information flows processed between various sites by communication technologies, the space of the network society is made of the articulation between three elements: the places where activities (and people enacting them) are located; the material communication networks linking these activities; and the content and geometry of the flows of information that perform the activities in terms of function and meaning. This is the space of flows.

Time, in social terms, used to be defined as the sequencing of practices. Biological time, characteristic of most of human existence (and still the lot of most people in the world) is defined by the sequence programmed in the life-cycles of nature. Social time was shaped throughout history by what I call bureaucratic time, which is the organization of time, in institutions and in everyday life, by the codes of military–ideological apparatuses, imposed over the rhythms of biological time. In the industrial age, clock time gradually emerged, inducing what I would call, in the Foucauldian tradition, disciplinary time. This is the measure and organization of sequencing with enough precision to assign tasks and order to every moment of life, starting with standardized industrial work, and the calculation of the time-horizon of commercial transactions, two fundamental components of industrial capitalism that could not work without clock time: time is money, and money is made over time. In the network society, the emphasis on sequencing is reversed. The relationship to time is defined by the use of information and communication technologies in a relentless effort to annihilate time by negating sequencing: on one hand, by compressing time (as in split-second global financial transactions or the generalized practice of multitasking, squeezing more activity into a given time); on the other hand, by blurring the sequence of social practices, including past, present, and future in a random order, like in the electronic hypertext of Web 2.0, or the blurring of life-cycle patterns in both work and parenting.

In the industrial society, which was organized around the idea of progress and the development of productive forces, *becoming* structured *being*, time conformed space. In the network society, the space of flows dissolves time by disordering the sequence of events and making them simultaneous in the communication networks, thus installing society in structural ephemerality: *being* cancels *becoming*.

The construction of space and time is socially differentiated. The multiple space of places, fragmented and disconnected, displays diverse temporalities, from the most traditional domination of biological rhythms, to the control of clock time. Selected functions and individuals transcend time (like changing global time zones), while devalued activities and subordinate people endure life as time goes by. There are, however, alternative projects of the structuration of time and space, as an expression of social movements that aim to modify the dominant programs of the network society. Thus, instead of accepting timeless time as the time of the financial automaton, the environmental movement proposes to live time in a *longue durée*, cosmological perspective, seeing our lives as part of the evolution of our species, and feeling solidarity with future generations, and with our cosmological belonging: it is what Lash and Urry (1994) conceptualized as glacial time.

Communities around the world fight to preserve the meaning of locality, and to assert the space of places, based on experience, over the logic of the space of flows, based on instrumentality, in the process that I have analyzed as the "grassrooting" of the space of flows (Castells, 1999). Indeed, the space of flows does not disappear, since it is the spatial form of the network society, but its logic could be transformed. Instead of enclosing meaning and function in the programs of the networks, it would provide the material support for the global connection of the local experience, as in the Internet communities emerging from the networking of local cultures (Castells, 2001).

Space and time are redefined both by the emergence of a new social structure and by the power struggles over the shape and programs of this social structure. Space and time express the power relationships of the network society.

Culture in the Network Society

Societies are cultural constructs. I understand culture as the set of values and beliefs that inform, guide, and motivate people's behavior. So, if there is a specific network society, there should be a culture of the network society that we can identify as its historical marker. Here again, however, the complexity and novelty of the network society require caution. First of all, because the network society is global, it works and integrates a multiplicity of cultures, linked to the history and geography of each area of the world. In fact, industrialism, and the culture of the industrial society, did not make specific cultures disappear around the world. The industrial society had many different, and indeed contradictory, cultural manifestations (from the United States to the Soviet Union, and from Japan to the United Kingdom). There were also industrialized cores in otherwise largely rural and traditional societies. Not even capitalism unified its realm of historical existence culturally. Yes, the market ruled in every capitalist country, but under such specific rules, and with such a variety of cultural forms, that identifying a culture as capitalist is of little analytical help, unless by that we actually mean American or Western, which then becomes empirically wrong.

In the same way, the network society develops in a multiplicity of cultural settings, produced by the differential history of each context. It materializes in specific forms, leading to the formation of highly diverse institutional and cultural systems (Castells, 2004b). However, there is still a common core to the network society, as there was to the industrial society. But there is an additional layer of unity in the network society. It exists globally in real time. It is global in its structure. Thus, it not only deploys its logic to the whole world, but it keeps its networked organization at the global level while specifying itself in every society. This double movement of commonality and singularity has two main consequences at the cultural level.

On one hand, specific cultural identities become the communes of autonomy, and sometimes trenches of resistance, for collectives and individuals who refuse to fade away in the logic of dominant networks (Castells, 2004c). To be French becomes as relevant as being a citizen or a consumer. To be Catalan, or Basque, or Galician, or Irish, or Welsh, or Scottish, or Quebecois, or Kurd, or Shiite, or Sunni, or Aymara, or Maori becomes a rallying point of self-identification vis-à-vis the domination of imposed nation-states. In contrast to normative or ideological visions that propose the merger of all cultures in the cosmopolitan melting pot of the citizens of the world, the world is not flat. Resistance identities have exploded in these early stages of the development of the global network society, and have induced the most dramatic social and political conflicts in recent times. Respectable theorists and less respectable ideologists may warn against the dangers of such a development, but we cannot ignore it. Observation must inform the theory, not the other way around. Thus, what characterizes the global network society is the contraposition between the logic of the global net and the affirmation of a multiplicity of local selves, as I have tried to argue and document in my work (Castells, 2000a, c, 2004c; see also Tilly, 2005).

Rather than the rise of a homogeneous global culture, what we observe is historical cultural diversity as the main common trend: fragmentation rather than convergence. The key question that then arises is the capacity of these specific cultural identities (made with the materials inherited from singular histories and reworked in the new context) to communicate with each other (Touraine, 1997). Otherwise, the sharing of an interdependent, global social structure, while not being able to speak a common language of values and beliefs, leads to systemic misunderstanding, at the root of destructive violence against the other. Thus, protocols of communication between different cultures are the critical issue for the network society, since without them there is no society, just dominant networks and resisting communes. The project of a cosmopolitan culture common to the citizens of the world lays the foundation for democratic global governance and addresses the central cultural-institutional issue of the network society (Habermas, 1998; Beck, 2005). Unfortunately, this vision proposes the solution without identifying, other than in normative terms, the processes by which these protocols of communication are to be created or could be created, given the fact that cosmopolitan culture, according to empirical research, is present only in a very small part of the population, including in Europe (Norris, 2000; European Commission's *Eurobarometer*, 2007, 2008). Thus, while personally wishing that the culture of cosmopolitanism would gradually increase communication between peoples and cultures, observation of current trends points in a different direction.

To determine what these protocols of intercultural communication may be is a matter for investigation. This investigation will be taken up in this book, on the basis of the following hypothesis: *the common culture of the global network society is a culture of protocols of communication enabling communication between different cultures on the basis not of shared values but of the sharing of the value of communication.* This is to say: the new culture is not made of content but of process, as the constitutional democratic culture is based on procedure, not on substantive programs. Global culture is a culture of communication for the sake of communication. It is an open-ended network of cultural meanings that can not only coexist, but also interact and modify each other on the basis of this exchange. The culture of the network society is a culture of protocols of communication between all cultures in the world, developed on the basis of the common belief in the power of networking and of the synergy obtained by giving to others and receiving from others. A process of material construction of the culture of the network society is under way. But it is not the diffusion of the capitalist mind through the power exercised in the global networks by the dominant elites inherited from industrial society. Neither is it the idealistic proposal of philosophers dreaming of a world of abstract, cosmopolitan citizens. It is the process by which conscious social actors of multiple origins bring their resources and beliefs to others, expecting in return to receive the same, and even more: the sharing of a diverse world, thus ending the ancestral fear of the other.

The Network State

Power cannot be reduced to the state. But an understanding of the state, and of its historical and cultural specificity, is a necessary component of any theory of power. By state, I mean the institutions of governance of society and their institutionalized agencies of political representation and of management and control of social life; that is, the executive, the legislative, the judiciary, public administration, the military, law enforcement agencies, regulatory agencies, and political parties, at various levels of governance: national, regional, local, and international.

The state aims to assert sovereignty, the monopoly of ultimate decision-making over its subjects within given territorial boundaries. The state defines citizenship, thus conferring rights and claiming duties on its subjects. It also extends its authority to foreign nationals under its jurisdiction. And it engages in relationships of cooperation, competition, and power with other states. In the analysis presented above, I have shown, in accord with a number of scholars and observers, the growing contradiction between the structuration of instrumental relationships in global networks and the confinement of the nation-state's authority within its territorial boundaries. There is, indeed, a crisis of the nation-state as a sovereign entity (Appadurai, 1996; Nye and Donahue, 2000; Jacquet et al., 2002; Price, 2002; Beck, 2005; Fraser, 2007). However, *nation-states, despite their multidimensional crises, do not disappear; they transform themselves to adapt to the new context*. Their pragmatic transformation is what really changes the landscape of politics and policy-making in the global network society. This transformation is influenced, and fought over, by a variety of projects that constitute the cultural/ideational material on which the diverse political and social interests present in each society work to enact the transformation of the state.

Nation-states respond to the crises induced by the twin processes of the globalization of instrumentality and identification of culture via three main mechanisms:

1. They associate with one another and form networks of states, some of them multipurpose and sharing sovereignty, such as the European Union. Others are focused on a set of issues, generally trade issues (for example, NAFTA or Mercosur) or security issues (for example, NATO). Still others are constituted as spaces of coordination, negotiation, and debate among states with interests in specific regions of the world; for example, OAS (Organization of American States), AU (African Union), the Arab League, ASEAN (Association of South East Asian Nations), APEC (Asia-Pacific Economic Cooperation Forum), the East Asian Summit, the Shanghai Cooperation Organization, and so on. In the strongest networks, the states share some attributes of sovereignty. States also establish permanent or semi-permanent informal networks to elaborate

strategies and to manage the world according to the interests of the network participants. There is a pecking order of such groupings, with the G-8 (soon to become G-20 or G-22) being at the top of the food chain.

2. States have built an increasingly dense network of international institutions and supranational organizations to deal with global issues, from general purpose institutions (for example, the United Nations) to specialized ones (the WTO, the IMF, the World Bank, the International Criminal Court, and so on). There are also ad hoc international institutions defined around a set of issues (for example, the treaties on the global environment and their agencies).

3. Nation-states in many countries have engaged in a process of devolution of power to regional governments, and to local governments, while opening channels of participation with NGOs, in the hope of halting their crisis of political legitimacy by connecting with people's identity.

The actual process of political decision-making operates in a network of interaction between national, supranational, international, co-national, regional, and local institutions, while also reaching out to the organizations of civil society. In this process, we witness the transformation of the sovereign nation-state that emerged throughout the modern age into a new form of state – which I conceptualized as the network state (Castells, 2000a: 338–65). The *emerging network state* is characterized by shared sovereignty and responsibility between different states and levels of government; flexibility of governance procedures; and greater diversity of times and spaces in the relationship between governments and citizens compared to the preceding nation-state.

The whole system develops in a pragmatic way, by ad hoc decisions, ushering in sometimes contradictory rules and institutions, and making the system of political representation more obscure, and further removed from citizens' control. The nation-state's efficiency improves but its crisis of legitimacy worsens, although overall political legitimacy may improve if local and regional institutions play their part. Yet, the growing autonomy of the local and regional state may bring the different levels of the state into contradiction, and turn one against the other. This new form of state induces new kinds of problems, derived from the contradiction between the historically constructed nature of the institutions and the new functions and mechanisms they have to assume to perform in the network, while still relating to their territorially bound national societies.

Thus, the network state faces a *coordination problem*, with three aspects: organizational, technical, and political.

Organizational: agencies invested in protecting their turf, and their privileged commanding position vis-à-vis their societies, cannot have the same structure, reward systems, and operational principles as agencies whose fundamental role is to find synergy with other agencies.

Technical: protocols of communication do not work. The introduction of computer networking often disorganizes the participating agencies rather than connecting them, as in the case of the new Homeland Security Administration created in the United States in the wake of the declaration of the war on terror. Agencies are reluctant to adopt networking technology that implies networking their practices, and may jeopardize their ability to preserve their control over their bureaucratic turf.

Political: the coordination strategy is not only horizontal between agencies, it is also vertical in two directions: networking with their political overseers, thus losing their bureaucratic autonomy; and networking with their citizen constituencies, thus being obliged to increase their accountability.

The network state also confronts an ideological problem: coordinating a common policy means a common language and a set of shared values, for instance against market fundamentalism in the regulation of markets, or acceptance of sustainable development in environmental policy, or priority of human rights over raison d'état in security policy. It is not obvious that such compatibility exists between distinct state apparatuses.

There is, in addition, a geopolitical problem. Nation-states still see the networks of governance as a bargaining table at which they will have the chance to advance their interests. Rather than cooperating for the global common good, nation-states continue to be guided by traditional political principles: (a) maximize the interests of the nation-state, and (b) prioritize the personal/political/social interests of the political actors in command of each nation-state. Global governance is seen as a field of opportunity to maximize one's own interests, rather than a new context in which political institutions share governance around common projects. In fact, the more the globalization process proceeds, the more the contradictions it generates (identity crises, economic crises, security crises) lead to a revival of nationalism, and to attempts to restore the primacy of sovereignty. Indeed, the world is *objectively multilateral* but some of the most powerful political actors in the international scene (for example, the United States, Russia, or China) *tend to act unilaterally, putting their national interest first, without concern for the destabilization of the world at large.* So doing, they jeopardize their own security as well, because their unilateral actions in the context of a globally interdependent world induce systemic chaos (for example, the connection between the Iraq War, tensions with Iran, the intensification of war in Afghanistan, the rise of oil prices, and the global economic downturn). As long as these geopolitical contradictions persist, the world cannot shift from a pragmatic, ad hoc networking form of negotiated decision-making to a system of constitutionally founded, networked, global governance.

In the last resort, it is only the power of global civil society acting on the public mind via the media and communication networks that may eventually overcome the historical inertia of nation-states and thus bring these nation-states to accept the reality of their limited power in exchange for increasing their legitimacy and efficiency.

Power in the Networks

I have now assembled the necessary analytical elements to address the question that constitutes the central theme of this book: where does power lie in the global network society? To approach the question, I must first differentiate between four distinct forms of power:

- networking power;
- network power;
- networked power;
- and network-making power.

Each one of these forms of power defines specific processes of exercising power.

Networking power refers to the power of the actors and organizations included in the networks that constitute the core of the global network society over human collectives or individuals who are *not* included in these global networks. This form of power operates by exclusion/inclusion. Tongia and Wilson (2007) have proposed a formal analysis that shows that the cost of exclusion from networks increases faster than the benefits of inclusion in the networks. This is because the value of being in the network increases exponentially with the size of the network, as proposed in 1976 by Metcalfe's Law. But, at the same time, the devaluation attached to exclusion from the network also increases exponentially, and at a faster rate than the increase in value of being in the network. *Network gatekeeping theory* has investigated the various processes by which nodes are included in or excluded from the network, showing the key role of gatekeeping capacity to enforce the collective power of some networks over others, or of a given network over disconnected social units (Barzilai-Nahon, 2008). Social actors may establish their power position by constituting a network that accumulates valuable resources and then by exercising their gate-keeping strategies to bar access to those who do not add value to the network or jeopardize the interests that are dominant in the network's programs.

Network power can be better understood in the conceptualization pro-posed by Grewal (2008) to theorize globalization from the perspective of network analysis. In this view, globalization involves social coordination between multiple networked actors. This coordination requires standards:

The standards that enable global coordination display what I call network power. The notion of network power consists in the joining of two ideas: first, that coordi-nating standards are more valuable when greater numbers of people use them, and second that this dynamic – which I describe as a form of power – can lead to the progressive elimination of the alternatives over which otherwise free choice can be collectively exercised...Emerging global standards...[provide] the solution to the problem of global coordination among diverse participants but it does so by elevating one solution above others and threatening the elimination of alternative solutions to the same problem.   (Grewal, 2008: 5)

Therefore, the standards or, in my terminology, protocols of communication determine the rules to be accepted once in the network. In this case, power is exercised not by exclusion from the networks, but by the imposition of the rules of inclusion. Of course, depending on the level of openness of the network, these rules may be negotiated between its components. But once the rules are set, they become compelling for all nodes in the network, as respect for these rules is what makes the network's existence as a communicative structure possible. Network power is the power of the standards of the network over its components, although this network power ultimately favors the interests of a specific set of social actors at the source of network formation and of the establishment of the standards (protocols of communication). The notion of the so-called "Washington consensus" as the operating principle of the global market economy illus-trates the meaning of network power.

Power in the Network Society

But who has power in the dominant networks? How does *networked power* operate? As I proposed above, power is the relational capacity to impose an actor's will over another actor's will on the basis of the structural capacity of domination embedded in the institutions of society. Following this definition, the question of power-holding in the networks of the network society could be either very simple or impossible to answer.

It is simple if we answer the question by analyzing the workings of each specific dominant network. Each network defines its own power relationships depending on its programmed goals. Thus, in global capitalism, the global financial market has the last word, and the IMF or rating financial agencies (for example, Moody's or Standard and Poor's) are the authoritative interpreters for ordinary mortals. The word is usually spoken in the language of the United States Treasury Department, the Federal Reserve Board, or Wall Street, with some German, French, Japanese, Chinese, or Oxbridge accents depending upon times and spaces. Or else, the power of the United States, in terms of state–military power, and, in more analytical terms, the power of any apparatus able to harness technological innovation and knowledge in the pursuit of military power, which has the material resources for large-scale investment in war-making capacity.

Yet, the question could become an analytical dead-end if we try to answer it one-dimensionally and attempt to determine the Source of Power as a single entity. Military power could not prevent a catastrophic financial crisis; in fact, it could provoke it, under certain conditions of irrational, defensive paranoia, and the destabilization of oil-producing countries. Or, global financial markets could become an Automaton, beyond the control of any major regulatory institution, because of the size, volume, and complexity of the flows of capital that circulate throughout its networks, and because of the dependence of its valuation criteria on unpredictable information turbulences. Political decision-making is said to be dependent on the media, but the media constitute a plural ground, however biased in ideological and political terms, and the process of media politics is highly complex (see Chapter 4). As for the capitalist class, it does have some power, but not power over everyone or everything: it is highly dependent on both the autonomous dynamics of global markets and on the decisions of governments in terms of regulations and policies. Finally, governments themselves are connected in complex networks of imperfect global governance, conditioned by the pressures of business and interest groups, obliged to negotiate with the media which translate government actions for their citizenries, and periodically assailed by social movements and expressions of resistance that do not recede easily to the back rooms at the end of history (Nye and Donahue, 2000; Price, 2002; Juris, 2008; Sirota, 2008). Yes, in some instances, such as in the US after 9/11, or in the areas of influence of Russia or China or Iran or Israel, governments may engage in unilateral actions that bring chaos to the international scene. But they do so at their peril (with us becoming the victims of collateral damage). Thus, geopolitical unilateralism ultimately gives way to the realities of our globally interdependent world. In sum, the states, even the most powerful states, have some power (mainly destructive power), but not The Power.

So, maybe the question of power, as traditionally formulated, does not make sense in the network society. But new forms of domination and determination are critical in shaping people's lives regardless of their will. So, there are power relationships at work, albeit in new forms and with new kinds of actors. And the most crucial forms of power follow the logic of *network-making power*. Let me elaborate.

In a world of networks, the ability to exercise control over others depends on two basic mechanisms: (1) *the ability to constitute network(s), and to program/reprogram the network(s) in terms of the goals assigned to the network*; and (2) *the ability to connect and ensure the cooperation of different networks by sharing common goals and combining resources, while fending off competition from other networks by setting up strategic cooperation.*

I call the holders of the first power position the *programmers*; I call the holders of the second power position the *switchers*. It is important to note that these programmers and switchers are certainly social actors, but not necessarily identified with one particular group or individual. More often than not these mechanisms operate at the interface between various social actors, defined in terms of their position in the social structure and in the organizational framework of society. Thus, I suggest that in many instances *the power holders are networks themselves*. Not abstract, unconscious networks, not automata: they are humans organized around their projects and interests. But they are not single actors (individuals, groups, classes, religious leaders, political leaders), since the exercise of power in the network society requires a complex set of joint action that goes beyond alliances to become a new form of subject, akin to what Bruno Latour (2005) has brilliantly theorized as the "actor-network."

Let us examine the workings of these two mechanisms of power-making in the networks: programming and switching. The *programming* capacity of the goals of the network (as well as the capacity to reprogram it) is, of course, decisive because, once programmed, the network will perform efficiently, and reconfigure itself in terms of structure and nodes to achieve its goals. How different actors program the network is a process specific to each network. The process is not the same in global finance as it is in military power, in scientific research, in organized crime, or in professional sports. Therefore, power relationships at the network level have to be identified and understood in terms specific to each network. However, all networks do share a common trait: *ideas, visions, projects, and frames generate the programs*. These are cultural materials. In the network society, culture is mostly embedded in the processes of communication, particularly in the electronic hypertext, with global multimedia business networks and the Internet at its core. So, ideas may be generated from a variety of origins, and linked to specific interests and subcultures (for example, neoclassical economics, religions, cultural identities, the worshipping of individual freedom, and the like). Yet, ideas are processed in society according to how they are represented in the realm of communication. And ultimately these ideas reach the constituencies of each network, depending on the constituencies' level of exposure to the processes of communication. Thus, control of, or influence on, the networks of communication, and the ability to create an effective process of communication and persuasion along the lines that favor the projects of the would-be programmers, are the key assets in the ability to program each network. In other words, the process of communication in society, and the organizations and networks that enact this process of communication, are the key fields where programming projects are formed, and where constituencies are built for these projects. They are the fields of power in the network society.

There is a second source of power: *the control of the connecting points between various strategic networks*. I call the holders of these positions the *switchers*. For instance, the connections between political leadership networks, media networks, scientific and technology networks, and military and security networks to assert a geopolitical strategy. Or, the connection between political networks and media networks to produce and diffuse specific political-ideological discourses. Or, the relationship between religious networks and political networks to advance a religious agenda in a secular society. Or, between academic networks and business networks to provide knowledge and legitimacy in exchange for resources for universities and jobs for their products (aka graduates). This is not the old boys network. These are specific interface systems that are set on a relatively stable basis as a way of articulating the actual operating system of society beyond the formal self-presentation of institutions and organizations.

However, I am not resurrecting the idea of a power elite. There is none. This is a simplified image of power in society whose analytical value is limited to some extreme cases. It is precisely because there is no unified power elite capable of keeping the programming and switching operations of all important networks under its control that more subtle, complex, and negotiated systems of power enforcement must be established. For these power relationships to be asserted, the programs of the dominant networks of society need to set compatible goals between these networks (for example, dominance of the market and social stability; military power and financial restraint; political representation and reproduction of capitalism; free expression and cultural control). And, they must be able, through the switching processes enacted by actor-networks, to communicate with each other, inducing synergy and limiting contradiction. This is why it is so important that media tycoons do not become political leaders, as in the case of Berlusconi. Or that governments do not have total control over the media. The more the switchers are crude expressions of single-purpose domination, the more power relationships in the network society suffocate the dynamism and initiative of its multiple sources of social structuration and social change. Switchers are not persons, but they are made of persons. They are actors, made of networks of actors engaging in dynamic interfaces that are specifically operated in each process of connection. *Programmers and switchers* are those actors and networks of actors who, because of their position in the social structure, hold *network-making power*, the paramount form of *power in the network society*.

Power and Counterpower in the Network Society

Processes of power-making must be seen from two perspectives: on one hand, these processes can enforce existing domination or seize structural positions of domination; on the other hand, there also exist countervailing processes that resist established domination on behalf of the interests, values, and projects that are excluded or under-represented in the programs and composition of the networks. Analytically, both processes ultimately configure the structure of power through their interaction. They are distinct, but they do, however, operate on the same logic. This means that resistance to power is achieved through the same two mechanisms that constitute power in the network society: the programs of the networks, and the switches between networks. Thus, collective action from social movements, under their different forms, aims to introduce new instructions and new codes into the networks' programs. For instance, new instructions for global financial networks mean that under conditions of extreme poverty, debt should be condoned for some countries, as demanded, and partially obtained, by the Jubilee movement. Another example of new codes in the global financial networks is the project of evaluating company stocks according to their environmental ethics or their respect for human rights in the hope that this will ultimately impact the attitude of investors and shareholders vis-à-vis companies deemed to be good or bad citizens of the planet. Under these conditions, the code of economic calculation shifts from growth potential to sustainable growth potential. More radical reprogramming comes from resistance movements aimed at altering the fundamental principle of a network – or the kernel of the program code, if you allow me to keep the parallel with software language. For instance, if God's will must prevail under all conditions (as in the statement of Christian fundamentalists), the institutional networks that constitute the legal and judicial system must be reprogrammed not to follow the political constitution, legal prescriptions, or government decisions (for example, letting women make decisions about their bodies and pregnancies), but to submit them to the interpretation of God by his earthly bishops. In another instance, when the movement for global justice demands the re-writing of the trade agreements managed by the World Trade Organization to include environmental conservation, social rights, and the respect of indigenous minorities, it acts to modify the programs under which the networks of the global economy work.

The second mechanism of resistance consists of blocking the switches of connection between networks that allow the networks to be controlled by the metaprogram of values that express structural domination – for instance, by filing law suits or by influencing the US Congress in order to undo the connection between oligopolistic media business and government by challenging the rules of the US Federal Communication Commission that allow greater concentration of ownership. Other forms of resistance include blocking the networking between corporate business and the political system by regulating campaign finance or by spotlighting the incompatibility between being Vice-President and receiving income from one's former company that is benefiting from military contracts. Or by opposing intellectual servitude to the powers that be, which occurs when academics use their chairs as platforms for propaganda. More radical disruption of the switchers affects the material infrastructure of the network society: the material and psychological attacks on air transportation, on computer networks, on information systems, and on the networks of facilities on which the livelihood of societies depend in the highly complex, interdependent system that characterizes the informational world. The challenge of terrorism is precisely predicated on this capacity to target strategic material switches so that their disruption, or the threat of their disruption, disorganizes people's daily lives and forces them to live under emergency – thus feeding the growth of other power networks, the security networks, which extend to every domain of life. There is, indeed, a symbiotic relationship between the disruption of strategic switches by resistance actions and the reconfiguration of power networks toward a new set of switches organized around security networks.

Resistance to power programmed in the networks also takes place through and by networks. These are also information networks powered by information and communication technologies (Arquilla and Rondfeldt, 2001). The improperly labeled "anti-globalization movement" is a global–local network organized and debated on the Internet, and structurally switched on with the media network (see Chapter 5). *Al-Qaeda*, and its related organizations, is a network made of multiple nodes, with little central coordination, and also directly aimed at their switching with the media networks, through which they hope to inflict fear among the infidels and raise hope among the oppressed masses of the believers (Gunaratna, 2002; Seib, 2008). The environmental movement is a locally rooted, globally connected network which aims to change the public mind as a means of influencing policy decisions to save the planet or one's own neighborhood (see Chapter 5).

A central characteristic of the network society is that both the dynamics of domination and the resistance to domination rely on network formation and network strategies of offense and defense. Indeed, this tracks the historical experience of previous types of societies, such as the industrial society. The factory and the large, vertically organized, industrial corporation were the material basis for the development of both corporate capital and the labor movement. Similarly, today, computer networks for global financial markets, transnational production systems, "smart" armed forces with a global reach, terrorist resistance networks, the global civil society, and networked social movements struggling for a better world, are all components of the global network society. The conflicts of our time are fought by networked social actors aiming to reach their constituencies and target audiences through the decisive switch to multimedia communication networks.

In the network society, power is redefined, but it does not vanish. Nor do social struggles. Domination and resistance to domination change in character according to the specific social structure from which they originate and which they modify through their action. Power rules, counterpowers fight. Networks process their contradictory programs while people try to make sense of the sources of their fears and hopes.

Conclusion: Understanding Power Relationships in the Global Network Society

The sources of social power in our world – violence and discourse, coercion and persuasion, political domination and cultural framing – have not changed fundamentally from our historical experience, as theorized by some of the leading thinkers on power. But the terrain where power relationships operate has changed in two major ways: it is primarily constructed around the articulation between the global and the local; and it is primarily organized around networks, not single units. Because networks are multiple, power relationships are specific to each network. But there is a fundamental form of exercising power that is common to all networks: exclusion from the network. This is also specific to each network: a person, or group, or territory can be excluded from one network but included in others. However, because the key, strategic networks are global, there is one form of exclusion – thus, of power – that is pervasive in a world of networks: to include everything valuable in the global while excluding the devalued local. There are citizens of the world, living in the space of flows, versus the locals, living in the space of places. Because space in the network society is configured around the opposition between the space of flows (global) and the space of places (local), the spatial structure of our society is a major source of the structuration of power relationships.

So is time. Timeless time, the time of the network society, has no past and no future. Not even the short-term past. It is the cancellation of sequence, thus of time, by either the compression or blurring of the sequence. So, power relationships are constructed around the opposition between timeless time and all other forms of time. Timeless time, which is the time of the short "now," with no sequence or cycle, is the time of the powerful, of those who saturate their time to the limit because their activity is so valuable. And time is compressed to the nano-second for those for whom time is money. The time of history, and of historical identities, fades in a world in which only immediate gratification matters, and where the end of history is proclaimed by the bards of the victors. But the clock time of Taylorism is still the lot of most workers, and the *longue durée* time of those who envision what may happen to the planet is the time of alternative projects that refuse to submit to the domination of accelerated cycles of instrumental time. Interestingly, there is also a mythical "future time" of the powerful which is the projected time of the futurologists of the corporate world. In fact, this is the ultimate form of conquering time. It is colonizing the future by extrapolating the dominant values of the present in the projections: how to do the same, with increased profit and power, twenty years from now. The ability to project one's own current time, while denying the past and the future for humankind at large, is another form of establishing timeless time as a form of asserting power in the network society.

But how is power exercised within the networks and by the networks for those who are included in the core networks that structure society? I will consider first the contemporary forms of exercising power through the monopoly of violence and then through the construction of meaning by disciplinary discourses.

First, because networks are global, the state, which is the enforcer of power through the monopoly of violence, finds considerable limits to its coercive capacity unless it engages itself in networking with other states, and with the power-holders in the decisive networks that shape social practices in their territories while being deployed in the global realm. Therefore, the ability to connect different networks and restore some kind of boundary within which the state retains its capacity to intervene becomes paramount to the reproduction of the domination institutionalized in the state. But the ability to set up the connection is not necessarily in the hands of the state. The power of the switch is held by the switchers, social actors of different kinds who are defined by the context in which specific networks have to be connected for specific purposes. Of course, states can still bomb, imprison, and torture. But unless they find ways to bring together several strategic networks interested in the benefits of the state's capacity to exercise violence, the full exercise of their coercive power is usually short-lived. Stable domination, providing the basis for the enforcement of power relationships in each network, requires a complex negotiation to set up partnerships with the states, or with the network state, that contribute to enhancing the goals assigned to each network by its respective programs.

Second, discourses of power provide substantive goals for the programs of the networks. Networks process the cultural materials that are constructed in the variegated discursive realm. These programs are geared toward the fulfillment of certain social interests and values. But to be effective in programming the networks, they need to rely on a metaprogram that ensures that the recipients of the discourse internalize the categories through which they find meaning for their own actions in accordance with the programs of the networks. This is particularly important in a context of global networks because the cultural diversity of the world has to be overlaid with some common frames that relate to the discourses conveying the shared interests of each global network. In other words, there is a need to produce a global culture that adds to specific cultural identities, rather than superseding them, to enact the programs of networks that are global in their reach and purpose. For globalization to exist, it has to assert a disciplinary discourse capable of framing specific cultures (Lash and Lury, 2007).

Thus, switching and programming the global networks are the forms of exercising power in our global network society. Switching is enacted by switchers; programming is accomplished by programmers. Who the switchers are and who the programmers are in each network is specific to the network and cannot be determined without investigation in each particular case.

Resisting programming and disrupting switching in order to defend alternative values and interests are the forms of counterpower enacted by social movements and civil society – local, national, and global – with the difficulty that the networks of power are usually global, while the resistance of counterpower is usually local. How to reach the global from the local, through networking with other localities – how to "grassroot" the space of flows – becomes the key strategic question for the social movements of our age.

The specific means of switching and programming largely determine the forms of power and counterpower in the network society. Switching different networks requires the ability to construct a cultural and organizational interface, a common language, a common medium, a support of universally accepted value: exchange value. In our world, the typical, all-purpose form of exchange value is money. It is through this common currency that power-sharing is most often measured between different networks. This standard of measurement is essential because it removes the decisive role of the state, since the appropriation of value by all networks becomes dependent on financial transactions. This does not mean that capitalists control everything. It simply means that whoever has enough money, including political leaders, will have a better chance of operating the switch in its favor. But, as in the capitalist economy, besides monetized transactions, barter can also be used: an exchange of services between networks (for example, regulatory power in exchange for political funding from businesses, or leveraging media access for political influence). So, switching power depends on the capacity to generate exchange value, be it through money or through barter.

There is a second major source of power: networks' programming capacity. This capacity ultimately depends on the ability to generate, diffuse, and affect the discourses that frame human action. Without this discursive capacity, the programming of specific networks is fragile, and depends solely on the power of the actors entrenched in the institutions. Discourses, in our society, shape the public mind via one specific technology: communication networks that organize socialized communication. Because the public mind – that is, the set of values and frames that have broad exposure in society – is ultimately what influences individual and collective behavior, programming the communication networks is the decisive source of cultural materials that feed the programmed goals of any other network. Furthermore, because communication networks connect the local with the global, the codes diffused in these networks have a global reach.

Alternative projects and values put forward by the social actors aiming to reprogram society must also go through the communication networks to transform consciousness and views in people's minds in order to challenge the powers that be. And it is only by acting on global discourses through the global communication networks that they can affect power relationships in the global networks that structure all societies. In the last resort, the power of programming conditions switching power because the programs of the networks determine the range of possible interfaces in the switching process. Discourses frame the options of what networks can or cannot do. In the network society, discourses are generated, diffused, fought over, internalized, and ultimately embodied in human action, in the socialized communication realm constructed around local–global networks of multi-modal, digital communication, including the media and the Internet. Power in the network society is communication power.

Chapter 2

Communication in the Digital Age

A Communication Revolution?

Communication is the sharing of meaning through the exchange of information. The process of communication is defined by the technology of communication, the characteristics of the senders and receivers of information, their cultural codes of reference and protocols of communication, and the scope of the communication process. Meaning can only be understood in the context of the social relationships in which information and communication are processed (Schiller, 2007: 18). I shall elaborate on the elements of this definition in the context of the global network society.

Beginning with the *scope of the process* itself, interpersonal communication must be differentiated from societal communication. In the former, the designated sender(s) and receiver(s) are the subjects of communication. In the latter, the content of communication has the potential to be diffused to society at large: this is what is usually called *mass communication*. Interpersonal communication is interactive (the message is sent from one to one with feedback loops), while mass communication can be interactive or one-directional. Traditional mass communication is one-directional (the message is sent from one to many, as with books, newspapers, films, radio, and television). To be sure, some forms of interactivity can be accommodated in mass communication via other means of communication. For example, viewers can comment on talk radio or television programs by calling in, writing letters, and sending e-mails. Yet, mass communication used to be predominantly one-directional. However, with the diffusion of the Internet, a new form of interactive communication has emerged, characterized by the capacity of sending messages from many to many, in real time or chosen time, and with the possibility of using point-to-point communication, narrowcasting or broadcasting, depending on the purpose and characteristics of the intended communication practice.

I call this historically new form of communication *mass self-communication*. It is mass communication because it can potentially reach a global audience, as in the posting of a video on YouTube, a blog with RSS links to a number of web sources, or a message to a massive e-mail list. At the same time, it is self-communication because the production of the message is self-generated, the definition of the potential receiver(s) is self-directed, and the retrieval of specific messages or content from the World Wide Web and electronic communication networks is self-selected. The three forms of communication (interpersonal, mass communication, and mass self-communication) coexist, interact, and complement each other rather than substituting for one another. What is historically novel, with considerable consequences for social organization and cultural change, is the articulation of all forms of communication into a composite, interactive, digital hypertext that includes, mixes, and recombines *in their diversity* the whole range of cultural expressions conveyed by human interaction. Indeed, the most important dimension of communication convergence, as Jenkins writes, "occurs within the brains of individual consumers and through their social interaction with others" (2006: 3).

Yet, for this convergence to have happened, a number of critical transformations had to take place in each one of the dimensions of the communication process, as defined above. These various dimensions constitute a system, and one transformation cannot be understood without the others. Together, they form the background of what Mansell (2002) and McChesney (2007) have labeled a "communication revolution," what Cowhey and Aronson (2009) characterize as "the inflection point," or what, some time ago, Rice et al. (1984) identified as the emergence of new media through the interaction of technological change and communication. For the sake of clarity, I will examine the transformations under way separately, without implying any causality in the order of my presentation. Then I will analyze their interaction.

First, there is a *technological transformation* that is based on the digitization of communication, computer networking, advanced software, the diffusion of enhanced broadband transmission capacity, and ubiquitous local/global communication via wireless networks, increasingly with Internet access.

Secondly, the definition of senders and receivers refers to *the organizational and institutional structure of communication*, particularly of societal communication, where the senders and receivers are the media and their so-called audience (people who are identified as consumers of media). A fundamental transformation has taken place in this realm in the past two decades:

- widespread commercialization of the media in most of the world;
- globalization and concentration of media business through conglomeration and networking;
- the segmentation, customization, and diversification of media markets, with emphasis on the cultural identification of the audience;
- the formation of multimedia business groups that reach out to all forms of communication, including, of course, the Internet;
- and increasing business convergence between telecommunication companies, computer companies, Internet companies, and media companies.

The formation of these global multimedia business networks was made possible by public policies and institutional changes characterized by liberalization, privatization, and regulated deregulation, nationally and internationally, in the wake of the pro-market government policies that have become pervasive throughout the world since the 1980s.

Thirdly, the *cultural dimension of the process of multilayered transformation of communication* can be grasped at the intersection between two pairs of contradictory (but not incompatible) trends: the parallel development of a global culture and multiple identity cultures; and the simultaneous rise of individualism and communalism as two opposing, yet equally powerful, cultural patterns that characterize our world (Norris, 2000; Castells, 2004c; Baker, 2005; Rantanen, 2005). The ability or inability to generate protocols of communication between these contradictory cultural frames defines the possibility of communication or miscommunication between the subjects of diverse communication processes. The media, from culturally diverse television broadcasting (for example, Al Jazeera in Arabic/English or CNN American/International/CNN en Español) to Web 2.0, may be the protocols of communication that either bridge cultural divides or further fragment our societies into autonomous cultural islands and trenches of resistance.

Lastly, each one of the components of the great communication transformation represents *the expression of the social relationships, ultimately power relationships, that underlie the evolution of the multimodal communication system.* This is most apparent in the persistence of the digital divide between countries and within countries, depending on their consumer power and their level of communication infrastructure. Even with growing access to the Internet and to wireless communication, abysmal inequality in broadband access and educational gaps in the ability to operate a digital culture tend to reproduce and amplify the class, ethnic, race, age, and gender structures of social domination between countries and within countries (Wilson, 2004; Galperin and Mariscal, 2007; Katz, 2008; Rice, 2008). The growing influence of corporations in the media, information, and communication industries over the public regulatory institutions may shape the communication revolution in the service of business interests. The influence of the advertising industry over media business via the transformation of people into a measurable audience tends to subordinate cultural innovation or entertainment pleasure to commercial consumerism. Freedom of expression and communication on the Internet and in the global/local multimedia system is often curtailed and surveilled by government bureaucracies, political elites, and ideological/religious apparatuses. Privacy is long forgone in a flurry of "cookies" and personal data-retrieving strategies, with the partial exception of those users with a high level of technical sophistication (Whitaker, 1999; Solove, 2004).

Yet, at the same time, *social actors and individual citizens around the world are using the new capacity of communication networking to advance their projects, to defend their interests, and to assert their values* (Downing, 2003; Juris, 2008; Costanza-Chock, forthcoming a). Furthermore, they have become increasingly aware of the crucial role of the new multimedia system and its regulatory institutions in the culture and politics of society. Thus, we are witnessing in some areas of the world, and particularly in the United States, social and political mobilizations aiming to establish a degree of citizen control over the controllers of communication and assert their right to freedom in the communication space (Couldry and Curran, 2003; Klinenberg, 2007; McChesney, 2007, 2008).

So, *the new field of communication in our time is emerging through a process of multidimensional change shaped by conflicts rooted in the contradictory structure of interests and values that constitute society.* Next, I identify in more precise terms the process of change in each one of these dimensions that, together, define the transformation of communication in the digital age.

Technological Convergence and the New Multimedia System: From Mass Communication to Mass Self-communication

A process called "the convergence of modes" is blurring the lines between the media, even between point-to-point communication, such as the post, telephone, and telegraph, and mass communications, such as the press, radio and television. A single physical means – be it wires, cables or airwaves – may carry services that in the past were provided in separate ways. Conversely, a service that was provided in the past by any one medium – be it broadcasting, the press, or telephony – can be provided in several different physical ways. So the one-to-one relationship that used to exist between the medium and its use is eroding.

(Ithiel de Sola Pool, 1983, cited by Jenkins, 2006: 10)

The trend identified in 1983 by Ithiel de Sola Pool's pioneering work is now a reality that has redesigned the communication landscape. It is hardly surprising that the emergence in the 1970s of a new technological paradigm based on information and communication technologies would have a decisive influence in the realm of communication (Freeman, 1982; Perez, 1983; Castells, 2000c; Mansell and Steinmueller, 2000; Wilson, 2004). From the technological point of view, telecommunication networks, computer networks, and broadcasting networks converged on the basis of digital networking and new data transmission and storage technologies, particularly optic fiber, satellite communication, and advanced software (Cowhey and Aronson, 2009).

However, different technologies and business models, supported by the policies of regulatory agencies, induced various transformative trends in each of the components of the communication system. Throughout the 1980s and 1990s, broadcasting evolved along a trajectory that emphasized continuity in the form of communication, while increasing the diversity of delivery platforms and the concentration of media ownership (Hesmond-halgh, 2007). Broadcasting and the print press remained, by and large, mass media. By contrast, computer networking and telecommunications rapidly exploited the potential of digitization and open source software to generate new forms of local/global interactive communication, often initiated by the users of the networks (Benkler, 2006). Technological and organizational convergence between the two systems began to take place in the first decade of the twenty-first century and led to the gradual formation of a new multimedia system (Jenkins, 2006).

Mutant Television: The Eternal Companion

Since the early 1990s, television, the archetypical medium of mass communication, has escaped the limits of spectrum allocation by developing new forms of broadcasting via cable and satellite transmission. The medium has gone from a highly centralized one-way communication system, based on a limited number of networks of stations, to a highly diverse and decentralized broadcasting system based on enhanced transmission capacity (Croteau and Hoynes, 2006). Digital technologies allowed for the multiplication of the number of channels that could be received (Galperin, 2004). While digital television enhances the capacity of the medium by freeing up spectrum, it only began operating in most advanced countries in the period 2009–2012. Yet, even before the advent of digital television, there was an explosion of television channels and diverse television programming throughout the world. In 2007, the average American home had access to 104 television channels, 16 more than in 2006 and 43 more than in 2000 (Nielsen, 2007).[3] According to the European Audiovisual Observatory, in European OECD countries the total number of available television channels (including terrestrial, broadcasting, and satellite) rose from 816 in 2004 to 1,165 in 2006, an increase of 43 percent (OECD, 2007: 175). Incomplete data for the world at large show similar increases (Sakr, 2001; Hafez, 2005; Rai and Cottle, 2007).

Television penetration has also held steady in the US at 98 percent for the past 20 years. In Europe, the number of households with television access grew from 1,162,490.4 in 2002 to 1,340,201.3 in 2007 (Euromonitor, 2007). The number of hours of television viewing has grown steadily in most countries. In the US, the average household spent 57 hours and 37 minutes watching television each week in 2006, an increase of 20 minutes from 2005, and nearly 10 hours since Nielsen began using "people meters" two decades ago (Mandese, 2007). And between 1997 and 2005 the amount of time dedicated to television viewing by the average viewer increased in almost all OECD countries (except for New Zealand, Spain, and South Korea; OECD, 2007: 176). So, television is alive and well, and

---

[3] But the number of channels actually tuned in to by the average household in America remained about the same, moving to 15.7 in 2006 from 15.4 in 2005 and 15.0 in 2004, the first year for which Nielsen reports that statistic (Mandese, 2007).

remains the foremost mass communication medium in the early twenty-first century. What has changed is television's fragmentation into multiple channels, often targeted to specific audiences, in a practice of narrowcasting that tends to increase cultural differentiation in the mass media world (Turow, 2005). Furthermore, the practice of digital video recording and computerized programming of television viewing, with the introduction of devices such as TIVO, has individualized and customized the reception of programming. So, television remains a mass communication medium from the perspective of the sender, but it is often a personal communication medium from the point of view of the receiver. The growing capacity to control the reception of television includes software able to program recordings and skip advertising, a fundamental threat to the main source of revenue for television broadcasting.

Thus, although television is still the dominant medium of mass communication, it has been profoundly transformed by technology, business, and culture, to the point that it can now be better understood as a medium that combines mass broadcasting with mass narrowcasting. In 1980, an average of 40 percent of US television households tuned in to one of the three major network news broadcasts on a given night. By 2006, this number had declined to 18.2 percent (Project for Excellence in Journalism, 2007).[4] According to Nielsen Media Research, by 2006 more than 85 percent of US households had utilized cable or satellite television, up from 56 percent in 1990. The primetime audience for broadcast television (8–11 p.m.) fell from 80 percent in 1990 to 56 percent in 2006 (Standard and Poor, 2007a).

However, while the new technological infrastructure and the development of cable and satellite broadcasting increased product customization and targeted segmentation of the audience, the vertical integration of local television stations in national networks owned by major corporations (as in the United States, but also in Italy, India, Australia, and elsewhere) induced growing standardization of content under the semblance of differentiation (Chatterjee, 2004; Bosetti, 2007; Flew, 2007; Hesmondhalgh, 2007; Schiller, 2007; Campo Vidal, 2008). Thus, Eric Klinenberg (2007), in his path-breaking study of the political debates surrounding the transformation of the media in the United States, has documented how local affiliates of television networks saw their ability to decide on the content of their programming diminish, and were compelled to broadcast products that

---

[4] However, according to Nielsen Media Research, despite the rapid increase in the number of available channels, the average consumer only watches 15 channels per week (OECD, 2007: 175).

were centrally produced, often on the basis of largely automated systems, including "local" weather reports presented in a familiar tone by reporters who have never been to the locality on which they were reporting.

Radio: Networking the Imagined Locality

Radio, the medium of mass communication most adaptable to individual schedules and audience locations during the twentieth century, followed a similar path of vertical integration. Technological change, under the conditions of ownership concentration, has led to a growing control of local content by centralized studios that serve the entire network. Digital recording and editing allow for the integration of local radio stations in corporate national networks. Most of the content of local news is, in fact, not local, and some "exclusive" investigative reporting is a generic program tailored to the context of each audience. Automated music broadcasting on the basis of pre-recorded catalogues brings radio stations closer to the iPod model of music on demand. Here again, the potential for customization and differentiation allowed by digital technologies was used to disguise central production of locally distributed products customized for specific audiences on the basis of marketing models. In the United States before the Telecommunications Act of 1996 removed many of the restrictions on ownership concentration, there were more than 10,400 individually owned commercial radio stations (see below). During 1996–8, the total number of station owners was reduced by 700. In the two years that followed the passing of the Act in Congress, corporate groups bought and sold more than 4,400 radio stations and established major national networks with an oligopolistic presence in the largest metropolitan areas. Thus, technologies of freedom and their potential for diversification do not necessarily lead to differentiation of programming and localization of content; rather, they allow for the falsification of identity in an effort to combine centralized control and decentralized delivery as an effective business strategy (Klinenberg, 2007: 27).

The Rise of the Internet and Wireless Communication

Computer networking, open source software (including Internet protocols), and the fast development of digital switching and transmission capacity in telecommunication networks led to the dramatic expansion of the Internet after its privatization in the 1990s. The Internet is, in fact, an old technology: it was first deployed in 1969. But it diffused on a large scale 20 years later because of several factors: regulatory changes, greater bandwidth in telecommunications, the diffusion of personal computers, user-friendly software programs that made it easy to upload, access, and communicate content (beginning with the World Wide Web server and browser in 1990), and the rapidly growing social demand for the networking of everything, arising both from the needs of the business world and from the public's desire to build its own communication networks (Abbate, 1999; Castells, 2001; Benkler, 2006).

As a result, the number of Internet users on the planet grew from under 40 million in 1995 to about 1.4 billion in 2008. By 2008, rates of penetration had reached more than 60 percent in most developed countries and were increasing at a fast rate in developing countries (Center for the Digital Future, various years). Global Internet penetration in 2008 was still at around one-fifth of the world's population, and fewer than 10 percent of Internet users had access to broadband. However, since 2000, the digital divide, measured in terms of access, has been shrinking. The ratio between Internet access in OECD and developing countries fell from 80.6:1 in 1997 to 5.8:1 in 2007. In 2005, almost twice as many new Internet users were added in developing countries as in OECD countries (ITU, 2007). China is the country with the fastest growth in the number of Internet users, even though the penetration rate remained under 20 percent of the population in 2008. As of July 2008, the number of Internet users in China totaled 253 million, surpassing the United States, with about 223 million users (CNNIC, 2008). OECD countries as a whole had a rate of penetration of around 65 percent of their populations in 2007. Furthermore, given the huge disparity in Internet use between people aged over 60 years and those under 30, the proportion of Internet users will undoubtedly reach near saturation point in developed countries and increase substantially throughout the world as my generation fades away.

From the 1990s onward, another communication revolution took place worldwide: the explosion of wireless communication, with increasing capacity of connectivity and bandwidth in successive generations of mobile phones (Castells et al., 2006b; Katz, 2008). This has been the fastest diffusing communication technology in history. In 1991, there were about 16 million wireless phone subscriptions in the world. By July 2008, subscriptions had surpassed 3.4 billion, or about 52 percent of the world's population. Using a conservative multiplier factor (babies do not use mobile phones [yet], and in poor countries, families and villages share one subscription), we can safely evaluate that over 60 percent of the people on this planet have access to wireless communication in 2008, even if this is highly constrained by income. Indeed, studies in China, Latin America, and Africa have shown that poor people give high priority to their communication needs and use a substantial proportion of their meager budget to fulfill them (Qiu, 2007; Katz, 2008; Sey, 2008; Wallis, 2008). In developed countries, the rate of penetration of wireless subscriptions ranges from 82.4 percent (the US) to 102 percent (Italy or Spain) and is moving toward saturation point.

There is a new round of technological convergence featuring Internet and wireless communication, including Wi-Fi and WiMAX networks, and multiple applications that distribute communicative capacity throughout wireless networks, thus multiplying points of access to the Internet. This is particularly important for the developing world because the growth rate of Internet penetration has slowed due to the scarcity of wired telephone lines. In the new model of telecommunications, wireless communication has become the predominant form of communication everywhere, particularly in developing countries. In 2002, the number of wireless subscribers surpassed fixed-line subscribers worldwide. Thus, the ability to connect to the Internet from a wireless device becomes the critical factor for a new wave of Internet diffusion on the planet. This is largely dependent on the building of wireless infrastructure, on the new protocols for wireless Internet, and on the diffusion of advanced broadband capacity. From the 1980s, transmission capacity in telecommunication networks expanded substantially. The global leaders in broadband width and deployment are South Korea, Singapore, and The Netherlands. The world at large has a long way to go to reach their level. However, the technological possibility of a global quasi-ubiquitous wireless broadband network already exists, thereby increasing the potential for multimodal communication of any kind of data in any kind of format from anyone to anyone and from everywhere to everywhere. For this global network to actually function, however, appropriate infrastructure has to be built and conducive regulation has to be implemented, nationally and internationally (Cowhey and Aronson, 2009).

Mass Self-communication

Note that our discussion has moved from broadcasting and mass media to communication in general. The Internet, the World Wide Web, and wireless communication are not media in the traditional sense. Rather, they are means of interactive communication. However, I argue, like most other analysts in the field, that the boundaries between mass media communication and all other forms of communication are blurring (Cardoso, 2006; Rice, 2008). E-mail is mostly a person-to-person form of communication, even when carbon-copying and mass-mailing are taken into account. But the Internet is much broader than that. The World Wide Web is a communication network used to post and exchange documents. These documents can be texts, audios, videos, software programs – literally anything that can be digitized. This is why it does not make sense to compare the Internet to television in terms of "audience," as is often the case in old-fashioned analyses of media. In fact, in the information economy, most of the time spent on the Internet is working time or study time (Castells et al., 2007). We do not "watch" the Internet as we watch television. In practice, Internet users (the majority of the population in advanced societies and a growing proportion of the third world) *live* with the Internet. As a considerable body of evidence has demonstrated, the Internet, in the diverse range of its applications, is the communication fabric of our lives, for work, for personal connection, for social networking, for information, for entertainment, for public services, for politics, and for religion (Katz and Rice, 2002; Wellman and Haythornthwaite, 2002; Center for the Digital Future, 2005, 2007, 2008; Cardoso, 2006; Castells and Tubella, 2007). We cannot carve entertainment or news out of this relentless use of the Internet and compare them to the mass media in terms of hours of "viewing" because working with the Internet includes occasional surfing of non-work-related web sites or the sending of personal e-mails as a result of widespread multitasking in the new informational environment (Montgomery, 2007; Katz, 2008; Tubella et al., 2008). Furthermore, the Internet is increasingly used to access mass media (television, radio, newspapers), as well as any form of digitized cultural or informational product (films, music, magazines, books, journal articles, databases).

The web has already transformed television. The teenagers interviewed by researchers at the USC Center for the Digital Future do not even understand the concept of watching television on someone else's schedule. They watch entire television programs on their computer screens and, increasingly, on portable devices. So, television continues to be a major mass medium, but its delivery and format are being transformed as its reception becomes individualized (Center for the Digital Future, "World

Internet Survey," various years; Cardoso, 2006). A similar phenomenon has taken place with the print press. All over the world, Internet users under 30 years of age primarily read newspapers online. So, although the newspaper remains a mass medium, its delivery platform changes. There is still no clear business model for online journalism (Beckett and Mansell, 2008). Yet, the Internet and digital technologies have transformed the work process of newspapers and the mass media at large. Newspapers have become internally networked organizations, globally connected to networks of information on the Internet. In addition, the online components of newspapers have induced networking and synergy with other news and media organizations (Weber, 2007). Newsrooms in the newspaper, television, and radio industries have been transformed by the digitization of news and its relentless global/local processing (Boczkowski, 2005). So, mass communication in the traditional sense is now also Internet-based communication in both its production and its delivery.

Furthermore, the combination of online news with interactive blogging and e-mail, as well as RSS feeds from other documents on the web, have transformed newspapers into a component of a different form of communication: what I have conceptualized above as *mass self-communication*. This form of communication has emerged with the development of the so-called Web 2.0 and Web 3.0, or the cluster of technologies, devices, and applications that support the proliferation of social spaces on the Internet thanks to increased broadband capacity, innovative open-source software, and enhanced computer graphics and interface, including avatar interaction in three-dimensional virtual spaces.

The diffusion of Internet, wireless communication, digital media, and a variety of tools of social software has prompted the development of horizontal networks of interactive communication that connect local and global in chosen time. With the convergence between Internet and wireless communication and the gradual diffusion of greater broadband capacity, the communicating and information-processing power of the Internet is being distributed to all realms of social life, just as the electric grid and the electric engine distributed energy in industrial society (Hughes, 1983; Benkler, 2006; Castells and Tubella, 2007). As people (the so-called users) have appropriated new forms of communication, they have built their own systems of mass communication, via SMS, blogs, vlogs, podcasts, wikis, and the like (Cardoso, 2006; Gillespie, 2007; Tubella et al., 2008). File-sharing and p2p (i.e., peer-to-peer) networks make the circulation, mixing, and reformatting of any digitized content possible. In February 2008, Technorati tracked 112.8 million blogs and over 250 million pieces of tagged social media, up from 4 million blogs in October 2004. On average, according to the information collected within a 60-day time frame, 120,000 new blogs are created, 1.5 million posts are published, and approximately 60 million blogs are updated per day (Baker, 2008). The so-called blogosphere is a multilingual and international communication space. Although English dominated the early stages of blog development, by April 2007 only 36 percent of blog posts were in English, while 37 percent were in Japanese, and 8 percent were in Chinese. The majority of other blog posts were divided between Spanish (3%), Italian (3%), Russian (2%), French (2%), Portuguese (2%), German (1%), and Farsi (1%) (Sifry, 2007; Baker, 2008). Blogs are becoming an important domain of self-expression for Chinese youth (Dong, 2008a). A more accurate accounting of Chinese blogs would probably raise the proportion of Chinese in the blogosphere closer to that of the English or Japanese languages.

Around the world, most blogs are personal in nature. According to the Pew Internet and American Life Project, 52 percent of bloggers say that they blog mostly for themselves, while 32 percent blog for their audience (Lenhart and Fox, 2006: iii).[5] Thus, to some extent, *a significant share of this form of mass self-communication is closer to "electronic autism" than to actual communication*. Yet, any post on the Internet, regardless of the intention of the author, becomes a bottle drifting in the ocean of global communication, a message susceptible to being received and reprocessed in unexpected ways.

Revolutionary forms of mass self-communication have originated from the ingenuity of young users-turned-producers. One example is YouTube, a video-sharing web site where individual users, organizations, companies, and governments can upload their own video content.[6] Founded in 2005 by Jawed Karim, Steven Chen, and Chad Hurley,[7] three Americans who met while working together at PayPal, the American version of YouTube hosted 69,800,000 videos as of February 2008. For instance, during November 2007, 74.5 million people viewed 2.9 billion videos on YouTube.com (39

---

[5] Moreover, according to the same Pew survey, only 11 percent of new blogs are about politics (Lenhart and Fox, 2006: ii–iii).

[6] However, the Pew Internet Project also found that users overwhelmingly prefer professional video content (62%) compared to only 19% who prefer amateur content and 11% who have no preference (Madden, 2007: 7). As more and more media companies distribute their video content online, the trend seems to be moving away from user-generated video content (though this may be temporary).

[7] Jawed Karim is originally from Germany but moved to the US at the age of 13; Steven Chen moved to the US from Taiwan at the age of 8.

videos per viewer; ComScore, 2008). Moreover, national and international broadcasters such as Al Jazeera, CNN, Kenya's NTV, France 24, Catalan TV3, and numerous other media outlets maintain their own YouTube channel in order to build new audiences and connect interested members of their diasporas. Additionally, in July 2007, YouTube also launched 18 country-specific partner sites and a site specifically designed for mobile telephone users. This made YouTube the largest mass communication medium in the world. Web sites emulating YouTube are proliferating on the Internet, including ifilm.com, revver.com, and Grouper.com. Tudou.com is China's most popular video-hosting web site and one of its fastest growing sites, attracting more than 6 million individual viewers per day in August 2007, a 175 percent increase over the number of individual viewers just three months earlier (Nielsen/NetRatings, 2007). Social-networking sites such as MySpace.com also offer the ability to upload video content. In fact, MySpace was, in 2008, the second largest video-sharing site on the web. In November 2007, 43.2 million people viewed 389 million videos on MySpace.com (ComScore, 2008). Video streaming is an increasingly popular form of media consumption and production. A Pew Internet and American Life Project study found that, in December 2007, 48 percent of American users regularly consumed online video, up from 33 percent a year earlier. This trend was more pronounced for users under 30 years of age, 70 percent of whom visit online video sites (Rainie, 2008: 2).

Thus, YouTube and other user-generated content web sites are means of mass communication. However, they are different from traditional mass media. Anyone can post a video on YouTube, with few restrictions. And the user selects the video she wants to watch and comment on from a huge list of possibilities. Pressures are, of course, exercised on free expression on YouTube, particularly legal threats for copyright infringements and government censorship of political content in situations of crisis. Yet, YouTube is so pervasive that the Queen of England chose to issue her 2007 Christmas broadcast on the site. Also, the televised debates of the 2008 United States presidential candidates and the 2008 Spanish parliamentary elections were simulcast on YouTube and supplemented by video posts from interacting citizens.

Horizontal networks of communication built around people's initiatives, interests, and desires are multimodal and incorporate many kinds of documents, from photographs (hosted by sites such as Photobucket.com, which had 60 million registered users in February 2008) and large-scale cooperative projects such as Wikipedia (the open-source encyclopedia with

26 million contributors, although only 75,000 are active contributors) to music and films (p2p networks based on free software programs such as Kazaa) and social/political/religious activist networks that combine web-based forums of debate with global feeding of video, audio, and text.

For teenagers who have the ability to generate and distribute content over the net, it "is not 15 minutes of fame they care about, it is about 15 megabytes of fame" (Jeffrey Cole, personal communication, July 2008). *Social spaces in the web*, building on the pioneering tradition of the virtual communities of the 1980s and overcoming the shortsighted early commercial forms of social space introduced by AOL, have multiplied in content and soared in numbers to form a diverse and widespread virtual society on the web. As of June 2008, MySpace (with 114 million users) and Facebook (with 123.9 million users) stood as the world's most successful web sites for social interaction for users across different age and social demographics (McCarthy, 2008). Online communities engage in a whole range of projects, such as, for instance, the Society for Creative Anachronism, with over 30,000 paying members in December 2007, an historical re-enactment virtual community founded in 1996. For millions of Internet users under 30, online communities have become a fundamental dimension of everyday life that keeps growing everywhere, including China and developing countries, and their growth has only been slowed by the limitations of bandwidth and access (Boyd, 2006a, b; Montgomery, 2007; Williams, 2007). With the prospects of expanding infrastructure and declining prices of communication, it is not a prediction but an observation to say that online communities are fast developing not as a virtual world, but as a real virtuality integrated with other forms of interaction in an increasingly hybridized everyday life (Center for the Digital Future, 2008).

A new generation of social software programs has made possible the explosion of *interactive computer and video games*, today a global industry valued at $40 billion. In the US alone, the video and computer gaming industry amassed 18.7 billion in sales in 2007. In its first day of release in September 2007, Sony's *Halo 3* earned 170 million dollars, more than the weekend gross of any Hollywood film to date.[8] The largest online game community, World of Warcraft (WOW), which accounts for just over half of the Massively Multiplayer Online Game (MMOG) industry, reached over 10 million active members (over half of whom reside in the Asian continent) in 2008. These members carefully organize themselves into hierarchical guilds

[8] www.boxofficemojo.com/alltime/weekends (retrieved August 5, 2008).

based on merit and affinity (Blizzard Entertainment, 2008). If the media are largely entertainment based, then this new form of entertainment, based entirely on the Internet and software programming, is now a major component of the media system.

New technologies are also fostering the development of *social spaces of virtual reality* that combine sociability and experimentation with role-playing games. The most successful of these is *Second Life* (Au, 2008). As of February 2008, it had about 12.3 million registered users and about 50,000 visitors at any point in time on an average day. For many observers, the most interesting trend among *Second Life* communities is their inability to create Utopia, even in the absence of institutional or spatial limitations. Residents of *Second Life* have reproduced some of the features of our society, including many of its pitfalls, such as aggression and rape. Furthermore, *Second Life* is privately owned by Linden Corporation, and virtual real estate soon became a profitable business, to the point that the United States Internal Revenue Service started to develop schemes to tax Linden dollars, which are convertible to US dollars. Yet this virtual space has such a communicative capacity that some universities have established campuses in *Second Life*; there are also experiments to use it as an educational platform; virtual banks open and go bankrupt following the ups and downs of the US markets; political demonstrations and even violent confrontations between leftists and rightists take place in the virtual city; and news stories within *Second Life* reach the real world through an increasingly attentive corps of media correspondents. Disaffected utopians are already leaving *Second Life*, to find freedom in another virtual land where they can start a new life, as wandering immigrants have always done in the physical world. In doing so, they are expanding the frontier of virtuality to the outer borders of interaction between different forms of our mental construction.

Wireless communication has become a delivery platform of choice for many kinds of digitized products, including games, music, images, and news, as well as instant messaging that covers the entire range of human activity, from personal support networks to professional tasks and political mobilizations. Thus, the grid of electronic communication overlies everything we do, wherever and whenever we do it (Ling, 2004; Koskinen, 2007). Studies show that the majority of mobile phone calls and messages originate from home, work, and school – the usual locations where people are, often with a fixed phone line. The key feature of wireless communication is not mobility but perpetual connectivity (Katz and Aakhus, 2002; Ito et al., 2005; Castells et al., 2006a; Katz, 2008).

Communication in the Digital Age

The growth of mass self-communication is not confined to the high end of technology. Grassroots organizations and pioneering individuals are using new forms of autonomous communication, such as low-power radio stations, pirate television stations, and independent video production practices that take advantage of the low-cost production and distribution capacity of digital video (Costanza-Chock, forthcoming a).

Certainly, mainstream media are using blogs and interactive networks to distribute their content and interact with their audience, mixing vertical and horizontal communication modes. But there are many examples in which the traditional media, such as cable TV, are fed by autonomous production of content using the digital capacity to produce and distribute many varieties of content. In the US, one of the best-known examples of this kind is Al Gore's Current TV, in which content originated by the users, and professionally edited, accounts for about 40 percent of the content of the station. Internet-based news media, largely based on user feeding information, such as Jinbonet and Ohmy News in South Korea or Vilaweb in Barcelona, have become relatively reliable and independent sources of information on a mass scale. Thus, the growing interaction between horizontal and vertical networks of communication does not mean that the mainstream media are taking over the new, autonomous forms of content generation and distribution. It means that there is a process of complementarity that gives birth to a new media reality whose contours and effects will ultimately be decided by political and business power struggles, as the owners of the telecommunication networks position themselves to control access and traffic in favor of their business partners and preferred customers (see below).

The growing interest of corporate media in Internet-based forms of communication recognizes the significance of the rise of a new form of societal communication, the one I have been referring to as *mass self-communication*. It is mass communication because it reaches a potentially global audience through p2p networks and Internet connection. It is multimodal, as the digitization of content and advanced social software, often based on open source programs that can be downloaded for free, allows the reformatting of almost any content in almost any form, increasingly distributed via wireless networks. *It is also self-generated in content, self-directed in emission, and self-selected in reception by many who communicate with many*. This is a new communication realm, and ultimately a new medium, whose backbone is made of computer networks, whose language is digital, and whose senders are globally distributed and globally interactive. True, the medium, even a medium as revolutionary as this one, does not determine the content and effect of its messages. But it has the potential to make possible unlimited diversity and autonomous production of most of the communication flows that construct meaning in the public mind. Yet, the revolution in communication technology and the new cultures of autonomous communication are processed and shaped (although not determined) by organizations and institutions that are largely influenced by business strategies of profit-making and market expansion.

The Organization and Management of Communication: Global Multimedia Business Networks[9]

In the network society, the media operate mostly according to a business logic, regardless of their legal status. They depend on advertisers, corporate sponsors, and consumer fees to make a profit on behalf of their shareholders. Although there are some instances of relatively independent public service (for example, the BBC, Spanish TVE, Italian RAI, South African SABC, Canadian CBC, Australian ABC, and so on), these broadcasters face increasing pressure to commercialize their programming in order to maintain their audience share in the face of competition from the private sector (EUMap, 2005, 2008). Indeed, many public broadcasters, such as the BBC and South Africa's SABC, have launched corporate for-profit arms in order to fund their public initiatives. Meanwhile, in countries such as China, state-controlled media operations are moving from a propaganda-oriented model to an audience-centered corporate model (Huang, 2007).[10] Furthermore, while the Internet is an autonomous network of local/global communication, private and public corporations also own its infrastructure, and its most popular social spaces and web sites are fast becoming a segment of multimedia business (Artz, 2007; Chester, 2007).

Because *the media are predominantly a business, the same major trends that have transformed the business world – globalization, digitization, networking, and deregulation – have radically altered media operations* (Schiller, 1999, 2007).

[9] This section is based on an article co-authored with Amelia Arsenault (Arsenault and Castells, 2008b).

[10] The commercialization of the domestic Chinese media market is referred to as *"guan ting bing zhuan,"* which refers to a process in which state-owned media outlets that fail to perform economically are closed down or annexed, merged with commercial media organizations, or transformed into commercial corporate entities (Huang, 2007: 418). Between 2003 and 2007, 677 party or government newspapers were shut down and 325 were transformed into commercial newspaper groups.

something that could've affected Occupy?! media coverg?

These trends have removed most of the limits to corporate media expansion, allowing for the consolidation of oligopolistic control by a few companies over much of the core of the global network of media.[11] However, the largest media conglomerates are rooted in the West, but most media businesses around the world remain nationally and/or locally focused. Almost no media organizations are truly global and a decreasing number of media outlets are singularly local. *What are global are the networks* that connect media financing, production, and distribution within countries and between countries. *The major organizational transformation of media that we observe is the formation of global networks of interlocked multimedia businesses organized around strategic partnerships.*

Yet, these networks are organized around dominant nodes. A small number of mega-corporations form the backbone of the global network of media networks. Their dominance is predicated on their ability to leverage and connect to locally and nationally focused media organizations everywhere. Conversely, nationally and regionally focused media organizations increasingly rely on partnerships with these mega-corporations to facilitate their own corporate expansion. Although capital and production are globalized, the content of media is customized to local cultures and to the diversity of segmented audiences. So, in ways that are typical of other industries, globalization and diversification work hand in hand. In fact, the two processes are intertwined: only global networks can master the resources of global media production, but their ability to conquer market shares depends on the adaptation of their content to the taste of local audiences. Capital is global; identities are local or national.

The digitization of communication has prompted the diffusion of a technologically integrated media system in which products and processes are developed on diverse platforms that support a variety of content and media expressions within the same global/local communication network. The shared digital language allows economies of scale and, even more important, economies of synergy between these various platforms and products. By economies of synergy, I mean that the integration of platforms and products may yield a return greater than the sum of the parts invested in the merger or networking of

---

[11] The post-World War II Hollywood Studio era was also marked by vertical integration and disproportionate control over the world cinema market by a few privileged actors. However, digitization and globalization mean that contemporary multimedia conglomerates now control a much broader range of delivery platforms (Warf, 2007).

these platforms and products. Synergy takes place as a result of processes of creativity and innovation facilitated by the integration.

The diffusion of the Internet and of wireless communication has decentralized the communication network, providing the opportunity for multiple entry points into the network of networks. While the rise of this form of mass self-communication increases the autonomy and freedom of communicating actors, this cultural and technological autonomy does not necessarily lead to autonomy from media business. Indeed, it creates new markets and new business opportunities. Media groups have become integrated in global multimedia networks, one of whose aims is the privatization and commercialization of the Internet to expand and exploit these new markets.

The result of these variegated trends and their interaction is *the formation of a new global multimedia system*. To understand communication in the twenty-first century, it is necessary to identify the structure and dynamics of this multimedia system. To do so, I start by focusing on the global core of this structure, as well as on the key communication networks organized around this core. Then I analyze the organization and strategies of the largest multimedia organizations that constitute the backbone of the global media network. Thirdly, I examine the interplay between these "global media" organizations and regional and/or locally focused media organizations. Finally, I will unveil the dynamics of media networks by explaining how media organizations negotiate and leverage parallel networks and seek to control the connecting switches between media networks and financial, industrial, or political networks.

The Core of Global Media Networks

The core of global media networks is formed by multimedia corporations whose main source of revenue and diversified holdings originate from multiple regions and countries around the world. As stated above, "global media" organizations are not truly global; their networks are. However, some media businesses have a stronger international presence than others, and the globalizing strategies of local and regional media organizations depend on (and facilitate) the dynamics of this core of global media networks. Thus, I will examine the organization of the internal networks of the largest globalized media corporations (measured by revenue circa 2007): Time Warner, Disney, News Corporation, Bertelsmann, NBC Universal, Viacom, and CBS. I will then include in this analysis the interaction of these "Magnificent Seven" with the largest diversified Internet/computer companies: Google, Microsoft, Yahoo!, and Apple.

Looking at the configuration of this global media core, we can observe four inter-related trends:

1. *Media ownership is increasingly concentrated.*
2. At the same time, media conglomerates are now able to *deliver a diversity of products over one platform as well as one product over a diversity of platforms.* They also form new products by the combination of digital portions of different products.
3. *The customization and segmentation of audiences* in order to maximize advertising revenues is encouraged by the fluid movement of communication products across platforms.
4. Finally, the extent to which these strategies are successful is determined by the ability of internal media networks to find *optimal economies of synergy* that take advantage of the changing communications environment.

Let me elaborate on each one of these features of the core of global multimedia networks.

Concentration of Ownership

A number of analysts have documented the trend toward media corporatization and concentration at different points in time and in different areas of the world (for example, McChesney, 1999, 2004, 2007, 2008; Bagdikian, 2000, 2004; Bennett, 2004; Thussu, 2006; Hesmondhalgh, 2007; Campo Vidal, 2008; Rice, 2008).

Media concentration is not new. History is full of examples of oligopolistic control over communication media, including the priesthood's control of clay-stylus writing, the Church's control of the Latin Bible, the chartering of the presses, government mail systems, and military semaphore networks, among others. Wherever we look across history and geography, there is a close association between the concentration of power and the concentration of communication media (Rice, personal communication, 2008). In the twentieth century, in the United States, the "big three" networks, ABC, CBS, and NBC, dominated both radio and television into the 1980s. Through the early twentieth century, the British Reuters, French Havas, and German Wolff News agency formed a "global news cartel" that dominated the transmission of international news stories (Rantanen, 2006). Outside the United States, most governments have traditionally maintained a monopoly on radio and television networks. Control over the space of communication has thus always ebbed and flowed as a result of complementary and contradictory changes in regulation, markets, the political environment, and technological innovations. However, the digitization of information and the rise of satellite, wireless, and Internet communication platforms mean that traditional firewalls to ownership expansion are diminished. Beginning in the 1990s, media mergers and acquisitions accelerated to levels never seen before. For example, between 1990 and 1995, as many media mergers took place as from 1960 to 1990 (Greco, 1996: 5; Hesmondhalgh, 2007: 162).

In the first edition of his seminal book, *The Media Monopoly* (1983), Ben Bagdikian identified 50 media firms that dominated the US media market. Several revised versions of the book revealed an ever-shrinking number of dominant firms: 29 firms in 1987, 23 in 1990, 10 in 1997, six in 2000, and five in 2004 (cited by Hesmondhalgh, 2007: 170). While Bagdikian focused on the United States, this same concentration is evidenced globally (Fox and Waisbord, 2002; Campo Vidal, 2008; Winseck, 2008). For example, in 2006, Disney, Time Warner, NBC Universal, Fox Studios (News Corporation), and Viacom accounted for 79 percent of film production and 55 percent of film distribution globally (IBIS, 2007a, b).

This gradual tightening of the media field evolves not just from competition, but from the increased capacity of major firms to network both with each other and with regional actors (which will be discussed in greater detail in the following section). Figure 2.1 maps key partnerships and cross-investments between the global multimedia and Internet dominant firms.

As Figure 2.1 illustrates, the Magnificent Seven and the major Internet companies are connected through a dense web of partnerships, cross-investments, board members, and managers.[12] National Amusements, the

---

[12] Figure 2.1 reflects only relationships as of February 2008. It does not reflect numerous temporary partnerships conducted by these corporations. For example, while NBC Universal won the broadcast rights to the 2006 Turin Winter Olympics, it signed a content provision deal with ESPN.com (owned by Disney) and advertising deals with Google. Thus, Figure 2.1 provides only a time-specific snapshot of the interconnections between these companies. As their property portfolios ebb and flow, so do the form and content of these interconnections. However, the fact that these data are dated does not preclude the analytical interest of our contribution (Arsenault and Castells, 2008b). This is because we are suggesting a pattern of organization and strategy of global multimedia business networks that may change in its composition but may well remain the standard pattern for the multimedia business world for years to come. Indeed, we hope that researchers will update, expand, and correct our current assessment of these business networks.

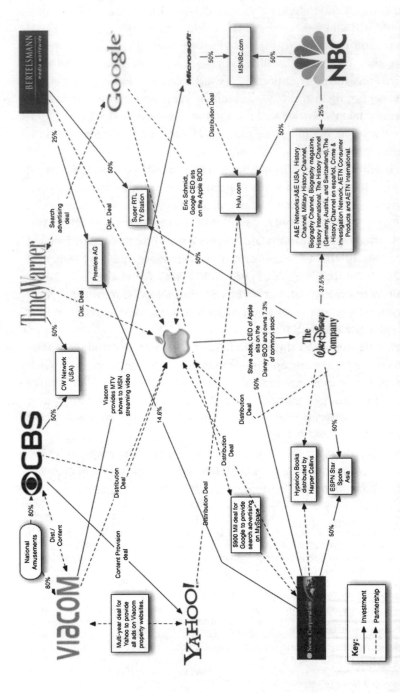

Fig. 2.1. Key interconnections between multinational media and diversified Internet corporations. Please note that this diagram represents key partnerships and cross-investments. It is not exhaustive. The relationships are as of February 2008

Source: Arsenault and Castells (2008a: 713).

family company of Sumner Redstone, maintains a controlling 80 percent stake in both CBS and Viacom. NBC Universal and News Corporation jointly own online content provider Hulu.com, launched in 2007 as a rival to Google's YouTube streaming video platform. Time Warner's AOL, Microsoft's MSN, News Corporation's MySpace, and Yahoo! also provide distribution for the Hulu platform. But while Hulu seeks to break YouTube's hold on the digital video market, its backers have elsewhere formed strategic partnerships with Google. Google provides advertising delivery for News Corporation's MySpace social-networking site. In February 2008, Microsoft made an ultimately unsuccessful offer to purchase Yahoo! for 44.6 billion dollars. Thus, these multimedia conglomerates simultaneously compete and collude on a case-by-case basis according to their business needs.

When certain corporations amass disproportionate control over particular content delivery or production mechanisms, such as YouTube's dominance over Internet video, other media properties seek to break this bottleneck through investment or development of rival properties. Diversification of properties thus works hand in hand with media concentration. The ability of media giants to successfully broker favorable deals, both with each other and with other key media businesses, depends on their ability to accumulate diversified media holdings through partnership, investment, or direct acquisition.

Diversification of Platforms

The largest media organizations now own more properties than ever, and also own more proprietary content that is delivered via different platforms. Figure 2.2 provides an overview of the main properties currently owned or partially owned by the seven largest global multimedia organizations as of 2008. As Figure 2.2 illustrates, all of the leading firms are vertically integrated. Time Warner, for example, controls Warner Brothers, which accounts for 10 percent of global film and television production. Time Warner also owns the second largest cable TV operator in the United States, 47 regional and international cable channels, and the AOL Internet platform over which these productions are distributed. News Corporation, perhaps the most vertically integrated company of all, owns 47 US television stations and the MySpace social-networking platform, has interests in satellite delivery platforms in five continents, and controls Twentieth Century Fox Studios and home entertainment as well as numerous regional television channels. Vertical integration has increased largely because the ability to distribute products is critical for the success of any cultural

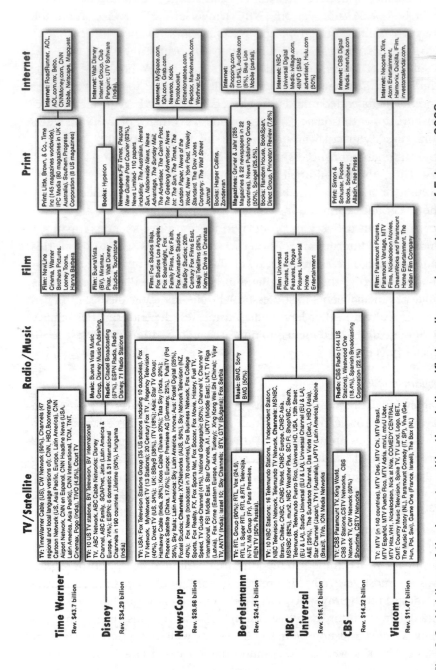

Fig. 2.2. Holdings of the largest multinational diversified media conglomerates as of February 2008

Source: Arsenault and Castells (2008a: 715).

product. Vertical integration of television and film production and distribution escalated in the 1980s with News Corporation's integration of Twentieth Century Fox with Metromedia and then took full flight when Disney purchased ABC in 1995.

Today, vertical integration of media companies includes the Internet. Media organizations are moving into the Internet, while Internet companies are creating partnerships with media organizations and investing in streaming video and audio functionality. Significantly, the largest acquisition of one media group by another to date was the $164 billion purchase of Time Warner, a major traditional media group by America Online (AOL), an Internet start-up. The deal was financed with inflated AOL shares at the peak of the Internet bubble in 2000. In recent years, the blurring of boundaries between Internet, media, and telecommunications companies has only accelerated. In 2005, News Corporation paid $560 million for Intermix, the parent company of the MySpace social-networking site. In 2007, Google bought YouTube for $1.6 billion. In 2007, Google, Apple, Yahoo!, and Microsoft began escalating attempts to compete with more traditional multimedia conglomerates for control over the increasingly lucrative online video market. NBC and News Corporation launched Hulu.com in an attempt to compete with Apple's iTunes video service and Google's YouTube, the dominant site for streaming video. Conversely, Internet companies moved to penetrate the offline media market. The US cable news channel MSNBC was launched as a joint venture by Microsoft and NBC in 1996. And in 2007, Google initiated a partnership with Panasonic to launch a high definition television set that would broadcast traditional television programming as well as Internet content (Hayashi, 2008).

The Past 5 years of social media dvlpt

Segmentation and Customization: Changing Patterns in Advertising as a Driver of Transformation in the Media Industry

Media organizations can maximize their advertising revenue by expanding their potential audiences by moving content across delivery platforms. In 2006, global spending on advertising topped $466 billion (Future Exploration Network, 2007). However, while spending on advertising continues to increase, media continues to fragment. For example, in 1995 there were 225 shows on British television that reached audiences of over 15 million; 10 years later there was none (Future Exploration Network, 2007: 4). So, advertising revenue is spread across an increasing number of platforms and channels (Gluck and Roca-Sales, 2008).

Moreover, traditional barriers between "old" and "new" media companies are disappearing as corporations seek to diversify their portfolios. As documented above, the digitization of all forms of communication means that the barriers between mobile, media, and Internet networks are dissolving. The ability to produce content via mobile devices and upload, exchange, and redistribute this content via the web both widens access and complicates the traditional roles of sender and receiver. Media organizations have more platforms with which to deliver audiences to advertisers, but the process of targeting, distributing, and controlling messages is simultaneously becoming more complicated. Platform diversification, particularly strategic acquisitions of online properties and partnerships with Internet companies like Yahoo! and Google, represents both an attempt to hedge their bets on the central gateway to audiences in a quickly shifting media environment and a movement to take advantage of the ability to segment and target audiences.

Media organizations are moving toward new and dynamic ways of identifying and delivering customized content that targets critical advertising markets. The advent of computer-controlled digital video recording means that television users can easily skip paid advertising. Content supported by embedded advertising is supplanting paid-content models (i.e., traditional 30-second commercials). In 2006, product placement within scripted media products rose to $3 billion, up 40 percent from 2004 (Future Exploration Network, 2007: 5).

Among the global media giants and other media organizations, the digitization of information and the expansion of networks of mass self-communication have facilitated a preoccupation with how to monetize these networks in terms of advertising. Figure 2.3 illustrates the rapid growth of the Internet advertising market between 2002 and 2007. In 2000, online advertising was not even included in advertising medium forecasts. In 2007, according to Zenith Optimedia, it accounted for 8.1 percent of all advertising. Although this remains a small piece of the pie in terms of percentages, translating this into dollars reveals that online advertising now accounts for almost $36 billion in revenue. Furthermore, Internet advertising revenue is growing an average of six times faster than revenue from traditional media (*The Economist*, 2008). In countries with high broadband penetration like Sweden, Norway, Denmark, and the United Kingdom, online advertising now accounts for 15 percent of the market. Zenith Optimedia and Bob Coen, two of the most reputable advertising forecasters, estimated that by 2010 there will be more advertising on the Internet than

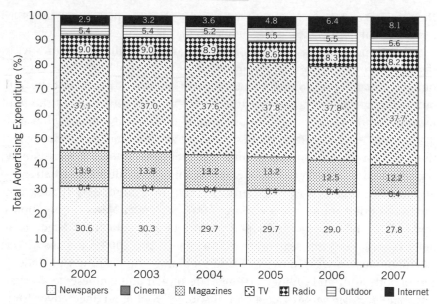

Fig. 2.3. Global advertising expenditure by medium, 2002–2007

Source: Compiled by Arsenault and Castells (2008a: 718) from Zenith Optimedia (2007).

on radio or in magazines. Predictably, media giants have invested in online advertising delivery mechanisms. In 2007, Microsoft bid $6 billion dollars for aQuantitative, and Yahoo! spent $600 million to acquire the 80 percent of remaining shares in Right Media.

Major advertisers are also investing in scripted online branded content as an alternative to conventional advertising. For example, Disney had one of its films written into an episode of *KateModern*, a series that debuted in July 2007 on the British social-network site, Bebo. And Volvo was featured in *Driving School*, a 2007 MSN 12-episode series, starring Craig Robinson of NBC's *The Office*. However, branded content applications still constitute a small part of the money spent on video advertising which, according to media consultant Veronis Suhler Stevenson, could be estimated at $600 million in 2007 (Shahnaz and McClellan, 2007).

The diversification of platforms also makes it critical to find ways to increase the attractiveness of the brand identity of media holdings. Despite the proliferation of blogs and other news and information sites, mainstream media organizations continue to dominate the online news market. In 2005, 16 of the top 20 most popular online news sites, as ranked by

Nielsen/NetRatings, were owned by the 100 largest media companies in terms of total net revenue generated in the US in 2005.

News Corporation has focused on buying and expanding properties with strong brand identity and a multimodal presence. The 2007 News Corporation Annual Report touted the purchase of the Dow Jones Company and other strategic digital properties as a move "to take advantage of the two most profound social and economic trends of our age, globalization and digitization." The Report continues: "We are at a moment in history when there is a confluence of content and of digital delivery and of increasingly sophisticated micro-payment systems, meaning that the value of analysis and intelligence to a business user can be far more accurately reflected in the price of that content" (NewsCorp, 2007: 8). Under News Corporation's ownership, MySpace has developed a hyper-targeted system of advertising delivery based on user search habits. Moreover, the 2007 purchase of *The Wall Street Journal* was a move to acquire a brand with a strong global identity in both print and online versions. The Indian and Chinese editions of *The Wall Street Journal* provide a critical source for elite targeted advertising in markets that could well be the center of future global advertising growth (Bruno, 2007).

Economies of Synergy

The ability to replicate content and consequently advertising across platforms generates economies of synergy, a fundamental component of the business strategy of corporate networks. Lance Bennett (2004) downplays the relevance of size and scale as criteria for domination in the media business scene because "corporate behemoths are anything but well-organized machines" (2004: 132). He points to the failure of AOL and Time Warner and Viacom and CBS to create profitable synergies. Synergy effects depend on adding value because of successful integration in a process of production that yields higher productivity, and thus profit, for its components. Thus, simply adding resources through mergers does not guarantee higher profits. Indeed, the inability of CBS and Viacom to smoothly meld their corporate cultures is a stunning example that illustrates that economies of scale are not always beneficial. The CBS and Viacom relationship dates back to 1973 when CBS was forced to spin off Viacom, its TV syndication unit, under new Federal Communications Commission (FCC) regulations forbidding US TV networks from owning TV syndication units. By 2000, Viacom was the more successful company and purchased its parent company CBS for $22 billion in what was the largest media merger to date. The companies split again in 2005, however, because there were few economies of synergy between them. National Amusements, one of the United States' oldest and largest movie theater chain companies and the family company of Sumner Redstone, retains controlling interest in both companies. After the split, CBS retained the majority of the content delivery platforms (for example, the CBS Network, CBS Radio, and the CW), while Viacom retained the majority of the content creation properties (for example, Paramount Studios and the MTV family of networks).

The key is *synergy*. Synergy is based on the compatibility of the merging networks. Production merges, not property. Networked organizations appear to be more successful business models in contemporary multimedia conglomerates than horizontal property integrations. Indeed, in recent years, several of the most highly capitalized media companies have begun to pare down their operations. Clear Channel, a US-based company with principally radio holdings, sold its television division. The New York Times Company also divested itself of its television broadcasting interests.

News Corporation's growing competitive advantage in the global market depends less on its size than on its organizational networking strategy, which supports economies of synergy. Louw (2001) saw News Corporation's global business model as an example of the global network enterprise, where "We can find multiple (and proliferating) styles of control and decision-making being tolerated in different parts of the network, so long as those at the centre of the web can gain from allowing a particular practice and/or organizational arrangement to exist in a part of their networked 'empire'" (Louw, 2001: 64). Even as Rupert Murdoch has maintained rigid vertical control, News Corporation has shown notable flexibility, particularly in specialization across platforms. Over the past 30 years, News Corporation has transformed from an enterprise whose assets were overwhelmingly in newspaper and magazine publishing in the 1980s to one that, in the 2000s, has 63.7 percent of its total corporate assets in the areas of film, television, and cable/satellite network programming (Flew and Gilmour, 2003: 14), and is now shifting toward Internet properties. News Corporation has focused on maximizing the profitability of individual segments of its network rather than integrating the day-to-day management of its diverse holdings (Fine, 2007). Thus, News Corporation is generally identified as both the most "global" media business in terms of holdings and the most sustainable in terms of its internal networking management strategy (Gershon, 2005).

In sum, *the companies that form the core of global media networks are pursuing policies of ownership concentration, inter-company partnerships, platform diversification, audience customization, and economies of synergy with varying degrees of success*. In turn, the internal configuration of these media businesses is heavily dependent on their ability to leverage and connect to the broader network of media businesses. Moreover, the fate of second-tier national media industries is largely a function of their ability to connect to these global media networks.

The Global Network of Media Networks

As noted earlier, the multinational, diversified media giants remain territorially anchored to their main markets. For example, News Corporation, perhaps the most global media conglomerate in terms of properties, makes 53 percent of its revenue from the United States and 32 percent from Europe (Standard and Poor's, 2007b). Yet, favorable positioning in the global network of media organizations involves much more than territorial expansion, ownership concentration, and platform diversity. The success of the internal networks of News Corporation and other similar properties rests on their ability to connect to the global network of mediated communication. While a few media organizations form the backbone of the global network of media networks, this is not tantamount to one-sided domination. Local and national media are not falling under the ruthless expansion of "global media" organizations. Rather, global companies are leveraging partnerships and cross-investments with national, regional, and local companies to facilitate market expansion *and* vice versa. Regional players are actively importing global content and localizing it, and global media organizations are pursuing local partners to deliver customized content to audiences. Processes of localization and globalization work together to expand a global network. I will try to identify more precisely the role of the structure and dynamics of this global network. To do so, I first analyze the formal structures of collaboration between the global media core and regional, local, and national media organizations. I then examine how these structures are dependent on processes of the localization of globalized products. Finally, I explore the dynamics of flows of media production and organization to document how the local influences and leverages the presence of global media companies.

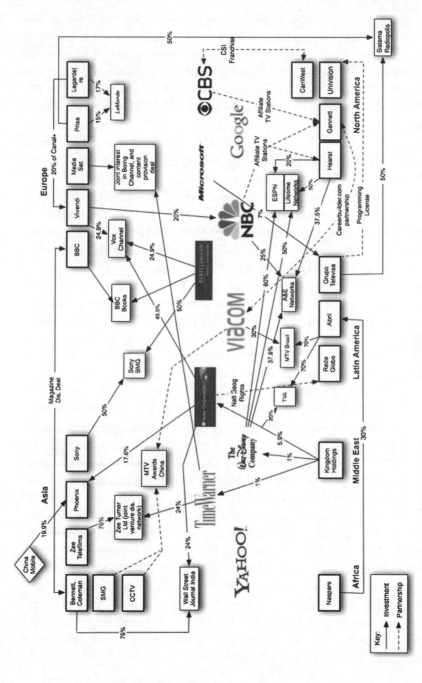

Fig. 2.4. Interconnections between select second-tier multinational media groups and the global core

Source: Arsenault and Castells (2008a: 723).

Communication in the Digital Age

Structures of Collaboration

Multinational media, in the form of news agencies like Reuters (established in 1851), have existed since the mid-nineteenth century, but policies of deregulation accelerated in the mid-1990s, paving the way for greater imbrication between multinational and local media organizations (see below). The 1996 US Telecommunications Act, the founding of the World Trade Organization in 1995, and support for media privatization from the International Monetary Fund (IMF) and other international institutions helped to denationalize the processes of media production and distribution (Artz, 2007). Global media networks are consolidated through the interplay of globalization and localization and the emergence of new production and distribution business models. The global reach of organizations like Time Warner and Disney cannot be measured solely in terms of their holdings. Partnerships and cross-investments extend their reach. Figure 2.4 provides an overview of the critical cross-investments and partnerships between major global media actors and key regional players.

Figure 2.4 only shows key investments and partnerships with second-tier companies. It reflects only a small percentage of the deals conducted between the Magnificent Seven and other players. For example, Disney has a large, but uneven presence in China. Its programs air on Chinese state television; Disney characters appear in Shanda video games; global retailers like Wal-Mart sell their merchandise in Chinese stores; and a percentage of the foreign films legally allowed to screen in China are also produced and distributed by Disney. The figure does not include a host of now defunct partnerships and cross-investments, such as Bertelsmann's partnership with Time Warner to deploy AOL Europe. However, Figure 2.4 provides an overview of the vast web of strategic partnerships and cross-investments upon which the expansion and corporate growth of the Magnificent Seven are predicated. Vivendi Universal SA, a French company, exchanged its share in Universal Entertainment for a 20 percent stake in NBC Universal. Vivendi also has a joint stake in the German Vox station with Bertelsmann. Bertelsmann, in turn, also has interests in the German Premiere TV with News Corporation. Saudi prince Al-Walid bin Talal's Kingdom Holdings is one of the largest media investors in the Middle East with a stake in LBC, Rotanna, and numerous other commercial media operations. Moreover, the company also owns stakes in many of the key global media properties such as News Corporation (as its third largest investor), Apple, Amazon, and Microsoft.

As Figure 2.4 illustrates, corporations like News Corporation and Time Warner are embedded within a larger network of more regionally and locally focused media organizations which themselves are fulfilling similar expansion and diversification strategies. These companies follow similar patterns of concentration of ownership and diversification. Figure 2.5 provides an overview of the key holdings of select media companies by region. As Figures 2.4 and 2.5 illustrate, what Lance Bennett (2004) refers to as the "second tier" of multimedia conglomerates is also pursuing strategies of diversification, concentration of ownership, and cross-investments. These processes are underscored by the ability of the global network of media networks to influence local and national conditions of production and distribution and vice versa.

The Global Influences the Local

Globalized conglomerates break into new markets and effectively reprogram the regional market toward a commercial format that facilitates the connection with its business networks. This influence is manifested in a number of trends.

First, an obvious example of global influence on local media markets is the direct import of programming and channels such as CNN, Fox, ESPN, HBO, and other transnational media channels. Secondly, multinational media companies have helped to diffuse a corporate-driven media model. The introduction of corporate media products creates a further demand for these products and propels players further down the media chain to participate in similar behavior. For example, CBS contracts with SABC (the South African government-owned corporation). Their programs are successful and induce consumer demand. SABC recognizes the success of this business model and creates programs modeled on the commercial rather than the public-service model and then markets those to smaller media players around Africa. Teer-Tomaselli et al. (2006: 154) argue that, "while the South African media occupy a marginal position in the global media arena, as a market for media products owned and produced outside its borders, they extend their influence (albeit on a much smaller scale) as a powerful role-player into the region and further on the continent." Iwabuchi identifies a similar trend in the Japanese media market where media companies actively seek to localize the format of Japanese television dramas and music for local markets around Asia. Once these formats become popular, they are further circulated by other media companies, as was the case of Korean

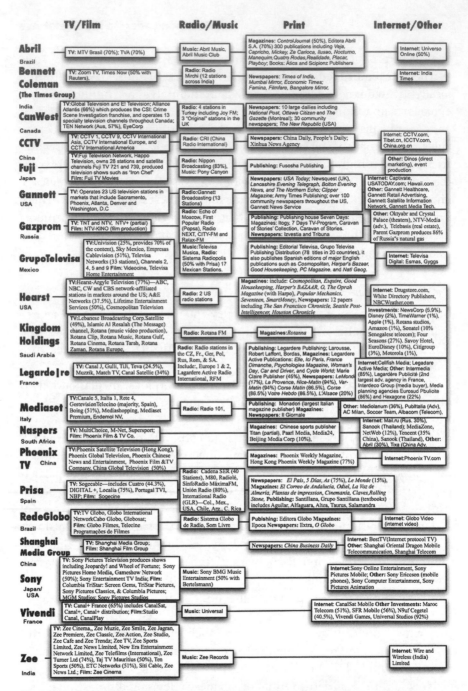

Fig. 2.5. Property map of "second-tier" multimedia conglomerates. Data collected from the latest available proxy statements and/or corporate web sites as of February 2008. The chart includes key holdings and is not an exhaustive list

Source: Arsenault and Castells (2008a: 725).

television producers who actively sought Japanese television formats to remake for the Chinese media market (Iwabuchi, 2008).

Several scholars have written about the diffusion of corporate and cultural formats from the global to the local sphere. Thussu (1998) describes the "Murdochisation of the media" in India as "the process which involves the shift of media power from the public to privately owned, transnational, multimedia corporations controlling both delivery systems and the content of global information networks" (1998: 7). This "Murdochisation" is characterized by "a tendency toward market-driven journalism thriving on circulation and ratings wars; transnational influence of US-inspired media formats, products, and discourse; and lastly, an emphasis on infotainment, undermining the role of the media for public infotainment." Lee Artz (2007) has analyzed the rise of "transnational media projects" or "enterprises that produce within one nation but are jointly owned by multiple corporations from multiple nations ... [and] have no national allegiance and bring together capitalist classes from two or more nations for the purpose of producing and profiting from media commodities" (2007: 148). For example, Germany's Vox television channel is owned by the Australian/American News Corporation (49.5%), France's Canal Plus (24.9%), and Germany's Bertelsmann (24.9%).

Thirdly, global media players export programs and content which are produced for local formats, but typically are based around standard formats popularized in the West. Iwabuchi (2008: 148) refers to this process as "local camouflaging." Shows such as *Pop Idol*, *Survivor*, and *Who Wants to Be a Millionaire* have been franchised to many countries. Viacom has been at the forefront of this process of localizing content. Its motto is "think globally, act locally." Its MTV (Music Television) property is perhaps the most customized media platform in the world with service in 140 countries and customized Asian, Middle Eastern, Latin American, African, and European channels featuring local talent and presenters. MTV also engages in partnerships with local outlets. For example, in China, MTV sponsors major award shows in cooperation with CCTV and the Shanghai Media Group (Murdock, 2006). Viacom has also created international versions of *America's Next Top Model*, a television show originally produced for the American UPN Network (now part of the CW network). *Top Model* franchises have been marketed to 17 countries, including Taiwan (*Supermodel #1*), Turkey (*Top Model Turkiye's*), Spain (*Supermodelo*), and Russia (*Russia's Next Top Model*). And, while not officially a *Top Model* franchise, an Afghani local TV station made headlines in the Fall of 2007 when it launched its own low-budget take on the format.

The Local Influences the Global

However, while global media corporations control a disproportionate number of distribution and production processes, they do not hold a monopoly over the markets in which they operate. Indeed, there are numerous "counter-flows" that impact on the form and structure of the operation of these media giants (Thussu, 2006).

The most obvious example of local/national influence over global media networks is through regulation and deregulation. The opening of China's and India's media markets spurred a wave of attempts by global multinationals to conquer these markets. Still, these states maintain a great deal of control over the structure and content of their entry. For example, when Microsoft and Yahoo! launched in China, they had to install software that automatically filters controversial words such as Tibet, Falun Gong, freedom, and democracy. Earlier, Murdoch's Star TV agreed to remove BBC World from its service in order to be allowed to launch in China. As Murdock (2006) points out, the localizing strategies of global media organizations must take into account the simultaneous rise of the globalizing strategies of regional media platforms. He cites India as the archetype of this process, where globalization is less an influx of Western culture into India than the outflow of Indian cultural products into the global sphere (2006: 25). Similarly, Cullity (2002: 408) identifies a new form of cultural nationalism based on the active and self-conscious indigenization of global media (for example, the tradition of Miss India wearing a sari in the Miss Universe pageant, which is owned by Donald Trump).

Moreover, while multinational conglomerates have helped transmit the formulas for shows like *Pop Idol* and *Top Model* worldwide, these programs have diverse origins. The *Big Brother* franchise originated from an independent production arm of Endemol, a Dutch media company. *Betty La Fea*, a Colombian *telenovela*, has been circulated to more than 70 markets around the world both as a prepackaged program and as a format (see below). Following *Ugly Betty*'s success in the US market, Disney-ABC International Television forged broadcasting deals with 130 territories around the world, making *Ugly Betty* the most popular franchise to date (World Screen, 2007). Similarly, the executive producer of *Who Wants to Be a Millionaire* first developed a similar program for ABC, which the company rejected. Only after the show succeeded in Britain and several other markets did it finally reach the US market. Thus, just as global media companies are trying to insert their content into local markets, other media organizations are pursing strategies to find ways to circulate their content globally, often via the core global media corporations. For instance, the story and characters of Disney's *Lion King* originated in Japanese Manga comics.

In many markets there is substantial inter-media agenda-setting in which the media agendas of global properties are influenced by other organizations. Studies by Van Belle (2003) and Golan (2006) demonstrate that "global media" corporations depend on key elite publications (that they do not own) to set their news agenda in the United States. For example, Golan (2006) found that the news agendas of CBS, NBC, and ABC evening news were dependent on the stories run by *The New York Times* that morning. This is why Murdoch's purchase of the Dow Jones company is critical – *The Wall Street Journal* is a key inter-media agenda-setter. Al Jazeera, the BBC World Service, and *The Economist* are also critical sources of both inter-media and public agenda-setting. Therefore, we cannot measure the influence of the Magnificent Seven in terms of sheer audience numbers and/or market revenue. These companies also help circulate and filter content produced by other members of the media organization network.

Identity Matters: The Limits of Competition and Cooperation

Many of the largest media firms share some shareholders, and/or own portions of each other, and/or have interlocking boards of directors (see Table A2.1 in the Appendix), and/or depend on one another for advertising revenue (McChesney, 2008). However, there are several counter-examples that illustrate that media industries built around cultural and political identities can grow in quasi-parallel networks.

Al Jazeera, which includes two international broadcasting networks (Arabic and English), as well as several specialty children's and sports channels, is heavily subsidized by the Heir Prince of the Emirate of Qatar. Because only 40 percent of Al Jazeera's operating revenue comes from advertising, it retains more latitude to utilize non-commercial formats. And it provides direct competition to channels like CNN, the BBC, and CNBC in the Middle East and Arabic-speaking populations abroad. However, Al Jazeera's presence outside the Middle East is also predicated on its ability to connect to other media networks either through content delivery deals and/or placement within satellite or cable television line-ups. For example, Al Jazeera's presence on the African continent is facilitated by content delivery deals with SABC and Multi-choice in South Africa.

The Indian film industry, popularly referred to as Bollywood, is another example of an industry that evolved largely independently from the global network of media networks. It now produces over 800 films a year compared to 600 by Hollywood (*The Economist*, 2008) and commands a significant portion of international film revenues. Bollywood films are heavily dependent on an Indian cultural format that largely eschews the Hollywood format. However, structures of collaboration between Bollywood and Hollywood are increasing. In November 2007, Sony Pictures Entertainment released its first Bollywood production, *Saawariya*, a film that cost $10 million to produce and grossed $20 million. Viacom, through its Viacom 18 arm, jointly owns the Indian Film Company with the Indian media company TV18. Bollywood filmmakers are also increasingly using cross-promotions and product tie-ins popularized by Hollywood-based studios to increase their revenues.

The Nigerian film industry, nicknamed Nollywood, produces over 1,000 video films per year, grosses $2.75 billion annually, and ranks as the third largest film industry internationally (UNCTAD, 2008: 5). Nollywood films are typically crafted for the domestic Nigerian market and are produced in several of Nigeria's 250 tribal languages and English (which accounts for 65 percent of the export market). The industry's success arose from a pool of creative talent and a low-cost production format requiring low start-up costs. Cheap production values offer high return on investment. These films are typically shot on video over a two-week period and distributed on video cassette around the country (Marston et al., 2007). Nollywood is an example of an industry that has thrived by developing a mainly national market predicated on a media format that is not readily marketable abroad. However, the success of Nollywood films has sparked interest from multinational conglomerates. In 2007, Time Warner and Comcast formed a partnership with IAD to distribute Nollywood films. In addition, members of the Nigerian government and film industry actively court Hollywood investors. In 2006, media actors and government officials invited movie insiders from around the United States to Los Angeles, California, for "The Nollywood Foundation Convention 2006: African Cinema and Beyond" in order to attract greater attention from international audiences and investors. Thus, although there are successful media industries and actors able to develop independently from the global core of media networks, these industries are beginning to forge stronger ties to the global network in order to enhance revenues and expand their audience share.

Switching Networks

Media networks do not exist in a vacuum. Their success is dependent on their ability to successfully leverage connections to other critical networks in finance, technology, cultural industries, advertising industries, suppliers of content, regulatory agencies, and political circles at large. Media businesses connect to other networks through multiple mechanisms. The cross-affiliations of board members and executives are perhaps the easiest of these mechanisms to document. Table A2.1 in the Appendix provides an overview of the affiliations of key executives and board members of global multimedia companies and Internet giants.

Interlocking boards of directors and managers are but one component of these connections. The solidification and expansion of the global business media network is also dependent on numerous other connections to non-media networks, which in turn also leverage their connections with media organizations. Thus, *the connection to financial networks is an essential component of media business networks*. Table A2.1 in the Appendix shows the personal connections between financial networks and media business networks. The boards of directors of media multinationals are heavily stacked with individuals who either sit upon the boards of other large non-media multinational corporations, investment banks, and private equity firms and/or have important positions in organizations such as NASDAQ and the New York Stock Exchange. These interconnections are not inconsequential. In its 2007 proxy statement, Time Warner, for example, reported that it had conducted transactions with a significant number of companies to which members of its board of directors were also affiliated. Although the specific role of each board member in facilitating these transactions is difficult to document, it suggests that this interlocking of directorates is not without consequence.

Media businesses and related industries are a significant component of the networks of financial capital. In 2007, one-fifth of the world's largest companies in terms of market capitalization as ranked by the *Financial Times* were media, Internet, or telecommunications companies.[13] The production of high-tech hardware and software to support the distribution and consumption of media products ranks among the world's largest industries. Although the popular press typically focuses on the leadership of these media multinationals (for example, Rupert Murdoch as CEO of News

[13] The *Financial Times*'s annual Global 500 companies rankings is available on http://www.ft.com/reports/ft5002007.

Corporation and Sumner Redstone as majority owner of CBS and Viacom), a number of non-media organizations also hold significant beneficial ownership in these firms (see Table A2.2 in the Appendix for a list of the major institutional investors in these properties). AXA, a French insurance company, for example, holds significant stakes in both Yahoo! (0.8%) and Time Warner (5.79%), and Fidelity maintains significant interest in both Google and News Corporation.

Between 2002 and 2007, media organizations were buoyed by a significant influx of investment from private equity firms and venture capitalists to finance their mergers and acquisitions. In 2007 alone, private equity firms invested $50 billion in media properties (Malone, 2007). Thus, it is not surprising that the management of global media companies is laden with individuals with close connections to private equity firms such as Bank of America (which manages a $2 billion investment fund), Highpoint Capital Management, and Templeton Emerging Markets Investments.

Media businesses are particularly attractive to private investors because they typically require little capital investment and generate large revenues. These investors typically seek maximum return on their investments,[14] but play no role in the day-to-day operations of their media investments. However, the participation of these private investors in media mergers and acquisitions can play a vital role in their success or failure. Sony's successful bid for Metro-Goldwyn-Mayer in 2004, for example, was financed by Providence Equity Partners and Texas Pacific Group, while Grupo Televisa's bid for the US Spanish-language channel Univision failed when it lost the backing of two private equity firms, Blackstone Group and Kohlberg Kravis Roberts.

Conversely, power players among the global entertainment elite participate in private equity firms and venture capital endeavors that invest in both media and non-media-related endeavors. For investments, Bill Gates uses a personal private equity firm, Cascade Investments. The firm has a stake in Gay.com, Planet Out, Grupo Televisa, and participated in a failed

[14] These investment firms remain largely unregulated as most media regulations, particularly in the United States, place limits on companies that demonstrate management control over the day-to-day operations of a media property. The increase in private equity investments has facilitated a corresponding concern with the ramifications of ownership because these firms are largely unregulated. Moreover, while they typically fail to become involved in the daily operations of these companies, questions of undue influence have arisen. For example, in 2007 Harbinger Capital Partners Funds and Firebrand private equity partners used their leverage of 4.9% combined holding in the New York Times Company to nominate four directors at the 2008 Annual Meeting.

bid for Univision in 2007. Its $4 billion portfolio also includes many non-media and technology properties such as the Canadian National Railway, Berkshire Hathaway, and Six Flags Amusement Parks (United States SEC File 28-05149). Cascade Investments also participated in a joint venture with Kingdom Holdings to purchase the Four Seasons Hotel chain in 2006. And in April 2007, Bertelsmann redirected 10 percent of its acquisition budget into a €1 billion joint private equity group with Citigroup Private Equity and Morgan Stanley Principal Investment to expand its holdings.

The importance of access to private capital is not unique to the Magnificent Seven. Firms such as Blackstone, Cisco, and 3i have invested heavily in Bollywood film productions. In addition, Indian companies, such as the Indian Film Company and other corporations, have raised cash on the British Alternative Investment Market (AIM) to fund projects. In another example, the venture capital arm of the Abu Dhabi Group headquartered in the UAE made a significant investment in Bertelsmann's Arvada Middle East Sales group to build a regional digital entertainment business.

The Advertising Industry

The advertising industry is another decisive network that connects with media business networks. Media companies depend on their ability to connect to the global advertising industry. In 2007 alone, corporations (including government corporations) spent $466 billion on advertising (US Optimedia data reported in the *Future of the Media Report 2007* [Future Exploration Network, 2007]).[15] The advertising industry includes agencies as well as graphic design services, display advertising, and media representatives (IBIS, 2008). Access to the advertising industry's network can determine a media organization's success or failure. It is no accident that a high number of affiliations listed in Table A2.1 in the Appendix are corporations that rank among the largest purchasers of advertising (these organizations are listed in italic). Even the film industry, which historically relied on box-office revenue, increasingly depends on consumer–product tie-ins and cross-promotions (Hesmondhalgh, 2007: 196). This process is further complicated by the fact that multimedia conglomerates are among the world's largest purchasers of advertising. Time Warner, Disney, GE (NBC's parent company), News Corporation, Viacom, and Microsoft are among the top global 100 purchasers of advertising. IBIS (2008) estimates that

---

[15] The United States government, for example, ranked as the twenty-ninth largest advertiser in the United States, spending $1,132.7 billion (*Advertising Age*, 2007).

entertainment media are the third largest advertising consumer base for the advertising industry, representing 16 percent of total industry revenue.

The diversification of media networks conditions changes in advertising expenditure and vice versa. Multinationals have competed for entry into the Chinese media market because it reflects one of the fastest growing advertising markets, estimated at a value of $14 billion for 2007 (Gale, 2008). Conversely, advertisers are attracted to the Chinese market precisely because there are now more delivery mechanisms available.

The advertising industry has also become increasingly concentrated. The majority of top agencies are owned by one of four major media holding companies: WPP Group, Interpublic Group of Companies, Publicis Groupe, and Omnicom Group (IBIS, 2008). In addition to owning the majority of the world's advertising and marketing agencies, these groups have also diversified their investments by purchasing Internet delivery technologies that are attractive to media and entertainment industry advertisers. In 2007, the WPP group, for example, purchased 24/7 RealMedia, a search engine marketing company; Schematic, an interactive Internet advertising agency; and BlastRadius, a company specializing in social-networking advertising. Media networks thus provide platforms for other corporations to promote their business interests, outlets for advertising, and critical sources of customers for advertising sales.

Internet, Wireless Networks of Communication, and Media Networks
The Internet and wireless networks have provided media conglomerates with new markets for advertising, but they are also heavily contested spaces. The movement of global media players into the Internet involves attempts to re-commodify media and information that flows out of convergence culture. In addition, YouTube, Facebook, MySpace, and other similar online properties may be emerging as critical connecting points between media networks, autonomous mass self-communication networks, business interests (advertisers), and political players (who want either to filter or to introduce content into all of these networks).

Google was the world's biggest media company by stock-market value in 2008, but it had a far smaller annual revenue than the other multimedia giants. However, the global reach of Google, Microsoft, Yahoo!, and their numerous partnerships with regional Internet and media companies means that the global Internet giants cannot be considered separately. Moreover, it appears that their actions are increasingly setting the agenda for other multimedia giants with fewer online properties. Now that Google owns

YouTube, Yahoo! owns Xanga, and Microsoft has a stake in Facebook, they control critical nodes between the media sphere and the online sphere. All the major players are trying to figure out how to re-commodify Internet-based autonomous mass self-communication. They are experimenting with ad-supported sites, pay sites, free streaming video portals, and pay portals.

As more and more media products are distributed and consumed online and intermeshed with social networking and other online user-generated content, individual user behavior plays a more central role in driving advertising. Online search engines are now configured in such a way that they feature tacit, if not necessarily conscious, end-user participation. Observers are pinpointing the growing importance of the Googlearchy, referring to the positioning of search items in search results (Hindman et al., 2003). Google, Yahoo!, and other web sites use a combination of keyword relevance, the popularity of search terms, links to other sites, and the behavior of end-users to determine the order of search results. As more and more users follow particular links, the higher these sources rise in the Googlearchy. Search-engine users are thus simultaneously consuming information and helping to determine the accessibility and dominance of that information source for other users in the Internet sphere. This triggers a domino effect. Users are most likely to click on a link among the first pages of results. Relevance thus breeds relevance. For instance, searches on African topics make little use of African sources since they are not among the first group of results. Only sophisticated users can reach sources that are not highly ranked as per Google's programmed criteria.

Strategic partnerships between media properties and Yahoo!, Google, Microsoft, and many regionally popular search engines are an attempt to harness end-user behavior to maximize advertising revenues. In 2007, News Corporation, for example, signed a $900 million deal with Google to provide targeted search advertising for its Internet properties.

Web 2.0 technologies empowered consumers to produce and distribute their own content. The viral success of these technologies propelled media organizations to harness the production power of traditional consumers. Almost every major news organization offers site visitors the opportunity to upload content that, if compelling enough, will be featured online and in an increasing number of television programs that feature user-generated content (for example, CNN's iReport and VH1's Web Junk 2.0). Similarly, newspapers now regularly cite and depend on members of the blogosphere as sources of cutting-edge social and political news. This blurring of boundaries has facilitated what Brian McNair (2006) refers to as a "chaos paradigm" in international communication.

Networks of Supply and Multimedia Networks

Supplier networks are fundamental to the operation of multimedia networks. These include, but are not limited to, news agencies, talent agencies, and labor networks. Media corporatization has encouraged cost-cutting measures that include the closing of regional and international news bureaus and the streamlining of journalistic practices. News agencies such as Reuters, Bloomberg, the Associated Press, and World Television news are thus critical suppliers for news content for many media properties around the world (Klinenberg, 2005). Wu (2007), for example, found that the news agencies were a critical determinant of the international news coverage of CNN and *The New York Times*.

Because news agencies are valued for their global reach, the industry is controlled by a small group of historically established players: the Associated Press, Getty Images, Bloomberg, Dow Jones, Reuters, and Agence France Press control 70 percent of the syndicated global news market (IBIS, 2007b: 17). Since 2000, these news syndicates have expanded their international presence in order to fulfill increased demand for their product. Digital convergence has expanded the demand for their syndicated content as newspapers seek to maintain dynamic and continually updated online versions. News agency profit margins continue to expand. Getty Images, for example, earned $484.8 million in revenue in 2000 and almost double that amount in 2006 (807.3 million; IBIS 2007b: 21). Moreover, television, magazine, and radio properties are also increasingly utilizing news wire services (IBIS, 2007b: 28). These organizations are diversifying their content offerings with images and video in order to provide for these platforms.

Connections to writers, actors, performers, and other creative professionals are also essential for the success of media business. In the United States alone, the network of agents for artists, athletes, and entertainers is a $6 billion a year industry (IBIS, 2007a). The financial losses resulting from the 2007–8 Writers Guild of America (WGA) strike showed the importance of these networks to the overall economic success of media businesses. The strike halted production on all major scripted television shows and prompted the cancellation of numerous other scripted live events. The ability to leverage networks that produce and supply the physical infrastructure of media production and delivery is also important. The production of radio and television broadcast equipment for the US market alone boasted an annual revenue of $38,225 million in 2006.

Beyond the networks I cite here, *there are numerous other networks with close connections to the media industry*. For instance, as I will argue below, the capacity to network with political actors that have influence on the regulation of media and telecommunication networks is a critical factor for media businesses to expand and build economies of scale and synergy. Thus, the growth and prosperity of global media networks depend not only on their ability to configure their internal networks and expand their market and supplier networks, but also on their capacity to set up switches that ensure their connection to pivotal networks in other areas of the economy, politics, and society at large. The configuration of old and new media business and communication companies ultimately depends on the politics of regulatory policies.

The Politics of Regulatory Policies

The technological and cultural transformation of societal communication has been channeled and shaped by business strategies that led to the formation of a globally networked multimedia business system, as analyzed in the preceding section. However, the process of formation of this business system has been guided and made possible by the evolution of regulatory policies throughout the world. Indeed, societal communication is a practice regulated by political institutions in all countries because of the essential role communication plays in both the infrastructure and culture of society. There is no technological necessity or demand-driven determination in the evolution of communication. While the revolution in information and communication technologies is a fundamental component of the ongoing transformation, its actual consequences in the communication realm depend on policy decisions that result from the debates and conflicts conducted by business, social, and political interest groups seeking to establish the regulatory regime within which corporations and individuals operate. For instance, Wu (2007b), in his analysis of the strategies of wireless communication operators in the United States, has shown how the strategies of vertical integration, which were intended to keep tight control over their networks, actually hampered technological innovation, shrunk the range of applications, and ultimately limited the expansion of the networks, thereby undermining their capacity to add value to the networks. Business interests, not technology or public service, are often the defining factors in the deployment of communication networks. This is not an iron rule. It all depends on the interplay between social actors that underlies the process of policy decision-making.

There has been a tectonic shift in the regulation of communication in all countries from the mid-1980s through the first decade of the twenty-first century, albeit with different orientations and emphases depending on the culture and politics of each country. Yet, overall, there has been a dominant trend toward the liberalization, privatization, and regulated deregulation of both broadcast and telecommunication industries.

It helps to differentiate between four main domains of regulation of communication: broadcasting, the print press, the Internet, and telecommunication networks. There is reciprocity among the four and they have converged to form a digital communication system. However, because regulatory institutions have a history, policies have developed differently in each one of these four domains. Furthermore, there are at least three different areas of regulation that are transversal to the four domains mentioned above: namely, regulation of content, including the enforcement of intellectual property rights; regulation of ownership; and regulation of service imposed on operators and broadcasters (for example, universal service of telephony, non-discriminatory access to the common carrier networks, and so on).

The matter is further complicated if we adopt a global perspective because the regulator is a plural actor, as different institutions assume specific responsibilities in each one of these four domains and these three areas. Even in the United States, where the supposedly independent Federal Communications Commission (FCC) has responsibility for both broadcasting and telecommunications (in contrast, for instance, with most European countries), the governance of the Internet was originally under the jurisdiction of the Defense Department, and is now the responsibility of the Commerce Department; the regulation of media and Internet company ownership comes partly under the anti-trust legislation enforced by the Justice Department; and surveillance of activity is conducted by the Homeland Security Agency, while Congress tries to legislate on a variety of issues (such as the failed attempt to impose censorship on the Internet in the 1996 Communications Decency Act) and the courts intervene decisively to resolve the growing number of conflicts derived from the implementation of communication policies. To make matters more complex, in Europe, the

European Commission has jurisdiction over national telecommunications and media operations, and the governance of the Internet is considered to be global, since the Internet is a global network of computer networks.

An analysis of this complex set of regulatory institutions, policies, and practices is beyond the scope of this book, and, in fact, is not needed because there are a number of excellent studies on the subject (Price, 2002; Wilson, 2004; Goldsmith and Wu, 2006; *International Journal of Communication*, 2007; Klinenberg, 2007; Rice, 2008; Terzis, 2008; Cowhey and Aronson, 2009). But I want to pinpoint the regulatory processes that shape the current multimodal digital communication system informing communicative practices nowadays. I will use the United States to ground my analysis before expanding the argument with reference to other contexts.

The Evolution of Regulatory Policies in the United States: Telecommunications, Intellectual Property, and the Internet

In the United States, there were three pivotal moments of evolution in the regulated deregulation of communication in the digital age. The first came in 1984, with the *divestiture of the monopoly of ATT in telecommunications*, ushering in managed competition in the communication industries, while preserving local monopolies for cable operators. As a result, the so-called "Baby Bells," originally established in different regional markets, became powerful national and global players that actively lobbied Congress and the FCC to assert their control over the "last mile" (now renamed the "first mile" by corporations like Verizon) in fierce competition with the cable companies before regulation permitted partnerships between the two. The relatively slow diffusion of broadband in the United States was partly the result of this early conflict between cable companies and telephone operators that led to failures of interconnection nationally and locally.

The second key legislative measure was the *1996 Telecommunications Act*, which substantially lifted the restrictions on concentration of ownership in the media industries. As a direct consequence of this Act, there was a swift movement toward corporate consolidation, leading to the formation of multimedia oligopolies, particularly in the major metropolitan areas, as documented in the preceding section of this chapter. This concentration of ownership affected television, radio, and the print press, although, in the case of the print press, the process of concentration predates the 1996 Act. For instance, in 1945, 80 percent of American newspapers were privately owned, often by families. In 2007, more than 80 percent of American newspapers were owned by corporations, most of which were subsidiaries of major multimedia groups (Klinenberg, 2007: 31). Furthermore, the 1996 Act authorized mergers and alliances between companies of different segments of the industry (for instance, between telecommunication operators and media companies, including Internet companies), thus opening the way for the interlocked business communication system that emerged in the early twenty-first century. The 1996 Act was also important because it reiterated the operators' obligation to allow sharing of the network under similar conditions for all users (the so-called unbundling policy). This limited the capacity of the new mega-corporations resulting from permitted mergers to appropriate the technological revolution for their benefit.

In terms of media content, the FCC has traditionally kept a low profile to avoid interfering with the principle of free speech set by the First Amendment, though it encouraged discretion to protect children from harmful programming and to limit pornographic broadcasting. Yet, Congress and the government became much more belligerent toward the control of content on the Internet. The key rationale for the Communications Decency Act of 1996 was the prevention of child pornography online. But after the courts overturned the provisions of the Act related to the control of free communication on the Internet, censorship attempts receded until 2001, when the terrorist threat facilitated the passing of new legislation authorizing government surveillance of the Internet and control of the diffusion of certain types of information. This proposition was almost impossible to execute, as proven by the proliferation of Bin Laden's proclamations and the materials of other terrorist groups over the Internet.

What became the most important issue in terms of content control on the Internet was the enforcement of technologically outdated copyright laws over digitized material circulating on the Internet, particularly via p2p networks. Under relentless pressure from the media and cultural industries, Congress enacted legislation extending and expanding copyright protection, and the courts were used as firewalls against the culture of sharing and remixing that had blossomed on the Internet. Indeed, the Digital Millennium Copyright Act of 1998 represented a serious threat to the remix culture that is at the heart of creativity in the digital age. Although this legislative arsenal had an intimidating effect on Internet users, it was not capable of preventing the mass insurrection (by the tens of millions) of users/producers of content against the media oligopolies' perceived capture of free digital culture (Lessig, 2004; Benkler 2006; Gillespie, 2007). Calling technology to the rescue, the entertainment industry developed a new system of "digital rights management" (DRM) to prevent the unauthorized copying of material. Yet, DRM only limits a small portion of the supposed infringement because it does not prevent the growth of p2p networks, nor does it stop the posting of remixed material on YouTube and other Web 2.0 sites with millions of users and producers of content.

The impromptu evolution of Internet regulation and management parallels the serendipitous maturation of the Internet as the communication commons of the network society (Abbate, 1999; Castells, 2001; Movius, forthcoming). When first deployed in 1969, ARPANET, the predecessor of the Internet, was an experimental computer networking program originated in DARPA, the US Defense Department research agency, and largely run by the scientists and engineers who created it. In 1970, the Defense Department offered to transfer its operation and property to ATT. After weighing the possibility for a few weeks, ATT did not see any commercial interest in ARPANET, and declined the offer (Abbate, 1999). Thanks to this monumental shortsightedness on ATT's part, and to the inability of Microsoft to understand the significance of the Internet, the world became what it is today. So much for technological determinism.

In 1984, as the Internet developed and began to be used around the world, DARPA, and the most prominent designers of the Internet, established the Internet Activities Board made up of a number of task forces. One of these became the Internet Engineering Task Force (IETF) created in 1986 to manage the development of technical standards for the Internet. Decisions made by the IETF were made by consensus, and involved a wide variety of individuals and institutions. By and large, the Internet emerged in a legal vacuum with little supervision from regulatory agencies, including the FCC. The agencies that were created developed on an ad hoc basis to solve the needs of the users of the network. The most critical decision was to set up a coherent system for assigning domains and IP addresses that would organize traffic on the Internet so that packets would reach their designated addressee. It was mainly a solo operation undertaken in the mid-1980s by University of Southern California engineering professor Jon Postel, one of the early co-designers of the Internet. He established the system under contract with DARPA and in connection with the Stanford Research Institute (SRI, not affiliated with Stanford University). The resulting organization became collectively known as the Internet Assigned

Names Authority (IANA). Postel administered the US government grants to IANA to maintain lists of unique reference numbers. Though the root servers of IANA were operated voluntarily by 13 different organizations, Postel made most of the key technical decisions out of his USC office. That one person, without financial profit for himself, and without direct control from a higher authority, created the Internet domain system unchallenged because of the trust deposited in him by the user community, is one of the most extraordinary stories of the Information Age.

By 1992, the National Science Foundation (NSF) had assumed responsibility for coordinating and funding the management of the Internet, while leaving the small military components of the network under the jurisdiction of the Defense Department. In 1993, the National Science Foundation contracted the administration of the Domain Name System (DNS) to the private US company Network Solutions, Inc. (NSI), although Postel continued to play a role until his death from cancer in 1998 at the age of 55. Then, at the expiration of NSI's contract with the NSF in 1998, and without Postel present to function as the trusted guarantor of the assignment of IP addresses, pressure increased to formalize the institutional management of the Internet. The ensuing controversy led IANA and the autonomous organization created by the first community of users, the Internet Society (ISOC), chaired by another trusted "father" of the Internet, Vint Cerf, to organize the International Ad Hoc Committee (IAHC) to resolve DNS management questions. The invention of the World Wide Web and the free diffusion of its web server program by its creator Tim Berners-Lee in 1990 provided the technological foundation for the development of a user-friendly Internet. As the Internet became a hugely profitable opportunity for business investments, President Clinton directed the Secretary of Commerce to privatize the DNS on July 1, 1997, in a way that increased competition and facilitated international participation in its management. The US Department of Commerce implemented the directive and established ICANN (the Internet Corporation for Assigned Names and Numbers) in November 1998.

As soon as the Internet was recognized as an extraordinarily important form of networked communication with a wide range of potential applications, corporate appetites for the commercialization of the Internet grew exponentially. Yet, the history, culture, and architecture of the Internet made it difficult to appropriate it privately or to regulate it exclusively for the sake of business profits. Furthermore, because it was a global network, and because this was precisely one of its main attractions for users and business alike, the Commerce Department had to share some control with international regulatory agencies and the user community, leading to the unprecedented electronic election of the ICANN board by more than 200,000 registered Internet users in 2000, an expression of grassroots participation in spite of the lack of representativeness of this electorate. A coalition formed by an active user community, civil libertarians, and the US courts became the guardian of the Internet's autonomy, so that much of the Internet remained a vast social space of experimentation, sociability, and autonomous cultural expression. Every attempt to tame or parcel out the Internet was countered with such determination that governments and corporations had to learn to use the Internet to their benefit without subduing its autonomous development. Not only was the genie out of the bottle, but the genie's genes rejected confinement of this newly found freedom of communication, as per the deliberate design of its creators, exemplified by Tim Berners-Lee's decision to release into the open the software of the World Wide Web. Yet, when the expansion of broadband and the rise of Web 2.0 opened up new opportunities for profit-making in the first decade of the twenty-first century, a new set of regulatory policies was introduced, aiming at the private appropriation not of the Internet itself but of the network infrastructure on which the Internet relies.

Enclosing the Commons of the Information Age (or Trying to)

The third major step toward the creation of a new regulatory environment for digital communication in the United States took place in the 2000s: a series of bills approved in Congress and decisions adopted by the Federal Communications Commission (FCC) that rewrote the provisions of the 1996 Act, thus *enabling companies to invest in different industries and to proceed with vertical integration between carriers, manufacturers, and providers of content, while curtailing public scrutiny over business practices* (Benkler, 2006; Klinenberg, 2007; McChesney, 2007; Schiller, 2007). In 2004, the FCC introduced a policy called "spectrum flexibility," which aimed to increase available spectrum, particularly for wireless communication, and to authorize the free resale of spectrum by companies that were operating within regulated frequencies, thus creating a market for spectrum that increased the purview of major corporations. The FCC also ended the unbundling requirement, thus liberating the Bell operators from their network-sharing obligations while still permitting cable television operators to introduce broadband into their networks and sell services over their proprietary networks. This new policy gave carriers and operators ample freedom to manage access and prices on the networks of their property.

In a logical continuation of this devolution of power to network operators, the latest stage of US deregulation points toward the reversal of the traditional policy of "net neutrality," that is, the consideration of the carrier network as a common-use infrastructure, access to which cannot be blocked, subject to conditions, or discriminated against by the carrier operator vis-à-vis different users.[16] The key decision that opened the debate on net neutrality was the FCC's Cable Modem Order of 2002, which stated that broadband service was no longer considered a telecommunication service (and thus subject to regulation) as it was under the Telecommunications Act of 1996, but as an "information service" beyond the scope of the regulator. The Supreme Court upheld this decision in 2005, thus opening a major debate between two groups. On one side, Internet users, innovative high-tech companies, and Internet content providers, such as Google, Yahoo!, Amazon, and e-Bay, argue for open access to the networks. On the other side, network operators wish to differentiate access and pricing to leverage their private control of the communication infrastructure.

The conflict is about more than a dispute between different industries with specific interests. As Clark (2007: 702) has written, "right now, what they are fighting over is the future of television." This is so because the digitization of all content (bits are bits) opens the way for the Internet to become a carrier for TV. For example, Hulu.com is used by almost all of the largest media conglomerates to stream their television content to audiences free of charge, and Joost.com, a service launched in January 2007, streams television programming using peer-to-peer technology. The Internet already carries substantial voice communication traffic (e.g., Skype), thus fundamentally altering the revenue model of broadcasting companies and telecommunication operators. So, although liberalization and deregulation stimulated the development of Internet-based communication throughout the 1980s and 1990s (largely because they did not interfere with the self-managed development of the Internet), the change of rules attempted by the FCC under the Bush administration in the 2000s was tantamount to re-regulation in favor of the telecommunication, cable, and broadcasting companies which kept resisting the challenges that the

---

[16] For a diverse, well-documented analysis of this fundamental policy development, see the Special Issue on Net Neutrality published by the *International Journal of Communication* in its 2007 volume.

diffusion of broadband Internet and related Web 2.0 content and services posed to their entrenched business model.

Thus, while the attention of the world was focused on freedom of expression on the Internet, the transformation of the communication infrastructure into a series of "walled gardens" managed by network operators, with respect to their specific business interests, imposed fundamental constraints upon the expansion of the new digital culture. The pipes of the Internet Galaxy are being privatized and left to their own fragmented management. While we were concerned about protecting the free electronic frontier against the intrusion of Big Brother (the government), the Big Sisters (major network operators), who appropriate and manage the broadband traffic circulating through the Information Superhighways, have become the ones responsible for restricting free virtual space.

The evolution of regulatory policies was the result of power-making strategies through the articulation of business and political interests, dressed up in discourses about technological wonders and consumer choice and supported by economic models worshipping the higher authority of the Invisible Hand. While there were intra-business conflicts in the 1990s between the supporters of the "Baby Bells" (long-distance carriers) and cable operators, when it came to the main decision of letting the market (i.e., big business) decide the shape of the communication revolution, most of the political class espoused the strategy. The 1996 Act, under Clinton, received the support of the Republican Congress, and many of the measures allowing vertical integration and cross-industry investment recruited supporters from both parties. This is because the telecommunications industry plays a major role in financing political campaigns, while the broadcasting industry is essential in facilitating media coverage of political candidates. The nascent Internet companies took some time to develop political clout and they were too self-satisfied with the mantra of their innate superiority as technological innovators to worry about the future. Furthermore, the public was largely unaware of the importance of the issues that were being decided without consultation or debate. Communication regulation was an obscure field reserved to lawyers, economists, and engineers which did not seem to be related to the concerns of the commons, except in pricing and service abuse claims against monopoly cable operators, matters that were more often than not blamed on the licenses issued by local governments with little information about what they were doing.

Things changed dramatically in the 2000s, partly due to the arrogance of Michael Powell, the new chair of the FCC appointed by President Bush in 2001. A military man, and the son of the then Secretary of State Colin Powell, he was (and is) a free market fundamentalist, who after leaving the FCC in 2004 went to work for Providence Equity Partners, an investment firm managing equity for the media and telecommunication companies that Powell had been in charge of regulating. The President gave him personal support so that he could lift restrictions on media cross-ownership and re-regulate in favor of the big companies in the telecommunication and broadcasting industry. Rupert Murdoch's News Corporation was a major beneficiary of this new policy. The media concentration in television, cable, radio, and the print press that followed the FCC's decision triggered a flurry of protests which mobilized progressive activists, civic associations, civil libertarians, and defenders of local government in America, including powerful conservative groups such as the National Rifle Association. From this protest emerged a potent, multifaceted, social movement, including organizations such as Free Press, the Center for Digital Democracy, Media Access Project, Reclaim the Media, Media Alliance, Media-Tank, the Prometheus Radio Project (calling for "low power to the people" in reference to autonomous LP radio), and many others who successfully fought the FCC's attempt to disenfranchise citizens from communication policy. These groups stirred up an unusual level of public interest in the FCC's public hearings. They protested over the Internet, pressured Congress, and filed law suits in federal courts, making the new Democratic majority in Congress more receptive to the demands for citizen control of communication. This widespread mobilization was concurrent with other factors leading to Powell's resignation from the FCC (Costanza-Chock, 2006; Klinenberg, 2007; McChesney, 2007; Neuman, personal communication, 2007). When a new debate on communication policy emerged in 2005–7 on the issue of "net neutrality," an informed citizenry entered the communication policy arena, pushing it to the forefront of public debate. In the words of Robert McChesney, "what was crucial in 2003 was that the light switch went on for millions of Americans. They did not have to accept all the problems with media as an 'unalterable' given. The media system was not natural; it resulted from policies" (2007: 159). However, to put this awakening experience into perspective, it is worth pointing to a sobering reminder of the power of the communication industry: in the 2008 electoral campaign, as in all other campaigns, no major presidential candidate highlighted the issue of citizen control over the media and communication networks.

Deregulating the World (but not the American Way)

Throughout the world, there has also been a widespread trend toward liberalization, privatization, and deregulation of broadcasting and telecommunications since the 1980s, but at a slower pace than in the United States. However, the regulatory regime was, and still is, to a large extent, different from the United States. In fact, the United States represents the exception in the history of communication regulation from a global perspective. This is because, in the world at large, communication has always been considered too important to be left to private business. Throughout history, communication was seen as a critical domain in which to assert government control, sometimes on behalf of the public interest, and sometimes as a naked expression of state power, with business interests coming in second. Furthermore, there has been a distinctive separation between regulation of the media and regulation of telecommunications throughout the world. The latter was seen as a public-service infrastructure, while the former was considered a key instrument of political and cultural control. Thus, generally speaking, the media were regulated by the political and ideological institutions of the state. Television and radio were usually government owned and government operated, although some room was left for private ownership, though this was always kept under the close eye of the would-be censors. By contrast, newspapers and the print press were usually trusted to the various elites so that they could have their own voice in the public sphere, with the exception of countries under rightwing or leftwing dictatorships, in which all the media were kept under control of the party or the dictator. But even in democratic countries, the print press was subject to political inclinations so that the idyllic notion of an independent professional press was usually belied by the political and ideological alignment of most media, often the expression of religious affiliations, ideological preferences, business interests, and political parties. Overall, the state and ideological apparatuses were the matrix of the media more than the market. Of course, business was present in the media, but commercial strategies had to operate under the umbrella of the holders of political-ideological power.

This state of affairs changed in most parts of the world from the 1980s onward. At the source of the change was the wave of liberalization policies linked to new economic strategies in the context of globalization, the rapid technological change that opened up a new universe of communicative capabilities, and the cultural change toward individualism and freedom of choice that weakened the foundations of ideological conservativism, particularly in developed countries. How this translated into new forms of regulation varied between countries. In some of the most important countries in the world (China, Russia, India), in spite of a growing business presence in the media, there is still, in the twenty-first century, tight direct (China, Russia) or indirect (India) government control over the media. But in most countries, the regulatory regime is exercised by a combination of government ownership and government licenses to business groups that must follow rules that limit their power as fully independent media groups. The usual method of submitting business to political will in the media industry is to distribute spectrum licenses between different business partnerships related to a plurality of political orientations. Thus, whoever is in power always has some access to some media group. The vertical integration of television, radio, and the print press facilitates this division of labor in the media under the control of the political system at large. In addition, in all countries there are still some networks that are owned by the government and in which the independence of the media is limited.

There are exceptions to this general pattern, on both sides. For instance, in the UK, the BBC has been hailed around the world as a model of a public corporation asserting its independence from direct government interference, although some acts by the Blair government tarnished this image without destroying the reputation of the BBC as a reference for independent public media around the world. However, the BBC had to compete with private television networks and the satellite and cable companies that won a substantial market share of the audience, so that it lost its dominant position. On the other extreme of the liberalized media world, Italy, under the government of Berlusconi, produced a most original model of public–private partnership. The Italian government owned the three RAI networks, historically known for their professionalism, that were subjected to heavy political pressures in spite of determined resistance by journalists and producers. On the other hand, Berlusconi, a real-estate businessman, with the support of the Socialist prime minister Bettino Craxi, used a loophole in the Italian Constitution to build three private national television networks on the basis of the local stations that he owned. Berlusconi leveraged his media power from these networks to be elected prime minister in 1994, and then re-elected. So, in the 1990s and 2000s, all national television networks, public or private, were under his control, with obvious consequences for the impoverishment of cultural and political diversity of Italy (Bosetti, 2007). France privatized most public television (TF1 was sold to a construction company), while reserving control over some channels, such as TV7, and partly dedicating one public network (Antenne 2) to cultural programming for the solace of French intellectuals.

Germany, Portugal, and Spain took similar paths. Spain, during the Socialist government of Felipe González in the 1980s, kept two national networks under government control and licensed two open television networks and one satellite television channel to three consortia of private investors, conveniently distributed between different business groups with the proviso that no one shareholder should own more than 25 percent of the open networks. In 1996, González's successor, the conservative prime minister José María Aznar, followed the Berlusconi model and used his control of Telefonica, the Spanish multinational in telecommunications, to acquire one of the private channels and put pressure on the other, effectively monopolizing most of the national television networks during the period 1996–2004. In 2006, a new Socialist government licensed two additional television networks to friendly groups of investors and accelerated the transition to digital television, which freed additional spectrum and made room for a wider range of national and international media companies (Campo Vidal, 2008). However, the most profound transformation of the Spanish media system came as a result of the constitutional refoundation of the Spanish state, from 1978 onward, into a quasi-federal state. The Spanish Autonomous Communities (the equivalent of the German *Länder*) were granted the possibility of developing their own public television and radio networks within the boundaries of their territory. They used this capacity to its full potential, with the result that in Catalonia and in other areas of Spain the regional television networks captured most of the audience, and in Catalonia, the Basque Country, and Galicia they became a key instrument for strengthening national identity via the preservation of their own languages, among other means (Tubella, 2004).

In short, the most important regulatory policy in Europe and in most of the world has been the gradual, yet limited, release of the national government's control over radio and television, and indirectly over the print press, in favor of a diversity of private business groups and regional governments. Media businesses often used this relative autonomy to link up with global business networks, thereby increasing their independence vis-à-vis the government.

The commercialization of the media around the world has received widespread support from public opinion because they have largely escaped (and are still in the process of doing so, in many countries) the iron cage of political bureaucracies. Up-to-date entertainment is a winner over propaganda supplemented with old films and national folklore. This feeling of relative liberation from the political grip in the past two decades may explain the quasi-absence of social protests against media policy in most countries, save for the self-interested claims of business groups losing out in the licensing process. Indeed, when and where media-oriented social movements have taken place, they are not directed toward media business but toward the state to fight its censorship. This is particularly the case in Russia under Putin, where journalists and citizens are fighting an authoritarian media regime guided by political motivation from the highest levels of the state (see Chapter 4).

In most of the world, *telecommunication regulation has changed dramatically* from a monopoly regime (legally or de facto) to a policy of re-regulation and competition that started to take hold in Europe in 1998 and in Japan in 2000 (Rutherford, 2004; OECD, 2007; Cowhey and Aronson, 2009). Supposedly independent telecommunication regulators were established in most countries, and in the European Union, the European Commission assumed oversight of the national regulators. Regulatory authorities prevent monopolistic practices and abusive pricing, submitting companies to fines and mandatory directives. Yet, the original monopolies, even after their privatization, have leveraged their resources and political connections to retain a dominant position in their national territories while embarking on ambitious policies of global expansion and strategic partnerships.

Wireless communication is a more competitive field because it is a newer industry, and in some countries, like China, private wireless operators are used by the government to put pressure on the old wireline operators (Qiu, 2007). However, this policy of managed competition in Europe, Japan, and South Korea seems to have won the upper hand over the disorganized competition induced in the US by the FCC with its free-for-all policies. Broadband penetration is higher in Northern Europe, Japan, and South Korea than in the United States, and its cost per bit is lower. The unbundling rule is still in effect in Europe, thus keeping, for the time being, the principle of network neutrality. Furthermore, the agreement on standards and pricing schemes imposed by the European Commission to wireless communication operators in Europe has led to a higher penetration of wireless communication, higher usage, and higher quality service in Europe than in the United States. The competitive edge of Europe and Asia in this area was also helped by the quality of wireless communication technology and manufacturing design in Europe (particularly in Nordic countries) and

East Asia. In short, regulation in telecommunication networks in the world at large has kept a greater degree of government control over the operators than in the United States, while unleashing managed competition. The net result has been an expansion of broadband and wireless communication, laying the groundwork for a global diffusion of the infrastructure of the digital communication age, and particularly of the Internet in its new Web 2.0 and Web 3.0 incarnations.

Regulating Freedom: When the Red Hood Internet Meets the Big Bad Corporate Wolves

The Internet is a global network, so its regulation could not be left to the US Department of Commerce, even in the form of an ICANN board elected by Internet users. But since there is no global government, the Internet diffused globally, restrained only by limits that each national government could impose within its territorial jurisdiction. Yet, short of unplugging the Internet, it is difficult to control its networking capabilities because they can always be redirected to a backbone somewhere else on the planet. True, it is possible to block access to some designated sites, but not the trillions of e-mail messages and the millions of web sites in constant processes of renewal. Yes, the Internet can be supervised and is, in fact, being actively supervised by all governments in the world (Deibert et al., 2008). But the best governments can do to enforce their legislation is to prosecute a few unfortunate culprits who are caught in the act, while millions of others enjoy their merry ride over the web. Hundreds of Internet freedom fighters (plus a few crooks and child pornographers) end up in real jails to pay for their virtual vagaries. Yet, while a few of the messengers are punished, the messages go on, most of them surfing the ocean of global, seamless communication (see Chapter 4).

This is why the only legitimate body with responsibility for global governance, the United Nations, took up the issue of the Internet in two consecutive World Information Summits, one in Geneva, Switzerland, in 2003 and one in 2005 in Tunis, Tunisia (a country known for its Internet censorship and where journalists covering the meeting were arrested). In December 2003, a number of goals were discussed in Geneva, focusing on information and communication technologies for the benefit of the world's population. Naturally, the Internet became a focal point in many of these discussions. The Geneva Declaration of Principles and Geneva Plan of Action were adopted on December 12, 2003, but participants were unable to agree on a definition of Internet governance. Debates centered on the distinction between a "narrow" definition that encompassed only ICANN-related functions (Internet resource allocation and assignment) and a "broad" definition that would include, ultimately, control over the content circulated through the Internet. As is usually the case in United Nations' meetings, when faced with disagreement over the very concept of "Internet governance," the UN established a Working Group on Internet Governance (WGIG) whose objective was to define the term and provide input to the second phase of the World Summit in Tunis in November 2005. After two years of hard labor by the 40 members of the group, who represented stakeholders from governments, the private sector, and civil society, the August 2005 WGIG Report gave birth to the following working definition: "Internet governance is the development and application by Governments, the private sector and civil society, in their respective roles, of shared principles, norms, rules, decision-making procedures, and programmes that shape the evolution and use of the Internet."

Enlightened by this path-breaking definition, the 2005 UN World Summit on the Information Society (Second Phase) in Tunis, after a debate on policy principles, confirmed the role of ICANN and the overseeing capacity of the US Commerce Department, defined an agenda for the global information society, and established the Internet Governance Forum (IGF). IGF is an international organization whose purpose is to "support the United Nations Secretary-General in carrying out the mandate from the World Summit on the Information Society (WSIS) with regard to convening a new forum for multi-stakeholder policy dialogue." The UN Secretary-General established an Advisory Group and a Secretariat as institutional bodies of the IGF. Subsequently, the IGF held several meetings in Greece in 2006, in Rio de Janeiro in 2007, in Hyderabad in November 2008, and, at the time of writing, a meeting is planned for Cairo in October 2009. There has been an identification of the key policy areas under discussion. These are:

1. Internet infrastructure and resource management (physical infrastructure; VoIP; spectrum policy; technical standards; resource management; administration of Internet names and addresses; administration of root-server system and root-zone files).
2. Issues relating to the use of the Internet (security of network and information systems; spam; national policies and regulations; critical infrastructure protection).

3. Issues with wider impact than the Internet (electronic authentication; competition policy, liberalization, privatization, regulations; access protection, consumer/user protection, privacy; unlawful content and practices; dispute resolution; intellectual property rights; e-commerce and taxation of e-commerce; e-government and privacy; freedom of information and media).
4. Issues with developmental impact (Internet-leased line costs; affordable and universal access; education, human-capacity building; national infrastructure development; social dimensions and inclusion; content accessibility; open source and free software; cultural and linguistic diversity).

According to reliable sources, the policy debate is proceeding at the usual pace for this kind of institutional setting, although there is no conclusion yet to report at the time of writing. I hope to be able to analyze the structure and policy of global Internet governance emerging from this debate in the second, or perhaps tenth, edition of this book.

My skepticism about the results of these debates stems from my own experience on a number of national and international advisory boards on Internet policy. I came to the conviction (leading, of course, to my withdrawal from all these bodies, including those related to the United Nations) that the fundamental concern of most governments is to establish regulations to control the Internet and find mechanisms to enforce this control in the traditional terms of law and order. Regardless of my personal feelings about such a policy (I am against it), there are serious reasons to doubt the effectiveness of the proposed controls when they are not directed toward specific corporations or organizations but at the user community at large (unless there is a generalized attack on Internet service providers that would cripple the entire Internet communication system – never say never). Yet this is an unlikely hypothesis given the extent of business interests already invested in the Internet and the widespread support that the Internet enjoys among most of the 1.4 billion users for whom it has become the communication fabric of their lives. Therefore, the regulation of the Internet has shifted its focus from the Internet itself to specific instances of censorship and repression by government bureaucracies, and to the privatization of the global communication infrastructure that supports Internet traffic. So, in spite of regulation, the Internet thrives as the local/global, multimodal communication medium of our age. But it submits, as everything else in our world, to relentless pressure from two essential sources of domination that still loom over our existence: capital and the state.

The relationship between capital and the state is indeed the source of the policies of liberalization and deregulation that induced the rise of global capitalism and the formation of global multimedia business networks at the heart of the new digital communication system. But because business interests seem to prevail in their interaction with the state, and because business sees a major new field of investment in the expansion of digital communication, regulatory policies have been conducive to the global diffusion of new forms of communication, including mass self-communication. Under such conditions, the media audience is transformed into a communicative subject increasingly able to redefine the processes by which societal communication frames the culture of society. Paradoxically, the yielding of the state to the interests of capital leads to the rise of a new form of communication that may increase the power of citizens over both capital and the state.

Cultural Change in a Globalized World

For communication to happen, senders and receivers need to share codes. In the media business, there has been a strategic shift from broadcasting to a generic audience (assuming its ability to identify with a homogeneous message) to targeting specific audiences, thus adapting the message to the intended receiver. As analyzed above, this has been made possible by the networking of global media business and by new digital technologies that allow the combination of mass production and customized distribution of content. The identification of the audience requires an understanding of its diverse cultural codes. Therefore, the evolution of the format and content of media messages, whether generic or specific, depends on the cultural evolution of societies. Each society has its own path and pace in such evolution. But because the network society is global, there are commonalities and interdependencies in the process of cultural transformation. Lash and Lury (2007), in their analysis of the global culture industry, emphasize the qualitative change represented by globalization in the cultural realm. As they write:

Culture has taken on another, different logic with the transition from the culture industry to *global* culture industry; globalization has given culture industry a fundamentally different mode of operation. Our point is that in 1945 and in 1975 culture was still fundamentally a superstructure...Cultural entities were still exceptional...But in 2005 cultural objects are everywhere: as information, as communication, as branded products, as financial services, as media products, as transport and leisure services, cultural entities are no longer the exception: they are the rule. Culture is so ubiquitous that it, as it were, seeps out of the superstructure and comes to infiltrate, and then take over the infrastructure itself. It comes to dominate both the economy and experience in everyday life...In global culture industry, production and consumption are processes of the construction of *difference*.

(Lash and Lury, 2007: 3–5; emphasis added)

How is this difference constructed? What are the cultural materials that permeate throughout the different domains of experience and structure the frameworks of meaning in which media operate? As a working hypothesis, I propose that the process of cultural transformation in our world evolves along two major bipolar axes: *the opposition between globalization and identification* and *the cleavage between individualism and communalism* (Inglehart, 2003; Castells, 2004c; Tubella, 2004; Baker, 2005; Cardoso, 2006; Qvortrup, 2006).

Cultural globalization refers to the emergence of a specific set of values and beliefs that are largely shared around the planet.

Cultural identification refers to the existence of specific sets of values and beliefs in which specific human groups recognize themselves. Cultural identification is largely the result of the geography and history of human organization, but it can also be formed on the basis of specific projects of identity-building.

Individualism is the set of values and beliefs that gives priority to the satisfaction of needs, desires, and projects of each individual subject in the orientation of her/his behavior.

Communalism is the set of values and beliefs that places the collective good of a community over the individual satisfaction of its members. Community is defined, in this context, as the social system organized around the sharing of a specific subset of cultural and/or material attributes.

Let us examine the actual content of this process of cultural change. *What is a global culture?* Are we in a world of increasing cultural homogeneity? Yes and no. For the most part, we are not (Lull, 2007; Page, 2007). The World Values Survey of the University of Michigan shows the prevalence of national and regional identities over the cosmopolitan identity that is adopted by only a small minority of the world's population (Norris, 2000; Inglehart, 2003; Inglehart et al., 2004). European citizens feel much less European than national or local (Castells, 2004b). Similarly, data from the Latinobarometer indicate the strength of national, regional, and ethnic identification in Latin America (Calderon, 2006). Religion is a major source of collective identification in parts of the world, particularly in the United States, Latin America, India, and Islamic societies, but not in most of Europe (with some exceptions: for example, Poland or Ireland), nor in East Asia, where it is idiosyncratic and not very influential (Norris and Inglehart, 2004).

Yet, *there is indeed a global culture* that can be observed at three levels. First, for a small but influential minority of people, there is the consciousness of the shared destiny of the planet we inhabit, be it in terms of the environment, human rights, moral principles, global economic interdependency, or geopolitical security. This is the principle of *cosmopolitanism* supported by social actors who see themselves as citizens of the world (Beck, 2005). Survey data show that they are overwhelmingly members of the most educated and affluent segments of society, although age is also a factor: the younger people's age, the more open they are to a cosmopolitan view of the world (Inglehart, 2003). Secondly, there is a *multicultural global culture characterized by the hybridization and remix of cultures* from different origins, as in the diffusion of hip hop music in adapted versions throughout the world or the remixed videos that populate YouTube. Thirdly, what is perhaps the most fundamental layer of cultural globalization is the *culture of consumerism*, directly related to the formation of a global capitalist market (Barber, 2007). For capitalism to globalize, the culture of commodification must be present everywhere. And the very fact that capitalism is global and that all countries now live under capitalism (save North Korea at the time of writing) provides the foundation for the planetary sharing of market values and consumer culture.

At the same time, *the existence of diverse sources of cultural identification* creates a complex pattern of interaction between global consumerism, cosmopolitanism, and global hybridization, on one hand, and diverse sources of cultural identification (national, religious, territorial, ethnic, gender, self-selected identities) on the other (Inglehart et al., 2004).

Another *axis of cultural differentiation opposes individualism to communalism*. Wayne Baker's empirical analysis of the evolution of American values shows the parallel development of both trends in the minds of American people over the past three decades (Baker, 2005). The United States is a bipolar culture, made of a Me culture (Mitchell, 2003) and of a God culture (Domke and Coe, 2008). In both cultures, there are extreme positions toward libertarian individualism, on one hand, and submission to God's law (whoever God may be), on the other. The culture of familialism is also a defining set of values bridging the individual and her/his contribution to the moral principles of society. Me, my family, and my God constitute the holy trinity of American values.

In a different context, the study that I and my colleagues conducted on a representative sample of the population of Catalonia in 2002 shows the importance of family identification as the primary organizing principle of life for 56 percent of the population, followed by "myself" (8.7%) and peers (4.9%; Castells and Tubella, 2007). All sources of collective iden-tification together (nation, ethnicity, religion, and territoriality) were the main self-identifying principle for only 9.7 percent of the sample. However, when people were asked to choose in terms of their primary national affiliation, 37.5 percent considered themselves primarily Catalans, with 19.7 percent identifying themselves primarily as Spanish, 36.2 percent as both Catalan and Spanish, and 6.6 percent identifying with the world at large (Castells and Tubella, 2007). Religion was the primary factor of identification for only 2.5 percent. Meanwhile, 13.1 percent of the popu-lation cited a combination of nature, humankind, and the world at large (indicators of cosmopolitanism) as their main self-identifying principle. Interestingly enough, this is the same percentage of people who primar-ily identify with cosmopolitanism in the world at large, according to the World Values Survey (Norris, 2000), with these values becoming more pronounced in the younger age groups. This is to say that in societies in which religion is not a primary source of identification (as is the case in Catalonia and in most of Europe), the individual and her/his family, on one hand, and cosmopolitanism, on the other hand, emerge as the main cultural references for people, particularly for young people. National, regional, and local identification (or non-state national identities as in the case of Catalonia) remain a principle of identification as resistance identities when facing challenges either from globalization or from dominant nation-states (Castells, 2004c; Castells and Tubella, 2007).

If we combine the two bipolar axes of cultural identification, we can detect four significant combinations that are expressed in definite forms of cultural patterns, as shown in Figure 2.6. I shall elaborate on the content of the typology presented here. The articulation between globalization and individualism leads to the diffusion of *consumerism* as the individual form

	GLOBALIZATION	IDENTIFICATION
INDIVIDUALISM	*Branded consumerism*	*Networked individualism*
COMMUNALISM	*Cosmopolitanism*	*Multiculturalism*

Fig. 2.6. Typology of cultural patterns

of relationship to a process of globalization dominated by the expansion of capitalism (Barber, 2007). A particularly important expression of this individual relationship to a global capitalist culture, as proposed by Scott Lash and Celia Lury (2007), is *branding*. Branding is the cultural dimension of the global market, and the process by which individuals assign meaning to their consumerism (Banet-Weiser, 2007).

The combination of identification and individualism is at the source of the culture of *networked individualism* found by sociologists to be the pattern of sociability in the network society (Wellman, 1999; Castells, 2001; Hampton, 2004, 2007). In the age of the Internet, individuals do not withdraw into the isolation of virtual reality. On the contrary, they expand their sociability by using the wealth of communication networks at their disposal, but they do so selectively, constructing their cultural world in terms of their preferences and projects, and modifying it according to the evolution of their personal interests and values (Katz and Aakhus, 2002; Center for the Digital Future, 2005, 2007, 2008; Castells, 2007).

At the intersection of communalism and globalization, we find the culture of *cosmopolitanism*, or the project of sharing collective values on a planetary scale and thereby building a human community that transcends boundaries and specificity on behalf of a superior principle. This is, of course, the case of the Islamic *Umma* (Moaddel, 2007), but could also be the environmental culture (Wapner, 1996), worshipping Gaia on behalf of the past and the future of humankind, or the cosmopolitan culture, affirming the collective values of democracy in a new space of global citizenship (Beck, 2005).

Finally, the fusion of communalism and identification leads to the recognition of multiple identities in a world constituted by a diversity of cultural communities. This is tantamount to recognizing *multiculturalism* as a decisive trend of our interdependent world (Al-Sayyad and Castells, 2002; Modood, 2005).

120

Thus, four cultural configurations emerge from the interaction between the two major bipolar cultural trends that characterize the global network society: *consumerism* (signified by brands), *networked individualism, cosmopolitanism* (be it ideological, political, or religious), and *multiculturalism*. These are the basic cultural patterns of the global network society. And this is the cultural space in which the communication system must operate.

The Communication Vectors of Cultural Patterns

There is not an exclusive, direct connection between each one of the four cultural patterns defined above and specific technologies or forms of communication. The four cultural patterns are present in the mass media and in mass self-communication, and they all underlie communicative practices throughout the whole range of technologies and delivery platforms. However, each one of these cultural patterns is better suited to whichever form of communication is more likely to construct the cultural codes that maximize the communication effect in the minds of the audience. That is, to frame the process of communicative action.

The harbinger of *branded consumerism* is the *global entertainment industry* in the diverse array of its products: films, music, shows, soap operas, video games, massively multiplayer online games, newspapers, magazines, book publishing, and the entire paraphernalia of supporting icons, from clothing to designed consumer goods. The global, vertical integration of the industry facilitates the delivery of brands through multiple channels that reinforce each other. Furthermore, the evolution of news toward infotainment broadens the scope of consumerism to the entire social and political realm, as world events and local politics become mixed with the theatrics of weather reports and the display of goods and services to be consumed. The Hollywood industrial complex has come to be identified as the source of much of this global cultural production and distribution (Wasko, 2001; Miller et al., 2004). Such an historically rooted business dominance has led to the ideologically charged thesis of cultural imperialism, usually assimilated to the one-sided domination of American culture over all of the world's other cultures (Hesmondhalgh, 2007). In fact, cultures resist and evolve on their own, as I will argue below. But there is something else that is more important in analytical and practical terms: global culture is *not* an American culture in spite of the disproportionate share of American-based businesses in the cultural industries. Global is global. It means that the layer of global culture, built around consumerism and branding, processes cultural products of all origins, and delivers them in customized packages to maximize their communicative power in each targeted market (Straubhaar, 1991; Waisbord, 2004a). An example will clarify this analysis: the *telenovelas* industry and one particular *telenovela*: *Ugly Betty* (Miller, 2007).

Telenovelas, serial melodramas for television, while originally produced in Latin America, mainly in Venezuela, Mexico, Brazil, and Colombia, have become export products around the world, sometimes as canned products, just translated; sometimes newly produced and reformatted to the taste of each culture (Sinclair, 1999; La Pastina et al., 2003; Martinez, 2005). *Telenovelas* have been able to engage international audiences better than American soap operas, from whose format they differ substantially, in countries as diverse as Russia, India, Italy, and Germany, as well as their language-specific markets of Latin America and Spain. Successful *telenovelas*, once proven in their domestic market, are bought, produced, and distributed by global television companies, often based in the United States. *Telenovelas* first reached the large Hispanic market in the United States but later made significant inroads into the mainstream American market. The turning point of this market penetration was the success of *Ugly Betty* in 2006.

First produced in Colombia as *Betty la Fea* in 1999, the show reached a primetime audience of 70 percent in its home country, and then went on to obtain similar levels of popularity in Latin America. Thereafter, it was globally exported as both a canned program and a newly produced series, and was shown in 70 countries. Given its global impact, ABC decided, not without hesitation, to air its adapted American version in primetime. The opening of *Ugly Betty* in the Fall of 2006 attracted 16.3 million viewers and became one of the most successful shows in the American market. Jade Miller has conducted an investigation into the significance of the *Ugly Betty* phenomenon. She concluded that:

Telenovelas can best be understood as localizable yet universally appealing cultural products traversing global networks of capitalist cultural concerns. Betty la Fea serves as an example of the way in which a seemingly-domestic product is inherently a global product. The global is present not only in the universally-appealing Cinderella-style plot, but also in the multi-directional paths along which the show has been imported and exported, and the globally-interlinked structure of the corporations involved in Betty la Fea's production and distribution. Whether she is named Betty, Lisa, or Jassi, and whether she speaks Spanish, German, Hindi, or English, Betty serves as a window with which to look at the telenovela industry not as a South-to-North contra-flow of culture but as a global network of culturally-specific content with both local and global appeal. (Miller, 2007: 1)

In sum: the global entertainment industry, which supports and is supported by advertising, is the main channel for the construction of a consumerist, branded culture. The United States industry, as exemplified by the Hollywood industrial complex, is a major player in this industry, but not the only one by any means. Besides, the global entertainment industry does not diffuse just American culture, but any cultural product that sells both at the global level and in its customized, culturally specific form.

Global consumer culture is not the only cultural pattern with an intended global reach. *Cosmopolitanism*, at the intersection of globalization and communalism, aims to construct a global public sphere around shared values of global citizenship. *Global media news networks, in their diversity, aim for the construction of this communicative public sphere that brings countries and cultures together in the space of 24-hour global information flows*, as Ingrid Volkmer (1999) has shown in her study of CNN. However, following Volkmer and other analysts, *the construction of this global information is not neutral. It is biased toward certain values and interests*. Nonetheless, if we consider not just CNN but the entire set of global news networks that distribute the news and faces of the world globally, in real or chosen time, there is indeed a diverse global communicative sphere in the making. This is the case with the BBC, Venezuela-based TeleSur (at a much more modest level), South Africa's A24, EuroNews, and, most significantly, Al Jazeera and several other Arabic networks. While some of these networks started as culturally specific, they tend to diffuse globally; for instance, Al Jazeera began English-language programming in 2007. Al Jazeera is indeed a meaningful development because it was created, and is still owned, as noted above, by the Heir Prince of Qatar, the emirate that is home to the largest US military base in the Arabian Peninsula. Yet, it was more trusted than the Western news, and soon became an alternative source of information for the Arabic-language audience (El-Nawawy and Iskandar, 2002; Miles, 2005; Sakr, 2006). The network paid for its independence with the lives of its journalists and technicians killed during the US bombing of Al Jazeera's offices in Iraq. And it faces the continuing hostility of the United States and of Saudi Arabia, which have gone to substantial lengths to boycott advertising revenue in Al Jazeera.

Even CNN broadcasts in different versions depending on its audience. CNN International is very different from American CNN; CNN en Español (in Latin America) has specific programming and information policies; and CNN+ in Spain is openly critical of US foreign policy, a precondition for attracting audience among the majority of Spaniards in a country in which 93 percent of people opposed the Iraq War from its inception. It is through this diversity of global networks of news and information that an embryonic cosmopolitan culture finds the support of a media delivery platform.

Other types of communication system promoting other forms of cosmopolitanism, namely religious cosmopolitanism, are the global religious television networks, whose programming is broadcast around the world to include the believers of each religion scattered around the planet. The cultural boundaries of religion are now defined by the global networks that reunite the faithful beyond political boundaries throughout the world. In a sense, they are not cosmopolitan because they address the community of believers. But, in a more fundamental sense, they are indeed cosmopolitan because they aim to include everybody in their religious community. This is to say that cosmopolitanism is defined from the perspective of the would-be cosmopolitans.

Multiculturalism is the norm rather than the exception in our world. And so there is extraordinary diversity of cultural production and distribution of content. As stated above, Nigeria has a thriving film industry that reaches a huge audience in Africa, and is more often than not distributed through videos sold through informal networks (Dessa, 2007). India, not the United States, is the largest producer of films in the world. True, they are culturally specific and were for a long time confined to India. But Bollywood is extending its distribution networks to the very large Indian diaspora (Bamzai, 2007; Gopal and Moorti, 2008). And the gigantic Indian television market is dominated by Indian-produced content (Chatterjee, 2004). Home-produced content also dominates the television market in China, Japan, South Korea, Russia, Latin America, Europe, and the world at large (Abrahamson, 2004). Research has shown that audiences are more sensitive to content that is specific to their culture (Miller, 2007). So, while there is a layer of global culture in all media industries, most cultural products are local rather than global. Indeed, a study by Tubella (2004) has shown the decisive importance of television in constructing national identity under the conditions of cultural domination by another nation, as revealed by the important example of Catalan television in Spain after the post-Franco democratic regime devolved political autonomy to Catalonia in 1980. Interestingly enough, one of the strategies of the new Catalan television, in order to diffuse the Catalan language among Spanish immigrants to Catalonia, was to acquire the Spanish and Catalan language rights for popular global television series, such as *Dallas*, and broadcast them only in Catalan. So, the icon of the globalization of American culture became an instrument for the identification of Catalan culture in the media sphere.

Finally, *the culture of networked individualism* finds its platform of choice in the diverse universe of mass self-communication: the Internet, wireless communication, online games, and digital networks of cultural production, remixing, and distribution. Not that the Internet is the exclusive domain of individualism. The Internet is a communication network, and as such it is also an instrument for the diffusion of consumerism and global entertainment, of cosmopolitanism, and of multiculturalism. But the culture of networked individualism can find its best form of expression in a communication system characterized by autonomy, horizontal networking, interactivity, and the recombination of content under the initiative of the individual and his/her networks.

It has been shown that the cultural roots of the Internet are in the culture of freedom and in the specific culture of hackers (Castells, 2001; Himanen, 2001; Thomas, 2002; Markoff, 2006). There is, indeed, a cultural resonance between the culture of the designers of the Internet, the features of their practice as a relatively autonomous network of communication, and the rise of a culture of experimentation that finds its way into the minds of millions on the basis of the multidirectional networking constructed by these millions of senders/receivers of messages.

Protocols of Communication in a Multicultural World

There is still a major issue to be examined in the analysis of cultural change. In this globalized world, characterized by distinct cultural patterns, *how does communication happen?* How, in spite of the fragmentation, differentiation, customization, and segmentation of communication processes, is communication reintegrated in a communicative action that transcends all these cleavages? Is culture fragmented or integrated in the process of communication? In reality, it is both. It is fragmented in the delivery of messages and integrated in the production of meaning through a series of protocols of communication that make intelligibility possible in a communication-centered culture. The construction of the new public sphere in the network society proceeds by building protocols of communication between different communication processes. How does this construction take place? And what are these protocols of communication?

Protocols of communication, in this context, refer to practices and their supporting organizational platforms that make the sharing of meaning possible between the cultural fields of the global network society (consumerism, networked individualism, cosmopolitanism, and multiculturalism). Protocols of communication are transversal practices that are intertwined with the practices embodied in each one of the four cultural patterns that I have identified. The main protocols of communication are the following:

Advertising is the backbone of global and local media business networks (Gluck and Roca-Sales, 2008). Thus, it is present everywhere, in all cultural patterns, and uses all platforms, from television and radio to the Internet and mobile phones. It is through advertising that the *culture of commodification*, at the heart of global capitalism, influences all cultural expressions and their media support.

The construction of a common media *language*, by means of reformatting a shared formula of storytelling and the integration of genres (e.g., infotainment), is made possible by the versatility of *digitization* (McClean, 2007).

Branding (whether commercial or otherwise) structures the relationship between individuals and collectives vis-à-vis diverse cultural patterns. Branding becomes most effective under the condition of vertical integration of media products, facilitated by the globalization and networking of cultural industries (Lash and Lury, 2007).

The constitution of a *networked digital hypertext* made of multidirectional feeds of everything and based on interactive connecting patterns from everyone to everyone induces a common culture: *the culture of co-production of the content that is consumed*, regardless of the specific content.

In our society, the protocols of communication are not based on the sharing of culture but on the culture of sharing. This is why, ultimately, the protocols of communication are not external to the process of communicative action. They are built in people's minds through the interaction between the multiple connecting points in the communication system and people's own mental construction in their communicative multitasking. It follows that the so-called audience is at the origin of the process of cultural change, reversing its historical dependence on the media during the mass communication era.

The Creative Audience

The process of mass communication has been misconstrued around the artificial notion of "the audience." This is directly adopted from the mind-setting of the media industries, and of the advertisers who support them, who need to define their would-be consumers as passive targets for their messages in order to program content assumed to sell in the marketplace. As with any sale, measures of consumer reaction are taken into consideration to refine the adaptation of the merchandise to consumer preferences. Yet, the audience remains the object, not the subject of communication (Burnett and Marshall, 2003).

As I documented above, with the multiplication of channels and modes of communication permitted by new technologies and changes in regulation, the industry has evolved from a predominantly homogeneous mass communication medium, anchored around national television and radio networks, to a diverse media system combining broadcasting with narrowcasting to niche audiences. Yet, even a fragmented audience consuming customized programming remains a subordinate addressee whose preferences are interpreted by media corporations on the basis of sociodemographic profiling.

Interestingly enough, critical theorists of communication often espouse this one-sided view of the communication process (Mattelart, 1979; Postman, 1986; Mattelart and Mattelart, 1992; De Zengotita, 2005). By assuming the notion of a helpless audience manipulated by corporate media, they place the source of social alienation in the realm of consumerist mass communication. And yet, a well-established stream of research, particularly in the psychology of communication, shows the capacity of people to modify the signified of the messages they receive by interpreting them according to their own cultural frames, and by mixing the messages from one particular source with their variegated range of communicative practices (Neuman, 1991). Thus, Umberto Eco, in a seminal text with the suggestive title "Does the Audience Have Bad Effects on Television?" (Eco, 1994), emphasizes the capacity of people at large to add their own codes and subcodes to the codes of the sender that constitute the signifiers of the message. He proposes a scheme of representation of the communication process that adds complexity to the simple one-way communication scheme (see Figure 2.7).

By defining her own signifier in the reception process of the signified message, the addressee constructs the meaning of the message for her practice, working on the materials of the sent message but incorporating

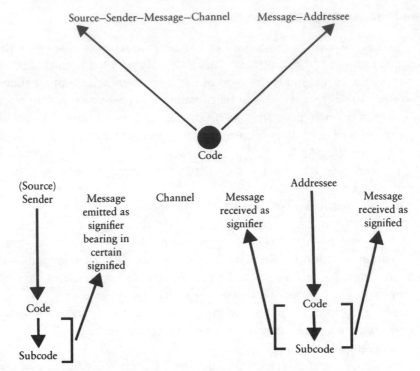

Fig. 2.7. Schematic representation of the communication process according to Umberto Eco. The upper schema represents the classic model of communication; the lower schema represents the model redefined

Source: Eco (1994: 90).

them into a different semantic field of interpretation. This is not to say that the communicative subject is not influenced, and even framed, by the content and format of the message. But the construction of meaning is complex, and depends on mechanisms of activation that combine different levels of involvement in the reception of the message. As Russell Neuman writes, in his path-breaking study of the future of the mass audience:

The audience member is both passive and active at the same time. The mind is such that new information, ideas and impressions are taken in and evaluated and interpreted in the light of cognitive schema and the accumulated information from past experience...The accumulated research of the past several decades confirms that the average audience member pays relatively little attention, retains only a small fraction, and is not the slightest bit overloaded by the flow of information or the choices available among the media and messages. (Neuman, 1991: 114)

With the diversification of the sources of messages in the mass communication world, the audience, while remaining confined to its role as a receiver of messages, increased its range of choice and used the new opportunities offered by the media to express its preferences. With a larger number of television channels, the practice of zapping intensified over time. Loyalty to specific networks and programs declined. Viewers, listeners, and readers constructed their own baskets of news and entertainment, and thereby influenced the content and format of programming. The transformation of programs for children is a good example of the evolution of messages to fit into the diversity of children's cultures (Banet-Weiser, 2007). Yet, diversity of channels and programs does not necessarily mean diversity of content. In the United States, as mentioned above, studies have shown that a typical household only watches 15 channels per week (Mandese, 2007). Much content is reiterative. The capacity to consume sexual and violent movies with very similar plots is rather limited. So, the promised viewers' paradise of 100 or 500 channels becomes a down-sized reality when confronted with unimaginative content and constrained money and time budgets.

However, the potential for the audience to take charge of its communicative practices has increased substantially with the related developments of the culture of autonomy and the rise of mass self-communication. On one hand, a growing number of people, and particularly young people, affirm their autonomy vis-à-vis the institutions of society and the traditional forms of communication, including the mass media (Banet-Weiser, 2007; Caron and Caronia, 2007; Montgomery, 2007). On the other hand, the diffusion of the Internet and of wireless communication supports and strengthens the practices of autonomy, including user-produced content that is uploaded on the web. For instance, in the research that Imma Tubella and I conducted on a representative sample of the Catalan population (3,005 individuals) using factor analysis, we identified six different, and statistically independent, dimensions of autonomy: personal, entrepreneurial, professional, communicative, sociopolitical, and bodily. By studying the uses of the Internet of the surveyed individuals and comparing them to their indexes of autonomy, we found that the higher the level of autonomy, in any dimension, the higher the frequency and intensity of the use of the Internet. And the more people used the Internet, the more they increased their level of autonomy. So, the common view of the Internet as an instrument of autonomy-building has been empirically tested by our study (Castells and Tubella, 2007).

Other studies of the uses of the Internet (Katz and Rice, 2002; Wellman and Haythornthwaite, 2002; Cardoso, 2006; Center for the Digital Future, 2008) and of wireless communication (Castells et al., 2006b; Katz, 2008) show similar results. The Internet-based horizontal networks of communication are activated by communicative subjects who determine both the content and the destination of the message, and are simultaneously senders and receivers of multidirectional flows of messages. Following Eco's terminology, the senders are also addressees, so that a new subject of communication, the sender/addressee emerges as the central figure of the Internet Galaxy. In Figure 2.8, I propose a model of communication that follows Eco's logic but places it in the context of mass self-communication.

Let me explain the meaning of the process represented in Figure 2.8. Senders and addressees are collectively the same subject. Specific individuals or organizations do not necessarily correspond with each other: one sender/addressee may not necessarily receive messages from the sender/addressee to whom she sent a message. But taking the communication process as a shared, multidirectional network, all senders are addressees and vice versa. Communication in the new technological framework is multichannel and multimodal. Multimodality refers to various technologies of communication. Multichannel refers to the organizational arrangements of the sources of communication. If a message is multimodal, it is carried through the Internet (wireline or wireless), wireless devices, television (with its different broadcasting technologies), radio, VCRs, the print press, books, and the like. Furthermore, this multimodality may mesh in a particular process of communication (for example, IPTV, interactive television shows, MMOGs, online newspapers, and so on). Each one of these modes, and their composites, organizes a particular code of communication, to be identified specifically in each context and process. For instance, we know that IPTV is not the same as broadcast TV, but the specific differences in terms of the implicit code of each medium is a matter for investigation rather than the application of a general principle.

Communication also proceeds through multiple channels: a variety of television channels and radio stations (global, national, and local) and their networks, multiple newspapers in print or online, and a seamless ocean of web sites and web-based social spaces that organize the communication networks of millions of senders and receivers. Each one of these channels represents a code. For instance, a network based on 24-hour television news sets a particular frame of reference. YouTube defines its code by a mixture of video and free posting and downloading, with comments and

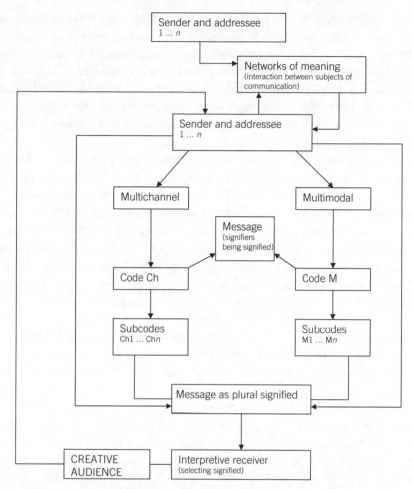

Fig. 2.8. The process of communication by the creative audience

rankings. Religious television networks or porn stations pre-select their viewers by their own self-definition. Each one of these channels has specific characteristics that define a given code (religious, pornographic, free video, social networking as in Facebook, virtual citizenship as in *Second Life*, and the like).

So, following my adaptation of the schema of communication proposed by Eco to the new communication context, I propose the notion that different modes of communication can be defined as Code M and different channels of communication as Code Ch. Code M (e.g., television or the web) operates through a number of subcodes that are the specific modes

131

of a given communication process (e.g., cable television versus specialized television or IPTV versus online games). Similarly, Code Ch (e.g., global television news or religious channels) operates through various subcodes (Islamic networks versus Fox News, Sports IPTV versus IPTV diffusion of clips of broadcast television programming). Thus, Code M operates through a $1 \ldots n$ number of M subcodes and Code Ch operates through a $1 \ldots n$ number of Ch subcodes. They operate by producing and sending messages (signifiers bearing signified).

But, unfortunately, I must add another level of complexity to the understanding of the new communication process. As in Eco's formulation, senders and addressees interpret the codes and subcodes by involving their own codes which decouple the relationship between the signifier and the signified in the message that was sent, and filter the signifier to obtain a different signified. The problem is that, in the world of mass communication, senders and addressees merge in the same subject, so this subject will have to negotiate the meaning between the code of the message she sent and the code of the message she received in order to produce her own signifier (the meaning of the message for the individual engaged in communication). So, the complexity of the communication process is as follows.

The sender/addressee has to *interpret* the messages she receives from multiple modes of communication and multiple channels of communication by engaging her own code in interaction with the code of the message originated by the sender and processed in subcodes of modes and channels. In addition, she has to negotiate her meaning as addressee on the basis of her experience as sender. Ultimately, there is a self-selected meaning that works with the diverse materials of the communicative process. Furthermore, communicative subjects are not isolated entities; rather, they interact among themselves by forming networks of communication that produce shared meaning. We have shifted from mass communication addressed to an audience to an active audience carving out its meaning by contrasting its experience with the one-directional flows of information it receives. Thus, we observe the rise of the interactive production of meaning. This is what I call *the creative audience, the source of the remix culture that characterizes the world of mass self-communication.*

While this is admittedly an abstract representation of the communication process, it can provide a framework to understand the actual complexity of the new communicative practices observed by communication researchers. Thus, Tubella et al. (2008) explored the interplay between different modes of communication in the practice of a focus group of 704 individuals in

Catalonia in 2007. They first analyzed the data (including their own original surveys) relating to the uses of media and the Internet in the population at large. Their field of observation (Catalonia) is interesting because it is an advanced economy and has a developed multimedia system, with about 51 percent of households connected to the Internet, the large majority of them with DSL lines. Fifty-six percent of the population are Internet users, and among Internet users, 89 percent are under 24 years of age. At the same time, it is a society in transition in which there is a mix between an aged, uneducated population and a dynamic, well-educated, Internet-savvy, young population. Thus, while only 8.9 percent of people over 60 years of age were *daily* users of the Internet in 2006, the percentage of the group between 16 and 29 years of age was 65.7 percent.

On one hand, television (mainly open broadcast television) continues to be the dominant mass medium, with almost 87 percent of people watching it every day. Furthermore, both for Catalonia and for Spain, the average number of hours spent watching television remained stable between 1993 and 2006 at a level of 3.5 hours per day. On the other hand, the subset of active Internet users, most of them under 40, shows a very distinct profile of communicative practice. To investigate this new pattern of relationship to the media, the Catalan researchers constructed a focus group of 704 subjects who were observed, using different techniques, with their full consent, for several months. They are active users of new communication technologies, including the Internet, wireless communication, and video-game consoles. The 18–30 years of age segment of this focus group is connected to the Internet, on average, for 4 hours per day, mainly from home. They watch less television than the average viewer, and sleep less as well. But the time they spend on the Internet is intertwined with the time they watch television. More importantly, they belie the notion of "prime time." They manage their communication time, they communicate throughout the day by different means, and they often do it simultaneously. Multitasking is the norm rather than the exception for this group. They simultaneously watch television, are online, listen to music (or radio), check SMSs on their mobile phones, and play on their consoles. In their use of the Internet, they send e-mail, surf web sites, read newspapers online, work and study in the same time-frame. Furthermore, they are not passive recipients of messages and information. A significant subgroup is also a producer of content. They remix videos and upload them, download and share music and films, and create and participate in blogs. Their use of the Internet is highly diversified.

The intense use of the Internet has an effect on other communicative practices. Thus, about 67 percent of the members of the focus group say that they watch less television as a consequence of their activity on the Internet. And 35 percent read less print press (they read the newspapers online). On the other hand, 39 percent listen to more music (downloaded), and 24 percent listen to more radio, the two channels of communication that can be included without too much interference in an Internet-based activity of communication. Indeed, those activities that are incompatible with the use of the Internet (reading books, sleeping) or require visual attention (traditional television) decline in the time allocated to them by active Internet users.

Thus, on the basis of this investigation of the interaction between traditional media and Internet-based media, it appears that active use of the Internet in its various modes leads to three major effects:

1. Time substitution of Internet-based communication for incompatible activities.
2. Gradual dissolution of "prime time" in favor of "my time."
3. Growing simultaneity of communicative practices, integrated around the Internet and wireless devices, by the generalization of multitasking and the capacity of the communicative subjects to combine their attention to different channels, and to complement sources of information and entertainment by mixing modes and channels according to their own interests.

These interests define their own communicative codes. As Tubella et al. (2008) write:

With the Internet at home, audiovisual consumption becomes specialized and diversified, evolving toward a universe that is *multimodal, multichannel and multiplatform*. New technologies allow greater flexibility and mobility, thus supporting the management of any activity in any space anywhere. With the diffusion of the tools that make participation possible in the processes of production, editing and distribution of information and content, the consumer becomes, at the same time, an active creator with the capacity to contribute to and to share multiple visions of the world in which he/she lives.   (2008: 235; my translation)

Granted, this pattern of communication is not predominant in either Catalonia or the world at large. However, if we consider that it is widely diffused among the population under 30 and among active Internet users, it may well be a harbinger of future communication patterns. Indeed, the one thing we know about the future is that the young people of today will make the world of it, and that Internet usage will become generalized on the basis of wireless Internet in the world at large, considering the inevitability of the disappearance of the older generations, among whom the rate of penetration of the Internet is lower.

The results of the Catalan study can be extrapolated in their analytical meaning. The grand convergence in communication, as Jenkins (2006) has proposed, is not just technological and organizational, although these are key dimensions that create the material basis for the broader process of convergence. Convergence is fundamentally cultural and takes place, primarily, in the minds of the communicative subjects who integrate various modes and channels of communication in their practice and in their interaction with each other.

Communication in the Global Digital Age

I am now able to weave together the threads that compose the communication fabric of the global digital age. Micro-electronics-based information and communication technologies make the combination of all forms of mass communication possible in a digital, global, multimodal, and multichannel hypertext. The interactive capacity of the new communication system ushers in a new form of communication, mass self-communication, which multiplies and diversifies the entry points in the communication process. This gives rise to unprecedented autonomy for communicative subjects to communicate at large. Yet, this potential for autonomy is shaped, controlled, and curtailed by the growing concentration and interlocking of corporate media and network operators around the world. Global multimedia business networks (including government-owned media) have taken advantage of the tidal wave of deregulation and liberalization to integrate the networks of communication, the platforms of communication, and the channels of communication in their multilayered organizations, while setting up switches of connection to the networks of capital, politics, and cultural production.

However, this is not tantamount to one-sided, vertical control of communicative practices for four reasons: (1) corporate communication is diverse and, to some extent, competitive, leaving room for some choice as a marketing strategy; (2) autonomous communication networks need a certain breathing space to be attractive to the citizens/consumers, thus expanding new communication markets; (3) regulatory policies are in the hands of institutions that, in principle, are supposed to defend the public interest, but they often betray this principle, as in the past two decades in the United States; and (4) the new technologies of freedom increase people's ability to appropriate the new forms of communication in ways that relentlessly try, not always with success, to run ahead of commodification and control.

Furthermore, the organizations of communication operate within the diverse cultural patterns of our world. These patterns are characterized by the opposition between globalization and identification, and by the tension between individualism and communalism. As a result, the global culture of universal commodification is culturally diversified and ultimately contested by other cultural expressions. Media organizations use new technologies and new forms of management, based on networking, to customize their messages to specific audiences, while providing a channel for the global exchange of local cultural manifestations. Therefore, the global digital communication system, while reflecting power relationships, is not based on the top-down diffusion of one dominant culture. It is diverse and flexible, open-ended in the content of its messages, depending on specific configurations of business, power, and culture.

Because people are recognized for their diversity (as long as they remain consumers) and because technologies of mass self-communication allow greater initiative to the communicative subjects (as long as they assert themselves as citizens), a creative audience emerges, remixing the multiplicity of messages and codes it receives with its own codes and communication projects. Thus, in spite of the growing concentration of power, capital, and production in the global communication system, the actual content and format of communication practices are increasingly diversified.

Yet, precisely because the process is so diverse, and because the technologies of communication are so versatile, the new global digital communication system becomes more inclusive and comprehensive of every form and content of societal communication. Everybody and everything finds a way of existence in this intertwined, multimodal, interactive communication text, so that any message external to this text remains an individual experience without much chance of being socially communicated. Because our brains' neural networks are activated through networked interaction with their environment, including their social environment, this new communication realm, in its variegated forms, becomes the main source of signals leading to the construction of meaning in people's minds. Since meaning largely determines action, communicating meaning becomes the source of social power by framing the human mind.

Chapter 3

Networks of Mind and Power

The Windmills of the Mind[17]

Communication happens by activating minds to share meaning. The mind is a process of creation and manipulation of mental images (visual or not) in the brain. Ideas can be seen as arrangements of mental images. In all probability, mental images correspond to neural patterns. Neural patterns are arrangements of activity in neural networks. Neural

[17] This section is largely based on research in neuroscience as theorized and systematized by Antonio Damasio. In support of the analysis presented here, I refer the reader to some of his published work: Damasio (1994, 1999, 2003); Damasio and Meyer (2008). I have also learned some basic notions in the field of research on emotion and cognition from my ongoing interaction with Professors Antonio Damasio and Hanna Damasio over the years. I am deeply indebted to Antonio Damasio for his advice on the analysis presented here. I would also like to acknowledge the influence throughout this chapter of my conversations with, and readings of, George Lakoff and Jerry Feldman, distinguished cognitive scientists and colleagues of mine at Berkeley. I refer the reader to George Lakoff's analysis as presented in Lakoff (2008). It should be obvious that I am not claiming any special competence in neuroscience or cognitive science. My only purpose in introducing this element as a layer in my analysis is to connect my knowledge of political communication and communication networks to the knowledge we now have on the processes of the human mind. It is only with such an interdisciplinary scientific perspective that we may move from description to explanation in understanding the construction of power relationships by human action on the human mind. Naturally, any error in this analysis is my exclusive responsibility.

networks connect neurons, which are nerve cells. Neural patterns and the corresponding images help the brain to regulate its interaction with the body-proper and with its environment. Neural patterns are shaped by the evolution of the species, the original brain equipment at birth, and the learned experience of the subject.

The mind is a process, not an organ. It is a material process that takes place in the brain in interaction with the body-proper. Depending on the level of wakefulness, attention, and connection to self, the mental images that constitute the mind may or may not be conscious. To be conscious of something means: (a) to have a certain level of wakefulness; (b) to have focused attention; (c) to connect the object of attention with a central protagonist (self).

The brain and the body-proper constitute one organism connected by neural networks activated by chemical signals circulating in the blood stream and electro-chemical signals sent through nerve pathways. The brain processes stimuli received from the body-proper and from its environment with the ultimate purpose of ensuring survival and increasing the well-being of the brain's owner. Mental images, for example, ideas, are generated through the interaction between specific regions in the brain and the body-proper responding to internal and external stimuli. The brain constructs dynamic neural patterns by mapping and storing activities and the responses they elicit.

There are two kinds of images of the body: those of the body interior, and those from special sensory probes that capture alterations in the environment. In all cases, these images originate from a body event or *from an event that is perceived as relating to the body*. Some images relate to the world within the body, others to the world outside. In all cases, images correspond to alterations in the body and its environment, transformed in the brain through a complex process of constructing reality by working on the raw materials of sensorial experience through the interaction of various areas of the brain and the images stored in its memory. The construction of complex images from different sources occurs by neural binding that is achieved by simultaneous neuronal activity in different areas of the brain to bring the activity from various sources together in one single time interval. Networks of associations of images, ideas, and feelings that become connected over time constitute neural patterns that structure emotions, feelings, and consciousness. So, the mind proceeds by networking patterns in the brain with patterns of our sensorial perception that derive from coming into contact with the networks of matter, energy, and activity that constitute our experience, past, present, and future (by anticipation of consequences of certain signals according to images stored in the brain). *We are networks connected to a world of networks.* Each neuron has thousands of connections coming from other neurons and thousands of outgoing connections to other neurons. There are between 10 billion and 100 billion neurons in the human brain, so connections are in the trillions. Binding circuits create experience, either immediate or accumulated over time.

We construct reality as a reaction to actual events, internal or external, but our brain does not merely reflect these events. Instead, it processes them according to its own patterns. Most of the processing is unconscious. So, reality for us is neither objective nor subjective, but a material construction of images that mix what happens in the physical world (outside and inside us) with the material inscription of experience in the circuitry of our brain. This takes place through a set of correspondences established by neural binding over time between the characteristics of events and the catalog of responses available to the brain to fulfill its regulatory function. These correspondences are not fixed. They can be manipulated in our mind. Neural binding creates new experiences. We can establish spatial and temporal relationships between the objects that we sense. The construction of time and space largely defines our construction of reality. This requires a higher level of manipulation of images. That is, it requires the conscious mind; a mind that symbolizes correspondences between events and mental maps; for instance, with the use of metaphors, many of them derived from the experience of the body-proper. Indeed, the body-proper is the source of the mind's activity, including the conscious mind. But the processing of these signals at higher levels of abstraction becomes a fundamental mechanism for the preservation and well-being of the body-proper. As Damasio writes: "The brain's body-furnished, body-minded mind is a servant of the whole body" (2003: 206).

Consciousness possibly emerges from the necessity of integrating a greater number of mental images from perception with images from memory. The greater the integration capacity of a mental process, the greater the capacity of the mind for problem-solving on behalf of the body. This greater recombining capacity is associated with what we call creativity and innovation. But the conscious mind needs an organizing principle to orient this higher-level activity. *This organizing principle is the self*: the identification of the specific organism that should be served by the process of manipulation of mental images. From the generic purpose of survival and well-being, my brain defines a specific mental manipulation for survival and well-being for myself. Feelings, and therefore the emotions from which they arise, play a fundamental role in determining the orientation of the mind in assuring the destination of activity toward the proper body-proper. In fact, without consciousness, the human body cannot survive.

Consciousness operates on the processes of the mind. Integration of emotions, feelings, and reasoning that ultimately lead to decision-making determine these processes. Mental representations become engines of meaningful action by incorporating the emotions, feelings, and reasoning that define the way we live. We need to understand this mechanism in order to be able to grasp what we actually mean when we speak of emotional politics or when I say that I want to do what I feel like doing. Emotions, feelings, and reasoning all originate in the same neural patterning between the brain and the body-proper, and follow the same rules of association and multilayered representation that characterizes the dynamics of the mind.

Antonio Damasio (1994, 1999, 2003) has demonstrated, experimentally and theoretically, the prominent role of emotions and feelings in social behavior. Emotions are distinctive patterns of chemical and neural responses resulting from the brain's detection of an emotionally competent stimulus (ECS), that is, changes in the brain and in the body-proper induced by the content of some perception (such as the emotion of fear when confronted with an image of, or evoking, death). Emotions are deeply wired in our brain (and in most species' brains) because they have been induced by the drive to survive throughout the process of evolution. Ekman (1973) identified six basic emotions recognized everywhere. Experimental research shows that the operation of these emotions can be related to specific systems in the brain. The six basic emotions are: fear, disgust, surprise, sadness, happiness, and anger. Species or individuals that are not equipped with the proper emotional sensing system are unlikely to survive.

Emotions are perceived in the brain as feelings. "A feeling is the perception of a certain state of the body along with the perception of a certain mode of thinking and of thoughts with certain themes" (Damasio, 2003: 86). Feelings derive from emotionally driven changes in the brain that reach a level of intensity sufficient enough to be processed consciously. However, the process of feeling is not a simple transcription of emotions. Feelings process emotions in the mind in the context of memory (i.e. feelings include associations to other events, either directly experienced by the individual or transmitted genetically or culturally). Furthermore, emotional patterns derive from the interaction between the characteristics of the emotionally competent stimulus and the characteristics of the brain maps of a specific individual.

The images in our brain are stimulated by objects or events. We do not reproduce events, we process them. Neural patterns lead to mental images rather than the other way around. The primary images on which the mind operates originate in the body or through its peripheral sensors (e.g., the optic nerve). These images are based on neural patterns of activity or inactivity related to the body interior or to its external environment.

Our brain processes events (interior or exterior) on the basis of its maps (or established networks of association). These events are structured in the brain. By connecting these maps with events, neural binding creates emotional experiences by activating two emotional pathways defined by specific neurotransmitters: the dopamine circuit conveys positive emotions; the norepinephrine circuit conveys negative emotions. These emotional pathways are networked with the forebrain, where much of the decision-making process takes place. These convergent pathways are called *somatic markers* and they play a key role in linking emotions to event sequences.

The brain activity necessary to produce the proto-self, a necessary step to constitute the self, shares some mechanisms with the production of feelings in the brain. Thus, feelings and the constitution of the self emerge in close relation, but only when the self is formed are emotions processed as feelings. By becoming known to the conscious self, feelings are able to manage social behavior, and ultimately influence decision-making by linking feelings from the past and the present in order to anticipate the future by activating the neural networks that associate feelings and events. This associative capacity extraordinarily amplifies the ability of the brain to learn by remembering emotionally competent events and their consequences.

Emotions and feelings are linked in the mind to orient the self toward decision-making in relation to the self's internal and external networks. The human mind is characterized by its capacity for future-thinking, which is its ability to relate foreseeable events with the brain maps. For the brain to connect these maps with external events, a communication process must take place. In simple terms, the human mind is activated by accessing the brain maps via language.

For this communication to happen, the brain and its sensorial perceptions need protocols of communication. The most important protocols of communication are metaphors. Our brain thinks in metaphors, which can be accessed by language but *are physical structures in the brain* (Lakoff and Johnson, 1980; Lakoff, 2008). In Lakoff's analysis:

As neuroscientists say, "Neurons that fire together wire together." As the same circuit is activated day after day, the synapses on the neurons in the circuit get stronger until a permanent circuit is formed. This is called neural recruitment... "Recruitment" is the process of strengthening the synapses along a route to create a pathway along which sufficiently strong activation can flow. The more neurons are used, the more they are "strengthened." "Strengthening" is a physical increase in the number of chemical receptors for neurotransmitters at the synapses. Such a "recruited" circuit physically constitutes the metaphor. Thus, metaphorical thought is physical... Simple metaphors can then be combined via neural binding to form complex metaphors. (2008: 83–4)

Metaphors are critical to connect language (thus human communication) and brain circuitry. It is through metaphors that narratives are constructed. Narratives are composed of frames, which are the structures of the narrative that correspond to the structures of the brain that resulted from the brain's activity over time. *Frames are neural networks of association that can be accessed from the language through metaphorical connections. Framing means activating specific neural networks.* In language, words are associated in semantic fields. These semantic fields refer to conceptual frames. Thus language and mind communicate by frames which structure narratives that activate networks in the brain. Metaphors frame communication by selecting specific associations between language and experience on the basis of brain mapping. But frame structures are not arbitrary. They are based on experience, and they emerge from social organization that defines social roles within culture and then becomes wired in the brain circuits. Thus, the patriarchal family is based on the role of father/patriarch and the mother/homemaker derived from evolution and established through domination and the gendered division of labor throughout history, which is then inscribed in brain networks through biological evolution and cultured experience. From there, if we follow Lakoff's proposition, emerge the frames of the strict father and the nurturing parent (not mother, since gendered metaphors are cultural) on which many social and institutional structures are based. While there is a debate over the universality of this proposition (actually Lakoff refers specifically to American culture), the framing mechanism unveiled by Lakoff stands by itself.

Narratives define social roles within social contexts. Social roles are based on frames that exist both in the brain and in social practice. Goffman's (1959) analysis of role-playing as the basis of social interaction also relies on the determination of roles that structure organizations in society. Framing results from the set of correspondences between roles organized in narratives, narratives structured in frames, simple frames combined in complex narratives, semantic fields (related words) in the language connected to conceptual frames, and the mapping of frames in the brain by the action of neural networks constructed on the basis of experience (evolutionary and personal, past and present). As a reminder, language is not simply verbal language; it can also be non-verbal communication (e.g., body language), as well as a technologically mediated construction of images and sounds. Most communication is built around metaphors because this is the way to access the brain: by activating the appropriate brain networks that will be stimulated in the communication process.

Human action takes place through a process of decision-making that involves emotions, feelings, and reasoning components, as represented in Figure 3.1 proposed by Damasio. The critical point in this process is that emotions play a double role in influencing decision-making. On one hand,

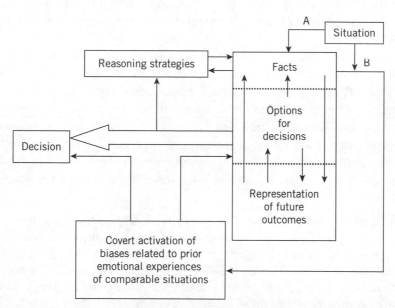

Fig. 3.1. The process of decision-making according to Antonio Damasio

Source: Damasio (2003: 149).

they covertly activate the emotional experiences related to the issue that is the object of decision-making. On the other hand, emotions can act directly on the process of decision-making, by prompting the subject to decide the way she feels. It is not that judgment becomes irrelevant, but that *people tend to select information in ways that favor the decision they are inclined to make.*

Thus, decision-making has two paths, one based on framed reasoning, the other directly emotional. But the emotional component may act directly on the decision or indirectly by marking the reasoning with a positive or negative signal that narrows the decision-making space on the basis of past experience. Signals relate in one way or another to the body, *so these signals are somatic markers*. The experiments conducted by Kahneman and Tversky (1973) on economic decision-making appear to support the existence of this shortcut from emotions and feelings to decision-making without indirect processing in strategic thinking.

Communication, in its different modalities, plays a major role in activating relevant neural networks in a process of decision-making. This is because "some of the same neural structure in the brain that is used when we live out a narrative is also used when we see someone else living out that narrative" (Lakoff, 2008: 40). Although there is a difference between the two processes, our brain uses the same structures for perception and for imagination.

One way in which exposure to communication can influence behavior is through *the activation of so-called mirror neurons in our brain* (Gallese and Goldman, 1998; Gallese et al., 2004; Rizzolatti and Craighero, 2004). Mirror neurons represent the action of another subject. They enable processes of imitation and empathy. They make it possible to relate to the emotional states of other individuals, a mechanism that underlies cooperation in animals and humans. *However, mirror neurons do not act alone. They depend on broader processes in the brain's networks.* According to Damasio and Meyer:

Cells in mirror-neuron areas do not themselves hold meaning, and they alone cannot carry out the internal simulation of an action . . . Mirror neurons induce widespread neural activity based on learned patterns of connectivity; these patterns generate internal simulation and establish the meaning of actions. . . . The neurons at the heart of this process . . . are not so much like mirrors after all. They are more like puppet masters, pulling the strings of various memories . . . Mirror neurons pull the strings, but the puppet itself is made of a large brain network.

(Damasio and Meyer, 2008: 168)

Emotions are not only critical for feeling and reasoning, they are also essential for communication in social animals. Mirror neurons, by activating certain neural patterns, appear to play an important role in emotional communication because *the same neural networks are activated when I feel fear, and when I see someone else feeling fear, or when I see images of humans feeling fear, or when I watch events evoking fear. Furthermore, simulation processes generated by patterns activated by mirror neurons facilitate the construction of language because they assist the transition from observation and action to general representation, that is, the process of abstraction. The capacity for abstraction introduces symbolic expression, the source of communication through language.*

The effects of mirror neurons and their activated neural patterns assist the mind in the representation of the intentional states of others (Schreiber, 2007). Mirror neurons will fire when performing an action and when observing another subject's action. However, for this action to have a meaning in my brain I need to assess what the subject is doing. The medial parietal cortex is activated by emotionally competent events (ECS) resulting from its evaluation of the environment (Raichle et al., 2001). Because these medial regions are active in the detection, representation, assessment, and integration of self-referential stimuli, a number of neuroscientists think that *this region of the brain is critical to the construction of the self* (Damasio, 1999; Damasio and Meyer, 2008). Experiments have shown that the capacity to evaluate the intentional states of others and to send signals to manipulate these intentions can assist evolution toward higher cooperation, inducing better individual and group outcomes (Schreiber, 2007: 56).

Activation of our brain through neural patterns induced by mirror neurons is at the source of empathy, identification with or rejection of narratives in television, cinema, or literature, and with the political narratives of parties and candidates. As Lakoff (2008) asserts, the use of the same neural structure for experience and representation of experience has "enormous political consequences" (p. 40). In Westen's words: "political persuasion is about networks and narratives" (2007: 12) because "the political brain is an emotional brain" (2007: xv). This is why "the states that really determine elections are voters' states of minds" (2007: 4).

Indeed, a growing body of research in political science and political communication has established a complex set of connections between mind and power in the political process. Power is constructed, as all reality, in the neural networks of our brain. Power is generated in the windmills of the mind.

Emotion, Cognition, and Politics

Political cognition has been a key factor in the evolution of humankind, helping to foster cooperation and collective decision-making in the quest toward survival and well-being. An increasingly influential stream of research demonstrates the integration of cognition and emotion in political decision-making. Political cognition is emotionally shaped. There is no opposition between cognition and emotion, but there are different forms of articulation between emotion and cognition in decision-making. Information processing (cognition) can operate with or without anxiety (emotion), leading to two different forms of decision-making: rational decision-making as a process of evaluating new information or routine models of decision based on past experience as processed in brain maps.

The theory of affective intelligence provides a useful analytical framework that inspires a diversified body of evidence in political communication and political psychology supporting the notion that emotional appeals and rational choices are complementary mechanisms whose interaction and relative weight in the process of decision-making depend on the context of the process (Marcus et al., 2000; MacKuen et al., 2007; Neuman et al., 2007; Marcus, 2008). Indeed, emotional impairment disables the ability to make proper cognitive judgments. Evaluation of events is emotional, and shaped by somatic markers (Spezio and Adolphs, 2007: 71–95). According to MacKuen et al., "Rationality is appropriate only in some situations" (2007: 126). Increasing anxiety is indicative of uncertainty and uncertainty is associated with rationality:

Ideology dominates the choice of complacent voters – voters who feel no uneasiness about their candidate. On the other hand when engaged by their emotional alert mechanisms, people do change their behavior ... When emotionally stimulated to reasoned consideration, that is to say, highly anxious about their party's candidate, citizens reduce their reliance on disposition and increase their weighing of contemporary information. (MacKuen et al., 2007: 136)

Thus, interestingly enough, strong emotions trigger alert mechanisms that increase the significance of rational evaluation of the decision (Schreiber, 2007). Emotion highlights the role of cognition while influencing the cognition process at the same time.

According to affective intelligence theory, the emotions that are particularly relevant for political behavior are *enthusiasm* (and its opposite, depression) and *fear* (with its counterpart, calm). But what are the sources of these political emotions? And how are emotions colored positively or negatively vis-à-vis a specific event?

Political behavior is conditioned by two emotional systems: (a) the *disposition system* induces enthusiasm and organizes behavior to achieve the goals of the enthusiastic subject in a given environment; (b) the *surveillance system*, when experiencing fear or anxiety as a result of the presence of a given ECS, calls upon the reasoning mechanism to carefully evaluate the adequate response to the perceived threat. So, acting on behavioral predispositions should trigger enthusiasm, while anxiety should increase consideration of the complexity of specific circumstances. Enthusiastic citizens follow the party line, while anxious citizens take a closer look at their options.

According to the analysis of Huddy et al. (2007), positive and negative affects are linked to two basic motivational systems that result from human evolution: *approach* and *avoidance*. The approach system is linked to goal-seeking behavior that produces positive emotions by directing an individual toward experiences and situations that produce pleasure and reward. The negative affect is linked to avoidance intended to protect an individual against negative occurrences. Their analysis is based on reported evidence that shows the activation of both systems in different regions of the brain and different neurochemical pathways (Davidson, 1995). There is a weak link between positive and negative emotions; one is not the reverse of the other. Positive emotions are more common. Negative emotions are heightened when it is time to move from decision to action. However, this analytical model does not account for the difference among types of negative emotions, such as *anxiety and anger*. Neurological research connects anger and approach behavior and anxiety and avoidance behavior. Furthermore, there is an association between anxiety and risk aversion and anger and risk-taking (Huddy et al., 2007: 212). *Anxiety is associated with heightened vigilance and the avoidance of danger*. But anger is not. Anxiety is a response to an external threat over which the threatened person has little control. *Anger is a response to a negative event that contradicts a desire. Anger increases with the perception of an unjust action and with the identification of the agent responsible for the action. Anxiety and anger* have different consequences. *Anger* leads to an imprudent processing of events, reduction of risk perception, and greater acceptance of the risks linked to a given action. *Anxiety* is connected to avoidance and induces a higher level of threat evaluation, a higher concern about risks involved, and a cautious assessment of information. For instance, some studies on negative emotions and the Iraq War did not find a relationship between these feelings and attitudes toward the war. But this is because they have conflated anger and anxiety. A study conducted by Huddy et al. (2002) found a link between anger toward Saddam Hussein and terrorists and American support for the Iraq War, and a link between anxiety about the same subjects and opposition to the war. Anxiety leads to risk-aversive behavior. Anger leads to risk-taking behavior. Anxiety is associated with unknown objects. Aversion is associated with well-known negative objects (Neuman, personal communication, 2008).

Emotion influences political judgment via two paths: (a) loyalty to parties, candidates, or opinion-leaders based on an attachment to these leaders (when circumstances are familiar); (b) critical examination of parties, candidates, or opinion-leaders based on rational calculations influenced by heightened anxiety (when circumstances are unfamiliar). In both cases, rationality alone does not determine decision-making; it is a second-level processing of information that depends on activated emotions.

The emotional component of political cognition conditions the effectiveness of information processing related to issues and candidates. To understand how citizens process their political knowledge, Redlawsk et al. (2007) conducted an experiment using dynamic process voting techniques on a group of students. Their findings show that anxiety operates only for preferred candidates and depends on the environment. *In a high-threat environment, anxiety leads to careful information processing, more effort to learn about the candidate who generates anxiety, and more attention to the candidate's position on issues*. But in a low-threat environment, anxiety does not have much effect on information processing and learning. There appears to be an anxiety threshold: with *too little anxiety in the environment, learning is not activated; but too much anxiety undermines learning*. In both environments, anxiety does not affect the processing of information about the less-favored candidate(s). Anxiety is associated with unknown objects. Aversion is associated with well-known negative objects. (Neuman, 2008, personal communication).

Anger, it is worth repeating, *is different from anxiety in its affect effect. In low-threat environments, more attention is paid to information that evokes anger*. When that anger is directed toward a previously liked candidate, aversion follows, as voters support other candidates and tend to inaccurately remember the positions of the candidate that they rejected after an initial moment of support. On the other hand, *greater enthusiasm results in more frequent searches for information*, although more frequent searching does not always result in a more accurate assessment of the issues. Higher levels of political experience increase emotional connections to candidates and parties, as citizens rely on their stored, implicit association. On the other hand, politically inexperienced people are more inclined to use their cognitive mechanisms to evaluate their options (Redlawsk et al., 2007).

A classic study by Zaller (1992) found that uncertainty prompted attention to political information and increased the probability that information would actually be retained. When seeking information, people begin with their values, and then look for information to confirm their values. Similarly, Popkin (1991) has shown that individuals are "cognitive misers" who look for information that confirms their existing beliefs and habits, a cognitive shortcut that reduces the mental effort required to perform a task (Popkin, 1991; Schreiber, 2007). For instance, people will make judgments based on information they can recall from memory rather than on a complete set of information gathered from various sources. This memory-recall engages the reflective system. The reflexive system, meanwhile, plays a subconscious role in the formation of attitudes.

Explicit attitudes construct a limited set of information. Implicit attitudes result from automatic associations among many factors, and are susceptible to stereotypes. Implicit and explicit attitudes often conflict. Implicit attitudes have a strong role in political decisions because they help construct the coalitions that foster cooperation. Coalition and cooperation were fundamental to the survival of early humans and provoked the evolution of human intelligence by inducing cognitive competition. Humans establish coalitions around shared characteristics; one of these characteristics is race, which leads to racial stereotypes. Multiracial coalitions must establish cooperation around other shared characteristics besides race. So, cooperation rather than the specific features of the cooperators is the key to political bonding that is able to transcend racial or gender stereotypes (Schreiber, 2007: 68).

All politics are personal. Social networks play an important role in defining political behavior. If people find congenial attitudes in their social network, they are more active politically, while contradictory ideas in the social network reduce participation. Strong partisans are more likely to be in homogeneous political networks. Subjects' attitudes are influenced by feelings toward other people in the network. Attitudes are produced in shared practice, and therefore can be changed if the practice changes (MacKuen et al., 2007). Attitudes depend on feelings, and feelings are constructed through the perception of emotions. As stated above, studies show the recurrence of a number of emotions across cultures. Some of these emotions play a particularly important role in the political process. One of these emotions is fear. Another is hope (Just et al., 2007). Since hope involves projecting behavior into the future, it is accompanied by fear of failing to find fulfillment. Since a distinctive feature of the human mind is the ability to imagine the future, hope is a fundamental ingredient in activating brain maps that motivate political behavior oriented toward achieving well-being in the future as a consequence of action in the present. So, hope is a key component of political mobilization.

But hope is also mixed with the fear of the preferred candidate losing, or deceiving her constituents. Hope and fear combine in the political process, and campaign messages are often directed to stimulate hope and to instill fear of the opponent. Fear is essential for self-preservation, but hope is essential for survival because it allows individuals to plan the outcome of their decisions and it motivates them to move toward a course of action from which they expect to benefit. Both fear and hope encourage people to seek more information about their decisions. Hope and enthusiasm are not the same. Hope involves a level of uncertainty about the subject through which that hope is mediated (i.e. the party or the candidate). Enthusiasm is simply a positive evaluation and does not necessarily require the projection of social change. But the critical matter is that evaluation of candidates or political options is processed in relation to the goals of the self. There is no politics-in-general; it is always "my politics," as processed by my brain's neural patterns and enacted through the decisions that articulate my emotions and my cognitive capabilities, communicated through my feelings. This is the framework of human action in which the political process operates.

Emotion and Cognition in Political Campaigns

As Brader (2006) remarks, for a long time scholarly research minimized the impact of media and political campaigns on the outcome of elections (e.g. Lazarsfeld et al., 1944), a contradiction of the majority of political consultants' beliefs and practices. However, since the 1990s, a substantial body of political communication studies has provided evidence of the influence of news, political campaigns, and political advertising on citizens' decision-making processes (e.g. Ansolabehere et al., 1993; Ansolabehere and Iyengar, 1995; Zaller, 1992; Valentino et al., 2002). Most of these studies identified message content and policy issues as the primary factors in political decision-making. However, an increasing number of studies emphasize the role of emotional appeals contained in political campaigns (Jamieson, 1992; West, 2001, 2005; Richardson, 2003). Marcus and his colleagues (Marcus et al., 2000; Marcus, 2002), building on discoveries in neuroscience and cognitive psychology as reported in the previous sections, have demonstrated the connection between emotion and purposive thinking in the process of political decision-making. Their research on US presidential elections from 1980 to 1996 showed that two-thirds of the vote could be explained by two variables: feelings toward the party and feelings toward the candidate, while policy issues weighed much less in voters' decisions. Moreover, policy issues become important primarily when they arouse emotions among the voters.

Brader (2006) built on this body of evidence, as well as on Damasio's theory of somatic markers (1994), and on the theory of affective intelligence (Marcus et al., 2000), to test empirically the role of emotions in determining the effects of political advertising on voting behavior, focusing on two basic emotions considered to be key motivational sources: *enthusiasm* and *fear*. He first conducted experiments designed to replicate real decision-making as closely as possible in order to identify the mechanisms by which emotions embedded in political advertising, and particularly in music and images, would affect voting patterns. His findings show that advertising eliciting enthusiasm mobilized voters. Yet, it also polarized their choices, by reaffirming the choices they had already made and inducing a stronger rejection of the opposite candidate, regardless of which candidate's ad they had watched. On the other hand, exposure to fear advertisements introduced uncertainty in the voter's choice, thereby increasing the likelihood of changing the viewer's political preferences. Fear ads tend to erode the opponent's base of support among voters, while heightening the importance of voting for those viewers made anxious by the ad. But fear advertising may also demobilize voters. So, ads designed to instill fear do have a powerful effect in favor of the advertisement's sponsor in two ways: by mobilizing the concerned supporters of the ad's sponsor and by discouraging the potential voters of the opponent. Interestingly, the most knowledgeable citizens are also the most responsive to emotional appeals. This is consistent with the argument of the theory of affective intelligence, according to which emotions serve as "relevance detectors." There is heightened scrutiny of the positions of a candidate when a message triggers the fear of negative consequences of an electoral outcome. Thus, the hypothesis presented in the previous section is verified empirically: emotion is not a substitute for analysis in the process of decision-making; it is a factor activating a higher level of reflective behavior.

On the basis of the findings of his experiment, Brader proceeded to perform a content analysis of 1,400 congressional and gubernatorial electoral advertisements produced during the 1999 and 2000 US electoral campaign seasons. He found that most ads had strong emotional content and that enthusiasm and fear were the dominant frames in the sample. There was a tendency for the incumbents to rely on enthusiasm and for the challengers to resort to fear. The more voters are concerned with the consequences of a given policy, the greater the probability of partisan ads using fear in their message. However, both fear and enthusiasm were often mixed within the same ad, and they were connected to policy issues. In other words, Brader found that there was no opposition between emotional ads and reasoning ads. Emotions are a channel to convey arguments. As he writes:

Emotion and information are related. Substance and arguments are often required to give the overall message . . . The message must provide voters with a sense of what to feel scared or hopeful about, and in many cases what voters should do with those feelings . . . Emotions are not mere extension of argument. They lend force to the argument, not so much by making it more convincing, but rather by helping to redirect attention and motivate thought into action. Our emotions send us signals to say: "This is important!" And the rapidity of our emotional responses allows this process to bias what we make of the information we are receiving, for better or for worse.   (2006: 185)

Thus, emotions simultaneously prompt reasoning, frame understanding, and mobilize action under the frames conveyed by the constructed message. Yet, the effects of emotional messages vary according to the context of their reception. They depend on the feelings of the receivers of the message at the time and place of the message's reception. It is the capacity of one given set of stimuli to activate a given frame that defines its impact. While frames are pre-existing conditions in our brain, their association with specific images depends on the meaning of images in a given cognitive environment: for example, the bombing of the World Trade Center becomes associated with a political message related to the war on terror in a context of still being at war; while the vision of an abandoned factory may resonate differently in an economic depression (unemployment) than it would in a booming economy (leaving behind the old industrial past for higher-paying jobs in new technologies). Information and emotion are mixed in the construction of political messages as well as in people's minds.

Since people's minds are constructed through their experience, political advertising and political campaigning aim to connect specific images with specific experiences to activate or deactivate the metaphors that are likely to motivate support for a given political actor. Citizens make decisions by managing conflicts (often unconscious) between their emotional condition (how they feel) and their cognitive condition (what they know). Emotional politics is but one dimension of affective intelligence, the reflective act of selecting the best option for our reflexive being.

The Politics of Beliefs

The basic materials that form public opinion are of three kinds: values, group dispositions, and material self-interests (Kinder, 1998). Available research shows that predispositions and values (the ingredients of symbolic politics) have a greater say in the formation of political opinion than material self-interest (Brader and Valentino, 2007).

What happens when the conflict between cognition and emotion sharpens? A plurality of studies seems to indicate that *people tend to believe what they want to believe*. Indeed, experiments show that people are much more critical in evaluating facts that contradict their beliefs than those that support what they think. This biased selectivity of the critical mind appears as early as in the first years of schooling (Westen, 2007: 100). The more citizens are educated, the more they are capable of elaborating interpretations of available information in support of their pre-determined political preferences. This is because a higher level of knowledge provides people with more intellectual resources for self-rationalization in support of their emotionally induced misperceptions. In a study conducted by Westen and his colleagues between 1998 and 2004 on people's judgment about judicial and political leaders (including presidents) during three political crises, they were able to predict people's judgments 80 percent of the time from emotional constraints alone. As Westen writes, "When people make judgments about emotionally significant political events, cognitive constraints matter, but their effects are trivial. When the stakes are high people prefer what Stephen Colbert has called 'truthiness' over truth" (2007: 103).

In the same line of argument, the theory of motivated reasoning effects maintains, on the basis of experiments, that individuals exhibit a widespread tendency to hold on to their evaluation of events even when confronted with information that contradicts their assessment (Kunda, 1990; Lodge and Taber, 2000). Individuals are more likely to recall information that confirms their desired outcome(s) or goals. They are also likely to draw upon their intellectual resources in order to search for information that supports rather than contradicts their goals. Motivation is thus a key factor in shaping how individuals process information leading to their judgments, particularly when they are dealing with important issues. Conflicting emotions simultaneously increase attention to some pieces of information while diminishing the perception of new, contradictory information.

Sears and Henry (2005) have systematized evidence from three decades of research that documents the fact that economic interests do not have much effect on voting patterns, except when those economic interests represent the values and beliefs of voters. This does not hold when there is a major economic crisis or an event that deeply upsets everyday life. However, even in an economic crisis, it is an individual's emotional response to the crisis, rather than a reasoned calculation of how best to respond to the crisis, that organizes people's thinking and political practice. In *What's the Matter with Kansas?*, Frank (2005) analyzes the mechanism leading to the disjuncture between citizens' material interests and their political behavior. Values shape citizens' decisions more often than their interests do. The mediating structures between values and interests are parties and candidates. People see their politics through the eyes of their candidates, and they act on the basis of their feelings, positive or negative, toward these candidates. Summarizing the body of research on this matter, Westen writes: "the data from political science are crystal clear: people vote for the candidate that elicits the right feelings, not the candidate that presents the best arguments" (2007: 125). And when they do not have a clear feeling, or do not trust the connection between their feelings and the mediating instances enough, they drop out from the electoral process or turn to political cynicism, as I will analyze in Chapter 4.

A key source of citizens' emotional constraint is partisanship, or loyalty to the party they have voted for in the past. This is simultaneously an institutional feature and an emotional factor. It is institutional because it is rooted in the history of the country. It is emotional, however, because experiences of partisanship, often received from the family during childhood, are wired into the brain, as they are associated with a number of emotional events. This is even more important in institutional contexts, such as Western Europe, Chile, India, or South Africa, in which organized, mass political parties have a stronger tradition than in the United States. There is, however, a universal trend toward growing disaffection vis-à-vis traditional parties everywhere, as I will document in Chapter 4. Thus, while feelings of party affiliation are important in determining political choices, citizen beliefs appear to be the key factor in determining political behavior. And these beliefs are largely dependent on what citizens desire. To change their beliefs, they have to change what they want. Thus, according to Westen's research, partisan Republicans adapted their rationale to support the Iraq War in the 2003–6 period to fit new evidence into new arguments in support of the war. They first were convinced that there were weapons of mass destruction. When this claim was dismissed, they reshaped their argument around the defense of freedom in Iraq. It was only when the human and economic pain of the war became too blatant to ignore that the majority of Americans began to accept the harsh reality and adapt their emotional processes. However, as I will argue in the next section, conservative partisans' desire for victory led them to adopt a new set of beliefs in 2007–8 that drew upon information compatible with their emotional preference for victory as a test of national pride and power. For these citizens, as long as they continue to associate patriotism with military victory, and as long as they live in the frame of the war on terror, news about the war is automatically filtered according to the victory narrative.

However, the connection between political messages and political decision-making is not direct. It is processed by the mind on the basis of stimuli received from its communication environment. Therefore, I will now turn to examine the specific mechanisms through which communication systems activate the mind.

The Framing of the Mind

The mechanisms of information processing that relate the content and format of the message to the frames (patterns of neural networks) existing in the mind are activated by messages generated in the realm of communication. Of particular relevance to the analysis of power-making is an understanding of how news stories are produced in the media and how they are selected and interpreted by people.

Indeed, audiences pay markedly different levels of attention to different news stories. A study by Graber (2007) documents that, according to a 1986–2003 Pew survey, only 7 percent of stories reported in the US media attracted a great deal of attention. The most salient stories were those that threatened the media consumer's safety or violated social norms. Fear-arousing situations attract the largest audiences (Graber, 2007: 267). These are reactions to events that threaten survival, and these reactions mobilize cognitive resources inducing attention. Graber reports, along the lines of the analyses of cognitive scientists discussed in the preceding sections, that there is no need to experience the situation personally. News (particularly images) can operate as sources of stimuli equivalent to lived experience. Hatred, anxiety, fear, and high elation are particularly stimulating and are also retained in long-term memory. As I have indicated in this chapter, when the information suggests that no unusual reaction is required, individuals adopt routine responses to the stimuli that refer to their disposition systems. But when emotional mechanisms are triggered in the brain's surveillance system, higher-level decision capacities are activated, leading to more attention to information and a more active information search. This is why deliberate framing is typically based on the arousal of emotions.

Nelson and Boynton (1997) analyzed fear-inducing political advertisements on television. Fear and other strong emotions motivate people to search for information but also determine news choices. Thus, according to Graber (2007), television news (the main source of political information) sets the agenda on specific topics by reporting the story repeatedly, placing it in the headlines of the broadcast, increasing the length of coverage of the story, stating the importance of the story, selecting words and pictures to represent the story, and pre-announcing the stories that are coming up in the broadcast. Framing proceeds by the structure and form of the narrative and by the selective use of sounds and images. Drawing upon data from Pew surveys, Graber (2007) analyzed the mechanisms underlying news attention. She proposed a typology of seven groups of media stories and measured the attention paid to each story by viewers. Her findings show that fear-arousing elements, stimuli portending imminent harm to the self or significant others, and signals of journalistic importance increased attention to news stories. Fear of harm at the individual level interacts with the perception of potential damage at the societal level. Her data dismiss the need for supportive context in terms of social and political events. The stimulus acts by itself. In other words, there is no need to add an explicit interpretation: framing works by activating the mind with a proper stimulus. Once a frame is conveyed, the magnitude of the danger in the narrative is the critical source of impact, rather than its visual effects. The key is the recording of information, even if the presentation is not spectacular. Lengthier coverage allows for more stimuli and increases the effectiveness of framing.

Because the media constitute the main source of socialized communication – that is, communication with the potential to reach society at large – *the framing of the public mind is largely performed through processes that take place in the media*. Communication research has identified three major processes involved in the relationship between media and people in the sending and receiving of the news through which citizens perceive their selves in relation to the world: agenda-setting, priming, and framing.

Agenda-setting refers to the assignment of special relevance to one particular issue or set of information by the source of the message (e.g. a specific media organization) with the expectation that the audience will correspond with heightened attention to the content and format of the message. Agenda-setting research assumes that, even if the media may not be able to tell people how to think, they have a major role in influencing what they think about (Cohen, 1963). Research on agenda-setting has established that public awareness of issues, particularly of political/policy issues, is closely linked to the level of coverage of the issues in the national media (Iyengar and Kinder, 1987; McCombs and Zhu, 1995; Kinder, 1998). Furthermore, media agenda-setting is particularly salient when it relates to the viewer's everyday life (Erbring et al., 1980). Thus, the political views of both elites and people in general seem to be largely shaped by the information made available by the mass media or by other sources capable of wide diffusion, such as the Internet (McCombs et al., 1997; Gross and Aday, 2003; Soroka, 2003).

Priming occurs:

when news content suggests to news audiences that they ought to use specific issues as benchmarks for evaluating the performance of leaders and governments. It is often understood as an extension of agenda setting... By making some issues more salient in people's mind (agenda setting), mass media can also shape the considerations that people take into account when making judgments about political candidates or issues (priming).   (Scheufele and Tewksbury, 2007: 11)

The priming hypothesis draws on the cognitive model of associative networks presented in the preceding sections of this chapter. It proposes that stories on particular issues that affect one memory node can spread to influence opinions and attitudes on other issues. Thus, the more frequently an issue is covered, the more likely people are to draw on information presented in the coverage to make their political evaluations.

Framing is the process of "selecting and highlighting some facets of events or issues, and making connections among them so as to promote a particular interpretation, evaluation and/or solution" (Entman, 2004: 5). Framing is a fundamental mechanism in the activation of the mind because it directly links the structure of a narrative conveyed by the media to the brain's neural networks. Remember that frames are associative neural networks. Framing as a chosen action by the sender of the message is sometimes deliberate, sometimes accidental, and sometimes intuitive. But it always provides a direct connection between the message, the receiving brain, and the action that follows. According to Lakoff (2008), framing is not just a matter of slogans; it is a mode of thought, a mode of action. It is not just words, although words or images are necessary to construct the frame and to communicate it. The critical issue is that frames are not external to the mind. Only those frames that are able to connect the message to the pre-existing frames in the mind become activators of conduct. Entman (2004) argues that frames that employ the most culturally resonant terms have the greatest potential for influence: words and images that are noticeable, understandable, memorable, and emotionally charged. Frames are effective by finding resonance and increasing the magnitude of their repetition. The greater the resonance and magnitude, the more likely the framing is to evoke similar thoughts and feelings in a larger audience. Framing operates by leaving gaps in the information that the audience fills with their preconceived schemas: these are interpretive processes in the human mind based on connected ideas and feelings stored in the memory. In the absence of counter-frames in the information provided by the media, the audience will gravitate toward the frames that are suggested. Frames are organized in paradigms: networks of habitual schemas that provide the application of analogies from previous stories to new developments. For instance, frames can reiterate a well-known narrative with strong emotional content, such as the paradigm of terrorism, thus evoking death and inducing fear.

While agenda-setting, priming, and framing are key mechanisms in the construction of the message, the delivery of messages in the media also depends on specific operations that diminish the autonomy of the audience interpreting the message. One such operation is *indexing*. Bennett (1990, 2007; Bennett et al., 2006) has investigated the importance of indexing in the practice of professional journalism. Publishers and editors tend to index the salience of news and viewpoints according to the perceived importance of a specific issue among the elites and in public opinion. More specifically, media professionals tend to rank the importance of a given issue according to government statements. This is not to say that they simply reproduce the government's point of view. Rather, it means that the government is the primary source of information on major issues, and the body responsible for actually implementing a proposed policy or plan of action. Therefore, it is understandable, albeit regrettable, that the material provided by government policy or statements from government officials receive special attention in the indexing process.

The capacity of the media to decide on indexing depends on the level of agreement or disagreement on an issue among the elites and opinion-leaders. If there is little dissent, the media will index according to a single set of evaluation on a given issue (for example, 9/11 in its immediate aftermath in the United States, inducing the acceptance of the "war on terror" frame). On the other hand, the more there is division and ambiguity in elite responses to a crisis (for example, the aftermath of Hurricane Katrina in the United States), the more the media exercise their own diverse judgments in the indexing of an event. According to Bennett (personal communication, 2008), indexing by journalists does not depend on the importance of an issue for the public, but on the level of engagement by the elites. Public opinion polls are selected to support the narrative that fits into the news story. Furthermore, indexing depends not only on the positions of the elites, but also on the degree of division among the elites in power.

An analysis of indexing is essential to complement the perspective of study in terms of agenda-setting because it sheds light on the source of the news. News organizations structure their narratives on the basis of indexing that favors those issues and frames that originate in the power circle to influence the public. Thus, Hallin (1986), in an influential study of public opinion on the Vietnam War, showed that the vast majority of American media were usually not critical of the war until the 1968 Tet Offensive, and that this turn was "intimately related to the unity and clarity of the government itself, as well as to the degree of consensus in society at large" (1986: 213). In another study of the indexing of political events, Mermin (1997) documented how the US decision to intervene in Somalia in 1993 was not prompted by the media. Instead, the bulk of media coverage of the crisis on television networks followed rather than preceded the decision of the US government to focus on Somalia's unrest (Mermin, 1997: 392). Livingston and Bennett (2003) analyzed eight years of international stories on CNN and found that, while new technologies have increased the amount of reporting on event-driven stories, officials "seem to be as much part of the news as ever" (2003: 376).

However, when and if opinion-leaders split in their judgment positions, the media provide the space for the expression of their debate and dissent. In turn, the differentiation of elite attitudes on policy issues may reflect to some extent how people feel about the issues. Yet, for citizens to have an informed opinion, they need information and counter-frames to exercise a choice in interpretation. Herbst (1998) has analyzed the framing of public opinion by political elites. She shows how staff members of political leaders, activists, and journalists construct data on "public opinion" and call upon representatives of interest groups and media pundits for interpretation. Howard (2003) argues that a small, professional elite compiles data on public opinion to influence leaders as well as the public – data that are presented to the public with its own aggregate opinion as if it were its own self-generated verdict on issues.

Framing should not be understood as systematic political bias in the media. A number of studies show that there is no evidence of consistent political bias in the media. But, as Entman (2007) argues, this is contradicted by analyses that show how news and reporting favor certain interpretations. Thus, it may be that the question is incorrectly formulated. Instead, "The consolidating question, then, is whether the agenda setting and framing content of texts and their priming effects on audiences fall into persistent, politically relevant patterns. Powerful players devote massive resources to advancing their interests precisely by imposing such patterns on mediate communications" (2007: 164).

Entman goes on to propose an analytical integration between agenda-setting, framing, and priming under *the notion of bias*. Bias has three meanings. *Distortion bias* refers to news that deliberately distorts reality. *Content bias* refers to "consistent patterns in the framing of mediated communication that promote the influence of one side in conflicts over the use of government power" (Entman, 2007: 166). *Decision-making bias* refers to the motivations of media professionals who produce the biased content. Entman argues that, by bringing together the three mechanisms of influencing popular opinion, the media not only tell the audience *what to think about*, as in the classical proposition of Cohen (1963), but also *what to think*. And:

It is through framing that political actors shape the texts that influence or prime the agendas and considerations that people think about . . . Because the best succinct definition of power is the ability to get others to do what one wants (Nagel, 1975) "telling people what to think about" is how one exerts political influence in non-coercive political systems (and to a lesser extent in coercive ones).

(Entman, 2007: 165)

The power of framing in the media can be exemplified by the study of Bennett et al. (2006) of the case of American troops torturing Iraqi prisoners in Abu Ghraib prison in 2003–4. In spite of overwhelming photographic evidence of practices that were at the very least condoned by the military wardens of the prison, the media quickly adopted the frame that Abu Ghraib represented isolated abuses on the part of a few troops. A key mechanism was the absence of the word "torture" in most of the news reports. The story quickly disappeared from the headlines of the news, as officials downplayed its relevance and the mainstream media were reluctant to engage in criticism of American troops in the middle of a war. In order to limit public exposure to the realities of torture conducted by US troops, it was essential to limit exposure to "offensive" images. The pretext was that their content could be excessively shocking for sensitive viewers. The Internet provided a global platform to expose the brutality of the Abu Ghraib jailers. Yet the American media were much more reserved in the presentation of these images than their counterparts in Europe and the rest of the world.

The effort to limit the exposure of Abu Ghraib images in the American public sphere at times involved extraordinary lengths. For example, when the celebrated Colombian artist Fernando Botero exhibited his stunning paintings of the Abu Ghraib tortures in leading European art galleries, his repeated offers to bring the exhibit to the United States were politely rebuffed by all major galleries in the country. Finally, the Center of Latin American Studies at the University of California, Berkeley, exhibited the paintings at the university's library to the acclaim of art critics and visitors alike. Botero then donated the paintings to Berkeley, where they are still on display. But Botero's artistic testimony was carefully removed from the public debate in America because of its controversial nature, in spite of being inspired by a well-known reality. Yet a reality without images is a faded reality.

Media framing represents a multilayered process that begins with a negotiation between key political actors or interest groups and the media before reaching citizens' minds. Entman has proposed an influential analytical model known as *cascading activation*. It is schematically represented in

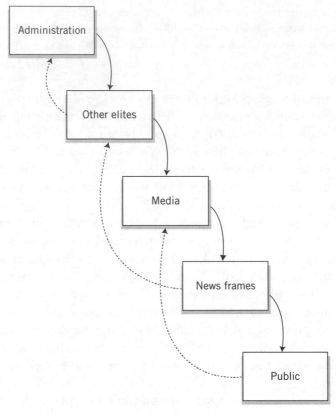

Fig. 3.2. Cascading network activation

Source: Adapted from Entman (2004:10, figure 1.2).

Figure 3.2. The model, based on Entman's (2004) research on the relationship between news framing, public opinion, and power in issues of US foreign policy, highlights the sequential interaction between different actors in a hierarchy of influence that combines the mechanisms of agenda-setting, priming, framing, and indexing in a single process characterized by the asymmetrical relationships between the actors tempered by feedback loops. Statements and stories generated at the top of the political hierarchy (high-ranking administration officials) more often than not initiate national and international political news stories. There are two main reasons for this: they are the holders of privileged information and their policy choices are the ones with the greatest likelihood of generating consequences (for example, decisions between war and peace in certain cases). The agenda-setting process is filtered by second-tier political elites or first-tier foreign elites, until reaching the media which provide the frames to the public on the basis of messages received from the political elites. Frames spread through the media and interpersonal networks and are activated in people's minds. But the public also reacts by influencing the media, either with their comments or simply with their level of attention, as measured by media audiences.

It is important to note that news frames, once constructed, feed back to the political elites. For instance, once the "war on terror" frame became well established in the media, it was highly risky for the second-tier political elites to counteract it with their statements and votes. Robinson (2002) has demonstrated that the influence of media frames on political elites is most pronounced when policy decisions are uncertain. Robinson proffers a media–policy interaction model based on an analysis of six different humanitarian crises in which the dominant media frames addressed the issue of US intervention. Across all six cases he found that the level of policy uncertainty combined with media framing were the best predictors of whether the US ultimately decided to intervene. These findings are in line with the discussion presented earlier in this chapter: uncertainty induces anxiety that calls for heightened attention in public opinion as well as in the political establishment, thus predisposing the government to act on a highly salient issue.

In the cascading activation model of analysis, the public is equated with perceived public opinion, as reflected in opinion polls, voting patterns, and other indicators of aggregate behavior. In this sense, the logic of the model is internal to the political system. The public is seen as a mixture of political consumers and reactive audience. This is, of course, not the opinion of the researchers, let alone Entman's view. It reflects the construction of the process of agenda-setting and framing from the standpoint of the political elites and the media. The model allows a measure of frame dominance, from complete dominance of one frame in the news to "frame parity" in which "two or more interpretations receive roughly equal play," which are "the conditions that free press theories prefer" (Entman, 2004: 48). Research suggests, however, that frame parity is the exception to a rule of frame dominance when it comes to foreign policy, although a degree of frame contestation does arise in a significant minority of cases (Entman, personal communication, 2008).

Mainstream political elites wield the greatest control over news frames. Their level of control intensifies when news frames refer to culturally congruent events (for example, defense of the nation against the enemy after 9/11 or in times of war). Indeed, Gitlin (1980), Hallin (1986), and Luther and Miller (2005) have found that, during times of war, the American press tends to marginalize dissenting voices (e.g., the anti-war movement), privilege political insiders, and often focus on the spectacle of the protest itself rather than the positions of the protestors. This is not unique to the American case. Studies of Iraq War coverage have found that actors in official political positions are consistently granted more media time than those who dissent from them in the United Kingdom (Murray et al., 2008), in Sweden (Dimitrova and Strömbäck, 2005), and in Germany (Lehmann, 2005; Dornschneider, 2007).

Counter-frames have greater sway when they refer to culturally ambiguous events; for example, the management of the catastrophe caused by Hurricane Katrina, when the government's protective role was contradicted by reports from the ground. However, there is a possibility that the media accept the administration's framing of a problem but not the interpretation of the action that follows, as shown in the cases of the invasion of Grenada (1983), the bombing of Libya (1986), and the invasion of Panama (1989–90; Entman, 2004).

In the cascading activation model, media are also stratified. Thus, *The New York Times* and other leading publications cascade down to other media through a process of inter-media agenda-setting (Van Belle, 2003; Entman 2004: 10; Golan, 2006). Variations of frame processing in the cascading model depend on two main factors: the level of unity or dissent among the political elite, and cultural congruence or incongruence of the frames proposed at the top of the cascade. Media professionals have much broader opportunities to introduce counter-frames or a variety of interpretive schemas when there is a discrepancy between the elites and/or cultural incongruence between the decision-makers and the culture of the country (e.g., blatant human rights violations). For the counter-frames to be powerful enough to challenge the elite-induced frames, they need to be culturally resonant with the public – or at least with the journalists' perceptions of public opinion.

Activation at each level of the cascade depends on how much information is communicated in a particular set of framings. What passes from one level to another is based on selective understanding. Motivations play a key role in the effectiveness of framing at each level of the cascade. Participants in the process of communication are cognitive misers who will select information on the basis of their habits, as stated previously in this chapter. Elites select the frames that advance their political careers. Media professionals select the news that can be most appealing to audiences without risking retaliation from powerful players. People tend to avoid emotional dissonance, thus they look for media that support their views. For instance, when people try to escape the cascading process in one media system because of their disagreement with the frames, they search for online news from foreign sources. Best et al. (2005) have shown that individuals who are dissatisfied with the dominant frame in their own country seek out confirmatory information (usually via the Internet) from foreign media sources. Thus, cascading activation works within specific polity systems and in relation to specific media environments. The global network of news media offers the public an alternative when framing in one particular media context fails to win acceptance or subdue resistance. Indeed, media framing is not an irresistible determination of people's perceptions and behavior. As important as it is to unveil the mechanism by which social actors influence human minds through the media, it is equally essential to emphasize the capacity of the same minds to respond to alternative frames from different sources or to switch off the reception of news that does not correspond to their way of thinking.

To investigate the interplay between framing and counter-framing in the shaping of the human mind through the process of communication, I will now proceed to a case study of particular relevance for our understanding of communication and power: the framing of the American public in the process that led to the Iraq War.

Conquering the Minds, Conquering Iraq, Conquering Washington: From Misinformation to Mystification[18]

In March 2004, the US House Sub-Committee on Government Reform (2004) released a report (*The Waxman Report*) that included a searchable database of 237 false or misleading statements about the reasons for the US war in Iraq, made by President George Bush, Vice President Richard Cheney, Defense Secretary Donald Rumsfeld, Secretary of State Colin Powell, and National Security Advisor Condoleezza Rice in 125 separate public appearances.[19] These statements included references

---

[18] This section expands and updates the analysis published in 2006 in an article co-authored with Amelia Arsenault (Arsenault and Castells, 2006).

[19] http://oversight.house.gov/IraqOnTheRecord/

to Iraq's nuclear capabilities, its links to *al-Qaeda*, and Saddam Hussein's involvement in 9/11. In June 2004, the *9/11 Commission Report* stressed the lack of evidence of a link between Saddam Hussein and *al-Qaeda*. The next month, in July 2004, the Senate Select Committee on Intelligence released a similar report contradicting the administration's claims. In October 2004, Charles Duelfer, handpicked by the Bush administration to investigate the issue, released a report saying that investigations had found no evidence of a comprehensive weapons program after 1991 (Duelfer, 2004). To date, no evidence of weapons of mass destruction has been found and no pre-war connection between Iraq and *al-Qaeda* has been established.

American and international media widely reported these findings in due time. Yet, in October 2004, according to a Harris poll, 38 percent of Americans still believed that the United States had located weapons of mass destruction (WMDs) in Iraq. Moreover, 62 percent believed that "Iraq gave substantial support to al-Qaeda" (Harris, 2004b). What is even more extraordinary is that in July 2006, after years of official information and media reports documenting the falsification of the pre-war situation in Iraq, a survey conducted by Harris (2006) found that the number of Americans who believed that WMDs had been found in Iraq had risen to 50 percent (from 36 percent in February 2005) and that beliefs that Saddam Hussein had close ties with *al-Qaeda* had returned to 64 percent (from a low of 41 percent in December 2005; see Table 3.1).

A series of polls from a different, equally reliable source, the Program for International Policy Attitudes (PIPA, 2004) also detected widespread misperceptions about the circumstances that led to the Iraq War. Thus, according to PIPA, in August 2004, after multiple governmental sources had confirmed that these perceptions were wrong, 35 percent of Americans still believed that the United States had located weapons of mass destruction (WMDs) in Iraq and an additional 19 percent believed that, while no weapons had been found, Iraq did possess a developed program for creating them. Moreover, 50 percent believed either that "Iraq gave substantial support to al-Qaeda, but was not involved in the 11 September attacks" (35%) or that "Iraq was directly involved in the 11 September 2001 attacks" (15%). Furthermore, in December 2006, after years of official information and media reports documenting the falsification of the pre-war situation in Iraq, a new survey conducted by PIPA found that 51 percent of Americans still believed that WMDs had been found or that Iraq had a significant program for making them, and 50 percent of Americans believed

Table 3.1. American misperceptions about the Iraq War, 2003–2006

	Iraq had WMDs(%)	Saddam Hussein had close links with *al-Qaeda*(%)
Jun-03	69	48
Aug-03	67	50
Oct-03	60	49
Feb-04	51	47
Apr-04	51	49
Jun-04	–	69
Oct-04	38	62
Feb-05	36	64
Dec-05	26	41
July-06	50	64

Margin of error ±3%.

Source: Harris Poll (2004a, b, 2005, 2006).

that Saddam Hussein had close ties with *al-Qaeda* or was directly involved in 9/11.[20]

How and why could such a significant percentage of the population have remained so misinformed for such a long time? What was the social process leading to the widespread adoption of misinformation? And what were the political effects of these misperceptions, particularly with respect to attitudes toward the war? How was support for the war obtained through misperceptions played out in the presidential and congressional elections? In dealing with these questions, I will build on the theory and research presented in this chapter, without further reference to what I have already cited and documented.

I will start by restating that *people tend to believe what they want to believe*. They filter information in order to adapt it to their predisposed judgments. They are considerably more reluctant to accept facts that challenge their beliefs than those that coincide with their convictions. Moreover, despite all information to the contrary, the Bush administration continued to release

[20] A Zogby International Poll of US troops stationed in Iraq conducted in February 2006 found that 85 percent of the troops polled said that they were there because the US mission in Iraq was "to retaliate for Saddam's role in the 9/11 attacks," and 77 percent said they also believed "the main or a major reason for the war was to stop Saddam from protecting al-Qaeda in Iraq."

misleading statements that played on existing misperceptions for years after the war began. For example, in June 2004, in response to the *9/11 Commission Report*, President Bush told reporters that "the reason I keep insisting that there was a relationship between Iraq and Saddam and al-Qaeda [is] because there was a relationship between Iraq and al-Qaeda." In another example, Republican Senator Rick Santorum, reading from a report by the National Ground Intelligence Center, told a press conference on June 22, 2006 that:

We have found weapons of mass destruction in Iraq, chemical weapons. Since 2003, coalition forces have recovered approximately 500 weapons munitions, which contain degraded mustard or sarin nerve agent. Despite many efforts to locate and destroy Iraq's pre-Gulf War chemical munitions, filled and unfilled pre-Gulf War chemical munitions are assessed to still exist.   (Fox News, 2006)

Researchers have found that emotional and cognitive connections between terrorism and the Iraq War were critical in raising levels of popular support for the war. A number of studies have illustrated that people with a greater fear of future terrorism, and/or who were concerned about their own mortality, were more likely to support President Bush, the War in Iraq, and the broader war on terror (e.g., Huddy et al., 2002; Hetherington and Nelson, 2003; Kull et al., 2003–4; Landau et al., 2004; Cohen et al., 2005; Valentino et al., 2008). Thus, in a survey of attitudes toward the Iraq War conducted by Huddy et al. (2007), anxious people were more likely to oppose the war than angry people. Anxiety heightened perceived risk and reduced support for the war, while anger reduced perception of risk and increased support for military intervention. Anger also diminished the connection between knowledge about Iraq and support for the war. Angry people were not less informed, but information did not undermine their support for the war compared to non-angry people. Meanwhile, a higher level of information reduced support for the war among anxious people. However, while anxiety propels individuals to seek out new information, it also has the effect of degrading their ability to assess and/or recall information. Huddy et al. (2005) found that, *while those most anxious after 9/11 and the beginning of the war in Iraq were more attentive to politics, they were also less accurate in their recall of these events.*

These findings have powerful implications when coupled with studies that suggest that individuals who had fewer facts and more misperceptions about the war were more likely to support it (Kull et al., 2003–4; Valentino et al., 2008). Thus, people who were angry were most likely to underestimate the consequences of the war, while people who were anxious were more likely to seek out information. However, considering that the circulation of inaccurate information by the administration was distributed via the media, anxious people were also relying on inaccurate information and thus less likely to recall disconfirming information when it was introduced (Valentino et al., 2008). In other words, anxious people may have been *less* likely to support the war, but anxious people who *did* support the war were less likely to have their opinions influenced by the introduction of corrective information.

It appears that *information per se does not alter attitudes unless there is an extraordinary level of cognitive dissonance. This is because people select information according to their cognitive frames*. Stimuli aimed at producing emotional effects that condition information processing and shape decision-making can activate certain frames. Efforts to mobilize Americans in support of the Iraq War *activated two main frames: the war on terror* and *patriotism*. The Bush administration and the media clearly and consistently formed connections between the war on terror and the Iraq War (Fried, 2005; Western, 2005). The war on terror and its associated images and themes (*al-Qaeda*, Afghanistan, the Iraq War, radical Islamism, Muslims in general) *constructed a network of associations in people's minds* (Lakoff, 2008). *They activated the deepest emotion in the human brain: the fear of death*. Psychological experiments in a plurality of countries provide evidence that connecting issues and events with death favors conservative political attitudes in people's brains (Westen, 2007: 349–76). Once death is evoked, people hold on to what they have and what they believe in as a refuge and a defense, thus reaffirming traditional values, values tested by history and collective experience. People become less tolerant of dissent and more inclined toward law and order policies, more nationalistic, and more supportive of the patriarchal family. The reasons are deep.

As Ernest Becker (1973) argued in his classic book *The Denial of Death*, and as I elaborated in my own analysis on the transformation of time in the network society (1996: 481–91), individual psychology and collective cultures have developed mechanisms to avoid confronting death as our only certainty. Refusing the consciousness of non-being is a condition for being. Testing Becker's ideas through research, Cohen et al. (2005), as reported by Westen (2007), showed the effects of the salience of mortality on people's attitudes and behavior. By investigating the impact of the ensuing anxiety on political decisions, they showed that the presence of death in the minds of voters led to strong support for Bush and for his policy in Iraq in the 2004 election, even among people with liberal ideology. In a designed survey, voters in the Northeast voted 4 to 1 in favor of Democratic presidential candidate John Kerry when not reminded about death, while those who filled out a "death questionnaire" voted 2 to 1 for Bush (Westen, 2007: 367). The findings fit with the theory of terror management developed by Solomon and his colleagues, according to which the evocation of death is a powerful strategic tool in politics, and particularly in conservative politics (Solomon et al., 1991; Landau et al., 2004).

Both frames, *war on terror* and *patriotism*, were particularly effective in the psychological climate resulting from the 9/11 attacks. But they are distinct. The *war on terror metaphor* activated a fear frame, which is known to be associated with anger and anxiety (Huddy et al., 2007). The *patriotism metaphor* acted on the emotion of enthusiasm, eliciting mobilization in support of the country, literally rallying people around the image of the American flag waving on television screens, on the trucks of firefighters and ordinary citizens, and on the pins displayed by opinion-leaders (Brewer et al., 2003).

But who framed whom? By and large, the political agency framed the media, which, in turn, conveyed the frames to their audience. Indeed, people depend on the media to receive information and opinion. Studies of the influence of mass-mediated coverage of terrorism have found a correlation between increased coverage and public perceptions of the threat of terrorism (Kern et al., 2003; Nacos, 2007; Nacos et al., 2008). But this information, when it refers to major policy issues, originates within the political system and is provided in the form of frames. Frames also define the relationship between different components of the political agency. This relationship is asymmetrical. The presidency is only one component of this agency, albeit the most important one because of its constitutional capacity to implement executive power (Entman, 2004). The political agency also includes Congress (differentiating between Republicans and Democrats), the military as an institution, the United Nations, and foreign leaders, differentiating between the administration's allies and other governments. The administration's initial success in imposing the war on terror and patriotism frames on the American political elites (Republican and Democrat alike) disabled their potential opposition. By associating the Iraq War with the war on terror and the defense of the nation, any significant dissent would be easily labeled as un-American, either by the administration or by their surrogates in the media, thus jeopardizing politicians' careers

(Jamieson and Waldman, 2003; Western, 2005: Bennett, 2007; Lakoff, 2008).[21]

George Lakoff has analyzed how the Bush administration used successive frames to neutralize the Democrats' criticism of the war, even when the Democrats won control of both houses in November 2006. In Lakoff's words, "the political battle was a framing battle" (2008: 148). The Bush administration fought the framing battle in stages, changing the narrative according to the unexpected evolution of the war. The original frame, based on the threat posed by weapons of mass destruction, was built on a *self-defense narrative*. In the first weeks of the war, as US troops moved into Baghdad, the *victory frame* was evoked in order to distract the agenda away from the heavy fighting in and around Baghdad. In a photo-opportunity staged by the military, US soldiers helped Iraqi citizens topple a prominent statue of Saddam Hussein in order to evoke a victory frame. Aday et al. (2005), in a content analysis of American broadcast news coverage of the statue incident, illustrate how eagerly the media adopted the "victory frame" conveyed by the event. They also found that, following this event, the number of stories documenting continuing violence in Iraq declined sharply, suggesting that the victory frame superseded the potentially competitive narratives in the media sphere. As previously mentioned, the propensity for the press to echo the narrative set by the administration during war time is not unique to the United States. In a cross-national study of images accompanying newspaper stories about the Saddam Hussein statue, Fahmy (2007) found that papers published in coalition countries used more images of the event overall and more images that supported the victory frame than non-coalition countries. This victory frame was similarly evoked when President Bush landed on an aircraft carrier before a crowd of soldiers (later discovered to be in San Diego) against the backdrop of a banner announcing, "Mission Accomplished." Critics point to the fact that the event was clearly theatrical in nature. Bush landed in a flight suit

---

[21] Journalists also conformed to the patriotic frame. Then anchorman of CBS News and veteran reporter, Dan Rather told the BBC in 2002 that the US media (including himself) had compromised journalistic principles in reporting on the Bush administration following 9/11 out of a fear of appearing unpatriotic. In an interview on the program *Newsnight*, he lamented: "In some ways, the fear is that you will be necklaced here, you will have a flaming tire of lack of patriotism put around your neck. It's that fear that keeps journalists from asking the toughest of the tough questions and to continue to bore-in on the tough questions so often. Again, I'm humbled to say I do not except myself from this criticism."

aboard a fighter plane even though his helicopter was in easy range of the carrier.

When no WMDs were found, a *rescue narrative* was introduced: the US was in Iraq to rescue the Iraqis and provide them with the gift of democracy. When it quickly became clear that the "mission" was anything but "accomplished," and resistance to the occupation and civil war escalated violence in Iraq, the supposedly liberated Iraqis suddenly became "insurgents" or "terrorists" and the *war for self-defense narrative* was reinstated. *Al-Qaeda* was now introduced into the frame with more evidence to support it, as the overthrow of Saddam Hussein and the dismantlement of the Iraqi army facilitated an active presence of *al-Qaeda* in Iraq *after the invasion* of the country. In the first half of 2004, when support for the war began to wane, US causalities began to mount, and evidence of US torture of prisoners at Abu Ghraib surfaced, precisely at the time of the upcoming presidential campaign, the administration escalated its attempts to frame the war in Iraq in connection with 9/11 and *al-Qaeda*. Harris polls conducted just after the 9/11 Commission released its findings show that the number of Americans who believed that Saddam Hussein had strong links to *al-Qaeda* actually jumped 20 percentage points from 49 percent in April 2004 to 69 percent in June 2004.

For the president to assume war powers, it was essential for the administration to avoid mentioning *occupation*, and to keep *the war frame as part of the war on terror* for the safety of America. But once the war began, the key for a successful framing strategy was to introduce the *patriotic frame* into the debate, as embodied by "support for our troops." Any attempt by Congress to disengage the country from the occupation of Iraq became susceptible to accusations of treason against the country at war and betrayal of the troops in combat. President Bush was able to use these frames to fight off any serious challenge from the Democrats to curtail funding of the war, and even succeeded in May 2007 in convincing 90 percent of the representatives in the "Out of Iraq" caucus in Congress to vote to continue funding, in full contradiction of their own stated position and the wishes of their electorate in November 2006.

Foreign leaders and the United Nations were either co-opted as a coalition of the willing or denounced as unreliable partners. Because the political choice was to proceed down the path of unilateralism as a display of American superpower, the intended effect was to cater to American public opinion, regardless of the world's public opinion. To counter the notion of isolation, the patriotic frame was activated: we, as Americans, are defenders of freedom regardless of the indecision or irresponsibility of other countries. In the months preceding the war, the framing went so far as to rename French fries as "Freedom fries" in the restaurant of the US Congress.

The administration's successful framing of political elites set the stage for the effectiveness of *the process of agenda-setting*. Agenda-setting is directed toward the media, and is transmitted through the media to affect public opinion. Agenda-setting entails two related operations: to highlight certain issues and to define a narrative for the issues. In this case, the Bush administration set the agenda by linking the Iraq War to the war on terror, and by mobilizing the country around the sacrifices and heroic acts of American troops. As stated above, the original narrative was based on misinformation: Saddam Hussein had developed weapons of mass destruction and was holding on to them; Saddam was connected to *al-Qaeda*; *al-Qaeda* had attacked the US and had vowed to escalate the devastation of future attacks. Ergo, Iraq represented a direct threat to the survival of the American people as the nurturer of the terrorist networks that were about to bring havoc to America and destroy the Western way of life around the world. Pre-emptive action was a moral imperative and a defensive necessity. As George Bush told soldiers in a speech at Fort Lewis in June 2004,

This is a regime that hated America. And so we saw a threat, and it was a real threat. And that's why I went to the United Nations . . . The members of the United Nations Security Council looked at the intelligence and saw a threat, and voted unanimously to send the message to Mr. Saddam Hussein, disarm or face serious consequences. As usual, he ignored the demands of the free world. So I had a choice to make – either to trust the word of a madman, or defend America. Given that choice, I will defend America every time.

Of course, the protection of oil supplies and the liberation of the Iraqi people were additional lines of argument, but they were cognitive arguments, and thus subordinated to the emotional impact sought by the reference to weapons of mass destruction in the hands of 9/11 terrorists.[22]

Following *the theory of cascading activation*, I propose that agenda-setting is mainly directed toward the media because it is through the media that

[22] In this chapter, I am not analyzing the causes and consequences of the Iraq War from a social and political perspective. I proposed my own interpretation of the war in its geopolitical context in other writings (Castells, 2004b, 2007). In the analysis presented here, I am using the case study of the Iraq War to put to work the conceptual tools proposed in this chapter to understand the relationship between mind-framing and power-making.

frames and narratives reach people at large. As Entman (2004, 2007), Bennett et al. (2007), and others have shown, the media react differently depending on the level of agreement among political elites. The greater the dissent, the more diversified the treatment of the narrative, with the increased possibility of introducing counter-frames in the reporting and debating of the issues. The media respond to the political climate by priming events and indexing the news. In the 2002–3 period, there was little dissent in the US Congress vis-à-vis the Iraq War and the war on terror. As long as the media did not perceive a major split in assessing the war, they remained largely confined within the narrative provided by the administration. This is why the analysis must differentiate between the 2002–3 period and the period leading to and following the presidential election of 2004, when political dissent started to emerge in terms of the narrative, although without challenging the predominant frames that had been activated in people's minds.

But before introducing a dynamic perspective to the analysis, there is a critical consideration to be made: media are diverse. In their diversity, there is a fundamental difference that dominates all others: *partisan media* versus *mainstream media*. However, both are dominated by business considerations. As I argued in Chapter 2, in some cases partisan reporting constitutes an effective business model as it captures an important segment of the market by attracting people who want their views confirmed by media reporting. In the United States, this is particularly the case for conservative and liberal talk show radio and the Fox News television network. Conservative partisan media embraced the two frames, patriotism and the war on terror, and linked them to the Iraq War. Accordingly, the coverage of the war was characterized by *distortion bias*. Table 3.2 presents data from a study conducted by Kull et al. (2003–4) using data collected by PIPA during June,

Table 3.2. Frequency of misperceptions per respondent by news source (percentages)

Misperceptions per respondent	Fox	CBS	ABC	CNN	Print media	NPR/ PBS
One or more misperceptions	80	71	61	55	47	23
None of three	20	30	39	45	53	77

Source: Kull et al. (2003–4: 582).

July, and August of 2003. It illustrates the association between the source of news on the Iraq War and the level of misperception in the audience, with Fox News viewers being significantly more prone than others to follow the administration's narrative. On the other side of the spectrum, news from the non-commercial networks, NPR and PBS, seems to have been conducive to greater scrutiny of the official story.

The effects of media bias on misperceptions are not explained by political ideology. While Republicans were more likely to follow the version of the Republican administration, their level of misperception varied with the source of their news. So, in June–September 2003, 43 percent of Republicans still thought that there were weapons of mass destruction in Iraq. But this belief was held by 54 percent of those Republicans whose news source was Fox, compared to 32 percent of Republicans whose news source was either NPR or PBS (PIPA, 2004). This media bias was not unique to the exceptional moments post-9/11 and in the early period of the Iraq War. Moving forward in time, the study of Jacobson (2007b), three years later, using data from the 2006 Cooperative Congressional Election Study, shows the correlation between news source and misperceptions (Table 3.3). Table 3.3 also highlights how Fox viewers were more likely to associate the Iraq War with religious beliefs (i.e. that Bush was chosen by God to lead the war on terror).

Terror management theories find that subliminal death stimuli increase people's tendency to support policies and actions that sustain their world-view or cultural orientation (e.g., the war on terror; Landau et al., 2004). There is also evidence that under these conditions, individuals gravitate toward leaders who seem to reflect their own worldview and culture. In an experimental study, for example, Cohen et al. (2005) found that subjects with high levels of mortality salience were much more likely to gravitate toward Bush, a leader whom they considered to be charismatic and reflective of their worldview, rather than John Kerry, a candidate who was perceived as "task-oriented." By extension, we may surmise that Americans seeking a confirmation of their worldview also sought out Fox News Channel, a station that consistently reaffirmed the primacy of American political and cultural supremacy (Iskandar, 2005). The issue then becomes one of causality. Are viewers influenced by media biases or are they attracted to the media outlets that they think are more in tune with their views? Kull et al. (2003–4) lean toward the hypothesis of an independent effect of media sources on misperceptions. But it is likely that both processes are at work. People who are motivated by their predispositions listen to

Table 3.3. Television news source and beliefs about Iraq and Bush (percentages)

	PBS, CNN, MSNBC	ABC, CBS, NBC	Fox
US has found WMDs in Iraq	2	5	36
Iraq probably has WMDs, US has not found	30	23	36
Iraq probably does not have WMDs	83	48	13
Don't know	10	23	15
Iraq War is part of the war on terrorism	9	27	79
Iraq War is separate from the war on terrorism	89	69	20
Was Bush chosen by God to lead a global war on terrorism?			
Yes	2	6	37
Don't know	5	11	22
No	93	83	40

Source: CCES, elaborated by Jacobson (2007b: 28, table 11).

what they want to listen to (Gentzkow and Shapiro, 2006). For people inclined toward greater scrutiny because of the anxiety induced by negative emotions, exposure to specific media sources may tilt their opinion one way or the other.

For the mainstream media, content bias dominated as long as the opinions of political elites remained consistent with the frames set up by the administration.[23] When elites became more divided in their opinions about the war, decision-making bias was introduced, as professional journalists interpreted signals from the audience and from their own criterion to differentiate viewpoints, albeit without challenging the fundamental frames of patriotism and the war on terror. As political criticism of the conduct of the war emerged among Democrats and intensified around the world, mainstream media stopped following the agenda set by the Bush administration, and disassociated the Iraq War from the dominant frames that

[23] One of the most direct examples of the administration's attempt to control news framing was the policy of embedding reporters within military units on the ground.

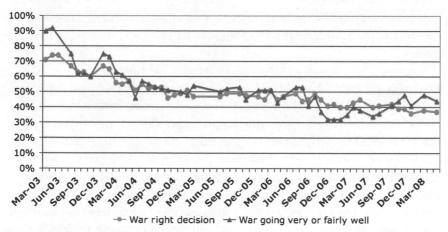

Fig. 3.3. Support for, and evaluation of the success of, the war in Iraq, March 2003–April 2008

Source: Compiled and elaborated by Amelia Arsenault.

had until then continued to influence their reporting. They began report-ing misinformation, thus introducing counter-frames into the process. The more political competition transformed the landscape of agenda-setting, the more journalists in the mainstream media used *decision-making bias* (i.e., exercised their own professional preferences in the priming and indexing of the news) to produce different patterns of slant, depending on the inter-actions of elite politics and "facts on the ground." However, administration frames dominated for a significant period of time until the presidential campaign of 2004. To examine the evolution of support for the war and the evaluation of its conduct, and to detect the points of inflection in this evo-lution, Amelia Arsenault and I have constructed Table A3.1, located in the Appendix. Table A3.1 provides an overview of changes in public opinion about the war as documented by the Pew Research Center for the People and the Press and the actual changes on the ground in Iraq as presented by the Brookings Institution Iraq Index between March 2003 and April 2008. The data from Table A3.1 are charted in Figure 3.3.

I will be basing my analysis on the reading of these data. In January 2004, 65 percent of Americans still believed that the US invasion of Iraq was the right decision and 73 percent thought that the war was going well. In February 2004, opinion began to turn against the war: sup-port dropped significantly in May to the 51 percent level and reached, for the first time since the war began, a minority level of approval in

177

October 2004 (46%). To explain how this change occurred and how it was related to misinformation, we must refer to theory and recall specific events.

Because 2004 was a presidential election year, the media were receptive to a differential source of agenda-setting from the political elites. President Bush identified the Iraq War as his central campaign issue at a period when he was enjoying wide support, including some support among the Democrats in early 2004. On the other hand, the insurgent primary campaign of Howard Dean, who was the Democratic front-runner until his defeat in the Iowa caucuses in January 2004, rallied the opposition against the Iraq War and widened the space available for the inclusion of counter-frames in the public debate. Because Dean organized his campaign largely around the Internet (Teachout and Streeter, 2008), the discussion of the war became particularly intense in the blogosphere, and some of this discussion opened up the field of reporting in the media. Citizen journalism started to play a role. Some information made it through the maze of agenda-setting, which was, until then, largely controlled by the administration.

In April 2004, a photograph of military staff discreetly unloading coffins containing the bodies of American soldiers from a cargo plane in Seattle made it to the front page of *The Seattle Times*, and to the Internet, courtesy of conscientious workers who lost their jobs in the process of exposing the photos. And on April 28, 2004, CBS's *60 Minutes* broke the Abu Ghraib torture story, which was reported by Seymour Hersh (2004) in *The New Yorker* two days later, on the basis of a leaked internal military report. While we do not know the source of the leak, it indicated the existence of internal dissent among the military establishment on the tactics used in the war on terror. This dissent created the opportunity for some of the media to depart from what was, until then, the dominant frame on the war. However, the criticism of the war itself remained largely subdued in the media. Bennett (2007: 72–107) has analyzed in detail the effort by the media to water down the Abu Ghraib episode by deliberately not using the word "torture" and by depicting it as an isolated incident. Yet, the Internet networks and some outlets of the print press, led by the Seymour Hersh article in *The New Yorker*, and followed by *The Washington Post*, chose not to dilute the report. Thus, 76 percent of Americans ended up seeing the pictures within a month of their publication, although one-third believed that they were excessively publicized, and most of the pictures were considered too sensitive to be presented on television (Pew, 2004b).

The presidential campaign of 2004 amplified the trend toward a broader array of positions on the war in the media in spite of the fact that John Kerry, the Democratic presidential candidate, had supported the war and was very cautious about not being labeled as soft on the war on terror. In fact, he tried to counter Bush's advantage as a wartime president by using his Vietnam War hero credentials and "reporting for duty" (in his words) at the 2004 Democratic Convention, implying that he would be a more effective commander-in-chief than the draft dodger (Bush) had been. However, he changed his position on the war during the campaign in order to satisfy the growing anti-war sentiment among the Democrats. The perception of his flip-flopping on Iraq undermined his credibility and made him vulnerable to the devastating Republican Swiftboat Veterans attack-ad which, in a brilliant exercise of extreme political manipulation, contributed to the failure of his electoral bid. The ad was effective because it negated Kerry's war-hero narrative, which had been the basis for his image at the onset of the campaign. However, by introducing a debate about the war in the 2004 campaign, the Democrats created an opening for a more independent examination of the war in the media.

Although Kerry and his vice presidential running mate, John Edwards, did not directly oppose the war for fear of negative political fall-out (a decision that Edwards came to publicly regret thereafter), a growing number of Democrats did. This provoked Kerry and Edwards to adopt a more critical position in the last stage of the campaign. And so, the combination of a greater awareness of the process of manipulation that led to the war, and the introduction of negative information about the war in the media, opened up the possibility for committed Democrats (and, to some extent, for independents) to escape the administration's frame, the respectful media corps, and a decidedly cautious Democratic leadership who had rallied around the flag. In October 2004, the last month before the election, support for the war fell below 50 percent (to 46 percent) for the first time. However, the loss of the election by Kerry stabilized the trend against the war until the Fall of 2005. The courageous solo campaign by Cindy Sheehan (the mother of a soldier killed in Iraq) for peace in the summer of 2005 reinvigorated the peace movement.[24] But what really changed the overall

---

[24] Sheehan left the peace movement and the Democratic Party on May 27, 2007 in protest of the decision by the majority of Democrats to vote for the funding of the war in a reversal of their promises to the voters in the November 2006 congressional election. She justified her decision in a written statement: "The first conclusion is that I was the darling of the so-called left as long as I limited my protests to George Bush and the Republican Party. Of course, I was slandered and libeled by the right as a 'tool'

political climate was the mismanagement of the aftermath of the Hurricane Katrina disaster by the Bush administration (Bennett, 2007).

Bush's failure to rescue his own people, as well as his apparent lack of concern, undermined the effectiveness of a fundamental frame in politics: the president as a protective father and efficient leader in a crisis. While hardcore Republicans continued to support the president and his war, Democrats and independents felt increasingly free from their loyalty to a wartime President; and Democrats, in a time of uncertainty, reaffirmed their traditional values in terms of solidarity and war prevention. The media took the opportunity to diversify their sources and make for more interesting debates both in domestic and foreign affairs. Even Fox News Channel joined the bandwagon and became more critical of the administration, although at a lower level than other networks, while still maintaining its patriotic frame (Baum and Groeling, 2007). Bad news from the war front found appropriate resonance in the context of the electoral campaign in 2006.

Moving toward the mid-term congressional elections in November 2006, the Democrats seized on the war as the major issue to undo the dominance of both Bush and the Republican candidates. They benefited from crises of confidence in the president in the aftermath of Hurricane Katrina and from a string of political scandals that shook the administration (see Table A4.1 in the Appendix).

While Democrats mobilized, Republicans hardened their support for the president. In Jacobson's (2007a, b) terms, Democrats and Republicans found themselves in separate cognitive worlds concerning their assessment of the war. In the fall of 2006, only 20 percent of Democrats supported the war, compared to almost 80 percent of Republicans: partisan sentiments had dictated beliefs and positioning about the war. With only 40 percent of independents supporting the war, the 2006 congressional elections returned the Democrats to a majority status in the US Congress for the first time in 12 years, the first political casualty for Republican incumbents of the misinformation that led to the Iraq War. Indeed, at that time, 80

of the Democratic Party. This label was to marginalize me and my message. How could a woman have an original thought, or be working outside of our 'two-party' system? However, when I started to hold the Democratic Party to the same standards that I held the Republican Party, support for my cause started to erode and the 'left' started labeling me with the same slurs that the right used. I guess no one paid attention to me when I said that the issue of peace and people dying for no reason is not a matter of 'right' or 'left,' but 'right and wrong.' "

percent of Democrats believed that the president deliberately misconstrued information about Iraq (Jacobson, 2007b: 23).

Aided by the changing political climate, the unpopularity of the Iraq War, which had exploded in March 2006, became the major point of contention among the political elites. Accordingly, the media broadened the range of issues and narratives to be conveyed to the public, thus increasing the opportunity for citizens to either reaffirm their opinion against the war or examine the arguments that supported their judgments. However, in 2007, the media again followed a new agenda set by the Bush administration: the success of the "surge strategy" in Iraq. In a desperate but brilliant maneuver to salvage his legacy of the Iraq War, Bush fired Paul Wolfowitz, and then Donald Rumsfeld, the architects of the failed war strategy, and shifted the responsibility for conducting the war to commanders in the field. He ordered a surge in combat troops and gave command to General Petraeus, thereby granting him the capacity of recommending the timing and extent of future troop movements in Iraq. By so doing, Bush was giving the responsibility for agenda-setting to the military, the most trusted institution in the country.[25]

Indeed, an attempt by the grassroots organization MoveOn.org to delegitimize General Petraeus as "General Betray us" in full-page advertisements in several American newspapers completely backfired and forced the Democrats to publicly rebuke an organization that had been credited with a major contribution to the revival of Democratic politics. While some of the top brass objected in private to the bypassing of the Joint Chiefs of Staff in the decision-making process, General Petraeus soon made his mark on public opinion via the media and the political class. An educated officer, with a PhD in international relations from Princeton, the general understood that the key to influencing public opinion was to reduce

[25] A September 2007 CBS/New York Times poll found that 68 percent of respondents trusted the military the most to resolve the war issue, compared to 5 percent who trusted President Bush, and 21 percent who trusted Congress most ($n =$ 1035, +/−3%; ?, ?). A poll conducted by the Pew Research Center for the People and the Press in August 2007 found that more than half the respondents (52%) believed that the military was a trustworthy source for accurate information about the Iraq War, while only 42 percent expressed similar confidence in the press (42%; Pew, 2007b). Moreover, this trend was more pronounced among Republicans, 76 percent of whom said that they trusted the military a great deal or a fair amount as a reliable source of information (Pew, 2007b). However, trust in both institutions has declined sharply from the beginning of the war when 85 percent expressed confidence in the military and 81 percent expressed confidence in the media coverage of the war.

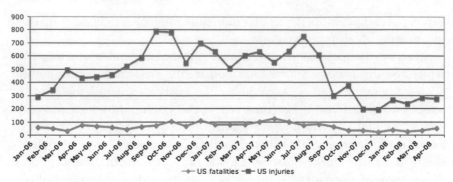

Fig. 3.4. US troop fatalities and injuries in Iraq, January 2006–April 2008

Source: Compiled and elaborated by Amelia Arsenault.

American casualties and violence in the country at large. To obtain this result as quickly as possible, he reversed the unconditional alliance with the Shiites, formed an alliance with the Sunnis, and gave the tribal leaders and the Sunni militias resources, training, and legitimacy to defend their own territories, thus operating a de facto partition of the country. He negotiated with al-Sadr's Mahdi Army, obtaining a truce and allowing this influential Shiite faction the control of a large number of localities, including Sadr City in Baghdad and most of Basra, its port, and its smuggling networks. He reiterated support for the autonomy of Kurdistan at the risk of intensifying tensions with Turkey. Having deactivated much of the civil strife, Petraeus turned the bulk of American forces against the militant, small groups organized around *al-Qaeda* in Iraq, thus damaging their operational capacity. With his record of improvement in hand (see Figure 3.4), his testimony to Congress in September 2007 gave credibility to a new agenda, this time set by the military on the ground, with the support of the president.[26]

The new agenda appeared under the mantle of a reasonable strategy to leave Iraq in due time after accomplishing stability and achieving victory over *al-Qaeda*. As long as the gains of the surge could not be consolidated, troop deployment would be maintained at a sufficient level, and the commanders in the field should be left to evaluate the timing of a phased withdrawal themselves. The media at large bought into this agenda-setting, and

[26] In April 2008, the US Army reversed this policy, leading to an upward trend in US troop casualties and injuries, and calling into question the immediate rationale for, and the long-term viability of, the surge strategy.

so, to some extent, did many of the Democrats. The Bush administration successfully, if temporarily, bolstered the war's legitimacy by shifting its agenda-setting power to a more credible and traditionally well-esteemed source: the military commanders responsible for engaging in direct combat with the enemy. This represented a resurrection and repackaging of the victory frame, a difficult one to reject. Victory incorporates both the patriotic frame and the war on terror frame. It also played into general fears of American fallibility that had dominated public opinion since 9/11. If the war in Iraq was the key battle against *al-Qaeda*, achieving victory in Iraq was a decisive step toward winning the war on terror. By imbuing invisible terror networks with territoriality, the surge strategy suggested that security could be achieved by the traditional means of military combat. Because territorial control requires continuity of military presence, the vigilance of victory implies a long-term presence of US armed forces, albeit at a reduced level, in the most critical region of the world.

Lost in this narrative was the inability of the surge strategy to deal with the reconstruction of Iraq, the democratization of the country, the coexistence of irreconcilable religious communities, institutional instability, lack of reliability of the Iraqi military and police forces, difficulties in the preservation of the unity of Iraq, the resettlement of millions of displaced people, the viability of an economy in shambles, and the continuation of the presence of tens of thousands of mercenaries handsomely paid by US taxpayers. Reduced casualty statistics provided the key agenda-setting mechanism. With images of violence substantially reduced in the news, the emotional aspects of the Iraq War were downplayed, while the cognitive aspects of the war, including the original responsibility for the war, became the topic for little-read op-ed pieces and occasional comments from professional journalists (Project for Excellence in Journalism, 2008b). Figure 3.5 gives an approximation of the news media's failure to adequately serve the public demand for news about the Iraq War. The line reflects the difference between the percentage of respondents reporting that they were more interested in news about Iraq than any other news story and the percentage of the news agenda devoted to war coverage.

As Figure 3.5 illustrates, the only period in which the media significantly overserved American interest in news about the Iraq War was during General Petraeus's testimony, a period in which the administration was in a privileged position to champion the war's successes and recalibrate the news frame. In this period, mystification replaced misinformation as the principal mechanism through which the administration garnered a

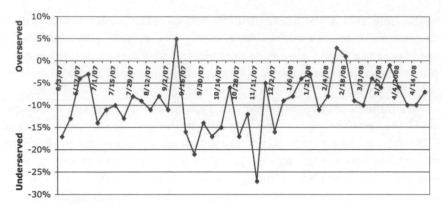

Fig. 3.5. War coverage in the media versus likely voter interest in war news, June 2007–April 2008

Source: Figures collected from the Pew News Interest Index and the Project for Excellence in Journalism News Index June 2007–April 2008, elaborated by Amelia Arsenault.

continuing supportive environment for the war effort. The majority of the US population remained opposed to the war, but the surge strategy encouraged a subtle shift. During this period, evidence of the surge's successes downgraded the importance of the war for many Americans, thereby allowing the administration more operational independence.

This operational independence was aided by the media's shifting attention from the Iraq War toward the deterioration of the US economy and to the presidential electoral campaign in 2008, which downplayed the relevance of the Iraq War in the news. This was, in fact, the result of a fundamental mechanism of decision-making bias in the media. Fragments of information, characterized as "stories," compose the narrative in the media, and particularly in television. Each story has its own features, format, and delivery. They are indexed according to their perceived relevance for the audience. Each story relates to a domain of information. The meaning of the relationship between different stories is treated as opinion or news analysis. Thus, unless the viewer herself establishes the connection between different stories, they are independent, and lead to independent assessments. In reality, there was an obvious connection between the Iraq War, the economy, and the presidential campaign. I do not consider it necessary to provide support for this statement (see Stiglitz and Bilmes, 2008) because I am focusing here on the mechanism of media bias. But the key is the disjunction between the news and what is intimately linked in reality. However, the economic consequences of the war were highlighted by several Democratic political candidates, particularly by Barack Obama, thus providing a counter-frame that could garner support to end the war. Yet, in terms of media reporting, news about the link between the war and the economy was folded under the election campaign story. As for the campaign itself, in the 2008 presidential primaries Iraq was not a focus of debate because there was basic agreement within the Republican camp and within the Democratic camp (save for Hillary Clinton's reversal of her initial support for the war in 2002), so that there was little material to be primed under the frame of horse-race politics.

A different matter was, of course, the presidential campaign leading to the November 2008 election. But by the time the campaign was engaged, considering the unusually lengthy Democratic primary, the narrative of the success of the surge had become dominant in the media, in spite of the fact that both Obama and Clinton committed to a phased withdrawal from Iraq, in direct contradiction to the warnings of General Petraeus in his testimony before Congress in April 2008. The general was promoted to Chief of the Central Command that supervises Iraq and Afghanistan, while the Democratic presidential contenders shifted their focus to the rampant economic crisis. Thus, while over two-thirds of Americans opposed the war in the spring of 2008, the victory frame set up by the administration continued to operate among the core of war supporters, and the counter-frame introduced by the Democratic leaders made the conduct of the war a derivative of economic policy. Because of conflicting frames, induced by the changing needs of political expediency, beginning in December 2007 public opinion about the evolution of the war was characterized by volatility rather than by a clear trend of evaluation of the conduct of the war. As previously mentioned, Sears and Henry (2005) found that, over the past three decades, economic concerns rarely influenced voting and political attitudes except when there was a major economic crisis or an event that deeply upset everyday life. In 2008, skyrocketing gas prices, the downturn in the housing market, massive home foreclosures, and ultimately the collapse of financial markets and an economic crisis unprecedented since the 1930s, propelled a greater awareness among the American people of the United States' precarious economic condition. For the first time, the economy surpassed the Iraq War as the "most important problem" facing America according to Gallup polls. In September 2006, only 7 percent of respondents listed economic concerns as paramount, while 39 percent listed the Iraq War. In March of 2008, these trends were reversed. Only 15 percent believed that the Iraq War was the most important problem, and 39 percent listed the economy.

Thus, five years of framing and counter-framing had led the American public from misinformation to mystification. To link this case study to the analysis of the effects of frames, narratives, agenda-setting, and various forms of media bias in people's minds, *I will summarize the argument here and I will present a synthetic view of the analysis in Figure 3.6.*

The conclusions of this analysis of the social production of misperceptions on the Iraq War are the following. In the process leading to the Iraq War, American citizens were submitted to the frames of the war on terror and patriotism through the media, and then misinformed by the agenda set by the administration, with the consent of the political elites, as portrayed by the media. Their positive emotions (enthusiasm) mobilized support for the troops and ultimately for the war in the form of national pride and patriotic feelings. People responded according to their ideological routines. Thus, conservatives rallied in favor of the war and rejected information that challenged their beliefs. Democrats reacted cautiously and sought alternative information as soon as they could rely on counter-frames that would anchor their beliefs (Jacobson, 2007b). Negative emotions, such as fear, had different consequences depending on the circumstances under which they triggered anger or anxiety. Anger mobilized action and diminished the scrutiny of information. Anxiety, on the other hand, increased uncertainty and activated the surveillance mechanism of the mind to search more carefully for information to limit the level of risk. Therefore, partisan conservatives and angry citizens affirmed their beliefs in support of the administration's narrative and resisted any alternative information from sources such as the Internet, NPR, foreign sources, or dissenting op-eds in the mainstream media. Partisan Democrats were torn between their acceptance of the initial frames and their distrust of a president who, for many of them, had been elected through fraud in 2000. Anxious citizens searched for better information to support their judgments. However, as long as the majority of the media largely conveyed the narrative originally set by the agenda of the administration, the results of their search were necessarily limited. Misperceptions concerning the war lasted for years. Indeed, a CBS News poll conducted in March 2008 found that 28 percent of Americans still believed that Saddam Hussein had been directly involved in 9/11 (pollingreport.com).

The intensity and frequency of misperceptions were strongly correlated with support for the war, belief that the war was going well, support for

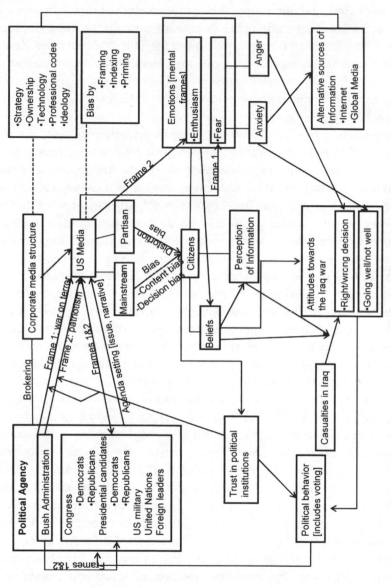

Fig. 3.6. Social production of mediated perceptions of the Iraq War, 2001–2008

the president, and support for the Republicans. While Republicans were most likely to hold misperceptions, these were also widespread among the Democrats. Once these attitudes were set in people's minds, additional information did not change their perception when rooted in partisan beliefs. Indeed, among those ready to vote for Bush in the 2004 election, the more they followed the news, the more they consolidated their views, and the greater their support was for the president. However, for people in general, the effect of the news varied according to the source of the news, as demonstrated by the aforementioned studies of Kull et al. (2003–4) and Jacobson (2007a, b).

Misinformation has been shown to largely determine support for the war. In the PIPA polls conducted in July–August 2003, among people who had none of three major misperceptions about the circumstances of the war (absence of links between Saddam Hussein and *al-Qaeda*, absence of weapons of mass destruction, and hostility of the majority of world public opinion toward the US-led invasion) only 23 percent supported the war. Among those who had at least one misperception, support for the war reached 53 percent; among those with two misperceptions, support for the war reached 78 percent; and among those with all three misperceptions, support reached 86 percent (Kull et al., 2003–4). The link between misperceptions and support for the war continued in the following years, even though the level of misperception was reduced, particularly among those who were not partisan Republicans (PIPA, 2005, 2006; Harris, 2006).

Since the war was the most salient policy issue, support for the war led to support for the president who had launched the war, framed the media, and misinformed the citizenry. But this changed over time. Dissent among the political elites diversified the agendas proposed to the media. Citizen journalism and the Internet broke through the dominant frames that had constrained information. Loss of trust in the president, Hurricane Katrina, and a stream of political scandals affecting the administration and the Republican Party prompted greater scrutiny of information and narratives about the war. Casualties began to be perceived as senseless rather than the inevitable consequences of heroic sacrifice for the defense of the nation. Support for the troops was interpreted by many as support for the withdrawal of the troops sent into harm's way for either obscure or mistaken reasons. The 2006 November election translated opposition to the war into political change.

Yet, support for the war did not wane following this election (see Table A3.1 in the Appendix). This is because a core of conservative citizens retained their beliefs and to a large extent held on to their misconceptions because their mental frames would not accept information that would contradict their views. Thus, at the lowest point of support for the war, in December 2007, there were still 36 percent of Americans who thought that the war was the right decision (it went up to 38 percent in February 2008). Even more importantly, a growing proportion of public opinion in the second half of 2007 and early 2008 (between 40 and 45 percent) thought the war was going well. This can be attributed to two mechanisms. One was the successful agenda-setting by the US military in Iraq and its acceptance by most media. The second was a certain ambiguity among Democratic politicians, including the leading presidential candidates, who were reluctant to put themselves on a collision course with the military, particularly since there is no easy way out from Iraq in the short term. Thus, the influence of the new Republican narrative, embodied by Senator John McCain, was based on the notion of responsibility: even if it was a mistake to go to war in the first place, now that we are in Iraq we must stay there until matters are resolved. The Democratic leadership was caught between the desire of 81 percent of their 2006 voters to leave Iraq within a year, and their electability and responsibility if elected.

Yet, the most fundamental transformation throughout the whole process took place in people's minds. A large majority of American citizens became more isolationist than at any time since the Vietnam War. They were ready to trade the imperial role of their country in world affairs for health care and secure jobs. Patriotism was being redefined in terms of society's well-being, and the war on terror frame lost much of its spectral power of intimidation. As Baum and Groeling write, after proceeding to a statistical analysis of the relationship between media frames, political agenda-setting, and attitudes toward the Iraq War: "Sooner or later, it would seem, the public can discern the true merits of a conflict to at least some degree, regardless of elite efforts to the contrary" (2007: 40). However, the issue remains that the later the public breaks through the frames of misinformation, the more the actions of mystifying elites result in destruction and pain "when the press fails" (Bennett et al., 2007).

The Power of the Frame

Power-making proceeds by shaping decision-making, either by coercion or by the construction of meaning, or both. The centuries-old struggle for democracy was aimed at elaborating rules of power-sharing on the basis of citizenship. People became citizens by assuming their role and their rights as sovereign subjects of power, then delegating their power to representatives accountable to the citizenry. The imperfect, yet indispensable mechanism for representation was based, in theory, on political elections, controlled by an independent judiciary, and made competitive by a free press and the right to free speech. Historical variations and manipulation of political institutions by the power-holders made the ideal of democracy unrecognizable more often than not if we take a long-term, worldwide perspective. Yet, continuing attempts to improve democracy still focus on approaching this ideal type of procedural democracy. It was, and it is, assumed that if the openness of the political system is preserved, if pressure groups do not control access to elected office, if parties and governments do not have a free hand to manipulate the system in their favor, free, informed people, confronting their views in an unfettered manner, will ultimately come close to a transparent process of shared decision-making. This will not ensure good government, but it will preserve good governance, with the possibility of rectifying eventual mistakes in the choices made by the majority and in respect of the rights of the minority.

But how does the common good emerge from the plurality of free, self-directed individuals? Through open debate of policy options presented to citizens by their aspiring leaders. So, in this view of the political process, the key is how policies are decided. There are good policies and bad policies for specific groups and for the collectivity at large. The process of aggregation of interests by debating policy choices implies the existence of a superior rationality that will ultimately reveal itself by the free confrontation of ideas. Naturally, the plurality of social interests and values must be taken into consideration. Nonetheless, the common goal is to reach the common good, the choices that a majority of citizens can live with at least for a while. Liberal politics is the politics of reason. Indeed, for a brief period in the heyday of the French Revolution, the goddess Reason was worshipped, and enthroned in Notre Dame Cathedral on November 10, 1794, as churches were converted to temples of the goddess. Reason became the new transcendency, annulling the power of God because it appealed to the best in people's minds, to their uniqueness as a conscious species capable of understanding and controlling life, anticipating the future, and appropriating nature after millennia of being subject to it. Reason made us superior, while "instincts" or emotions would downgrade our humanity to the level of animals. The politics of reason was modeled upon this principle,

190

and still is. Of course, there was, and there is, a clear understanding that this is not a perfect world, and that emotional behavior pollutes the realm of rationality. Therefore, the purity of political ideals is being sought out in the confrontation of well-designed policies in order to solve the problems of the collectivity, while repressing the irrational, emotional behavior that could drift into the turbulent waters of demagogy and fanaticism. Yet, what if emotions and feelings are essential components of the decision-making process? What if emotions and feelings ultimately decide the way in which politics, and power-making in general, construct meaning, and thus behavior, to determine action that is rationalized rather than rationally decided? As Leege and Wald (2007), write:

Meaning is "an attribute of symbolism" and is "a function of the context in which the symbol or the individual himself, was located." The most powerful symbols are found not in complicated theories of taxation and economic growth, or in efficient structures for health care delivery or in strategies for fighting terrorists or winning a war. They are found in pictures and sounds that tap into primary group experiences of things that promote pride or satisfaction or tap into reservoirs of fear or revulsion...Meaning is invested with emotion. It is far distant from cool rationality.

(Leege and Wald, 2007: 296–7)

This is not a normative call for the triumph of emotional politics, let alone for irrational decision-making. Rather, this is a recognition of the actual way in which people process signals on the basis of which they make their decisions, for themselves and for the world at large on behalf of themselves. Since democracy is essentially procedural, how people decide does not determine what they decide. To elaborate and implement a policy – for instance, a policy on war and peace – is a most important process that should be conducted in the full exercise of the best cognitive capacity available to us. But to reach the level of policy decision-making, democratic procedures have to be followed with the full understanding of the processes involved. And these processes are largely emotional, articulated around conscious feelings and connected to choices that elicit a complex array of responses dependent on the stimuli received from our communication environment. Because professional politicians or naturally born leaders know how to solicit the proper emotions to win the minds and hearts of people, the process of actual power-making overlays the formal procedures of democracy, thus largely determining the outcome of the contest. The

191

rational analysis of power-making processes starts with a recognition of the limits of rationality in the process. Instead, the discussion and analysis presented in this chapter show how, by activating networks of association between events and mental images via communication processes, power-making operates in multilayered dynamics in which the way we feel structures the way we think and ultimately the way we act. Empirical evidence and political communication theories converge toward emphasizing the power of the frame in the process of power-making. But who frames whom, how and why? If you really want to know, read on.

Chapter 4

Programming Communication Networks: Media Politics, Scandal Politics, and the Crisis of Democracy

Power-making by Image-making

Politics is the process of allocation of power in the institutions of the state. As I have argued and documented in this book, power relationships are largely based on the shaping of the human mind by the construction of meaning through image-making. Remember: ideas are images (visual or not) in our brain. For society at large, as distinct from a given individual, image-making is played out in the realm of socialized communication. In contemporary society, everywhere in the world, the media are the decisive means of communication. By media, I mean the whole array of communication organizations and technologies analyzed in Chapter 2, thus including both mass communication and mass self-communication. Media politics is the conduct of politics in and by the media. In this chapter, I will try to show that, in our historical context, politics is primarily media politics.

Messages, organizations, and leaders who do not have a presence in the media do not exist in the public mind. Therefore, only those who can convey their messages to the citizens at large have the chance to influence their decisions in ways that lead to their own access to power positions in the state and/or maintain their hold over political institutions. This is certainly the case in democratic politics: that is, politics based on competitive, supposedly free elections as the primary mechanism of access to political office. But it is also the case in non-democratic regimes, as control over the media is a potent form of domination. Without breaking through the organizational and technological barriers that structure information and socialized communication, the windows of hope for change are too narrow to allow effective resistance to the powers that be. Indeed, when their control of communication fails, authoritarian regimes evolve toward their demise, with different levels of violence and human trauma depending on the circumstances of political change (Randall, 1993; Sreberny-Mohammadi and Mohammadi, 1994; Castells and Kiselyova, 1995; O'Neil, 1998; Price, 2002). Moreover, the majority of countries on the planet exist in a variety of intermediate states between textbook democracy and evil authoritarianism. The definitional criteria of democracy need to be contextualized because the global diversity of political cultures is not reducible to the original ideas of liberalism as they emerged in the eighteenth century in a small, if influential, area of the world. Democracy as a social and institutional practice is not the same as the ideology of democracy, let alone the equivalent of the ideals of liberal democracy.

The fact that politics is essentially played out in the media does not mean that other factors (for example, grassroots activism or fraud) are not significant in deciding the outcome of political contests. Neither does it imply that the media are the power-holders. They are not the Fourth Estate. They are much more important: they are the space of power-making. The media constitute the space where power relationships are decided between competing political and social actors. Therefore, almost all actors and messages must go through the media in order to achieve their goals. They have to accept the rules of media engagement, the language of the media, and media interests. The media, as a whole, are not neutral, as the ideology of professional journalism asserts; neither are they direct instruments of state power, with the obvious exception of mass media under authoritarian regimes.

Media actors construct communication platforms and engage in message production in line with their specific organizational and professional interests (Schudson, 2002). Given the *diversity of media actors*, these interests are also diversified. As I illustrated in Chapter 2, corporate media are primarily businesses, and most of their business is entertainment, including the news. But they also have broader political interests, as they are directly invested in the dynamics of the state, a key part of their business environment. So the rules for political engagement in the media will depend on their specific business models and their relationship to political actors and to the audience.

For all media organizations, whether they are focused on mass communication or on mass self-communication, or both, the key is to expand their influence and resources by expanding and deepening their audience. Different media outlets identify their audiences according to specific strategies. So, it is not simply a matter of winning audience share, but also of winning the target audience. This is the critical rationale behind the partisan media model, as in the case of Fox News in the US, Antena 3 TV in Spain, or Mediaset in Italy. They target ideologically specific audiences interested in having their views confirmed rather than being informed from alternative sources. In a different model of audience targeting, independent political blogs aim to disseminate opinions and information that are not found in the mainstream media to build a support base for their specific approach to political issues. Yet, for the mainstream media, their key asset is credibility. Of course, this is always in relative terms, as the credibility of the media has been in a tailspin in recent years. For instance, in the United States, in 2007, 36 percent of people believed that the American press actually hurts democracy, up from 23 percent in 1985. And only 39 percent believed that the press accurately presents facts, down from 55 percent in 1985 (Pew, 2007b: 2).[27] People rely largely on the mass media to obtain most of their politically relevant information and, in spite of the growing importance of the Internet, television and radio remain the most trusted sources of political news (Paniagua, 2006; Eurobarometer, 2007; Public Opinion Foundation, 2007; Pew, 2008c). The reason is obvious: if

[27] However, these trends are not as pronounced in Eastern Europe and in developing countries where the *Edelman Trust Barometer* (Edelman, 2008), the Eurobarometer (2007), and other studies find rebounding levels of trust in the media. There is speculation that these trends reflect a change in definition of the media (i.e., a faith in the introduction of the Internet and new media technologies). It is also possible that lack of trust in government institutions leads to searching for alternative sources of information. Moreover, this is changing for the Internet generation.

you see it, it must be true, as television news editors know only too well (Hart, 1999).[28]

Graber (2001: 11–42) has shown that the effectiveness of audiovisual messages in conveying political information is related to the way in which our brain processes messages, following the logic of image production and stimulation that I analyzed in Chapter 3. Even when the Internet is cited as a key source of news, the most visited web sites are those of mainstream media, with the BBC news web site being the most visited news site in the world, with over 46 million visitors per month, 60 percent originating from outside the UK. Excluding Yahoo! News and Google News (which aggregate but do not produce news), the other most visited news web sites are, in decreasing order, CNN, *The New York Times*, Weather.com, MSNBC, and Reuters.[29]

However, to say that politics in our age is media politics is not the final word but the opening question. How does this translate into the mechanisms of political conflict, political competition, political participation, and decision-making? How does political agency transform itself to be more effective in the realm of media politics? What is the specific effect of media politics on political campaigns, leadership, and organization? To what extent do horizontal networks of mass self-communication, and particularly the Internet and wireless communication, modify political practices as compared to the conduct of politics in the mass media? What is the connection between media politics and the use of scandal politics as the weapon of choice in power struggles? And what are the observable consequences of the new brand of politics on democracy as a form of relationship between state and society?

The Killing (Semantic) Fields: Media Politics at Work

What are the actual nuts and bolts of [the] process used by the political hitman?

Step I: The political hitmen dig up the dirt.
Step II: The dirt is then given to the pollsters, who through sophisticated polling can determine which pieces of dirt are the most damaging in the minds of the voters.

---

[28] According to the Eurobarometer (2007: 54), more Europeans express trust in radio (66%) and television (56%) than in the written press (47%) or Internet (35%).
[29] According to Alexa.com traffic rankings, June 2008.

Step III: The pollsters give their results to the media advertising folks, who put the most damaging two or three negative issues into the TV, radio, and direct-mail pieces that do their best to rip their political opponent into shreds. The third step is truly impressive. I marvel at the unbelievable talents of campaign media spinsters...When it's all over, the truth has been exposed – and quite often the opponent has suffered a serious blow to his or her campaign, one from which sometimes they never recover.

The central role of media politics in political strategies is observed in countries around the world, as argued and documented by Swanson and Mancini (1996), Plasser (2000), Graber, (2001), Curran (2002), Hallin and Mancini, (2004a, b), Bosetti (2007), Hollihan (2008), and others. *The practice of media politics implies the performance of several key tasks*:

1. The first is to secure access to the media by the social and political actors engaged in power-making strategies.
2. The second is the elaboration of messages and the production of images that best serve the interests of each power-player. Formulating effective messages requires an identification of the target audience(s) as it fits the political strategy. To execute this strategy, it is essential to obtain information that is relevant both to the audience and to the message, as well as to generate knowledge about the best possible use of this information to achieve the goals of the political actor. Indeed, media politics is, in fact, one major component of a broader form of politics – informational politics, the use of information and information processing as a decisive tool of power-making.
3. Next, the delivery of the message requires the use of specific technologies and formats of communication, as well as the measure of its effectiveness through polling.
4. And last, but not least, someone must pay for all of these increasingly expensive activities: the financing of politics is a central connecting point between political power and economic power.

I will analyze each of these operations and draw the implications of the analysis for the exercise of power in society. However, before proceeding with this inquiry, I need to introduce two preliminary remarks.

First, media politics is not limited to electoral campaigns. It is a constant, fundamental dimension of politics, practiced by governments, parties, leaders, and non-governmental social actors alike. Affecting the content of the news on a daily basis is one of the most important endeavors of political strategists. Although, in democracy, electoral campaigns are indeed the decisive moments, it is the continuing process of information and the diffusion of images relevant to politics that conform the public mind in ways that are difficult to alter during moments of heightened attention, unless some truly dramatic event or message takes place near the time of decision-making. In fact, it is a frequent practice of governments and politicians to create events or to highlight events as a form of political ploy, such as starting a crisis with another country, hosting a major international gathering (for example, the Olympic Games), or revealing financial corruption or personal misconduct. Policies are largely dependent upon politics. Not only because political power determines the capacity to implement policies, but because policies are more often than not designed with their political effects in mind.

My second introductory remark concerns the diversity of media politics according to the institutional and cultural specificity of each country (Hallin and Mancini, 2004a). For instance, paid television advertising is central to electoral campaigns in the United States. This is a major factor in explaining the key role of political finance, and therefore the ability of lobbyists to influence American politicians. On the other hand, in most European countries, media advertising in electoral campaigns is highly regulated, and governments often provide paid access to the public television networks (often those with the largest audience), following strict rules of time allocation. Debates and propaganda are also typically controlled by electoral commissions, and the forms and extent of this control vary greatly in each country. However, while acknowledging this diversity, and accounting for it in my analysis through case studies in different contexts, it is possible to find regularities in the practice of informational politics and media politics around the world. These regularities define contemporary political processes. As Hallin and Mancini (2004a) write:

A powerful trend is clearly underway in the direction of greater similarity in the way the public sphere is structured across the world. In their products, in their professional practices and cultures, in their systems of relationships with other political and social institutions, media systems across the world are becoming increasingly alike. Political systems, meanwhile, are becoming increasingly similar in the patterns of communication they incorporate . . . It is reasonable to say that homogenization is to a significant degree a convergence of world media toward forms that first evolved in the US. The US was once almost alone among industrialized countries in its system of commercial broadcasting; now commercial broadcasting is becoming the norm. The model of information-oriented, politically-neutral professionalism that has prevailed in the US and to a somewhat lesser degree in Britain increasingly dominates the news media worldwide. The personalized, media-centered forms of election campaigning, using techniques similar to consumer product marketing, that again were pioneered in the US, similarly are becoming more and more common in European politics.   (2004a: 25)

(Stephen Marks, Confessions of a Political Hitman, 2007: 5–6)

I would add that Latin American political campaigns are even closer to the American practice, since they focus on personalized leadership, often use American consultants, and make extensive use of commercial media (Scammell, 1998; Plasser, 2000; Castells, 2005a; Sussman, 2005; Calderon, 2007).

In fact, rather than Americanization, this convergence pattern of politics toward media politics is a feature of globalization, as Hallin and Mancini (2004a) point out. The global concentration of media business that I documented in Chapter 2, and the growing interdependence of societies around the world, lead to the rise of a global media culture and global professional practices that are mirrored in similar forms of media politics. American political consultancy has become a global business, with direct influence in elections in Russia, Israel, and many other countries (Castells, 2004b; Hollihan, 2008). Therefore, while paying attention to the specificity of each media politics regime, and providing some illustration of this diversity, for the sake of the analysis presented here, I will review each of the key components of informational and media politics in generic terms.

Gatekeeping Democracy

Access to the media is provided by gatekeepers (Curran, 2002; Bennett, 2007; Bosetti, 2007). This dimension of media politics is essential because without such access messages and messengers cannot reach their intended audience. This is also the dimension that differs most amongst media regimes, particularly when it comes to broadcasting. From tight government control, based on ownership or censorship, to private, commercial media business, and through all intermediate scenarios and mixed regimes, there is a broad range of variation in the mechanisms of media access.

First, there is a distinction to be made between political access to the media through regular news and media programming and access through paid political advertising. Paid political advertising is more important in the United States than in other countries, and refers essentially to political campaigns (a relentless activity in America). Its widespread practice places an extraordinary burden on political democracy in America, as it makes finance the centerpiece of political campaigns. Media politics benefits media businesses twofold: through advertising revenue and increased viewership during hard-hitting political competitions (Hollihan, 2008). I will elaborate on this fundamental topic below while analyzing political campaigns. In Europe, paid advertising is either banned or plays a minor role in the electoral process, although financing is also a significant matter for reasons I will explain later. Political campaigns in Latin America, Asia, and Africa offer a diverse mixture that combines government control over the media, paid advertising in the commercial media, and clientele networks fed with cash and promises of favors (Plasser, 2000; Sussman, 2005; CAPF, 2007).

However, for the world at large, including the United States, I suggest that political access to regular television and radio programming and the print press is the most important factor in the practice of media politics. There are four components to the process (Tumber and Webster, 2006; Bosetti, 2007; Bennett et al., 2007; Campo Vidal, 2008): (1) the overseeing organizational control of either government entities or corporate businesses (or, in some rare cases, nonprofit corporations); (2) editorial decisions; (3) the choices of the professional journalism corps; and (4) the logic embedded in the adequate performance of the task assigned to the media organization, namely to attract the audience to the media product's message. The latter component is fundamental because it introduces flexibility into an otherwise one-directional flow of information. It requires paying attention to the credibility of the medium by reporting on issues that people perceive as important and/or entertaining. The absence of reporting on well-known events, or the blatant manipulation of information by the sender, undermines the capacity of the media to influence the receiver, thus limiting its relevance in media politics.

Access politics is played out in the interaction between these four levels of the gatekeeping process. Thus, the more independence the medium has from government control, whether through statutory independent public broadcasting (such as the BBC) or by private ownership, the more access will be influenced by commercial interests (advertising as a function of audience share) and/or by the professional corps. The more the medium is dominated by commercial logic, the more journalists will have to play within these limits. The more journalists have a say in programming, priming, and framing, the more they will rely on attracting the public as a source of their professional influence. And the more the actual course of events permeates into the media, the more media influence expands, as people recognize themselves in what they read or watch. If we combine these different effects, what we find in the analysis is *a common denominator effect* and *two filters operating in the selection of media access.*

The *common ground* is that what is attractive to the public boosts audience, revenue, influence, and professional achievement for the journalists and show anchors. When we translate this into the realm of politics, it means that the most successful reporting is the one that maximizes the entertainment effects that correspond to the branded consumerist culture permeating our societies. The notion of a deliberative democracy based on in-depth exposés and civilized exchanges about substantive issues in the mass media is at odds with the broader cultural trends of our time (Graber, 2001). Indeed, it is the mark of a small segment of elite media that caters primarily to decision-makers and to a minority of the highly educated strata of the population.[30] This does not mean that people in general do not care about substantive issues. It means that for these issues (for example, the economy, the war, the housing crisis) to be perceived by a broad audience, they have to be presented in the language of infotainment, in the broadest sense: not just laughing matters, but human drama as well. Seen from this perspective, politics becomes horse-race politics: who is winning, who is losing, how, why, and what is the latest gossip or the dirtiest trick (Ansolabehere et al., 1993; Jamieson, 2000; Sussman, 2005)? Media political language reproduces competitive sports jargon (Gulati et al., 2004).

---

[30] Postman (2004, in a speech published posthumously) argues that the glut of information sources has degraded the authority of societal institutions such as the family, the church, the school, and political parties that traditionally served as gatekeepers and agenda-setters. Overwhelmed with information, individuals are now less equipped to identify and participate in democratic processes. However, the image of a literate society engaging in deliberative democracy in the past seems to be more myth than reality. Thus, Postman, in his classic book *Amusing Ourselves to Death* (1986), depicted eighteenth-century colonial America as a society of active readership with a culture based on the print press. Without challenging Postman's important contributions to the analysis of the relationship between media, culture, and democracy, this nostalgia clearly refers to the educated, propertied segments of society; that is, the educated white male. In fact, African Americans were not allowed to read. As for overall literacy rates, the data used by Postman has been shown by historians to be biased in terms of sampling, over-representing older adults, males, and wealthy people. Herndon (1996), after correcting for biases using data from Rhode Island and different sources of signatures, found overall literacy rates in New England in the mid-eighteenth century to be 67% for males and 21.7% for females. The literacy rates were lower in the Middle and Southern colonies. And as late as 1870, 20% of the entire adult population and 80% of the African American population were illiterate (Cook, 1977; Murrin et al., 2005). This is to say that the imagined cultural past and the notion of the loss of deliberative democracy are often the result of a nostalgic, elitist bias.

While most pronounced in American elections, the tendency to reduce elections to horse-race politics is evident in countries around the world (Sussman, 2005).[31]

Moreover, sensationalism drives political reporting: exposing the wrong-doing of the powerful has always been the solace of the populace, and nowadays it can be interpreted on a mass-communicated theatrical stage (Plasser, 2005). A key feature of theatrical politics is its personalization (Bosetti, 2007). A mass audience requires a simple message. The simplest message is an image; the simplest image, and the one with which people can identify the most, is a human face (Giles, 2002). This does not only mean the physical traits of a person or the color of her clothes. More important is the person's character, as it is manifest in her appearance, words, and the information and memories that she embodies. This is partly because understanding complex policy issues can be taxing for many citizens, while most of them have confidence in their ability to judge character, which is an emotional response to the behavior of persons embedded in political narratives (Hollihan, personal communication, 2008). Thus, media politics is personalized politics, or what Martin Wattenberg (1991, 2004, 2006) refers to as "candidate-centered politics." As Wattenberg points out, media technologies such as "television, direct mail, and now the Internet have freed candidates from reliance on political parties, thereby allowing campaigns to be run independently of party affiliation" (2004: 144). This is perhaps the most important effect of media politics on the political process because it provokes parties, unions, NGOs, and other political actors to rally around one person and bet on her chances alone in the political media market.

This was always the case in the United States and Latin America. But in the past 20 years, coinciding precisely with the growing centrality of media politics, personality politics has characterized the political process in the entire world, to the detriment of stable parties, ideological affinities, and political machines. The question is who selects whom. The media make the leaders known, and dwell on their battles, victories, and defeats, because narratives need heroes (the candidate), villains (the opponent), and victims to be rescued (citizens). But the would-be leaders have to position themselves as media-worthy, by using any available opening to display their tricks (or their virtues, for that matter). They can do so by creating events that force the media to pay attention to them, as in the case of

---

[31] For this trend in Canada, see also Trimble and Sampert (2004); for Australia, see Denemark et al. (2007).

an underdog political candidate unexpectedly winning a primary election. Media outlets love stories of unlikely success. The more a political figure fits into a celebrity frame, the easier it is for the media to incorporate news about that candidate into the increasingly popular infotainment format of news provision. However, "success story" frames are commonly reversed, as chronicles of falls from grace are as juicy as fairy tales of improbable triumph. Yet, it is important to remember the principle: political material (persons, messages, events) is processed as exciting infotainment material, formatted in sports language and couched in narratives as close as possible to tales of intrigue, sex, and violence. Naturally, while maintaining noble themes about democracy, patriotism, and the well-being of the nation on behalf of the common folk (the man in the street, this mythical creature who has replaced citizenship in the media world).

This logic of access selection is deeply modified by the activation of *two filters*. The first filter is *direct government control*, either by explicit censorship or by hidden directives. This, of course, refers to authoritarian governments, such as China or Russia, which I will analyze later in the chapter because of the specificity of their media regimes. But even in democratic regimes, governments often interfere with the operation of national broadcasters or with other media outlets over which they wield financial or indirect influence. I would even say that this practice is typical. Sometimes, control is intensified, as in the cases of Berlusconi in Italy in the 1994–2004 period (Bosetti, 2007), and of Spain during the Aznar government in 1996–2004 (Campo Vidal, 2008). In this case, gatekeeping is strictly political and caters to the interests of the government, a political party in government, or a particular politician.

The second filter is one imposed by *corporate ownership and leadership in terms of editorial criteria*, usually corresponding with their business interests rather than their ideological preferences (Fallows, 1996; Tumber and Webster, 2006; Bennett et al., 2007; Arsenault and Castells, 2008b; McClellan, 2008). There is an abundance of reported evidence on such practices in various media outlets in both the print press and television networks.[32]

---

[32] On May 28, 2008, in CNN's evening news program *Anderson Cooper 360*, Cooper interviewed a CNN correspondent regarding a claim made by Scott McClellan, former Whitehouse spokesman for President Bush, that the press corps was guilty of failing to adequately investigate misinformation claims made by the White House regarding the Iraq War. To Cooper's surprise, the correspondent relayed her own experience of being advised by CNN corporate executives to support Bush's version. She posited that the corporate directive evolved out of a belief that President Bush's then high popularity ratings would translate into similarly high channel ratings.

This is to be differentiated from the practice of partisan journalism that does not preclude access to opposed political views since this is the salt and pepper of their infotainment appeal. In some cases, there is a direct editorial decision to block access to political views or political actors because they are incompatible with business media strategies. In fact, most radical political critiques in democratic societies are banned from the mainstream media because they are considered to be out of touch with the country, and thus with the interests of the audience. Only by generating news (for example, colorful demonstrations, preferably turned violent by police action) can the radicals break through the media barrier. Of course, this marginalizes them further as they are equated with violence and hooliganism, a second-order level of political exclusion from the public mind.

One important observation concerning access is that the analysis presented so far refers exclusively to media of mass communication. Yet, I have emphasized in Chapter 2 *the growing significance of mass self-communication in reaching people's minds*. In this case, traditional forms of access control are not applicable. Anyone can upload a video to the Internet, write a blog, start a chat forum, or create a gigantic e-mail list. Access in this case is the rule; blocking Internet access is the exception. The Internet and mass media are two distinct, albeit related, platforms of communication that share a key common feature in the construction of the political field: in both cases the process of communication is shaped by the message.

The Message is the Medium: Media Politics and Informational Politics

The key features of media politics are: the personalization of politics, electoral campaigns focused on use of the media, and the daily processing of political information through the practice of spin. Bosetti (2007) defines *spin* as "the activity of politicians, usually through consultants, consisting of communicating matters in a form that favors their interests, while looking to inflict damage on the opponent" (p. 18, my translation). I would also include the practice of spin by media pundits, who play diverse roles in formatting political information according to their specific biases.

The goal of media politics, as with all politics, is to win and to hold on to the spoils of victory for as long as possible. This does not mean that political actors are indifferent to the content of politics. But, as I was repeatedly reminded during personal conversations with political leaders around the world, reaching a position of power is the prerequisite to enacting any policy proposal. Winning actually results in the control of political office and its attached resources by the person who embodies a political project (including his or her own ambitions), supported by a political party or coalition. Thus, the message to citizens is simple: support this candidate and reject her opponents (or vice versa: reject her opponents more vehemently than you support her candidacy, a more frequent instance in contemporary politics). Because the message is clear and simple, and embodied in one person, the communication process is constructed around this message. In this sense, the message is the medium because formats and platforms of communication, in their diversity, will be selected in terms of their effectiveness in supporting this specific message, namely a given politician.

Political messages must overcome a major difficulty to reach the minds of citizens. As Doris Graber (2001) has documented, "Information processing research shows that average Americans [and I would add people in the world at large: M.C.] pay close attention only to news about significant topics that clearly relate to their lives and experiences. Many news stories fail to meet these criteria" (p. 129). Indeed, most political news is peripheral to the concerns of everyday life and, often, too complex for citizens to follow with the interest required to process them, let alone remember them. However, when news is presented as infotainment, which includes personalizing the news via a particular political figure, and in ways that relate to the receiver's emotions and interests, it is more easily processed and stored in the memory.

Therefore, the production of the message has to proceed as an interface between the characteristics and values of the politician and the characteristics and values of the intended target audience. This is the case for both electoral campaigns and day-to-day politics. Political actors devise their strategy by tailoring messages to bring about the most favorable connection between their political leader and the electorate, taking into consideration the specific format of a variety of media platforms: television, radio, print press, Internet, SMS, paid advertising, media interviews, political debates, and the like. The accuracy of the strategy depends on a careful, social-science-based analysis of the potential electorate. True, it is also contingent upon the characteristics of the political figure. But politicians are the ones who master the resources in order to compete, so they will adapt their strategy to who they are rather than the other way around. Until they lose, naturally. Then their troops will find promising new lords.

How does the strategy work? For a long time, it was largely based on a mixture of intuition, hope, advice from experts, and feedback from networks of supporters. The development of the tools of political science and communication psychology has led to the diffusion of a new form of professionalized political practice, which I call *informational politics*.

Designing the Message: Political Think Tanks

Informational politics begins with *the articulation of messages depending on the interests and values of the sociopolitical coalition constructed around specific political actors*. The content and format of political projects is increasingly decided with the help of *think tanks* that bring together experts, academics, political strategists, and media consultants in the conduct of politics and policy-making. The use of databases, targeted messaging, and polling tracking must be understood within the context of a broader perspective that took hold in America three decades ago, but later spread to most of the world: the formation of strategic, political think tanks responsible for analyzing trends, understanding people's cognitive mechanisms, and applying the results of their studies to devise efficient tactics to win elections, hold office, and win major policy battles, such as health-care policy, energy policy, or abortion rights in America, or the reform of the welfare state in Britain. Most of these think tanks in the United States were linked to conservative groups and, ultimately, to the GOP[33] candidates. They received high levels of financial support from corporations and from religious movements.

Their origin can be traced back to the social and political turmoil of the late 1960s. At that time, American society was in the process of losing its political innocence. During this period, public opinion began to turn against the atrocious Vietnam War, formally escalated on the pretext of fabricated evidence (the Gulf of Tonkin incident in August 1964). The post-World War II generation called into question the legitimacy of the government's call for the ultimate sacrifice for the first time in American history. Domestic upheaval amplified these trends. The civil rights movement, urban ethnic riots, and the rise of counter-cultural social movements shook the foundations of social and political conservatism. While Nixon won the 1968 and 1972 elections largely as a result of the inability of the Democrats

[33] GOP (for the Grand Old Party) is the American expression for the Republican Party.

to transform social protest into a new brand of politics, the writing of the political crisis was on the wall. It materialized soon after with the Watergate scandal and the resignation of Nixon, and with the collapse of US power in Vietnam. Compounded by an economic crisis that halted the model of economic growth that had brought prosperity after World War II (Castells, 1980), political uncertainty appeared to open the door to a period of Democratic dominance in politics, and to a society escaping the influence of conservative values. A small elite of Republican strategists decided it was time to bring academic knowledge and professional expertise into the practice of politics. The situation in the world and in America required deep thinking, a long-term political vision, and the instruments to translate thinking into tactics, and tactics into political power. Republican political power, that is. A series of "think tanks" were created, and lavishly funded as the conservative elites decided to take matters into their own hands, pushing aside the amateurish politics of individual candidates and betting instead on those political campaigns that would respond to targeted conservative strategies.

The Powell Memo is usually credited with launching the rise of right-wing think tanks and the "new right approach" to American politics. In August 1971, Lewis Powell, a corporate lawyer (who was appointed Supreme Court Justice by Nixon two weeks later), distributed a "Confidential Memorandum: Attack on the American Free Enterprise System" (later known as "the Powell Memo"), outlining the dangers of liberal control of academic and media resources. The memo inspired the creation of the Heritage Foundation, the Manhattan Institute, the Cato Institute, Citizens for a Sound Economy, Accuracy in Academe, and other influential organizations. Key funders of these new think tanks included the banking and oil money of the Mellon-Scaifes of Pittsburgh, the manufacturing fortunes of Lynde and Harry Bradley of Milwaukee, the energy revenues of the Koch family of Kansas, the chemical profits of John M. Olin of New York, the Vicks patent-medicine empire of the Smith Richardson family of Greensboro, NC, and the brewing assets of the Coors dynasty of Colorado, among others. Joseph Coors provided the initial funding for the Heritage Foundation inspired by the memo. Heritage Foundation trustees have included Joseph Coors, former Treasury Secretary William E. Simon, Richard M. Scaife, Grover Coors, Jeb Bush, and Amway Corporation co-founder Jay Van Andel. The memo remained "confidential" for more than a year after Powell wrote it. But months after his Senate confirmation to the Supreme Court, it was leaked to Jack Anderson, a liberal syndicated columnist. He published two columns about it in September 1972, stirring nationwide interest in the document. The role of these right-wing think tanks became increasingly critical over the following years, and is often credited with contributing to the election of Ronald Reagan in 1980, reversing the Democratic domination of Congress in 1994, and shaping key aspects of George W. Bush's candidacy and presidency, including the design of the "war on terror" and the initiation of the second Iraq War (Rich, 2004, 2005a, b).

Seeking to provide a counterweight to these conservative institutions, Democrats followed suit, albeit at a lower level of funding and with less political impact. There was even an attempt by the leading cognitive scientist George Lakoff to establish a think tank to develop progressive frames to counter the conservative dominance in framing politics. His Rockridge Institute, in spite of its remarkable intellectual performance and substantial political influence, closed in 2008, at the peak of the presidential campaign when it was most needed, due to lack of support from a Democratic establishment that still did not "get it."

Overall, according to Rich (2005b), between 1970 and 2005 the number of think tanks in the US quadrupled, and state-based think tanks grew at an even faster pace, reaching 183 organizations. Of these 183 state-based organizations, 117 had research agendas focused primarily on state policy issues, more than a tenfold increase over the ten that existed in 1970. Among these 117 think tanks, conservative ideology dominates. In a survey conducted by Rich among conservative think tanks, a significant plurality – almost 40 percent – of those who were the organizations' first leaders came from the private sector; they were either former lobbyists or business executives (38.2%). By contrast, almost two-thirds of those who formed liberal think tanks came out of state government or from the nonprofit advocacy community (63.1%). Among the top priorities for the leaders of conservative think tanks were issue expertise (61.8%), media and public affairs experience (35.3%), and a record of publication (32.3%). Three-quarters of the leaders of conservative think tanks named shaping public opinion as important (73.5%), while only half of the leaders of liberal think tanks reported this issue as important (52.6%).

A key component of these conservative think tanks is the systematic use of the media to shape public opinion, an expensive endeavor. Studies of interest groups have shown that the single most important organizational attribute leading to media visibility is the budget size of the organization seeking it. A number of conservative foundations have poured substantial amounts of money into conservative think tanks, including the Lynde and Harry Bradley Foundation, the Carthage Foundation, the Earhart Foundation, the Charles G. Koch, David H. Koch, and Claude R. Lambe charitable foundations, the Phillip M. McKenna Foundation, the JM Foundation, the John M. Olin Foundation, the Henry Salvatori Foundation, the Sarah Scaife Foundation, and the Smith Richardson Foundation. The strong funding support provided by these foundations has had important influence on the visibility of right-wing think tanks. Edie Goldenberg (1975), in her study of "resource-poor groups," finds that more resources equate with the improved ability of groups to gain media visibility. Lucig H. Danielian (1992) similarly finds the economic strength (i.e., larger size) of interest groups to be among the strongest predictors of their visibility in network news, and suggests that the proportion of resources that an organization devotes to public affairs and media-related efforts affects its visibility. Studies conducted during the 1980s and 1990s found that conservative think tanks devoted significantly more resources to promoting their products and seeking visibility (Feulner, 1986; Covington, 1997). In contrast, liberal think tanks were deemed to be more resource-poor and less supportive of visibility-generating projects (Callahan, 1995, 1999; Shuman, 1998). In a study of conservative think tanks and media visibility during the 1990s, Rich and Weaver (2000) found that, depending on the ideological leanings of the specific publication, high-spending think tanks received many more citations (i.e., in *The Wall Street Journal* and *The Washington Post*).

Although conservative think tanks used to be better funded, left-leaning organizations began to catch up in the 2000s (Rich, 2005a). The most well-funded liberal or "no-ideology" think tanks are now often better funded than places like the Heritage Foundation. What is different is that liberal and independent think tanks continue to spend most of their money on policy analysis, while conservative think tanks dedicate significant proportions of their resources to media relations and government lobbying. As an illustration of the contrasting strategies, Brookings, one of the leading independent think tanks, in 2004 spent 3 percent of its $39 million budget on communications; in 2002, the most recent year for which information is available, the conservative Heritage Foundation spent 20 percent of its $33 million budget on public and government affairs (Rich, 2005a: 25). According to Herb Berkowitz, Heritage's former vice president for communication:

Our belief is that when the research product has been printed, then the job is only half done. That is when we start marketing it to the media . . . We have as part of our charge the selling of ideas, the selling of policy proposals. We are out there actively selling these things, day after day. It's our mission.   (quoted in Rich, 2005a: 25)

Thus, *while liberal and independent think tanks are mainly engaged in policy analysis, following their belief in rational politics, the conservative think tanks are primarily oriented toward shaping minds by the means of media politics.*

Interestingly enough, in Britain, the most active and insightful political think-tank scholars rose to prominence during the early days of Tony Blair's ascent to Prime Minister. For example, Geoff Mulgan (1991, 1998), one of the most innovative analysts of the network society, co-founded Demos in 1993 and later went on to lead Tony Blair's Forward Strategy Unit in the Prime Minister's office in 1997. Yet, the political shock suffered by many of these tank thinkers as a result of Blair's alignment with Bush following 9/11 led to a separation between the most insightful think tanks and the leadership of the Labour Party during Blair's tenure. In other countries, policy-oriented foundations are usually linked to major political parties. Such is the case, for instance, in Germany, with the Friedrich Ebert Foundation, associated with the Social Democrats, and the Konrad Adenauer Foundation, linked to the Christian Democrats. Or, in Spain, with the Fundación Alternativas and the Fundacion Pablo Iglesias in the Socialist area of influence, and the FAES Foundation led by former conservative leader José María Aznar. But most of these foundations primarily play a role in policy analysis and ideological elaboration rather than a direct operational function in designing the politics of the party. The practice of informational politics is usually left to political consultants, a growing global industry with deep roots in the soil of American politics, as I mentioned above (Sussman, 2005; Bosetti, 2007).

Targeting the Message: Profiling Citizens

Once the policies and political strategies are formulated, media politics goes into a new phase of operation: *the identification of values, beliefs, attitudes, social behavior, and political behavior (including voting patterns) for segments of the population identified by their demographics and spatial distribution.* Mark Penn, one of the leading American pollsters, and chief advisor to Hillary Clinton's 2008 primary presidential campaign, proceeds in his book *Microtrends* (Penn and Zalesne, 2007) to carefully dissect the American electorate by social profiles. He illustrates how, by looking for statistical associations between demographic characteristics, beliefs, media inclinations, and political behavior, it becomes possible to target each specific group and to tap into their predispositions, thus honing the political message. How does this translate into political strategy? The following example will reveal the method.

In an interview with *Vanity Fair*, Karl Rove, whom many considered to be the chief architect of George W. Bush's communications strategy, reported that when the Bush campaign learned that the television sitcom *Will & Grace*, about a gay man Will and his best friend Grace sharing an apartment together in New York City, was extremely popular with young Republicans and swing voters, particularly women, they saturated the program with 473 campaign commercial placements. The campaign purchased these ads on a program that provided a sympathetic portrait of contemporary urban gay life, while seeking to increase voter turnout among other conservative populations through a proposed constitutional amendment banning gay marriage (Purdum, 2006).

Thus, *the message is unique: the politician*. The incarnations of the candidate in different formats vary with the target population (Barisione, 1996). Of course, within the limits of avoiding exposure to blatant contradictions between the images projected in different groups, spaces, and times. Focus groups help to refine the messages, and polling provides a way of measuring the effectiveness of the message in real time and of following the evolution of public opinion. However, polling per se is not a very sophisticated tool of political navigation because it only reveals the politician's standing in public opinion and the positives and negatives of his or her message. *It is the combination of polling and social data analysis* that provides an interpretation of the trends in real time and enhances the opportunity to modify unfavorable evolution by acting on latent attitudes through new rounds of targeted messages differentiated for each social category (Hollihan, 2008). The construction of databases has another direct, operational effect on political strategies. Data can be calculated for each electoral precinct, thus offering a political geography of choice that allows personalized political propaganda through automated or live phone calls to the homes of prospective voters, direct e-mailing, and canvassing, as I will discuss below while analyzing political campaigns.

That this sophisticated form of political marketing is a derivative of commercial marketing is a clear indication of the rise of the citizen-consumer as a new persona in public life. In fact, politicians and businesses use the same databases because there is an active commerce of data-selling which originated from the use of massive computer power applied to processing data from government and academic sources with the huge collection of data resulting from the invasion of privacy by credit-card companies, telecommunication companies, and Internet companies selling information about those of their customers (the majority) who, unaware of the fine print in their contracts, do not opt out of the companies' policy of selling their customers' data.

Indeed, the large and sophisticated system of voter targeting, propelled by the construction of the "Voter Vault," a database containing detailed information about target populations, was one of the key factors in the success of the Republican Party in the United States over the 2000 and 2004 election cycles. Karl Rove, the brilliant, if unscrupulous, brain behind the conservatives' rise to power in American politics, is considered one of the key architects of the adaptation of corporate marketing techniques to American political campaigning. I will dwell briefly on this analysis as it is one of the most revealing cases of informational politics. To follow Karl Rove's career as a political operative provides a window into the *evolution of political practice in the early years of the Information Age*.

Karl Rove was the chief architect of the Bush administration's political strategy until his resignation in August 2007 to avoid indictment in the Plame Affair (see Table A4.1. in Appendix). He also guided Bush's 1994 and 1998 runs for Texas Governor, John Ashcroft's successful 1994 run for Senate, and the successful Senate bids of John Coryn (2002) and Phil Gramm (1982 for House and 1984 for Senate). He was considered to be "Bush's Brain" and, along with Lee Atwater,[34] is credited with the transformation of the political campaigning strategies of the Republican Party.[35]

Rove began his formal work for the Republican Party in 1971 when he dropped out of college to serve as the Executive Chairman of the College Republicans. He first worked with Lee Atwater in 1973, when Atwater managed his campaign for National Chairman of the College Republicans. During this campaign, an opponent who had dropped out of the race

[34] Atwater was advisor to both Reagan and Bush I and later RNC Chairman. He was the creator of the infamous Willie Horton revolving door ad that played a large role in Dukakis's defeat. Atwater died in 1991.

[35] Rove has a colorful history of dirty tricks. In his early years, while working for the campaign of a US Senate Republican candidate from Illinois, he pretended to volunteer for a Democrat named Alan J. Dixon, who was running for state treasurer (and later a Senator). Rove stole some stationery from Dixon's office, wrote a flyer promising "free beer, free food, girls and a good time for nothing," and distributed a thousand copies at a commune, a rock concert, and a soup kitchen, and among drunks on the street; a throng showed up at Dixon's headquarters (Purdum, 2006).

(Terry Dolan) leaked tapes to *The Washington Post* featuring Rove talking about dirty campaign techniques such as searching through the opponent's garbage. The *Post* broke the story – "Republican Party Probes Official as Teacher of Tricks" – at the height of the Nixon Watergate scandal. George H. W. Bush resolved the matter of whether Rove should win the election given these revelations and ruled in Rove's favor. This is how Rove first met George W. Bush. Rove moved to Texas a few years later and served as an advisor for George W. Bush's first run for Congress in 1978. Two years later, George H. W. Bush hired Rove to work on his 1980 campaign – but fired him in the middle of the race for leaking information to the press. After Rove left the White House, he became a political analyst for Fox News Channel, as did Dick Morris, who is given similar credit for encouraging Bill Clinton to approach politics as a lifestyle, consumer-driven, marketing process.[36]

Under Rove's leadership, the Republican Party led the way in the use of MLM (multi-level marketing) techniques, or what the Republicans and Rove refer to as "metrics." MLMs are traditionally corporate firms that build businesses through pyramid-style recruiting and marketing techniques (selling candidates as one would sell Tupperware). One of the leading names in corporate multi-level marketing is Amway. Richard De Vos founded Amway in 1959, a company that in 2004 had sales in excess of $6.2 billion. The De Vos family has long had an affiliation with GOP politics. Ubertaccio (2006a: 174) argues that the formal entrance of the De Vos family into electoral politics is only the latest evidence of the synergy between parties and MLM. According to Ubertaccio (2006a), the Republican Party commissioned studies to test the effectiveness of these MLM techniques, beginning in 2002, in recognition of the need to increase voter turnout among specific voter populations if they were to succeed once more, considering the very close margin of victory in 2000. MLM research in the corporate world had illustrated that volunteers are more effective at recruiting and managing other volunteers, particularly in the area of their targeted interest. They made political use of these techniques through two projects that represent informational politics at its best: the 72-Hour Task Force and the Voter Vault project.

Under Rove, the Republican Party first set up the 72-Hour Task Force in 2001 in order to drive Republican voter turnout. Drawing upon MLM

---

[36] Morris in 2008 was running vote.com, a webportal that asks users to vote on certain issues and then e-mails the results to relevant legislators.

data during each election, the Force focuses on increasing Republican voter turnout through a targeted campaign for the three days before a given election day. They do so by drawing upon carefully chosen volunteers who then activate their specific networks (for example, churches, gun clubs, PTA members, and so on).

Yet, the most ambitious and effective strategy was the construction of the Voter Vault, an extensive voter database built by the Republican Party in anticipation of the 2004 presidential election. The database contains information on specific groups, including consumer data, hunting license registrations, and magazine subscriptions considered to be "Republican" in nature. This system has information on over 175 million individuals and includes a web-based grassroots organizing tool that allows campaign volunteers to establish their own "precincts." The Vault is available to national and state parties. Bush's pollster and strategist Matthew Dowd (who reported to Rove) launched the Vault. The Voter Vault uses a point system which, based on certain demographic canvassing criteria, can tabulate if a constituent is a likely Republican or Democratic voter. The database – mostly processed in India – comes from various sources of public information. Data is legally bought in bulk on the web or gathered by tens of thousands of dedicated field workers. Statistics come from credit reports and ratings, magazine subscriptions and records traded among monthly and weekly publications, vehicle registrations, consumer polls that people answered or mailed in exchange for a free gift, records of consumer buying preferences captured by discount cards at the grocery store, lists of every local Evangelical church with a bus, as well as census figures about the racial and financial makeup of a particular neighborhood.

The Voter Vault helped to expand the Republican National Committee's (RNC) use of micro-targeted direct mail and phone calls. In 2004, the Republican Party spent almost $50 million on direct mail (up from $22 million in 2000). They spent $8.6 million on phone banks in 2004 (up from $3.6 million in 2000; La Raja et al., 2006: 118). Simultaneously, expenditures on party staff decreased from $43 million in 2000 to $33 million in 2004, possibly due to increased reliance on automated systems of targeting voters. In the 2006 election, the RNC Chairman, Ken Mehlman, expanded the Vault, as he explained to *Vanity Fair*: "We target voters the way that Visa targets credit-card customers. That's the difference from before. We used to target them based on their geography. We now target them based on what they do and how they live" (Purdum, 2006).

The Voter Vault allowed for greater micro-targeting of the media. In 2004, the Bush team identified which web sites its potential voters visited and which cable channels they watched. It spent its money accordingly, advertising on specialty cable outlets such as the Golf Channel and ESPN, whose audiences tended to be Republican. This allowed the party to target Republican voters living in otherwise "liberal areas" who would have been missed in traditional "get out the vote" drives. Between 2004 and 2006, the RNC expanded access to the Vault to organizers in all 50 states and trained approximately 10,000 volunteers how to use it.

Not to be outdone, beginning in 2002, the Democratic Party developed two databases: DataMart, containing the records of 166 million registered voters, and Demzilla, a smaller database used for fund-raising and organizing volunteers. But in contrast to the Voter Vault, the DNC data only covered the two previous elections and only 36 states had access, and the process of data input was far inferior to the Republican system. In February 2007, as a personal initiative by Howard Dean, DNC chairman at the time, the DNC replaced these systems with VoteBuilder. Described as a "state-of-the-art nationwide voter file interface," the web-based tool was designed to ensure that Democratic candidates, from the national party to the state parties, had access to the tools needed to help win elections. Yet, it was not until the 2008 election cycle that the Democrats instituted a centralized database, with continuous updating.

To what extent did these new informational strategies affect the political process? Panagopoulos and Wielhouwer (2008) examined National Election Study (NES) surveys for 2000 and 2004, the years that saw the greatest amount of "personal contact campaigning" since the survey began. They found that, across the board, campaigns targeted prior voters. By 2004, voters in swing states were highly coveted by both parties. The focus was on securing the party's own electoral basis, while still paying attention to the independents. Databases were critical in identifying both groups of voters. Voter turnout increased sharply in 2004 – arguably as a result of the increased focus on voter mobilization. Of 202.7 million eligible voters, 60.3 percent voted in the 2004 presidential election, a substantial increase over the 54.2 percent voting figure in 2000, and the second highest voter turnout rate since the 1960s (McDonald, 2004, 2005; Bergan et al., 2005). This increase is notable particularly given the overall decline in voter turnout in Western democracies in recent decades (Dalton and Wattenberg, 2000). Voter mobilization strategies, coupled with ideological polarization (also a Rove trademark), may have been the decisive combination for Republican victories in 2000 and 2004. Indeed, according to the 2004 American National Election Study, respondents perceived the candidates to be more ideologically distinct in 2004 than in 2000 (Bergan et al., 2005).

There is a darker side to informational politics. This is the search for information damaging to political opponents. It is a highly elaborated activity, labeled in the trade *"opposition research"* (Marks, 2007). Because it plays an essential role in political campaigning and in the development of scandal politics, I will address the issue in detail in the following sections of this chapter.

Data gathering, information processing, and knowledge-based analysis yield a crop of politically potent messages built around the promotion of the central message: the politician him or herself. Once messages are constructed, the process of communicating them to the target audiences proceeds through a variety of platforms and formats, of which regular television programming and electoral campaigns are the most relevant. I analyzed the former in Chapter 3, referring to the mechanisms of agenda-setting, framing, indexing, and priming that determine different forms of media bias. In this chapter, I will review the practice of political campaigns as a key instrument of winning political power, largely through media politics. However, I must first address the mother of all media politics: finance schemes.

The Money Trail

Informational politics is expensive, and in most countries cannot be supported by the regular financing of political organizations. Most spending is linked to political campaigns, and particularly to paid television advertising in countries, like the United States, where this is the main channel for candidates to communicate directly with the voters. The cost of electoral campaigns in the US has skyrocketed over the past few decades, with a significant acceleration since the mid-1990s. Figure 4.1 depicts the total contributions raised by US presidential candidates over the past nine election cycles.

Skyrocketing campaign costs are not limited to presidential candidates. In the US, in 2004, the cost of winning a seat in the Senate was, on average, $7 million, and a seat in the House was $1 million, an eleven-fold increase since 1976 (Bergo, 2006). However, Hollihan (2008) argues convincingly that the growth of political financing is not only a result of the increasing

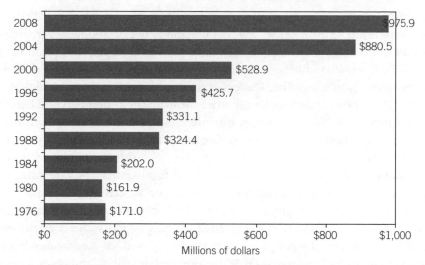

Fig. 4.1. **Total contributions to US presidential candidates' election cycle, 1976–2008**

Notes: These totals include primary receipts, general election public funding, and convention public funding. The dollar amounts have not been adjusted for inflation. The 2008 figure reflects total contributions through June 6, 2008.

Source: Federal Election Commission filings compiled by the Center for Responsive Politics.

needs of cash-strapped political campaigns. It is, in fact, a mechanism for the influence of corporate actors and other special interests on policy-making at all levels of government (Hollihan, 2008: 240–73). The supply seems to be even more significant than the demand. Politicians can afford to practice expensive politics because there is an abundance of funds from lobbyists and donors. Indeed, some politicians cannot even spend all the money they receive; so instead, they use it for extravagant lifestyles justified through creative accounting. Since 1974, a number of campaign finance reforms have been implemented in the United States, but they are quickly circumvented each time by new practices. Thus, US election laws now limit the amount that individual donors can contribute to candidates during an election cycle. For example, during the 2007–8 election cycle, individuals were allowed to contribute up to $2,300 to their candidate of choice during the primary election and up to the same amount for the general election. To circumvent these limits, Political Action Committees (PACs) were created and allowed to raise higher amounts. When PAC funding was capped, a new

217

possibility arose: soft money donations directly to the parties were allowed without limits. Since parties work for candidates, it ultimately reaches the candidates. Furthermore, there is the widespread practice of bundling donations, which allows some individuals (for instance, the CEO of a company, partners in a law firm, leaders of a union) to collect individual donations (for instance, from their employees or from their members) on behalf of a candidate. Often, companies provide bundled donations for both parties, to hedge their bets. Paid advertising in the media – the main expense of an electoral campaign – is often the initiative of so-called 527 groups (from the name of the tax code that confers their legal status), private citizens, or organizations that exercise their right to free speech by advertising on behalf of, or against, a given candidate. They cannot solicit the vote, but their message is unambiguous, and usually highly negative. Naturally, these groups develop on the periphery of the campaigns of the main candidates, so they are, in fact, subrogates that can pursue particular candidates' agendas outside the boundaries of formal fund-raising restrictions.

Furthermore, individuals pay thousands of dollars to attend fund-raising events and/or dinners that often raise millions of dollars. In the 1990s, President Clinton raised funds by inviting wealthy patrons to pay for the privilege of staying in the White House or what was called in the media "Motel 1600" (from 1600 Pennsylvania Avenue). While searching for donors for the 1996 presidential re-election campaign, his advisors came up with the idea of using the prestige of the presidency and the appeal of the White House to invite potential donors in exchange for a set donation. For as little as $12,500, the donor would be offered a fancy dinner in a Washington Hotel and a photo with the president. For coffee at the White House with the president and administration officials, the donor was asked to donate $50,000. If the enthusiasm of the president's supporter should reach the $250,000 mark, he or she would be invited to a whole day at the White House and enjoy its amenities, such as swimming in the pool, playing tennis, bowling in the presidential alley, or munching over a barbecue on the lawn. For an undisclosed, exceptionally generous donation, deluxe donors were able to spend a night in the Lincoln bedroom to reflect comfortably on the fate of American democracy. This select group became, in fact, a mass market: between 1993 and 1996 there were 103 fund-raising breakfasts at the White House and 938 overnight guests. About half of them were relatives and personal friends, but the others were among the rich and infamous of the world, including a Chinese arms company official, a financial broker convicted of fraud, a multimillionaire convicted of spying on his employees, an Indonesian banking family peddling US trade policy toward Indonesia, a Chinese beer company executive, and John Huang, the Democratic National Committee fund-raiser, later to be found guilty of breaking campaign finance laws by soliciting funds from foreign Asian donors. But there was no legal trouble for Clinton's funding: all of the soliciting was done with due respect to the rules. The donors were not asked for contributions within the White House or in any other government property, and their payments were not requested until a later time (Fineman and Isikoff, 1997; Frammolino and Fritz, 1997; both cited by Hollihan, 2008: 246).

Individual candidates can also contribute unlimited personal funds to their own campaigns. As a result, any wealthy American can attempt to run for office, circumventing parties or any other intermediary by buying access to citizens through the media and direct political advertising. This political finance system in the US has not been seriously challenged, since the Supreme Court has protected the right to donate to political campaigns as part of the right to free speech, emphasizing that corporations also have such right. Besides, politicians themselves are unlikely to put limits on a system from which the incumbents benefit. Thus, the Federal Electoral Commission (FEC) has remained an ineffective bureaucracy, basically fulfilling the function of window dressing to direct attention away from the uncomfortable truth of an American democracy literally for sale. In the case of the United States, money rules politics, and politicians who do not follow this rule have no chance to compete (Center for Responsive Politics, 2008c; Garrett, 2008).

However, it is still possible to draw upon grassroots financing for campaigns, as I will argue below. But with two caveats: for grassroots financing to be significant, it needs to be the result of massive support from a political movement following a charismatic leader; even under such circumstances, this is never enough, and forces the politician, regardless of his or her values, to look for sources of funding in the corporate and special interest worlds.

The case of the United States is unique because it combines the direct influence of private political financing with a legal system that encourages lobbying, a major industry in Washington, DC, with the indifference or resignation of the public at large (Hollihan, 2008). By contrast, in most, but not all, of the world money buys its way into politics, from local governments to the presidential office, without any effective legal framework to insulate government from special interests. A case in point is *Kenya*, a democracy since independence, where the contested, and ultimately violent, 2007 election was the most expensive in the country's history. Indeed, between 1963 and 2007, the average expenditure per parliamentary candidate increased by 200,000 percent without any regulatory framework to account for the flow of money (CAPF, 2007). The funds were used to buy votes, to bribe journalists and polling companies, to launch youth campaigns and women's campaigns in the country, to pay for media advertising, to cover inflated travel expenses, to pay for campaign staff, and the like. Funding came from a variety of sources. Some of the government party's money came from covert use of public funds through phony accounting. A larger share came from companies securing contracts with the government in exchange for their financial and logistical support. Substantial donations were given to the opposition party by foreign sources. Wealthy persons were relentlessly solicited by the would-be MPs of both parties and required to pay them off handsomely, to the point where the Kenyan elites increasingly created their own parties in order to have direct access to parliament without having to pay intermediaries (it is apparently a more cost-effective method).

In 2007, the lucrative Kenyan political business attracted record numbers of democracy lovers: 130 political parties fielded 2,500 parliamentary candidates. In many cases, they had to raise their own money, but the expected payoff, in the event of a successful bid, was worth the effort. A study showed that investment in previous elections resulted in a legal return of seven times the investment five years later, in terms of compensation, plus benefits.[37] This is without counting the bribes that permeate the political system. After the election, in 2007, a regulatory framework for campaign finance was established, but independent observers consider it to be ineffective. A-legal financing and money-driven political dealings are a systemic feature of Kenyan democracy (CAPF, 2007).

Kenya is the rule rather than the exception when it comes to money and politics in a global perspective. Reports from the rest of Africa, from Latin America (with the exception of Chile), and from Asia, all point in the same direction (see the section on scandal politics below).

---

[37] In fact, the substantial financial benefits of political office are also prevalent in the United States. However, levels of legal compensation from politics in the US and in most Western democracies pale in comparison with the privileges and pay enjoyed by Italian politicians of all political affiliations, as has been documented in an explosive book by two Italian journalists (Rizzo and Stella, 2007).

In a few other countries, particularly in Western and Northern Europe, Canada, Australia, and New Zealand, the situation is more complex, as public financing of politics is the norm, paid media advertising is limited or forbidden, and there are strict regulations about direct funding for politicians holding office. And yet, the money trail does not stop at their shores. To illustrate the argument, *I will consider two democracies that appear to be above suspicion: the UK and Spain.*

Regulatory bodies govern the financing of political parties in both Britain and Spain. In both countries, as in the US, there is provision for disclosure of contributions to political parties. In the UK, donors and parties have to disclose contributions over a certain threshold, and political parties have to disclose contributions received. In Spain, all contributions received must be declared. Furthermore, unlike the US, there is a ceiling on party election expenditure, and parties must provide detailed information about their spending. The key difference with the US is that in both countries political parties, not candidates, receive direct public funding during the election period and between elections. The purpose of the funds is for general party administration and policy analysis and proposal, besides defraying the costs of campaigning. Funding is proportional to the parties' performance in the last election, which, of course, favors the continuing dominance of major political parties. Costs of campaigning are significantly reduced in comparison to the US because political parties are entitled to free media access in the UK and Spain. The criteria for allocating broadcast time are the number and geographic distribution of candidates put forward in a given election for the UK, and performance at a previous election for Spain. On the other hand, paid political advertising on television is banned in both countries. During election periods, Spanish and UK parties are allocated broadcast spots on terrestrial television channels and national radio stations. In Spain, political news on the government channels is also regulated during election campaigns, by allocating time of exposure to political leaders proportionally to their past electoral performance.

In the UK, paid advertising is largely used on billboards, pamphlets, leaflets, and other materials. Conservatives spend more on advertising (46% versus 29% for Labour in 2005), while Labour spends more than the Tories in rallies and events, using the remnants of its grassroots infrastructure. While spending in political campaigns increased substantially in the UK between 2001 (£23.7 million for all parties) and 2005 (£42 million), it pales in comparison with the United States (see Figure 4.1), even when taking into account the disparate size of their electorates. Indeed, parties in the UK usually respect the ceiling placed on campaign spending. Thus, one fundamental difference between the United States and most Western European democracies is that the overwhelming dominance of lobbyists in American politics is in sharp contrast to the regulated separation between business and interest groups in the European polity.

Yet, the tension between money and politics is as real in Europe as in the rest of the world. In fact, the current UK regulatory environment resulted from widespread public concern in 1998 about the funding of political parties arising from a number of high-profile political funding scandals, particularly after Tony Blair went on television, in 1997, to apologize for taking a £1 million donation to Labour from the Formula One tycoon, Bernie Ecclestone. Henry Drucker, the Labour fund-raiser who quit his job soon after Labour came to power, criticized the now outlawed "blind-trust" arrangements, which allowed multimillionaires to make secret donations to Labour without leading politicians realizing where the money had come from. These donations did not have to be declared until the law was changed in 2001. The Committee on Standards in Public Life (a supposedly independent body established by John Major) recommended a new system of regulating the financial activities of political parties. The Political Parties, Elections and Referendums Act (PPERA) was passed in 2000, and the 2001 UK general election marked the first election where party campaign expenditure was controlled. Nonetheless, problems with donors continued to recur in British politics, and to plague the Labour Party. The scandal became significant during the 2005 election when a commission of the House of Lords found that Labour had received tens of millions of pounds in loans from wealthy donors that had not been declared to the Electoral Commission. This prompted Scotland Yard to investigate the so-called "cash for honours". In short, Tony Blair was accused of selling peerages for the benefit of the party. Each country has its traditions, and now traditions were for sale. Clinton had been renting out, as mentioned above, the Lincoln suite at the White House with its presidential memorabilia. Now, English nobility was becoming a commodity. Nothing could infuriate the kingdom's surviving hereditary peers more. Other forms of hidden financing surfaced when it was disclosed that property developer David Abrahams had given more than £600,000 to the Labour Party, using other persons to hide his identity, in direct violation of the Electoral Commission rules (Hencke, 2007).

As for the young and vibrant Spanish democracy, in the 2004 parliamentary elections, all parties combined spent 57.2 million euros in their two-week campaigns. Electoral campaign spending was even lower in 2008, at

50 million euros. The main reason for such thrifty behavior is that the Ministry of Economy caps the maximum spending for each party: in 2008, the two major parties, Socialists (PSOE) and Conservatives (PP) were allowed to spend a maximum of 16.7 million euros each. On the other hand, the government financed the parties at the rate, in 2008, of 0.79 euros per vote received and 21,167.64 euros per elected seat in the Congress, plus transportation and accommodation costs for the candidates. Most of the funds were used for billboard advertising, mailing, printed material, the organization of political rallies, and advertising on radio and in the print press (Santos, 2008). Yet, Spanish parties actively seek private donations, some of them in a gray area in terms of their legality (Bravo, 2008; Murillo, 2008; Santos, 2008).

Why do parties, whose basic media advertising, campaigns, and management needs are satisfied by public funding, still need to tap into private donors? To be sure, there is never enough money to satisfy all political needs. But because all parties are similarly constrained, the playing field is somewhat leveled. This is precisely the matter. Wealthy individuals, special interests, and large corporations aim to tilt one of the political options in their favor by providing extra cash. Since the operation must be hidden, these kinds of favors to leaders and parties have a very personal connotation. This is not a generic contribution to a political cause, but a specific line of political credit to be used when the donor requires. This is cronyism as an alternative to lobbying (of course, the United States' political scene is marked, in addition to lobbying, by widespread cronyism, as allegedly exemplified, according to media reports, by Vice President Dick Cheney and his Halliburton Corporation). However, why do the parties need to access this extra cash outside the legal system? *Because they need to spend the funds flexibly and confidentially.* Flexibly, because to be innovative in politics requires spending in areas and on projects that escape the definition of political activity in the strict regulatory terms of electoral commissions. Confidentially, because some decisive political operations outside campaign periods (for example, illegal fundraising, spying, fabricating scandals against the opponent, bribing journalists, paying blackmail, and the like) require substantial underground funding. Furthermore, the more the use of funds is discretionary, the greater the number of opportunities for political intermediaries in and around the party and its leadership to take a personal cut. Political office is the basis for the personal primitive accumulation of capital for democratic power-holders: precisely those who accept the rule of democratic alternation are the ones who have to make good use of the good times when they are in power, either for themselves or for the struggle on behalf of their ideals (Rose-Ackerman, 1999; International Foundation for Election Systems, 2002).

Spinning the News

People make their decisions, including their political decisions, on the basis of images and information that, by and large, are processed through the media, including the Internet. This is a continuing process. In fact, electoral campaigns – the theatrical moment of choice in democracy – work on the predispositions stored in people's minds through their practice in everyday life. Therefore, *the politics of news media is the most significant form of media politics*. To be sure, information with political implications is not limited to the news (Delli Carpini and Williams, 2001; Banet-Weiser, personal communication, 2008). And television news (the main source of news for most people) is staged as entertainment: it constitutes "the politics of illusion" (Bennett, 2007). But it is precisely because the news media are formatted in ways that attract the average viewer that they are influential in establishing the connection between people's predispositions and their assessment of the issues that are the stuff of political life.

As analyzed in Chapter 3, political strategies aim primarily at setting the agenda, framing, and priming information in the news media. But the methods of doing so vary greatly within the media regime, depending on the interaction between governments, corporate business, and media companies. In order to identify the logic of political framing in the media, I will first rely on an analysis of the Italian experience, largely following the study of Giancarlo Bosetti (2007). Indeed, Italian television is particularly suited to the analysis. First, because television is the pre-eminent source of political news: over 50 percent of Italians depend on television as their exclusive source of political information. This proportion jumps to 77 percent during political campaigns, with 6.6 percent mainly following the campaign in the newspapers. Second, the Italian case is revealing because, while formally maintaining the ideology of independent, professional journalism, Italy's television regime is, in fact, the most politicized in the democratic world (except Russia insofar as it can still be considered a democracy). This is because historically, before the 1990s, Italy's three government television channels (those belonging to the RAI, the public corporation) were assigned to the three major political families, in decreasing order of importance: the

Christian Democrats (RAI Uno), the Communists in their sequential re-incarnations (RAI Due), and the Socialists (RAI Tre). In the 1990s, taking advantage of the European wave of liberalization and privatization of television, Silvio Berlusconi, a real-estate entrepreneur turned media tycoon, was able to establish three private national networks managed by his Mediaset company. He parlayed his television power into victory in the 1994 national elections. Therefore, since Berlusconi was elected Prime Minister in 1994 and then elected again on two additional occasions (the last one in 2008), he has controlled all Italian television networks, public and private, with the exception of a brief and chaotic period of an unstable center–left coalition government. While local cable networks and satellite television maintain diversity in the media landscape, the bulk of politically relevant information has gone through the filters of Berlusconi's appointees.

Analyzing the evolution of Italian television news over the past two decades, Bosetti (2007) finds similarities between Italy and the United States in some of the key features of news reporting: personalization, dramatization, fragmentation of information, and solicitation of a predominant schema constructed around the notion of order versus disorder. Indeed, the theme of order was the main political appeal of Berlusconi, in spite of his suspected Mafia links, for an electorate deeply tired of endless partisan infighting, and of a polity built around the interests of a political class that indulged in privileges and compensation without parallel in the democratic world (Rizzo and Stella, 2007). Bosetti adds an Italian specialty to the menu: personal attacks between politicians in the daily news shows, thus increasing the disgust of the audience toward politics in general, while providing colorful material for newscasts. Reporting is largely constructed around the behavior and statements of party leaders, emphasizing the personalization of politics, even if, in the Italian political scene, this includes a wide variety of political shops, some of them serving the interests of just one politician (as long as his vote would decide control of the parliament).

Bosetti's content analysis shows no major difference between public and private television channels in the formula underlying political reporting under Berlusconi (Bosetti, 2007: 62). Berlusconi used this media domination to conduct his personal fights against the judges and parliamentarians who tried unsuccessfully to bring him to trial. He skillfully launched several media political offensives that discredited his adversaries while cultivating his image as a self-made man above party politics, and defending the essence of the Italian nation, the virtues of the free market, and the

Christian roots of Europe (Bosetti, 2007: 85). By bypassing parties and addressing public opinion and ultimately voters directly through the media, Berlusconi was able to establish the power of a media oligarchy that gradually took the place of the party oligarchy that had previously characterized Italian politics. Staging politics became more significant than priming news, as specialized 24-hour news channels could not counter the mainstream culture of political entertainment, often couched in terms of farce and comedy that came to permeate the Italian media scene.

While admittedly an extreme example of political manipulation of news media, the Italian case offers a raw version of the spinning games that characterize the mass media, and particularly television, around the world. Thus, characterizing the politics of news media in America, Bennett (2007: 14) writes:

In the view of CNN pollster and pundit William Schneider, Washington is increasingly a town of individual political entrepreneurs who rely less on parties for their political support than on their own media images . . . The public enters this mediate reality at select moments, when targeted audience segments are rallied to vote, participate in polls, or send e-mail barrages to Congress. More often, the public is addressed at the end of the policy process when results need to be "sold" through news images. Governing with the news is thus also about controlling what gets to the public.

Not even the poster child of public service television, the BBC, could escape the spinning schemes of the Blair government, as illustrated by the notorious "Dodgy Dossier" affair. In early 2003, Alistair Campbell, the Prime Minister's Office's spinner-in-chief, concocted a briefing document for the Blair government under the title "Iraq: Its Infrastructure of Concealment, Deception and Intimidation." The document, thereafter known as the "Dodgy Dossier," was released to journalists in early February 2003. Colin Powell praised the document as it constituted a strong basis for support of the already-made US decision to attack Iraq. The dossier claimed evidence of Iraqi concealment of its possession of weapons of mass destruction drawing "upon a number of sources, including intelligence reports." In fact, as Cambridge University scholar, Glen Rangwala, exposed it, a section of the document was plagiarized from an article written by a California graduate student, Ibrahim al-Marashi. Sections of the article appeared verbatim, with even typographic mistakes in the original article repeated in the government document. BBC Radio 4 reported on the incident after its reporters learned of the plagiarism. Together with an earlier September dossier ("Iraq's Weapons of Mass

Destruction: The Assessment of the British Government"), these documents were used by the government to justify involvement in the 2003 invasion of Iraq, and were cited by President Bush in support of his decision to go to war. Claims in the 'September' and 'Iraq' dossiers were called into question when weapons of mass destruction were not found in Iraq. All of the allegations in the dossiers were proved to be untrue by the Iraq Survey Group.

The exposure of the Blair government scam by the BBC led to a controversy between Downing Street and the BBC. BBC correspondent Andrew Gilligan filed a report for BBC Radio 4's *Today* program on May 29, 2003. Gilligan stated that an unnamed source had told him that the September dossier had been "sexed up," and that the intelligence agencies were concerned about the truthfulness of the claim that Saddam Hussein could deploy weapons of mass destruction within 45 minutes of an order to use them. On June 1, 2003 Gilligan wrote in the *Mail on Sunday* newspaper that Alistair Campbell was responsible for the insertion of the 45-minute claim, a most dramatic example of scare tactics. Campbell demanded an apology, but the BBC stood by Gilligan's story. Campbell appeared on Channel 4 news to respond to the accusations. Blair stated that the BBC was wrong in reporting that the government had deliberately "sexed up" the dossier and defended his aide's efforts to refute the BBC charge. Blair's public opinion ratings fell, and a majority of citizens surveyed declared that they would no longer trust Blair to tell the truth. The efforts of the government to refute the BBC charge led to the government's identification of Dr. David Kelly, a scientist working for the Ministry of Defense, as the BBC's probable source. In July 2003, a few days after his identification, Dr. Kelly was found dead in what appeared to be a suicide. These events led to the appointment of the Hutton Inquiry to investigate the death of Dr. Kelly. The Hutton Inquiry report cleared the government, partly because Gilligan's reporting did not follow sound journalistic practices. The report found that Gilligan's accusation was "unfounded" and that the BBC's editorial and management processes were "defective." The BBC was strongly criticized in the report, leading to the resignation of the BBC's Chairman and Director-General. Thereafter, national newspapers accused Hutton of participating in a "whitewash" because the report did not dare to bring the government under serious scrutiny.

While political spinning and framing operations are not usually as blatant and dramatic as the manipulations of Campbell and his operatives, they are the daily staple of media news and media politics in every country. It is not clear, however, who uses whom. While politicians feed the media, the media often feast on raw politics, either to cook it for the audience or to let it rot, so that the feeders become exposed, thus attracting the interest of the public in both cases. Indeed, media politics is a composite social practice made of media and politics.

The Moment of Untruth: Electoral Campaigns

Electoral campaigns are the key instances that enable access to institutional power positions by appealing to the citizens' formal delegation of power by means of their vote. They are the wheels of democracy. However, elections are specific moments of political life that operate on the basis of the day-to-day construction of meaning that structures the interests and values of citizens. Election campaigns act on the predispositions of the voters by activating or deactivating the processes of emotion and cognition that I analyzed in Chapter 3, with the purpose of achieving the goals of the campaign. Regardless of ideology and rhetoric in political discourse, only one thing matters for political parties and candidates in campaigning – winning. Everything else is a derivative. This implies that policy proposals have to be constructed as political messages seeking to obtain the support of the electorate. Naturally, candidates and parties position themselves in the polity of the country and relate to the interests and values of their supporters, so their political platforms must be credible in terms of the cognitive congruence between who the candidate is and what her message is.

Yet, the margins of variation between the history of parties and candidates and their programs for a given election have widened over time because of the need to adjust the political message to a diverse and increasingly volatile electorate. Indeed, most campaigns use a three-pronged strategy. First, they try to secure their historical base of support, the party loyals. In most countries, feelings for a given party or political tradition constitute one of the key factors in determining voting behavior (Montero et al., 1998; Winneg and Jamieson, 2005; Westen, 2007). Therefore, a candidate cannot depart excessively from the policy positions that were fundamental in establishing the party's influence in the past without eroding the much-needed support of the core constituencies, such as women's choice in abortion policies for the left or tax cuts for the right. The second component of a successful strategy is to demobilize or confuse the core constituency of the opponent, particularly by pinpointing her flaws or wrongdoing, or the contradiction between the political opponent and the values of her potential voters; for example, her support for gay rights in a homophobic context. Then comes the third and most decisive strategic move: to win the support of the independents and undecided. This is the group that determines the election result, provided that the core constituency is mobilized. This does not mean that elections are won by courting the center of the political spectrum. Sometimes, going left or right from the center is what convinces people who were on the sidelines because they did not connect with the message of any candidate. The critical matter in winning the support of independents is to heighten their scrutiny of the candidates. Thus, independents have been shown to be particularly sensitive to negative messages (Ansolabehere and Iyengar, 1995; Hollihan, 2008: 159). Since they do not have pre-established loyalties, they tend to mobilize against the potential negative consequences of electing a given candidate. This explains the significance of negative messages, through the media or political advertising, in shaping elections (see Chapter 3).

The Professionalization of Political Campaigns

To enact these basic strategies, candidates and parties must first build a *campaign infrastructure*. Electoral politics is now a highly professionalized activity with high entry barriers for any challenger, which explains why maverick candidates must usually operate within the limits of established party politics. The infrastructure starts with financial solvency: without sufficient funding, there is no credible campaign to the point that the level of funding for candidates is one of the key criteria for electability. It is a virtuous (or vicious) circle: the more money, the greater the potential for winning the election, which attracts more funding from people and groups betting on a specific candidate. Money and politics are intertwined. The campaign also depends on the quality of consultants, and on the accuracy of their informational politics. This includes the construction of a reliable database that allows targeting of the social characteristics and spatial distribution of specific groups of voters, and adjusting the message of the campaign to each context. It also relies on the establishment of a grassroots campaign, made up of a mixture of volunteers and paid workers, whose function differs from country to country. In the United States, it appears essential to contact potential voters on behalf of candidates, either by phone or by door-to-door canvassing, providing printed material, registering new voters prior to the election, advising early voting by mail, and getting out the vote by soliciting support from supposedly committed voters on election day. The more a campaign counts on the support of ideologically dedicated supporters, the more the potential appeal of a candidate bears fruit in the ballot box. In other countries, such as Spain, it would be counterproductive to knock on doors, and phone banks are deemed ineffective. Distributing electoral propaganda in public places or by direct mailing, local rallies, festive parades, and major political meetings, gathering thousands of supporters, are largely the means of energizing the core constituency, while displaying the strength of the party in front of the cameras, rather than the means of attracting new voters. In most instances, and in all countries, campaigns are essentially based on communicating through the media, either by direct advertising or by feeding the media with their messages. Indeed, political rallies are staged for the media, and timed on the basis of media programming to increase the chances of live coverage of the candidate, who is instantly warned of the media presence and typically changes the content and tone of his or her speech accordingly, in the middle of a sentence, to go live on TV.

An increasingly important dimension of political campaigning *is the use of the Internet to manage the campaign and relate to supporters*. In countries like the United States that authorize individual campaign donations, the Internet has become the main vehicle to solicit and process these donations. In the most expensive presidential primary in history, the Democratic contest between Barack Obama and Hillary Clinton, a significant percentage of the candidates' funding was raised over the Internet, particularly by the Obama campaign (see Chapter 5). Furthermore, candidates now make use of the Internet to coordinate activities, provide campaign updates, and receive input from concerned citizens. Forums of debate and networks of information on the Internet have become essential organizational tools for contemporary campaign politics. The attractiveness and functionality of campaign web sites have become a trademark for successful political projects, both in terms of their effect on the conduct of the campaign and in projecting an image of modernity, interactivity, and efficacy on behalf of the candidate. Furthermore, for candidates wishing to affirm their autonomy vis-à-vis the traditional bureaucracy of the party, the Internet provides a platform to reach militants and voters while bypassing political machines (Bimber, 2003; Sey and Castells, 2004; Howard, 2005; Chadwick, 2006). In many countries, mobile phones have become a critical medium for reaching out to both supporters and the public at large. SMS offers a cheap, direct, and real-time form of spreading information, rallying support, and directing attacks toward political opponents (Castells et al., 2006a; Katz, 2008).

Campaigning in a Multimedia Digital Environment

The essence of campaigning is communicating, which requires identifying the proper communication channels. *People rely on the media for most of their political information*, particularly television, as shown in figure 4.2 for the United States, a feature that is common to almost all Western democracies (Bosetti, 2007). In Spain, for instance, in 2005, television was the main source of daily political news for 71.5 percent of people, followed by the radio (39.5%), newspapers (15.2%), and the Internet (2.9%) (Paniagua, 2006). However, Figure 4.2 also illustrates the decline of television and the increasing significance of the Internet as a source of campaign news in the United States, with the Internet growing from 2 percent as the primary source of election news in 1992 to 15 percent in 2007. Indeed, when the first and second sources are combined, the use of the Internet as a source climbs to 26 percent. The trend is particularly accentuated for young people: for 18- to 29-year-old citizens, the relevance of the Internet as the main source of election news increased from 21 percent in January 2004 to 46 percent in December 2007, while television declined from 75 percent to 60 percent (Pew, 2008c: 4). Younger people who get campaign news online cite a wider variety of election news sources than do older people. When asked to offer web sites they use, 41 percent of 18- to 29-year-olds listed more than one web site, compared with just 24 percent of people aged 30

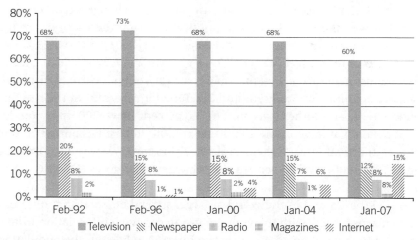

Fig. 4.2. Main source of campaign news in the United States, 1992–2007

Note: $n = 1430$, +/− 3%.

Source: Pew (2008c).

and over. Both MySpace and YouTube are sources of campaign information unique to younger people (Pew, 2008c: 7).

Furthermore, about one in six Americans (16%) have sent or received e-mails among friends and family regarding candidates and the campaign, and 14 percent have received e-mail messages from political groups or organizations about the campaign (Pew, 2008c: 8). Fully two-thirds of Americans aged 18 to 29 say that they use social networking sites, and more than a quarter of this age group (27%) say that they have received information about candidates and the campaign from them. Nearly one in ten people under the age of 30 (8%) say they have signed up as a "friend" of one of the candidates on a site (Pew, 2008c: 9). Nearly a quarter of Americans (24%) say they have seen something about the campaign in a video online – a speech, interview, commercial, or debate. For each of these four types of video, approximately 12–13 percent of those surveyed report seeing it online. Among younger respondents, the numbers are even higher. Fully 41 percent of those under the age of 30 have viewed at least one type of video (Pew, 2008c: 9–10).

These findings are echoed in Catalonia, according to a study conducted on the uses of the Internet and multimedia in 2006–7 (Tubella et al., 2008). The Internet is a key source of information for younger segments of the population, and because young voters represent the main basis for innovative, proactive political projects (regardless of their ideology), the role of Internet communication in supporting political change becomes decisive. However, the main sources of political news on the Internet are the web sites of mainstream mass media (e.g., MSBNC, 26%; CNN, 23%), as well as web sites such as Yahoo! News and Google News, which link to other mainstream media, and this holds true for younger citizens, although MySpace accounts for 8 percent and YouTube for 6 percent of their online political news, and "others" account for 20 percent (Pew, 2008c: 7). Yet, for the population at large in the US, 40 percent in 2008 still reported getting political information from their local television news (it was 42% in 2004 and 48% in 2000), and 38 percent cite cable news networks (MSNBC, CNN, and Fox).

Both in the US and in the world at large, a trend emerges that differentiates citizens by age, with the younger group receiving information from a variety of sources, often accessed via the Internet, while, for the population over 30 years of age, it appears that mainstream mass media continue to be the main channels of political information, even if they are increasingly accessed via the Internet. A different matter is how new information is generated in the first place, and this is where the Internet plays a novel and significant role, as I will analyze in Chapter 5. But in terms of message distribution, the bulk of campaign politics is still mass media politics.

Dancing with the media requires *adapting to their language and format*. This means that campaign strategists have to be able to provide attractive footage and exciting information to the media. Campaign events, such as speeches by the candidate and visits to neighborhoods, schools, factories, farms, coffee shops, markets, and political rallies, have to be colorful to the point of entertaining if they want to make it onto the news. Statements must abide by the rule of sound bites: they must be striking, and as short as possible. In the US, the average sound bite for candidates shrunk from 40 seconds in 1968 to 10 seconds in the 1980s (Hallin, 1992), then to 7.8 seconds in 2000 (Lichter, 2001) and to 7.7 seconds in 2004 (Bucy and Grabe, 2007). Similar trends have been reported in the UK (Semetko and Scammell, 2005), New Zealand (Comrie, 1999), and Brazil (Porto, 2007), though these sound bites are on average a few seconds longer than those in the US. Reporters and anchors have dominated the time allotted to campaign reporting in the US, with an average of 34.2 seconds per story in contrast to 18.6 for the candidate (Bucy and Grabe, 2007).

Image bites are replacing sound bites as the predominant message, and You Tube videos (named "sound blasts" by some observers) have become a potent campaign tool. Because YouTube posts are spread virally, they have the potential to significantly affect political campaigns by shaping the candidate's image. For example, in the 2006 US senatorial election, Republican Senator Allen, who was considered a promising presidential candidate until that moment, was defeated after a video of him using a racial epithet against one of his opponent's supporters during a campaign rally was posted on YouTube and then picked up by the evening television news around the country. His defeat was the decisive event contributing to the loss of the Senate majority for the Republicans in 2006. During the 2008 Democratic presidential primaries, the widely popular campaign of Senator Obama was almost derailed from its victorious trajectory by YouTube postings featuring his former pastor Reverend Wright engaged in inflammatory rhetoric in his South Chicago church. Although ABC News was the original source of these videos, their diffusion over the Internet prompted all media outlets to replay the damaging images for the rest of the campaign.[38]

---

[38] Because of its significance for the theme of this book, I will analyze in detail the Obama campaign in Chapter 5.

Programming Communication Networks

It is this interaction between mainstream media and the Internet that characterizes media politics in the digital age. While the media are still the primary conveyors of the images and sounds that shape the minds of the voters, entry points into the mass audiovisual universe have multiplied. Anyone can upload a video, write a blog, or disseminate information. The potential impact of their message depends on how it resonates with people's perceptions, as well as how relevant the mass media perceive it to be for their audience. This is why the two forms of communication, mass communication and mass self-communication, are increasingly integrated with the views of the audience. The key difference is the level of control at the point of entry into the audiovisual system. While the filters established by owners, advertisers, editors, and professional journalists prime or block information and images, the Internet remains the domain of choice for unsupervised messages that broaden the scope of sources of information and misinformation, trading lesser credibility for greater diversity.

Political campaigns navigate the troubled waters of this variegated media world by feeding the Blackberries of mainstream media journalists with breaking news, while posting and counter-posting on the Internet. They also try to place pundits and surrogates on spin shows that frame the actual news and follow the race as if it were a sports competition. At the same time, they must mobilize their support in the blogosphere that engulfs the mainstream media, while paying attention to the amateur pundits that comment on the news on their own web sites, often in unfriendly terms. There is no time or format for substance in media politics; it is a matter of scoring points. Thus, stories have to be couched as entertainment, climaxing in face-to-face, live political debates.

Staging Political Choice: Electoral Debates

Televised political debates are less decisive than people think. Typically, these debates consolidate people's predispositions and opinions (Riley and Hollihan, 1981). This is why the debate winners are often the election winners: people are more likely to side with their preferred candidate as the winner, rather than voting for the candidate who debated more persuasively. Thus, in the 2008 Spanish electoral campaign, there were two debates broadcast on television and over the Internet between the leading candidates, the Socialist Rodríguez Zapatero, and the Conservative Rajoy. According to the majority of phone polls, Rodríguez Zapatero won in both cases by a comfortable margin, nearly the same margin by which he would later win the actual election. Yet, when those following the debate over the Internet were polled, their opinion reflected the ideological inclination of the web site that they used to follow the debate, as these web sites were those of the main newspapers, usually with unambiguous political leanings.

Political debates can, however, have a potentially significant effect: making mistakes and, consequently, losing support, unless the candidate can use the error to his or her advantage by using humor or inciting empathy among the viewers. The goal of error-free performance leads to caution and diminishes the likelihood of a true exchange. Rules of engagement are carefully negotiated by the campaigns of each candidate, including the stage, the seating, the sequence of the questions, the moderators and interviewers, and, in some cases, the camera angle. It is usually understood that the challenger will attack to erode the dominant position of the front-runner. Often, what happens before and after are the most significant moments of the debate. Madsen (1991) analyzes televised political debates as a discourse composed of three elements: the debate itself, the post-debate spin by commentators, and the media response, including polling of audience reactions. Thus, rather than a forum for contrasting policy options, debates are displays of personality and material for elaboration by the media, according to the rules of political story-telling (Jamieson, 2000; Jamieson and Campbell, 2006).

The Politics of Personality

The fundamental feature of media politics is *the personalization of politics*, and the key factor in deciding the outcome of the campaign is the positive or negative projection of the candidate in the minds of the voters. A number of combined factors explain the critical role of the personality projected by the candidate or by the leader of a party in a political contest: a decline in the direct influence of political parties in society at large; the typically short time periods of elections that activate the perception of contrasting political messages to be established within a few weeks (with some exceptions, such as the 2008 US Democratic presidential primary); widespread reliance on the media, and particularly television, as the main source of political news; the role of political advertising, modeled on commercial advertising spots, intended to produce an immediate attraction to, or rejection of, a candidate based on physical characteristics, posture, or musical/image background; a tendency to avoid specificity on issues that may alienate some voters, which leads to a general solicitation of trust in the candidate's ability to find solutions to the problems affecting the populace (Paniagua, 2005; Hollihan, 2008: 75–99).

But perhaps the most fundamental mechanism linking media politics and the personalization of politics is what Popkin (1994) identified as "low information rationality" in voters' behavior. He shows that voters tend to be "cognitive misers" who are not comfortable handling complex political issues and consequently base their voting decisions on everyday life experiences, including information obtained from the media and judgments based on daily interaction with their environment. He labeled this process the "Drunkard's Search," a quest to find easier ways of information acquisition. The easiest way to acquire information about a candidate is to make a judgment based on his or her appearance and personality traits, particularly in terms of trustworthiness, the paramount quality that is appreciated in a would-be leader, since elections are ultimately delegations of power from citizens to a particular person (Keeter, 1987). On the other hand, the image of the candidate must also convey leadership potential, as people do not trust themselves to be leaders. Voters look for someone like them, yet with a superior capacity to lead them. In fact, they proceed in two stages: first, they evaluate the honesty and human qualities of the candidate; second, they look at her decisiveness, competence, and effectiveness (Kendall and Paine, 1995). Hollihan (2008: 94) cites research by Tannenbaum et al. (1962), which reported that when people are asked about the most important qualities in a candidate, the three features most frequently cited are honesty, intelligence, and independence. This is to say, a person I can trust with the capacity to lead my country, and me.[39]

How do personal images shape voter decision-making? Hollihan (2008: 85–99), summarizing research on the matter, emphasizes the role of emotions, a finding that directly relates to the analysis I presented in Chapter 3. Positive emotional evaluation is driven by homophily between candidates and voters. A candidate's ability to relate to voters is critical, and often leads to biographical accounts emphasizing his or her humble origins or, if this fails, folksy ways of behavior, as in the case of George W. Bush, whose image was mutated by his image-makers from privileged brat-boy to goofy Texan rancher joking about his low reading ability. Indeed, the reconstruction of George W. Bush's image from a draft-dodging, alcoholic, drug-abuser into a rehabilitated, born-again Christian following God's guide toward a "mission accomplished" was a masterful example of spinning. This example shows how successful political personalities are often made rather than discovered.

[39] Studies show that people often vote on referendum initiatives according to the persons who support or reject the propositions (Aronson, personal communication, 2008).

But, of course, image-makers need good human material to start with. Their art consists of working with this material in different ways and adapting what the candidate (selected by money or party connections) has to offer. Thus, personalization does not tend to rely on how good-looking or even articulate a person is (although this is important, it is not decisive), but on how well a person is able to relate to his or her voters.

In countries where there is greater influence of party politics over self-declared candidacies, the personalization of politics is not irrelevant. It simply modifies the mechanism of selection. Thus, Nicolas Sarkozy did not have the support of the conservative coalition *in France*, and was met with the hostility of "his" president Jacques Chirac. Yet, his public image, and his effective campaigning while Minister of the Interior (based on an anti-immigration stance and law and order themes), yielded such a level of popularity that his party and, later, the broader coalition around it, built on his charisma to ensure a victory over the Socialist candidate, Ségolène Royal, in the 2007 presidential election. Their calculations were proved to be correct.

In Spain, at the dawn of democracy in the late 1970s, the Socialist Party sought to establish itself as a viable governing party by counting on the enthusiasm of Spaniards for their newly gained political freedom, while stoking their fears of a Fascist backlash (indeed, a military coup attempted in 1981 nearly succeeded). The party strategists decided to bet on the personality of their young leader, Felipe González, a labor lawyer from Seville, who was charismatic, intelligent, handsome, pragmatic, and a brilliant communicator. In sum, González was a natural born leader. In spite of all his qualities, the first democratic election in 1979 saw the triumph of the centrist party (UCD) which was also counting on a young and determined leader, Adolfo Suárez, who broke ranks from the Franquist party to guide the transition from dictatorship to democracy. Still, the Socialists were not discouraged. They proceeded to enhance the image of their leader, while methodically destroying the image of the respected Prime Minister Suárez, conveniently nicknamed "the Mississippi gambler" (alluding to the image of sinister characters in popular Western movies) in reference to his supposed dirty tricks in government. The negative campaign worked, and, combined with pressures from the right wing of the government party, led to Suárez's resignation in early 1981.

In 1982, Felipe González led the Socialists to the largest landslide victory in Spanish history. The entire campaign was built around him. This was a major departure from the party's history, since the dominance of the party machine had characterized the Socialists throughout their long journey from the 1880s. The same strategists who had propelled González to victory were concerned about their choice. They knew they were relinquishing control of the government, and ultimately of the party, to their leader. They were acutely aware of the dangers of such a move, both in terms of party democracy and in terms of electoral vulnerability, should the leader fail. However, they keenly perceived the transformation of democratic politics into image politics, and so continued to cultivate the image of the leader, now supported by tight control of the national television networks and the work of a highly professional image department established at the Prime Minister's office, a new feature in Spanish politics. It worked, again and again, as the Socialists were re-elected three times, and remained in power for the following 13 years, in spite of relentless attacks from the opposition and a section of the media (see below).

License to Kill: Attack Politics

The personalization of politics has extraordinary consequences for campaign tactics. If the chances of a political option depend on the perceived qualities of a person, effective campaigning enhances the qualities of the candidate while casting a dark shadow on her opponent. Furthermore, negative images have a more powerful effect on voting behavior than positive images, as I have documented and analyzed both in Chapter 3 and in this chapter. Character assassination is therefore the most potent weapon in media politics. This can proceed in various ways: by questioning the integrity of the candidate herself, both in private and public life; by reminding voters, explicitly or subliminally, of negative stereotypes associated with the personality of the candidate (e.g. being black or Muslim in America or in the UK); by distorting candidates' statements or policy positions in ways that appear to conflict with fundamental values in the electorate; by denouncing wrongdoings, or controversial statements by persons or organizations linked with the candidate; or by revealing corruption, illegality, or immoral conduct in the parties or organizations supporting a candidacy. In all cases, the goal is to raise doubts among potential candidate supporters and to mobilize opposition voters. Because of the effectiveness of negative image-making, there has been a widespread trend around the world toward the use of destructive information as the predominant tactic in political campaigns. Damaging information may be found, fabricated, or twisted around a fact taken out of context. Thus, a key component of any political campaign is what has come to be known in the United States as "opposition research."

Stephen Marks, an American Republican consultant, ardently embraced *opposition research* as his professional specialty for over 12 years (1993–2006). He spent this time, in his own words, "digging dirt" to destroy the electoral chances of opponents of his clients – usually Democratic candidates, but also Republicans during primary elections. After some personal and moral fatigue, he revealed his tactics, and those of his profession, in his remarkable *Confessions of a Political Hitman: My Secret Life of Scandal, Corruption, Hypocrisy and Dirty Attacks that Decide Who Gets Elected (and Who Doesn't)* (Marks, 2007). Marks makes no apologies. He considers exposing the true nature of politicians as tantamount to public service. And there are no illegalities, either – at least not as presented in his book. His testimony, however self-serving, opens a rare window on the world of the "rat fuckers," the name that the Watergate operatives proudly used to label themselves. The task is relatively simple. It requires identifying, through polling and the advice of political consultants, all of the damaging issues for a given candidate in a given election. Specificity matters. Then the search begins, using archival documents such as voting records, media statements, biographical episodes supplemented with graphic material, financial investments, commercial interests, tax returns, property assets, campaign donation sources, and the like. In some instances of opposition research (not revealed in Marks's book but noted in other accounts), digging up personal information, such as credit card records, telephone call listings, and travel locations and expenses, yields a wealth of details that help reconstruct the private and public life of the targeted politician (Hollihan, 2008). Since no one is perfect, and since professional politics requires frequent ethical compromises for the sake of expediency, close scrutiny rarely comes up empty-handed. This occurrence is even rarer if the search extends to the parent political organization, be it the party, close allies, or the campaign itself. The information retrieved is then processed in light of what would be most damaging according to the polls, and is then transformed into a media message, either a damning advertising spot or a confidential leak to a well-placed journalist, with supporting visual evidence whenever possible.

Because of the effectiveness of negative attacks, politicians or parties need to be ready for them, even if they would otherwise be unwilling to engage in these tactics, because, as Truman said and Hillary Clinton endlessly repeated in her 2008 presidential primary campaign, "if you cannot stand the heat, get out of the kitchen." Therefore, any campaign must stockpile retaliatory ammunition in case it is needed, often as a deterrent to the opponent. Similar to opposition research is "vulnerability assessment," or an information search for one's own candidate to discover potential problems in his or her life and behavior before his or her adversary can uncover them. In fact, political consultants usually include these skills in their services (and in their fees). Halfway between detective work, legal blackmailing, and political marketing, the profession has become increasingly popular and sought after, first in America, and then around the world, with some of its pros becoming legendary figures. For instance, Averell "Ace" Smith, the consultant widely credited with briefly turning around Hillary Clinton's 2008 presidential primary campaign for a modest $140,000, was referred to by a fellow Democratic consultant who worked in the Clinton White House as "one of the few balding, bespectacled guys who I wouldn't like to run into in a dark alley" (Abcarian, 2008: A14).

Nonetheless, negative campaigning has its costs, as it can provoke a backlash among voters who do not necessarily like dirty tricks, in spite of their fascination with the dark side of celebrity. There is a need for fine-tuning between negativity vis-à-vis the opponent and fairness on part of the candidate. This is why the most effective route to image destruction is leaking information to the media and staying above the fray, while the opponent is flamed by respectable journalists suddenly turned into tabloid paparazzi. This is why, in spite of the abilities of Oppo Men and Women, they cannot claim major victories without some help: help from the media, always ready to broadcast juicy information to bring down political figures; help from the political organizations themselves, which supply much of the material and often leak information to eliminate competition within their own party; and help from an obscure army of information dealers who provide both opposing sides with similar ammunition, for themselves to prosper in the killing fields of media politics.

The Politics of Scandal

> Scandals are struggles over symbolic power in which reputation and trust are at stake.
>
> (Thompson, 2000: 245)

Beijing, 1723. Emperor Yongzheng, the fourth son of Emperor Kangxi, has just assumed power, as per his father's will. Or was it by his father's will? No, says a rumor spread around the four corners of the Empire. In reality, as the story goes, the old emperor favored his fourteenth son. But a high-ranking official of the court helped Yongzheng to revise the dying emperor's will. Although never proved, these allegations shadowed Yongzheng throughout his otherwise successful reign which lasted until 1735. Doubts about his legitimacy were particularly troubling for most Chinese because the Qing emperors and their court were not Han Chinese but Manchurians. The anti-Manchurian rebels found support for their cause in revolting against a Son of Heaven that could have been inducted by the devilish conspiracies populating the secluded Manchu court. The rumor spread to the vassal kingdoms of the Empire, including Korea, fueling popular resentment and tarnishing the legacy of the reformist Emperor Yongzheng in the minds of his subjects. No one knows the origin of the rumor, as it is likely that any witnesses to the alleged fraud or any indiscrete purveyors of the gossip were taken care of. Yet, the story followed Yongzheng to his grave and made it into contemporary Chinese historical soap operas, the template by which history lives in the public mind (Chen, 2004).

Paris, 1847. Segments of the propertied classes excluded from representation by an oligarchic political system batter the monarchy established by the 1830 Revolution on behalf of Louis Philippe d'Orléans with demands for democratization and reform. François Guizot, a brilliant academic–politician who was the brains of the government throughout the regime, then served as Prime Minister. He resisted pressure, convinced as he was that democracy was to be restricted to a selected elite guided by the "notables," the politicians of the monarchy. Guizot had already coined his trademark statement by encouraging the French to enrich themselves as a guiding principle for the country (an example to be followed 150 years later by Deng Xiaoping at the beginning of capitalism in Communist China). While Guizot did not indulge in such banal pursuits, busy as he was in making history and writing about it, his colleagues in the political class earnestly proceeded to put the principle into practice. They competed fiercely to appropriate the wealth being generated by the incipient process of industrialization and the expansion of international trade in proto-capitalist France. Access to ministerial posts was key to primitive accumulation of personal resources.

To undo their rivals, they used the press that they had created and financed as a way to shape and control the opinion of the educated classes, excluded from political power yet increasingly influential in society. In 1845, there were 245 newspapers in France, many of which were highly profitable, such as *Le Journal des débats*, secretly subsidized by the Ministry of Finance to manipulate trade in stocks for the benefit of the Minister's cronies. Most of the press reports concerned political matters, with Guizot a favorite target of criticism. Guizot was indifferent to such innuendo and was not unhappy to see the unruly crowd of his colleagues rip each other apart in the headlines of the press, denouncing political scandals, so that they could not coalesce in a conspiracy against the king or himself. Yet, in 1847, scandal politics went too far. An opposition newspaper, *La Presse*, reported widespread corruption, even criminal practices, among the highest circles of the regime, including financial speculation, assassination, bribery, and the sale of titles of nobility. The leaks to the press, intended to bring down competitors among the notables, had the effect of throwing into discredit the entire aristocratic class (a society that Balzac admirably chronicled in *Splendeurs et misères des courtisanes*). The scandals further antagonized the politically marginalized petty bourgeoisie, the most avid readers of this burgeoning press. A few months later, the 1848 Revolution was in full swing, ending forever the monarchy in France and sending Guizot to a comfortable intellectual exile in London (Jardin and Tudesq, 1973; Winock, 2004).

This is to say that, well before the advent of the network society, scandal politics was a critical feature in determining power relationships and institutional change. Indeed, anywhere we look into the history of societies around the world, the politics of scandal is a more rooted and typical form of power struggle than the conduct of orderly political competition as per the rules of the state. And yet, if it is true that nothing is new under the sun, it is also true that formally similar processes take new shapes and new meaning with the transformation of cultural, political, and communication contexts. *The specificity of scandal politics in the network society, and its centrality in media politics, is the object of this section.*

Let us start with late twentieth-century France in historical sequence with the vignette I have presented. Chalaby (2004) focuses on the role of judges and the media in reporting scandals in France, in a symbiotic relationship that has been often noticed in other countries as well (Ramírez, 2000; De Moraes, 2005; Bosetti, 2007; Heywood, 2007). Regardless of who first uncovers wrongdoing, be it journalists or judges, they support one another in their initiatives to the point that, once the scandal resonates with the public, the media tend to elevate judges to the role of enforcers of justice against the ill will of politicians, in a frame of defenders of morality versus the unaccountably powerful that resonates in the minds of the common people. Chalaby (2004) dates the rise of scandal reporting in contemporary

France to the October 1979 exposé by the satirical weekly *Le Canard enchaîné* of the donation of diamonds by General Bokassa, the self-proclaimed Emperor of the Central African Empire, to President Giscard d'Estaing in 1973. In spite of governmental pressures, *Le Monde* and other publications followed suit, a major blow for a political leader who had based his career on honesty and efficiency in managing the finances of the country. Thereafter, the French media created several investigative reporting units that, in spite of the economic and legal limitations they suffered, were instrumental in uncovering corruption over the years, including the Dumas/Elf Oil affair involving the Minister of Foreign Affairs and his mistress, which inflicted a potent blow to the administration of President Mitterrand in the last period of his 14-year presidency, as well as allegations of corruption against his successor, President Chirac, during his tenure as Mayor of Paris.

Ari Adut (2004) illustrates the rise of scandal politics in France in the 1990s in the context of the declining credibility of politicians and a growing sentiment that ideological differences do not matter in politics (see Figure 4.3). He reports on hundreds of cases of politicians investigated between 1992 and 2001 (see Table 4.1) for their involvement in cases of political corruption, such as the Dumas-Elf Affair. He highlights the role of magistrates in prosecuting political corruption as an expression of the independence of the judiciary vis-à-vis the political system, with magistrates taking it upon themselves to enforce the norms of public interest that are central to French culture, yet are frequently ignored by the political class. To say that this series of scandals and investigations negatively impacted upon citizens' trust in government would be an understatement. Figure 4.3 provides an overview of French views of elected officials between 1977 and 2001 as documented by TNS Sofres polls compiled by Adut (2004: 542).

In the United States, the Watergate scandal ushered in a new era of investigative reporting with direct consequences for the practice of politics and the process of governance (Markovits and Silverstein, 1988; Ginsberg and Shefter, 1999; Liebes and Blum-Kulka, 2004). One of the longest lasting effects of Watergate was the passing by Congress of the Ethics in Government Act of 1978, which contributed to the regulation of political life by setting procedures for the investigation of potentially unlawful practices by the executive branch. It resulted in a long series of investigations in the following decades and became the instrument of choice for political opponents to call into question the legitimacy of government and, in some

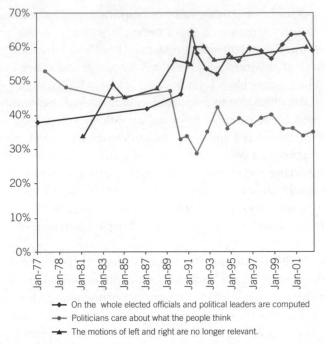

—▲— On the whole elected officials and political leaders are computed
—●— Politicians care about what the people think
—▲— The motions of left and right are no longer relevant.

Fig. 4.3. The increasing vulnerability of French politicians to scandal

Source: TNS Sofres polls compiled by Adut (2004: 542).

cases, to paralyze its action (Schudson, 2004). Furthermore, Watergate provided a mode of investigative reporting that became the standard of excellence in the US and around the world, with aspiring "deep throats" and entrepreneurial reporters joining forces in their self-righteous crusade, thus reaping the benefits of their power over the powerful. On the other hand, US politicians responded by intimidating the whistle-blowers and the press by proposing a bill in 2000 that would have penalized the disclosure and reporting of classified information (defined in very broad terms) with prison sentences. Only a last-minute effort by the media lobbies prompted President Clinton to veto the bill, in spite of his original support for the proposal (Nelson, 2003).

Since scandal politics is the weapon of choice for the party of opposition, in the 1990s Bill and Hillary Clinton were subjected to an endless barrage of accusations and investigations by the Republicans – some of them with serious consequences, others dismissed in the legal process. Clinton was

Table 4.1. Outcome of corruption investigations in France during the 1990s

	High-status politicians (1992–2000)	Highest-status politicians (1992–2001)
Total no. of politicians investigated	346	53
Under investigation 2004	90	12
Investigations concluded	256	41
Charges dropped during investigation	40 (16%)	12 (29%)
Indictments	216 (84%)	29 (71%)
Awaiting trial 2004	18 (7%)	5 (12%)
Acquittal	43 (17%)	8 (20%)
Fined only	20 (8%)	2 (5%)
Suspended sentence	40 (16%)	6 (15%)
Ineligibility sentence with or without suspended prison sentence	73 (28%)	5 (12%)
Prison sentence	22 (9%)	3 (6%)

Notes: Figures in parentheses specify the percentage of investigations that resulted in legal outcomes by the end of the period specified.

Adut (2004) defines "high-status politicians" as deputies in the National Assembly, senators in the Senate, and mayors. "Highest-status politicians" include national politicians; sitting or former prime ministers, ministers, National Assembly and Constitutional Council presidents, and the general secretaries of political parties. *Source*: Adut (2004: 564).

ultimately impeached by the House of Representatives, then saved by a Senate apparently influenced by threats from the president's men to reveal some of the senators' own scandals (Marks, 2007: 216–49). During the Bush administration, it was the Democrats' turn to expose a series of damaging wrongdoings by the president's administration and by several leading Republican leaders, as documented in table A4.1 in the Appendix. Thus, it is fair to say that American politics in the past two decades has been largely dominated by the reports and counter-reports of scandals and damaging information, directly aimed at specific political leaders or their proxies (for example, Scooter Libby as a proxy for Karl Rove and Dick Cheney). Political battles have been largely conducted by means of scandal politics (Sabato et al., 2000).

The prevalence and significance of scandal politics in recent years has been documented and analyzed along similar lines in the United Kingdom, Germany, Italy, Spain, Argentina, China, India, and an endless list of countries around the world (Arlachi, 1995; Rose-Ackerman, 1999; Thompson, 2000; Anderson and Tverdova, 2003; Esser and Hartung, 2004; Jimenez, 2004; Tumber, 2004; Tumber and Waisbord, 2004b; Waisbord, 2004b; Chang and Chu, 2006). Rather than burdening this chapter with a detailed discussion of all this evidence, I refer to the extensive (but not exhaustive) list of political scandals in recent times elaborated by Amelia Arsenault and presented in table A4.2 in the Appendix. Furthermore, Transparency International (accessible online) keeps records of published corruption, including political corruption, for countries around the world, showing both the pattern's universality and variance of intensity according to cultures and institutions. The most advanced democracies do not escape the general rule of scandal politics as a standard political practice. Table A4.3 shows the extent of scandal politics and the significance of its political effects in the G-8 countries, the exclusive club steering the world.

Why is scandal politics so prevalent? Where does it come from? Is it different from the past in its frequency and in its effect on political life? And why? I will discuss these critical issues on the basis of the limited evidence that is available from scholarly research. *Scandal politics is not the same as political corruption* (Thompson, 2000). Political corruption, understood as the unlawful selling of services by politicians and officials in exchange for personal or party benefits (or both), is a standard feature of political systems throughout history (King, 1989; Allen, 1991; Bouissou, 1991; Fackler and Lin, 1995; Rose-Ackerman, 1999). Political scandals include other alleged wrongdoings, such as improper sexual activities, as per the norms of a given society. The distribution of scandals between different categories of behavior varies between countries. For instance, in an historical perspective, the proportion of unlawful and not unlawful political scandals is roughly equal in France and the US, while sex and espionage is more prevalent than financial corruption in the UK (Barker, 1992). Historical data compiled in the Longman International Reference volume, *Political Scandals and Causes Célèbres since 1945* by Louis Allen (1991), and Transparency International's Global Corruption Barometer Survey administered by the Gallup International Association since 2003, do not show a consistent trend in terms of the frequency and intensity of scandal and corruption. They vary by country and by period according to political conjunctures and the media's reporting capabilities. However, most analysts seem to agree that the use of scandals in politics is on the rise (Thompson, 2000; Chalaby, 2004; Jimenez, 2004; Tumber, 2004; Tumber and Waisbord, 2004a, b; Chang and Chu, 2006). Indeed, it appears that it is the instrument of choice in political contention. Thus, Ginsberg and Shefter (1999), analyzing political trends in the United States, write:

In recent years elections have become less decisive as mechanisms for resolving conflicts and constituting governments in the United States ... Rather than engage in an all out competition for votes, contending political forces have come to rely upon such weapons of institutional combat as congressional investigations, media revelations, and judicial proceedings to defeat their foes. In contemporary America, electoral success often fails to confer the capacity to govern, and political forces have been able to exercise considerable power even if they lose at the polls or, indeed, do not compete in the electoral arena. (1999: 16)

Several trends concur in placing scandals at the heart of political life in countries around the world: *the transformation of the media; the transformation of politics; and the specificity of media politics.*

Scandal Politics in a Digital Communication Environment

Concerning the media, news as infotainment favors stories of scandal as prime material to attract the audience. This is particularly significant with the advent of the 24-hour news cycle, with relentless "breaking news" to feed the appetite for sensationalism and novelty (Fallows, 1996; Sabato et al., 2000). Since all major media outlets are on the web, the perpetual news cycle is not limited to television or radio news networks: information is constantly updated on the web sites of newspapers and magazines. Furthermore, Boczkowski (2007) has shown the process of imitation that characterizes headlines on media web sites: as soon as stories appear on one web site, they are immediately picked up, reformatted, and discussed on all the others.

Internet-based communication contributes powerfully to the rise of scandal politics in two main ways (Howard, 2003; McNair, 2006). First, it opens up mass communication to allegations and denunciations from multiple sources, thus bypassing the gatekeeping capacity of mainstream media. The most notorious example was the wave of anxiety set off among mainstream media editors when an Internet newsletter (the Drudge Report) broke the story that President Clinton had had an affair with Monica Lewinsky, a White House intern (Williams and Delli Carpini, 2004). The ability to directly access mass communication platforms via mass self-communication platforms feeds a vast ocean of rumors and conspiracy theories. It also opens up the possibility for anyone to expose the improper or unlawful behavior of politicians, often with audiovisual support on YouTube or other platforms. There is no longer any privacy for political leaders. Their behavior is constantly vulnerable to exposure by small, digital recording devices, such as cell phones, and capable of being instantly uploaded to the Internet.

Second, any news released in any form from any source has the potential of being immediately virally diffused over the Internet (McNair, 2006). Additionally, blogger and audience comments in general feed the controversy instantly, bringing objectionable conduct into the electronic agora of open, public debate, thus triggering "blog wars" (Perlmutter, 2008). Indeed, an increasing number of bloggers work as political consultants, as the blogosphere has become a critical communication space in which public images are made and remade (*The Economist*, 2008). Digital networked gossip constitutes an amplifier of gigantic proportions, igniting allegations of scandal in a matter of hours.

Scandal Politics and the Transformation of Politics

The centrality of scandals is also a function of the transformation of politics. Tumber (2004) considers the weakening of party identification and the decline of partisanship to be the source of the rise of scandal politics, with a corresponding rise in a *"culture of promotionalism"* in which politicians, governments, and corporations promote their own interests over the interests of the collective (Tumber, 2004: 1122). Analysts point to the fact that political competition is marked by the struggle to occupy the center of the electorate's political spectrum in terms of the perceived message, thus downplaying ideological contrasts, as parties and candidates, having secured their core supporters, strive to adopt their opponents' themes and positions to lure away potential voters. From this follows a tendency for citizens to rely more on the personal characteristics of the leaders and the honesty of their parties than on their programs and statements (Edwards and Dan, 1999). Thus, politicians involved in scandals make for better news because these scandals undermine their entitlement to the delegation of power from citizens (Thompson, 2000; Chalaby, 2004; Tumber and Waisbord, 2004a, b).

There are also a number of factors that affect the growing vulnerability of the political system to scandals. Some are related to structural trends in the *relationship between globalization and the state that affect the morality of politics*. Thus, some time ago, Guehenno (1993) suggested an interesting hypothesis: given the limits to the power of nation-states imposed by globalization, and considering the gradual fading of ideological commitments, the rewards for being in office are no longer distinct from those offered in society at large: money, which usually means money received outside the formal channels of compensation.

Furthermore, *in a growing number of countries, the global criminal economy has deeply penetrated the institutions of the state*, thus offering the possibility of exposing the criminal connections of the political system, a frequent source of political scandals in Latin America or Southeast Asia, but also in other countries, such as Japan, Italy, or Russia (Castells, 2000c; Campbell, 2008; Glenny, 2008). Illegal financing of political parties becomes a source of corruption, thus increasing the chances that damaging information will be used by the opponent (Ansolabehere et al., 2001). Because all parties engage in this practice, they all have their intelligence units and their army of intermediaries who trade threats and counter-threats, inducing a political world characterized by the possibility of mutually assured destruction. According to this political logic, once the market for damaging material is created, if there is not enough clear-cut material for scandals, then insinuations or fabrications fill the gap. Indeed, the strategy in scandal politics does not necessarily aim for a decisive blow by one scandal alone. Rather, a continuing flow of scandals of different kinds, and with different levels of evidence, weave the thread with which political ambitions are fulfilled or doomed by image-making in the citizens' minds.

Scandal Politics and Media Politics

Scandal politics is inseparable from media politics. First, because it is through the media (including, of course, the means of mass self-communication) that scandals are revealed and disseminated to society at large. But, more importantly, it is inseparable because the characteristics of media politics make the use of scandals the most effective tool in political contests. This is primarily because media politics is organized around the personalization of politics, as analyzed above. Since the most effective messages are negative messages, and since character assassination is the most definitive form of negativity, the destruction of a political leader by leaking, fabricating, formatting, and propagating scandalous behavior that can be attributed to him or her, whether personally or by association, is the ultimate goal of scandal politics. This is why tactics such as "opposition research," which I described above, are based on finding damaging information that could be used to bring down the popular appeal of a politician or a party. The practice of scandal politics represents the highest level of performance in the strategy of inducing a negative affect effect. Because media politics is the politics of the Information Age, scandal politics is the instrument of choice to engage in the political struggles of our time. However, are scandals always as effective as their promoters wish them to be? The evidence on the matter is inconclusive if, by effective, we mean the defeat of a political leader, party, or government.

The Political Impact of Scandal Politics

There is considerable debate about how and if the politics of scandal influences political behavior. Some researchers argue that scandal politics damages politicians rather than the political system. Because politicians market themselves on personality traits such as honesty and integrity, when they are caught behaving reprehensibly voters may lose trust in the individual culprit, but their respect for the political system is not necessarily affected. Welch and Hibbing (1997), for example, find that incumbents charged with corruption involving questions of morality can see their support diminish by as much as 10 percent of the two-party vote. Similarly, other studies have found that approval of individual congressmen or politicians has little to do with citizens' level of trust or regard for political institutions in general (Hibbing and Theiss-Morse, 1995). For example, during the 1990s in the United States, according to a number of Pew surveys, after an initial slump in political trust levels, the Monica Lewinsky scandal seemed to have had limited impact on levels of political trust.

Thus, empirical evidence suggests that political scandals influence voter behavior differently depending on the country and the level of political office. In the United States, congressional and state elections typically attract little voter interest, and voters have scant knowledge about the names of their representatives or their challengers. A growing body of research suggests that, for these politicians, particularly during primaries, being implicated in a scandal may actually be beneficial (Burden, 2002). This benefit is particularly pronounced for office challengers. As Mann and Wolfinger (1980) first noted, people are better at recognizing a candidate's name than spontaneously recalling it. This is important because voting only requires that voters recognize a name on a ballot. Thus, participation in scandal may be beneficial at these lower levels because it increases name recognition, which may translate into a higher percentage of the vote. However, for major political candidates, scandals are detrimental because voters already possess information about them and are more inclined to follow the details of the scandal.

Pew surveys conducted in the United States also suggest that partisanship may influence how scandal affects political trust. Independents appear to be more influenced by political scandal than either Democrats or Republicans. Independent voters who think their representatives have taken bribes are more than twice as likely as those who do not (46% vs. 20%) to say that he or she should be voted out of office in the following election (Dimock, 2006). The poll also suggested that while independents tend to follow news stories less closely than their partisan counterparts, their interest in congressional corruption is similar to their Democrat counterparts and exceeds Republican interest. Considering the importance of the independent vote in most US elections, this suggests that scandal reporting can play a crucial role in influencing the outcome of elections. Moreover, 77 percent of independents who have been following stories of congressional corruption believed that most sitting members of Congress should be voted out in the following election. In an international comparison, Simpser (2004) analyzed the political consequences of voter perception of corruption. Using an original dataset with a new measure of electoral corruption for 88 countries in 1990–2000, Simpser found that electoral corruption and high margins of victory were associated with lower turnout across a wide array of countries. Therefore, scandals may affect trust in elections and not just in politicians.

A key question is the role played by the media in enhancing the impact of scandals. Granted, without the media, there is no scandal. But does media reporting of scandals induce specific political effects? In the United States, a study by the Project for Excellence in Journalism and the Pew Research Center (2000) of 2,400 major newspaper, television, and Internet news stories and commentaries on the 2000 presidential election found that 76 percent of them focused on two themes: Al Gore lies/exaggerates and is marred by scandal. Despite allegations of cocaine use and business irregularities, the study found that George W. Bush was far more successful at conveying his campaign message that he was a "compassionate conservative" and "a different kind of Republican." The study also found that negative depictions did not seem to resonate strongly with voters. While depicting Gore as scandal-tainted was the most prevalent media frame, only 26 percent of people surveyed made this association.

Looking specifically at the Monica Lewinsky scandal, John Zaller (1998) expresses similar doubts that mediated political communication played a role in influencing public interpretations of the scandal. He explains continued public support for Clinton, despite overwhelmingly critical press coverage, by referring to three variables not linked to the media: (a) peace (the lack of any major security threats to the United States); (b) prosperity (the strong economy); and (c) Clinton's moderate policy positions. Zaller (1998) also notes that the political ramifications of the scandal were largely eclipsed by its sheer entertainment value as a drama of sex and power in the Oval Office. However, Lawrence and Bennett (2001) disagree with Zaller. According to their analysis, while the Lewinsky scandal had no negative impact on voter approval and trust levels, it did have a larger effect in that it caused a public deliberation about the role of sexual conduct in American public life. In other words, post-Monica, sexual behavior by politicians matters less to the American public in terms of political engagement and trust. Lawrence and Bennett (2001) note that support for the impeachment of Clinton, if he had lied under oath about his sexual conduct, declined from 50 to 31 percent over the course of the scandal. Samuelson (1998) credits Clinton's continued high approval ratings to general fatigue over political attack culture in general. He defines "attack culture" as the corruption of normal public investigations – by congressional committee, the press, and independent counsels and prosecutors. They become less concerned with uncovering wrongdoing than in ruining the accused politically. People instinctively find the process baffling, unfair, and (to the nation) self-destructive. They did not wish to reward and perpetuate it by making Clinton the latest and largest kill (Samuelson, 1998: 19). Samuelson also cites the fact that Republican disapproval ratings doubled from 22 percent in January 1998 to 39 percent in December 1998 as further evidence of attack culture fatigue. Clinton's apparent immunity from public indignation surrounding the scandal may also have been a function of his strong personal charisma: a *Washington Post* poll found a 17 percent jump (44 to 61%) in the percentage of Americans who approved of the direction the country was going immediately after his televised public confession (Renshon, 2002: 414). Waisbord (2004b) also draws upon Keith Tester's work on desensitization by the media to explain how pervasive media coverage of a scandal can result in the "banalization of corruption" and "scandal fatigue" in audiences.

However, other studies suggest that the major consequence of the Lewinsky scandal took place in the decisive 2000 presidential election when 18 percent of voters listed morality as the most important characteristic they were looking for in a president (Renshon, 2002). Renshon points to the fact that, while voters exhibited high job approval ratings of President Clinton, an overwhelming majority (74%) of Americans agreed with the statement: "I am tired of all the problems associated with the Clinton administration." Among those who expressed such fatigue, 60 percent said they would vote for George W. Bush, and 35 percent said they would vote for Al Gore (Renshon, 2002: 424). Similarly, Morin and Deane (2000), writing about Clinton fatigue, found that one in three voters who liked Clinton's politics but not his persona defected to Bush. Moreover, the researchers found that "honest" ranked as the single most important trait that voters in 2000 were seeking in the next president – and eight in ten of these voters supported Bush (Morin and Deane, 2000: A10). In other words, Clinton's approval ratings survived the series of scandals during his presidency and his impeachment vote because his policies received wide support, and his personal conduct was considered typical of most politicians. However, Al Gore paid the price for Clinton's immorality as he was tainted by association in an election against a candidate who was at the time perceived to be moral and honest. Ironically, in the minds of many Americans, George W. Bush will go down in history as one of the most egregious liars in the American presidency.

In sum: the effects of scandal politics on specific political outcomes are largely undetermined. They depend on the cultural and institutional context, the relationship between the kind of scandal and the politician involved in the scandal, the social and political climate of the country, and the intensity of the fatigue effect detected among citizens after endless reiteration of scandal stories in the media. Effects must also be measured over time, and are often indirect in their manifestations; for example, another politician suffering consequences by association.

But we do have evidence about two important political effects. First, *a growing number of major political changes in governments around the world are directly associated with the effects of scandals*, as shown in table A4.2 in the

Appendix. In other words, while many of the political scandals have minor direct political effects, there are so many scandals exploding constantly in the media that some of them do have a major impact, sometimes bringing down governments or even regimes.

Second, *because of the prevalence of scandal politics, regardless of specific outcomes in a given context, the entire political landscape is transformed everywhere* because the generalized association of politics with scandalous behavior contributes to citizen disaffection vis-à-vis political institutions and the political class, *contributing to a worldwide crisis of political legitimacy*. Indeed, it is precisely because all politicians are lumped together under the same negative judgment of their morality and trustworthiness that specific scandals related to specific politicians may have little impact: since politicians are considered to be generally unreliable by a majority of people, the disenchanted citizen must choose the unreliable person who is most akin to her/his values and interests. This observation raises *the most relevant question concerning power relationships: the relationship between media politics, scandal politics, and the crisis of political legitimacy*. I will go deeper into an examination of the dynamics of scandal politics by focusing on a case study full of lessons for the practice of democracy: the demise of the Spanish Socialists in the 1990s as a result of a well-designed strategy of scandal politics.

Targeting the Achilles' Heel: Scandal Politics in Socialist Spain

González won three elections with an absolute majority, and even a fourth one when all signs were pointing to a loss. Thus, we had to raise the stakes to extremes that sometimes affected the state itself. González was blocking something essential in democracy: political alternance... González's capacity to communicate, his political strength, his extraordinary ability, led many people to the conclusion that it was necessary to bring his era to a close. As the very harsh attacks launched against him in 1992–3 could not finish him off... we realized the need to step up the criticism. Then, we searched in this whole world of irregularities, of corruption... There was no other way to break González.

(Luis María Anson, then chief editor of the newspaper *ABC*, interviewed in the weekly *Tiempo*, February 23, 1998; my translation)

The series of orchestrated scandals that ultimately undermined the dominance of Felipe González and his Socialist Party in Spain, leading to their electoral defeat in 1996, represent a textbook case of scandal politics

(Anson, 1996; Ramírez, 2000; Amedo, 2006; Heywood, 2007; Villoria Mendieta, 2007). In 1982, only five years after the establishment of democracy, following four decades of General Franco's bloody dictatorship, the Socialists won a landslide victory. They were re-elected in 1986, in 1989, and, by a smaller margin, in 1993. Among the reasons for their success was the voters' rejection of the Conservatives, many of whom had been associated with the discredited Franco regime; the center–left orientation of the majority of the Spanish electorate; and the mobilization of "nations without states," such as Catalonia and the Basque Country, in defense of their fullest possible autonomy, a demand that the Conservatives opposed (Alonso-Zaldívar and Castells, 1992). Once elected, the Socialist government implemented a series of efficient policies that stimulated economic growth and employment, developed a welfare state of sorts, modernized the country, constructed a semi-federal state, brought the armed forces under control, and paved the way for joining the European Community in 1986.

But the skillful use of media politics was also a factor in helping the Socialists win the elections and stay in power for 13 successive years. At the core of the strategy was the personalization of politics in the party's Secretary General, Felipe González. González, a moderate social democrat and 40 years old when he came to power, was haunted by the dangers of a democratic transition in a country that throughout its tormented history had never known democracy, save for five years in the 1930s. His pragmatism stabilized the country and ensured the continuity of his government. He benefited from an efficient political team that used media politics and image-making in innovative ways unparalleled at that time in European politics. It helped that Spain inherited a media system in which the government had a monopoly of television stations, owned key radio networks, and had indirect influence on sections of the print press. To his credit, it was precisely the González government that decentralized, liberalized, and privatized the media, which allowed for two private national television networks, opened the way for cable and satellite television, and authorized regional television networks controlled by regional governments. In the process, the main Spanish newspaper, created at the dawn of democracy as a pro-democratic voice, *El País*, became the foundation of the major media group in the country, and developed a reciprocally fruitful cooperation with the Socialists (Machado, 2006).

In the early 1990s, such a concentration of power and media in the hands of the Socialists and their allies prompted González's adversaries to opt to take the battle outside the electoral realm. They adopted a strategy of image destruction aimed at the gradual erosion of the reputation for honesty and democracy at the source of the Socialists' appeal for voters. But who were these adversaries? Certainly, they included the Conservative political bloc that underwent several transformations before creating the Partido Popular (PP), affiliated with the European conservative parties. But in the 1980s, the PP was weak, with its influence limited to a minority of the electorate anchored in the ideological right. So, their radical opposition to the Socialists was joined by the Communist-led United Left coalition, a small but militant and influential group in some segments of society. It also counted on the discreet support of some business groups (in spite of González's pro-business policies), and was helped by the Catholic Church, which was fighting to preserve its financial and institutional privileges. Yet, actual leadership of the informal network of González's opponents was assumed by groups of journalists who, for personal, professional, and ideological reasons, entered the battle. Highly regarded journalist Pedro J. Ramírez, director of *Diario 16*, a second-tier, middle-of-the-road newspaper, was the key player. Ramírez, after a period in Washington, became fascinated by Watergate, and nurtured his obsession with political investigative reporting. After he supported his journalists investigating the GAL (Grupos Anti-terroristas de Liberación) affair (see below) and published several articles revealing government illegalities, he was fired on March 1989, allegedly at the suggestion of the Socialists. He vowed revenge. He obtained financial support and a few months later started publication of *El Mundo*, which would become the relentless inquisitor of the Socialist government and, in the end, a media mainstay for the Conservatives. The professional quality of the newspaper and its independence vis-à-vis the Socialist government, while also providing a platform for the left-wing critics of González, made it the second largest daily in terms of readership and guaranteed its good business standing.

El Mundo became the explicit harbinger of scandal politics and developed an efficient media format. The paper would obtain compromising information about the party or the government with exclusive rights to publication. It would then publish a series of articles with explosive headlines over several days. From its pages, information would diffuse to the rest of the media. The media were compelled to quote *El Mundo* and publish these stories because of their scandalous appeal to the public. Of course, this strategy required good scandal material, and there was an abundance of it. The Socialists were so self-assured of political control in the country that they engaged in careless illegal operations without taking the most elementary precautions. Teams of investigative reporters sometimes unearthed the damaging information with a crusader's mentality, asserting the power of the free press, a hard-fought conquest in Spain, over politicians. In most cases, though, the media, and particularly *El Mundo* because of its visibility, benefited from interested leaks from various participants in unlawful operations, as a way to pay back aggravations or to save face or freedom when schemes turned sour. This was the case in the Filesa affair, revealed in 1991, which exposed the Socialist Party's creation of a fake consulting firm to extract payments from businesses for the party's coffers. Several high-ranking party bureaucrats were found guilty and served time in prison after their accountant's request for extra payment was denied. Yet, the most significant scandal, and the one that I will use as illustrative of a long series of affairs that it is unnecessary to detail for the sake of the analysis, is the GAL episode.

The major domestic political challenge the Socialists faced after assuming power was the same challenge that all other Spanish governments have faced in the past 50 years, and continue to face: the Basque struggle for independence, and particularly the terrorism practiced by the most militant independent organization, ETA, with over 800 killings on its record at this point. Because of the military and law enforcement agencies' sensitivity to the issue, the Socialists decided to confront ETA head on from the beginning of their administration. By and large, the Socialist offensive was political, parlaying its support among the Basque working class into various forms of collaboration with the democratic and moderate Basque National Party, elected to govern the Basque institutions. But there was also a determined police action to eradicate ETA. It failed, as it has failed with all other governments, in spite of dozens of militants killed and hundreds jailed. Then, someone, a certain Mr. X, to use the terminology of Judge Garzón, who investigated the case, imagined a sort of "final solution:" kill them all. Why bother with legalities? (Does this sound familiar in the early twenty-first century?)

According to the documentation that provided the basis for judicial sentences years later, a special unit was created in the Ministry of the Interior using the government's secret funds. Several police officers were assigned to the task, who then contracted professional killers from France, as the safe refuge for ETA was in French territory. A shadow organization was set up and the "Antiterrorism Liberation Group" (GAL) went into action. It was a disaster. They began by kidnapping and assassinating two Basque activists in October 1983. But their second kidnapping, three months later, was a case of mistaken identity. And then, in 1984, they erroneously assassinated a dancer with no connection to ETA. The lack of professionalism and the supervising policemen's use of secret funds to enjoy the nightlife of criminal milieus led to the arrest of the two police officers in charge of the conspiracy, Amedo and Dominguez. They were judged and sentenced to long prison terms in September 1991. But they did not reveal their high-level connections because, according to their statements later on, "someone" in the Socialist government had promised them pardon in exchange for their silence.

In October 1994, when they realized that this promise was empty and there would be no pardon, they changed their allegiance and accused several high-ranking officials in the Ministry of the Interior and the Minister himself. Before going to the judge, they talked with leaders of the opposition Partido Popular, with the help of their lawyer, since (according to Amedo's version) they were promised pardon in the future if the PP came to power. They also gave an interview to the editor of *El Mundo*, possibly in exchange for money (although *El Mundo* has denied the allegation). On the basis of this new evidence, the leading judge in cases of terrorism, internationally renowned Baltasar Garzón (the same judge who issued an order of arrest in London against the then Dictator of Chile, Pinochet), reopened the case. Fueling the prosecution was the fact that Mr. Garzón had been seduced by Prime Minister González to be part of his candidacy in the 1993 elections, and then felt disappointed by his experience in the government, returning to his post in the court just in time to take on the procedure against the GAL. Between 1995 and 1998, a number of trials were conducted against Ministers, Secretaries of State, the General Director of Police, high-ranking government officials, and the Secretary General of the Socialist Party in the Basque Country. Several of them were found guilty and sentenced to prison, although through various pardons and generous application of parole benefits they did not stay in jail long. In spite of allegations from some of the convicts that led the judge to send a request to the Supreme Court accusing the Prime Minister, nothing could be proved, as Felipe González asserted that he had been unaware of the GAL operation, and denounced the political motivation of the prosecution. The Supreme Court did not pursue the accusations against him.

Throughout this tragic soap opera, *Diario 16*, and later *El Mundo*, kept feeding public opinion and other media with details and evidence of the

GAL conspiracy. The inside track of information originally came from the work of two investigative reporters of *Diario 16*, working under Pedro J. Ramírez. In August 1987, a few days after a new GAL assassination, these reporters found a secret GAL bunker full of documents, police reports, photographs, and guns and ammunition of the type used by the Spanish police. *Diario 16* went on to publish a series of five articles exposing the findings. Other media followed by publishing interviews with several people involved in the affair. As I mentioned above, it was precisely the exposure of the GAL that led ultimately to the firing of Ramírez by the publisher of *Diario 16* and to the creation of *El Mundo*, the relentless purveyor of political scandals in the following years.

The ensuing deterioration of the government image, together with a downturn in the economy, brought the Socialists to the edge of defeat in the parliamentary elections of March 1993. However, a forceful campaign by their leader, the legendary Felipe González, reversed the predictions of the polls and the pundits and gave the Socialists enough seats to govern in minority with the support of nationalist parties in Catalonia and the Basque Country. It was too much for the coalition that had tried for years to bring down González. It was time to launch a frontal attack by digging dirt from wherever it could be found with the support of discontented personnel in the government and police. To do so, a real media conspiracy was organized featuring, naturally, an *El Mundo* team with Ramírez at its helm, but adding to it a number of powerful players: Luis María Anson, the editor of *ABC*, the oldest and most prestigious conservative newspaper, and a towering figure in the right-wing circles of Spanish journalism; the director of the largest private television network, Antena 3; the director of another newspaper, *El Independiente*; the COPE, the radio network owned and operated by the Catholic Church; and several influential journalists, and occasional co-conspirators from different circles, including high-ranking politicians from the Partido Popular. They formalized their alliance by establishing an Association of Independent Journalists and Writers (AEPI in the Spanish acronym) which attracted all those who wanted to contribute to the demise of González. Then, the conspirators went to work.

From 1993 to 1996 a series of major political scandals shook the government and the country. In November 1993, *Diario 16* revealed that Luis Roldan, the first civilian appointed Director General of the paramilitary Guardia Civil (an elite force with a long tradition in Spanish history), had substantially increased his assets during his tenure. In April 1994, *El Mundo* provided evidence of the sources of this wealth obtained through illegal payments from suppliers and contractors to the Guardia Civil, funds that Roldan shared with the party in the Navarre region, while pocketing much of it. In addition, he appropriated some of the secret funds destined for clandestine law enforcement operations. Thereafter, the parliament opened an investigation. Roldan denied the accusations but a few days later escaped to Paris, and gave an interview to *El Mundo*, acknowledging receipt of payments from the government's secret funds, while adding that the Minister of the Interior and other officials of the security forces had been doing the same for years. When the government requested his extradition from France, he vanished. In 1995, he reappeared in Laos, and was finally duped by the Spanish police with false extradition documents from Laos and returned to Spain, where he was sentenced and imprisoned. His accusations aggravated the charges against the high-level officials from the Ministry of the Interior under investigation for the GAL affair. Several other officials were also sentenced for embezzlement of public funds.

Furthermore, in April 1994, *El Mundo* revealed that the Governor of the Bank of Spain, Mariano Rubio, as well as other personalities, including a Minister, had secret accounts to evade taxes through a financial company (Ibercorp) established by a former chairman of the Madrid Stock Exchange. They ended up in prison, and were soon freed on parole, although Mr. Rubio died shortly after his ordeal. Again, *El Mundo*, in June 1995, documented the fact that the Spanish military intelligence agency (CESID) had been illegally wiretapping political personalities, businessmen, journalists, and even the King of Spain. Thereafter, the chief of the agency, and the overseeing Ministers resigned.

The list of mishaps and corruption is even longer, but the scandals I have mentioned should suffice to illustrate the analysis. Several analytical points must be emphasized:

(1) There is a *direct relationship between the level and intensity of illegality and corruption in a political agency and the capacity to induce political scandals*. While skillful manipulation of information, and shrewd weaving of facts and fabricated evidence, increase the impact of the scandal, it is the raw material provided by the extent and significance of the wrongdoing that ultimately determines the effect of scandals on the public mind. In the case of the Spanish Socialists, corruption and illegal practices went undeniably out of control in high levels of government. It is exceptional in democracy that, in just two years, the Minister of the Interior, the head of the main security force, the head of military intelligence, and the Governor of the Central

Bank, among other authorities, were caught red handed. The arrogance of the Socialists, after one decade in power without a real challenge from the opposition, clearly played a role in creating a climate of loose morals and personal enrichment. While González and his closest collaborators did not participate in corruption (judicial investigations did not uncover wrongdoing on their part), his permissiveness on these matters, occupied as he was in changing Spain and the world, left the spread of unethical and delinquent behavior unchecked in a few, but significant, circles of the Socialist administration.

(2) *The media, and particularly one major newspaper, were decisive in uncovering government illegality.* Emphasis on investigative reporting, and the personal vendetta of *El Mundo*'s director, played a major role in the source of the damaging information. Journalists discovered some of the information, and then it diffused throughout the media. The profession of journalism asserted itself, after decades of living under censorship, by striving to find evidence of corruption in political circles, both local and national. Yet, the very actors involved in the corruption facilitated most of the documents that came to form the basis for the accusations in the courts of justice. Personal conflicts internal to the conspiracies prompted a strategy of winning personal advantage by framing a certain version of the story in the press that would allow those revealing the conspiracy to save face and escape indictment while it was still possible to do so. Furthermore, it was often the case that leaking damaging information to the press about opponents in the party was the weapon of choice in the fights among factions within the Socialist Party. In other words, *scandals became the hidden expression of political struggle by other means than debates and votes, both between parties and within parties.*

(3) *Business conflicts between media groups were also layered over political conflicts.* Conflict was particularly pronounced between the Prisa group, which was the publisher of *El País* and close to the Socialists, and *El Mundo*, the ABC group, and Antena 3 TV, which were closer to the Conservatives (Machado, 2006; Campo Vidal, 2008). Besides ideology, major business competition was at work, with *El Mundo* trying to increase audience share by depicting itself as the independent critic of a corrupt government. Faced with such a fierce rivalry, *El País*, and its multimedia group, had to echo some of the damaging information against its allies.

(4) Brought by the anti-corruption campaign to the forefront of public opinion, the judicial establishment indulged its role as the country's moral

savior, creating a de facto *alliance between judges and journalists that has come to be the core of the mechanism of scandal politics everywhere.*

As a result of the onslaught of media-driven, judicially supported, scandal politics, Felipe González and his Socialist Party were finally voted out of power, by a slim margin, in the parliamentary elections of April 1996. But the cognitive and political processes underlying this outcome were complex and deserve examination (Barreiro and Sanchez-Cuenca, 1998, 2000; Montero et al., 1998; Boix and Riba, 2000; Cainzos, 2000; Barreiro, 2001; Jimenez, 2004; Rico, 2005; Fundación Alternativas, 2007).

Spanish political behavior throughout the short history of its democracy has been marked by the difference of ideological positions between center-left, center-right, and "without ideology." Between 1986 and 2004, the proportion of citizens positioning themselves in the center-left oscillated between a low 53 percent (in 2000) and a high 60 percent (both in 1986 and 2004). On the other hand, those embracing a center-right position represented a much lower level of the electorate, between 17.5 percent in 1986 and 26.5 percent at its highest point in 2000, to decline again to 21 percent in 2004 (Fundación Alternativas, 2007). Given the minority status of the right-wing vote, the Conservative Party's chances of winning an election were dependent on its capacity to attract voters without declared ideology (between 18 and 24% of the electorate), and in the differential mobilization between center-left and center-right voters in terms of electoral participation. Throughout the 1980s and 1990s, the personal leadership of Felipe González provided the key factor in the capacity of the center-left to mobilize its voters and attract independents.

There is a strong correlation between the ranking of leaders in the citizens' opinion and their voting choices. González was consistently ranked at the top of the list, and voters who held him in high esteem have been shown to be 23 percent more likely to vote Socialist (Barreiro and Sanchez-Cuenca, 1998). Additional factors in explaining voters' behavior were personal ideology, the ideology of a partner or of close friends, and, far behind in the causality effect, the television network most frequently watched, and the opinion formed after televised electoral debates. In 1993, the economic downturn and the widespread opinion of pervasive corruption in the Socialist government (in November 1992, 75% of Spaniards thought that "the level of corruption was intolerable") appeared to doom the Socialists' electoral chances. Yet, with González committing personally to the campaign in March 1993, his leadership mobilized the center-left electorate (abstention was contained at about 23%) and attracted the independent vote. Indeed, his personal ranking among the undecided increased from 5.58 to 7.58 (on a scale of 0–10) before and after the campaign. The personalization of politics, a charismatic leader, and a skillful use of media politics were stronger determinants of political behavior than the acknowledged wrongdoings of the party in government. Voters decided to give González a new chance to regenerate his administration, as they were ideologically reluctant to switch their support to the Conservatives, and continued to identify with an exceptional leader. The flurry of scandals between 1993 and 1996 altered the political equation, to the point that González called early elections in 1996. In his version, the reason was to submit himself to the verdict of the citizens. In the version of some of his collaborators, he did it as a result of personal and political fatigue at withstanding a constant, and increasingly virulent, media assault, compounded by his bitterness about the betrayal and corruption in his entourage. The media conspiracy described above eventually produced its effects. In June 1994, 19 percent of Spaniards thought that almost all high-level political appointees were involved in corruption, 38 percent considered that this was the case for the majority of them, and another 38 percent thought that at least some of them were corrupt. Less than 2 percent thought that the administration was clean. Similar opinions were expressed in 1995 and 1996 (Villoria Mendieta, 2007).

As a result, in spite of a renewed mobilization of the Socialist vote, which increased by 3 percent, and a similar level of abstention to 1993 (22.6%), the non-ideological vote was sensitive this time to the perception of corruption, and switched to the Conservative Party, which consequently increased its vote by 18.5 percent and won the election for the first time in democratic Spain. These political trends were accentuated in the 2000 election, when the majority of the independent voters chose the PP over the PSOE, consolidating the power of the Conservative Party which felt free to then tilt its policies toward the right, a move that would eventually frustrate its expectations of continuing in power. Yet, in the short term, the strategy of scandal politics, designed in 1993 by a conspiracy of media leaders, politicians, and businessmen, with the blessing of the Catholic Church, was effective in delegitimizing the Socialists (who made themselves an easy target by the behavior of several of their officials), and in pushing an exhausted Felipe González out of the Spanish political scene.

González is still revered by many, and has continued to play a significant role in world politics over the years. Yet, the Socialist Party faced the challenge of regenerating itself. The wounds inflicted by scandal politics persist in the memory of citizens, and particularly in the perception of young citizens reluctant to concede to political cynicism. Furthermore, all Spanish politics became tarnished with the stigma of corruption. In spite of the absence of an equivalent political scandal strategy from the opposition after the Conservative victory in 1996, corruption among the new government elites, now Conservatives, continued to be exposed in the media, albeit with much less militant fervor from *El Mundo* to denounce the corrupted. In December 1997, 92 percent of Spaniards thought that corruption continued to be a very serious problem, and in December 1998 over 50 percent thought that corruption had significantly increased during 1997 (Centro de Investigaciones Sociológicas, 1998). In July 2003, 74 percent of those surveyed considered that corruption "was affecting significantly public life" (Transparency International, 2003). Consequently, the crisis of legitimacy of the political system deepened in Spain, in line with trends in the rest of the world. In the process, a young democracy lost its innocence.

The State and Media Politics: Propaganda and Control

The state remains a critical actor in defining power relationships through communication networks. While we have analyzed the complexity of the interaction between media and politics, we should not overlook the oldest and most direct form of media politics: propaganda and control. This is: (a) the fabrication and diffusion of messages that distort facts and induce misinformation for the purpose of advancing government interests; and (b) the censorship of any message deemed to undermine these interests, if necessary by criminalizing unhindered communication and prosecuting the messenger. The extent and forms of government control over communication networks vary according to the legal and social environment in which a given state operates. Thus, I will analyze three distinct contexts in which the state exercises control of communication following different procedures adjusted to its rules of engagement with society at large: the United States, Russia, and China.

Government Propaganda in the Land of Freedom: Embedding the Military in the Media

The US government has a well-established tradition of fabricating intelligence to justify its actions, particularly in moments of decision between war and peace in order to sway public opinion (Kellner, 2005). Yet, even by US standards, the multifaceted strategy of misinformation leading to the 2003 Iraq War, and sustaining the war effort for years afterwards, stands out as a textbook case of political propaganda. In Chapter 3, I have analyzed the process of social production of misinformation and mystification around the Iraq War. Here, I refer to a different form of communication strategy: the direct penetration of media networks by the Department of Defense to script the reports and commentaries of supposedly independent analysts working for the networks.

On April 20, 2008, *The New York Times* published the results of an investigative report exposing, with detailed precision and properly sourced information, how the Pentagon organized a group of 75 military analysts working for the main television networks, such as Fox, NBC, CBS, and ABC, between 2002 and 2008, in addition to contributing to syndicated newspaper networks (Barstow, 2008). The effort started in early 2002, as the march toward the war began in spite of public hesitation to engage in military action. Tori Clarke, Assistant Secretary of Defense for Public Affairs, designed a program that would recruit retired military officers to work as commentators with the media networks. Because of the credibility usually associated with the military, they were considered more effective conveyors of the Pentagon's view on the war. Their collaboration was made easier by the fact that they were usually eager to be associated with the armed forces, the institution to which they had devoted most of their lives. It also helped that many of these analysts were, and are, working with military contractors or lobbying for them. While the Pentagon did not pay them (except for occasional trips to Iraq), there was a quid pro quo: report as we tell you and you will receive access to sources, and, more importantly, access to contracts from the Defense Department. Indeed, occasional criticism of the conduct of the war was punished with the loss of a potential contract, prompting the dismissal of the independently minded officer from his job as a lobbyist. The group of analysts met regularly with staff from the department, and on the most relevant occasions with Rumsfeld himself who, according to transcripts of the sessions, instructed them directly on the content of their commentaries.

Programming Communication Networks

At each critical juncture of the war, when bad news reports were coming in and casualties mounted, special meetings would be held to coordinate reports that would provide an upbeat view of the war, or would emphasize its need in the context of the war on terror and the threat from Iran. When, in April 2006, several generals openly criticized Rumsfeld for his incompetent leadership, a campaign was staged in defense of Rumsfeld, including an op-ed contribution to *The Wall Street Journal* by two of the leading analysts of the group, Generals McInerney and Vallely, who, according to *The New York Times*, requested input from Rumsfeld's staff for their article (Barstow, 2008). A media monitoring company was paid hundreds of thousands of dollars to follow up on the effectiveness of these analysts' media commentaries. One of General Petraeus's first actions after taking command in Iraq in 2007 was to meet with the analysts group. Indeed, he placed a conference call with these media analysts during a recess in his testimony before Congress. The media networks knew of the existence of the Pentagon's analysts group and of the participation of their commentators in such meetings. It was, however, justified under the pretext of obtaining access to information. But it is unclear how much the networks were aware of the trading of propaganda for access on behalf of military contractors which seemed to be key to the operation. At the very least, several networks knew of the professional activities of their military experts and they chose not to ask questions. Indeed, as soon as rumors spread, and it appeared that there were obvious conflicts of interest, some of the analysts lost their jobs with the media, although most of them continued to sustain, against all evidence, that they were separating their three identities – as employees of military contractors, propagandists for the Pentagon, and independent analysts for the media, without forgetting, of course, their patriotic service to the nation.[40] Moreover, despite Barstow's (2008) revelations of the Pentagon's domestic propaganda campaign, a study by the Project for Excellence in Journalism (2008a) revealed that the major media outlets who had previously featured these military analysts systematically failed to cover the story.

---

[40] After the affair came to light, the Pentagon made 8,000 pages of documents relating to the analysts' activities public via the web site: http://www.dod.mil/pubs/foi/milanalysts/. Moreover, in May 2008, Democratic Congresswoman Rosa L. DeLauro and 40 colleagues delivered a letter to the Department of Defense Inspector General calling for an investigation into this "propaganda campaign aimed at deliberately misleading the American public."

Cases of direct US government intervention in media reporting, both in America and in the world, are too numerous to be detailed here, but they constitute a pattern. Thus, the Bush administration hired actors to pose as journalists. It produced mock news bulletins (Video News Releases referred to as VNRs) to promote its view of the Iraq War. VNRs first gained notoriety in early 2005, when *The New York Times* reported that many local stations aired prepackaged segments produced by federal agencies under the Bush administration. The VNRs cheered the Iraq War, the Bush Medicare plan, and various programs. And conservative commentator Armstrong Williams confessed that the Department of Education paid him $240,000 to go on television to promote President Bush's education policies (Kirkpatrick, 2005). These propaganda interventions are not unusual. They are justified by their enactors on behalf of the superior interest of the country and, when necessary, of democracy in the world. In analytical terms, what is relevant to emphasize is the awareness by the American state that the battle over information, the construction of public opinion through the media, is the necessary condition to obtain support for its actions. The experience of the Vietnam War showed that this support is the most important condition for the exercise of American power. General Paul Vallely, an analyst with Fox News until 2007, and a specialist in psychological warfare, wrote a paper in 1980 blaming American media for the defeat in the Vietnam War. According to *The New York Times*'s Barstow, Vallely wrote that "We lost the war – not because we were outfought, but because we were Psyoped," and went on to propose psychological strategies for future wars aimed at domestic opinion, which he termed a "MindWar" strategy centered on televison and radio networks (Barstow, 2008: A1). This is why, in the legal environment of the United States, in which state power to censor is limited, the control of information usually takes the form of generating messages and placing them with credible messengers who, willingly or not, convey untruth to an increasingly mystified audience.

Other institutional and cultural contexts appear more prone to direct government control of the media. Indeed, this is the case for most countries in the world. Governments tend to combine various strategies: political control over public media (often the most influential); government pressure on media owners; legislation empowering government control over all forms of communication; and, if everything else fails, personalized intimidation of journalists or bloggers. This is critical in the attempts to control Internet-based communication in countries in which the state is the dominant instance of society. To explore strategies of direct government control of communication networks, I will analyze processes in two countries that are particularly relevant for our understanding because of their pivotal role in the world and because of their explicit emphasis on controlling communication in the Internet Age: Russia and China.

Russia: Censor Yourself

The Russian state in democratic transition never forgot the fundamental lessons of its Soviet past: information is power and control of communication is the lever for keeping power.[41] But, of course, the situation changed after the peaceful democratic transition that ended the Communist regime. Russia was now under the rule of law, and the law was under the rule of the market. Censorship was banned, except when legally authorized censorship was appropriate, particularly under the Russian version of the war on terror. Journalists were free to report, though their companies could fire them when deemed necessary. Media managers could manage on their own, but they were expected to abide by the same bottom line as corporate media around the world – profit-making through media advertising by winning audience shares – which is tantamount to a focus on entertainment and infotainment.

Thus, the key mechanisms of state control over the media take place through bureaucratic and financial controls of media networks, either directly or indirectly. The establishment of these mechanisms was the decisive fight of Putin against the Yeltsin oligarchs, who had taken advantage of Yeltsin's weakness to exact control of key national television networks, such as NTV. Putin reasserted his control over government-owned media, and made sure that his oligarchs prevailed over unfriendly oligarchs in other national media. As for the regions, it was simpler. Regional governments, ultimately dependent on the President's delegate, would control regional media, and major resource companies bought regional television networks, as in the case of Lukoil taking control of Languepas, a network typical of what is called "pipe television" in Russia. The defining moment in this battle for media control was the aftermath of Putin's election to the presidency in 1999. As soon as he was elected, Putin wrested away from Berezovsky's

[41] Some of the data presented in this analysis have been obtained from the reliable web sources listed below. Additional sources are referred in the text. http://www.fapmc.ru, http://www.freedomhouse.org, http://www.gdf.ru, http://www.hrw.org, http://www.lenta.ru, http://www.oprf.ru, http://rfe.rferl.org, http://www.ruj.ru, http://sp.rian.ru

ownership the main television network (Channel 1) and returned it to the state. He also instructed Gazprom (the energy giant controlled by the government) to claim the debt contracted by MediaMost, the conglomerate owned by another Yeltsin oligarch, Gusinsky, which included one of the most influential television networks, NTV. In fact, NTV was the only major media outlet to oppose Putin during the electoral campaign. The retribution was swift. Gusinsky ended up in prison (accused of fiscal fraud, a typical practice among Russian oligarchs) and ultimately joined Berezovsky in deluxe exile in London, while his media empire was absorbed by Gazprom Media.

Gazprom became one of the most powerful media conglomerates in Russia today. It owns NTV (the third largest network in terms of audience), as well as NTV-satellite, NTV-studio production, entertainment network TNT, the classic newspaper *Izvestia*, major radio stations (e.g., Echo Movsky, City FM, Popsa), the *Itogy* magazine, advertising companies, and a variety of media outlets throughout the vast Russian geography. The Russian state organized another major conglomerate, VGTRK, with Rossiya TV Network, Kultura network, Sport network, 88 regional television networks, the news agency RIA Novosti, a 32 percent share in the European network Euronews, and major investments in the film production and export industry (Kiriya, 2007). The Russian state also kept control of Channel 1, the main television network, with 21.7 percent of the audience in 2007, and used it to attract private investors, led by Roman Abramovich, allowing them 49 percent of the network's shares, to be managed from offshore financial centers. The two state-dominated networks account for 50 percent of total advertising revenues (Kiriya, 2007). Other minor networks, such as Domashny (focusing on family programs), part of the holding STS Media, have specialized programming with only limited news reporting. TV-3 and DTV focus entirely on films. The only surviving media oligarch from the Yeltsin era, Vladimir Potanin, adopted a cautious business strategy, concentrating his properties in the Profmedia holding and focusing on entertainment, while selling his most politically sensitive properties, particularly the newspapers *Komsomolskaya Pravda* and *Izvestia*. Overall, all media groups are either under direct control of the state or dependent on the good will of the state and its inspectors.

The range of *bureaucratic pressures on the media* is as diverse as it is creative. According to reliable sources that I cannot identify because of their justified concern with retribution, the publication of reports unpalatable to the authorities (national, regional, or local) may trigger a number of consequences. It may be a visit by the fire marshals, or by the public hygiene agency, that would lead to cancellation of the permit to operate in the premises. Or, if the pressroom is housed on a high floor in the building, the elevator may suddenly stop working and its repair would be indefinitely delayed. If the independent-minded media outlet does not fall into line, the retaliation will escalate and the tax inspectors will wreck the company's finances. Thus, facing such a multi-pronged strategy of intimidatory actions, independent media can hardly put up a real fight, as denunciations of tampering with the free press can easily be derided if the problems come from the electricity company or from the landlord who suddenly decides to increase the rent. Furthermore, the few legal protections that journalists had in the past have been gradually phased out. The so-called Legal Chambers on Information Claims were dissolved after showing a degree of independence. New institutions, such as Public Chambers and Regional Councils on Information Claims, were put into place in 2006, stacked with bureaucrats and depleted of journalists' representation. Under such conditions, the control mechanism over the media is simple. It relies on the wise judgment of responsible journalists, and ultimately of their managers, if they want to keep their jobs and preserve their working conditions. *Self-censorship is the rule*.

Yet, if pushed by their drive to attract audience, or by their professionalism, journalists venture into politically sensitive information, they are *forcefully reminded of the commercial powers overseeing their task*. A case in point was the temporary suspension of the publication of the newspaper *Moskovsky Korrespondent* (owned by billionaire Alexandr Lebedev) in April 2008 after the paper's director general experienced major financial problems. The newspaper owners denied any connection between the suspension and the paper's publication of news concerning an alleged affair between President Putin and the gymnast and member of parliament, Alina Kabayeva.

While corporate oversight and bureaucratic harassment are the main mechanisms of control over the media, *the Russian government also counts on a wide range of legal tools, aimed at both the media and Internet communication*. In principle, censorship is forbidden, but a number of laws and decrees provide for exceptions to protect national security and to fight against cybercrime. Particularly relevant are the 1996 Sorm 1 and 1998 Sorm 2 laws authorizing the FSB, the security agency, to monitor communications; the 2000 "information security doctrine," which was added to Sorm 2 law to penalize Internet piracy, protect the telecommunications industry, and prevent "propaganda" and "disinformation" over the Internet; the 2001 law on "mass media" and "combating terrorism," apparently aimed at blocking terrorist access to communication networks; and the 2006 law on "information technologies and protection of information," which updated and strengthened the measures against unwarranted use of these networks. But perhaps the most controversial law was the one approved in July 2007 to fight "extremism." This law includes restrictions on certain types of criticism against public officials aired in the media, with penalties such as publication closure and prison sentences of up to three years. Cases of application of this law include sanctions to the portals Pravda.ru, Bankfax.ru, and Gazeta.ru, as well as a fine handed out to the editor of the online newspaper *Kursiv* for the publication of an article on Putin that was considered "offensive."

Then there is the *control of political programming content by media outlet managers*. Leading political opponents, such as Gary Kasparov, Vladimir Ryzhkov, representatives of the main opposition party (Communist party), and even Putin's former political allies, such as Mikhail Kasyanov or Andrei Illarionov, have all but vanished from television. One of the most popular political satirists, Viktor Senderovitch, saw his puppets program cancelled; rock groups performing for the opposition parties saw their television bookings cancelled; and jokes about Putin and Dmitry Medvedev are no laughing matters as their authors are swiftly removed from the telecast (Levy, 2008). According to Levy's interviews with Russian journalists, the Kremlin did not keep a formal, master list of persons who were not to appear on television. They said that, in fact, the networks themselves operated on the basis of an informal blacklist, following their own interpretation of the government's potential displeasure.

Furthermore, when some daring journalists venture into the murky waters of political corruption, or, even worse, into reports on terrorism and counter-terrorism, or into the clandestine operations of the Chechnya War, hired assassins may silence their voice, as was the case with the most respected Russian journalist, Anna Politkovskaya, murdered in St. Petersburg on October 7, 2006, in circumstances that remain mysterious. Indeed, since 2000, 23 journalists have been killed in Russia, creating a situation that has been labeled by Reporters without Borders as "difficult" for the press and for freedom of expression. In the World Freedom Press Index, Russia ranks 144th in a list of 169 countries (Reporters without Borders, 2002–8).

Programming Communication Networks

The *bright spot for free expression in the Russian media lies with some radio stations*, in spite of the informal rule in state-controlled Russian radio networks that at least 50 percent of the news must be positive for the government (Kramer, 2007). The widely popular *Echo Moskvy*, in spite of being owned by Gazprom, features interviews with opposition leaders, including Gary Kasparov, although after his performance Kasparov was summoned for a follow-up interview with the FSB. There are also a number of media outlets that assert a certain level of political independence, such as the small national network REN TV, and a few national and regional newspapers. The Internet is not censored in terms of user-produced content (see below) and displays frequent criticism of the government in its online communities and blogs. In fact, Masha Lipman writes:

The government has radically curtailed broadcast freedom, but it does not totally control speech. Some broadcast, print and online outlets with smaller audiences have maintained relatively independent editorial lines, which serves to let off steam. These outlets may create an appearance of media freedom, but they are tightly insulated from national television, effectively marginalized and kept politically irrelevant. (Lipman, 2008: A13)

However, as in the rest of the world, the most important forms of *control over the media concern the network infrastructure and programming content*. In Russia, the state owns over 80 percent of radio and television infrastructure. It also has decisive influence over the main telecommunication companies, owns some of the largest film studios (Mosfilm), as well as the print presses of 40 percent of newspapers and 65 percent of books.[42] As for the content of programming, in major television networks the dominant trend since 2000 has been to follow the Western model by tilting content toward entertainment. A study by Ilya Kiriya (2007) on the distribution of programming by genres in 16 television networks shows that the percentage of entertainment and games programs increased from 32 percent in 2002 to 35 percent in 2005, and sports doubled from 4 to 8 percent, while news programs were halved from 16 to 8 percent. However, in a distinctive feature of the Russian culture, cultural and educational programs increased from 3 to 9 percent, although they remain concentrated in specialized networks. Films

[42] The material control of the print press is an old tradition in Russia. Among Lenin's first measures after seizing power in 1917 were the nationalization of telephone and telegraph networks, and printing paper production.

and television series still dominate programming (37% in 2005), with the majority of films being foreign films.

While most Russians hold critical views of American foreign policy, American sitcoms (such as *Married with Children*) are among the top programs in audience share. According to analyst Elena Prohkorova, this is a reflection of the changes in Russian society because "sitcoms require a very stable social life" (quoted in Levy, 2007). On the other hand, Danii B. Dondurei, chief editor of Cinema Art magazines, warns that "television is training people to not think about which party is in Parliament, about which laws are being passed, about who will be in charge tomorrow" (quoted in Levy, 2007). However, foreign domination of television programming may be changing, as Russian television networks are now producers of films and teleseries that, together with entertainment and games, occupy most of prime-time broadcasting.

However, while media programming is increasingly depoliticized, Russian interest in politics continues to be high. According to a nationwide poll conducted by the Public Opinion Foundation in July 2007, 48 percent of Russians were interested in political news (although only 35% of the younger group shared this interest). Forty-eight percent were also interested in international relations, and 40 percent in arts and culture. National television is the main source of news for 90 percent of the population (less so in Moscow: 82%), followed by national newspapers (30%) and regional television (29%). Interest in print news, however, is declining: 27 percent of Russians do not read any newspaper, and the most popular newspapers, such as *Komsomolskaya Pravda*, have adopted the tabloid genre, focusing on scandalous reporting of sex and violence (Public Opinion Foundation, 2007; Barnard, 2008).

Furthermore, the Russian public's disenchantment with Yeltsin's democrats, and Putin's popularity, after he restored order in the country while benefiting from energy-led economic growth, makes the use of the legislative, administrative, and corporate arsenal of media control mechanisms in the hands of the Russian state largely unnecessary. In the aforementioned Public Opinion Foundation poll, 41 percent of respondents found national television's political coverage satisfactorily objective, while 36 percent considered it biased (though Moscovites and college-educated people where more critical of the reporting). Political support for Putin influenced opinion on political news. The perception of objective reporting was much higher among the 47 percent of people who declared total trust in Putin than among the minority (21%) who distrusted the president. *In sum: rather than political censorship, in a situation of direct and indirect control over the media, and of majority support for the presidency, self-censorship largely accounts for state control of Russian media.*

And yet, there were no risks taken when it came to the presidential campaign of February 2008. In spite of the guaranteed victory of Putin-backed presidential candidate Dmitry Medvedev, the multifaceted control of the media was put at the service of the candidate. A study by the Center for Journalism in Extreme Situations (CJES; Melnikov, 2008) of presidential campaign television coverage showed that 60 percent of the airtime on Channel 1, the main network, was allocated to President Putin. Eighty-seven percent of these reports were positive toward Putin, and the rest were neutral. Medvedev accounted for another 32 percent of the coverage, usually with a positive tone. Similar biased distribution of airtime was found in the state-run channels Rossiya and TV Tsentr. As for the private television networks, NTV (remember, owned by Gazprom) allocated 54 percent of airtime to Putin and 43 percent to Medvedev, while REN TV was more balanced: Putin was given 31 percent of air time, but the three main candidates, Medvedev, Zyuganov, and Zhirinovsky all received about 21 percent each, and the tone of the reporting was generally neutral, except for Zhirinovsky whose coverage was negative. Yet, given the overwhelming dominance of state-controlled networks, the relative neutrality of REN made little difference. Thus, the CJES report concluded that the biased media coverage of the campaign was one of the major flaws of the election. It attributed it to political control of state-run national networks, as well as the pressure put on the majority of broadcasters in the regions. This media bias reproduced the situation that critics denounced in the parliamentary elections of December 2007. It appears that, through a wide range of procedures and practices, media control remains the mainstay of state power in Russia.

Does the Internet alter this environment of communication control? Although only about 25 percent of Russians are Internet users, excepting the use of email (Levada Center, 2008), and only 9 percent of the population cites the Internet as a source of political news, netizens are concentrated in the younger, more educated, more active, and more independent segments of the population. Indeed, in the Moscow region, the percentage of people citing the Internet as their source of political news increases to 30 percent (Public Opinion Foundation, 2007). Social spaces and blogs are quickly becoming a key domain of expression and interaction for Russia's new generation. Sites like Odnoklassniki.ru, created for former classmates to keep in touch around the country, or vkontakte.ru, the Russian equivalent of Facebook, are building social networks of users who feel free to communicate among themselves. Blogs are also rapidly springing up. According to Technorati, Russian blogs now represent about 2 percent of blogs in the world. The leading blog site is *Zhivoi Zhurnal* (Live Journal), created in the US in 1999, and acquired in 2005 by the Russian company SUP, and owned by the banker Aleksander Mamut. As in the rest of the world, only a handful of blogs are directly political, but political conversations take place in the blogosphere. In December 2007, bloggers exposed fraud and political pressures in the parliamentary elections: in one instance, a blogger uploaded a cell phone-recorded video of two officials stacking ballot boxes in a St. Petersburg polling office. Marina Litvinovitch, a communication expert supporting Gary Kasparov, asserted that "blogs are one of the most important supports for us ... There are a small number of internet users, maybe 2 percent, who use the net for political purposes, but they make a difference" (quoted in Billette, 2008).

Moreover, the global nature of the Internet, and the relative openness of its networks, represent a major challenge for a state historically obsessed with the control of information. The Russian state's first reaction, when observing the fast diffusion of the Internet, was to arm itself with the legal and technical means to control the net. As mentioned above, the Sorm 1 (1996) and Sorm 2 (1998) laws provided the ground for surveillance of the Internet, and instructed the Internet service providers to install a device in their servers, at their expense, to enable the FSB to track email, financial transactions, and online interactions in general. In 2000, a new directive was incorporated to Sorm 2 to include the surveillance of wired and wireless telephone communications, while updating controls over the Internet. The justification in every case is the fight against crime and cybercrime. While there is a provision for judicial control of surveillance, it is usually disregarded. In 2008, at the time of writing, the Duma was debating a "Model Law on the Internet" which, according to reports in the news portal lenta.ru, "will define the system of government support for the Internet, designate participants in the process of regulating the Internet as well as their functions when regulating and define the guidelines designating places and times of the performance of legally significant actions upon the use of the Internet." In reality, Russian laws do not censor content on the Internet. They simply allow surveillance to enforce in cyberspace whatever laws and decrees exist on any domain of activity, including national security laws, property laws, anti-pornographic decrees, anti-libel laws, and laws banning racist and anti-Semitic propaganda, although they are rarely enforced. Yet, from time to time, something happens, as in the case of a young man in Syktyvkar, arrested in April 2008 for posting an anti-Semitic comment on a friend's blog aimed at inciting violence against the police.[43] Regardless of the judgment on the content of the blog, it became clear that private conversation online is not private in Russia, and if it irks the police it does have consequences.

In spite of limited government action against Internet communication, it appears that *the Russian government is bracing itself for a battle in cyberspace*, using methods similar to those that have worked so well with the media. First: creating a legal environment in which surveillance is legal and enacted. Second: spreading intimidation through publicized exemplary punishments. Third: recruiting Internet service providers and webmasters into surveillance activities, by making them responsible for punishable content on their web sites. Fourth: using state-owned companies to buy popular web sites to make sure that their managers keep political matters under control. Thus, RuTube, the equivalent of YouTube, created in December 2006, with 300,000 users a day, was acquired by Gazprom Media in March 2008. Gazprom Media is planning to invest heavily in Internet media. And fifth, and foremost, the state is responding to the challenge of free communication networks by intervening in discussions and postings on the Internet through hired hands, or government moles posing as independent bloggers, an issue that was brought up in the online Russian forum of *The New York Times* in 2008. Indeed, corporate Internet executives dispute the notion of censorship on the Russian Internet. Thus, Anton Nosik, a leading figure of the Russian Internet since the 1990s, and director of Live Journal in 2008, asserts that:

There is no censorship in Live Journal...They are not that stupid in the Kremlin. They have seen that the Chinese or Vietnamese practice of censoring the Internet does not bring any good. They prefer a different method, trying to saturate the Russian net with their own propaganda sites and intervening with their own bloggers on the web.   (quoted in Billette, 2008)

Marina Litvinovitch, a liberal politician, seems to agree: "Internet is a natural reserve for the small Russian intellectual elite. The power sees it

[43] The blog read: "It would be a great idea if in the central square of each Russian city a furnace were built like in Auschwitz, and a faithless cop is burned once, or better twice a day" (quoted in Rodriguez, 2008).

this way, and tolerates this space of freedom considering that their capacity to make trouble is limited" (quoted in Billette, 2008). Medvedev, in contrast to Putin, is said to be a habitual reader of blogs and web sites.

However, should Russian society become more restive vis-à-vis the state, as a new generation overcomes the frustrations of the transition period and takes democracy and freedom of expression as citizens' rights, the state appears ready to extend its control of communication to the Internet and wireless networks. It is uncertain, though, how much actual political, cultural, and technical capacity for proceeding with systematic control the state will have in a world of global interactive networks. It is probable that if and when the time comes for such an effort, Russian bureaucrats will pay careful attention to the most determined and sophisticated attempt to date in controlling communication in the Internet Age: the Chinese experience.

China: Taming the Media Dragon, Riding the Internet Tiger

China's history has been marked by the relentless effort of the state to control communication. This obsession went so far as to forbid the building of ocean-going vessels in 1430 to curtail interaction with foreign countries, a move that, together with a number of other isolationist measures, is considered by some historians to have contributed to the technological retardation of what was probably until then the most knowledgeable civilization on earth (Mokyr, 1990). The advent of the Communist party-state in 1949 refined and deepened the systematic control of information and communication by the party apparatus with a primary focus on the media which became the property of the state. But the party leadership paid heightened attention to communication control from 1979 onward, as the post-Mao Communist leaders engaged in a vast transformation of the economy and society while hanging on to the party's monopoly of power and the primacy of Marxist-Leninist ideology, regardless of its anachronistic meaning in a China deliberately integrated into global capitalism (Hui, 2003). Moreover, the dramatic failure of Gorbachev, in his attempt to steer a similar economic and political transition, alerted the Chinese leaders to the perils of *glasnost*, deemed to be the critical blunder that brought Soviet society out of control. The stakes were made even higher when the issue of controlling communication was compounded by the need to modernize the infrastructure in information and communication technologies as a prerequisite to compete globally, a dilemma that lies at the heart of the collapse of the Soviet Union (Castells and Kiselyova, 1995). The Chinese leadership confronted the matter head on, with a clear purpose that would guide their action in the two following decades: to assert uncontested political dominance over society through communication control, while modernizing the telecommunications and information technology capabilities of the new China as the foundation of its economic competitiveness and its military power.

To do so, the party organized two sets of institutions (Zhao, 2008: 19–74). In December 2001, it established the State Leadership Group on Informatization (which included telecommunications), a supra-ministerial body chaired by the Prime Minister (Zhu Rongji at the time, other premiers subsequently). The group included the heads of most relevant communication and information agencies in technology industries, infrastructure, and security, establishing an "information cabinet" above the authority of the State Council to coordinate the entire range of policies dealing with the information economy and information security. When the Internet diffused in China in the early 2000s, an Internet Information Management Bureau was added to the group, as were all relevant agencies and commissions directing the building and management of communication networks. Under the guidance of this high-level group, various government agencies (particularly the General Administration of Press and Publications and the State Administration of Radio, Film, and Television) set regulations for the different sectors that comprise the media: newspapers, periodicals, publishing, electronic publications, film management, radio and television management, and management of satellite ground-reception facilities. Regulations concern both the industry itself and the content of its products. In addition, each government agency issued "stipulations" applying the general guidelines to its specific realm of activity.

To modernize the media industry and to focus it on commercialization and entertainment, while keeping tight political control, the government enacted a vast reform of the media in 2003, closing down multiple publications and stations, and reorganizing others. Media were open to commercialization, but with a specific status under which the rule of ownership by investors does not apply. Only the sponsoring organization (always dependent on the Communist Party) is acknowledged as investor. All other funding is treated either as a charitable donation or as a loan, so that media companies received commercial investment that can be rewarded with profits but the ownership and control remain in the hands of a party-controlled organization. Furthermore, any form of information dissemination must be licensed by the central government (Qinglian, 2004).

In addition, the party's traditional Propaganda Department strengthened its power and perfected its methods, a process that began by renaming the department the Publicity Department, a term considered to be more professional than "propaganda." This department covers all areas of potential diffusion of ideas and information in China, including, in addition to the media, cultural institutions, universities, and any form of organized ideological or political expression. It extends its activities to day-to-day control of media operations, television, radio, print press, news agencies, books, and the Internet. Yuezhi Zhao (2008) has analyzed and documented the actual operation of the control system by the Publicity Department. It works on a "directive mode," with specific instructions on specific information and guidelines conveyed by leaders' statements and reports from the Xinhua News Agency. A key mechanism is the so-called "brief meeting" that takes place regularly in all media organizations, in which the officials in charge of controlling information give instructions from the party and evaluate possible deviations from the party line. When journalists working for Chinese media organizations are not present at their "brief meetings," it is often the case that they receive an SMS from their supervisors telling them what not to report. This is the practice that Qiu calls "the wireless leash" (Qiu, 2007). According to Yuezhi Zhao, under Hu Jintao's leadership political discipline in the media has been reinforced through micro-management of information. Personnel control is also important, as journalists must be certified, and political ideology and acceptable social behavior are major requisites for certification.

However, as Yuezhi Zhao and other analysts have observed, the controlling process is more complex than it appears at first sight. It is unthinkable that in the most populated country in the world, and in a highly complex society, party committees could suppress any deviation in the elaboration and diffusion of media messages, particularly when, in most matters, directives cannot be precise to the smallest detail. And details matter, particularly in local contexts. This is why *its distributed structure is the critical mechanism through which communication control operates*. Political appointees closely surveil the entire media system in a cascade of controls that ultimately places responsibility on the shoulders of the immediate supervisor in charge of the production and distribution of each media message, so that generalized self-censorship is the rule.

Individual mistakes have a price. Historically, journalists would lose their jobs and, depending on the seriousness of their error, would be dealt with by the political police or the party's re-education programs. In recent, capitalism-obliging times, minor slips would result in the culprit seeing his or her meager salary cut in proportion to his/her fault. For instance, in China Central Television, according to a reliable account, each discrepancy of an anchor from the cue machine results in a fine of 250 yuan as of 2008. Therefore, in case of doubt, the journalist, or the anchorperson, or the writer, tends to opt for the politically correct version of his or her rendering. Alternatively, they can check with their supervisor who will proceed accordingly, thus distributing throughout the command and control hierarchy the internalization of censorship. Furthermore, those who have the power to interpret the guidelines apply the principle of party control with flexibility. This flexibility is critical for the system to work realistically, and also for the system to maintain its capacity for regeneration through relative openness to criticism. Thus, there are matters that are considered strategically important and others that are open to moderate criticism. For instance, the Communists have been for some time (less so recently) extremely worried about Falun Gong, as the cult appeared to be capable of triggering a messianic movement for the restoration of Chinese traditions (ironically under the guidance of a leader living in New York and organizing the movement via the Internet; Zhao, 2003). So, any reference to Falun Gong that is laudatory or even neutral is sure to ring all the alarms. Taiwan's independence is a sensitive matter. The memory of the Tiananmen massacre should be buried in history. Specific debates on democracy and on the leadership of the party are not welcome subjects. Human rights is a suspicious phrase in China unless clarified. The Tibetan question remains usually off limits for public debate, unless it is to reassert the sovereignty of the Chinese state or to remind the populace of the Dalai Lama's Nazi connections in World War II. And reports of catastrophes, be it SARS epidemic or earthquakes, have to be sanitized to avoid public alarm, albeit during both the SARS outbreak and the Sichuan earthquake there were moments when government censorship could not be fully enforced.

So, what is left? In fact, almost everything else, which is the overwhelming proportion of topics and ideas that are of concern to the Chinese people. So, criticism of local or provincial government officials is often published in the media as it is, in fact, one of the forms of political in-fighting in the party (Guo and Zhao, 2004; Liu, 2004). Citizens' claims to their rights, as well as reports about peasants' protests and displaced city-dwellers, populate the Chinese press in a filtered mode, albeit less so in television (Hsing, forthcoming). And debates on social problems, within the rhetorical limits of respect for the party, are the daily staple of the Chinese media.

Furthermore, what is forbidden, and what is not, changes with context and with the interpretation of party line by specific censors. In an indicative expression of the reality of Chinese censorship on the ground, Zhao (2008: 25) writes that:

Some topics are either completely forbidden or to be reported under strict control...Other taboo topics are of more transient nature and are "defined situationally." Thus in the words of one cyber essayist, the party line is "not a straight line, but an ever-changing and hard-to-grasp curve." A range of factors, including the shifting focus of the party's policy priorities at a given period, intra-elite power struggles, domestic and international political climates, and, indeed, changes in the political season...are all possible variables. Rather than undermining the effectiveness of party control, however, the ever shifting and unpredictable nature of the party line ensures its continuing relevance and its disciplinary power.

How do journalists, media executives, and bloggers alike manage the uncertainty and complexity of the rules governing communication? Fan Dong (2008b) points to the fact that there is lifelong training through the education system in interpreting the signals from political oversight, so that people sense in each context what is politically correct. Reporting on her study of the control of Chinese media, she states that her interviewees are capable of concretizing the ambiguity of general regulations and instructions in the reality of their professional environment. They learn by doing on the basis of their experience. She refers to a Chinese saying: "people can always find a way to cope with Chinese government policies" (Dong, 2008b: 8).

However, while the Chinese model of control of traditional media is both comprehensive and reasonably effective, *the issue of the feasibility of extrapolating this model to the Internet arises*. Indeed, this is a question that dominates the debate about the true freedom of the Internet throughout the world. How contradictory is, in Qiu's (2004) terms, the diffusion of technologies of freedom in a statist society? Because the actuality of this diffusion exists: while in 2007, there were 210 million Internet users in China, compared to 216 million in the US, according to government statistics in July 2008, there were 253 million Internet users in China, which now makes it the country with the highest number of Internet users in the world (CNNIC, 2008). The Chinese government has fully embraced the Internet as a business, as well as an educational, cultural, and propaganda tool. For instance, on June 25, 2008, President Hu Jintao interacted with netizens for four minutes on the People's Net, which belongs to the Xinhua News Agency, and emphasized

281

the importance of the Internet as a tool of democracy, while calling on government officials to engage in similar dialogues with citizens. Yet, the Chinese government, like many governments in the world, is unyielding in its long-standing practice of surveilling content, blocking unwanted messages, and punishing the messengers accordingly. But how can the government exercise control over such a gigantic, decentralized network of communication, connected to global networks, in which Chinese users spend over two billion hours a week?

Since the late 1990s, the Chinese government has attempted to control the Internet with the same determination that it displayed for decades vis-à-vis the media industry. The same agencies in charge of controlling communication set up specific units to police the Internet. As early as February 1996, a decree was issued, and revised in May 1997, establishing measures for the purpose of channeling international Internet traffic through approved gateways; to license Internet service providers; to register all Internet users; and to ban harmful information. Additional decrees aimed to improve "network security" and to ban unlicensed encryption. Over the years, flurries of new regulations and intimidating measures have accompanied the irresistible rise of the Internet as a mass self-communication network in China. Technically, a "Great Firewall" was set up to block web sites considered to be potential sources of unwanted information; according to some sources, this includes as many as 10 percent of sites on the World Wide Web. Advanced Internet and tracking technologies were implemented, and the most sophisticated blocking system in the world (the Golden Shield Project) was contracted to Cisco, although its expected deployment is still to be completed at the time of writing in mid-2008.

On the human side of political repression, dozens of Internet users have been tracked down, arrested, and punished (some jailed) for Internet hacking, propagating Falun Gong, "inciting subversion," or spreading rumors that cause public alarm, such as the SARS epidemic (Qiu, 2004: 111). Furthermore, a number of web sites around the world, including some of the main Western media (for example, *The New York Times*), have been blocked for a period of time, and major sites such as YouTube have been shut down in China during critical times. Besides, cyber cafés, considered to be the hub of free Internet use, are regularly closed, and relentlessly harassed and surveilled. And yet, the technical effectiveness of controls is questionable. This is because, as a last resort, surveillance mechanisms are based on automated content analysis systems that track key words. Thus, if people do not use "dirty words" (such as Falun Gong, porn, Tiananmen, Taiwan, or democracy), the robots are unlikely to detect a punishable message, even with new semantic context analysis systems of the latest generation of surveillance technologies. People can use "tricks," finding ways to say what they want without saying the word. Only the most notorious web sites are blocked. Most other web sites, including those of mainstream Western media, are only blocked for limited periods of time. Chinese Internet users can also use "proxy" sites, using peer-to-peer networks, rather than link directly to suspected web sites. While there is an obligation for every Internet user to be registered, as Qiu (2004: 112) writes:

There is no systematic way to ensure that each of China's 59 million Internet users is registered or that the registration information is verified. Usually one can access the Net at a cybercafé without showing an ID card; and it is a common practice for people to use "Get Online Cards (*shangwangka*)" that provide dial-up connections without asking for any personal information. Although the censorship regime tries to block, filter, and track, most determined users in China can access outlawed information via encrypted messages, FTP, and most recently, peer-to-peer technologies.

This is why *the most effective system of controlling the Internet in China* is the one that reproduces the time-tested method used over the years to control the media: *the cascading hierarchy of surveillance that ultimately induces self-censorship at all levels*, and makes the culprit pay at each level when a significant failure of control is detected (Dong, 2008b). Thus, the property of Internet access providers is in the hands of the government. Internet service providers are licensed, and are liable for the diffusion of any undue content over the Internet. Internet content providers are also liable, and additionally must attend government-training sessions and obtain a certificate to operate their service. They must also keep records of their traffic and yield all content provided by their users, as well as their logs, to the authorities upon request. This also applies to Internet cafés. Yet, user-generated content is more difficult to control. This is why the ultimate, and most effective, level of control lies with the webmasters. But here lies the secret flexibility of the control system, following the analysis of Dong (2008b). According to Guo Liang, the author of the *Academy of Social Sciences' Internet User Report in China*, in an interview with Dong, the personality, age, and background of the webmasters have a direct impact on the style and content of online interaction. While older webmasters are stricter about deleting content, those who belong to the new generation of Internet users better understand the meaning of what people (usually young people) say, and the limits of what could be offensive to the higher powers. There follows a mixture of complicity and self-censorship that makes Internet life livable for the overwhelming majority of Internet users, those who do not have a political agenda, even if they sometimes interact about politics. This is, in fact, the fundamental point to be made concerning the control of the Internet in China.

In her study on "The actual effectiveness of Internet control in China," Dong (2008b) observed online interaction in two Chinese forums for several weeks in the spring of 2008, recording comments, including those exchanged with the webmasters. One of the forums was in China, while the other was in the United States and thus free of government control. She used key words to search for interaction concerning issues divided into three categories: the most politically sensitive (e.g., Falun Gong, Tiananmen); those considered moderately sensitive (e.g., Tibet, Taiwan, democracy, human rights); and the least sensitive, though still controversial issues, such as corruption and freedom. She found that the most sensitive issues were not directly treated in either forum, although Falun Gong was referred to indirectly in the American-based forum. The webmaster submitted to a vote regarding the issue, and after it was approved, he let it go, actually prompting a flurry of criticism against "the wheels" (the followers of Falun Gong) from the forum's participants. For the second kind of issues, both Tibet and Taiwan, there were heated discussions in both forums, and in both forums the same mechanism operated: the content of the political position did not determine whether the message was blocked, but its tone did. For instance, "we should liberate Taiwan now!" was deemed too controversial. As for the third level of issues debated, corruption was freely discussed in both forums, but while in China the focus was on specific corruption cases by local officials, in the US-based forum the discussion referred to corruption as a problem of Chinese society.

Although the results of this interesting, but limited, case study cannot be extrapolated, their implications are meaningful. Political debate on the Internet is steered flexibly by webmasters, and is largely self-managed by the participants in online forums. The overwhelming proportion of user-produced content on the Internet is apolitical, and thus does not come under the aegis of censors. As for the small number of political debaters, support for China as a nation, often identified with the government, accounts for the majority of opinions. This observation was vindicated in the spring of 2008 when Western criticism of Chinese repression of political demonstrations in Tibet triggered a political storm on the Chinese Internet, particularly intense among Chinese students abroad, which denounced the Western media for image manipulation and defended China, and the government, against what they considered to be colonialist attacks. Although it is probable that the Chinese government fueled the flames of the students' indignation, there are indications that it was a genuine movement. Indeed, the Chinese government blocked access to YouTube to appease the controversy, thus censoring the videos that the students had posted in support of China.

There is, indeed, a major question underlying the relationship between China and the Internet. It is often assumed that large proportions of Chinese people suffer under Communism and cannot voice their criticism. In fact, survey data show that in 2005, 72 percent of Chinese were satisfied with the national conditions of their country, a proportion higher than any other country in the world (Pew Global Attitudes Project, 2005). Among students and youth in general, the main political ideology that generates large support is nationalism, particularly against Japan and Taiwan. The Communist Party, who came to power as a nationalist movement in the "patriotic war" against Japan before vanquishing the Kuomintang, has been able to depict its leadership as the expression of the independence and future greatness of China. Thus, while democracy, which has never been known in the country, remains an abstract ideal, espoused by a tiny intellectual minority, the wounds of colonialism and foreign humiliation remain vivid, and promote support for the nation, and its government, among the young generation. If we add the fact that over two-thirds of Internet use in China concerns entertainment, and that the main preoccupation of the educated urban-dwellers who are the bulk of Internet users is the enjoyment of consumerism (Chinese Academy of Social Sciences, 2007), it may well be that the gigantic system deployed by the Chinese government to control the Internet results more from a reflex of the past than from a current necessity. As for the future, it appears that the uprising of peasants and displaced city-dwellers against the speculative land grab at the heart of China's primitive accumulation may be a much more serious threat than the salon gossip chitchatting of the Internet (Hsing, forthcoming).

And so, *state power, in its most traditional manifestation, that is manipulation and control, is pervasive in the media and the Internet throughout the world*. It constitutes yet another layer of media politics aimed at influencing behavior by constructing meaning. But it does not cancel the processes of power-making examined in this chapter. In fact, scandal politics often relates to the capacity of the state itself, and not just of political actors, to fabricate, reveal or block damaging information regarding its opponents. In some instances, the conflicts within the state are fought over the media, at times through the use of scandal politics. Thus, there are multiple forms of media politics, but they all share two fundamental features: they are aimed at power-making by shaping the public mind; and they contribute to the crisis of political legitimacy that is shaking the institutional foundations of our societies.

The Demise of Public Trust and the Crisis of Political Legitimacy

As documented in Figures A4.1–A4.8 (see Appendix at the back of the book), a majority of citizens in the world do not trust their governments or their parliaments, and an even larger group of citizens despise politicians and political parties, and think that their government does not represent the will of the people. This includes advanced democracies, as numerous surveys show that public trust in government and political institutions has substantially decreased in the past three decades: for example, the World Economic Forum's Voice of the People Survey (2008), the Eurobarometer (2007), the Asian Barometer (2008), the Latinobarometro (Corporación Latinobarometro, 2007), Accenture (2006), Transparency International (2007), the BBC (Globescan, 2006), the World Values Survey (Dalton, 2005b) and worldpublicopinion.org (Kull et al., 2008). According to WorldPublicOpinion.org (Kull et al., 2008), an average of 63 percent of respondents in all 18 nations included in the survey believed that their country was "run by a few big interests looking out for themselves" and only 30 percent thought that it was run "for the benefit of all people" (p. 6). In September 2007, only 51 percent of Americans exhibited a "great deal" or a "fair amount" of trust in the federal government, the lowest percentage since Gallup began fielding the question in 1972 (Jones, 2007a). In the European Union, according to the Eurobarometer (2007), over 80 percent of citizens do not trust political parties, and over two-thirds do not trust their national government. In Latin America, 77 percent of Voice of the People Survey respondents thought that their political leaders were dishonest (World Economic Forum, 2008).

Why is this so? To be sure, dissatisfaction with specific policies, and with the state of the economy and society at large, are important factors in accounting for citizen disaffection. Yet, survey data find that *perception of corruption is the most significant predictor of political distrust*. While the rate of decline of trust varies by country, the overall downward trend is evidenced in almost all of the more developed countries (except The Netherlands between the 1970s and 1990s). Hetherington (2005), Warren (2006), and others argue that trust in government by itself has now become an important and independent predictor of support for government policies, and is more important than partisanship or ideology alone. Different forms of political trust interact with each other. Lack of trust toward specific incumbents, for instance, can transform itself into a distrust of different political institutions, and, ultimately, of the political system as a whole. Political trust is closely linked to general social trust. Social capital studies (e.g., Putnam, 2000) argue that civic engagement and interpersonal trust contribute to overall social and thus political trust. Overall, while trust in societal institutions has declined sharply (with slight fluctuations) in the post-World War II period, the impact of this decline is not uniform or straightforward. For example, declining political trust does not necessarily mean lower voter turnout or declining civic engagement, as I will analyze below. However, there is consensus that prolonged periods of distrust in government breeds dissatisfaction with the political system and may have critical implications for democratic governance.

Acknowledging the problem, governments around the world have established new regulations to mitigate appearances of corruption, and increased the number of political inquiries and judicial controls. Despite these efforts, perception of corruption is on the rise everywhere. A 2007 survey conducted by Transparency International (Global Corruption Barometer Survey, pp. 8, 9, and following) found that:

- The general public believes that political parties, parliament, the police, and the judicial/legal system are the most corrupt institutions in their societies.
- Political parties (about 70%) and the legislative branch (about 55%) are perceived by people around the world to be the institutions most tainted by corruption.
- The poor, whether in developing or highly industrialized countries, are the most penalized by corruption. They are also more pessimistic about the prospects for less corruption in the future.
- About 1 in 10 people around the world had to pay a bribe in the past year. Reported bribery has increased in Asia-Pacific and South-east Europe.
- Bribery is particularly widespread in interactions with the police, the judiciary, and registry and permit services.

- Half of those interviewed – and significantly more than four years earlier – expect corruption in their country to increase in the next three years, with some African countries being the exception (probably a function of the current level of corruption).
- Half of those interviewed think that their government's efforts to fight corruption are ineffective.
- NGOs, religious organizations, and the military are perceived by citizens to be the least affected by corruption.
- In general, citizens' perceptions about corruption in key institutions did not change dramatically between 2004 and 2007. But opinion about some institutions, such as the private sector, has deteriorated over time. This means that the public now has more critical views of the role of business in the corruption equation than it did in the past. Comparing 2004 and 2007 data, there was an increase in the proportion of people around the world who consider NGOs to be corrupt. However, the proportion of people around the world who consider the judiciary, parliament, the police, tax revenue authorities, and medical and education services to be corrupt decreased slightly in the 2004–7 period, although the majority of people still had a negative view of the government and judicial institutions.

Why is the perception of corruption so important for political trust? After all, it is a pervasive practice as old as humankind. Yet, since democracy is essentially procedural, as I argued in Chapter 1, if the process of power allocation in state institutions and the management of governing institutions can be modified by extra-procedural actions in favor of specific interest groups or individuals, there is no reason why citizens should respect the orderly delegation of power to their rulers. *What follows is a crisis of legitimacy; that is, a widespread lack of belief in the right of political leaders to make decisions on behalf of citizens for the well-being of society at large.* Governance becomes a practice to be endured with resignation, or resisted when possible, rather than supported after deliberation. When citizens think that government and political institutions cheat on a regular basis, everybody feels entitled to become an equal-opportunity cheater. Consequently, the seeds of institutional disintegration are sown. In moments of social explosion, people in many countries join the rallying cry of the Argentinian protesters who brought down their government in 2001: "*Que se vayan todos!!!* [All should go away]," referring to the entire political class.

Furthermore, while corruption may not have increased substantially in recent history (the opposite is more likely), what has increased is the publicity of corruption, the perception of corruption, and the impact of such perception on political trust. According to Warren (2006: 7), psychological political trust involves an assessment of the moral values and attributes associated with a certain government, political institution, and/or individual political leaders. As such, it refers to the perspective that people might have on the trustworthiness of their political representatives. In political trust based on psychological reasoning, people search for sincerity and truthfulness in the personality, public appearance, speech, and behavior of their political leaders.

Therefore, *the connection between exposure to political corruption and the decline of political trust can be directly related to the dominance of media politics and the politics of scandal in the conduct of public affairs.* A number of studies have found evidence of the relationship between the decline of general political trust and the recurrence of scandal politics. Treisman (2000) analyzed a sample of countries, using data from the University of Michigan's World Values Survey, and found a direct correlation between perceived corruption and lower political trust, when the effects of GNP and political structure are controlled. However, looking at Germany, Herbert Bless and colleagues (Bless et al., 2000; Schwarz and Bless, 1992; Bless and Schwarz, 1998) found that the impact of scandals on young adults' judgments is not as simple as it would appear at first glance. They showed that the effect of a German political scandal on political judgment depended on who was being judged. More precisely, the activation of a negative frame on the politician involved in a scandal (i.e., an untrustworthy politician) decreased judgments of trustworthiness of politicians in general (the category) but increased judgments of trustworthiness of other specific politicians not involved in the scandal. Regner and Le Floch (2005) replicated Bless's research design in the French context. While they found similar outcomes in participants with high levels of knowledge about the Dumas/Elf Oil Affair, they found the reverse to be true for participants with little knowledge. Those with a high level of knowledge displayed contrast effects and ranked other politicians more highly in contrast to politicians involved in the scandal. Those with lower levels of knowledge displayed no such effects: they found all politicians, as well as politics in general, less trustworthy.

While there is a consensus that general societal trust and institutional trust has decreased (Putnam, 1995; Brehm and Rahn, 1997; Robinson and Jackson, 2001), there is debate about the role of the media in this process. A number of scholars argue that negative media coverage leads to "media malaise" among citizens, increasing feelings of ineffectiveness, cynicism, and isolation (for example, Patterson, 1993; Putnam 1995, 2000; Cappella and Jamieson, 1997; Mutz and Reeves, 2005; Groeling and Linneman, 2008). They argue generally that, while it is unclear whether civil discourse has changed dramatically over time, the proliferation of media platforms, particularly television, means that citizens are increasingly exposed to uncivil political actions, which leads to declining estimations of political institutions. Robinson (1975) was the first to coin the term "videomalaise" to refer to this phenomenon. The current trend is to refer to "media malaise" as negative coverage on television that is mimicked across mediums.

On the other hand, a smaller but influential group of scholars, such as Inglehart (1990), Norris (1996, 2000), and Aarts and Semetko (2003), argue that the increase in media coverage creates a stronger connection between the governed and the governors, leading to a "virtuous circle" of increasing civic engagement. However, the terms of the debate need clarification. What Norris's data show is that people who are more politically engaged are more attentive to the media. But this does not say much about the direction of their engagement. Politically active citizens are eager to retrieve information from all possible sources. However, if a growing bulk of political information comes under the terms of scandal politics, greater exposure to this information undermines trust in the political system, although it may lead to mobilization for systemic change. In other words, it appears that *scandal politics is more directly related to the crisis of trust than media politics per se*. Yet, because scandal politics operates through the media, and because it is the consequence of the dynamics of media politics, as I have argued above, the majority of studies find a correlation between media coverage (both slant and volume) and evaluations of social and political institutions. Thus, Fan et al. (2001) found that press coverage of the press itself, the military, and organized religion has an effect on confidence in these institutions as measured by General Social Survey data. Hibbing and Theiss-Morse (1998) found, in the US context, that those citizens who rely mainly on television or radio to evaluate political institutions had significantly more negative emotional evaluations of the US Congress than people who are exposed to the media less, though their cognitive perceptions were the same. In an experimental study, Mutz and Reeves (2005) found that television exposure to uncivil political discourse significantly reduced trust in politicians in general, trust in Congress, and trust in the American political system, while exposure to a televised civil discourse increased trust (see Figure A4.8 in Appendix).

Other studies suggest that individuals who rely on television as their main source of news are more likely to experience "media malaise" because the visual medium enhances the importance of personality characteristics (Keeter, 1987; Druckman, 2003). So, arguably, *it appears that news coverage of political scandals has a greater impact in the pervasive, audiovisual media environment that characterizes our society.*

The relationship between media-driven scandals and public distrust extends beyond the realm of politics to the institutions of society at large. Thus, in an experimental study, Groeling and Linneman (2008) found that individuals who were exposed to media stories about sexual scandals in the Catholic Church (specifically the Boston cardinal scandal) in the treatment group exhibited significant declines in trust in the church as an institution as well as in other institutions not directly involved in the scandal.

However, the relationship between scandal politics and political trust is mediated by the cultural and ideological context in which the scandals play out. For instance, analyzing the political effects of the Argentinian arms scandal, Waisbord (2004b) found that perceived corruption is critical to the sociopolitical ramifications of scandal. In order for scandals to grab the public imagination, "scandals require the publicity of information that contradicts widely held ideas about individuals" (2004b: 1090). So, if the public already perceives that the government is corrupt, as was the case of 96 percent of people in Argentina, then scandals like the Argentinian arms deal fail to attract attention because these stories merely confirm what people already suspected/expect.[44] Perceived widespread corruption thus fosters the "banalization of corruption," resulting in what Waisbord calls "scandal fatigue," which reduces the reformative and transformative potential of scandals (2004b: 1091). This is not to say that scandal politics and public distrust are not related. It means that when distrust is already ingrained in people's consciousness, any additional revelation simply reaffirms disaffection with political institutions.

A decisive mediation is *the ideological context in which scandal politics takes place.* Thus, in the United States, between 1980 and 2004 political trust generally evolved in a similar pattern among distinct ideological groups, suggesting a low correlation between ideological self-placement and trust. After 9/11, this relationship changed fundamentally. Although it is unclear

---

[44] Waisbord's (2004b) work raises definitional issues. Should major instances of revealed corruption like the Argentinian arms deal be labeled as scandals even if the public remain largely uninterested in the story? Or can we differentiate between elite-centered mediated scandals and public-opinion-centered mediated scandals?

whether this pattern will hold in the future, the period between 2000 and 2004 saw political trust in the government surge among conservatives, and slightly increase among non-ideologues, while political trust among liberals and moderates plummeted (Hetherington, 2008: 20–2). Hetherington believes that these patterns demonstrate that "without question the Bush presidency and the lockstep support the president received from the Republican majority in Congress has politicized what it means for ordinary citizens to trust the government in Washington" (2008: 22). Therefore, while scandal politics and media politics tend to negatively affect political trust in a given context characterized by sharp ideological polarization, militant support or opposition to the government finds arguments in the revelations of scandals or dismisses them as propaganda, following the cognitive mechanism of selective information processing that I analyzed in Chapter 3.

The irony is that, *as the media play their role in propagating scandals and delegitimizing institutions, they confront the risk of losing their own legitimacy vis-à-vis their audience.* Trust in the media as an institution declined by 21 percent between 1973 and 2000 (Fan et al., 2001: 827). In the words of Fan and his colleagues (2001: 826–52), *the media may have become "the suicidal messenger."* In their study, they examined the relationship between press coverage of the media itself and subsequent public opinion of the press. For contrast, they also examined the same trends for coverage and public opinion of the military and organized religion. They found that coverage of religious scandals reduces confidence in religious institutions and that military trust was relatively stable at a high level, with a spike around the first Gulf War. They also found that, unlike trust in other institutions, trust in the press is predicted by a rise in media stories about the general failure of the press and their loss of reporting credibility – in other words, they are their own suicidal messenger. This builds upon their previous work, which shows that press stories featuring conservatives complaining about liberal press bias increase perceptions that the overall press is biased (Watts et al., 1999). Along a similar line of argument, Wyatt et al. (2000) found that the best predictor of both press confidence and media credibility was overall confidence in other institutions as measured by the General Social Survey.[45] Their findings suggest that both confidence and credibility of the press are measures of affect toward institutions in general rather than

---

[45] They also found a significant relationship between general confidence in the press and the specific credibility rating of the news medium that respondents used most.

indicators of whether audiences believe simple factual statements made in particular stories or programs (Fan et al., 2001). In other words, while negative reporting about the press does not appear to call the press itself into question, negative news on social institutions at large may undermine the credibility of all institutions, including the media.

Thus, *there appears to be a connection, however mediated and complex, between media politics, scandal politics, and the decline of trust in political institutions.* Yet, the decisive question is: how does this growing distrust among the citizenry affect political participation and political behavior? The answer to this question is highly differentiated, depending on political contexts and institutional regimes.

Everywhere in the world we perceive a trend of discontent vis-à-vis political parties and political institutions. *But this does not necessarily translate into withdrawal from the political system.* Citizens have a number of alternatives. First, they may mobilize against a given political option, following the general pattern of negative politics, as Spaniards did in 1996, 2004, and 2008. Second, they may mobilize in terms of their strongly felt ideology and put their organizational strength to the service of a mainstream party and capture it by becoming an indispensable constituency, as Evangelicals have done with the Republican Party in the United States. Third, they may support third-party candidacies as a protest vote, as was the case in France during the presidential elections of 2002, Ross Perot's candidacy in the US in 1992, and (repeatedly) with the Liberals, Social Democrats, and Liberal Democrats in the UK, in spite of constraints established in the British electoral system. Fourth, they rally around an insurgent candidacy that challenges the political establishment from within the system, as with the 2003 Lula candidacy in Brazil and the 2008 Obama campaign in the United States, or from outside the system, as in the cases of the first candidacies of Chávez in Venezuela, Morales in Bolivia, or Correa in Ecuador. Fifth, if none of the above is feasible, they may vote with their feet (except in countries, such as Italy or Chile, in which voting is mandatory), though this is clearly the last choice for people who still try to make their voices heard in spite of the little hope they harbor about how much change politics can bring to their lives. Then, they still have a sixth possibility: to increase social mobilization outside the political system. Indeed, this type of movement outside the system was documented by Inglehart and Catterberg (2002) who, using data from the World Values Survey, measured indicators of elite-challenging action outside the institutional system for 70 countries. They observed increased social mobilization throughout the 1990s. This is consistent with the study we conducted with Imma Tubella in Catalonia, which showed that, while only 2 percent of the population participate in the activity of political parties (although they do vote in general elections), and a majority of citizens do not trust political parties, over two-thirds think that they can change society by self-reliant mobilization (Castells, 2007).

Even in the United States, considered, until 2008, an extreme case of voter apathy among advanced democracies, Mark Hetherington (2005, 2008) and others have shown that, despite the polarization of elites and heightened levels of distrust, political participation and engagement is actually on the rise. Popkin (1994) argues that voter turnout as a percentage of the voting-age population is not a reliable indicator of change over time. In the contemporary United States, in the context of massive minority criminalization and widespread undocumented immigration, a much higher proportion of the voting-age population than in other countries is ineligible to vote because people have been disenfranchised by their pasts as convicts or by virtue of their citizenship status (see Chapter 5). Therefore, the voting-eligible population (VEP) is a more appropriate denominator in calculating voter turnout. When this statistic is used, it shows that voter turnout has increased over the past three presidential elections, from about 52 percent in 1996 to over 60 percent in 2004, and it reached 63 percent in the 2008 presidential election (Center for the Study of the American Electorate, 2008). VEP-based turnout was almost exactly the same in 2004 as it was in 1956, and only about 3.5 percentage points lower than in 1960 (Hetherington, 2008: 5). Moreover, in the United States there has been increased citizen involvement in the political process in the 2000–2004 period, as shown in Tables A4.4 and A4.5 in the Appendix, largely due to efforts by political parties to connect with their constituencies. Hetherington (2008) also finds that those with heavy ideological slants are much more likely to be contacted by a political party (see Figure A4.9 in the Appendix). The Democratic presidential primary of 2008 saw unprecedented levels of political mobilization in the United States (see Chapter 5).

This increased capacity of political parties to mobilize support may be linked to the use of the tools of informational politics analyzed above in this chapter. Moreover, the Internet is playing a major role in facilitating both autonomous mobilization and direct linkage between parties, candidates, and potential supporters (see Table A4.5 and Table A5.6 in the Appendix). Thus, Shah et al. (2005) found that informational media use encourages citizen communication, which in turn induces civic engagement. What is most intriguing about these findings is the role played by the Internet.

Online information seeking and interactive civic messaging – uses of the web as a resource and a forum – both strongly influence civic engagement, often more so than do traditional print and broadcast media and face-to-face communication (Shah et al., 2005: 551).

The relationship between political trust and civic engagement appears to be different in new and established democracies. While increased civic engagement brings enhanced social and political working trust in the industrialized world, Brehm and Rahn (1997) found a negative relationship between civic engagement and political trust in the developing world. In other words, those who are more civically involved in the developing world show lower political trust. This finding converges with the results of the cross-cultural study by Inglehart and Catterberg (2002). Their data show that in the new democracies of Latin America and Eastern Europe, once people had experienced democracy after regime change, there was a decline in political participation during the following years, prompting what they label a post-honeymoon decline in democratic support. However, disenchantment with democracy, and the consequent reduction in political participation, lead in many cases to accrued sociopolitical mobilization (Inglehart and Catterberg, 2002), thus increasing the gap between political institutions and political participation.

So, *the international experience shows the diversity of political responses to the crisis of political legitimacy*, often depending on electoral rules, institutional specificity, and ideological situations, as I tried to document in my analysis of the crisis of democracy in the network society (Castells, 2004c: 402–18). In many cases, the crisis of legitimacy leads to an increase in political mobilization rather than to political withdrawal. *Media politics and scandal politics contribute to the worldwide crisis of political legitimacy but a decline in public trust is not tantamount to a decline in political participation.* Challenged by citizens' disaffection, political leaders search for new ways to reach out and activate their constituencies. Distrustful of political institutions, but dedicated to asserting their rights, citizens look for ways of mobilizing within and outside the political system on their own terms. *It is precisely this growing distance between belief in political institutions and desire for political action that constitutes the crisis of democracy.*

Crisis of Democracy?

While there is no doubt about the worldwide crisis of political legitimacy, it is unclear if and how this translates into a crisis of democracy. To assess this fundamental issue, we need to be precise about the meaning of democracy. Indeed, democracy as an historical practice, in contrast to democracy as a concept of political philosophy, is contextual. In the early twenty-first century, in a globally interdependent world, democracy is usually understood as the form of government resulting from the will of citizens choosing between competitive candidacies in relatively free elections held at mandated intervals of time under judicial control. I introduce relativity to signal the wide range of interpretations of the notion of free elections. To be generous and realistic, let us set the 2000 US presidential election in Florida as a minimum standard. In addition, for the practice of governance to be perceived as democratic, a certain level of freedom of expression, association, and respect for human rights, as well as some mechanisms of administrative and judicial controls on government, must be asserted by the laws and constitution of the country. Even by this low level of institutional requirements for democracy, numerous countries in the world do not fit these criteria, and some important nations, such as China, would not recognize the definition of democracy in those terms, or would interpret it in ways that sharply depart from the ideal type of representative democracy. Furthermore, countries accounting for a large proportion of the world population established formally democratic institutions only in the past 60 years, and in many countries these institutions remain highly unstable. This is to say that, in a global perspective, democracy is in perma-crisis. The real question is: how democratic are the self-proclaimed democracies, and how stable are their institutions when confronted with the growing gap between their constitutional rules and the beliefs of their citizens? It is from this vantage point that I will assess the potential crisis of democracy as it relates to media politics.

To a large extent, the crisis of legitimacy and its consequences for democratic practice is related to the crisis of the nation-state in the global network society, as a result of the contradictory processes of globalization and identification, as analyzed in Chapter 1. Since modern representative democracy was established in the realm of the nation-state by constructing individual citizens as legally based political subjects, the efficiency and legitimacy of the state have been diminished by its inability to control global networks of wealth, power, and information, while its representation is blurred by the rise of identity-based cultural subjects. Attempts to reassert the power of the nation-state by the traditional means of the use of force, particularly intense in the post-9/11 period, quickly found the limits of global interdependency and culturally based counter-domination strategies.

The gradual building of global governance networks still remains dependent on national political institutions in interaction with local and global civil society. Thus, the relationship between people's beliefs and political institutions continues to be central to power relationships. The greater the distance between citizens and governments, the lower the capacity of governments to conciliate their global endeavors with their local/national sources of legitimacy and resources.

It is in this specific context that we must understand the consequences of media politics for the practice of democracy. Media politics, and its corollary, scandal politics, have deepened the crisis of legitimacy at the very moment when the nation-state is most in need of the trust of its citizens to navigate the uncertain waters of globalization, while incorporating values of identity, individualism, and citizenship. However, in spite of massive citizen disaffection vis-à-vis the political class, and vis-à-vis democracy as they experience it, more often than not people around the world have not given up on their democratic ideals, though they interpret them in their own way. What we observe is that citizens at large have adopted a variety of strategies to correct or challenge the malfunctioning of the political system, as I analyzed above. These different reactions/proactions have distinct effects on the practice and institutions of democracy.

Thus, the vote to punish incumbent politicians, rather than hoping for the future, may correct the mismanagement of politicians by sending a powerful warning that their power and their careers depend on listening to their constituents. Yet, when repeated warnings have limited effect, and when the parties brought to power by the protest vote reproduce the same neglect of public decency, a downward spiral develops, adding negativity and cynicism to a fatigued citizenry. However, rather than abandoning their rights, citizens often turn to third parties, or to new leaders outside the mainstream, in what has come to be labeled as *insurgent politics*. If their support results in new projects, and eventually in new policies more closely aligned with their values and interests, democratic institutions could be regenerated, at least for awhile, as long as some new political blood flows through the veins of democracy, precisely because of the adaptability of democratic institutions to new actors and new ideas. Yet, in other instances, challenging the failure of democratic politics to address the concerns of society may lead to political change outside the institutional system. This change is often led by populist leaders who break with the past on behalf of new popular legitimacy, usually resulting in a re-foundation of institutions. In cases of radical protest, discontent may produce revolution; that is, political change independent of the formal procedures of political succession. This process results in a new state, transformed by the new power relationships embedded within it. In extreme situations, military force may directly or indirectly intervene in the transformation or restoration of political institutions, thus breaking with democratic practice. In all cases of institutional rupture deviating from constitutionally mandated practices, media politics and scandal politics play a major role in brewing discontent and articulating challenges. In this sense, they are directly linked to the crisis of democracy.

Yet, there is another, less apparent, form of crisis. If we accept the idea that the critical form of power-making takes place through the shaping of the human mind, and that this process is largely dependent on communication, and ultimately on media politics, then *the practice of democracy is called into question when there is a systemic disassociation between communication power and representative power*. In other words, if the formal procedures of political representation are dependent on the informal allocation of communication power in the multimedia system, there is no equal opportunity for actors, values, and interests to operate the actual mechanisms of power allocation in the political system. It follows that the most important crisis of democracy under the conditions of media politics is the confinement of democracy to the institutional realm in a society in which meaning is produced in the sphere of media. Democracy can only be reconstructed in the specific conditions of the network society if civil society, in its diversity, can break through the corporate, bureaucratic, and technological barriers of societal image-making. Interestingly enough, the same pervasive multimodal communication environment that encloses the political mind in the media networks may provide a medium for the diverse expression of alternative messages in the age of mass self-communication. Is this really so? Or is this another utopia that could transform into dystopia when placed under the lens of scholarly scrutiny? The following chapter investigates the issue.

Chapter 5

Reprogramming Communication Networks: Social Movements, Insurgent Politics, and the New Public Space

Change, be it evolutionary or revolutionary, is the essence of life. Indeed, the still state for a living being is tantamount to death. This is also the case for society. Social change is multidimensional, but is ultimately contingent on a change in mentality, both for individuals and collectives. The way we feel/think determines the way we act. And changes in individual behavior and collective action gradually, but surely, impact and modify norms and institutions that structure social practices. However, institutions are crystallizations of social practices of prior moments in history, and these social practices are rooted in power relationships. Power relationships are embedded in institutions of all sorts. These institutions result from the conflicts and compromises between social actors, who enact the constitution of society according to their values and interests. Therefore, the interaction between cultural change and political change produces social change. Cultural change is a change of values and beliefs processed in the human mind on a scale large enough to affect society as a whole. Political change is an institutional adoption of the new values diffusing throughout the culture of a society. Of course, no process of social change is general and instantaneous. Multiple changes proceed at different paces in a variety of groups, territories, and social domains. The ensemble of these changes, with their contradictions, convergences, and divergences, weaves the fabric of social transformation. Changes are not automatic. They result from the will of social actors, as guided by their emotional and cognitive capacities in their interaction with each other and with their environment. Not all individuals engage in the process of social change, but throughout history there are always individuals who do, thus becoming social actors. The others are "free-riders" as the theory would put it. Or, in my own terminology, selfish parasites of history-making.

I conceptualize social actors aiming for cultural change (a change in values) as *social movements*, and I characterize the processes aiming at political change (institutional change) in discontinuity with the logic embedded in political institutions as *insurgent politics*. I posit as a hypothesis that insurgent politics operates the transition between cultural change and political change by incorporating subjects mobilized for political or cultural change into a political system they were not previously a part of, for a variety of reasons (for example, those who were not allowed to vote, or could not participate, or withdrew from the political system because they could not see the possibility of connecting their values or their interests with the system of political representation). Furthermore, both social movements and insurgent politics may originate either from the assertion of a cultural or political project, or from an act of resistance against political institutions, when the actions of these institutions are perceived as unjust, immoral, and ultimately illegitimate. Resistance may or may not lead to the rise of projects enacted by social movements or insurgent politics. But only when such projects arise can there be structural transformation. Thus, nobody can predict the outcome of social movements or insurgent politics. Therefore, to some extent, we only know if collective actions were actually subjects of social change in the aftermath of the action.

This introduces the question of a timetable to determine when there is such an aftermath: a question that can only be specifically answered by research on a given process of social change, focusing on how, when, and how much new values are institutionalized in the norms and organizations of society. *In analytical terms*, there cannot be a normative judgment on the directionality of social change. Social movements come in all formats, as societal transformation is not predetermined by a-historical laws operating on the basis of divine fate or ideological prophecies, let alone the personal taste of the analyst. Any structural change in the values institutionalized in a given society is the result of social movements, regardless of the values put forward by each movement. And so, the collective drive to establish a theocracy is as much a social movement as the struggle for the emancipation of women. Regardless of personal preferences, social change is the change that people seek to achieve by their mobilization. When they succeed, they become the new saviors. When they fail, they become fools or terrorists. And when they fail but their values eventually triumph in a future institutional rebirth, they are enshrined as the founding mothers of a new world or, depending on their fate, as the proto-martyrs of a new gospel.[46]

Social movements are formed by communicating messages of rage and hope. The specific structure of communication of a given society largely shapes social movements. In other words, social movements, and politics, insurgent or not, spring up and live in the *public space*. Public space is *the space of societal, meaningful interaction where ideas and values are formed, conveyed, supported, and resisted; space that ultimately becomes a training ground for action and reaction*. This is why, throughout history, the control of social-ized communication by ideological and political authorities, and by the wealthy, was a key source of social power (Curran, 2002; see also Sennett, 1978; Dooley and Baron, 2001; Blanning, 2002; Morstein-Marx, 2004; Baker, 2006; Wu 2008). This is now the case in the network society, more so than ever before. In this book, I hope to have shown how multimodal

---

[46] I have presented my theory of social movements elsewhere, and I do not find it necessary to reproduce it here in detail. The analysis of the case studies presented in this chapter will provide a better method of communicating the theory than its abstract formulation. For readers interested in the presentation of the theoretical background of the study of social movements, I refer to my analysis in *The Power of Identity* (Castells, 2004c: 71–191). For an analysis of social movements as "symbolic struggles," focusing on anti-war mobilizations and the use of new media in the UK, see Gillan, Pickerill, and Webster (2008).

communication networks constitute, by and large, the public space in the network society. And so, different forms of control and manipulation of messages and communication in the public space are at the heart of power-making, as documented in Chapters 3 and 4. Politics is media politics, and this extends to forms of power relationships rooted in the business world or in cultural institutions. Yet, the public space is a contested terrain, however biased toward the interests of the builders and caretakers of this space. Without contesting the images created and projected in the public space by the powers that be, individual minds cannot reconstruct a new public mind, and so societies would be trapped in an endless process of cultural reproduction, walling off innovation, alternative projects, and ultimately social change.

In sum: in the network society, the battle of images and frames, at the source of the battle for minds and souls, takes place in multimedia communication networks. These networks are programmed by the power relationships embedded within the networks, as analyzed in Chapter 4. Therefore, the process of social change requires the reprogramming of the communication networks in terms of their cultural codes and in terms of the implicit social and political values and interests that they convey. It is not an easy task. Precisely because they are multimodal, diversified, and pervasive, communication networks are able to include and enclose cultural diversity and a multiplicity of messages to a much greater extent than any other public space in history. Thus, the public mind is captured in programmed communication networks, limiting the impact of autonomous expressions outside the networks. But in a world marked by the rise of mass self-communication, social movements and insurgent politics have the chance to enter the public space from multiple sources. By using *both horizontal communication networks and mainstream media to convey their images and messages*, they increase their chances of enacting social and political change – even if they start from a subordinate position in institutional power, financial resources, or symbolic legitimacy. However, their accrued power as alternative messengers comes with a servitude: they must adapt to the language of the media and to the formats of interaction in the communication networks. On balance, the rise of networks of mass self-communication offers greater chances for autonomy. However, for this autonomy to exist, social actors must assert the right to mass self-communication by preserving freedom and fairness in the deployment and management of the networked infrastructure of communication and in the practice of the multimedia industries. Liberty, and ultimately social change, become entwined with the institutional and organizational operation of communication networks. Communication politics becomes dependent upon the politics of communication.

I will elaborate on the process of social change in the new public space constituted by communication networks by focusing on two different types of social movements and two significant cases of insurgent politics. First, the construction of a new environmental consciousness leading to universal awareness of the reality, causes, and implications of climate change by a science-based social movement acting on and through the media and the Internet. Second, the challenge to corporate globalization enacted by networked social movements around the world using the Internet as an organizational and deliberative medium to encourage citizens to put pressure on governments and corporations in their quest for a just globalization. Third, the burgeoning, instant movements of resistance to political wrongdoing, often able to transform indignation in insurgent politics by seizing the versatility and networking capabilities of mobile phones. While I will refer to multiple cases of these "mobil-izations," I will dwell on one of the most significant of such movements: the spontaneous outcry against the manipulation of information by the Spanish government following the Madrid bombing by *al-Qaeda* in March 2004. Finally, I will analyze the 2008 Obama campaign in the presidential primary election in the US as it epitomizes the rise of a new form of insurgent politics with the potential of transforming the practice of politics altogether. As I will document, it was characterized by the recasting of traditional forms of community organizing in the communicative conditions of the Internet Age, arguably with considerable success, including the substitution of citizen financing for lobby financing. I will then try to bring together the meaning of these diverse movements into a common analytical thread: *the potential synergy between the rise of mass self-communication and the autonomous capacity of civil societies around the world to shape the process of social change.*

Warming Up to Global Warming: The Environmental Movement and the New Culture of Nature

We have now come to accept, by and large, that the climate of the planet is changing, and that this potentially catastrophic process is primarily man-made. If corrective measures and policies follow from this recognition, we may still be able to prevent a disastrous course of events in the twenty-first century, although much time has been lost and much damage has already been done to livelihood on the blue planet. The facts are well known: since the mid-1970s, the average surface temperature has warmed by about 1°F. The Earth's surface is currently warming at a rate of about 0.32°F per decade or 3.2°F per century. The eight warmest years on record (since 1850) have all occurred since 1998; the warmest was 2005. Since 1979, when satellite measurements of troposphere temperatures began, various satellite data sets for the mid-troposphere showed similar rates of warming – ranging from 0.09°F per decade to 0.34°F per decade, depending on the method of analysis (National Aeronautics and Space Administration, 2007; National Oceanic and Atmospheric Administration, 2008).

The large majority of scientists in the field, on the basis of two decades of research published in peer-reviewed journals, agree that human activity is an essential contributor to global climate change. The United Nations-sponsored Intergovernmental Panel on Climate Change (IPCC) concluded in its 2007 report, presented at a conference in Paris attended by over 5,000 scientists, that the global warming trend is "unequivocal" and that human activity is "very likely" (meaning a likelihood of at least 90%) the cause. The executive director of the United Nations Environment Program, Achim Steiner, said the report represented a tipping point in the accumulation of data on climate change, adding that February 2, 2007, the closing day of the conference, will perhaps be remembered as the day when global thinking about climate change moved from debate to action (Rosenthal and Revkin, 2007). The formal recognition of the gravity of the problem, and the international community's call to act on it, came half a century after scientists had alerted the public to the matter and environmental activists had begun to put pressure on governments, until then oblivious to the issue.

The Long March of Environmentalism

For the awareness of climate change and its consequences to settle in the public mind, and ultimately in decision-making circles, a social movement was necessary to inform, to alert, and, more importantly, to change the way we think about our collective relationship to nature. In fact, a new culture of nature had to be socially produced because, despite the signals coming from the scientific community for a long time, the power relationships embedded in the institutions and culture of our societies were adamant about defending the culture of productivism and consumerism at all costs, because the logic of profit-making, at the source of the market economy, and the pursuit of mass consumption, the bedrock of social stability, rest on the premise of using nature as a resource rather than as our living environment. The way we think of nature determines the way we treat nature – and the way nature treats us. Throughout the industrial revolution, humankind took its historical revenge on the forces of nature that for millennia appeared to dominate our survival without possible control. Science and technology enabled us to subdue the limits imposed by nature. Or so we thought.

There followed a largely uncontrolled process of industrialization, urbanization, and technological reconstruction of the living environment that has resulted in our way of life. Because standards of living in health, education, food production, and consumption of everything improved dramatically, reassuring our belief in GDP growth as a measure of progress, we kept going in a linear path of development within a productivist model whose statist version was even more extreme than the original capitalist matrix. Indeed, *as late as 1989*, the US National Association of Manufacturers, together with the oil and automotive industries, organized the Global Climate Coalition to *oppose* mandatory regulations from governments regarding global warming, a position still echoed in the 2000s by many governments, including the Bush administration. In April 1998, *The New York Times* published an article reporting on a memo of the American Petroleum Institute designing a strategy vis-à-vis the media to make "recognition of uncertainty [about climate change] . . . part of the conventional wisdom . . . and thereby educate and inform the public, stimulating them [the media] to raise questions with policy makers" (Cushman, 1998: 1). Lance Bennett has documented the strategies of Republican leaders in the US to spin the media with denials of the human responsibility for the generation of climate change (Bennett, 2009: ch. 3).

However, it is fair to say that, in recent years, a number of major corporations, including some in the oil and automotive industries, have changed their positions substantially, including BP, Shell, Texaco, Ford, and General Motors. Since 2000, the Carbon Disclosure Project has been working with corporations to disclose their carbon emissions, and in 2008 the Project published the emissions data for 3,000 of the largest corporations in the world. The World Business Council for Sustainable Development, an association of 200 major corporations, has even called on governments to agree on global targets. The collective effort of environmental activists and scientists, who used the media to change the opinion of the public and influence decision-makers, prompted business to change its attitude, or at least the public image it would like to project. This is precisely what epitomizes the role of social movements in transforming the culture of society, in this case the culture of nature. Governments, however, were reluctant to acknowledge the gravity of the problem, and even more reluctant to accept human activity as a major cause of climate change. Moreover, no effective measures were taken, as conferences met, committees were assembled, and reports were issued in a parade of rhetorical statements without significant policy consequences.

Yet, the scientific community had been investigating global warming, and discussing its implications, since the nineteenth century (Patterson, 1996). In 1938, a British scientist, G. D. Calendar, presented evidence of the relationship between fossil fuels and global warming, although his findings were met with the skepticism of climate change experts: belief in the balance of nature was ingrained in the minds of science (Newton, 1993; Patterson, 1996).[47] A pivotal moment in spreading the word beyond the small group of researchers stubbornly investigating the matter came in 1955 when Roger Revelle, a scientist with Scripps Laboratories, alerted the public about reported trends in global warming, and testified before the US Congress on the future consequences of these trends. In 1957, Charles Keeling, a young researcher at Harvard, began measuring atmospheric CO_2 and produced the "Keeling Curve," which showed the increase of temperature over time. Revelle hired Keeling to work with him at Scripps and, together, they established that the baseline CO_2 level in the atmosphere had risen at approximately the rate that Revelle had calculated (Weart, 2007).[48]

Keeling's findings had an impact on scientists in the field. The Conservation Foundation sponsored a 1963 conference on climate change, and scientists issued a report warning of "potentially dangerous atmospheric increases of carbon dioxide" (Conservation Foundation, 1963). In 1965, a panel of the US President's Science Advisory Committee stated that

[47] Global warming is a type of "climate change" and the terms are often used interchangeably. The United Nations Framework Convention on Climate Change uses the term "climate change" for human-caused change and "climate variability" for other changes (United Nations, 1992). The term "anthropogenic global warming" is also used when focusing on human-induced changes.

[48] Al Gore was a student of Keeling at Harvard, and he recalls seeing the "Keeling Curve," writing that this moment changed his views of the world (Gore, 1992).

global warming was a matter of national concern. But the panel's report mentioned it only as one brief item among many other environmental problems. Despite these warnings, research such as Keeling's remained under-funded. At this critical juncture, scientists were aided by the environmental movement that had surged in the US and around the world, as symbolized by the first Earth Day celebration in April 1970. With the movement's support, an emboldened scientific community forcefully requested more research and more monitoring of how human actions affected the natural environment. Several scientists, led by Carroll Wilson, organized a group at MIT in 1970 to focus on "The Study of Critical Environmental Problems." The group's final report listed global warming as a very serious issue that needed to be studied further (SCEP, 1970). Yet, while there was some media attention paid to this report, the study of global warming was largely overlooked (Weart, 2007). Wilson followed up the MIT study by organizing a meeting of experts in Stockholm, the "Study of Man's Impact on Climate," which is considered a landmark in the development of climate change awareness. The final report, which was widely read, ended with a Sanskrit prayer: "Oh, Mother Earth... pardon me for tramping on you" (Wilson and Matthews, 1971).

Weart (2007) argues that during this time the rhetoric and attitudes of the environmental movement spread rapidly among climate researchers, and a new view of the relationship between science and society started to emerge in the media. This trend was indicated by a rise in press articles in American magazines related to global warming: the number of articles in the 1970s rose from three to more than 20 articles per year. As a result of this growing attention, bureaucrats put carbon dioxide into a new category: "Global Monitoring of Climatic Change." Under this title, research funding, which was stagnant for many years, doubled, and doubled again between 1971 and 1975. By the end of the 1970s, scientists largely agreed that warming was occurring, and some scientists went to the public to demand action. In many countries, environmentalists put pressure on their governments to regulate on behalf of environmental protection, and governments responded by enacting laws to reduce smog and clean the water supply, among other measures (Weart, 2007). In the early 1980s, global warming had become well known enough to be included in public opinion polls for the first time. In March 1981, Al Gore held a congressional hearing on climate change, where scientists such as Revelle and Schneider testified. This hearing drew attention to the Reagan administration's plan to cut funding for CO_2 research programs. Embarrassed by the media attention, the administration reversed its decision. Pressures from the environmental organizations saved the newly created Department of Energy, which was under direct threat of dismantlement.

At the international level, in 1985 a joint conference was convened in Villach, Austria, by the United Nations Environment Programme (UNEP), the World Meteorological Organization (WMO), and the International Council of Scientific Unions (ICSU) on the "Assessment of the Role of Carbon Dioxide and of Other Greenhouse Gases in Climate Variations and Associated Impacts." The Advisory Group on Greenhouse Gases was then established by UNEP, WMO, and ICSU to ensure periodic assessments of scientific knowledge on climate change and its implications. A 1986 report by the WMO and NASA discussed how the atmosphere was being changed significantly by human activity. In the United States, James Hansen, a climate scientist, testified during the hearings held by Senator John Chaffee in 1986 and predicted that climate change would be measurable within a decade. Hansen created a stir among scientists with his statements, although the media paid little attention to his testimony. The US Congress continued to hold hearings on global warming in 1987, and Senator Joseph Biden submitted the Global Climate Protection Act, signed by President Reagan, which elevated climate change to the level of a foreign policy issue. Yet, concern over global warming was still largely confined to a narrow group of scientists and interested law-makers.

Then, a heat wave hit the United States in the summer of 1988, one of the hottest summers on record. No one can be sure about the relationship between a hot summer and global warming, but this is not the point. For people, and also the media, to connect atmospheric warming to their daily experience, they must feel it in some way, as was the case years later with particularly active seasons of hurricanes and tornados that became, in the minds of many, messengers of apocalyptic climate change. And so, the hot summer of 1988 "galvanized the environmental community" as no other event had done since the first Earth Day in 1970 (Sarewitz and Pielke, 2000). As the summer began, only about half of the US public was aware of global warming (Weart, 2007). Then Senator Wirth, seizing the opportunity presented by the heat wave, called a hearing on global warming in June 1988 and summoned several key witnesses. Though science hearings were usually not well attended, this one was packed with reporters (Trumbo, 1995). James Hansen, the NASA scientist who had already testified in 1986 and 1987, testified again during this hearing,

Table 5.1. Awareness of global warming in the United States, 1982–2006: Percentage answering yes to the question "have you heard anything about the greenhouse effect/ global warming?"

Year	Yes(%)	Source
1982	41	Cambridge
1986	45	Harris
1988	58	*Parents Magazine*
1989	68	Cambridge
1990	74	Cambridge
1992	82	Cambridge
1997	85	CBS
2000	89	Harris
2001	88	Harris
2002	85	Harris
2006	91	Pew

and argued that data proved that temperature increases were not due to natural variation. Hansen argued that global warming was occurring and that it was a critical problem in need of immediate action. This time, his testimony was front-page news around the world, since it was the first time a respected scientist had stated so definitively that global warming posed a direct threat to the Earth. A flurry of media coverage brought the debate on global warming into the public realm (Ingram et al., 1992). Between the spring and fall of 1988, articles about global warming tripled (Weart, 2007). The number of Americans who had heard of the greenhouse effect jumped from 38 percent in 1981 to 58 percent in September 1988 (see Table 5.1), and polls showed that Americans had begun to worry a great deal about global warming. Such public concern prompted politicians to add global warming to their agendas. There was an increase in global warming-related congressional activity in the US, and 32 bills were introduced in the second session of the 100th Congress, such as the Global Warming Act and the World Environmental Policy Act.

The year 1988 was also the time when intergovernmental action on climate change began to gather steam. This is, of course, essential, as global warming is, well, global. The key decision that would have considerable institutional impact on future policy-making was the establishment of the Inter-Governmental Panel on Climate Change (IPCC), under the sponsorship of the United Nations. The IPCC is a scientific body that evaluates the risk of climate change caused by human activity. The panel was established by the WMO and UNEP. Its main activity is to provide regular reviews of climate science and issue assessment reports on the evolution of the climate. The first assessment report was published in 1990, and played a key role in the development of the United Nations Framework Convention on Climate Change (UNFCCC), which was opened for signature in the Rio de Janeiro summit of 1992 and enforced in 1994. This convention provided the policy framework for addressing the climate change issue. In 1991, the IPCC expanded its membership to all member countries of the WMO and UNEP. The Second Assessment Report was published in 1995 and provided input for the Kyoto Protocol negotiations in 1997. The Third Assessment Report was initiated in 1997 and published in 2001. It contributed further information for the development of the UNFCCC and the Kyoto Protocol.

The Fourth Assessment Report was released in Paris on February 2, 2007, as mentioned above, and received the approval of officials from over 130 countries after three days of negotiations regarding wording (Kanter and Revkin, 2007). During this meeting, government delegates adopted the report's "Summary for Policymakers" line by line, and then accepted the underlying report (IPCC, 2007a). While the panel members met behind closed doors for a week, they were flooded with messages from hundreds of outside experts who sought to alter the presentation of findings or the wording in one direction or another. Some scientists said that the US delegation tried to downplay language that suggested a link between hurricane intensification and warming caused by human activity (Kanter and Revkin, 2007). There were also present at the meeting a number of observers from industry groups, such as the International Chamber of Commerce, the International Petroleum Industry Environmental Conservation Association, and the International Aluminum Institute, as well as environmental NGOs like Greenpeace and Friends of the Earth. Before the report was released, all of the lights on the Eiffel Tower were shut off for five minutes. Environmental activists had advocated the darkening of the Eiffel Tower as part of a "lights out" campaign aimed at raising public awareness about global warming (BBC, 2007b). The IPCC shared the 2007 Nobel Peace Prize with Al Gore. The Peace Prize was awarded "for their efforts to build up and disseminate greater knowledge about man-made climate change, and to lay the foundations for the measures that are needed to counteract such change" (Nobel Foundation, 2007).

Although less noble than the IPCC endeavors, the report (classified) that the US National Intelligence Committee presented to Congress in June 2008 is just as indicative of governmental agencies' change of mind regarding climate change. The report not only acknowledged the reality of global warming, but also labeled it a threat to the national security of the United States, as its consequences were likely to increase global terrorism. The convoluted argument asserted that the devastation caused by future climate change in many poor countries of the world would throw millions into poverty, to the point where these countries would become fertile ground for recruiting terrorists. Thus, although, according to the report, the US could obtain economic benefits from global warming (because of a higher yield of agricultural crops!), climate change would "jeopardize the national interest because the United States depends on a smooth-functioning international system ensuring the flow of trade and market access to critical raw materials, such as oil and gas, and security for allies and partners. Climate change and climate change policies could affect all of these" (CNN, 2008).

The fact that global warming was elevated to the level of a national security issue by US intelligence agencies is indicative of a global attitude adjustment regarding climate change, a problem that had been largely ignored three decades earlier. And while the Bush administration remained reluctant until the very end of its term to engage in policy measures to confront global warming (probably because of the influence wielded by the oil industry on both the president and the vice president), the state of California, led by a Republican Governor (remember *Terminator*?) announced, in June 2008, a plan to bring down greenhouse emissions to 1990 levels by regulating the way electricity is generated, setting standards for car-making and building construction, and establishing a carbon-credit trading market. As for the European Union, on March 9, 2007 at a summit in Brussels, the European Union's government leaders agreed on a binding target to reduce greenhouse-gas inducing emissions by at least 20 percent from 1990 levels by 2020 (see below). Thus, toward the end of the first decade of the twenty-first century, global warming had become a major global policy issue. To a large extent, this was the consequence of the changes that took place in the minds of citizens around the world.

The Rise of the Environmental Mind

Since the first Earth Day celebration in April 1970 there has been a dramatic shift in the public mind concerning the environment in general and the reality and implications of global warming in particular. *This change of mentality has taken place all over the world.* Indeed, early studies of environmentalism in the United States and Europe considered public concern over the environment to be a consequence of economic wealth, and therefore an issue unique to Western industrialized countries. However, as more cross-national research was conducted, this perception has been proved to be inaccurate. For example, a 1992 Gallup poll, which surveyed 24 countries in different socio-economic conditions, found high concern for environmental issues, including global warming, in most countries (Brechin, 2003). In the US, awareness of global warming has increased considerably since the issue was first brought to the public's attention in 1988 (see Table 5.1). By combining a variety of survey results, we observe a steady increase in the awareness of global warming as a problem, with only 41 percent of the US public aware of global warming in 1982, increasing to 58 percent in 1988, over 80 percent since 1992, and 91 percent in 2006 (see also Table A5.1 in the Appendix).

In recent times, and on the global scale, analysis of 11 international polls conducted by World Public Opinion (2007b) found widespread and growing concern about climate change worldwide. Every international poll found that the majority of respondents felt global warming was a problem or threat. For example, a 2007 Pew poll found that a majority of all 37 countries surveyed agreed that global warming is a serious problem. Majorities in 25 countries and pluralities in six countries rated the problem as "very serious." Seventy-five percent of Americans rated the problem as serious, with 47 percent rating it very serious. In China, 88 percent considered global warming a serious problem, while 42 percent called it very serious. A Pew 2006 survey found that about two-thirds of Japanese (66%) and Indians (65%) responded that they personally worry "a great deal" about global warming, while about half of the respondents in Spain (51%) and France (45%) were greatly worried. In contrast, in the UK, only 26 percent worried a great deal. In the US in 2006, only 19 percent of respondents worried a great deal about global warming, and approximately the same did so in China (20%). Thus, in 2006, the two largest producers of greenhouse gases, the US and China, were also the countries with the lowest level of concern over global warming, despite acknowledging that it was indeed a serious problem. However, a 2007 ABC News/Washington Post/Stanford poll found that the proportion of Americans identifying global warming as the world's biggest environmental problem had doubled in just a year, with 33 percent citing it as the world's top environmental issue in 2007, compared to 16 percent in 2006.

Concern about climate change appears to be growing fast worldwide. GlobeScan conducted polls across countries in 2003 and 2006, and found that the percentages calling climate change/global warming a "very serious" problem increased by an average of 16 points. For example, in the UK, the percentage rose from 50 percent in 2003 to 70 percent in 2006, and in the US the percentage rose from 31 percent in 2003 to 49 percent in 2006. The German Marshall Fund also detected increasing concern about global warming: in ten European countries polled in 2005 and 2007, the average percentage of citizens saying that global warming is an extremely important threat increased by 5 points (from 51 to 56%). A similar increase was observed in the United States (from 41 to 46%).

More importantly in terms of policy consequences, various international polls found that large majorities of respondents perceive climate change to be caused by human activity. However, the belief that humans have contributed significantly to climate change was accepted more rapidly in Europe than in other parts of the world, especially the United States (Pew, 2006). In 1999, GlobeScan found that a large majority of respondents around the world were somewhat or totally convinced that human activities are a cause of climate change, except for the US (Leiserowitz, 2007). This is probably because the belief that humans cause global warming is deeply polarized along political lines in the US, with 24 percent of Republicans, 54 percent of Democrats, and 47 percent of independents responding that global warming is due to human activity in 2006 (Pew, 2006). Nonetheless, a 2008 Pew survey found that 47 percent of American respondents said global warming is caused by human activity. This is a six-point increase from 2006 and a huge jump from the mid-1990s, when few Americans considered it a problem deserving their personal concern (Pew, 2008g). Hurricanes Katrina and Rita may have had an impact upon American perception of the role of human causes in extreme weather patterns. For example, in 2004 before a very active hurricane period, 58 percent of respondents viewed "extreme weather patterns, including violent storms, flooding, and drought" as "part of a natural pattern." In 2005, after the hurricanes devastated the country, the percentage of respondents who attributed extreme weather to natural

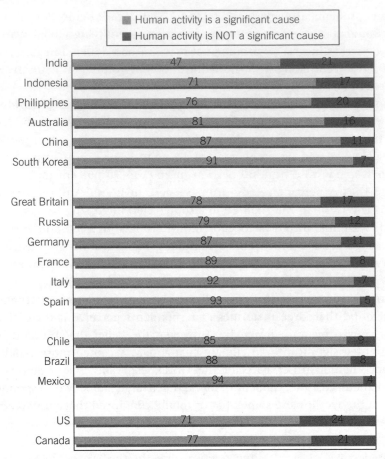

Fig. 5.1. Views of human activity as a significant cause of climate change

Source: BBC/GlobeScan/PIPA poll 2007, elaborated by Lauren Movius.

patterns dropped 19 points to 39 percent (World Public Opinion, 2006). Environmental campaigns on global warming seem to be more effective if people have been affected by images or experience of disasters that make them more receptive to changing their deep-seated opinions, and thus more likely to relate to environmentalist messages. From a global perspective, the 2007 BBC/GlobeScan/PIPA poll (World Public Opinion, 2007a) found that in 20 out of 21 countries polled (the exception is India), two-thirds or more of people believed that human activity is a significant cause of climate change (see Figure 5.1).

In sum: the data show that from the late 1980s to the late 2000s there has been a dramatic shift in the world's public opinion in terms of global warming awareness and concern regarding its potential consequences. Global warming, once an obscure scientific issue, has come to the forefront of public debate. Why and how? What happened between 1988 and 2008? Who were the actors and what were the communication processes that brought people and institutions around the world to face the crisis of global warming?

The Greening of the Media

As documented throughout this book, people make up their minds according to the images and information they retrieve from communication networks, among which the mass media were the primary source for the majority of citizens during the two decades when awareness of global warming increased. Media research in the United States, as summarized by Nisbet and Myers (2007), has shown a relationship between media attention and changes in public opinion on environmental issues. For example, during the first half of the 1980s, with little news coverage of the issue, only 39 percent of respondents had heard anything about the greenhouse effect. By September 1988, after the hottest summer on record and an increase in media attention, 58 percent of people were aware of the issue. By the early 1990s, as media attention continued to increase, 80 to 90 percent of the public had heard of global warming.[49] However, while the majority of Americans believe in the reality of global warming, there is some hesitation concerning whether or not scientists are in accord with one another. Nisbet and Myers (2007) note that, depending on the specific question and poll, the percentage of Americans who think scientists have reached consensus ranges from 30 percent to 60 percent. Nonetheless, even by this indicator, there has been a clear shift in public acknowledgment of global warming. The Cambridge and Gallup surveys, using consistent wording, found the

[49] Results vary based on question wording and different surveys. Nisbet and Myers (2007) note that other polls show 65% of the public had heard "a lot" or "some" about global warming in 1997, and this increased to 75% of the public during the summer of 2001, to 66% in 2003, 78% in 2006, and 89% in 2007. Another survey, by the Program on International Policy Attitudes (PIPA Knowledge Networks Poll: Americans on Climate Change, 2005), with different measures, found 63% of the US public had heard "a great deal" or "some" about global warming in 2004, and 72% in 2005.

percentage of the public who answered "most scientists believe that global warming is occurring" was 28 percent in 1994, 46 percent in 1997, 61 percent in 2001, and 65 percent in 2006. The Program on International Public Attitudes (PIPA), using different wording, found that 43 percent of the public in 2004 and 52 percent in 2005 responded that there was a consensus among scientists regarding the existence and potential damage of global warming.

In fact, media reporting may have induced more doubt about the scientific community's consensus on global warming than is warranted by the current level of dispute on the issue. This is because news coverage of global warming has portrayed heated debate and disagreement between scientists, despite the fact that a strong scientific consensus about global warming does exist (Antilla, 2005). This discrepancy is due to the journalistic norm of "balance" (Trumbo, 1995; Boykoff and Boykoff, 2007). Boykoff and Boykoff (2004) surveyed 636 articles from four top United States newspapers between 1988 and 2002, and found that most articles gave as much time to the small group of climate change doubters as to the scientific consensus. Dispensa and Brulle (2003), analyzing news articles in major newspapers and scientific journals during 2000, found that the US media presented a biased view of global warming by portraying it as controversial, whereas the press in New Zealand and Finland published the story as consensus.

The mass media play a key role in the identification and interpretation of environmental issues, since scientific findings must often be formatted in media language for the public to understand (Boykoff and Boykoff, 2007). While international conferences may raise the profile of environmental issues among the world's political elite, it is through the mass media that the public learns about the scientific findings relating to issues that may affect people's lives. Thus, media visibility of global warming was crucial in moving global warming from a condition to a public issue to a policy concern. According to Dispensa and Brulle (2003: 79), "without media coverage it is unlikely that an important problem will either enter the arena of public discourse or become part of political issues . . . Media is key to forming a framework for global warming . . . " A 1995 study by Kris Wilson, cited in Dispensa and Brulle (2003), found that the mass media were a key source of knowledge about global warming. Krosnick et al. (2006), analyzing results from a representative sample of US adults collected in 1996, found that greater television exposure was associated with increased belief in the existence of global warming. As documented in Chapter 4, priming by the media can increase the salience of a topic and cause shifts in attitudes. For this specific issue, we can observe the agenda-setting mechanism at work, as research has established a significant link between how the media constructs the issue of global warming and the nature of international policy responses. Thus, Newell (2000) reports that the peaks of environmental awareness in the 1960s and the mid-to-late 1980s strongly correlate with high points of media coverage of environmental issues, just as pressure on governments to take action declined in tandem with media coverage in the 1990s. In Newell's analysis, the media may have a direct agenda-setting effect (politicizing an issue and bringing it to public attention, which results in government activity) or an indirect public opinion-shaping effect (framing of the debate). Guber (2003) found that media attention over time partially explained the constant but fluctuating level of support for environmentalism. Trumbo and Shanahan (2000), analyzing opinion polls, show that the level of respondents' concern regarding global warming rose and fell with increases and decreases in television coverage of the issue, and conclude that changes in public attention to global warming can be seen as "reflecting the development of a specific plot within specific narrative outcomes" (2000: 202).

Thus, it is clear that media reporting has been essential in creating global awareness of global warming at an unprecedented level in the long march from the culture of productivism to the culture of environmentalism. But *why have the media so decisively highlighted the issue of global warming?* As analyzed in Chapter 2, the bottom line for the media is to attract audience. The audience gravitates toward news that raises their emotions. Negative emotions have greater effect on focusing attention than positive ones. And fear is the most potent negative emotion. The catastrophic connotation of the consequences of global warming instills deep fear in the public. Indeed, in some projections, global warming may lead to the disastrous rise of ocean levels in many areas of the world, droughts that would devastate water resources and agricultural production, a recurrent pattern of storms, hurricanes, tornados, and typhoons bringing widespread destruction to a largely urbanized planet, relentless forest fires, desertification, and a long series of Apocalyptic horsemen, amplified by the imagination of image producers and image consumers in our culture of special effects. This is not to deny the seriousness of the threat of global warming, but simply demonstrates how scientific projections and carefully worded warnings are translated into media language in ways that alert the public to danger by visualizing a catastrophic future. Indeed, Boykoff (2008) analyzed US television coverage of climate change from 1995 through 2004 and found that news coverage did not reflect the scientific perspective on climate change, but followed the occurrence of events that people experience in their lives. Boykoff and Boykoff, analyzing media reporting on television and in the newspapers in the US from the perspective of the "public arena model" of interpretation, argue that, for an issue to become salient in the media agenda, it has to piggyback on real world events. Thus, over time, politicians, celebrities, and environmental activists have replaced scientists as the main source of news on global warming (Boykoff and Boykoff, 2007).

In other words, the media are essential in the process of awareness-raising, and a number of journalists have invested themselves, professionally and ideologically, in the project of raising environmental consciousness. However, the construction of the global warming issue in the media has been conducted along the bottom line of media business: *attract audience by scripting narratives that raise concern among citizens*. And the media have been alerted to the drama involved in the trends of global warming largely as the result of *a multi-pronged environmental movement, whose main components are scientists, celebrities, and environmental activists*. The media are simultaneously *the conveyors of the movement's messages and the producers of these messages in a format that fits the rules and goals of their business trade*.

Science to the Rescue

If there is a core value in science, it is that the pursuit of truth is a fundamental contribution to the betterment of humankind, and sometimes critical to its survival. However self-serving this statement may be, from time to time scientists can make a case for their argument. The discovery of the process of climate change, along with the evaluation of its consequences, is one of these instances. So, for the past 50 years, and with rising intensity and growing success, scientists have committed themselves to the task of warning citizens and their leaders about the worrisome implications of the results of their arcane research.

First, I want to emphasize that scientific research on climate change has benefited extraordinarily from two major developments: the revolution in computational modeling and the evolution of systemic thinking. The ability to build gigantic databases and proceed with high-speed calculations has made possible the construction of dynamic simulation models that are able to analyze and predict a wide range of atmospheric processes. Meanwhile, while theories of complexity are still in their infancy, a number of scientists are using system thinking as a key methodological tool to understand the planet as an eco-system of eco-systems, laying the foundations for mapping the relationship between human activity and the transformation of the natural environment (Capra, 1996, 2002; National Science Foundation, 2007).

However, despite the rapid progress of scientific research in the area of climate change and environmental interdependence, most scientists publish their findings in scientific journals, of which only a few are covered by the media, and in a very fragmented form. And so, when some scientists became seriously worried about their findings on global warming, they sought to address the public and politicians in the first person; for instance, by writing popular books. This occurred for a long time with little impact. In a few countries, a few bills regarding the climate were proposed, but most politicians showed scant interest. In 1974, scientists in the US urged the government to fund a National Climate Program. When their demands were ignored, scientists sought allies in the environmental community and associated themselves with the Environmental Defense Fund, the World Resources Institute, and other groups. Together they began to issue reports and lobby Congress about global warming.

In the mid-1980s, concern over global warming continued to rise among climate scientists, and computer models of the climate won the trust of experts (Weart, 2007). Science and scientists played a key role in the environmental movement and in the evolution of how the public viewed global warming (Ingram et al., 1992). As mentioned above, Hansen's 1986–8 testimonies shocked his colleagues and awakened a few minds. Ingram et al. (1992) propose that, even earlier than Hansen, Revelle was the archetype of the scientist advocate, since his 1957 discovery was one of the first to call attention to global warming. Revelle was also key in putting together a study of global climate change and disseminating it to the public. Another pioneer in activist science was Stephen Schneider, who simultaneously conducted research and conversed with the media and politicians to make climate change a public policy issue. Beyond these individual personalities, it was the growing scientific community of researchers on global warming who framed the issue of climate change as a major problem for humanity. Scientists who decided to directly stir up the public had to "learn some tricks," since Senators would brush them off – unless they saw the scientist speak on television (Weart, 2007). Some scientists used public relations techniques to produce short statements for journalists. So, though scientists were responsible for the discovery of global warming and made the first attempt to alert the public to the gravity of the issue, they also had to become activists themselves, and take part in the environmental movement, to be able to reach out to the world. The fundamental role of scientific knowledge in the global movement to prevent global warming is widely acknowledged, as environmental organizations appoint scientists to influential positions, and governments view scientists as their privileged interlocutors. Indeed, global warming as a natural phenomenon could only be identified and defined by science. The discourse on appropriate responses to global warming has been a scientific discourse, just as counter-claims have been. Both sides of the global warming debate enlist the work of scientists to support their arguments.

The groups of scientists involved in the IPCC can be conceptualized as an epistemic community (Patterson, 1996; Newell, 2000). An epistemic community is a network of individuals or groups with a claim to policy-relevant knowledge (Drake and Nicolaidis, 1992; Haas, 1992). The international epistemic community constituted by researchers on climate change played a key agenda-setting role: it identified the problem of global warming, fostered consensus on the nature of the problem, and pushed for a political response (Patterson, 1996). Without influential voices from the scientific community, global warming may not have entered the realm of international policy-making (Patterson, 1996; Newell, 2000). As mentioned above, the IPCC has had a clear influence in setting the terms of the debate on global warming. In September 1995, the IPCC issued a report that "changed everything" (Krosnick et al., 2000). The report stated that "the balance of evidence suggests that there is a discernible human influence on the global climate" (IPCC, 1995: 3). With this shift from lack of evidence to a certain level of scientific consensus, the media covered the report, and public alarm began to mount. In 2001, the IPCC furthered its conclusion by writing that "most of the warming observed over the last 50 years is attributable to human activities" (IPCC, 2001: 5). This process climaxed in 2007 when the IPCC report, as mentioned above, mobilized international public opinion and brought global warming to the top of decision-makers' policy agenda. So, scientists moved global warming from an "objective issue" to an "explicit issue" in public discourse, and then into a global policy debate. Once global warming entered public discourse, the media reported on it, which impacted upon public opinion and ultimately put pressure on governments to act. Of course, it is not *just* science that moved

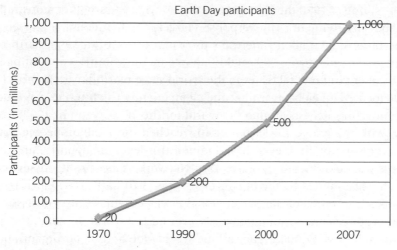

Fig. 5.2. Number of Earth Day participants, 1970–2007

Source: US Environmental Protection Agency, Earth Day network.

global warming from an objective problem to an explicit policy issue. It was the networking between the scientific community, environmental activists, and celebrities that brought the issue to the media, and communicated it to the public at large via multimedia networks.

Networked Environmental Action and Global Warming

The alliance between scientists, environmentalists, and opinion leaders that ultimately put global warming on the public agenda cannot be understood without situating it within the context of the environmental movement, one of the decisive social movements of our time.[50]

Given the diversity of the movement and its differential evolution throughout the world, it is difficult to provide a synthetic overview of its development. Yet, I think a significant indicator of the growth of the movement is participation in Earth Day activities from 1970 to 2007. Figure 5.2 provides an estimate of the number of Earth Day participants. Earth Day has been celebrated annually since 1970. It started in America, before quickly reaching global proportions. Senator Nelson of Wisconsin announced that

[50] For my analysis of the environmental movement as social movement, see my book *The Power of Identity*, 2nd edn. (Castells, 2004c: 168–91).

in the spring of 1970 there would be a nationwide grassroots demonstration on the environment. The response, largely spontaneous, surpassed all expectations: 20 million Americans took part in 1970. In 1990, Earth Day went global, mobilizing 200 million people in 141 countries and lifting the status of environmental issues to the world stage (earthday.net). Earth Day 2000 focused on global warming and clean energy. The Internet was crucial in connecting activists around the world for the 2000 event. In 2007, Earth Day, with the whole world joining in, reached the 1 billion people mark. No event of any kind, ever, has obtained this level of support. Earth Day events are coordinated by Earth Day Network, a nonprofit organization which was founded by the organizers of the 1970 Earth Day. Earth Day is significant in terms of the rise of global environmental consciousness as it is an event celebrated simultaneously around the world. In 2008, the network mobilized 17,000 organizations worldwide and 5,000 organizations in the US. In 2007, global warming was one of the main issues submitted to the participants for debate. Earth Day 2008 focused on global warming as the key issue.

From the first Earth Day in 1970 onward, national environmental organizations in the United States and around the world have had remarkable growth (Mitchell et al., 1992; Richardson and Rootes, 1995). The widespread rise of deep ecological awareness explains why global warming could immediately be seized by grassroots organizations, environmental NGOs, and media activists and made into a major policy issue. After three decades of militant work in all domains of environmental activism, environmental organizations are the most trusted sources of information about the environment. In the European Union, both environmental associations and scientists rank above television as the most trusted source of environmental information (Eurobarometer, 2008). Leveraging the legitimacy they enjoy in public opinion, environmental activists use a range of strategies to influence policy and decision-making processes, such as lobbying politicians, staging media events, and taking direct action.

As I will discuss below, environmental groups/campaigns often use a celebrity to gain more news attention. Thrall et al. (2008) argue that celebrities are not only used to break into and attract news media attention, but also to break into the *entertainment* media world, since viewers increasingly turn to entertainment media for their news. Thus, environmental groups strategically use entertainment venues as channels to communicate their messages, all of which is made easier with new technology and digital networks. Half of the environmental groups studied by Thrall et al. (2008) used a form of entertainment to disseminate their message, and tactics included staging concerts, inserting messages into entertainment broadcasts, and streaming videos with celebrity interviews. The most well-known example of this type of environmental entertainment advocacy is Live Earth, the concert series sponsored by Al Gore and environmental groups to combat climate change (see below). There has been a shift in the tactics of environmental organizations from broadcasting to narrowcasting to communicate their message. Approaches to narrowcasting include: creating web sites, setting up channels on YouTube, establishing pages on social networking sites, and using mobile phones to send SMSs. With horizontal networks of communication, people can communicate directly with environmental advocacy groups. Interactive features can be as simple as allowing a web site visitor to e-mail a link or web page to a friend, or they could be chat rooms, or social networking sites which create networks of interested individuals. For instance, the Alliance for Climate Protection and Current TV chose not to hire an agency for their campaigns and instead produced their own ecospots. Celebrities such as Cameron Diaz, George Clooney, and others served on the judges' panel. Using a combination of grassroots organizing, media-oriented activism, and Internet networking, environmental action has taken shape all around the world in multiple forms, and with increasing clout in public influence.

Taking advantage of the dense and intense network of environmental action, *organizations and activists around the world are coming together to work on the issue of global warming.* A case in point is *Stop Climate Chaos*, a coalition of over 70 NGOs. Stop Climate Chaos was launched in Britain in September 2005 to highlight the potential dangers of climate change. There is a diversity of members in the coalition, from the UK's leading environmental organizations to international development agencies to national campaigning bodies, and includes, among others, Greenpeace, Islamic Relief, Oxfam, UNA-UK, WWF-UK, and Youth Against Climate Change. Stop Climate Chaos is funded by the subscriptions of its members. Seed funding was provided by the Network for Social Change, Friends of the Earth, Greenpeace, the Royal Society for the Protection of Birds (RSPB), and WWF-UK. The stated purpose of Stop Climate Chaos is: "To build a massive coalition, that will create an irresistible public mandate for political action to stop human-induced climate change." In order to meet this objective, Stop Climate Chaos launched its "I Count" campaign in October 2006. The "I count" campaign was supported by web-site postings, newspaper ads, and SMS campaigns. The launch was marked by the unveiling of a four-foot high ice sculpture of Tony Blair's head encasing a first edition of their book *I Count: Your Step-by-step Guide to Climate Bliss*. The notion was that, as Blair's premiership melted away, climate change became the most important issue on which he could act and leave a legacy. In November 2006, 20,000 people rallied in Trafalgar Square demanding that the government should act on global warming. Stop Climate Chaos's 16-step *I Count* pocket book was published by Penguin and featured in the *Independent* to coincide with the rally. Subsequently, the coalition organized over 200 events around the UK during the "I Count Climate Change Bill Week of Action," asking for a more decisive Climate Change bill (www.icount.org.uk).

The use of the Internet is crucial for Stop Climate Chaos for both media strategy implementation and organizing purposes. The Internet connects member organizations of the coalition and their web sites. The network of web sites includes information about global warming, the Coalition's manifesto, a list of events, and links to the "I Count" campaign web site. The campaign web site features video, news, lists of events, podcasts, e-newsletters, background reading, and ways to get involved, such as sending messages to ministers who make decisions about climate-related programs. Individuals can sign up "to say I count" on the web site. The campaign urges users to sign up since "The bigger the count gets, the more we get noticed. And the more we get noticed, the more politicians will listen. And the more the politicians listen, the more they do" (www.icount.org.uk). Users can also pledge online to take action in their personal lives, and the data are collected by the web site. Action reminders are sent by e-mail and SMS. The actions listed on the web site periodically change, and users can personalize their experience by creating a "My Actions" account, which tracks their own activity.

Another major organization that has mobilized public opinion to act on global warming is the Alliance for Climate Protection founded by Al Gore in the United States. The self-assigned task of the Alliance is to educate the public about the importance of climate change and the role of human activity, since public opinion polls show that, despite awareness of climate change in the US, a significant minority of people still do not understand its connection to human activity. The Alliance's $300 million three-year campaign, launched on April 2, 2008, is one of the most costly public advocacy campaigns in US history (Eilperin, 2008). The "we" campaign uses online organizing and television advertisements on popular shows such as *American Idol* and *The Daily Show with Jon Stewart*.

On a global scale, Friends of the Earth have national member groups in 70 countries and unite 5,000 local activist groups. It has over 3 million members and supporters, and identifies itself as "the world's largest grassroots environmental network." Having identified climate change as "the biggest environmental threat to the planet," it has engaged in a major campaign to demand "climate justice." Friends of the Earth aims to join with communities that are affected by climate change to "build a global movement." Stopping climate change is also one of the main focuses of activity for Greenpeace International, who seeks new energy policies and encourages individuals to change how they use energy. Greenpeace views climate change awareness as a critical task. It is very self-conscious about the networked character of its movement, as it works with other environment organizations, companies, governments, and individuals. Another major player in climate change awareness and action is the World Wide Fund for Nature, or World Wildlife Fund (WWF), one of the largest environmental organizations, established in Switzerland in 1961. WWF has over 2,000 conservation projects, most of which focus on local issues where they team up with local partners. Climate change is one of their priorities in their campaigns. WWF promotes Earth Hour, which is discussed below.

The Internet has played an increasingly important role in the global movement to prevent global warming. As I will develop in the next section of this chapter, social movements addressing global issues are transnational in scope and depend on the Internet for the diffusion of information, communication, and coordination. Internet-mediated social networks are key ingredients of the environmental movement in the global network society. The Internet has extraordinarily improved the campaigning ability of environmental groups and increased international collaboration. Thus, Warkentin (2001) analyzed the uses of the Internet by several environmental NGOs and determined its critical role in enhancing member services, disseminating information resources, and encouraging political participation. For instance, the Internet helped the Earth Island Institute expand its membership by including tools in its web site such as "Take Action" and "Get Involved" pages and an "Activist Toolbox." He identified similar practices in the Rainforest Action Network and Greenpeace. Greenpeace has a network of web sites to coordinate actions globally and to urge people to act through the act of bearing witness. These acts are publicized and visually documented in the web site's network.

Bimber (2003) studied the greater efficiency obtained by the Environmental Defense Fund by using the Internet. In 1999, it reinvented itself over the Internet, cutting its staff to 25 full- and part-time employees and transforming into a network of grassroots organizations coordinated and informed over the Internet. Bimber points out that a web-based organization is better equipped to build coalitions by adding groups and partners for ad hoc campaigns. This is exactly what Environmental Defense did with considerable success. In the UK, Pickerill (2003) analyzed the British environmental movement and emphasized the role of the Internet in strengthening the movement. He lists five processes through which organizations and groups mobilized participation using computer networking: to provide a gateway to activism, to raise their campaign profile, to mobilize online activism, to stimulate local activism, and to attract participants to protests. For instance, Friends of the Earth had 4,000 links to itself on other sites, and its web site provided a number of entry points for users to become active. The web site also used technology to draw attention to campaigns: for example, an interactive map of a proposed bypass in the UK with photos of the threatened areas posted on the site, together with an online petition against the bypass for people to sign.

Many environmental NGOs have pages on MySpace, Facebook, or similar social networking sites, with links to these pages from their web site. In addition to using the Internet to mobilize participation in activism such as protest attendance, organizations also use the Internet to encourage participation in *online* activism. For example, the Friends of the Earth UK Climate Change online campaign was based on a network of individuals who, at the request of Friends of the Earth, sent e-mails to world leaders attending the UN Climate Change Kyoto summit. Likewise, the Internet is used to stimulate local action. Environmental groups provide local data and information relevant to local populations. Web sites contain advice on how to lobby large corporations and how to link to local groups. Friends of the Earth UK encourages citizens to engage in local activism by providing contact details and links to local groups on their web site. To support campaigns on specific issues, environmental organizations provide draft letters on their web site. In the US, the Safe Climate Act's coalition uses its web sites to encourage local groups or individuals to start a campaign or link their neighborhood campaign to a larger network. Being able to simply download campaign materials, from scientific background to promotional materials, greatly simplifies the process of mobilization.

The Internet increases the ability of an organization to disseminate its message. Not only do web sites provide information for visitors to the site, but visitors are encouraged to engage in viral diffusion of the information.

For example, many sites allow visitors to e-mail a story to a friend from their site, to e-mail friends a form message to encourage them to sign up for a campaign, to tag a story using Delicious or Digg, and to embed videos or banners and add an organization's feed to an individual's web site or blog. The Stop Global Warming site has a "promotion" page, where promotional banners and images are made available for use on web sites, blogs, and online community pages. Visitors to the site are asked to help spread the word about the Stop Global Warming virtual march by encouraging others to join or by hosting a banner or button. In many cases, the organization's web site introduces people to online tools of which they were possibly not aware.

However, the uses of the Internet are integrated in a *broader multimedia strategy* that characterizes the actions of the environmental movement. For example, Greenpeace has a network of web sites, podcasts, a blog, pages on social networking sites, and broadband television (GreenTV). WWF has a well-developed web site, coupled with its e-newsletter and YouTube videos, though it also uses television spots, radio spots, and print advertisements to spread its message regarding global warming. *In sum*, the versatility of digital communication networks has allowed environmental activists to evolve from their previous focus on attracting attention from the mainstream media to using different media channels depending on their messages and the interlocutors they aim to engage. *From its original emphasis on reaching out to a mass audience, the movement has shifted to stimulate mass citizen participation by making the best of the interactive capacity offered by the Internet.* Thus, environmental organizations act on the public and on decision-makers by bringing issues to their attention in the communication realm, both in the mainstream media and on the Internet. To pursue this strategy, they often count on the support of a potent source of social influence: *celebrities*.

When Celebrities Save the World (and Why)

Celebrities use their fame and their sometimes charismatic following to draw attention to a number of issues. In the past decade, some of the most environmentally active celebrities have fully engaged in raising awareness of global warming. While celebrities have historically supported political and ethical campaigns, today's celebrity activists have more incentive to adopt global causes and are more likely to be successful in pushing the agenda (Drezner, 2007). This has less to do with the celebrities' fame and more to do with how people consume information. For example, an increasing number of Americans get their information about world politics from soft-news shows, which celebrities dominate (such as *Entertainment Tonight*, *Access Hollywood*, and *The Daily Show*). A similar trend can be observed around the world (Bennett, 2003b; Baum, 2007).

This shift to soft news affects the formation of public opinion. For any issue, a significant challenge is to maintain public attention long enough to influence policy. As the audience for entertainment-centered, soft news grows, one way to sustain attention is to leverage celebrity appeal. As celebrity activists have access to this wider range of outlets, and thereby audience, celebrities may have an advantage over political activists in getting their message across. Drezner explores how celebrities are taking an active interest in world politics: "these efforts to glamorize foreign policy are actually affecting what governments do and say. The power of soft news has given star entertainers additional leverage to advance their causes. Their ability to raise issues to the top of the global agenda is growing" (2007: para. 2). Celebrity advocacy is a type of star-powered "outside strategy" of social protest, in which groups operating outside the formal policy process turn to celebrities to gain media attention which they would have greater difficulty obtaining otherwise (Thrall et al., 2008).

As for celebrities' own interest, besides the sincere commitment that many of them have toward creating a better world, espousing well-meant, popular causes, such as environmentalism, has a huge pay-off in terms of free publicity. By linking their name to the aspirations of millions of people around the world, they reach new audiences and consolidate their support among their fans. Thus, it is a win-win situation: celebrity status lends popularity to certain campaigns whose success, in turn, enhances and dignifies the celebrities themselves. Indeed, celebrities have been highly influential in raising the profile of global warming as a relevant public issue. Some of the well-known actors who support environmentalism include Leonardo DiCaprio, Matt Damon, Brad Pitt, Angelina Jolie, Orlando Bloom, and Sienna Miller. DiCaprio established the Leonardo DiCaprio Foundation in 1998 and has an environmental web site to reach, inform, and interact with a wide global audience. The Foundation spearheaded the production of the feature-length environmental documentary, *The 11th Hour*, which DiCaprio produced and narrated. Brad Pitt is the narrator of a series on green architecture.

Leonardo DiCaprio, Orlando Bloom, KT Tunstall, Pink, The Killers, Razorlight, and Josh Hartnett have thrown their weight behind the effort of

"Global Cool," a UK foundation established in 2006 with the goal of reaching out to one billion people to reduce carbon emission by one tonne for the next ten years. Laurie David, wife of comedian Larry David, is another well-known environmental activist. She founded the Stop Global Warming Virtual March with Senators John McCain and Robert F. Kennedy, Jr. Laurie David is also the producer of the Academy Award-winning *An Inconvenient Truth* (see below). In 2007, David launched the "Stop Global Warming College Tour" with Sheryl Crow, where they visited college campuses to raise awareness and inspire students to become part of the movement to stop global warming. David was declared the Bono of climate change by *Vanity Fair*; she has been featured several times on *The Oprah Winfrey Show* and appeared on the Fox News one-hour special "The Heat is On." David was also the guest editor of *Elle Magazine*, which was the first fashion magazine to devote an entire issue to the environment and print its pages on recycled paper.

Although certainly not an actor (in fact, his electoral campaign performance was mediocre), Al Gore is one of the most influential global warming celebrity activists. Drezner argues that "Gore has been far more successful as a celebrity activist than he ever was as vice president" and points to his limited success in global warming issues as a conventional politician, and his significant successes (including an Oscar and the Nobel Peace Prize) as a "post-White House celebrity" (2007: 4). Al Gore has played a key role in the global warming debate as a prominent environmental activist. As mentioned above, Al Gore is the founder of the Alliance for Climate Protection. He also organized the Live Earth benefit concert for global warming in 2007. When awarding the Nobel Peace Prize to Al Gore, the Nobel committee stated that Gore was "probably the single individual who has done most to create greater worldwide understanding of the measures that need to be adopted [to counter global warming]." The Sierra Club awarded Gore its top award, the John Muir Award, in 2007 for his 30 years of generating awareness of the dangers of global warming. In 2008, the Tennessee House of Representatives passed "The Gore Resolution," which honors Gore's efforts to curb global warming. In 2007, the International Academy of Television Arts and Sciences awarded Gore the Founders Award for Current TV and work in the area of global warming.

Gore represents an interesting, and rare, case of professional politician turned celebrity activist. But his interest in environmental issues began long ago. Al Gore was one of the earliest legislators to "see the potential in the global climate change issue" (Ingram et al., 1992: 49). He held the first congressional hearings on the subject in 1981. Gore wrote that once legislators heard the evidence, he was sure they would act. They did not. As a member of the House of Representatives in 1981, Gore supported the American Association for the Advancement of Science's proposal for research on global climate change. As Vice President, Gore argued in favor of a carbon tax, which was partially implemented in 1993. He also helped broker the 1997 Kyoto Protocol, although it was not ratified in the US. Gore pledged to ratify the Kyoto Protocol during his presidential campaign in 2000. When Gore "lost" to Bush in 2000 (by a 5 to 4 decision of the US Supreme Court), he returned to his work on global warming and went around the world presenting a slide show documenting the matter. Laurie David, the founder of the Stop Global Warming Virtual March, saw the slide show in New York in 2004 after the premiere of the feature film *The Day After Tomorrow*, a film about global warming. David met with Gore to propose making the slide show into a movie (Booth, 2006). She became the producer of Al Gore's documentary, *An Inconvenient Truth*, which has significantly popularized the global warming debate. The film was first shown at the 2006 Sundance Film Festival and went on to win an Oscar for best documentary in 2007. Gore also wrote a companion book, which was a bestseller in 2006. Gore has devoted 100 percent of his profits from the film and book to the Alliance for Climate Protection campaign, and Paramount Classics, the film's distributor, has pledged 5 percent of the film's profit to the Alliance (Eilperin, 2008). It is unclear how and to what extent the film has influenced public opinion, but it did strongly impress the elites and policy-makers who saw the documentary (Weart, 2007).

Films and television programs have significantly contributed to increased awareness of global warming. Before *An Inconvenient Truth* was released, there was media attention surrounding *The Day After Tomorrow*, a 2004 environmental disaster film. Although it was a fiction film, with a tenuous relationship to scientific fact, commentators still hoped that the film would heighten awareness of global warming (Semple, 2004). Environmental groups were keen to offer commentary on the film, hoping to use it to leverage their agenda. A study by Lowe et al. (2006) found that *The Day After Tomorrow* influenced viewers' attitudes in the UK, with viewers being more concerned about climate change than non-viewers. *In sum*: celebrities of various origins seem to have converged around the one common cause that appears to transcend partisan politics (although it does not) to use their reputation and ascendance to call people to the defense of our livability on the planet. To do so, they create events, a potent form of media politics.

Events as Environmental Media Politics

The environmental movement in general and the mobilization against global warming in particular create events to raise consciousness by attracting media attention. Furthermore, these events are often global, either through coordinated performances staged in different countries around the world or by ensuring global coverage of the event. As described above, Earth Day was the first of such events in 1970, and continues to be the icon of the global environmental movement. But, as the multifaceted campaign on global warming intensified in the first decade of the 2000s, global events have become both a tool of action and an organizing ground. A few *examples* will illustrate the contemporary contours of this event-mediated social movement.

Stop Climate Chaos was one of the chief coalitions participating in the 2007 *Global Day of Action against Climate Change* event, along with the Campaign against Climate Change, Greenpeace, and independent grassroots efforts. The Global Day of Action coincided with the UNFCCC's conference in Bali and with marches and rallies organized simultaneously in over 80 countries. The Global Day of Action started in 2005 to coincide with the date of the legal enforcement of the Kyoto Protocol. The Internet was instrumental in coordinating international events, with web sites that listed various international demonstrations on climate change and information on how to get involved.

Another global event, the Live Earth concert, was promoted by Al Gore in 2007. Many celebrities, including Kelly Clarkson and Lenny Kravitz, partnered with Gore and showed their support by performing. Live Earth was a series of worldwide concerts held on July 7, 2007. Al Gore said that the concerts began a three-year campaign to combat climate change and "to make everyone on our planet aware of how we can solve the climate crisis in time to avoid catastrophe" (Gore, 2007). The concerts brought together more than 150 musical acts in 11 locations around the world and were broadcast through television and radio, and streamed via the Internet. Live Earth had over 15 million video streams during the live concert alone. Live Earth acted in association with Save Our Selves, founded by

Kevin Wall, which included partners such as Al Gore's Alliance for Climate Protection, Earthlab, and MSN.

Another major global event was Earth Hour, sponsored by WWF, which took place from 8 p.m. to 9 p.m. on March 29, 2008. The concept was to turn off one's lights for 60 minutes to inspire people to take action on climate change. The event is individual-centered in nature, as the goal is to "create a symbolic event that could become a movement" and a "simple act that would create a positive tipping point" (Earth Hour 2007 video). Earth Hour started in Australia in 2007, when 2.2 million people and 2,100 Sydney businesses turned off their lights for one hour – Earth Hour – on March 31, 2007. As icons such as Sydney Harbour Bridge and the Opera House joined in, the event drew considerable attention. The event was promoted through radio, various advertisements, banners on city streets, and text message reminders. In 2008, people in six continents and more than 400 countries participated, turning the event into a worldwide manifestation. Corporations and landmarks participated in the event, from the Colosseum in Rome to the Sears Tower in Chicago to the Golden Gate Bridge in San Francisco. Google displayed a message against a blackened homepage: "We've turned the lights out. Now it's your turn."

The founder of Earth Hour said that he was amazed at how far the initiative had spread since it was launched a year earlier (AFP, 2008). Indeed, the Internet provided the tools to widely disseminate the message. Google's dark homepage brought awareness to many. Earth Hour's official web site, www.earthhour.org, received over 2.4 million visitors on March 29 alone (Reuters, 2008). The Earth Hour site posts background material, encourages users to sign up and pledge to participate in Earth Hour, and allows people to send e-mail messages with helpful links to friends, encouraging them to participate. There is a "supporters' download kit" with brochures and posters so individuals can spread the message to their neighborhood. The web site also has links to add their friend page on MySpace, join their fan page on Facebook, post photos on their Flickr group, follow along on Twitter, and post videos on their YouTube channel. A video about Earth Hour was posted on the site, and several versions of the video and others from around the world were posted on YouTube, with one such post having 748,531 views as of March 30, 2008. The video discusses climate change and its negative effects on the world and shows how "social activism took hold" in March 2007 for Earth Hour.

StopGlobalWarming.org is a self-described online grassroots movement that supports the *Stop Global Warming Virtual March*. The site states that "the Virtual March is creating one, loud collective voice that will be heard around the world. By spreading the word, we are building a movement to stop global warming." Site visitors can join the Virtual March by clicking on an icon and inputting their names and e-mail addresses. Stop Global Warming has organized a virtual march with 1,037,744 individual, verified marchers who have signed up from all 50 states in the United States, and over 25 countries around the world. More than 35 US legislators and governors have joined, including John McCain and Arnold Schwarzenegger (www.stopglobalwarming.org). Another event, which is organized through the Internet but takes place in locations around the United States, is a program of Internet-connected climate change rallies called *Step It Up*. In 2007, Bill McKibben, a scholar at Middlebury College, put a call online for locally run demonstrations under the "Step It Up" banner to occur on April 14, 2007. The campaign's goal is to provoke the US Congress to reduce carbon emissions by 80 percent by 2050. McKibben's online call generated plans for hundreds of events in all 50 states. The actions and rallies are organized online by a half-dozen Middlebury graduates who "filter a kind of passion and fashion reminiscent of the 1960s through a YouTube lens." McKibben said: "It's a source of eternal pleasure for me to turn on my computer every morning and see what people have come up with the night before" (Barringer, 2007).

Thus, with the help of celebrities and the use of the interactive capacity of global communication networks, environmentalists reach out to citizens around the world by acting on the media. While grassroots organizations play a large role in the movement, outreach often works on the basis of media events, whereby activists create events that draw media attention, thereby reaching a larger audience. Many activists rely on event creation tactics that will draw attention and provoke debate, from being arrested for disrupting meetings to staying atop trees for several months (in Berkeley, for over a year). Events and stunts can capture global media attention and help popularize environmental issues with the public. Indeed, an important role of environmental organizations is to educate and raise environmental consciousness, "even transforming global culture," as Greenpeace has been able to transform the image of whaling from a heroic action to slaughter (Clapp and Dauvergne, 2005: 79).

However, while the media play a key role in constructing images of global warming, the media is diverse, and therefore may present different social constructions of global warming. Thus, environmental organizations often take the construction of the message into their own hands. For instance, the Environmental Defense Fund, a nonprofit organization established in 1967, partnered with the Ad Council, another nonprofit organization, to launch a campaign of public service television ads on global warming in 2006. The advertisements were accompanied by a public education effort, which included information about simple action steps for individuals. The campaign's web site also offered interactive tools where users could calculate the amount of carbon pollution they produce. The global warming ads created a media buzz, with coverage from *Forbes*, *Newsweek*, *Time*, and various radio stations.

Books, specialized magazines, and other channels of communication have also contributed to the new environmental consciousness. Clapp and Dauvergne (2005), in discussing the evolution of global environmental discourse, note the public impact of Rachel Carson's 1962 bestseller *Silent Spring*, which had a simple and powerful message about the destructive effects of pesticides on nature. Clapp and Dauvergne discuss how public concern changed its focus as environmentalists worried about the cumulative effect of local problems. Pictures of the Earth from space became more common and more people viewed life on the planet as interconnected (Clapp and Dauvergne, 2005: 49). Clapp and Dauvergne conclude that certain publications were important in the diffusion of environmentalism, including *Silent Spring* (1962), *The Population Bomb* (1968), *The Limits to Growth* (1972), *Small is Beautiful* (1973), the Founex Report, and the Brundtland Report. There are also a number of media outlets that have been highly influential in creating a global environmental consciousness. A case in point is the National Geographic Society, which for more than a century has promoted global understanding of the planet, the people who inhabit it, and the ways to protect it. In recent years, its popular television shows and web sites have been among the strongest advocates for conservation of the planet. And so, though the paths to mind change originated in multiple sources, most of them were opened by those who first heard the call from Gaia.

Action in the End: Policy Changes as a Result of Changes in the Public Mind

Political leaders are aware of the increased public concern regarding global warming. Calls for action on climate change lift public approval ratings for politicians. After the 2007 IPCC assessment report, it became difficult to object to the need to take action on global warming. Indeed, the debate today is less centered on whether or not humans are affecting global warming, but on what to do about it. The public view of global warming influences how far politicians, who are dependent on an election cycle, are willing to go in terms of policy.

While in some countries, like the United States, there has traditionally been a political cleavage in opinions about global warming, this is lessening. Pollster John Zogby says that there is a growing consensus that global warming must be addressed, not only among left-leaning and young voters, who were among the first to embrace the issue, but increasingly among all citizens (Horsley, 2007). According to Zogby, in the 2006 US midterm elections, the very existence of global warming was a "wedge" that divided Democrats and Republicans. This is no longer the case. Even President Bush acknowledged the problem in his 2007 State of the Union speech, although his actual policy remained, by and large, indifferent to the issue. In April 2007, the US Supreme Court made its first decision related to global warming, and in a 5 to 4 vote rejected the Bush administration's argument that the Environmental Protection Agency was not authorized to regulate carbon dioxide. The decision has been described as a landmark victory for environmental activists. Other indicators of climate change policy in the US, during the wait for a new, environmentally conscious president, included intense congressional activity regarding greenhouse gas emissions. As of March 2008, law-makers in the US had introduced more than 195 bills, resolutions, and amendments specifically addressing global climate change in the 110th Congress (2007–8), compared to 106 pieces of legislation submitted during the previous congressional two-year term from 2005 to 2006 (Pew Center on Global Climate Change, 2008). Lieberman and Warner's Climate Security Act of 2007 was approved by the Senate Environment and Public Works Committee on December 5, 2007. The act was described in the press as a significant piece of legislation to reduce global warming, and is considered evidence of how far Congress has moved on the issue of climate change (Kelly, 2008).

Global warming played an important role in the 2008 presidential election. Historically, environmental issues have not been decisive topics of contention in US national elections. For the 2008 US presidential election, however, the environment emerged as a significant issue, with more than 30 percent of voters saying that they would take a candidate's green credentials into account, which is up from only 11 percent of voters in 2005. All major presidential candidates discussed the issue at length and supported proposals to cut carbon emissions. The League of Conservation Voters created a web site (www.heatison.org) to keep track of the candidates' views on global warming and to keep the "heat on" the issue through the election. Senators Clinton, McCain, and Obama supported, at least in general terms, policies to curtail global warming in sharp contrast with the Bush administration – although McCain and Obama simultaneously supported intensifying oil drilling to respond to the rise in oil prices.

In the European Union, as mentioned above, on March 9, 2007, at a summit in Brussels, government leaders agreed on a binding target to reduce greenhouse-gas inducing emissions by at least 20 percent from 1990 levels by 2020. While the overall target is 20 percent, the deal allows individual targets for each of the 27 members. For example, Sweden plans to reduce its greenhouse gas emissions by at least 30 percent by 2020. On January 23, 2008, the EU agreed to a comprehensive package of proposals: the "Climate Action and Renewable Energy Package." Commission President José Manuel Barroso called the targets "20/20 by 2020." Two key targets were set by the European Council: a reduction of at least 20 percent in greenhouse gases by 2020 – rising to 30 percent if there is an international agreement committing other developed countries; and a 20 percent share of renewable energies in EU energy consumption by 2020. The package also includes updating the Emissions Trading System. The EU has the world's first carbon dioxide cap-and-trade program. In the UK, in response to intense pressure from environmental campaigners, including Friends of the Earth and the Stop Climate Change Coalition, the government agreed to plan for a bill introducing legislation to restrict greenhouse gas emissions (BBC, 2006; Wintour, 2006). The Climate Change Bill was introduced in March 2007.

The international community is also acting on global warming. The Kyoto Protocol, negotiated in 1997, entered into force in 2005, establishing binding emission limits for industrialized countries through 2012 (except the United States, which did not ratify). As of August 2008, the US and Kazakhstan were the only signatory nations not to have ratified the Kyoto Protocol. The first commitment period of the Kyoto Protocol ends in 2012, and international talks began in May 2007 on a subsequent commitment period. The UN Climate Change Conference 2007, held in Bali, culminated in the adoption of the Bali Roadmap by the Kyoto Protocol member countries. The Bali Roadmap set up a two-year process aiming to secure a binding deal at the 2009 UN summit in Denmark. And in July 2008, at the G-8 meeting in Sapporo, in a context of serious crises in energy prices and food supply, the host country (Japan) placed a new round of global warming measures at the top of the agenda. However, no corrective measures were adopted at the meeting due to the indifference of lame-duck president Bush, who decided to leave the task to his successor.

Thus, after decades of effort by the environmental movement to alert the public to the dangers of climate change by reprogramming the communication networks to convey its message, the world has finally awakened to the threat of self-inflicted destruction that global warming represents, and it seems to be moving, albeit at an uncertain, slow pace, toward adopting policies to reverse the process of our collective demise.

The New Culture of Nature

The social movement to control climate change has largely succeeded in raising awareness and inducing policy measures, albeit woefully inadequate to this point, by joining the broader environmental movement that has produced a new culture of nature over the past four decades. A comparison between Figure 5.2 and Figure 5.3 provides a good indication of the close association between the rise of environmental activism and the rise in awareness of global warming.

Thus, a multi-pronged movement made up of activists, scientists, and celebrities, acting on the media and networking via the Internet, has transformed the way we think about nature and about our place on the planet. The change is three-dimensional: it concerns our notion of space, our notion of time, and the very notion of the boundaries of society. The *space of our existence has become global and local at the same time*. We realize that we have a global home whose survivability depends on what we do in our local homes. The time horizon of our collective life, as proposed by the environmental movement, could be characterized as *glacial time*, the notion that I borrowed from Lash and Urry to apply to my analysis of the network society: "[Glacial time is] a notion in which the relation between humans and nature is very long term and evolutionary. It moves back out of immediate human history and forwards into a wholly unspecifiable future" (Lash and Urry, 1994: 243). The slow-motion time of the natural environment and of the evolution of our species, in contrast to the fast-paced time of our daily life as ephemeral individuals, underlies the project of environmentalism to redefine the parameters of our existence.

337

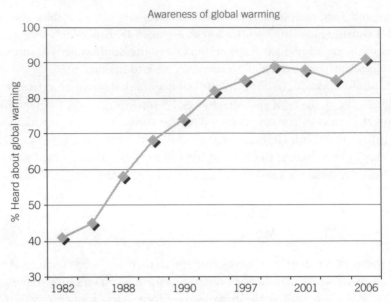

Fig. 5.3. Index of awareness about global warming in the US, 1982–2006, as per the sources in Table 5.1

The boundaries of society have to be rethought as well. Our social organization cannot be solely conceived in terms of our present or our past, but must also include the vision of our future. The vision of *intergenerational solidarity* bonds us with our grandchildren and with the grandchildren of our grandchildren, as the consequences of our action will reverberate over generations. As I wrote in 1997 (with all due apologies for exceptionally citing myself):

The holistic notion of integration between humans and nature, as presented in "deep ecology" writers, does not refer to a naïve worshipping of pristine natural landscapes, but to the fundamental consideration that the relevant unit of experience is not each individual or, for that matter, historically existing human communities. To merge ourselves with our cosmological self we need first to change the notion of time, to feel "glacial time" running through our lives, to sense the energy of stars flowing in our blood, and to assume the rivers of our thoughts endlessly merging in the boundless oceans of multiformed living matter.

(Castells, 2004c: 183)

Ten years after writing this, we are seeing the beginnings of a deep, cultural transformation of societies around the world. And we are acting on global warming now, or starting to do so. But to be able to act, we had to change the way we used to think. We had to reprogram the networks of our minds by reprogramming the networks of our communication environment.

The Network is the Message: Global Movements against Corporate Globalization[51]

> We are building autonomous counterpower by networking movements and creating our own alternatives without waiting for the government... and helping others to achieve them as well.
>
> (Pau, an activist of Infoespai, Barcelona, quoted by Juris, 2008: 282)

Since the late 1990s, a multifaceted, globally networked movement has challenged the inevitability and orientation of corporate globalization, understood as the priority given to markets over societies in the process of asymmetrical liberalization of markets around the world under the guidance of the so-called Washington consensus, enacted by the G-8 club, the World Trade Organization (WTO), the International Monetary Fund (IMF), the World Bank, and other international institutions (Stiglitz, 2002). Starting with the demonstrations against the WTO meeting in Seattle in December 1999, the protests spread thereafter throughout a global symbolic geography, mirroring the time and space of the gatherings of global power-holders with the presence of thousands who contested the values and interests reflected in the new global order in the making. These protesters were not anti-globalization, as the media quickly labeled them. They were against the policies that supported one-sided economic globalization without social and political control, and, moreover, against the discourse presenting this specific form of globalization as an irresistible historical trend. Resisting the summons to adapt to the only possible world, *they asserted*, in a variety of ideologies and organizations, *that another world was possible*.

---

[51] This section is largely based on the pioneering study conducted by my former Berkeley student and now Northeastern University Professor, Jeffrey Juris, for his PhD dissertation in Anthropology, on the basis of his ethnography of the movements in Barcelona and in various protests. The investigation, which was carried out with the full knowledge and consent of the activists, provided the basis for a major book on the development and meaning of the social movements against corporate globalization (Juris, 2008). Naturally, this section reflects my own interpretation of his findings, although I think we are not too far apart in our conclusions. For my own analysis of the movements against corporate globalization, see Castells (2004c, ch. 2). Other sources used in this section are cited in the text.

And so, activists from around the world converged on Washington in April 2000, Quebec City in April 2001, Genoa in July 2001, New York (in more modest proportions after 9/11) in January 2002, Barcelona in June 2001 and March 2002, Cancún in September 2003, Gleneagles, Scotland, in July 2005, and in Prague, Gothenburg, Nice, Geneva, Brussels, Durban, Fortaleza, Monterrey, Quito, Montreal, São Paulo, Johannesburg, Florence, Copenhagen, Athens, Miami, Zurich, Sapporo, and numerous other sites in which global networks of power and counter-power landed simultaneously to confront each other under the spotlight of the media. But these global events were just the tip of a much bigger iceberg of social discontent and cultural critique of the directions taken by the emerging global world. Thousands of local struggles on a whole range of issues became connected by the Internet and broadcast over the media, both mainstream media and the alternative media networks that had sprung up around the planet (Melucci, 1989; Keck and Sikkink, 1998; Waterman, 1998; Ayres, 1999; Ray, 1999; Riera, 2001; Appadurai, 2002; Klein, 2002; Calderon, 2003; Hardt and Negri, 2004; della Porta et al., 2006).

The World Social Forum, first organized in Porto Alegre in 2001, countered the corporate-dominated World Economic Forum, meeting annually in Davos, by convening a massive gathering to debate alternative projects at the same time. After its 2005 meeting, the World Social Forum migrated to different locations, rotating its venues to reach out to areas of the world that were less involved in the movement, from Hyderabad to Bamako. Regional social forums were also organized in Europe and Latin America. Over time, the movement became more diffused in its iconic expressions, and less present in the media. But it actually took a stronger hold in the daily struggles of people everywhere, and in its articulation over the Internet, which became both its organizational form and its mode of action. In fact, the movement as such is mainly visible on the Internet, and it is on the Internet that we find, ten years after Seattle, the variegated, global expressions of its existence.

The early attempts to build a permanent organization dissolved because of the reluctance of most activists to accept new command and control centers in charge of their collective action. Indeed, the composition of the movement, starting with the demonstrators in Seattle, defied uniformity, either in terms of social characteristics, ideologies, or goals. Environmentalists and feminists joined indigenous movements fighting for the survival of their identity; labor unions claimed their right to a global social pact alongside French farmers defending their cheese; human rights advocates coalesced with dolphin saviors; critique of capitalism mixed with critique of the state; and the unanimous demand for global democracy was entwined with the utopian search for networked self-management. There was convergence in the protest, yet divergence in the projects emerging from the negation of globalization as experienced in this early twenty-first century. But no major component in this diverse, mass movement ever pretended to unify it, to organize it, or to lead it (save for a few survivors of the old left, always ready to apply for a job in the vanguard leading the masses). To no avail. *until now*

In my personal observation of the Porto Alegre's World Social Forum of 2005, attended by over 150,000 participants, about 50,000 were camping in the "free city" of the International Youth Camp, a self-managed area with little involvement from the host municipality. There was no central program for the event. More than 5,000 roundtables and debates were held, under the initiative of specific people or groups that simply informed the coordinating center and were assigned a time and a place. And while the self-designated organic intellectuals of the movement insisted on writing and publicizing a manifesto, read in the presence of Hugo Chávez, in an attempt to recruit rebels for their cause, many participants ignored the proclamations and continued with their own local networking, a mixture of sharing life, hacking ideas, plotting actions, setting up future networks, exploring cool alternative media, and enjoying communal partying.

The extreme decentralization and diversity of the movement made it relatively opaque to the media once the militant demonstrations against fixed targets had receded. But by the time the movement metamorphosed into a myriad of local struggles and ad hoc global networks, it had brought the pitfalls of globalization to the public's attention, and many of its themes were incorporated into the policy debate. This included discussions in venues such as the World Economic Forum, which even tried, unsuccessfully, to arrange a joint meeting with the World Social Forum. As Stiglitz[52] writes:

[52] Joseph Stiglitz, a Professor of Economics at Stanford University, and the recipient of the Nobel Prize for Economics in 2001, left his post in the Clinton administration to become Chief Economist at the World Bank. His disagreements with the economic policies of the World Bank and IMF, which he considered disastrous (and proved to be so), led him to resign from the World Bank, take up a chair at Columbia University, and write and lecture around the world, documenting his critique, while

Reprogramming Communication Networks

As I moved to the international arena, I discovered that, especially at the International Monetary Fund, decisions were made on what seemed a curious blend of ideology and bad economics, dogma that sometimes seemed to be thinly veiling special interests ... It is the trade unionists, students, environmentalists – ordinary citizens – marching in the streets of Prague, Seattle, Washington and Genoa, who have put the need for reform on the agenda of the developed world.

(2002: xiii and 8)

The movement, however, could not, and never intended to, present a blueprint for a new set of global policies. Some of its components (for example, the trade unions) had a very specific agenda, and often successfully defended their interests, since in most countries, including the United States, public opinion turned against the understanding of globalization as an adaptation to global markets at the cost of jobs and living standards. Trade unions, allied to other actors in the movement and in society at large, succeeded in putting pressure on politicians to temper the strictly capitalist logic of globalization. But for the militant wing of the movement, for those who wanted not just a better place in the world as it is, but another world organized around the supremacy of human values, the movement itself was the harbinger of the society to come, a society of self-managed communities coordinated and activated over the Internet. The *networking form* of the movement, a decisive organizational tool, became the *networking norm* of the movement, in a process that Jeff Juris (2008) has thoroughly documented and analyzed.

The multiple components of the movement against corporate globalization were/are local and global at the same time. They are largely based on militants rooted in local communities, such as the movements in Barcelona, one of the most active and innovative nodes of the global movement, which Juris observed and participated in. But, at the same time, these militant organizations, as well as thousands of individual activists who mobilize for specific campaigns, connect with each other over the Internet to debate, to organize, to act, and to share. Furthermore, when a symbolic protest is planned for a particular location – for example, the meeting place of the G-8 club – Internet networks are essential to bring together the hundreds of local organizations and the thousands of activists that come to the local from the global. Therefore, organizing over the Internet relies on prior instances of face-to-face interaction, which, by converging on one eventful

proposing alternative policies oriented toward economic stability and social equity (see Stiglitz, 2002).

locale, create new occasions for broader face-to-face interaction. The Internet is central in this organizational and cultural logic that articulates global networks and local communities. Thus, Bennett (2003b: 164) concludes his study of these activist networks by stating that:

various uses of the Internet and other digital media facilitate the loosely structured networks, the weak identity ties, and the issue and demonstration campaign organizing that define a new global politics...It seems that the ease of creating vast webs of politics enables global activist networks to finesse difficult problems of collective identity that often impede the growth of movements...The success of networked communication strategies in many issue and demonstration campaigns seems to have produced enough innovation and learning to keep organizations emerging despite (and because of) the chaos and dynamic change in those organizations...The dynamic network becomes the unit of analysis in which all other levels (organizational, individual, political) can be analysed most coherently.

The networking practice of the movement goes beyond the instrumentality of coordinating actions and leveraging flexibility in distributed networks of activism. *Internet-based networking is critical at three different levels: strategic, organizational, and normative.*

What Juris (2008) conceptualizes as *the rise of informational utopics* starts in the tactics and strategy of the movement, which finds, in Internet use and alternative media, privileged tools to organize, inform, and counter-program the media networks. A key instrument in this regard is the development of *Indymedia*, a network of hundreds of media centers, some temporary, some permanent, that provide activists with the technical means to create their own information material and distribute it over the net or over hundreds of radio and community television stations, while Indymedia reporters and editors also work on stories about the movement, and on the issues raised by the movement (Downing, 2003; Costanza-Chock, forthcoming a). Open-source digital publishing has been critical in facilitating the capacity to generate and distribute information in different formats without needing to go through the mainstream media. High-quality, inexpensive video-recording and producing equipment has put communication power into the hands of activists. The ability to upload videos on YouTube and other social spaces on the Internet, or the possibility of setting up links to the movement on popular web sites, such as MySpace or Facebook, have amplified the uses of mass self-communication as the expression of new values and new projects. Alternative media are at the core of alternative social movement action (Coyer et al., 2007; Costanza-Chock, forthcoming a).

But the movement also gained coverage from the mainstream media by staging spectacular demonstrations, such as the aesthetics of the Italian group Tutte Bianche who, completely dressed in white, would advance in massive ranks against police lines under white plastic shields, a striking choreography made more appealing to the media when the blood of the demonstrators clubbed by the police would occasionally stain the immaculate purity of their peaceful protest. Or else, the Black Block, dressed in black, masked, and ready for action, would engage in a symbolic form of urban guerrilla action that was sure to draw the attention of television cameras. The media exposure that these tactics received came at the price of a "violent" tag from the media, even though violent actions were displayed by only a small minority of those involved. Street theater performances, such as those conducted by the British Reclaim the Streets group or the American group Art & Revolution, were more effective. So were festive parades with clowns, musicians, and dancers that reinvented the "flower power" revolution of the 1960s. Yet, as imaginative as these forms of communication were, they yielded the image-making of the movement to the editors of the mainstream media, limiting their impact on a public amused but distanced from the antics of the young rebels.

This is why the movement, from its beginning, was adamant about producing its own messages, and distributing them via alternative media, either community media or the Internet. The networks of information and communication organized around Indymedia are the most meaningful expression of this counter-programming capacity. Such capacity, while rooted in the creativity and commitment of the activists, is inseparable from the revolution in digital technologies. Hackers and political activists came together in the networks of alternative media. Besides Indymedia, numerous hacklabs, temporary or stable, populated the movement and used the superior technological savvy of the new generation to build an advantage in the communication battle against their elders in the mainstream media. In some cases, electronic guerrilla actions developed from these trenches of resistance, by hacking the web sites of organizations of the global establishment, posting messages from the movement in media networks, mocking globalizers with videos exposing their ideology and ridiculing their arrogance, and, more broadly, engaging in electronic civil disobedience in line with the strategy conceived some time ago by the Critical Art Ensemble and, later, by the Electronic Disturbance Theater (EDT).

Stefan Wray, the main theorist of the EDT, started in 1998 to organize virtual sit-ins by using FloodNet software that enabled large numbers of cyber activists to participate in protests by just clicking their web browsers. Since then, politically active hackers (a minority among hackers) have become a key component of the global justice movement. Their technological capacity to use computer networks for purposes different from those assigned by their corporate owners has placed hackers at the forefront of the movement, freeing activism from the limitations imposed on their autonomous expression by corporate control of the media networks. As Juris writes, "Key 'activist-hackers' operate as relayers and exchangers [of networked movements], receiving, interpreting, and routing information to diverse network nodes. Like computer hackers, activist-hackers combine and recombine cultural codes – in this case political signifiers, sharing information about projects, mobilizations, strategies and tactics within global communication networks" (2008: 14).

From media intervention and autonomous organization, the movement evolved, at least in some of its most self-reflexive components, into a *project of societal organization around networked self-management.* In some cases, the open-source movement and the movement against globalization came together to propose a new form of production and social organization based on the logic of open source, as in the German project Oekonux (a combination of *oekonomy* and Linux), an e-mail list of people committed to exploring a postcapitalist order based on the principles of free software. While Oekonux focuses on new forms of economic production, similar projects envisage forms of direct, electronic democracy (Himanen, 2001; Levy, 2001; Weber, 2004; Juris, 2008).

More broadly, the neo-anarchist current that has a strong presence in the movement against corporate globalization sees the expansion of global networks of communities and individuals as a political goal: "The self-produced, self-developed, and self-managed network becomes a widespread cultural ideal, providing not only an effective model of political organizing but also a model for reorganizing society as a whole" (Juris, 2008: 15). In a certain way, the networking dynamics present in the movement appears to bring to life the old anarchist ideal of autonomous communes and free individuals coordinating their self-managed forms of existence on a broader scale, and using the net as their global agora of deliberation without submission to any form of bureaucracy emerging from the mechanism of power delegation. Juris has the insight to cite the Russian anarchist, Voline, who, just after the Bolshevik revolution, and before the voice of anarchists were silenced in the Soviet Union, declared that:

Of course society must be organized . . . the new organization . . . must be established freely, socially, and above all, from below. The principle of organization must not issue from a center created in advance to capture the whole and impose itself upon but on the contrary it must come from all sides to create nodes of coordination, natural centers to serve all points.   (Voline, quoted by Juris, 2008: 10)

Could it be that the technological and organizational transformation of the network society provides the material and cultural basis for the anarchist utopia of networked self-management to become a social practice? This is at least what many activists in the movement against corporate globalization seem to think. While the realization of the communist prophecy under the form of statism built on vertical hierarchies directed by command-and-control centers was washed away by the test of history, the promise of self-managed networks enabled by technologies of freedom, such as the Internet and wireless communication, appears at the forefront of the new social movements of our age. And yet, we know, and Juris reminds us forcefully, that all technologies can be used for oppression as much as for liberation, and that networks connect and disconnect, include and exclude, depending on their programs and on their configuration. However, the simple fact that the movement itself, or at least a significant component of the movement, in Barcelona and elsewhere, is seizing the new technological medium to claim the historical possibility of new democratic forms of living together, without submitting to structures of domination, is a project in itself. Utopian, certainly. But utopias are not chimeras. They are mental constructions that by their existence inspire action and change reality. By advocating the liberating power of electronic networks of communication, the networked movement against imposed globalization opens up new horizons of possibility in the old dilemma between individual freedom and societal governance.

Mobil-izing Resistance: Wireless Communication and Insurgent Communities of Practice

Anger is one of the most potent emotions behind rebellious practices as it reduces the perception of risk and increases the acceptance of risk-taking behavior. Furthermore, anger intensifies with the perception of an unjust action and with the identification of the agent responsible for the action (see Chapter 3). Throughout history, anger has sparked protests, resistance, and even revolutions, starting from an aggravating event, and escalating into a rejection of the authority responsible, as the accumulation of injuries and insults suddenly becomes intolerable. The price of bread, the suspicion of witchcraft, or the injustice of rulers have been more frequent sources of revolts and social movements than the ideals of emancipation. In fact, it is often the case that these ideals only come to life by germinating in the fertile soil of popular anger against the unjust (Labrousse, 1943; Thompson, 1963; I. Castells, 1970; Spence, 1996).

Yet for resistance to emerge, individual feelings, such as anger, have to be communicated with others, transforming lonely nights of despair into shared days of wrath. And so, the control of communication and the manipulation of information have always been the first line of defense for the powerful to get away with their misdeeds. This is particularly relevant in the case of spontaneous indignation about a precise event at a given time and place. The narrower the circle of discontented, the easier the repression of their protest and the faster the restoration of order. Movements of solidarity among protesters scattered across distant locales have always had to confront the uncertainty of what actually happened as horizontal channels of communication were non-existent or broke down in moments of crisis. Furthermore, anger-driven actions surge instantaneously. They become a movement of resistance through an unforeseen chain of events. It is rarely the case that leaders plot the revolt. They usually become leaders by joining the movement on their own terms. It is precisely the unpredictable nature of these revolts that makes them dangerous and uncontrollable. They catch fire like a spark in the prairie, even if this requires a prairie dried out by the harshness of life under ruthless masters. Historically, modes of communication were critical factors in determining the extent and consequences of revolts and in explaining how isolated incidents could reach societal proportions (Dooley and Baron, 2001; Curran, 2002). This is why one of the oldest mechanisms of resistance – spontaneous revolts against allegedly unjust authority – take new meaning in the context of digital communication.

The existence of 3.5 billion mobile-phone subscribers in 2008 means that it is possible to reach out and diffuse a message anywhere, in real time. The notion of real time is of the essence in this case. It means that people can construct instant networks of communication which, by building on what they do in their everyday lives, can propagate information, feelings, and calls to arms in a multimodal and interactive manner (Rheingold, 2003). The message can be a powerful image, or a song, or a text, or a word. The image can be retrieved instantaneously by recording the despicable behavior of those in positions of power. A short SMS or a video uploaded on YouTube can touch a nerve in the sensitivity of certain people or of society at large by referring to the broader context of distrust and humiliation in which many people live. And in the world of networked mass communication, one message from one messenger can reach out to thousands, and potentially hundreds of thousands, through the mechanism of the "small world" effect: networks of networks exponentially increasing their connectivity (Buchanan, 2002). Furthermore, the networked form of message distribution matters, because if each receiver becomes a sender broadcasting via a mobile phone to many receivers by using his/her pre-programmed address book or his/her usual network of correspondents, the message is identified by the receiver as originating from a known source. In most cases, this is tantamount to receiving the message from a personally trusted source. Mobile-phone networks become trust networks, and the content transmitted through them gives rise to empathy in the mental processing of the message. From mobile-phone networks and networks of trust emerge networks of resistance prompting mobil-ization against an identified target.

In the 2000s, as wireless communication in its various modalities diffused around the world, spontaneous sociopolitical mobilizations have seized this platform of communication to enhance their autonomy vis-à-vis governments and mainstream media. In a number of countries, protesters and activists empowered by devices that allow them "perpetual connectivity" have used this communicative capacity to multiply the impact of social protests, in some cases activating revolutions, fueling resistance, propelling presidential candidates, and even bringing down governments and political regimes. To cite just a few examples, the use of mobile phones has been shown to have had significant effects in the People Power II movement, leading to the fall of President Estrada in the Philippines in 2001; in the voting into power of Korean President Moo-Hyun in 2002; in the "Orange Revolution" in Ukraine in 2005; in the movement of Los Forajidos, which ousted President Gutierrez in Ecuador in 2005; in the 2006 revolt in Thailand against intolerable corruption (precisely in the telecom business) under Prime Minister Shinawatra, ultimately prompting a military coup to cleanse the regime; in the resistance against the police repression of popular protests in Nepal in 2007, which forced free elections and resulted in the end of the monarchy; and in the pro-democracy demonstrations in Burma in 2007, which shook up the military dictatorship and prompted an international solidarity movement that put the extraordinary pressure of the international community on the Junta.

In less dramatic terms, mobile phones have become a key component in the organization and mobilization of social protests around the world, from ethnic youth battling the police in the French *banlieues* to the Chilean students' "Penguin movement" (Andrade-Jimenez, 2001; Bagalawis, 2001; Arillo, 2003; Demick, 2003; Fulford, 2003; Hachigian and Wu, 2003; Rafael, 2003; Rhee, 2003; Uy-Tioco, 2003; Fairclough, 2004; Salmon, 2004; Castells et al., 2006a; Brough, 2008; Ibahrine, 2008; Katz, 2008; Rheingold, 2008; Win, 2008). But perhaps the movement that best exemplifies the new relationship between communication control and communication autonomy at the root of current forms of protest and resistance is the March 2004 mobil-ization in Spain, when spontaneous indignation against the lies of the government concerning *al-Qaeda*'s terrorist attack in Madrid ignited a movement that resulted in the electoral defeat of Prime Minister Aznar, one of the staunchest supporters of the policies of President Bush. This is one movement in which the use of mobile-phone networks played a decisive role, as I will document below.

Of Terror, Lies, and Mobile Phones: Madrid, March 11–14, 2004

On March 11, 2004, in Madrid, a Madrid-based, mainly Moroccan, radical Islamic group associated with *al-Qaeda* conducted the largest terrorist attack to date in Europe, bombing four commuter trains, killing 199 people, and wounding over 1,400. The bombing was performed by the remote-controlled explosion of bags placed on the trains and activated by mobile phones. Indeed, it was the discovery of a mobile-phone calling card in an unexploded bag that led to the arrest and subsequent elimination of the terrorist cell. Some of the terrorists blew themselves up a few days later when the police surrounded their flat in a suburb of Madrid. Others were arrested in Spain and in other countries, and were brought to trial. Those who were found guilty received long prison terms, since in the European Union there is no death penalty. *Al-Qaeda* claimed responsibility for the bombing on the evening of March 11 by a message addressed to the London-based, on-line journal, *Al-Quds Al-Arabi*, explicitly relating the bombing to the role of Spain as one of the "crusaders" waging war in Muslim lands.

Reprogramming Communication Networks

The attack took place in a significant political context, three days before the Spanish parliamentary elections. The campaign had been dominated by the debate on the participation of Spain in the Iraq War, a policy opposed by the vast majority of citizens. Yet, the Conservative Party, the Partido Popular (PP), was considered likely to win the election, based on its record on economic policy and its tough stand on Basque terrorism. The evolution of political polls provides the political context for the story. After obtaining an absolute majority of seats in parliament in the 2000 elections, José María Aznar's PP maintained a sizeable lead over the main opposition party, the Socialist Party (PSOE) until early 2003. Then Bush, Blair, and Aznar met in the Azores shortly before the invasion of Iraq to symbolize their alliance and to plan the political aftermath of the war, as Bush was attempting to substitute a "coalition of willing countries" for the failed approval of the United Nations. Spanish public opinion was adamantly opposed to the war. Indeed, 75 percent thought, in April 2003, that "all wars are a disaster for everybody." As a result, the citizens turned against Aznar (67% did not trust him in 2003), as he was seen as a subordinate of the despised President Bush. Consequently, the Socialists jumped to a five-point lead over the Conservatives after the Azores meeting.

However, over the following year, the anti-war movement became demoralized, as in other countries, by the failure to stop the war, and the Conservative Party regained its strength, mainly as a result of two factors: economic prosperity with one of the highest growth rates in Europe, low unemployment, and low inflation; and the government policy of direct confrontation of the terrorism of ETA, the Basque radical separatist organization. So, at the start of the electoral campaign, one month before the election date set for March 14, 2004, a national poll from the Centro de Investigaciones Sociológicas (CIS) showed the Conservatives four points ahead of the Socialists among likely voters. In the Spanish electoral system, the winner translates its margin in the popular vote into a larger majority of seats, as per the D'Hondt rule aimed at facilitating stable governance. Shortly before the elections, all polls anticipated a victory by the Conservatives against a Socialist Party that was in disarray after the 2000 defeat and whose figurehead was a young, intelligent, but untested leader, José Luis Rodriguez Zapatero, whose campaign stressed his commitment to clean politics and his promise to proceed immediately with the withdrawal of Spanish troops from Iraq.

Then, in the early morning of Thursday, March 11, terror struck Madrid. The whole of Spain was in shock and disbelief, as was the world. But in the middle of the pain, fear, and anger that spread through people's minds, one persistent question immediately arose, as the media rushed to report from a background of images of bloody wreckage: who had done it?

As soon as the Madrid terror attack occurred, and before any evidence had surfaced, the PP government stated with complete conviction that the Basque terrorist group, ETA, was behind the bombing. Prime Minister Aznar went as far as to personally call the directors of the main newspapers of the country around 1 p.m. on March 11 (four hours after the attack) to assure them that, with the information in his hands, he had no doubt that ETA were the authors of the massacre. He called them a second time, at 8 p.m., to reiterate his claim. Based on this assurance, *El País*, the main newspaper of the country, whose political orientation is opposed to the Conservatives, changed the headline on its front page, which was already in the press, from *"Terrorist Massacre in Madrid"* to *"ETA Massacre in Madrid,"* thus contributing to the credibility of the government's version of events. Government ownership of the main television network, TVE, political control over one of the two private television networks, Antena 3 TV, and the ideological support of the other Madrid newspapers (*El Mundo, ABC, La Razón*) ensured the relentless reiteration of the government's message regarding responsibility for the attack. As late as Saturday, March 13, the government-owned news agency EFE distributed an article titled "Leads point at ETA and discard Al Qaeda." As the hours went by, it became increasingly likely, as early as March 12, that *al-Qaeda* was the culprit, since the police had found a van with detonators, and a tape with Islamic verses, and *al-Qaeda* had claimed responsibility for the attack. Yet, the Minister of the Interior and the government's spokesman continued to insist on ETA's responsibility until the evening of the 13th, and even then they only acknowledged reluctantly and conditionally what the police already knew. Indeed, on the afternoon of the 13th, while the Minister of the Interior kept singing along to his favorite Basque terrorist tune, the first Islamic arrests were taking place in Madrid.

Why should there be such a stubborn attempt to mislead public opinion, possibly jeopardizing security in other European capitals in the event of a coordinated offensive from *al-Qaeda*, in a moment of collective psychological trauma in the country? There is an obvious answer: the political stakes were high. The elections were three days away and, as the *Financial Times* wrote at the time, "If ETA were held responsible, it could bolster support for the ruling Popular party, which is already leading in the polls. However, any involvement by al-Qaeda could lead voters to question the government's staunch support for the US-led occupation of Iraq" (Crawford et al., 2004).

In the minds of millions of Spaniards (actually 65% of them) judging the events one week later (Instituto Opina, 2004), the government manipulated information about the attack to seek political advantage. The work of an investigative parliamentary commission produced evidence that, without explicitly lying, the PP government delayed the publication of some critical information concerning the actual events of March 11–14, and treated evidence that was still under scrutiny as indisputable fact. There was clearly a systematic determination to favor the hypothesis of Basque terrorism instead of pursuing the Islamic trail, despite early leads pointing police in this direction. The manipulation was particularly blatant on the government television station TVE1, which has the largest viewership for events, whose news anchorman, Mr. Urdazi, went to great lengths to omit or delay any information on the Islamic connection until it was officially acknowledged by the government. And even then, on the evening of March 13, hours before the polls would open on Sunday the 14th, TVE1 changed its programming for Saturday night to broadcast a special presentation: the film *Murder in February*, which tells the story of the assassination of a Basque Socialist leader by ETA terrorists.

Based on available documentation (Rodriguez, 2004; Spanish Parliament, 2004; de Ugarte, 2004), press reports, and personal knowledge, I think it is possible to reconstruct the sequence of events behind the Aznar government's effort at misinformation. It was a matter of timing. On March 11, emotions were too overwhelming for citizens and journalists to enter the fray over the source of the attack, even if international observers and some journalists in Spain were pointing to *al-Qaeda* and had started to question ETA's responsibility as ETA itself denied any connection with the attack. The government rejected the statement as it refused to give any credibility to ETA.

Friday, March 12, was dominated by the massive, and emotional, popular outpouring against terrorism of all origins. Over 11 million people marched in the streets of Spanish cities, with all political parties united in the demonstration, in a rare display of national unity. However, in spite of the unanimous feeling of grief, as the police were quickly assembling data that discredited the ETA hypothesis, and as this information began to leak into some of the media, many of the demonstrators demanded to know the truth. How could the government hope to get away with hiding information on such an important matter, while the police and independent media were uncovering the truth? In fact, Aznar and his Minister of the Interior had only to withhold information for a couple of days, as voting was scheduled for Sunday the 14th. The critical point was that Saturday the 13th was "reflection day," a date on which, under Spanish law, no campaign statements or public political demonstrations are allowed. And so, as the investigation unfolded on Friday and Saturday, the government stuck to its disinformation strategy to minimize any potential electoral impact by association between the terrorist attacks and Spain's participation in the Iraq War. It was probably decided to acknowledge *al-Qaeda*'s connection on Monday after the results of the election were in. While the calculation was shrewd, it backfired.

This is because, regardless of the extent of the manipulation that actually took place, what counts is that thousands of citizens were convinced on March 12 and 13 of the existence of this manipulation. A key factor in breaking through the government agenda-setting strategy in the media and in influencing public opinion was the report of the most important private radio network, SER, which, very early on in the process, questioned the government's version of events and broadcast information from police sources that pointed to Islamic terrorism. The determined information strategy of SER, which directly confronted the government and the media close to the government, reveals the relative autonomy of journalists vis-à-vis their corporations: SER is owned by Grupo Prisa, the same corporation that controls *El País* newspaper. And yet, while *El País*, in spite of being distant from the Conservatives, exhibited a cautious attitude toward informing the public about *al-Qaeda*, the radio network unearthed every possible piece of information and diffused it immediately (in one instance, erroneously giving credit to the rumor that the remains of a terrorist had been found in the train wreckage). By Saturday morning, various media began questioning the government's version of events, and so, the front page of *La Vanguardia*, the main Barcelona newspaper, was titled "Proofs point to Al-Qaeda but the government insists on ETA."[53]

---

[53] On a personal note, I was in Barcelona at that time, and I was among the skeptics regarding the government accusation against ETA, in part because I had studied *al-Qaeda* and the bombing fitted well into what I knew of its tactics. So, I published an article in *La Vanguardia* on the morning of Saturday the 13th arguing for the likelihood of the *al-Qaeda* connection, and exposing the government's misinformation strategy. This article, together with its second part one week later in the same newspaper, received the Godo Prize, one of the leading awards in Spanish journalism, and an unlikely one for me as I do not pretend to be a journalist.

So, by Saturday morning, streams of information from a variety of sources, including the Internet and the foreign media, had permeated among sections of public opinion, particularly among the young, educated, and politically independent, often mistrustful of governments and parties. The more people knew about possible political manipulation of something as tragic and significant as the terrorist attacks, the more anger surfaced and incited the public to do something about it. But what? No political demonstrations were allowed that day, the government media kept replaying stories about Basque terrorism (even though, by then, the police knew this was not the case), and political parties and opposition leaders were muzzled by electoral regulations and their own sense of caution a few hours before the vote. Thus, the unheard opinion on terror and the truth about terror had to find alternative communication channels to express its views, and ultimately call for action. People, particularly young people, used the Internet, as they use it everyday, to retrieve information, express their grief, share their opinions, and e-mail their networks.

Then, on the morning of Saturday the 13th, someone in Madrid sent an SMS to ten friends from his mobile phone. Although he had decided to remain anonymous, he was identified by journalists as being a 30-year-old man, educated and politically independent, though he never thought he could launch a movement. As he later explained in an interview,[54] his idea was to call his friends and the friends of his friends to protest in front of the Madrid headquarters of the Partido Popular, and if they could get 15 people together, then they would all go to the movies afterward. The message he sent was spontaneous and limited to the 160 characters of a standard SMS. It read (in Spanish of course): "Aznar off the hook? They call it day of reflection and Urdazi [the manipulative TVE anchorman] works? Today, 13 M, 18h. PP headquarters, Genova Street 13. No parties. Silent for Truth. Pasalo! [Pass it on!]" In fact, his ten friends happened to forward the message to their ten friends, who did the same with their ten friends, and on and on. SMS traffic in Spain increased by 30 percent over an average Saturday, at a much greater level than a weekday; additionally, the message was relayed via e-mail, so Internet traffic also increased by 40 percent (Campo Vidal, 2004, using sources from telecommunications operators). At 18 hours, there were hundreds of people, mostly young, sitting in the street at Genova 13, Madrid. One hour later, the crowd

[handwritten margin note: mobilizing communication]

[54] Available at: http://www.elpais.com/audios/cadena/ser/Entrevista/hombre/promovio/concentracion/sabado/frente/Genova/elpaud/20040316csrcsr_4/Aes/

had grown to over 5,000 people, according to media sources. Their slogans included: "Who was?!," "Before voting, we want the truth!," "The bombs of Iraq explode in Madrid," and the most ominous message for Aznar: "Liars! Liars! Tomorrow we'll vote, tomorrow we'll throw you out!!!"

Similar spontaneous demonstrations, prompted by the massive diffusion of the same or similar messages, took place in cities around Spain, particularly Barcelona. The riot police took up position around the PP buildings, but so did the media. Thus, while the demonstrations were technically illegal, the police were hesitant to beat up protesters peacefully sitting in the street a few hours before a general election. Besides, while most people stayed home, they were not indifferent to the protest. In the main Spanish cities, a form of protest adopted during the anti-war movement was spontaneously re-enacted in thousands of homes: banging pots and pans from their windows at an agreed time, also convened by SMS. With the sounds of protest filling the air of a Saturday evening, and as news of the arrests of Islamists diffused over a few media outlets and the Internet, the king of Spain himself intervened in the crisis. He issued an institutional declaration condemning the terrorist attack without mentioning ETA. But before doing this, he requested that, before he spoke to the country, the government should acknowledge what the police already knew: that al-Qaeda were responsible. To make sure his message was understood, he distributed his videotaped statement to the foreign television networks 15 minutes earlier than scheduled in the Spanish media, allowing the government enough time for the Minister of the Interior to make an announcement at about the same time. Aznar was forced to concede. At 20.20 hours on Saturday the 13th, less than 12 hours before the polls would open, the Minister of the Interior appeared on national television to announce the arrest of an Islamic cell and the identification of other Islamic militants in the attack. He still, however, insisted on the possibility of a connection between al-Qaeda and ETA, a conspiracy theory (which in some versions includes the Spanish socialists as well) that Aznar continues to defend to this day, in spite of its explicit and unequivocal dismissal by the police, the parliamentary commission of inquiry, and the courts that tried the case. Nonetheless, the acknowledgment by the Minister of the Interior of al-Qaeda's responsibility resulted in the worse possible political outcome for the PP. Not only were the dangers of supporting Bush in Iraq exposed, to the dismay of peaceful Spaniards content with their marginality in world conflicts, but the government's perceived scheme to lie to the country about the most tragic event of recent Spanish history was deeply resented by the citizens, and particularly by young citizens who tend to be more sensitive to moral issues than to political ideologies.

These feelings were directly reflected in the vote of March 14, 2004. Against the odds, the Socialists won the election by receiving 42.6 percent of the popular vote against 37.6 percent for the PP. The difference between the opinion polls taken before the terrorist attacks and the actual election results was more than ten points. But how do we know that the vote was connected to the crisis, and, more specifically, to the mobilization that denounced the government's manipulation of information? On this crucial matter, I largely rely on the thorough, statistical analysis of Narciso Michavila (2005) on the electoral impact of the Islamists' attacks of 2004, using the data from the Center of Investigaciones Sociologicas post-election survey, as well as exit polls from several polling firms. It is important to present the subtlety of this analysis because of its broader implications.

The first important effect of the drama surrounding the election was the mobilization of the electorate. Participation in the elections increased by 7 percentage points in 2004 over 2000, reaching over 75 percent of the electorate, the highest level since 1996 (participation rate fell again in 2008, to 69%). While a large majority of the voters (71%) did not acknowledge any influence of the March events on their voting decision, 21.5 percent declared that the events had a major or significant influence on their vote, a proportion of the electorate large enough to change the results of the election. Michavila (2005), following Lazarsfeld et al.'s (1944) classic paradigm, differentiates two mechanisms underlying such change. One is activation, or mobilizing the vote. The other is conversion, or changing the vote. Activation involved about 1.7 million voters, out of a total of 25,847,000. Activation was particularly intense among previous abstainers and among voters under 40. Conversion represented the behavior of about one million voters, mainly of middle age and most of whom were voting for the party they chose for the 2004 election for the first time. The Socialists received 8.7 percent of their votes from voters activated as a consequence of the attack and the incidents surrounding it, while only 3.5 percent of Conservative voters were activated by the attack. Of people converted as a consequence of the attack, those who changed their vote in favor of the Socialists represented 6.5 percent of the Socialist vote in contrast to only 1.2 percent of the Conservative vote. Thus, the party that received more support as a result of the attack and the subsequent process of information manipulation was the Socialist Party, particularly because the 951,000 voters who were not planning to vote did so as a result of the events preceding the election day. But even more important was the impact of 700,000 converted votes because these votes were subtracted from the parties that the voters deserted, and the majority of these votes were for the Socialists. A similar conclusion can be obtained from the analysis of the exit polls conducted by Sigma2 and according to which the increase in Socialist votes came from one and a half million previous abstainers, one and a half million voters from other parties, and half a million new voters.

A key element of these vote transfers was the electoral behavior of the younger segments of the electorate. Compared with the 2000 election, the Socialists increased their vote by 3 percent in the 18–29-year age group, and by 2 percent in the 30–44-year age group, while the Conservatives decreased their vote respectively by 7 percent and 4 percent (Sanz and Sanchez-Sierra, 2005)). Thus, it appears that young voters, who were at the origin of the mobil-izations, and who usually have a lower turnout on election day, increased their participation considerably, and did so in favor of the Socialists. This does not appear to be the result of ideological positioning. First, because there is widespread disaffection among Spanish youth vis-à-vis all established political parties, including the Socialists. Second, because the new contingent of voters actually tilted the Socialist electorate toward the center in ideological terms, in comparison with the 2000 election. This is because a pro-Socialist shift occurred among those voters without a defined ideological position. Third, a higher proportion of professional classes, and higher educated groups voted for the Socialists in 2004 than in previous years, another change in a segment of the electorate that may link the Socialist victory to a displacement from traditional voting patterns for reasons other than party influence. Fourth, people activated by the events, and voters who changed their vote as a result of these events, had a more neutral ideological profile than regular Socialist and Conservative voters. In other words, in situations of social stress, partisan voters stick to their ideological roots, while non-ideologues react with their feelings, and it appears that these feelings led them to vote, and to vote against the Conservatives. Indeed, among the voters who decided their vote at the last minute and chose to vote Socialist, 56 percent were ideologically conservative.

An interesting method of assessing the factors that decided the election is an analysis of the voting patterns of those who decided to vote or changed their vote at the last minute. The Socialists won a larger share of the vote than the Conservatives among those who were hesitating between parties; the Socialists received 4.1 percent of the votes of those who had originally decided not to vote, in contrast to the Conservatives who only received 1.6 percent of those voters. In other words; the events of March mobilized voters, and particularly independent and non-ideological voters, to participate in the election and to do so in order to vote against the Conservatives. The group of Socialist voters who hesitated most between voting Conservative or Socialist had a higher proportion of young people and educated people than those who decided to vote Conservative. Personal interviews I conducted with some of the young voters at the time illustrated the targeted anger of these voters against the "liars," to the point of voting for a party (the Socialists) for which they felt little sympathy as it is came within the general category of traditional politicians. Interestingly, the less "pro-establishment" party in the political spectrum, the Catalan nationalists of the ERC, received 17 percent of the vote of last-minute voters, significantly more than any other party, an indication that young voters were hesitating between their rejection of the system, their political allegiance to some new options, and the desire to efficiently use a Socialist vote to oust "the liars." Indeed, the polls taken two months before the March 2008 national election showed that young voters were likely to return to their lower participation rate, and that their voting inclinations favored the Socialists less than their vote in 2004 (*La Vanguardia*, 2008). While Rodriguez Zapatero was re-elected in 2008 in spite of lower support from young people than in 2004, he owed his victory to the mobilization of the Catalan voters against the threats of the PP to their cherished autonomy.

In the end, the more voters were influenced by the March 2004 events, the more they hesitated to vote until the last minute; and the more they were provoked to vote by March 11 and subsequent events, the more likely they were to vote for the Socialists on March 14, as graphically presented in Figure 5.4 elaborated by Michavila (2005). On the basis of his data analysis, Michavila concludes that "the association between the final election and the influence of the attacks is statistically significant" (2005: 29). Thus, a major political change took place in Spain with significant consequences for global geopolitics, as Bush lost a key ally in a critical moment of constructing his coalition to sustain the war in Iraq. Indeed, Prime Minister Rodriguez Zapatero honored his electoral promise and ordered the immediate withdrawal of Spanish troops from Iraq (but not from Afghanistan)

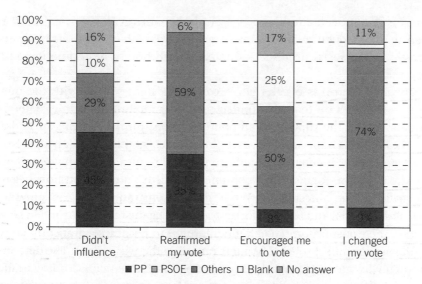

Fig. 5.4. Final vote for PP, PSOE, or others, among late-deciding voters in the Spanish parliamentary elections of March 14, 2004, according to the influence of the events of March 11 on voters' decisions

Source: Michavila (2005: 29).

on his first day in office, provoking a chill in the relationship with the White House that would last until the last day of Bush's tenure, while ex-prime minister Aznar became a habitual guest of the Bushes. It was the first crack in a coalition that would disintegrate over the following years.

This major political change resulted from a change of mentality in Spain that has taken place over the past three decades, as a young generation has largely embraced the desire for world peace, and yearns for authenticity and morality in the conduct of world affairs (notwithstanding its equally sincere passion for discos, sex, and drinking). The sadness of death, and rage against the assassins, was compounded by a deep sense of betrayal that was more personal than political, less ideological than moral. It triggered a movement of resistance that directly impacted upon the state, not only by changing the party in government, but by sending a message to the political class that it would ignore them at its peril in future. Indeed, the first Zapatero administration, in spite of multiple mistakes, appeared to put into practice the notion that honesty comes first in the minds of a new brand of citizens, and was re-elected in 2008.

Reprogramming Communication Networks

But for this movement to evolve from indignant revolt to civic protest it had to go through a process of communication that I consider characteristic of the social protests of our age. I will briefly underline its main features.

The actual process of alternative communication started with the outpouring of emotion that surrounded the government-called street demonstrations, with the support of all political forces, on the evening of Friday the 12th. This is important: it was in this physical gathering that people first started to react, independently of the political parties that remained silent for the occasion. Right there, spontaneous calls from demonstrators began to challenge the official story. While the demonstration was convened by established social and political forces to protest against terrorism and in support of the Constitution (an oblique reference to Basque separatism), many of the participants displayed banners opposing the war in Iraq. The demonstration was intended to mark the end of political statements, leading to the day of reflection on Saturday and to the election vote on Sunday. Yet, on Saturday morning, when a number of individuals, mostly without political affiliation and independent of the mainstream parties, started to circulate SMSs to the addresses programmed in their mobile phones, they created an instant network of communication and mobil-ization that resonated in the minds of thousands whose uneasiness had grown in the previous 48 hours. On Saturday, as mentioned above, traffic in SMS reached a record level. The critical matter is that while most messages were very similar, the sender for each receiver was someone known, someone who had the receiver's address in his/her mobile-phone address book. Thus, the network of diffusion was increasing at an exponential rate but without losing the proximity of the source, according to the logic of the "small world" phenomenon. And it is important to remember that the rate of penetration of mobile phones per person in Spain at the time was 96 percent. People also used the Internet to look for other sources of information, particularly from abroad. There were a number of initiatives to organize alternative communication networks, including some by journalists acting on their own, to set up a web site with information and debates from various sources. Interestingly enough, the Conservative Party (PP) started an SMS network of its own with a different message: "ETA are the authors of the massacre. Pasalo!" But it was diffused mainly through party channels, did not reach a critical mass of known person to known person, and, more importantly, was not credible to the thousands of people who were already doubting the government's word.

360

The context provided by the mainstream media was also significant. Major television networks were ignored as reliable sources very early on. Newspapers, because of their hesitation, became unreliable, although in some cases, particularly *La Vanguardia* in Barcelona, their Saturday editions began to legitimize the version linking *al-Qaeda* to the attack. On the other hand, as reported above, the major private radio network (SER), under the initiative of its journalists, immediately looked for evidence away from the Basque trail. Most, although not all, of SER's reports proved to be on target. As a result, many people referred to the radio as their primary source of information, and then interacted with SMSs and voice communication over mobile phones: voice communication with their close friends, and SMS to diffuse their own messages or those they were receiving and in agreement with.

Thus, the context of communication was provided by the physical gathering on the streets, at the origin of the formation of public space, and as a result of the process of political communication: being together in front of the PP buildings was the verification of the effectiveness of the message. The actions on the street attracted the attention of some radio and television networks (regional television, CNN-Spain), and ultimately forced the Minister of the Interior to publicly appear on national television to acknowledge *al-Qaeda*'s possible role. Later on, the angry leading candidate of the PP would also appear on television, denouncing the demonstrators and unwittingly diffusing the self-induced crisis of trust among the entire population. Thus, an error in political communication, largely provoked by demonstrators and partly assisted by the king, amplified the effect of the demonstrations. While the Internet was important in providing a source of information and a forum of debate in the days preceding the demonstrations, the critical events were the demonstrations of Saturday the 13th, a typical instant mobilization phenomenon prompted by a massive network of SMSs that exponentially increased the effect of communication through interpersonal channels. I will now elaborate on the deeper, analytical meaning of this and similar social movements.

Networked Individualism and Insurgent Communities of Practice

Mobile phones have become a fundamental medium of communication and intervention for grassroots movements and political activism around the world, as a growing literature on the matter shows, and as the case study of the Spanish mobil-ization against the shameful behavior of their government strikingly illustrates.

But as we learn from the social history of technology, the relevance of a given technology, and its acceptance by people at large, do not result from the technology itself, but from appropriation of the technology by individuals and collectives to fit their needs and their culture. The study I conducted with my collaborators on mobile communication and society (Castells et al., 2006b) showed the key role of wireless communication in supporting personal and cultural autonomy, while maintaining patterns of communication and meaning in all domains of social activity. The sociopolitical uses of wireless communication epitomize this analysis. If mobile phones and other wireless communication devices are becoming the privileged tools of grassroots-initiated political change in our world, it is because their sociotechnical features directly relate to the major cultural trends underlying social practice in our society.

As proposed in Chapter 2, two major trends define the basic cultural patterns of the global network society through their interaction: networked individualism and communalism. On one hand, the culture of individualism, inscribed in the social structure characteristic of the network society, reconstructs social relationships on the basis of self-defined individuals who aim to interact with others following their own choices, values, and interests, transcending ascription, tradition, and hierarchy. Networked individualism is a culture, not an organizational form. A culture that starts with the values and projects of the individual but builds a system of exchange with other individuals, thus reconstructing society rather than reproducing society. Networked individualism inspires project-oriented social movements that build on the sharing of new values among individuals who want to change their lives and need each other to fulfill their goals. On the other hand, in a world of values and norms constantly in flux, in a risk society, people who feel uncertain or vulnerable as individuals seek refuge in communities that respond to their identities, always constructed, either with the materials of history and geography, or with the desires from which projects are made. These communities often become trenches of resistance against a social order perceived as alien and imposed by force, when the institutions that used to provide security (the state, the church, the family) no longer function properly.

There are also social movements that result from the crossing of the two cultural patterns: networked individualism and communalism. These are movements that emerge from networks of individuals reacting to perceived oppression, and then transforming their shared protest into a community of practice, their practice being resistance. So, *networks of individuals become insurgent communities.* In proposing this conceptualization, I build on the analytical tradition that shows the decisive role of communities of practice in all domains of society (Wenger, 1999; Tuomi, 2002; Wenger and Synder, 2008). Communities of practice are communities; that is, social groupings of individuals sharing values, beliefs, and norms with those identified as belonging to the community. Specific communities are defined by specific criteria: territorial boundaries, religious affiliation, sexual orientation, national identity, and the like. Communities of practice are those that are constituted around a defined shared practice, such as a scientific project, a cultural creation, or a business venture. What is distinctive is that they form strong ties during the practice, but they do not remain as communities beyond the practice. They are ephemeral but intense. And so, they can reproduce and expand, forming different communities; for instance, scientists may meet their colleagues again in another research team formed upon a previous successful experience. But each community of practice is defined by the practice, and exhausts itself with the specific practice that was at the origin of the formation of the community.

These concepts may allow a better understanding of the novelty and significance of mobil-izations that constitute a practice of resistance by bringing together networks of individuals who join this particular instance of resistance in a given time and space. Because mobile phones enable people to be perpetually networked, anytime, anywhere, explosions of anger felt at the individual level have the potential of developing into an insurgent community by the instant networking of many different individuals who are united in their frustration, though not necessarily united around a common position or solution to the perceived unjust source of domination. Because wireless communication builds on networks of shared practices, it is the appropriate communication technology for the spontaneous formation of communities of practice engaged in resistance to domination; that is, *instant insurgent communities.* Since social actors select and use technologies depending on their needs and interests, people who react individually against institutional domination, and yet need to find support for their revolt, will turn naturally to the forms of communication that they use in their daily lives both to be themselves and to be together with those with whom they want to share meaning and practice. Under these cultural and technological conditions, social explosions of resistance do not need leaders and strategists, as anyone can reach everybody to share their rage. If the rage is, in fact, a purely individual feeling, the SMS will drift harmlessly in the ocean of digital communication. Yet, if the bottle thrown into the ocean comes to be opened by many, the genie will be out, and an insurgent community will grow by connecting minds beyond their solitary revolt. If you think this is too theoretical, ask José María Aznar about its practical consequences.

"Yes, We Can!" The 2008 Obama Presidential Primary Campaign[55]

> Hope – Hope in the face of difficulty. Hope in the face of uncertainty. The audacity of hope! In the end, that is God's greatest gift to us, the bedrock of this nation. A belief in things not seen. A belief that there are better days ahead. I believe that we can give our middle class relief and provide working families with a road to opportunity. I believe we can provide jobs to the jobless, homes to the homeless, and reclaim young people in cities across America from violence and despair. I believe that we have a righteous wind at our backs and that as we stand on the crossroads of history, we can make the right choices, and meet the challenges that face us.
>
> (Barack Obama, speech before the 2004 Democratic
> National Convention)

The crisis of political legitimacy, documented in Chapter 4, manifests itself in people's lack of trust in their political representatives, in the low level of citizen participation in the political process, and in the prevalence of negative motivations in voting behavior. On all counts, the oldest liberal democracy in the world, the United States, has fared poorly over the past three decades. However, in the 2007–8 primary presidential campaign, a surge of citizen participation and political enthusiasm signaled a revival of the American democracy against the backdrop of the dire realities of war and economic decline, and the hard truth of presidential lies about matters of life and death. Political mobilization increased across the board, among Democrats, Republicans, and independents alike. However, there is ample

[55] This section was written between April and August 2008, with the exception of the concluding part under the subheading "The Day After." It has not been updated because its purpose is analytical, not documentary, and should stand as it is. The outcome of the general election appears to be coherent with the trends identified in this case study. Yet, what is relevant from the perspective of this book is the role of the new relationship between communication and insurgent politics established by the Obama campaign, the first campaign in which the political uses of the Internet played a decisive role.

evidence that, during the primary season, Democratic voters mobilized at a much higher percentage than Republican voters. The length and the intensity of the primary competition between Barack Obama and Hillary Clinton may account for some of the difference in levels of engagement. However, I will make the case that the personalities of the leading Democratic candidates, Barack Obama and Hillary Clinton, and the mobilization they generated among large groups of disenfranchised or disenchanted voters, largely account for the difference. Furthermore, it was the Obama campaign's novelty and enthusiasm that activated the droves of citizens who had previously remained on the sidelines of democracy during long years of political skepticism. This is not to downplay Hillary Clinton's ability to induce mobilization, particularly among women, seniors, and Latinos. But I propose the hypothesis that the challenge the unlikely competitor, Obama, posed to her supposedly unstoppable candidacy provoked her campaign to change its tone, strategy, and impact. During the transition from pre-ordained victory to impending defeat, after losing in 11 primaries in a row, Hillary transformed herself into the leader of a movement (partially proactive and partially reactive to Obama), "finding her own voice" and altering the landscape of American politics for years to come. Yet, regardless of personal preferences, it was fitting that she lost the nomination in the end, after a most spirited fight, because her movement was at least partly the result of her determined effort to counter Barack Obama's improbable surge at the forefront of a campaign potentially leading to the White House.

Thus, this will be the focus of my analysis: how and why was a junior politician – an African American with a Muslim surname and Kenyan ancestry, with one of the most left-leaning Senate voting records, without significant support among the Democratic Party establishment, who explicitly rejected funding from the Washington lobbies – able to secure the Democratic nomination for president of the United States by a comfortable margin?[56] A partial answer to this intriguing matter is that he was able to move into the heart of American politics by bringing along a substantial

[56] Since the 1980s, the US Democratic Party has chosen its nominee for the presidential race through a combination of 2,000 delegates, who vote at the annual nominating Convention according to the results of the popular vote in their respective districts, and 800 super delegates, an unelected selection of Democratic Party elites, including senators, congressmen, and state governors. In the 2008 Democratic primary race, Obama won 1,763 pledged delegates against 1,640 for Hillary, and 438 super delegates against 256 for Hillary. However, most of Obama's super-delegate advantage came from a movement of support for his candidacy in the last stage of the campaign, when it became almost certain that he would secure the majority of pledged delegates.

number of citizens who had been either marginalized or discouraged by politics as usual. And he was able to do so through a combination of a charismatic personality, a new kind of political discourse, and an innovative campaign strategy that transferred the time-tested principles of community organizing in America into the specificity of an Internet environment. Following in the footsteps of Howard Dean's presidential primary campaign in 2003–4 (Sey and Castells, 2004), Obama successfully mastered the rules of engagement of what has been labeled "the first networked campaign" (Palmer, 2008). It is because of these features that the Obama campaign constitutes a paradigmatic case of insurgent politics in the Internet Age.

Voting Power for the Powerless

Democracy, in the last resort, resides in the capacity to counter the power of heritage, wealth, and personal influence with the power of the multitude, the power of numbers – the numbers of citizens, whoever they are. Insurgent politics is a key process in connecting the powerless segments of the population to power-making procedures. Political participation is essential to keep democracy alive. And so, let us start with the facts about electoral mobilization.[57] *Voter registration*, the Achilles' heel of American democracy,[58] increased in record numbers between 2004 and 2008 in 43

[57] Millions of American citizens cannot vote, either because they are not registered or cannot register properly or because they have lost their civil rights as a result of having been convicted of a crime, which largely affects minorities. In addition, the US is the country, with the exception of the Gulf Emirates, where the contradiction between living in the country, working and paying taxes, and participating in elections is the most extreme. Every US state (except Vermont and Maine) prohibits individuals convicted of a felony crime from voting either permanently or until they complete a complex and often arbitrary set of steps to have their vote reinstated. The Sentencing Project estimates that these felon laws keep approximately 5.3 million people from voting each election cycle (King, 2006). Moreover, new laws passed in 2006 require a government-issued photo ID to vote in some states, a regulation that disproportionately prohibits poor, naturalized immigrants and elderly voters from voting. Add to this, the approximately 4–6 million voters whose votes are not counted either due to technological or human error at the polls, and the numbers of American disenfranchised voters becomes extraordinary (CalTech/MIT Voting Technology Project, 2006: 7). There are serious consequences for civic life in terms of the discrepancy between being there and not having the right to participate. Although, in all fairness, the American naturalization system, as bureaucratic as it may be, is still the most open in the world in making citizens out of immigrants. The policy is still to facilitate access to citizenship, but the bulk of an estimated 12 million undocumented immigrants makes it difficult to implement the principle.

[58] According to the US Census Bureau, 126 million Americans voted in November 2004, a record high for a presidential election year. Approximately 72% of voting-age

out of 44 states for which comparable data are available (the exception was Idaho; Jacobs and Burns, 2008). Seventeen of the 43 states set records for turnout during primaries or caucuses held after "Super Tuesday"[59] (on February 5, 2008) when McCain had already locked down the Republican nomination, marking a period in which the Obama campaign moved from behind Clinton to garner a series of successive victories. The dramatic increase in voter registration in states generally considered to be "at play" (neither solidly Democrat nor solidly Republican) altered the electoral map of the United States. About one-quarter of new voter registration took place in these states. Ten states increased their voter rolls by 10 percent or more, including New Hampshire (24 percent), Nevada (20 percent), Arizona (18 percent), and New Mexico (11 percent; Jacobs and Burns, 2008).

A case in point is Pennsylvania, a critical state in the general election. A reported 306,918 new Democrats joined the Pennsylvania voter rolls between January 1 and the voter registration deadline on March 24. Moreover, 146,166 first-time voters joined the Democratic Party and 160,752 switched their registration from Republican or independent to Democrat (a mere 39,019 first-time voters joined the Republicans; Cogan, 2008). The Obama campaign itself reported registering 200,000 new Democrats in Pennsylvania, 165,000 in North Carolina, and more than 150,000 in

American citizens were registered to vote in 2004, according to the last US census. However, these rates do not reflect the demographic inequities of voter registration in the US. Although naturalized immigrants have been allowed to vote in all US elections since the 1920s, successive immigrant legislation has made it harder and harder for immigrant citizens to vote. Most states now require a valid government-issued photo ID or birth certificate, which disproportionately impacts upon the ability of minorities and naturalized immigrants to vote. In 2004, almost 93% of registered voters were born in the United States and only 61% of naturalized citizens were registered to vote (compared to 72% of native citizens). Age is also an important factor: 79% of citizens over 55 were registered to vote in 2004 compared to 58% of 18–24-year-olds. White Americans are also more likely to register to vote (74%) than African Americans (68.7%), Hispanics (57.9%), or Asians (51.8%). Education is also a critical factor. Only 52.9% of Americans without a high school degree are registered to vote, compared to Americans with an advanced college degree (87.9%). Moreover, only 48% of Americans living in families with incomes of less than $20,000 per year are registered to vote compared to 77% of those living in families earning over $50,000 per year. All these statistics are cited from an official release of the US Census Bureau (see Holder, 2006).

[59] "Super Tuesday" refers to the date in the spring of a primary election year when more US states hold their primary elections than on any other day. In the spring of 2007, 24 states, representing over half the elected delegates to the National Convention, voted to change their primary date to Tuesday February 5, 2008, creating the largest "Super Tuesday" to date, or what the press popularly referred to as "Super-Duper Tuesday."

Indiana during the primary season (Green, 2008). The newly registered Democrats in Pennsylvania were concentrated in African American neighborhoods, a demographic that went overwhelmingly for Obama, although he lost the Pennsylvania primary. This unusually intense registration drive was no accident. In the 1992 election between George H. W. Bush and Bill Clinton, Clinton came from behind to win Illinois, largely because of unprecedented new voter registration. In Chicago alone, 150,000 new voters were registered, the large majority of them African American. According to a 1993 report in *Chicago Magazine*:

The election, to some degree, turned on these totals:...Clinton had almost unanimous support among blacks. But just as important, if less obvious, are the implications black votership could have for future city and state elections: For the first time in ten years, more than half a million blacks went to the polls in Chicago. And with gubernatorial and mayoral elections coming up in the next two years, it served notice to everyone from Jim Edgar to Richard M. Daley that an African-American voting bloc would be a force to be reckoned with in those races.

None of this, of course, was accidental. The most effective minority voter registration drive in memory was the result of careful handiwork by Project Vote!, the local chapter of a not-for-profit national organization. "It was the most efficient campaign I have seen in my 20 years in politics," says Sam Burrell, alderman of the West Side's 29th Ward and a veteran of many registration drives. *At the head of this effort was a little-known 31-year-old African-American lawyer, community organizer, and writer: Barack Obama.* (Reynolds, 1993, my emphasis)

The *youth mobilization in the 2008 primary campaign was significant.* In the 2008 primaries and caucuses, over 6.5 million people under the age of 30 voted, so that the national turnout rate for primary elections almost doubled from 9 percent in 2000 to 17 percent in 2008 (Marcelo and Kirby, 2008: 1). For the first time since the voting age was lowered to 18, youth turnout in the United States increased for three elections in a row. Since general election turnout typically follows trends set in the primary elections, it appears that the youth vote will start playing a significant role in the United States, a factor of considerable importance for the renewal of the social values that candidates will have to reckon with in electoral contests. A spring 2008 survey by the Harvard University Institute of Politics (2008) on youth and politics, focusing on the age group 18–24 years, provides significant evidence of the political awakening of American youth. Among other responses, 76 percent said they were registered to vote (an increase of 7 points from November 2007); 64 percent said they would vote in the 2008 general election; 40 percent considered themselves to be politically active;

and 40 percent declared themselves Democrats, 25 percent Republicans, and 35 percent independent. By all measures, the civic engagement of the surveyed youth had increased from November 2007 after they followed the primary campaigns of 2008.

Indeed, this could be a turning point for the crisis of legitimacy in America. Analyzing trends of civic engagement among the youth, Robert Putnam (2008) wrote:

Throughout the last four decades of the 20th century, young people's engagement in American civic life declined year after year with depressing regularity. In fall 1966, well before the full flowering of Vietnam War protests, a UCLA poll of college freshmen nationwide found that "keeping up with politics" was a "very important" goal in their lives for fully 60 percent . . . Thirty-four years later that figure had plummeted to 28 percent. In 1972, when the vote was first extended to 18-year-olds, turnout in the presidential election among 18- to 24-year-olds was a disappointing 52 percent. But even beginning at that modest level, rates of voting in presidential elections by young people steadily fell throughout the '70s, '80s, and '90s, reaching barely 36 percent in 2000 . . . Last month [February 2008] the UCLA researchers reported "For today's freshmen, discussing politics is more prevalent now than at any point in the past 41 years." . . . In the 2004 and 2006 elections, turnout among young people began at last to climb after decades of decline, reaching the highest point in 20 years in 2006. As we approached the presidential season of 2008, young Americans were, in effect, coiled for civic action, not because of their stage of life, but because of the lingering effects of the unifying national crisis they had experienced in their formative years. The exceptionally lively presidential nominating contests of this year – and, it must be said, the extraordinary candidacy of Barack Obama – have sparked into white hot flame a pile of youthful kindling that had been stacked and ready to flare for more than six years . . . Turnout in this spring's electoral contests so far has generally been higher than in previous presidential nominating contests, but for twentysomethings the rise has been truly phenomenal – turnout often three or four times greater than ever before measured. The 2008 elections are thus the coming-out party of this new Greatest Generation.   (Putnam, 2008: D9)

Because of sky-rocketing voter registration rates, particularly among young people and African Americans (a key Obama constituency), millions of new voters were registered for the November election, setting the stage for a record voter turnout. Concerning *voting rates*, overall voter turnout in the 2008 primary was the highest since 1972. For all 34 primaries conducted as of May 10, 2008, 19.3 percent of registered Democrats voted in 2008 (up from 9.7% in 2004; it was 21.2% in 1972; Gans, 2008b). The turnout of African Americans increased by 7.8 percent in comparison with the primaries of 2004, but the turnout of Latino voters (who voted in majority for Hillary) increased by a whopping 41.9 percent. However, the highest increase in turnout rate concerns the youth vote (18–29 years), which exceeded the 2004 voting rate by 52.4 percent (Gans, 2008b; see Table A5.2 in the Appendix).

Obama may also have benefited from the Democratic Party's general growth in popularity. According to Pew (2008b), since 2004, identification with the Democratic Party has increased across all age groups. In 2004, 47 percent of all voters identified with or leaned toward the Democratic Party, while 44 percent identified with or leaned toward the GOP. In surveys from October 2007 through March 2008, Democrats held a 13-point party identification advantage (51% to 38%). Perhaps the most striking change since 2004 has been among voters born between 1956 and 1976 – members of the so-called Generation X and the later Baby Boomers. People in this age group tended to be more Republican during the 1990s, and the GOP still maintained a slight edge in partisan affiliation among this group in 2004 (Keeter et al., 2008). This is to say that the rise of Obama has to be placed within the context of the growing disaffection of the American people with President Bush, after having elected him twice (or at least one and a half times). Or, in other words, Obama's capacity to tap into the reservoir of Americans' desire for change.

Obama also counts, understandably, African Americans among his core supporters. However, this was not obvious at the start of the campaign because Bill Clinton had considerable influence among the politicized African American constituency, and Hillary Clinton benefited from this connection early in the campaign. However, as the campaign developed, three factors played in Obama's favor. First, the notion that an African American was a competitive candidate to go all the way, for the first time in history, mobilized and converted a large share of the previous Clinton constituency. Second, the racial undertone of some statements from the Clinton campaign, including Bill Clinton himself, turned many African American voters away from Hillary. Year-to-year data show that, among black Democrats, Clinton went from being competitive with Obama as first choice for the Democratic Party's nominee in 2007 – 42 percent for Obama, 43 percent for Clinton – to the point where an overwhelming majority of 82 percent of black Democrats favored Obama, compared to 15 percent for Clinton, in June 2008 (Gallup, 2008a). Third, the ability of the Obama campaign to mobilize new voters was particularly welcome among disaffected black voters. And so Obama's image among blacks was 68 percent favorable and 8 percent unfavorable in June 2007, and improved to 86 percent favorable and 9 percent unfavorable in June 2008.

But Obama's support reached a much broader spectrum of the American population, particularly among the most educated segments of the citizenry (see Table A5.3 in the Appendix). True, a first appraisal of the demographics of voters in the primaries would indicate a race divide. Obama carried the African American vote in every single primary state, while Clinton carried the white vote in all but eight states. However, while the Hispanic population backed Clinton during the primary, Hispanics supported Obama in larger numbers in the general election, with younger Hispanics slightly more supportive of Obama than the general population (see below). Yet, the apparent determining influence of race in the election is the result of a lack of appropriate multivariate analysis in interpreting the data. *The key variable explaining support for Obama in the primaries was age.* According to Edison/Mitofsky exit polls, for the overall vote of the primaries, Obama won over Clinton among voters aged 45 or younger, including a majority of the white vote. In the under-30 vote, Obama carried all but five states. He also carried 30- to 44-year-olds in all but seven states. Clinton, on the other hand, took all but six states in the 60+ age group, while the two candidates split adults aged 45–59 (Carter and Cox, 2008). Overall, in the 18–29 age group, Obama received 58 percent of the vote compared to Clinton's 38 percent, while among those over 65 years of age, Clinton out-voted Obama 59 percent to 34 percent. Because of the greater proportion of women among elderly voters, there appears to be a gender gap, with 52 percent of women voting for Clinton compared to 43 percent for Obama, while 50 percent of men voted for Obama and 54 percent voted for Hillary. But controlling for age, the gender gap is reversed as 56 percent of women under 30 voted for Obama compared to the 43 percent who voted for Clinton (Noveck and Fouhy, 2008).

So, Obama is clearly the political leader who has inspired young voters the most in recent decades. He has also broadened his appeal across racial and class lines, although his greater strength is among the most educated segments of the population and the new professional middle class, while Hillary received the overwhelming support of seniors, the majority of the women's vote (but not among the younger segments of women), and the symbolically meaningful support of segments of the Midwestern working class (but not in all states: Wisconsin, for instance). A quick reading of these descriptive results, waiting for scholarly analyses once the data become available, points to the fact that Obama was the candidate of the new

Table 5.2. Levels of Internet activism among online Democrats

Online activity	Obama supporters	Clinton supporters
Signed an online petition (%)	24	11
Forwarded someone else's political commentary or writing (%)	23	13
Contributed money to a candidate online (%)	17	8

n = 516 Internet users; margin of error ±5%.

Source: Pew Internet and American Life Project, Spring Survey (2008).

America, the younger, more educated, and more open-minded America of the twenty-first century. Moreover, *not only did new groups of citizens register and vote, but they became actively engaged in the campaign*. Thus, Table 5.2 illustrates the substantially higher level of involvement in Internet activism of Obama supporters in relation to Hillary supporters, themselves being quite an active group.

On Facebook – a social networking application used by the vast majority of Americans under 30 – as of July 2008, Obama had 1,120,565 supporters, compared with about 158,970 supporters for Clinton and 119,000 for McCain. In May 2008, the College Democrats of America endorsed Obama:

We've heard from thousands of youth voices through Facebook, MySpace, YouTube and e-mail. Without a doubt, college students are ready for change and a new kind of leadership. Senator Obama empowers our voices and makes us feel like an important part of the process. That is why we support him to be the next president of the United States.   (quoted in Halperin, 2008)

As for other forms of political participation in the campaign, in April 2008, 25 percent of those under 30, a strong Obama constituency, said they had worked on a campaign, joined a political club, or attended a political rally or march (CBS/MTV 2008). Thus, Barack Obama's campaign ignited a fire of passion and commitment among large segments of American society, including those who kept themselves distant from the political process or were kept in a passive role by professional political elites reducing politics to clientelism and image-making. Why so? Who is this man who came from the uncertain to wish upon the stars without wearing the stripes?

The Unlikely Presidential Nominee[60]

The facts of Barack Hussein Obama's life are now widely known, and do not need to be recounted in detail. I am simply summarizing here what is relevant for the purpose of my analysis. Understanding Obama's life could be a special assignment for students seeking to grasp the meaning of our multicultural world. He was born in Hawaii in 1961. His father, the son of a servant to a British family, was born in Kenya, a member of the Luo tribe, and grew up herding goats in his village, before excelling in school and winning one of the first fellowships to attend an American university that were given to a small group of young Kenyans preparing to become the professional elite of the country after its upcoming independence. He enrolled in the University of Hawaii where he graduated in econometrics, before winning another fellowship to pursue a PhD at Harvard, although he ultimately settled for a master's degree. Obama's mother, Ann Dunham, was the daughter of a Kansas oil-rig worker, who grew up in Kansas but later moved to Texas, Seattle, and finally to Hawaii with her parents. Ann and Barack met at the University of Hawaii in a Russian language class. They divorced when Obama was two. His father, after a period at Harvard during which he remarried, returned to Kenya to work for the government, and saw Obama only once more before his death. His mother, the person, according to Obama, most directly responsible for making him who he is, died of ovarian cancer in 1995. When Obama was six years old he moved to Jakarta with his mother and new stepfather, Lolo Soetoro (who was a practicing Muslim). While in Indonesia, Obama attended the Besuki School (now called Menteng 1), a non-denominational public school founded for Europeans and Indonesian elites with no Muslim affiliation. Religious studies are compulsory in all Indonesian schools and so his school day included a set time in which students practiced their various religions.

His mother, teaching English to Indonesian businessmen and working with American foundations to help poor families in Indonesia, felt that Indonesia was not safe for him or his education. And so, at the age of ten, Obama returned to Hawaii to live with his grandparents and to attend the Punahou School, a prestigious private school in Honolulu, on a scholarship. He went by the name Barry.[61] Obama has openly admitted

---

[60] This analytically oriented biographic account relies on press reports and on my reading of Obama's *Dreams From my Father* (1995, 2004), the book that, as for many people, first introduced me to the fascinating personality of Barack Obama.

[61] He was not poor. His family could be characterized as middle class. His grandfather was a modest salesman but his grandmother, working up the ranks, became

to experimenting with marijuana and cocaine in high school and has even poked fun at his miscreant past. When Jay Leno, the host of ABC's *Tonight Show* asked, "Remember, senator, you are under oath. Did you inhale?" Obama replied, "That was the point." Upon graduation, he moved to Los Angeles and attended Occidental College for two years before transferring to Columbia University. After graduation, he worked for a public interest research company and at Business International for four years before moving to Chicago in 1985 to become a community organizer as director of the Catholic organization Developing Communities Project (DCP), a critical experience that became his on-the-job training for community organizing. Three years later (at 29), he attended Harvard Law School and was the first African American president of the *Harvard Law Review*. It was at Harvard that he met his wife, Michelle, who was also a law student, after graduating from Princeton with the help of a scholarship. In 1991, he received a fellowship from the University of Chicago Law School to work on a book about race relations that would be published under the title *Dreams From my Father* in 1995. He taught constitutional law at the University of Chicago from 1992 to 2004. In Chicago, he engaged himself in local politics focusing on disadvantaged communities, such as Project Vote! (an African American voter registration project) in 1992. In 1993, Obama joined Davis, Miner, Barnhill and Galland, a 12-attorney law firm specializing in civil rights litigation and neighborhood economic development, where he was an associate for three years from 1993 to 1996. In 1996, he started his political career by successfully running for a seat in the Illinois State Senate.

From his student years to his engagement in the stormy waters of Chicago politics, Obama went through a process of constructing his identity. He firmly asserted his belonging to the African American community, without renouncing his mixed ancestry, as his mother and white grandparents were his immediate family. After his marriage, Michelle and his daughters became the rock of his life, in Obama's words. This dual ethnic background was the source of his perennial search for a bridge over the racial divide, the fundamental "American Dilemma" in Gunnar Myrdal's (1944) words. He often said that he embodied this overcoming of the racial divide. Unity between races, classes, and cultures became his horizon for action. In

vice president of a local bank in Hawaii. However, for three years in Hawaii he moved into a small apartment with his mother and sister Maya, while their mother was studying Anthropology, with the three of them living on the mother's meager fellowship, sometimes on food-stamps.

374

this sense, he places himself squarely in the tradition of Saul Alinsky, for whom people could find the community of their interests, transcending the ideological and social cleavages of history, by fighting and organizing together toward a common purpose (see below).

Obama started his formal political career in 1996 with a successful run for the Illinois Senate (representing the South Side of Chicago). He was re-elected in 1998 and then again in 2002. Following an unsuccessful bid for a seat in the US House of Representatives in 2000, he announced his campaign for the US Senate in January 2003. After winning a landslide primary victory in March 2004, Obama delivered the keynote address ("The Audacity of Hope") at the Democratic National Convention in July 2004, capturing the national spotlight for the first time. In his famous speech, he noted: "It is that fundamental belief: 'I am my brother's keeper. I am my sister's keeper' that makes this country work. It's what allows us to pursue our individual dreams and yet still come together as one American family." This theme resonates throughout his political career, and in many ways evokes the frame of nurturing parents discovered by Lakoff as being fundamental to democratic thinking in America (Lakoff, 2004). Excerpts from the speech were re-broadcast on major networks around the country, catapulting him to national prominence. Many credit this media frenzy with helping his Senate victory. He was elected in November 2004 with 70 percent of the vote. In 2008, he was the only African American US Senator, the fifth in American history, and the third since Reconstruction. In late March 2005, Obama announced his first proposed Senate bill, the Higher Education Opportunity through Pell Grant Expansion Act of 2005 (HOPE Act), which sought to raise the maximum amount of Pell Grant awards to help assist American college students with tuition payments. In April 2005, *Time Magazine* listed Obama as one of the world's 100 most influential people in a special report on "Leaders and Revolutionaries" (Bacon, 2005).

But Obama is no revolutionary; he never was and will never be. In fact, it is difficult to place him on a right/left axis, in spite of his left-leaning voting record. He more aptly presents himself along another set of coordinates: the future versus the past. His project is to build an American majority on issues that matter most to everybody's daily life and to engage in dialogue with all geopolitical actors, reversing the aggressive diplomacy of the neoconservatives, without hesitating at the same time to take on the terrorist threat where it is (for example, in Afghanistan rather than in Iraq). This pragmatism is reflected in his choice of advisors, whose seasoned political practice compensates for his limited experience in national and international policy-making. Thus, when entering the Senate, he hired Pete Rouse, former chief of staff to Senate Democratic Leader Tom Daschle, as his chief of staff, and economist Karen Kornbluh, former deputy chief of staff to Secretary of the Treasury Robert Rubin, as his policy director. He recruited Samantha Power, author of *Human Rights and Genocide*, and former Clinton administration officials, Anthony Lake and Susan Rice as foreign-policy advisors. For his presidential race, he worked with Zbigniew Brzezinski, Air Force General Merrill McPeak, Bill Daley (the brother of Chicago Mayor Richard Daley and former Clinton official), and Dennis Ross, who has advised Bill Clinton and the two Bushes as a Middle East negotiator for US policy toward Israel and Palestine.

Obama sees himself as a unifier, for his party and beyond his party. As soon as the bitter primary campaign ended, not only did he open up avenues of collaboration with Hillary and Bill (without going so far as to offer her the vice presidency, largely because of possible conflicts of interests with Bill) but also hired key members of the Hillary campaign, such as Clinton's director of national security, Lee Feinstein; her foreign-policy advisors Mara Rudman, the deputy national security advisor under Bill Clinton, and Robert Einhorn, a former assistant secretary for nonproliferation at the State Department; and Stuart Eizenstat, an international trade specialist who was policy director for Jimmy Carter's 1976 campaign. On the domestic side, Obama's policy team retained Clinton's top economic advisor, Gene Sperling, as a consultant.

During his Senate career, Obama also partnered with high-profile Republicans to pass legislation, such as the Secure America and Orderly Immigration Act (with McCain) and the Lugar–Obama initiative, which expanded the Nunn–Lugar cooperative Threat Reduction bill. The Democratic Republic of the Congo Relief, Security, and Democracy Promotion Act marked the first federal legislation to be enacted with Obama as its primary sponsor.

In a country as religious as the United States, Obama's beliefs are a defining feature in terms of his public projection. His religious evolution was as atypical as the process of his identity construction. In *Dreams from my Father* (1995, 2004), he describes his upbringing as mainly secular, although he attended church at Easter and Christmas with his grandmother. It was not until he moved to Chicago in his mid-twenties and began attending Trinity that he says he found religion. Interestingly enough, at about the same time, he fully embraced an African American identity, an identity that became strengthened later on by his marriage to Michelle, born in an African American family, unlike Obama who was from African and American descent. It is possible that joining Trinity was part of his decisive move to self-construct an identity after his cultural and personal wandering. The Trinity United Church of Christ is a nationwide, highly respected Church whose constituency is predominantly white. But in South Side Chicago, the Trinity Church was "the" church for African Americans in Chicago, beginning in the 1980s. Other famous parishioners included Oprah Winfrey, who stopped going in the mid-1990s because she found the sermons of the Church pastor, Reverend Wright, too extreme.

Wright had considerable influence on Obama's religious and political views, to the point that he came very close to ruining Obama's political chances. Wright was a highly educated theologian with a national reputation. He was among the group of religious leaders who were called upon to pray with the Clintons at the White House during Bill's period of atonement following the Monica Lewinsky affair and subsequent confession. He came from the tradition of black liberation theology, and he sometimes engaged in racially charged diatribes about social injustice in America. Without following Wright's extreme views in some matters, Obama considered him, for 20 years, as his moral mentor. He married Barack and Michelle, and baptized their daughters. Moreover, Obama titled the speech that propelled him to national fame (and his second book) with the words of one of Wright's sermons, "The Audacity of Hope."

And hope became the central theme of Obama's political discourse. It is intriguing and meaningful that Obama was able to merge a radical critique of American society with a moderate political practice. It is this ambivalence that simultaneously constitutes Obama's appeal and makes him vulnerable to political attacks from right and left. While the notion that ambivalence could be a trump card in building hope and trust appears to be counterintuitive, the theoretical analysis proposed by Simonetta Tabboni (2006), when analyzing the new youth culture in Europe, exposes the mechanism by which ambivalence opens up the realm of possibilities for people to project their hopes, thus identifying with the source of the ambivalence that frees them from artificial certainty. In Tabboni's words: "I speak of 'sociological ambivalence' when the actor is attracted to, or engaged by, aspirations, attitudes or conducts that are opposed to each other, yet they have the same origin and are inseparable from the point of view of the goals one wants to reach" (2006: 166, my translation). Ambivalence is not flip-flopping. It is not changing views and positions depending on opinion polls. Ambivalence is an open-minded approach to life; it is committing to an action's goals while remaining uncertain about the best means of achieving these goals. And so, I am not saying that Obama calculates ambivalence. He *is* ambivalent vis-à-vis standard ideological definitions. He sees himself as an African American transcending racial divisions in a country that he knows is built on racial divisions. He situates himself beyond class boundaries, while acknowledging social inequality, workers' hardship, and corporate greed. He wants to engage in a dialogue with everybody in the world, including the potential enemies of the country, while being implacably opposed to fanaticism and terrorism. This is not political posturing, it is embedded in his unusual life, in the simple but profound ethical principles that his mother brought to his heart, and in the down-to-earth philosophy of his grandmother, and later, his wife. As he writes in his book: "She [Michelle] doesn't always know what to make of me; she worries that...I am something of a dreamer. Indeed, in her eminent practicality and Midwestern attitudes, she reminds me not a little of Toot [Obama's grandmother's nickname]" (1995/2004: 439).

It is his life of experiencing discrimination and yet attending and succeeding in some of the best educational institutions of the country (starting with his school in Hawaii) that taught him that, yes, he could do it. And so, it is this mixture of ambivalence and self-confidence that made him a rare kind of personality, displaying a quiet charisma that suddenly would ignite him and his audience in a flare of passion transmitted with words and body language. Words learned from the pulpits of black liberation, body language inherited from a dignified Luo man and repackaged in the Harvard Law School. In the era of personalized politics, Obama has built his political project on an unusual, appealing personality that embodies the polyhedral experience of his life. Toward the end of his first book, he writes of the unanswered questions that trouble his nights:

What is our community, and how might that community be reconciled with our freedom? How far do our obligations reach? How do we transform mere power into justice, mere sentiment into love? The answers I find in law books don't always satisfy me...I find a score of cases where conscience is sacrificed to expedience or greed. And yet, in the conversation itself, in the joining of voices, I find myself modestly encouraged, believing that so long as the questions are still being asked, what binds us together might somehow, ultimately prevail.

(Obama, 1995, 2004 edn.: 438)

Obama searches for answers in the politics of conversation, the politics of asking questions rather than providing answers, the politics of looking for community beginning with the preservation of freedom, politics as both an ideal and a process, rather than policy proposals for electoral image-making. These are unusual approaches; appealing, but apparently impractical in the killing fields of media politics. And yet, when, on a cold February 10, 2007, Obama announced his candidacy for president, in front of 15,000 supporters on the steps of the Old State Capitol in Springfield, Illinois, the same building where Abraham Lincoln delivered his 1858 "House Divided" speech against slavery, he was explicitly connecting with that message. He was saying "We," and he was saying "We Can." But how was he able to mobilize support for his unlikely candidacy? How did his dream materialize into grassroots politics, into campaign financing, into media strategies, and into fending off attack politics and the politics of scandal? What are the lessons of the Obama campaign for our understanding of insurgent politics, or of politics for that matter, in the Internet Age? I will distill the most important of them, relating observation of the campaign to the analysis presented in Chapter 4 on the key features of political campaigning and political strategies.

Changing the Formula: From the Power of Money to the Money of the Powerless

Money largely dominates politics in general and American politics in particular. Fund-raising is essential, since without considerable sums of cash, there is no competitive campaign. This is the threshold that the best-intentioned campaigns (say, John Edwards in 2007–8) have failed to cross. The choice is simple: either corporate and wealthy interests finance your campaign, thereby indebting you to their interests (save a few philanthropists with enough money and personal values to be the exception), or you are on your own and the voters will never know how good you would have been for them.

Obama was able to cut through this apparently unsolvable dilemma. According to FEC records, for the overall primary campaign (through June 30, 2008), Obama raised a record-breaking $339,201,999. Including his fundraising for the general election, he raised a total, for both elections, of $744,985,655. In contrast, the initially well-funded

Hillary Clinton campaign raised $233,005,665 (excluding loans but including $10,000,000 from Clinton's personal funds). In comparison, John Kerry raised $233,985,144 and George Bush raised $258,939,099 across the entire 2004 primary season.[62] This is in spite of the fact that, unlike Hillary, Obama refused to accept money from federally registered lobbyists. He even went so far as to return $50,000 in contributions that slipped through the cracks. Obama did, however, accept contributions from lobbyists registered at the state level. Obama also refused money from Political Action Committees (PACs), but he did accept money from employees of corporations and other interests that employ lobbyists. Still, according to the Center for Public Integrity, Obama did receive significant funding through bundlers of donations (although he did publish their names online in the interests of disclosure). An analysis of his campaign's 328 bundlers, who raised anywhere from $50,000 to more than $200,000, reveals that they brought in at least $31.65 million, accounting for about 11.9 percent of Obama's total fund-raising haul of more than the $265 million raised as of April 31, 2008. Of those 328 bundlers, 78 individuals brought in about $15.6 million dollars to the campaign – at least 5.8 percent of his total funds (Ginley, 2008).

Surprisingly, Obama also stood out as the favored candidate among hedge fund managers according to a report by the Center for Responsive Politics (2008b). According to interviews with these managers conducted by *The New York Times*, while Obama is not the intuitive candidate for big business, he does offer one thing that Clinton does not: potential access (Sorkin, 2008). In contrast to the Clinton inner circle, which is longstanding and tightly contested, Obama, as a newcomer, offers an opportunity for relative newcomers in economic circles to make their way into the political sphere. This may be surprising given the fact that both Obama and Clinton favor increasing the tax on hedge-fund and private-equity profits from 15 percent to 35 percent. However, besides the obvious explanation of the opportunistic attitude of going with the wind, it must be remembered that these are *not* contributions from the corporations, but from individuals working or managing these financial corporations, whose donations may or may not be bundled. This is, in fact, an indication of Obama's wide appeal among the educated, professional class. You may be an investment banker and still want to put an end to the Iraq War. Indeed, the best minds in

[62] The totals for Bush and Kerry reflect funds raised through August 31, 2004. Both candidates accepted public funding for the 2004 general election and so these totals reflect only money raised for their primary campaigns.

the financial sector are convinced of the damage done to global economic stability, starting with oil prices, by the reckless foreign policy of the Bush administration. In other words, the critical measure of the independence of a candidacy is the arms-length distance from the Washington lobbies because their donations are directly or indirectly tied to policy decisions.

The class background of donors constitutes interesting information but cannot be taken as a predictor of the domination of class interests over a future president. Granted, no one, not even Obama, is going to challenge capitalism in the US, as well as, for the time being, in the world at large. But within the framework of capitalism, there is a wide range of policy options, and it is unlikely that this range has been restricted for Obama because of the origin of his campaign donations. This is fundamentally because, while accounting for the diversity of these donations, as reported above, *up to 88 percent* of Obama's total funds received for the primary campaign *came directly from individual donations* (the remaining 12% were from bundled donations), coming from *over 1.5 million individual donors* (official campaign numbers). *Approximately 47 percent of these donations were less than $200 and 76 percent were less than $2,000* (FEC Filings June 20, 2008). In contrast, 39 percent of Hillary Clinton's and 41 percent of John McCain's contributions were for $2,000 and over.[63]

How was the Obama campaign able to raise this unprecedented amount of money to support its political project? One key factor is the skillful use of the Internet for fund-raising. Although data are inconclusive, estimates of the proportion of Internet-processed donations over total donations range from 60 percent to 90 percent. This compares to an average of 6 percent of Americans donating for a variety of causes over the Internet. Most of these donations were from small donors who contributed in small amounts repeatedly over the duration of the campaign, without reaching the maximum limit of $2,300 per person, and were therefore able to react swiftly to the evolution of the campaign according to the requests and information posted on the campaign's web site. A report on Obama's funding by Norman Ornstein (2008) noted that:

Having this base of small donors through a process that is incredibly inexpensive to run, with fund-raising costs that are 5 to 10 cents on the dollar (compared with 95 cents for direct mail), frees Obama from the punishing, time-consuming burden

---

[63] For an up-to-date view of Obama's contributions see the Federal Election Commission Presidential Finance web site: http://www.fec.gov

of attending scores of fundraisers and making thousands of phone calls to potential donors. (Of course, Obama is not at the same time ignoring the $2,300 donors and bundlers, who may create more flak for him through the rest of the campaign. But he will certainly spend much less of his own time courting donors than will McCain.)

However, the most important matter, of course, was *the existence of a very large, popular movement behind Obama's candidacy*, with thousands of committed activists and literally millions of active supporters. The web site My.BarackObama.com counted about 15 million members in June 2008, although this is, of course, worldwide.[64] This is precisely the point: Obama's appeal extends beyond the boundaries of the United States. So, it is the existence of the movement that enabled Obama to considerably limit, if not eliminate, the influence of interest groups in his campaign. And this independence fed into greater support from his enthusiastic supporters, in a virtuous circle that propelled him to the Democratic nomination. How was this support generated? Why did people of fairly diverse social and ethnic backgrounds mobilize in unprecedented numbers and with unusual intensity for Barack Obama?

The Message and the Messenger

Let us, first, consider emotions, the stuff of which politics is made (see Chapter 3). According to a Pew Study conducted in March 2008, *white voters' views of Obama are more influenced by how he makes them feel than by specific characteristics voters attribute to him*. Those white Democrats who say that Obama makes them feel *hopeful and proud* give him higher ratings. And, of the personal traits listed in the survey, "*inspiring*" is most closely linked with perceptions about the Illinois senator than any of the others (see Table 5.3; Pew, 2008a).

I will focus on Obama, rather than commenting on Hillary. The critical findings here are that the most important emotions in inducing a positive opinion about Obama are: (a) the message from him is inspiring; and (b) the

[64] A survey of 24 countries, conducted by the Pew Global Attitudes Project (2008) from March through April 2008, found that respondents expressed greater confidence in Obama than McCain to do the right thing in world affairs in every country except for the United States, where the candidates' foreign-policy competence was ranked evenly, and Jordan and Pakistan, where few people had confidence in either candidate. Obama was viewed more favorably than Clinton in almost every country except in India (58% to 33%), South Africa (57% to 36%), and Mexico (36% to 30%).

Table 5.3. Perceptions that shape the opinions of white US Democratic voters about the candidates

	Impact on favorability for	
	Obama	Clinton
Think of as . . .		
Inspiring	0.43	0.14
Honest	0.35	0.37
Patriotic	0.34	0.30
Down-to-earth	0.23	0.31
Hard-to-like	−0.25	−0.08
Phony	−0.38	−0.50
Has made you feel . . .		
Hopeful	0.62	0.46
Proud	0.58	0.34
Uneasy	−0.19	−0.28
Angry	−0.21	−0.28
R^2	0.60	0.51

This table contains unstandardized regression coefficients for the effect of each trait or emotion on favorable ratings of the candidates by Democratic or Democratic-leaning registered voters.

Source: Pew (2008a: 4).

receiver of the message feels hopeful. This is the core of Obama's campaign message: *hope*, coupled with *change*. Yes, change is needed, but *hope* is the driving emotion. This is the emotion that, according to research in political cognition (see Chapter 3), stimulates *enthusiasm* for a candidate. Only on the condition of being hopeful, change becomes "change we can believe in" because the messenger lends credibility to the message, not necessarily because of his credentials but because of his ability to inspire hope and trust (honesty). In fact, the contest between Obama and Hillary was defined, from the onset of the campaign, by the opposition between change and experience (see Table A5.4 in the Appendix) and between hope and solutions (Comella and Mahoy, 2008). Hillary bet that people would value her experience ("ready on Day 1") and her capacity to find solutions to their problems. This strategy fitted well within the traditional frame of rational politics characteristic of the Democrats in the US and of the left around the world (Lakoff, 2008). In fact, in policy terms, the differences between Obama and Hillary were minimal, save for the fundamental contrast in the 2002 positioning against (Obama) or for (Hillary) the Iraq War. But even this difference had disappeared by the time of the electoral campaign (see Table A5.5 in the Appendix). In fact, the same March 2008 Pew poll provided evidence that 65 percent of Democrats did not believe that Obama and Clinton had different positions on the issues (Pew, 2008a: 16). The critical contrast was between Hillary's approach to the voters, positioning herself with a good résumé for the job, compared to Obama's message of hope, placing the possibility of change with people themselves. Hillary dismissed Obama's superior rhetorical capacity as being "just words." In fact, words matter. Or rather, the images induced in our minds by words, in a context of decision-making toward who will decide, matter a lot. We live by words and the metaphors they construct (Lakoff and Johnson, 1980). And so, hope finally nested in the minds and souls of millions of people who were yearning for change after the fear of terror, and the fear inflicted upon them by the war on terror. Hope, not fear. This is what ultimately translated into the most active political campaign participation in recent history.

An interesting fact is that the data presented in Table 5.3 refer to the attitudes of white voters. What happened to race in American politics? Did Obama actually transcend the injuries of race just by invoking the togetherness of his family and his extended family, a new, communal America? In fact, he benefited from a long process of cultural accommodation to the realities of a multi-ethnic society. As Figure 5.5 illustrates, American approval of an African American president is about as high as it is likely to get. In comparison, in 2007, only 88 percent of Americans said that they would vote for a female candidate for president and only 72 percent would vote for a Mormon candidate (Jones, 2007b). However, the Bradley Effect[65] is still in effect, although studies by the Pew Project Research Center suggested that this trend was about to change in 2008:

Analysis of primary counts and polling data from the early primaries, including those held before and on Super Tuesday (February 5), indicated that pre-election polls did

---

[65] Survey researchers first noticed the so-called "Bradley effect" in 1982 when black Los Angeles Mayor Tom Bradley had a solid lead in the pre-election gubernatorial polls, but lost in a close election to his Republican opponent. Results from that and other elections involving black candidates indicated that, for whatever reason, pre-election polling tended to overstate support for black candidates compared with their actual vote percentages.

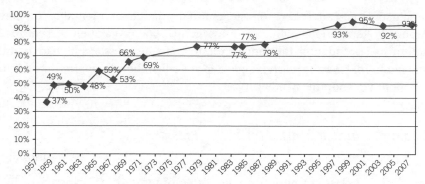

Fig. 5.5. Willingness to vote for an African American candidate, 1958–2007. (*Question*: If your party nominated a generally well-qualified person for president who happened to be African American would you vote for that person?)

Source: Gallup Organization.

indeed exaggerate support for Sen. Barack Obama in three states with relatively low black populations – New Hampshire, California and Massachusetts. But the reverse was true in South Carolina, Alabama and Georgia, where blacks make up a larger bloc of voters. The findings in South Carolina, Alabama and Georgia suggested to us the discovery of a new "reverse" Bradley effect, i.e., that in states with relatively large African American populations, pre-primary polls tended to underestimate support for Obama.   (Greenwalt, 2008)

Parks and Rachlinski (2008) argue that:

Though Senator Obama openly embraces the fact that he is a Black man, he does so in a way that does not overly alarm Whites. He often notes that though his father was from Kenya, his mother was a White woman from Kansas. He is not hesitant to call Blacks on the carpet about issues in the Black community. For example, he has spoken out on the lack of Black fathers in households, the notion among some Blacks that academic achievement is "White," and against anti-Semitism and homophobia in the Black community. Senator Obama, however, does not make frequent comments about race issues or his Blackness, particularly in front of White audiences. As a result, the goodwill he has built among Whites is not simultaneously eroded. He even managed to embrace a Black stereotype in an endearing, disarming fashion when he quipped that he did not know if Bill Clinton was truly the first Black President, because he had not yet had the chance to observe whether President Clinton could dance.   (2008: 14)

In sum, although there is probably more latent racism than the polls show, and the race factor is still present in American elections, Obama's

385

candidacy took advantage of the gradual change in mentality of new American generations, while his message of hope broadened the path for an unusual presidential messenger. Yet, to enact his message, he had to find an operational way to reach people and mobilize their hope. He found it in his adoptive land, the Windy City.

Obama's Chicago Roots: Alinsky for President

The key to the success of Obama's campaign strategy was his ability to translate the classic American model of community organizing, as elaborated half a century ago by Saul Alinsky, into the context of the Internet. Grassrooting the Internet and networking the grassroots, Obama, who learned his social organizational skills on the streets of Chicago's South Side, has probably invented a new model of mobilization that may be one of his lasting political legacies. By the time that Obama moved to Chicago, Alinsky had passed away.[66] However, a group of his disciples

[66] Saul Alinsky, a graduate student of sociology at the University of Chicago, devoted himself to organizing workers and low-income residents in their communities to improve their living conditions. Hired by a number of churches in Chicago and elsewhere to consolidate and mobilize their social programs, he established his Industrial Areas Foundation and developed a method of community organizing that became a reference for generations of community organizers throughout the United States. In a country sharply divided by race, ethnicity, and class, he argued for the unity of people as people, and toward that purpose his strategy was to find a concrete issue that was important for a community and organize a coalition of existing grassroots organizations to fight for the issue. As soon as the demands were satisfied, it was critical to find a new fighting target, and another, and yet another. This is because in his view the only resource that people could count on was their own organization, and this could only be maintained by mobilization. He called himself a radical, but he was critical of ideological positions, and distrustful of politicians that were a target to be pressured rather than the acknowledged leaders of the people. He used the word "radical" in its original sense, going to the roots. To the roots of American democracy, a democracy based on self-reliant communities and free individuals. He saw nothing wrong with the system, be it the market economy or liberal democracy. His critique concerned the imbalance of power between the rich, the organized, and the fragmented citizenry. Thus, by organizing the common people, he saw the possibility of restoring the balance of power between politicians and corporations, on the one hand, and citizens, on the other. Under such conditions, American democracy could function properly (see Alinsky, *Reveille for Radicals*, 1946). I analyzed the Alinsky experience of community organization in both theory and practice in my book *The City and the Grassroots* (1983: 60–5 and 106–37). I think that it would not be fanciful to say that the voice of Alinsky resonates in Obama's mind, although he naturally selected the themes and tones that would fit into his own understanding of politics. Interestingly, Hillary Clinton worked with Alinsky in 1968 and wrote her senior thesis at Wellesley about him. During her time as First Lady, she asked Wellesley to seal her senior thesis – speculatively because she didn't want the GOP to use it against the Clintons.

included Obama in their network and hired him to direct the Developing Communities Project (DCP) registering voters in the South Side of Chicago. It was here that he adopted the "Alinsky Method" of social organizing based, among other techniques, on winning the trust of the community by one-on-one conversations. The organizer's task is to draw out people's stories, listening for their goals and ambitions. Obama actually taught this method in his courses at the University of Chicago Law School. As director of the DCP, Obama helped build and guide a small network of grassroots groups that fought for better playgrounds, improvements in trash pickup, and the removal of asbestos from public housing. It was during his time with the DCP, Obama said during his presidential campaign announcement, "that I received the best education I ever had, and where I learned the true meaning of my Christian faith" (quoted in Slevin, 2007: A1). When Obama first ran for office in 1995, he echoed Alinsky's teachings, telling the *Chicago Reporter*, "It's time for politicians and other leaders to take the next step and to see voters, residents or citizens as producers of this change. What if a politician were to see his job as that of an organizer, as part teacher and part advocate, one who does not sell voters short but who educates them about the real choices before them?" (quoted in Slevin, 2007: A1). Though he told *The New Republic* that "Alinsky understated the degree to which people's hopes and dreams and their ideals and their values were just as important in organizing as people's self-interest" (Lizza, 2007), this is probably a healthy correction of Alinsky's pragmatism. And it is a distinctive trend of Obama's politics to mix reaching out to people's dreams with the nitty-gritty of grassroots organizing.

Some of Obama's key organizers were street-combat hardened veterans from the Alinskyte networks. Temo Figueroa was Obama's national field director and a long-time union organizer. Obama also enlisted Marshall Ganz, former Student Nonviolent Coordinating Committee (SNCC) organizer, and now a Harvard professor and one of the country's leading organizing theorists and practitioners, to help train organizers and volunteers as a key component of his presidential campaign. Ganz was instrumental in shaping the volunteer training experience. Many Obama campaign volunteers went through several days of intense training sessions called "Camp Obama." The sessions were led by Ganz and other experienced organizers, including Mike Kruglik, one of Obama's organizing mentors in Chicago. Potential field organizers were given an overview of the history of grassroots organizing techniques and the key lessons of campaigns that have succeeded and failed (Dreier, 2008). In the summer of 2008, the campaign launched the Obama Organizing Fellows program to train college students in organizing tactics. According to Dreier[67] (2008),

compared with other political operations, Obama's campaign has embodied many of the characteristics of a social movement – a redemptive calling for a better society, coupling individual and social transformation. This is due not only to Obama's rhetorical style but also to his campaign's enlistment of hundreds of seasoned organizers from unions, community groups, churches, peace, and environmental groups. They, in turn, have mobilized thousands of volunteers – many of them neophytes in electoral politics – into tightly knit, highly motivated and efficient teams.

While Alinsky's lineage to Obama can be easily established, his relationship to the Chicago political machine is less clear, though a frequent subject of commentary among analysts and pundits. The Internet is rife with speculation about illicit backroom deals between the Daley political machine and Obama. However, Obama's relationship with the Daleys is relatively recent and seemed to come only after he proved himself as a viable and charismatic candidate, although Axelrod, Obama's chief strategist, was Chicago Mayor Richard Daley's chief public relations strategist, and the representative who famously went on television to defend the mayor against corruption charges. The Daleys (Richard and Bill) consistently supported Obama's opponents until the 2004 Senate general election race. (They had supported State Comptroller Dan Hynes in the primary election. Hynes is the son of longtime Democratic machine politician Tom Hynes). But just hours after Obama declared his candidacy, Mayor Richard M. Daley announced his formal endorsement of Obama over Clinton, marking only the second time he has chosen to endorse a Democratic primary candidate in his 17 years as mayor. Around the same time, his brother Bill Daley signed on as a senior advisor to the Obama campaign. Obama then endorsed Mayor Daley's re-election run in January 2007, stating, "I don't think there's a city in America that has blossomed as much over the last couple of decades than Chicago – and a lot of that has to do with our mayor. He has a national reputation that's well-deserved . . . as somebody who's innovative, as somebody who's tough, as somebody who's willing to make the hard decisions, as somebody who is constantly thinking about how to make the city better" (quoted in Spielman, 2007).

In other words, Obama, the rising star in national politics from Illinois, made a strategic alliance with the Chicago political machine, but he was not

---

[67] Professor at Occidental College writing for *The Huffington Post*.

part of it. Incidentally, it is generally acknowledged among urban experts that Richard Daley's policies in Chicago are, indeed, among the most successful in the United States. It may well be the case that the legend of the Chicago political machine, based on the long reign of *the* Mayor Daley, the father of Richard and Bill, has survived its current reality, as Chicago has deeply transformed its social and political fabric in the past two decades.

Grassrooting the Internet: Obama's Competitive Advantage

In the early years of the twenty-first century, both in the US and in the world at large, politicians were reluctant to trust the fate of their campaigns to the Internet (Sey and Castells, 2004). Indeed, in his classic study, Bimber (2003) showed the limited influence of the use of the Internet on political behavior, with the major exception of increasing willingness to donate money to a candidate. However, the 2003–4 primary presidential campaign of Howard Dean, a frustrated case of insurgent politics, showed the potential of the Internet when coupled with a grassroots mobilization effort. It also showed the limits of the Internet when confronted with the broader impact of mainstream media on political campaigns (Sey and Castells, 2004).

However, it may well be that, as with other issues concerning the use of the Internet, it was too early to evaluate its actual impact, as it is only in the late 2000s that the new generation, who have grown up with the Internet, is coming of age, and that the diffusion of Internet use, and of broadband access for the majority of the population, makes the Internet a mainstream medium of communication. Indeed, in June 2008, according to a Pew Survey on a national sample, 46 percent of US adults were using either e-mail or SMS to get campaign information or discuss campaign-related information concerning the presidential election (Smith and Rainie, 2008: i). Online Democrats outpaced Republicans in their consumption of online video (51% vs. 42%). Furthermore, Democrats were significantly ahead among social networking site profile creators: 36 percent of online Democrats had such profiles, compared with 21 percent of Republicans and 28 percent of independents. The greatest jump in the use of the Internet for politics was with voters under 50. For voters over 50, there has only been a minor increase since 2004. However, 60 percent of Pew respondents thought that the Internet is full of misinformation and propaganda that too many voters believe is accurate (Smith and Rainie, 2008: iii).

Perhaps the most significant trend is the potential offered for online political interaction by the explosion of social networking sites. One in three Internet users has a profile on a social networking site, such as Facebook or MySpace, and 40 percent of these (representing 10% of all adults) have used these sites to engage in political activity of some kind. In keeping with the conversational nature of the online political debate, the most common of these activities is the simple act of discovering the personal interests or political affiliations of one's own friends – 29 percent of social networking users have done this, compared with one in ten who has signed up as a friend of one or more of the candidates or started/joined a political group. More than one-third of online Democrats (36%) have a profile on a social networking site, significantly greater than the comparable figures for both Republicans (21%) and independents (28%; Smith and Rainie, 2008: iii). Posting and watching videos with some relationship to political content is becoming an important form of political expression, particularly for the young segment of Internet users (see Tables 5.2 and 5.4).

However, in terms of general use of the Internet, there is considerable difference in the frequency and intensity of online activity depending on social characteristics, with the age factor being, again, the main source of differentiation. While 58 percent of the 18–29 group used the Internet for political purposes, only 20 percent of users over 65 did (see Table A5.6 in the Appendix.)

Obama supporters were considerably more active in using the Internet for political purposes than the supporters of any other political campaign in 2008. This is in part a function of age, as I have shown the considerable advantage of Obama over other candidates in the younger groups of the population, but it is also true across all age groups. According to the Pew Internet and American Life Spring 2008 Survey,[68] among Democrats, Obama's supporters were more likely than Clinton's supporters to be Internet users (82% vs. 71%), probably a function of age and education. But even among Internet users in both camps, Obama's supporters were more actively engaged online than Clinton's supporters – three-quarters of Obama's supporters (74%)

---

[68] Unless otherwise noted, these statistics are from Pew Internet and American Life (2008), $n = 2251$. For results based on the total sample, one can say with 95% confidence that the error attributable to sampling and other random effects is plus or minus 2.4 percentage points. For results based on Internet users ($n = 1,553$), the margin of sampling error is plus or minus 2.8 percentage points.

Table 5.4. Percentage of Internet users by age who are political online video watchers and content creators

	18–29 years (*n* = 212)	30–49 years (*n* = 565)	50–64 years (*n* = 470)	65+ years (*n* = 259)
Watched campaign commercials online	37	28	26	24
Watched candidate speeches or announcements online	35	29	20	19
Watched interviews with candidates online	35	27	20	21
Watched online video that did not come from a campaign or news organization	35	25	20	14
Watched candidate debate video online	33	23	17	16
Posted their own political commentary or writing	12	5	3	2

n = 1553; margin of error ±3%.
Source: Pew Internet and American Life Project, Spring Survey (2008). Table reproduced from Smith and Rainie (2008: 10).

obtained political news and information online, compared with 57 percent of Clinton's supporters. Among online Democrats, Obama's supporters were more likely than Clinton's supporters to have made online campaign contributions (17% vs. 8%), to sign online petitions (24% vs. 11%), to have forwarded political commentaries in blogs and other forms (23% vs. 13%), and to have watched campaign videos of any kind (64% vs. 43%). Obama's backers were also more likely than McCain's partisans to have engaged in a range of online campaign activities. Table 5.5 illustrates that Obama supporters were much more proactive Internet users than Clinton supporters.

Table 5.5. Percentage of Obama and Clinton supporters who are prolific consumers of online political content

	Obama supporters (n = 284)	Clinton supporters (n = 232)
Watched campaign speeches or announcements	45	26
Watched campaign commercials	41	31
Watched candidate interviews	41	26
Watched candidate debates	36	23
Watched video that did not come from a campaign or news organization	34	23
Have done any of these	64	43

$n = 516$; margin of error ±5%. All differences between Obama and Clinton supporters are statistically significant.

Source: Pew Internet and American Life Project, Spring Survey (2008). Table reproduced from Smith and Rainie (2008: 13).

This Internet following also explains the much greater attention given by the Obama campaign to spending money on Internet media in comparison with the other candidates. According to the Center for Responsive Politics (2008a), Obama's media expenditures as of July 2008 were as follows: broadcast media, $91,593,186; print media, $7,281,443; Internet media, $7,263,508; miscellaneous media, $1,139,810; and media consultants, $66,772. In contrast to Obama, by July 2008 Clinton had only spent $2.9 million, and McCain $1.7 million, on Internet media.

Thus, it is clear that the Obama campaign surpassed every major political campaign in the use of the Internet as a political mobilization tool both in the US and in the world at large. *Obama for America* used the Internet to disseminate information, to engage in political interaction on social networking web sites, to link these web sites to the web sites of the Obama campaign, to alert supporters of activities in their locale, to provide counterarguments to damaging rumors circulating over the Internet, to feed the mainstream media, to feed debates in the blogosphere, to establish a constant, personalized rapport with millions of supporters, and to provide an easy, accountable method for individual donations to support the campaign. Building on its core supporters' youth, education, and relative familiarity with the Internet, the Obama campaign demonstrated the extraordinary political potential of the Internet when transformed from a traditional billboard into an interactive medium geared toward stimulating political participation. The Internet provided a most useful platform to mobilize those yearning for change, and those who believed in Obama's potential to deliver change.

Mobilizing for Change in the Internet Age

The Obama campaign's success was predicated on its capacity to incorporate new political actors in large numbers and stimulate their active participation. This is, in fact, the key feature of insurgent politics. Among other strategies, the campaign created a number of voter mobilization tactics, including:

1. *My.BarackObama.com*, which had about 15 million members.
2. *Vote for Change*, a 50-state registration drive.
3. *Obama Organizing Fellows*: unpaid fellowships to train college students in mobilization tactics on behalf of the campaign.
4. *Centralized Funding Technology*: Obama's campaign attracted upward of 1.5 million individual donors, more than any other campaign in history. His donation system was computerized and *centralized,* so that his campaign staffers had, at their finger tips, access to the demographics, names, addresses, occupations, giving patterns, and social networking behaviors. His web of donors was also so vast that he was able to bypass Actblue,[69] and so become more self-reliant in terms of his political database.

Obama's campaign benefited from a combination of two important factors: centralization of fund-raising and data collection, and localization of mobilization tactics. He benefited from micro-targeting of voters through what his campaign director, David Plouffe, called a "persuasion army," as well as from a centralized system of communication and money collection through which he could mobilize his entire constituency or target sections of it. This infrastructure allowed him to work outside the confines of traditional Democratic structures (he built an alternative data-collection system to the Democrats' Demzilla and Datamart databanks, while at the

[69] A PAC allowing individuals and groups to channel their progressive dollars to candidates and movements of their choosing.

same time having access to those resources). Moreover, because he used grassroots organizing techniques and local volunteer networks, he could tailor messages to community concerns. In many ways, this process seems to have been a response to the Republican strategist Karl Rove's 72-Hour Task Force and use of MLM techniques (see Chapter 4).

In general, the message seems to be that, in American politics, voters crave personal connection and specialization of messages that address their individual concerns. However, the Obama campaign's novelty was to link people and communities among themselves, while centralizing knowledge about those communities, helping to coordinate their strategy by using the capacity of the Internet to be local and global, interactive and centralizing at the same time. He could do so because he and his politics had brought into the political realm a new generation that will be probably called by historians – regardless of Obama's fate – Generation Obama.

Generation Obama

Following the first caucuses, *Time Magazine* declared 2008 the Year of the Youth Vote (Von Drehle, 2008). Von Drehle (2008) notes that:

While enthusiastic Democrats of all ages produced a 90 percent increase in turnout for the first [Democratic] caucuses [in Iowa], the number of young voters was up half again as much: 135 percent. The kids preferred Obama over the next-closest competitor by more than 4 to 1. The youngest slice – the under-25 set, typically among the most elusive voters in all of politics – gave Obama a net gain of some 17,000 votes. He won by just under 20,000.

While Obama's message and style (and age) fits well amidst the open-mindedness of the new generation, the connection between Obama and young voters is no accident. Early on in his campaign, he brought a number of people on board with experience in mobilizing the youth vote, such as Hans Riemer, of Rock the Vote, who coordinated Obama's youth voting initiative; and Chris Hughes, co-founder of Facebook, who coordinated his social networking groups and helped craft My.BarackObama.com. Hughes actually took a leave of absence from Facebook with a significant pay-cut to work full time for Obama's campaign, and is widely considered to be the main inspiration behind Obama's networking strategies. Obama's new media chief was Joe Rospars, who was a writer and strategist for the Dean campaign before going on to found *Blue State Digital* (a multimedia firm that designs web campaigns for Democratic candidates including Dean and the DNC). The expertise of these, and other, digirati Obama supporters showed: in the first month of its existence (February 2007), Obama's social networking site logged 773,000 unique views, compared to McCain (the most web-savvy of the Republican candidates), whose web site clocked 226,000 views (Schatz, 2007).

However, an Internet-based campaign is largely a free campaign, and so the political strategists of any campaign, including Obama's, have to reckon with the dangers of autonomy exercised by those outside the formal campaign structures. A story may help illustrate these tensions. When Obama first clinched the Illinois Senate seat in 2004, Joe Anthony, a 29-year-old Los Angeles paralegal, launched a MySpace page for Obama. The rudimentary profile contained Obama's biographical information and a few photos. However, over the years, tens of thousands of MySpace users added Obama as their friend. After Obama officially launched his campaign, Obama's profile took off. Chris Hughes (see above) contacted Anthony about expanding the campaign's role in the profile. But as the number of visitors mounted, the campaign became concerned about their lack of control over the site and whether it might violate FEC limitations on in-kind contributions to political candidates (Schatz, 2007).

On his blog (on My.BarackObama.com), Joe Rospars (2007) worried: "What if someone put up an obscene comment during the day while Joe was at work?" (also cited by Schatz, 2007). When negotiations between the campaign and Anthony came to a standstill, the campaign contacted MySpace directly to shut down Anthony's Obama site, losing 160,000 "friends" in the process. That figure has since grown back to more than 418,535 friends as of July 2008. The team's decision to cut Anthony's page received criticism from many online activists. Anthony announced his withdrawal of support, complaining, "We're not a list of names and we're not inexpensive advertising. We are exactly the ordinary people you speak of, using the Internet to attempt to change the world" (quoted in Schatz, 2007). And so this is the real process of change, unleashing the force of the Internet and free spirits, while trying to rein them in according to the political realities.

Obama's influence on young people, while derived from deep cultural and social trends, was encouraged by the campaign's skillful use of video politics and pop culture. This is partly related to the support that Obama received from a large group of film, rock, and hip-hop stars (for example, will.i.am [sic] of the popular Black Eyed Peas, John Legend,

George Clooney, Jennifer Aniston, Will Smith, Nick Cannon, Jessica Biel, Nas, Jay Z, and many others). Coming as close as possible to an icono-clastic political figure, Obama was able to unite counter-cultural trends at the source of creativity in the entertainment industry. Furthermore, given the significance of African American musicians at the cutting edge of hip hop, Obama's appeal found a receptive attitude among people who are, in many cases, rebels without a cause. By embracing Obama, they solidified a connection with the youth culture, while at the same time connecting Obama with a politically active generation that will not disappear from the stage they have occupied for reasons of political convenience.

The success of the viral online video "Yes We Can," composed and produced by will.i.am, and directed by Jesse Dylan (son of Bob Dylan), is perhaps one of the best examples of the role of pop culture in rais-ing Obama's profile. The song/video overlaid Barack Obama's delivery of "Yes We Can," a speech that he delivered following the New Hampshire primary, with popular singers and actors singing the speech. Will.i.am released the song on February 2, 2008 on Dipdive.com and on YouTube under the username "WeCan08." Although the song's lyrics were entirely borrowed from Obama's speech, the campaign had no formal role in its production. By March 28, 2008, the video had been viewed over 17 million times (Stelter, 2008). In another example, in June 2007, the video "I've Got a Crush on Obama," created by 32-year-old advertising executive Ben Relles and starring a 26-year-old model named Amber Lee Ettinger, became the viral video hit of the summer. The video featured a mashup of footage of Obama in his bathing suit on vacation in Hawaii and footage of Ettinger dancing, sometimes in underwear with Obama written across the back.[70] The Obama campaign had a mutually beneficial relationship with its celebrity endorsers, as these videos proved to be extremely successful. In June 2008, the "Yes We Can" video won an Emmy Award in the first-time category, "New Approaches in Daytime Entertainment," and the pre-viously unknown Ettinger now makes a living from celebrity appearances. In another example, a relatively unknown hip-hop star named Taz Arnold (AKA TI$A), launched his solo career and dedicated his first single, "Vote Obama," to Barack Obama. The video featured numerous celebrity cameos,

[70] A few weeks after "Obama Girl" made headlines, Taryn Southern, a songwriter–singer–actress, released "Hott4Hill" on YouTube as a "response" to the earlier video. However, "Hott4Hill" gained more attention for its lesbian undertones than for any-thing else.

including Kanye West, Jay Z, Chris Brown, Travis Barker, Shepard Fairey, and Apple of the Black Eyed Peas.

From Media Politics to Scandal Politics

Much has been said about how the mainstream media became fascinated with Obama early on. There is no conspiracy behind the obvious focus on Obama during the early stages of the primary campaign. It was a sound business decision, coupled with the professional interest of reporters and political commentators. The presidential primaries can attract large media audiences or sink into the C-Span[71] mode of television, depending on voter interest in, and the uncertainty of, the outcome of the campaign. As analyzed in Chapter 4, the fusion of information and entertainment casts political campaigns into the narrative of horse races or competitive sports. So, in 2008, it quickly became apparent that the majority of the electorate was not ready to follow the Evangelicals (Huckabee) or a Mormon candidate (Romney), and the excitement surrounding the Republican campaign faded. As for the Democratic campaign, Hillary's presumptively inevitable victory forestalled media interest in the campaign before it had begun. Then, Obama's decisive victory in the Iowa caucuses opened up a world of possibilities in terms of appealing "horse-race" stories: the unlikely candidate against the establishment, the black man against the white woman, the Iraq War dissident against the one who voted for the war, with Bill Clinton and his paparazzi-friendly persona in the middle of the action. When, in less than two weeks, Hillary Clinton moved from dethroned commander-in-chief to a victorious weeping woman rescued by the women of New Hampshire, the soap opera formula was served. How much the media actually favored Obama over Hillary is arguable. For instance, to some critics, the ABC news debate moderated by George Stephanopoulos, Bill Clinton's former communications director at the White House, appeared to be biased against Obama.

But what soon became clear was that a long, contested primary season was on its way, with ups and downs and a charismatic candidate versus the comeback kid, the whole story spiced by its historical significance (it was, of course), and illuminated by the brilliance and intelligence of the

[71] C-Span is a commercial-free public service channel in the US, created in 1979, and supported by America's cable providers. The channel includes live, unedited, footage of governmental proceedings as well as public affairs programming.

two candidates (the candidacies of Edwards and Richardson did not survive against the tremendous drive of an inspiring Obama and a commandeering Hillary). Altogether, it became one of the most resonate storylines in the business of media politics in years. And the professional journalists, along with a legion of political pundits, went to work with dedication and skill to make the best of this colorful, yet meaningful campaign. The result was a six-month political show, the likes of which the world has rarely seen. Not that the race was without significance or that the exchanges lacked interest. Indeed, among other things, and in spite of some differences, this was the campaign that, in the footsteps of Michael Moore's documentary, established the priority of health care, one of the greatest social blunders of American capitalism, in the American mind. But the dynamics of the primary campaign were built on the candidates, on their joyful victories, on their heartbreaking defeats, and on the clash of will between two charismatic personalities and their legions of committed supporters. Hillary did not need more name recognition than she already had, although the last weeks of the campaign revealed a populist side that had been hidden behind the White House curtains. But for Obama, the intensity of the campaign propelled him to the status of media star, with all the pros and cons that this means for his future political career. His challenge was, and is, how to remain close to the grassroots he mobilized while remaining in the media spotlight. Overall, however, he mastered media politics because his personality and his manners came through in a very natural way. His self-confidence, depth of knowledge, and way with words helped him. He knows what he wants, he says it, and he communicates it.

Yet, this was only the first layer of media politics in the campaign. Because, as soon as it became clear that Obama was a viable candidate, he was subject to attack politics from his Democratic rival, and to scandal politics from unknown sources (Comella and Mahoy, 2008; Pitney, 2008). When Hillary saw the writing of her defeat on the wall, her centurions, and particularly Mark Penn and James Carville, used the time-honored tactics of attack advertising. It was more subliminal than blunt, but it mobilized the classic negative emotions: fear and anxiety. A typical example was the "3 a.m." ad, picturing a possible crisis in the night at the White House, while the children of American families were sleeping, and asking the rhetorical question: "Who do you want to answer the phone?" over the image of a presidential Hillary Clinton. It worked in the decisive primary of Ohio, as exit polls show, and it worked again, although less effectively, in Pennsylvania when Hillary issued a new version targeting McCain, but using the same 3 a.m. frame to remind voters about Obama's lack of commander-in-chief credentials. In another instance, Hillary, and the media, seized on Obama's supposedly private comment about the bitterness he discovered among the workers of small towns in Pennsylvania to accuse Obama of elitism, succeeding in creating a "bittergate."

In more subtle terms, Hillary also tarnished Obama using innuendo. When asked on television about Obama being a Muslim, she answered with a hesitant "Not that I know" rather than a clear response stating that he was, indeed, a Christian. Hillary did receive a great deal of negative media coverage. But more often than not, particularly after visual evidence surfaced showing that her claims to have landed in Sarajevo under sniper fire while she was First Lady were false, the Obama campaign, by and large, decided to take the high ground. This restraint was notable, particularly given the extreme animosity of many Obama supporters against "Slick Hillary." Yet the campaign refrained from engaging in attack politics, regardless of how principled its stand was, for two fundamental reasons: they knew that they would need Hillary's supporters in November; and they wanted to project the image that Obama represented a new kind of politician with a new kind of politics. It largely worked, in spite of the militancy of both candidates' supporters, and the toll that the harsh exchanges in the blogosphere probably took on Obama's chances in the general election.

Obama suffered, however, two major assaults on his candidacy. The first one was an insidious series of rumors and urban legends that circulated on the Internet and were picked up by the conservative talk shows around the country (see Table A5.7 in the Appendix). Depending on the source and on the medium, these were: Obama was a Muslim who swore his senatorial oath on the Qur'ān rather than the Bible; he had befriended former radicals; he was not patriotic (he did not wear the flag pin); he was married to a woman who was not proud of America; and a long litany of other allegations, a sample of which can be found in the Appendix (Table A5.8) on the attempted scandals against the Obama candidacy. Despite all evidence to the contrary and widespread media coverage about his relationship with Reverend Wright in Chicago, the belief that Obama was a Muslim still lingered: 14 percent of Republicans, 10 percent of Democrats, and 8 percent of independents thought he was a Muslim, according to a Pew survey conducted at the end of March 2008 (Pew, 2008b). Voters who did not attend college were three times more likely to believe that Obama was a

Muslim compared to voters who have a college degree (15% vs. 5%). And voters in the Midwest and South were about twice as likely as those in the Northeast and West to hold this belief. Nearly one-fifth of voters (19%) in rural areas said Obama was a Muslim, as did 16 percent of white Evangelical Protestants. However, largely because the main audience for these messages were conservative Republicans, this accusation did not work during the primary season. Doubts about Obama did have the effect of mobilizing the most conservative segment of Democratic voters against his candidacy, but it did little damage among independents and mainstream Democrats.

The Obama campaign skillfully managed defamation attempts. On one hand, it mobilized its vast network of grassroots organizations to stand up and correct the facts among people around them, in comments to the media, and on the Internet. They did not ignore the attacks; they confronted them with the conviction that "In the Internet age, there are going to be lies that are spread all over the place. I have been victimized by these lies. Fortunately, the American people are, I think, smarter than folks give them credit for" (Obama, MSNBC Debate, January 15, 2008). On the other hand, the Obama campaign maintained an instant reaction web site: Fact Check (http://factcheck.barackobama.com/). The Fact Check web site led with the quote: "I want to campaign the same way I govern, which is to respond directly and forcefully with the truth" (Barack Obama, 11/08/07). The page listed misleading or false claims made by other politicians and/or journalists followed by a brief correction. (Clinton also maintained a fact check web site called "Fact Hub.")

However, in the early days of the primary campaign, Obama went one step further, launching "Hillary Attacks" on December 3, 2007, a web site specifically focused on claims made by the Clinton campaign (the site was taken down by the Obama campaign at the end of the primary season).[72]

---

[72] The page launched with a letter from David Plouffe saying: "Today we're launching a web site that will keep track of all the attacks Senator Clinton has launched since she said she wasn't interested in attacking other Democrats at the Jefferson-Jackson Dinner on November 10th. We're asking all of you to be vigilant and notify us immediately of any attacks from Senator Clinton or her supporters as soon as you see them so that we can respond with the truth swiftly and forcefully. These attacks could be phone calls, literature drops, blog posts, mail pieces as well as radio and TV ads. Some could even be anonymous or designed to be. Please e-mail us at hillaryattacks@barackobama.com the moment you see something that concerns you. Senator Clinton has said her idea of fun is to attack Barack each day from here on out, and that's why we need you to help us stop those attacks and make sure that Barack

The site was unique in that it focused specifically on one candidate and was satirical in nature. In other words, the site used Hillary's attacks to frame the candidate as desperate. For example, it poked fun at the Clinton campaign's claim that Obama lied about the fact that his decision to run for president was not premeditated, using an essay he wrote as a Kindergartner entitled "I want to be President" as part of their evidence. The campaign also bought two other URLs, "desperationwatch.com" and "desperatehillaryattacks.com," which redirected visitors to the Hillary Attacks web site, hillaryattacks.barackobama.com. Many of her more damaging statements were also posted on the campaign's YouTube channel (http://my.barackobama.com/YouTube).

However, the near (political) death experience suffered by Obama came from the exposure of millions of viewers to video clips of fragments of the most extreme political sermons of his beloved pastor, Reverend Jeremiah Wright. I call it a scandal because it was a deliberate attempt to destroy Obama's credibility and reputation by emphasizing his association with a person whose extreme views he did not share. However, as all effective scandal politics strategies, the attack was founded on a selective presentation of facts. Reverend Wright was acknowledged by Obama as his pastor and a source of inspiration for his personal and political life. And while expressing his disagreement with the content of the videos, he did not disown him at first, until his repeated, provocative behavior forced Obama to denounce Wright and leave the Trinity Church. Since the story is widely known, I will simply focus here on some facts of analytical relevance. The videos of Reverend Wright were first shown on national television by ABC on *Good Morning America* on March 13, 2008, then spread virally on YouTube and throughout media networks in America and the world. But the ABC story may have stemmed from several prior publications. One of the first critiques of Wright appeared during the "Obameter" segment on the February 7, 2007 edition of MSNBC's *Tucker*. Host Tucker Carlson criticized Obama for being a member of the Trinity Church, a church that Carlson claimed "sounds separatist to me" and "contradicts the basic tenets of Christianity." The *Chicago Tribune* printed a similar critique around the same time (Boehlert and Foser, 2007). The final impetus may have come in the February 26, 2008 Democratic debate when moderator Tim

can continue to talk with voters and caucus-goers about the struggles they face and their hope for America."

Russert asked about Wright's support for Louis Farrakhan.[73] ABC aired the destructive piece on March 13, 2008. By March 16, 2008, a testimonial from Wright about Obama disappeared from the Obama campaign web site.[74] On March 18, 2008, Obama delivered his speech on race, referring to Wright as his former pastor, but cautioning that he could not disown the pastor just as he could not disown black America. His campaign insiders also released statements framing Obama's involvement in the Trinity Church as an exploration into his own African American identity, which he struggled to find because of his mixed race.

Obama's speech made a major impression, and his standing improved in the public mind. He was acknowledged as someone who would not escape controversy and would go to the substance of the matter, daring to refer to the open wounds that African Americans and their pastors still have because of lingering racism in US society. Obama's position is to start from the reality of the divide, from the recognition of the rage present in some black liberation theology, to overcome it by working together in building a multi-racial community. However, in the weeks following the controversy, Wright remained unrepentant, delivering speeches before the National Press Club (NPC) and the NAACP that only re-affirmed his earlier statements (in one instance he was invited by a prominent African American woman who was a Clinton supporter). He called the attacks on him "an attack on the black church." It was not until Wright's speech before

---

[73] Tim Russert said to Sen. Barack Obama, "The title of one of your books, *Audacity of Hope*, you acknowledge you got from a sermon from Reverend Jeremiah Wright, the head of the Trinity United Church. He said that [Nation of Islam leader] Louis Farrakhan "epitomizes greatness. What do you do to assure Jewish-Americans that, whether it's Farrakhan's support or the activities of Reverend Jeremiah Wright, your pastor, you are consistent with issues regarding Israel and not in any way suggesting that Farrakhan epitomizes greatness?" In fact, according to a Media Matters report (March 3, 2008), Wright never said that Farrakhan epitomizes greatness; it was another member of his church staff.

[74] *Interestingly, because churches are under the 513 chapter of the tax code concerning charities, it is actually illegal for them to endorse political candidates, so Wright's testimonial was actually legally questionable.* Here is the erased testimonial: Rev. Dr. Jeremiah A. Wright, Jr., Senior Pastor, Trinity United Church of Christ, Chicago, IL, Senator Obama's pastor: "I'm concerned with healthcare; the war in Iraq; the high rates of recidivism in our criminal justice system; the poor condition of the Illinois public school system. Many of the resources that go to support programs such as for those living with HIV/AIDS are now being spent to fund the war. We have to communicate . . . I support Barack because of his incarnated faith – his faith made alive in the flesh. He reaches across all faith communities and even to those who have no faith at all. He is building a community where everyone has worth. That kind of faith is not easy to find in 2007 and a man like Barack is a rarity."

the NPC on April 29 that Obama denounced his former pastor outright (on April 30).

In the weeks following the release of ABC's exposé of Wright's racist and anti-American rhetoric, nearly eight in ten Americans (79%) said that they had heard at least something about Wright's sermons (51% a lot, 28% a little) and about half (49%) had seen video of the sermons. Similarly, 54 percent said that they had heard a lot about Obama's speech and 31 percent had heard a little. A majority of the public (51%) said that they had watched videos of his speech, including 10 percent who had watched it on the Internet (Pew, 2008a). And as of June 10, Obama's speech on racial issues in the wake of the controversy, which was posted on the Internet by several people, had been viewed more than 6.5 million times on YouTube. However, while Obama's poll ratings slumped slightly in the immediate aftermath of the video, he had rebounded by March 22, moving ahead of Clinton again in Gallup daily tracking polls.

In fact, there were sizable partisan differences in the reaction to Wright's sermons: 75 percent of Republican voters who reported hearing at least a little about his sermons said that they found them offensive, compared with 52 percent of independents and just 43 percent of Democrats. Among Democratic and Democratic-leaning voters, far more Clinton supporters than Obama supporters reportedly found Wright's sermons offensive, though one-third of Obama's supporters found the sermons offensive. Among voters knowledgeable about the issue, just over half said that he had done an excellent (23%) or good (28%) job at handling the controversy. These numbers were higher among Democrats and African Americans (approximately two-thirds). Notably, a third of Republican respondents also said that Obama handled the issue well (Pew, 2008a). *In sum*: the Wright affair was a devastating attack that called the credibility of Obama as potential president of the United States into question. It was the work of mainstream media, specifically NBC and ABC, which considered everything related to presidential candidates fair game. This was indeed the case. Obama found himself in an almost unbearable contradiction between denouncing his most important mentor and renouncing his historical candidacy. He attempted to do neither, placing himself on another plane of the controversy, explaining and understanding, rather than hiding or condemning. He ultimately had to concede to depart from these roots, as Reverend Wright basked in the light of his unhealthy publicity. But he did it in a dignified manner. He survived, and his speech on race relations is being commented on in schools around the country, and it may remain as one of the most lucid confrontations with this unspoken reality of American society.

Yet, this is not the reason why Obama survived politically. As the data show, he survived because Democrats in general and his supporters in particular wanted to believe him, his version of the story, and his denial, while Republicans and conservative pundits, together with an opportunistic Hillary campaign, saw the window of opportunity to finish off the charisma of Obama. We know, however (see Chapter 3), that people believe what they want to believe for as long as they can. Since the good faith of Obama provided considerable proof by addressing the issue up front and not departing from his stated position of racial harmony in spite of racial injustice, he offered a haven for his own believers, and for most Democrats, to reject the Reverend while still hoping for Obama's candidacy. Comella and Mahoy (2008) document the negative impact of the scandal in the Pennsylvania primary, particularly among late-deciding voters. Yet, the desire of voters to believe in Obama, together with his eloquence and straightforwardness, propelled him past this formidable challenge to clinch the nomination. The skeleton, however, will remain in his closet for years to come.

The main analytical lesson of this episode is that words can be fought with words because words matter. Wright's sermons were words, offensive words for most Americans, accentuated with a body language that raised fear of racial rage. Obama's words were analytical, but also emotional, as when he recalled his grandmother's fear when crossing a black man in the street, and then looking at her grandson. Because he embodies the racial synthesis that he proposes to the country, his words earned credibility; at least enough credibility to keep the trust of those who needed to trust him.

The Meaning of Insurgency

Just a few weeks after his nomination, Obama made a calculated series of decisions that were considered by media observers to be a clear shift to the center of the political spectrum. He defended his stand by saying that he had not changed positions and that those criticizing him probably had not attentively followed his statements during the campaign. Although this is not entirely true (he actually changed his stance on the bill providing immunity to telecommunication companies eavesdropping on potentially terrorism-related activities), it is generally correct, and goes to the heart of the matter: Obama's structural ambivalence, in the terms I analyzed above. While his voting record in the Senate places him among the most liberal senators, he is not significantly to the left of a number of Democratic politicians. But he indeed represented a different kind of politician, a politician more attentive to the process of politics than to political outcome, more keen to be free of special interests and make decisions according to his own criteria, and more prepared to be held accountable for his actions, because this is where his political capital lies. History will ultimately judge his actions, as hope and betrayal of hope are often woven together in the fabric of politics, including insurgent politics. Though not always, so the jury is still out on this one.

Yet, this is not the concern of the analysis presented here, however strongly I feel about the matter myself as a concerned citizen. What is significant from the point of view of the relationship between communication and power is that a most unlikely candidate to the most important political office on the planet was able to break through the maze of vested interests surrounding the political establishment and the killing fields of scandal politics to reach the nomination for the presidency. Moreover, he succeeded by mobilizing millions of citizens, including many who were withdrawn from the political system or marginalized by the usual business of politics. And he did so by communicating a message of hope for credible change in a context of rage and despair about the country and the world. Yes, he was the first African American to be nominated by a major American party, and this alone is significant in a country in which identity politics is a fundamental dimension of civic life, and where the racial divide has been a defining feature throughout its history. However, I would argue that Hillary's nomination would have been an equally historic turning point. Because while a number of other countries have already elected women as their leaders, including Israel, Britain, India, Pakistan, Finland, Norway, the Philippines, Germany, Chile, Argentina, and others, in the United States in 2008 the polls showed that there was greater acceptance for an African American to be president than for a woman to be president.

And so, while the objective meaning of their primary campaign in identity terms is of extraordinary importance for the future of American politics (they both broke the glass ceiling of race and gender), this is not the most significant accomplishment of the Obama campaign. What makes it a case of insurgent politics in the Information Age was the capacity of the candidate to inspire positive emotions (enthusiasm, trust, hope) in a wide segment of society by connecting directly to individuals, while organizing them in networks and communities of practice, so that his campaign was largely theirs. It is this interactive connectivity that prompted millions to rebel against politics as usual. Of course, Generation Obama, the young citizens partly living on the Internet while yearning for community, the high-tech, high-touch subjects of the new culture, responded in droves to Obama's appeal. But the impact of the campaign was much broader. It tapped into the urge for positive politics felt inside so many, and it opened up avenues of political desire that everybody interpreted in a different way, but always as a hopeful project. In many ways, the campaign Obama inspired went far beyond himself and his specific political program. This is why the movement around the Obama candidacy was bound to fragment and conflict once the tactical urgency to beat McCain dissipated after the electoral process. In fact, even before the Democratic Convention, the first rumblings started to appear among Obama's faithful. Indeed, there is preliminary evidence that Obama's reliance on grassroots organizing may have serious ramifications for his presidency. The same networks that mobilized for him are also poised to mobilize against him when and if he adopts unprincipled policies. For example, as early as July 2008, "Senator Obama Please Vote NO on Telecom Immunity – Get FISA Right" became the largest network on MyBo (Obama's personal social network), within a week of launching. Organizations such as MoveOn, a major Internet-based grassroots movement with over three million members and donors, whose active support for Obama was decisive for his primary victory, was itself considerably strengthened as a result of the campaign, and vowed to stay focused on the target of citizen democracy without compromising with whoever is in office. This is the mark of insurgent politics, when insurgency does not end with the means (electing a candidate) but perseveres toward its goals: the change people hope for, and believe in.

The Day After

On November 4, 2008, Obama made history. He did so not just by becoming the first African American president of the United States, breaking the political glass ceiling of a country with a history of slavery and racial apartheid. He also made millions believe in democracy again, mobilized youth and minorities in unprecedented numbers,[75] contributed to an estimated increase in voter registration of more than 42 million since 2004,[76] and brought electoral participation to a remarkable level: 131,608,519 Americans cast their ballot for president in 2008, an increase of over ten million over 2004 (compared to a 6.5 million increase in eligible population; Center for the Study of the American Electorate, 2008). This number was tempered slightly by decreases in Republican voter turnout in comparison to 2004, however, at 63 percent of eligible voters, it still represented the largest voter turnout since 1960 (CSAE, 2008).[77] Obama was also the first Democratic candidate since Jimmy Carter in 1976 to win more than 50 percent of the popular vote. Particularly significant was the high level of participation by young people and minorities, many of whom had felt disenfranchised from the political system, and whose record numbers at the polls provided decisive support for Obama's candidacy.[78] But Obama's

[75] Obama almost quadrupled John Kennedy's lead over Richard Nixon among youth voters. Sixty-six percent of voters under 30 supported Obama, a 34 percentage point lead over John McCain. Moreover, it is estimated that 60% of all newly registered voters in 2008 were under the age of 30 (CIRCLE, 2008).

[76] On November 3, 2008 the US National Association of Secretaries of State (NASS) released preliminary voter registration numbers. The report documented record increases in voter registration in 20 states. However, final registration rates are likely to be higher as the preliminary report included numbers collected before many of the state registration deadlines. Final numbers were not available at the time of writing.

[77] Obama won the 2008 presidential election by securing 365 Electoral College votes against McCain's 173. He obtained 69,456,898 million votes (52.87% of total votes), while 59,934,814 million voters (45.62% of total votes) supported McCain. Eligible voter participation increased from 60.6% in 2004 to approximately 63% in 2008, an increase of 2.4% (Gans, 2008a). But this percentage underestimates the level of citizen participation, as voter registration increased from 143 million in 2004 to approximately 185 million in 2008, an increase largely attributed to the Obama campaign. He obtained more votes, in terms of absolute numbers, than any other American presidential candidate to date (Ronald Regan received 54,455,472 votes in 1984), motivated the highest electoral participation by young people in history, and induced the highest percentage of citizens voting in a presidential election at least since 1964.

[78] According to National Election Pool (NEP) exit poll data, Obama beat John McCain across a wide array of demographic, economic, and issue groups (NEP data reported by *The New York Times*, 2008). His most significant sources of support included: voters under 30 (66% to 32% who voted for McCain), first-time voters (69% to 30%), African Americans (95% to 4%), Hispanics (67% to 31%) and those making less than $50,000 per year (60% to 38%). He also won among women (56% to 43%), Catholics (54% to 45%), and Jews (78% to 21%). He carried citizens making more than $200,000 per year (52% to 46%), a marked contrast to John Kerry who only won 35% of this demographic in 2004. He also became the first Democrat since Bill Clinton in 1992 to carry, if only narrowly, the male vote (49% vs. 48%). In terms of issues, Obama won by significant margins among voters who considered the most important

victory went beyond his core base. He carried a large majority of the female vote, and a slight majority of the male vote. He redrew the electoral map of the United States, turning nine states from red to blue, including Virginia and Indiana, which had not voted for a Democrat since 1964. And he did it, by and large, without practicing the slash-and-burn form of politics that had characterized America for the past two decades, as documented in this book (Chapter 4). He broke the traditional hold of lobbies on presidential politics by raising an historically unsurpassed level of funding, over $744 million dollars, over half of which ($334,636,346) came from individual contributions of $200 or less.[79] According to statistics released by his social networking coordinator, Chris Hughes, on November 7, 2008, during the 21 months of the Obama campaign, his supporters, using the social networking infrastructure provided by My.BarackObama.com, created 35,000 local organizing groups and organized over 200,000 events. The campaign also pledged to keep the site up and running indefinitely as a platform for social organizing (Hughes, 2008). The Obama campaign showed that a new kind of politics, based on building trust and enthusiasm rather than inducing distrust and fear, can succeed under certain conditions.

However, his triumph in the general presidential election was decisively helped by other factors, the most important of which was the worsening of the economic crisis and the financial collapse in the fall of 2008. In early September, after the two conventions, the two candidates were statistically tied in most polls. The Sarah Palin effect had mobilized the conservative basis of the GOP and attracted the attention of the media to her picturesque personality. In the end, this media focus destroyed Palin's credibility, and her increasingly extravagant performance negatively affected the minds of

issue to be the economy (53% to 44%), Iraq (59% to 39%), health care (73% to 26%), and energy (50% to 46%). In contrast, McCain held a lead among voters who considered terrorism to be the most important candidate platform issue (86% to 13% for Obama; Pew 2008d). John McCain managed to hold on to certain demographic groups. Obama lost among white voters (43% to 55%), those older than 65 (45% to 53%), Protestants (41% to 50%), and among people living in small towns and rural areas (45% to 53%). However, in almost every case, Obama performed better with these populations than Democratic candidates in previous presidential election cycles. For example, the only other Democratic candidate to match Obama's performance among white voters since 1972 was Bill Clinton in 1996. He also won in all states that voted for Kerry in 2004, and added nine states that had voted Republican in 2000 and 2004, including such Republican strongholds as Indiana, Virginia, North Carolina, and Florida.

[79] Dollar amounts are from the official Obama campaign FEC Filing, November 24, 2008.

most voters. On election day, 60 percent of voters reported believing that Sarah Palin was not qualified to be president; 81 percent of those voters turned out for Obama (Pew, 2008d).

Furthermore, the McCain campaign was one of the worst managed presidential campaigns in recent memory. It shifted focus from one issue to another, alternated between dismissing Obama and attacking his policies, negated its key argument concerning Obama's inexperience by selecting Palin (a potential president given McCain's age and health), and wrongly targeted Hillary Clinton voters as potential supporters. Moreover, McCain's erratic behavior during the financial crisis undermined trust in his capacity to steer the country in the midst of economic uncertainty, in sharp contrast with Obama's steadiness. It must also be said that Obama was fortunate to confront John McCain, a candidate with a long track record of decrying attack politics. McCain's 2000 bid for the Republican primary derailed after unattributed flyers were circulated during the South Carolina primary, claiming that McCain's adopted child was actually his own whom he had fathered with an African American prostitute. In the aftermath of his defeat, McCain took the moral high ground, releasing statement after statement decrying this form of negative politics, and asserting that "sooner or later, people are going to figure out if all you run is negative attack ads you don't have much of a vision for the future or you're not ready to articulate it."[80] He also frequently criticized his opponents during the Republican presidential primary for going negative. He publicly attributed Mitt Romney's loss in Iowa to his negative tactics, telling members of a campaign rally, "People are not going to be fooled by negative campaigns."

In the early days of his 2008 general election campaign, while the Republican political action committees engaged in the usual lot of dirty tactics, and the conservative talk shows fanned demeaning rumors about Obama that circulated widely on the Internet, McCain attempted to keep negative attacks on Obama within the boundaries of personal respect. But given his frequent denunciations of attack politics during this period and throughout his career, any movement into the negative undermined perceptions of McCain more than those of Obama. McCain never adopted the form of deceptive politics that he himself had fallen victim to in South Carolina. However, when he ultimately moved toward more personal and aggressive

---

[80] This statement was made during an interview on the *NewsHour* with Jim Lehrer, on February 21, 2000.

attacks on Obama, both in his speeches and in his advertising, a tactic that had helped previous candidates mobilize voters, it backfired, and called into question McCain's claim that he was a "maverick" above traditional Washington mud-slinging.[81] A Pew poll conducted in October 2008 found that 56 percent of respondents viewed McCain as too personally critical of Obama (up from 26% in June; Pew, 2008f). Because the Republican attack machine could not operate fully within the logic of negative politics, which had been its trademark under Karl Rove's regime, a growing contradiction emerged between the candidate and the Republican advisors, and between McCain's advisors and Palin's advisors. The resulting chaos doomed the already slim electoral chances of McCain's candidacy.

Indeed, McCain's candidacy was seriously undermined by a financial crisis that climaxed during the most decisive moment of the campaign.[82] Obama had simply to point out the Bush administration's culpability in the crisis, and link McCain's voting record and economic policy proposals to Bush's economic philosophy and practice. A clear message, relentlessly broadcast through a media barrage in key states, and supported by a guarded performance in the presidential debates in which Obama prevailed largely by avoiding mistakes, were more than enough to secure victory. McCain's desperate attempts to distance himself from the Bush administration failed and this failure sealed his fate.

Thus, it is plausible to say that any serious Democratic candidate, such as Hillary Clinton, running a professional electoral campaign, would have won this election in the economic context in which it took place. Obama added a level of enthusiasm and mobilization, particularly among new voters, that propelled him to a decisive victory and gave him the mandate he was looking for to bring change to America and to the world. But he was no longer an improbable president once he became the Democratic candidate in a general election held in the middle of a major economic crisis and two unpopular wars. If we can still characterize the Obama election as a major

[81] A University of Wisconsin Advertising Project (2008) study found that only 26% of McCain ads contained no negative attacks on Obama compared to 39% for the Obama campaign.

[82] In September 2008, in what was widely perceived as a political gaffe, McCain "suspended his campaign" to return to Washington, DC, to help broker a congressional bailout of the American banking system. However, McCain was criticized for undermining rather than facilitating the quick passage of the bill. A Pew (2008e) poll conducted in October found that only 33% of respondents believed that McCain could better handle the economy, the most widely cited critical issue for voters on election day.

instance of insurgent politics, it is because he was the improbable nominee
of the Democratic Party. It was his unexpected victory over Hillary Clinton
and the formidable Clinton machine (using attack politics at its best) that
can be credited to Obama's new kind of politics, analyzed in this section,
which began as a movement generated by and large on the margins of
the political system and became an agent of transformation of the political
system itself. Moreover, the intensity and duration of the primaries honed
Obama's campaign operations, and greatly improved his standing, while
making him a household name in America and in the world. And so, what
is analytically relevant for the purpose of this book, namely the exploration
of the new avenues of social change opened up by a new relationship
between communication and power, is the study of the presidential primary
campaign as presented in this chapter. Because it was this campaign that
positioned Obama to become a decisive political agent of social change,
not only in America but in the world at large. And not just because of his
policies, but because of his inspiration, and his use of grassrooted Internet
politics.

By the time you read this text, the Obama administration will be in the
midst of one of the most challenging processes of governance in recent
times. He and his team (an ideologically and politically diverse team)
inhcritcd a country in ruins, a global economy in recession, a world at war,
and a planet in peril. Not even in the most messianic fantasies can anyone,
let alone Obama, believe that he will efficiently solve all the problems. For
some, he will succeed, for others, he will fail, and the balance will be for
historians and citizens to decide. He will probably try hard, with intelligence
and determination. He will surely disappoint many. Not only because such
is the nature of insurgent politics propelled by hope, once the insurgency
becomes institutionalized, but also because of Obama's ambivalence, as
understood in the terms analyzed in this chapter. Ambivalence permits one
to fill in the blanks with one's own dreams and wishes. Thus, on the one
hand, it is a major source of mobilization and belief, a generator of enthusiasm and positive feelings. On the other hand, precisely because people
project their own discourse onto Obama's discourse, without necessarily
concurring with his ideas and judgment, there will be many instances of
sharp contrast, disagreements, and feelings of betrayal. Yet, this potential
source of disenchantment cannot be equated with political manipulation
because, as I emphasized in my analysis of Obama's ambivalence, the uncertainty refers to the means, not to the goals. If Obama ends up changing his
goals (if he does not provide health coverage for everybody or if he does

not end the war in Iraq, for example), this would be politics as usual. If he tries to achieve his stated goals (e.g., job creation, new energy policies, international cooperation) by pragmatic means somewhat different from the traditional formulas of the political left, this is consistent with his stated program, albeit certain to be denounced by the most ideological of his supporters. How much he will have to deviate from his original ideas when confronted with the harsh economic and geopolitical realities of our world is a matter for future appraisal and further study. Yet, as I write this and you read it in another time/space warp, the fundamental analytical lesson to retain is how the insurgent politics of hope came to the forefront in the world's political scene at a critical moment when despair had descended upon us. We will always have Berlin. Or, for that matter, Grant Park.

Reprogramming Networks, Rewiring Minds, Changing the World

The case studies presented in this chapter are windows opening on the landscape of social change in our time. Acting on the cultural codes that frame minds, social movements create the possibility of producing another world, in contrast with the reproduction of norms and disciplines embedded in society's institutions. By bringing new information, new practices, and new actors into the political system, political insurgents challenge the inevitability of politics as usual and regenerate the roots of our fledgling democracy. In both instances, they alter existing power relationships and introduce new sources of decision-making about who gets what and what is the meaning of what we get.

Enacting social change in the network society proceeds by reprogramming the communication networks that constitute the symbolic environment for image manipulation and information processing in our minds, the ultimate determinants of individual and collective practices. Creating new content and new forms in the networks that connect minds and their communicative environment is tantamount to rewiring our minds. If we feel/think differently, by acquiring new meaning and new rules to make sense of this meaning, we act differently, and we end up transforming the way society operates, either by subverting the existing order or by reaching a new social contract that acknowledges new power relationships as a result of changes in the public mind. Therefore, the technology of communication that shapes a given communicative environment has important consequences for the process of social change. The greater the autonomy of the communicating subjects vis-à-vis the controllers of societal communication nodes, the higher the chances for the introduction of messages challenging dominant values and interests in communication networks. This is why the rise of mass self-communication, as analyzed in Chapter 2, provides new opportunities for social change in a society that is organized, in all domains of activity, around a meta-network of electronic communication networks.

Reprogramming networks of meaning substantially affects the exercise of power throughout all of the networks. If we think of nature as our fragile environment rather than our disposable resource, new forms of living prevail over the power relationships constructed in favor of the automobile, oil, and construction industries, their financial backers and their political appointees. If globalization is seen by a growing number of citizens around the world in a multidimensional way, in which markets, human rights, environmental safeguards, and a global social contract have to be harmonized and regulated in a new system of global governance, learning to live together in an interdependent world may prevail over the power of multinational corporations, financial traders, apologists for the flattening of the world, and bureaucratic enforcers of the proclaimed new global order. If citizens can catch their rulers in the act of lying to them, and if they can organize their resistance in an instant insurgent community, governments around the world will have to be on their guard and pay closer attention to the principles of democracy that they have largely disregarded for a long time. The powerful have been spying on their subjects since the beginning of history, but the subjects can now watch the powerful, at least to a greater extent than in the past. We have all become potential citizen journalists who, if equipped with a mobile phone, can record and instantly upload to the global networks any wrongdoing by anyone, anywhere. Unless the elites permanently withdraw to an invisible space, their actions are exposed to the decentralized surveillance of millions of eyes: we are all now potential paparazzi. And if a political outsider bets on becoming a political leader by mobilizing actors who were marginalized by the system, and by replacing the power of money with the money of the powerless, new avenues of democratic representation may be opened up by insurgent politics, using the information and communication power that makes it possible to grassroot the networks and to network the grassroots. Regardless of the possible betrayal of hope inscribed in the rules of politics, the case study in this chapter, as well as many other experiences around the world, shows that hope can be harnessed for change to the point that, if deception eventually happens, new actors may arise to chastise the false prophets and reclaim people's power.

All of these processes of social change, in values and in politics, have found a significant lever in the means offered by the networks of mass self-communication. It is through these networks that people at large can be reached, and the mainstream media, unable to ignore the buzzing world of multiple communication channels surrounding them, may be compelled to broaden the range of their messages. Of course, as I have reiterated to the point of being boringly repetitive throughout this book, technology per se does not produce cultural and political change, although it does always have powerful effects of an indeterminate kind. Yet, the possibilities created by the new multimodal, interactive communication system extraordinarily reinforce the chances for new messages and new messengers to populate the communication networks of society at large, thus reprogramming the networks around their values, interests, and projects. In this sense, the construction of communicative autonomy is directly related to the development of social and political autonomy, a key factor in fostering social change.

However, the technologies of freedom are not free. Governments, parties, corporations, interest groups, churches, gangsters, and power apparatuses of every possible origin and kind have made it their priority to harness the potential of mass self-communication in the service of their specific interests. Furthermore, in spite of the diversity of these interests, there is a common goal for this variegated mob of the powers that be: to tame the liberating potential of networks of mass self-communication. They are engaged in a decisive strategic project: the electronic enclosures of our time. As the potential of the industrial revolution was brought to the service of capitalism by enclosing land commons, thus forcing peasants to become workers and allowing landowners to become capitalists, the commons of the communication revolution are being expropriated to expand for-profit entertainment and to commodify personal freedom. History-making is not pre-scripted, and so the synergy I have documented in this chapter between the creation of new meaning and the rise of mass self-communication is only one episode in an ongoing struggle between the discipline of being and the freedom of becoming.

This is why perhaps the most decisive social movements of our age are precisely those aimed at preserving a free Internet, vis-à-vis both governments and corporations, carving a space of communication autonomy that constitutes the foundation of the new public space of the Information Age.[83]

[83] This essential area of investigation of the social movements that aim to shape the use and regulation of the Internet and other communication networks is becoming the focus of considerable attention of scholarly research, particularly among the new generation of communication scholars. Thus, my doctoral student Lauren Movius is investigating the global social movements aimed at the democratization of global Internet governance (Movius, forthcoming). Another of my doctoral students at the Annenberg School of Communication, Sasha Costanza-Chock, is conducting comparative analysis of the uses of new communication media by local social movements, considering both their local practice and their global networking (Costanza-Chock, forthcoming a). Among many other Annenberg students engaged in this field of research, I can mention Russell Newman (2008) and Melissa Brough (2008). Research by Downing (2000), Couldry and Curran (2003), Cardoso (2006), and McChesney (2008), among others, have pioneered this field of research. For a European perspective on this issue, see Milan (2008). For a Chinese perspective on the social conflicts related to the emerging network society, see Qiu (2009).

Toward a Communication Theory of Power

The analyses presented in this book provide, in my view, tentative empirical support for a number of hypotheses concerning the nature of power in the network society. Power is primarily exercised by the construction of meaning in the human mind through processes of communication enacted in global/local multimedia networks of mass communication, including mass self-communication. Although theories of power and historical observation point to the decisive importance of the state's monopoly of violence as a source of social power, I argue that the ability to successfully engage in violence or intimidation requires the framing of individual and collective minds. For instance, the Iraq War was made possible by the campaign of misinformation conducted under the frame of the "war on terror" by the Bush administration to conquer the minds of Americans as a way to conquer Iraq and retain the White House.

The smooth functioning of society's institutions does not result from their judicial and policing capacity to force citizens into compliance. In fact, in societies where institutions become dysfunctional because of their deep penetration by criminal networks, the police become a threat to law-abiding citizens who organize their lives as far as possible from the corridors of the state. How people think about the institutions under which they live, and how they relate to the culture of their economy and society, define whose power can be exercised and how it can be exercised. In the atrocious wars that proliferate around the planet, while economic interests and personal ambitions are played out in the carnage, people kill people because of what they feel: ethnic hostility, religious fanaticism, class hatred, nationalistic xenophobia, and individual rage. Messiahs, arms dealers, and foreign powers engage in symbolic manipulation to lead the masses to their self-destruction. Furthermore, political violence is a form of communication by acting on the minds of people through images of death to instill fear and intimidation. This is the strategy of terrorism, which resorts to spectacular manifestations of random destruction to induce a permanent state of insecurity among targeted populations. The security measures to counter the threat prolong fear and anxiety, eliciting citizens' uncritical support for their masters and protectors. Violence, broadcast over the communication networks, becomes the medium for the culture of fear.

Thus, violence and the threat of violence always combine, at least in the contemporary context, with the construction of meaning in the production and reproduction of power relationships in all domains of social life. The process of constructing meaning operates in a cultural context that is simultaneously global and local, and is characterized by a great deal of diversity. There is, however, one feature common to all processes of symbolic construction: they are largely dependent on the messages and frames created, formatted, and diffused in multimedia communication networks. Although each individual human mind constructs its own meaning by interpreting the communicated materials on its own terms, this mental processing is conditioned by the communication environment. Furthermore, while in the new world of mass self-communication and highly segmented audience there are few instances of simultaneous mass sharing of media messages, what is broadly shared is the culture of sharing messages from multiple senders/receivers. Precisely because the new communication system is so versatile, diversified, and open-ended, it integrates messages and codes from all sources, enclosing most of socialized communication in its multimodal, multichannel networks. Therefore, if power relationships are constructed largely in the human mind, and if the construction of meaning in the human mind is primarily dependent on the flows of information and images processed in the communication networks, it would be logical to conclude that power resides in the communication networks and in their corporate owners.

Conclusion

This conclusion may be logical, but it is empirically wrong. Because while communication networks are certainly the messengers, they are not the message. The medium is not the message, although it conditions the format and distribution of the message. The message is the message, and the sender of the message is at the source of the construction of meaning. In fact, it is one of the terms of this construction. The other is the receiving mind, both individual and collective. By collective mind, I mean the cultural context in which the message is received.

Referring to the conceptualization proposed in Chapter 1, the multimedia communication networks jointly exercise *network power* over the messages they convey because messages must adapt to the common protocols of communication (or standards, in Grewal's [2008] formulation) embodied in the structure and management of the networks. However, while standardized forms of mass communication may shape minds by their formatting of the messages (for instance, news as infotainment), in the world of mass self-communication the diversity of formats is the rule. Thus, apparently, standards are diminished as a source of network power. However, digitization operates as a protocol of communication. In principle, everything can be digitized, so it does not appear that this standard inhibits the message. Yet, it does have an opposite, significant effect: it amplifies the diffusion of the message beyond anyone's control. Digitization is tantamount to potential viral diffusion throughout global networks of communication. This is highly positive if you do want to diffuse the message, but devastating if you do not want to diffuse the message (if, say, the message is a video recording of your wrongdoing). In this case, the network power exercised by digital networks assumes a new form: the removal of control over message distribution. This is in contrast with the traditional network power of the mass media which reformats the message to be suitable for the audience in accordance with corporate strategy.

Yet, multimedia networks, as structures of communication, do not hold networking power, networked power, or network-making power, by themselves. They depend on the decisions and instructions of their programmers. In my conceptual framework (see Chapter 1), *networking power* consists of the capacity of letting a medium or a message enter the network through gatekeeping procedures. Those in charge of the operations of each communication network are the *gatekeepers*, and so they exercise networking power by blocking or allowing access to media outlets and/or to messages that are conveyed to the network. I call it gatekeeping the nodes and gatekeeping the messages. The rise of mass self-communication has deeply modified the gatekeeping capacity of the programmers of mass communication. Anything that reaches the Internet may reach the world at large. However, gatekeeping still yields considerable networking power because most socialized communication is still processed through the mass media, and the most popular information web sites are those of the mainstream media because of the importance of branding in the source of the message. Furthermore, government control over the Internet and the attempts of corporate business to enclose telecommunication networks in their privately owned "walled gardens" show the persistence of networking power in the hands of the gatekeepers.

Networked power, distinct from network power and from networking power, is the form of power exercised by certain nodes over other nodes within the network. In communication networks, this translates as the agenda-setting, managerial, and editorial decision-making power in the organizations that own and operate multimedia communication networks. In Chapters 3 and 4, I analyzed the multilayered structure of decision-making in the corporate media, albeit focusing on politically relevant information processing. I showed the complex interaction between different decision-makers of news production (the social actors that set up the communication agenda, e.g., governments or social elites; owners of communication networks and their corporate sponsors, through the intermediation of advertising agencies; managers; editors; journalists; and an increasingly interactive audience). It is at each one of these levels that *programmers* exercise power. There are multiple programmers in each network. While there is a hierarchy in the capacity to program the network, it is the whole set of programmers who jointly decide on the network's operations. Because they interact among themselves, as well as with the programmers of other communication networks, it can be said that *programmers constitute a network themselves*: a decision-making network to set up and manage the programs on the network. But their power is specific: it is geared to ensuring the fulfillment of the goals of the network, which is, primarily, to attract audience, regardless of whether the purpose of this goal is to maximize profits, or influence, or something else. *The overarching goal of network management by the networked power of programmers is to constitute the programmed*. The programmed are the subordinated subjects of the power-holders in the communication networks. However, the networked management of the communication networks operates under the conditions of a meta-program that has been designed by someone else from outside the network. This enigmatic "someone else" is the subject of the most determining form of power: network-making power.

Network-making power is the capacity to set up and program a network, in this case a multimedia, mass communication network. This mainly refers to the owners and controllers of media corporations, be they businesses or the state. They are the ones who have the financial, legal, institutional, and technological means to organize and operate mass communication networks. And they are those who, in the last resort, decide the content and format of communication, according to the formula that will best accomplish the goals they assign to the network: profit-making, power-making, culture-making, or all of the above. But who are "they?" I may name a few names: Murdoch, Berlusconi, Bloomberg, and, if I introduce Internet business corporations, Sergey Brin, Larry Page, Jerry Yang, David Filo, and the like. Yet, the analysis presented in Chapter 2 shows a highly complex picture of the reality of global multimedia business networks, the core of the entire communication system, global, national, and local. Network-making power is in the hands of a small number of conglomerates, their surrogates, and partners. But these conglomerates are formed by networks of multiple media properties operating in multiple modes and in multiple cultural and institutional environments. And multimedia conglomerates are intertwined with financial investors of various origins, including financial institutions, sovereign funds, private equity investment firms, hedge funds, and others. There are some exceptional cases of highly personalized decision-making capacity, but, as I will analyze below, even in the case of Murdoch, there is a dependence on various sources of network-making power.

In sum: the *meta-programmers* empowered with network-making capacity are themselves corporate networks, whose structure and dynamics I presented in Chapter 2. They are networks creating networks and programming them to fulfill the goals that these originating networks embody: maximizing profits in the global financial market; increasing political power for government-owned corporations; and attracting, creating, and maintaining an audience as the means to accumulate financial capital and cultural capital. Moreover, the range of investment of these global multimedia business networks increases with new possibilities of interactive, multimodal communication, particularly the Internet and wireless communication networks. In this case, the programming of the networks is less about content than about format. The Internet only becomes profitable if people use it, and people would use it less if it lost its fundamental features: interactivity and unfettered communication, regardless of how surveilled it is. The expansion of Internet networks, and the development of Web 2.0 and Web 3.0, offer extraordinary business opportunities for the implementation of the strategy I call the commodification of freedom: enclosing the commons of free communication and selling people access to global communication networks in exchange for surrendering their privacy and becoming advertising targets. However, once in cyberspace, people may have all kinds of ideas, including challenging corporate power, dismantling government authority, and changing the cultural foundations of our aging/aching civilization.

And so, there is a dialectical process that I documented in Chapter 2, and analyzed in terms of its political manifestations in Chapter 5: the more corporations invest in expanding communication networks (benefiting from a hefty return), the more people build their own networks of mass self-communication, thus empowering themselves. Therefore, network-making power in the communication realms is characterized by the action of multimedia corporate networks (including business and government) that interact with networked users who both consume media products and create their own culture. Networks interact with networks in the shared process of network-making.

But where is power in all of this? If power is the relational capacity to impose the will and values of social actors over others, who are these social actors? I have shown how power is made through communication networks, how these networks operate, and how and by whom these communication networks are established and programmed. But whose power do these networks process? If the meta-programmers are the owners of the multimedia business networks, are they the power elite of the network society? It would be tempting to play with words and characterize the transformation of power in the network society as a shift from the ownership of the means of production to the ownership of the means of communication since, as some theorists propose, we have shifted from the production of goods to the production of culture. This is, indeed, an elegant proposition but it leaves us hanging in discourse without precise reference to the actual drama of power struggles in our world.

The owners of global multimedia corporate networks (themselves networks, but networks of people at the helm of their organizations) are certainly among the power-holders of the network society because they program the decisive network: the meta-network of communication networks, the networks that process the ideational materials with which we feel, think, live, submit, and fight. Their relationship to the social actors over whom they exercise their power is also easy to identify: *they transform humans into audience by selling us the images of our lives.* So, they achieve their interests (money-making, influence-making) by designing the content of our culture according to their corporate strategies. This does not necessarily mean that they impose their values upon us (although they often do) because the effectiveness of the media depends on their adaptation to different cultural patterns and states of mind and to the differential evolution of each one of these patterns and moods. It means that the bottom line of what will be processed in the networks depends on what sells (or convinces, if the motive is politico-ideological), regardless of the congruity between what corporations want and what we want. There is consumer choice, but within a range of predefined products, and presupposing consumption rather than co-production. This is why the rise of mass self-communication, which increases the ability of us, the audience, to produce our own messages, potentially challenges corporate control of communication and may change power relationships in the communication sphere. However, for the time being, there is an unequal competition between professionalized media production and our low-quality home videos and blog gossip. Corporate media have adapted to the digital world and are extending their range of products by customizing them for individual profiles. Since we are unable to reinvent Hollywood by ourselves, we use the Internet for social networking (usually through corporate platforms), while most cultural production is globally concentrated and individually targeted. The power relationship between multimedia corporate networks and society at large is centered around the shaping of cultural production according to the will, values, and interests of corporate owners and their sponsors.

However, the range of power relationships is much broader, and includes, particularly, political power relationships, which provide access to, and management of, the institutions of governance. In this book, I have documented that communication networks are essential to the construction of political power and counterpower. The owners of corporate communication networks also provide the platform for the construction of meaning for other social actors. Thus, they exercise power through cultural production, and they exercise networking power over other actors by controlling access to communication networks; for example, vis-à-vis political actors who need access to communication to construct their power relationships with regard to the citizenry. However, in political power relationships, the meta-programmers, those who produce the message, are political actors. To be sure, political actors rely on the actors whose values and interests they represent (e.g., religious organizations, corporate businesses, the military-industrial complex). They articulate the diversity of interests supporting their project to maximize their autonomy as political actors while increasing their chances of seizing political power. But once in power, they are the programmers of political processes and policy-making. Their programs are diverse because different leaders and their coalitions vie for power in a political competition shaped by the procedures of each political system. However, they share some fundamental protocols of communication that aim to preserve the stability of state domination under constitutional rules. So, the programs embedded in political institutions exercise network power over citizens and political actors. The judiciary exercises networking power by gatekeeping access to political competition both in terms of actors and procedures. And the political system as a whole is based on networked power distributed at different levels of the relationship between the state and society.

Political network-making power, which is the power to define rules and policies in the political realm, depends on winning the competition to access political office, and on obtaining support or at least resignation from the citizens. I have shown in Chapters 3 and 4 that media politics is the fundamental mechanism by which access to political power and policy-making operates. Therefore, the programs embedded in multimedia networks shape and condition the implementation of the political networks' programs. Yet, media owners are not those who design and determine political programs. Neither are they passive transmitters of the programs' instructions. They exercise gatekeeping power, and they format and distribute the political programs according to their specific interests as media organizations. Thus, media politics is not just politics in general, and it is not the politics of the media: it is the dynamic interface between political networks and media networks. I call the management of this interface between two or more networks, *network switching*. The control of this switching capacity defines a fundamental form of power in the network society: switching power. I call the *holders of switching power, the switchers*. I shall illustrate this abstract, yet fundamental formulation with the findings of a case study of one significant switcher, Rupert Murdoch.

But I first need to broaden the scope of the analysis in terms of switching power by referring to other power networks in society. In particular,

Conclusion

I must consider the *structure and dynamics of financial networks* at the heart of capitalist power. Indeed, the network society, for the time being, is a capitalist society, as the industrial society was in most of the world (although in competition with statism). Furthermore, because the network society is global, we live in global capitalism. For the first time in history, the whole planet is capitalist. However, analysis of capitalism in general does not exhaust the understanding of the dynamics of power relationships because the brand of global capitalism we live in today is very different from previous historical forms of capitalism, and because the structural logic of capitalism is articulated in practical terms with the specific forms of social organization in societies around the world. And so, the dynamics of the global network society interact with the dynamics of capitalism in constructing social relationships, including power relationships. How does this interaction work to construct power relationships around communication networks?

Communication networks are largely owned and managed by global multimedia corporate networks. Although states, and their controlled corporations, are part of these networks, the heart of global communication networks is connected to, and largely dependent on, corporations that are themselves dependent on financial investors and financial markets. This is the bottom line of multimedia business, as analyzed in Chapter 2. But financial investors place their bets according to the expected performance of media business in the global financial market, the mother of all accumulations of capital and the dominant network of global capitalism, as I analyzed in my trilogy on the Information Age (Castells, 2000a, c, 2004c). The critical matter is that the global financial market is a network itself, beyond the control of specific social actors, and largely impervious to the regulatory management of national and international institutions of governance, to a large extent because the regulators chose to deregulate the financial networks and program the financial markets accordingly. Once financial markets became organized in a loosely regulated global network, their standards became applicable to financial transactions around the world, and therefore to all economic activities, since in a capitalist economy, production of goods and services begins with investment from capital and yields profits that are converted into financial assets. The global financial market exercises network power over the global economy, as became evident in the crisis of the global economy that exploded in the Fall of 2008 as a result of the absence of proper regulation of the financial markets.

This network power from financial markets is not in the hands of the invisible hand – the market. Because, as documented by a number of studies, financial markets only partly behave according to a market logic. What some scholars have called "irrational exuberance" and what I call "information turbulence" plays a major role in determining investors' psychology, and therefore their financial decisions. Furthermore, the global networking of financial markets means that any information turbulence from anywhere instantly diffuses throughout the network, be it political instability, saber-rattling in the Middle East, a natural catastrophe, or a financial scandal. Thus, while the global financial market exercises network power, and the governments of leading countries enacted network-making power by deregulating and liberalizing financial markets from the mid-1980s onward, there is a diffusion of networked power in the global financial networks. I have used the term "global automaton," in some of my writings, in reference to the global financial market, as it largely functions according to its own dynamic, without control from specific corporations or regulators, and yet it disciplines and shapes the global economy. I am not implying an automatic mechanism of power enforcement, or the existence of a dehumanized power. Corporate capitalism is embodied in financial tycoons, in financial managers, in securities traders and corporate lawyers, and in their families, personal networks, body guards, personal assistants, golf clubs, temples, secluded venues, and sinful playgrounds. All of these beautiful people are part of the networks that run the programs that run the world. But they are not alone in those networks, and they do not even control the financial networks that they inhabit, as they navigate their uncertain waters with their gut instincts rather than mathematical models, as Caitlin Zaloom (2006) showed in her wonderful ethnographic investigation of financial trading in the pits of Chicago and London.

The networking logic of financial markets is of utmost importance for the exercise of power in communication networks at two levels. First, because communication networks will be programmed, set up, reconfigured, and, eventually, decommissioned according to financial calculations – unless the function of the communication network is predominantly political. But even in this case, the power-making logic will apply to specific nodes of the global communication network, but not to the network itself, whose overarching principle is profit-making on the basis of financial valuation in the global financial market. Second, because financial institutions and financial markets are themselves dependent upon the information flows generated, formatted, and diffused in the communication networks. Not just in terms of financially relevant information, but in terms of the influence that information and communication networks exert on perception and decision-making by firms, investors, and consumers. There is no circularity involved in my argument. Yes, on the basis of observation, I say that global multimedia networks depend on global financial networks, and that global financial networks operate by processing signals produced and distributed in global multimedia networks. But there is nothing circular in this mechanism. It is, precisely, a network effect.

Global financial networks and global multimedia networks are intimately networked, and this particular network holds extraordinary network power, networking power, and network-making power. But not all power. Because this meta-network of finance and media is itself dependent on other major networks, such as the political network, the cultural production network (which encompasses all kinds of cultural artifacts, not just communication products), the military network, the global criminal network, and the decisive global network of production and application of science, technology, and knowledge management.

I could proceed with a similar exploration of the dynamics of network-making in each one of these fundamental dimensions of the global network society. But this task goes beyond the purpose of this book, which is focused on the role of communication networks in power-making, with an emphasis on political power-making. Furthermore, this is not really necessary to make the central argument I want to present, an argument that, to some extent, appears to be in accordance with the empirical analyses conducted in this book. My argument is threefold:

1. Power is multidimensional and is constructed around networks programmed in each domain of human activity according to the interests and values of empowered actors. But all networks of power exercise their power by influencing the human mind predominantly (but not solely) through multimedia networks of mass communication. Thus, communication networks are the fundamental networks of power-making in society.
2. Networks of power in various domains of human activity are networked among themselves. They do not merge. Instead, they engage in strategies of partnership and competition, practicing cooperation and competition simultaneously by forming ad hoc networks around specific projects and by changing partners depending on their interests in each context and in each moment in time.

3. The network of power constructed around the state and the political system does play a fundamental role in the overall networking of power. This is, first, because the stable operation of the system, and the reproduction of power relationships in every network, ultimately depend on the coordinating and regulatory functions of the state and political system, as was witnessed in the collapse of financial markets in 2008 when governments were called to the rescue around the world. Second, it is via the state that different forms of exercising power in distinct social spheres relate to the monopoly of violence as the capacity to enforce power in the last resort. So, while communication networks process the construction of meaning on which power relies, the state constitutes the default network for the proper functioning of all other power networks.

The multiplicity of power networks, and their necessary interaction for the exercise of power in the respective domains, raises a fundamental question: how can networks relate to one another without blurring the focus that ensures their specificity, and therefore the implementation of their programs? For instance, if media networks engage in a political crusade around one political option, their fate depends upon this option's success. They lose their relative neutrality, which thus diminishes credibility, the key factor in reaching out to a broad audience. If they gamble and lose, their political connections may be damaged, and they may pay for it in terms of regulatory advantage. If their personnel are appointed by political criteria, their professionalism will suffer. And, ultimately, if their political star fades, their financial results will deteriorate, and sound the bell for their corporate owners and their financial backers. True, there are a number of cases in which an ideological crusade (e.g., Fox News or Spain's *El Mundo*) also makes for good business, for a substantial period of time, and in a specific political context. But, in general terms, the "party press" is a defeating proposition in the business world. Furthermore, the more apparent the political autonomy of a media outlet is, the greater the service it can provide to its political constituencies.

And so, how do power networks connect with one another while preserving their sphere of action? I propose that they do so through a fundamental mechanism of power-making in the network society, as theorized in Chapter 1: *switching power*. This is the capacity to connect two or more different networks in the process of making power for each one of them in their respective fields. I will illustrate this analysis with the help of a case study that Amelia Arsenault and I conducted on the exercise of switching power by Rupert Murdoch and his News Corporation multimedia network (Arsenault and Castells, 2008b). To spare your reading effort, I will not dwell here on the empirical details of our findings, which can be found in the article accessible online. But I will summarize the analytically relevant content.

Murdoch is an ideologically conservative media tycoon who keeps personal control over the third largest and most profitable multimedia business conglomerate in the world. But he is, above all, a successful businessman who understood that his power would be maximized by keeping his options open. He is firmly anchored in the multimedia business networks, but he uses his media power to offer profitable connections to financial networks, and fruitful partnerships to political networks. Furthermore, he uses his media power to intervene in the construction of images and information in finance and in politics. His power resides in his capacity to connect the programming goals of media, business, and political networks in the interest of expanding his own media business network. He builds News Corporation's competitive advantage by maintaining tight control over the terms of its corporate connections and by leveraging his capacity to influence audiences around the world in order to gain political favors. Thus, politically, he hedges his bets by supporting a diversity of political actors in each country. For instance, in the United States, in the post-9/11 period, he put his media platforms, and particularly Fox News, at the service of the Bush administration's strategy for the war on terror and the war on Iraq, while donating more money to Democratic candidates than to Republicans. He also supported Hillary Clinton's campaign for the New York seat in the US Senate. But, as soon as Obama emerged as a leading presidential candidate, his *New York Post* endorsed Obama, and, later on, on the brink of his nomination, Murdoch praised Obama and welcomed his leadership, while referring to McCain as "my old friend." Similarly, in the UK, Murdoch was supportive of Blair, a move that infuriated many in the Labour Party, but kept his traditional ties with the Tories as an alternative means of political influence. The board of News Corporation includes political leaders as well as people with strong political influence in key areas of the world, such as the US, the UK, and China. They are paid handsomely, and so the promise of a News Corporation job for ministers or prime ministers after leaving office (e.g., Spain's José María Aznar) opens wide avenues of political influence for Sir Rupert.

Over the years, Murdoch has practiced a three-pronged strategy, providing propaganda platforms to those in power, cash to the opposition, and personal favors to a diverse crowd of politicians in need. As a result of this strategy, Murdoch influenced a number of regulatory measures in several countries in ways that greatly benefited his business. In 2007, he also made a strategic move to influence financial networks by acquiring Dow Jones, the parent corporation of the *Wall Street Journal*, one of the main financial bellwether media outlets in the world, thus placing himself squarely at the core of the production of financial information. Murdoch's strategy also embraced the communications revolution by positioning News Corporation in the social networking spaces of the Internet planet, as symbolized by his acquisition of MySpace.com, the largest social networking site in the world. He did it tactfully, by hiring professionals with knowledge of Internet culture and preserving the modes and practices of the Web 2.0 generation, consequently losing revenue but conquering the future – or so he believes.

The different networks – media, political, financial, and cultural – connected by Murdoch are separate and implement their specific programs. But he facilitates and enhances the performance of each program in each network by providing access and transferring resources between networks. This is the power of the switch. And this is the power of Rupert Murdoch, the most deliberate switcher, making power in various networks through his ability to connect them. However, his primary source of power remains his media power. He is simultaneously a meta-programmer in the global multimedia network and a switcher in the global network society. Switching functions, and therefore switchers, vary a great deal depending on the characteristics and programs of the networks they switch and on the procedures for exercising switching power. But their action is central to the understanding of power-making.

Thus, programmers and switchers are the holders of power in the network society. They are embodied by social actors, but they are not individuals, they are networks themselves. I deliberately chose the example of Murdoch because he epitomizes personalized programming power and switching power. And yet, Murdoch is a node, albeit the key node, in one particular network: News Corporation and its ancillary networks in media and finance.

This apparently abstract characterization of power-holding in the network society has, in fact, very direct empirical references. Of course, networks are formed by actors in their networking arrangements. But who these actors and what their networks are is a matter of the specific configuration of networks in each particular context and in each particular process. Therefore, I am not dissolving power relationships in an endless deployment of networks. Rather, I am calling for specificity in the analysis of power relationships and proposing a methodological approach: we must find the specific network configuration of actors, interests, and values which engage in their power-making strategies by connecting their networks of power to the mass communication networks, the source of the construction of meaning in the public mind. I would go as far as to say that what I consider a truly abstract, unverifiable proposition is the power of the capitalist class, of the military-industrial complex, or of the power elite. Unless we can specify who exactly holds power in a given context and in relation to a given process, and how his or her power is exercised, any general statement about the sources of power is a matter of belief rather than a tool of research.

And so, I am not identifying the concrete social actors who are power-holders. I am presenting a hypothesis: in all cases they are networks of actors exercising power in their respective areas of influence through the networks that they construct around their interests. I am also proposing the hypothesis of the centrality of communication networks to implement the power-making process of any network. And I am suggesting that switching different networks is a fundamental source of power. Who does what, how, where, and why through this multi-pronged networking strategy is a matter for investigation, not for formal theorization. Formal theory will only make sense on the basis of an accumulation of relevant knowledge. But for this knowledge to be generated, we need an analytical construction that fits the kind of society we are in. This is the purpose of my proposition: to suggest an approach that can be used in research, rectified, and transformed in ways that allow the gradual construction of a theory of power that can be disproved by observation. I have tried to show in this book the potential relevance of this approach by investigating the construction of meaning at the source of political power through the use of communication networks by a variety of actors and their power networks. Further research will certainly supersede the contribution submitted hereby, while hopefully finding some use for the effort spent cutting through the maze of networked social practices that weave the fabric of society in our time.

If power is exercised by programming and switching networks, counter-power, the deliberate attempt to change power relationships, is enacted by reprogramming networks around alternative interests and values, and/or disrupting the dominant switches while switching networks of resistance and social change. The case studies presented in Chapter 5 provide preliminary evidence of the relevance of this approach. It is up to the research community to test these hypotheses in social movements and political communities of practice in other contexts. What is theoretically relevant is that actors of social change are able to exert decisive influence by using mechanisms of power-making that correspond to the forms and processes of power in the network society. By engaging in the cultural production of the mass media, and by developing autonomous networks of horizontal communication, citizens of the Information Age become able to invent new programs for their lives with the materials of their suffering, fears, dreams, and hopes. They build their projects by sharing their experience. They subvert the practice of communication as usual by squatting in the medium and creating the message. They overcome the powerlessness of their solitary despair by networking their desire. They fight the powers that be by identifying the networks that are. This is why theory, necessarily grounded on observation, is relevant for practice: if we do not know the forms of power in the network society, we cannot neutralize the unjust exercise of power. And if we do not know who exactly the power-holders are and where to find them, we cannot challenge their hidden, yet decisive domination.

So, where can you find them? On the basis of what I have analyzed in this book, I can venture some answers. Look for them in the connections between corporate communication networks, financial networks, cultural industrial networks, technology networks, and political networks. Examine their global networking and their local workings. Identify the frames in the networks that frame your mind. Practice your critical thinking every day to exercise your mind in a culturally polluted world, the way you exercise your body to cleanse the poison of our chemical environment. Unwire and rewire. Unwire what you do not get, and rewire what makes sense to you.

Yet, the most important practical conclusion of the analysis presented in this book is that the autonomous construction of meaning can only proceed by preserving the commons of communication networks made possible by the Internet, a free creation of freedom lovers. This will not be an easy task – because the power-holders in the network society must enclose free

Conclusion

communication in commercialized and policed networks, in order to close the public mind by programming the connection between communication and power.

However, the public mind is constructed by networking individual minds, such as yours. Thus, if you think differently, communication networks will operate differently, on the condition that not only you, but I and a multitude choose to build the networks of our lives.

Appendix

Table A2.1. Connections between multinational media conglomerate leadership and other networks, c.2008[84]

Financial	Media/ICT	Global networks of creativity and innovation	Political
		Time Warner	
AllState, Altria (Philip Morris), American Airlines, AMR Corp., Appleton Partners, Axel Springer, *Bayer, Caesars, Citigroup, Colgate-Palmolive*, Continental Corp., Culbro Corp., *Estée Lauder*, Exclusive Resorts, FedEx, First Health Group, Gordon Brothers, Harrahs, Hilton, JER Partners, *Kellogg*, Kleiner Perkins, Caufield, &	ALM Media Holdings, Citadel Broadcasting Corp., *Dell*, Deutsche Presse-Agentur GmbH, Die Welt, Hamburger Morgenpost, Microsystems, Netscape, Proxicom, Sun, Wochenpost	American Museum of Natural History, Boston Museum of Science, Council on Foreign Relations, Fordham University, Harvard University, Howard University, Los Angeles World Affairs Council, Markle Foundation, Mayo Clinic, Memorial Sloan-Kettering Cancer Center, Partnership for the	Richard Parsons, formerly a member of the White House Domestic Council, NYC Housing Authority Board

(cont.)

84 The companies listed in *italic* rank among the 100 largest purchasers of advertising either in the United States and/or globally, as reported by *Advertising Age* (2007). (x2) indicates that more than one board member is affiliated with that corporation.

Table A2.1. (*Continued*)

Financial	Media/ICT	Global networks of creativity and innovation	Political
Byers, *Kraft*, Lazard, Leerink, Swann, & Co., *Macy's*, Morgan Stanley, New York Stock Exchange, Omnicom, Paratek Pharmaceuticals, Revolution Health Group, *Sears*, Westfield America		City of New York, Refugees International, Rockefeller Brothers Fund, Stanford University, San Francisco International Film Festival, Teach for America, University of Georgia, US/Russia Investment Fund, Yale University	

Disney

American International Group, *Bank of America*, Boeing, Boston Scientific Corp., Central Europe and Russia Fund, *Clorox*, Edison, *Estée Lauder*, European Equity Fund, FedEx, Gillette, Goodyear, Halliburton, Inditex,*Kraft*, McKesson Corp., Morgan Stanley, New Mountain Capital, *Nike*,	*Apple*, Archrock Corp., CIT Group, Jetix Kids Europe, *La Opinion* (largest Spanish language publication in the US), National Cable Telecommunications Association of America, Precision, Pyramid Technology (military computing), RSL Communications, Sun	American Film Institute, German-American Chamber of Commerce, Foreign Policy Association, Keck Foundation, Lincoln Center for the Performing Arts Inc., Museum of Television and Radio and of Ithaca College, Smith College, UCLA, University of Southern California	

Oakley, *Proctor & Gamble* (x2), *Sears*, Shinsei Bank (Japan), Starbucks, Transamerica Corp., US Chamber of Commerce, Washington Mutual, *Wells Fargo*, Western Asset Premier Bond Fund, WI Harper, Xerox, *YUM!* Microsystems, Sybase, Turbolinux, Vernier

News Corporation

Acumen, Allco, Allen & Co.., Altria Group, *American Express*, Ansell Ltd. (Aus.), Applied Materials, Centaurus Capital (UK), Chartwell Education Group, CLP Holdings, *Ford*, Genentech, Goldman Sachs, Hybridtech, Industrial and Commercial Bank of China Ltd., *JP Morgan*, Laura Ashley Holdings, LSI Corp., LLC, Pacific Century Holdings, Palamon European Equity, Beijing PDN Xiren Information Technology Co.., China Netcom (x2), Corning, Easynet Group, *Hewlett Packard*. Hughes Electronics, Intel, NDS Group, Reuters, Tickets.com Georgetown, Tsinghua University of Beijing, American Film Institute, Indian School of Business, Harvard National Lampoon, USC, KCRW NPR, Sundance Institute, Ditchley Foundation, Kirov Opera and Ballet, Victoria & Albert Museum, Imperial College of Science & Technology, Council, Royal Institute of International Affairs (Chatham House), Hoover Financial Control Board for the City of New York, Partnership for New York City, former Prime Minister of Spain, NY Citizens Budget Commission, former US Assistant Attorney General and chief architect of the Patriot Act, former member of US President's Foreign Intelligence Advisory

(*cont.*)

Table A2.1. (Continued)

Financial	Media/ICT	Global networks of creativity and innovation	Political
R. M. Williams Holdings, Knowledge Universe, Planet U, Templeton Emerging Markets Investment Trust Plc, Rio Tinto, Rolls Royce Group, Rothschild Investment Trust, Vietnam Motors Industry Corp.		Institution, Stanford, Oxford University, Brookings Institution, Yale, FAES Thinktank, Princeton, Howard University, Council on Foreign Relations	Board, former US Secretary of Education

Bertelsmann

Financial	Media/ICT	Global networks of creativity and innovation	Political
Air Berlin, Allianz (x2), Bayerische Landesbank, Bewag, *BMW* (x2), Commerzbank Deutsche Bank, E.On, Evonik, Festo AG & Co. KG, Fuchs Petrolub, Groupe Bruxelles Lambert, Hapag-Lloyd, HSBC Trinkaus & Burkhardt, John Deere, Linde, Lufthansa, Man (x2), *Merck, Metro*, NYSE	Activison, Amadeus Technology Group, Arvato, Audible, Avago Technologies, Basf, Barnesandnoble.com, Building B, Classic Media, DD Synergy, ebrary, Ediradio, Emotive Communications, Garner, Gruner, & Jahr AG & Druck- und Verlagshaus (x3), *Hewlett Packard*, Lycos Europe, Metropole Television	Princeton Review, Center for Communication, Children's Museum of Manhattan, Princeton University Press, the Bronx Lab School, American Association of Publishers, Art Directors Club Institute (x2), ZymoGenetics, American Society of Composers, Authors & Publishers, Fairfield	

Euronext, Oak Hill Securities Fund, Printer Industria Grafica, Powergen, RAG, RoyaltyShare, RWE, Shell, Silver Lake, Skandinaviska Enskilda Banken, Sportfive, Stinnes, Vattenfall Europe, WestLB	M6 (x2), Novo Nordisk, Oysterworks Software, SAP, Serena Software, *Sony BMG* (x4), Stern Magazine Corp., UFA Film & Fernseh	University, Council for the United States and Italy	Chairman of the Corporate Commission on Education Technology
Viacom			
Accenture, Banco Popular, Bear Stearns & Co., Consolidated Edison, DND Capital Partners (x2), Federal Reserve Bank of Boston, Harry Fox Licensing Association, Highpoint Capital Management, Hyperion, Intercontinental Exchange (x2), *Kodak, Kraft,* Lafarge (x2), LaBranche & Co., Marriot, Morgan Stanley, Oracle Corp., *Pepsi,* Rand-Whitney, Revlon, RWI Investments	Blockbuster, CBS, Genuity, National Cable and Telecommunications Association, Paramount, Black Entertainment Network, National Amusements, Midway Games, Matchmine Magfusion	Brandeis, New York City Ballet, National Cable Telecommunications Association, Board of American Society of Composers, Authors & Publishers, Tufts University, Boston College, Columbia	

Table A2.1. (*Continued*)

Financial	Media/ICT	Global networks of creativity and innovation	Political
		CBS	
AIG Aviation, Altria (Philip Morris), American International Group, Asia Global Crossing Ltd., Banco Popular, *Bank of America* (x2), Barrick Gold Corp. (Canada), Bear Stearns & Co., City National, Conoco Canada (oil company), Consolidated Edison, Granite Construction, Health Plan Services, Intercontinental Exchange, KB Home, *Kraft*, Massachusetts Mutual Life Insurance Co., NASDAQ, Neiman Marcus, Office Depot, *Pepsi*, *Sears*, Southwest Water, Stone Canyon Venture Partners, Topaz International Group	Actavision, AECOM, Akamai Technologies, Blockbuster (x2), Fusion Telecommunications International, Harcourt General, Midway Games, National Amusements (x3), Spectravision, *Viacom*, *Verizon*, *Vivendi*, Westwood One, Zenimax Media	Museum of Television and Radio, Boston University Law School, American Film Institute, Combined Jewish Philanthropies, John F. Kennedy Library Foundation, Tufts University, New York University, The 20th Century Fund, Urban Institute, Ditchley Foundation, New York and Presbyterian Hospital, Institute for Social and Economic Policy in the Middle East, NAACP, Northeastern University, Boston Symphony Orchestra, WGBH Public Broadcasting, Junior Achievement, Center for	Former Secretary of the United States Department of Health, Education and Welfare, former US Secretary of Defense, US Senator, NAFTAs North American Development Bank Community Adjustment Committee

(cont.)

SA, Travelers Group, Tyco International Ltd., Unilever, US China Business Council, US India Business Council, US Taiwan Business Council, Velocity Express Corp., Warnaco Group, Willis Group Holdings

Strategic and International Studies, Rand

NBC Universal

Alfa S.A.B., *Anheuser-Busch*, APBiotech, AP Capital Partners, Avon, BP, Carlyle Group, Chevron (x2), Chubb Corporation, *Coca-Cola*, Delphi, Detroit Diesel Remanufacturing Corporation, Federal Reserve Bank of New York, Fortsmann Little and Co, *General Motors*, Genpact Limited, Grupo Carso, Grupo Mexico, Grupo Sanborns, Gulfstream Aerospace, *Home Depot* (x2), ICG Commerce, America Movil, *Apple*, BSG Alliance, Cambridge Technology Partners, Carsdirect.com, Carso, Cingular, ClubMom, *Dell*, Dreamworks, Global Telecom, Grupo Televisa, Internet Brands, Internet Security Systems, ITM Software, Knight Ridder, *Microsoft*, Motorola, Scientific-Atlantic (x2), Telefonos de Mexico, Tube Media Company, *Verizon*

Art Center College of Design, American Film Institute, INSEAD, Georgia Tech., Robin Hood Foundation, Catalyst, Fairfield University, Memorial Sloan-Kettering Cancer Center, Robin Wood Johnson Foundation, MIT, S. C. Johnson Graduate School of Management, Carnegie Corp. of New York, Amersham, Wellcome, Museum of Natural History, World Wildlife Fund, Smith College, Columbia Business

Center for Strategic and International Studies, Council on Foreign Relations, Grocery Manufacturers Association

Table A2.1. (*Continued*)

Financial	Media/ICT	Global networks of creativity and innovation	Political
Inforay International, Investment Company of America, John Deere, *J. P. Morgan, Kellogg, Kimberly-Clark* (Mex.), Marvin and Palmer Associates, *Merck,* Momentive Performance Materials, Mutual Fund, Ogilvy Group, Partnership for New York City (x2), Pennsylvania International Raceway, Penske, Planet Hollywood, *Proctor & Gamble,* RRE Ventures (x2), Salomon Smith Barney International, Sustainable Performance Group, Texaco (x2), Unilever, United Auto Group, *Wal-Mart,* Xerox, Young & Rubicam (x2)		School, Boston Celtics, Phase Forward, Massachusetts Software and Internet Partners, Partners Healthcare System, Universal Technical Institute, Detroit Investment Fund, Detroit Renaissance, Business Council of New York State, Brookings Institution, Harvard Business School, Club of Greater New York, Rockefeller Foundation, NY Presbyterian Hospital, Princeton University, Stanford, Cornell, Research Foundation of the Medical College of Wisconsin, Massachusetts General Hospital	

(cont.)

Yahoo!

Fred Meyer (subsidiary of Kroger), Genuity, *Home Depot*, Hooker Furniture, KLM Airlines, MacManus Group, Morgan Stanley, Northwest Airlines, Occidental Petroleum Corp., Polo Ralph Lauren, Revlon, Starwood Hotels

Activision, Asia Global Crossings, Cisco, CNET, *Hewlett Packard*, Macromedia, *Microsoft* (Wilderotter used to work for them), Network Appliance, Red Hat, Reuters, Skyrider, *Walt Disney*, *Warner Brothers*, Xerox

Stanford University, Trinity College, the John F. Kennedy Center for the Performing Arts, the J. Paul Getty Trust, the National Urban League, the Los Angeles County Museum of Art, Committee for Economic Development

Google

American Independence Corp., Amyris, Biotechnologies Inc., Genentech (bio tech comp), *Kaiser Permanente*, Segway

Amazon.com, *Apple*, Atheros, Central European Media Enterprises, Cisco, Glu Mobile, Good Technology, GTI Group (ICT venture capital group), Intel, Intuit, Palm, Pixar (part of Disney), Plaxo, Siebel Systems, Tensilica (mobile aps), Zazzle.com

Carnegie Mellon, National Academy of Engineering, University of Michigan, the Aspen Institute, American Society of Microbiology, the New York Academy of Sciences, American Society for Biochemistry and Molecular Biology, Princeton University, Stanford University, Rockefeller University, Human Genome Project

Table A2.1. (*Continued*)

Financial	Media/ICT	Global networks of creativity and innovation	Political
	Microsoft		
Accenture, August Capital, *Bayer, Berkshire Hathaway,* Cambridge Tech., Chubb Corporation, Dubai International Capital, Hartford Financial Services, Minnosa System, Morgan Stanley, Northrop Grumman, *Pepsi,* Phase Forward, S.A. France Finance et Technologie, Scientific Atlanta, Six Apart, SkyPilot Networks, State Street Bank, Stele, *Wal-Mart*	*General Electric* (parent to NBC), GreenStone Media, Knight Ridder, Netflix, ITM Software, Thomson SA, Winstar Communication, Xirru	California State Board of Education	

Apple

Avon, Genentech, *General Electric*, Generation Investment Management GTI Group, *General Motors*, Highlands International, J. Crew, Kleiner Perkins, Caufield, & Byers, Lion Strategy Advisors, Metropolitan West Financial, *Nike*, Salomon Smith Barney International, Trancida Corp., Tyco, Waste Management

Common Sense Media, Current TV. Google (x3), Great Plains Software, Hostopia.com, Hyperion Solutions Corp., InSight Venture Partners, Intuit, Loudcloud, MGM, Motorola, Netscape, Novell, Opsware, Pixar, SanDisk, Siebel Systems, Software & Information Industry Association, Stellent Inc., Tilion, *Walt Disney*

Columbia University, Memorial Sloan-Kettering Cancer Center, California Institute for Quantitative Biomedical Research, Princeton University (x2), UCLA, Fisk University, Middle Tennessee State University, Carnegie Mellon, Menlo School, American Society of Microbiology, New York Academy of Sciences, American Association for the Advancement of Science, American Society for Biochemistry and Molecular Biology

Alliance for Climate Protection, Al Gore former U.S. Vice-President

Source: Latest company proxy statements as of February 2008.

Table A2.2. List of institutional investors with beneficial ownership in media conglomerates February 2008

Time Warner	Dodge & Cox (7.14%), AXA (5.79% common stock), Capital Group (4.6%), Fidelity (4.13%), Goldman Sachs (3.25%), Liberty Media (3%), Vanguard (2.95%), Muneef Tarmoom (UAE) (2.39%)
Disney	Steve Jobs (7.3%), Fidelity (5.5%), State Street (3.64%), AXA (2.9%), Vanguard (2.6%), Southeastern Asset Management (2.6%), Legg Mason (2.38%), State Farm (2.2%), Kingdom Holdings (1%)
News Corporation	Murdoch Family Trust (31.2% of class B common stock), Dodge & Cox (10.1% class A common stock), HRH Prince Al-Walid bin Talal bin Abdulaziz Alsaud, c/o Kingdom Holding Company (5.7%), Fidelity Management & Research Company (0.96% class A)
Bertelsmann	Bertelsmann Foundation (76.9%), Mohn Family (23%)
Viacom	National Amusements (71.2% class A), Mario J. Gabelli (8.44% class A), Sherry Redstone (8%), Franklin (7.8%), Morgan Stanley (6.81%), NWQ Investments (5.47%), Wellington (4.09%), State Street (3.46%), Barclays (3.5%), Templeton Growth Fund (2.51%)
CBS	Sumner Redstone (71.2% class A), AXA (France) (12.2% class B), Sherry Redstone (8%), Goldman Sachs (6.8%), State Street (4.12%), Barclays (3.24%), Capital Research (2.48%), Neuberger Berman (2.26%)
NBC (GE)	General Electric (80%), Vivendi Universal SA (20%)
Microsoft	Bill Gates (9.33%), Capital Research (5.95%), Steven A. Ballmer (4.9%), Barclays (4.05%), Vanguard (2.5%), AXA (1.26%), Goldman Sachs (1.2%)

Table A2.2. (*Continued*)

Google	Sergey Brin (President of Technology) (20.4% class B and 28.4% class A – assumes conversion), Larry Page (21.5% of class B convertible into 28.3% of class A), Eric Schmidt (13.7% class A, 7.7% class B), Fidelity Investments (11.49% class A common), SAC Capital Advisors (10%), Capital Research (8.3% class A common), Time Warner (8.2% class A), Citadel (4.6%), Sequoia Capital (3.2%), Legg Mason Focus Capital (2.2% common stock), Jennison Associates Capital Corp (1.75%)
Yahoo!	Capital Research and Management Company (11.6%), Legg Mason (8.86%), David Filo (5.89%), Jerry Yang (4.0%), Citigroup (2.08%), Goldman Sachs (2.02%), Fidelity (1.622%), AXA (0.8%)
Apple	Fidelity Investments (6.44%), AXA (3.86%), Barclays (3.69%), State Street (2.96%), Vanguard (2.80%), Marisco Capital Management (2.44%), Janus Capital Management (2.36%), Bank of New York Mcllon Corp (1.54%)

Source: Compiled from latest proxy and beneficial ownership statements filed with the US Security and Exchange Commission as of February 2008.

Table A3.1. Evolution of support for Iraq War and evaluation of its conduct in the context of war-related events, 2003–2008

	War right decision (%)	War going well (%)	US fatalities	US injuries	Iraqi civilians killed	Timeline
Mar-03	71	90	65	208	—	3/19 War begins
Apr-03	74	92	74	340	—	4/1 Jessica Lynch rescued, 4/9 Coalition forces enter Baghdad
May-03	74	—	37	55	866	5/1 Bush, "Mission Accomplished" speech, 5/22 UN lifts sanction, 5/31 CIA reports WMD trailer found
Jun-03	n.a.	—	30	147	1026	
Jul-03	67	75	48	226	935	
Aug-03	63	62	35	181	1292	8/20 Attack on UN headquarters
Sep-03	63	62	31	247	860	
Oct-03	60	60	44	413	825	
Nov-03	n.a.	—	82	336	677	
Dec-03	67	75	40	262	817	12/13 Saddam Hussein captured
Jan-04	65	73	47	187	831	
Feb-04	56	63	20	150	938	
Mar-04	55	61	52	324	1190	3/11 Madrid bombing, 3/16 *Waxman Report* released
Apr-04	57	57	136	1214	2014	Largest US losses in one month, 4/28 Abu Ghraib story breaks

May-04	51	46	80	759	1627	
Jun-04	55	57	42	588	1021	US transfers sovereignty to Iraq
Jul-04	52	55	54	552	932	7/9 Senate Select Committee on Intelligence Report on prewar intelligence failures, 7/22 *9/11 Commission Report* released
Aug-04	53	53	66	894	1517	
Sep-04	53	52	80	709	1434	
Oct-04	46	51	64	650	1329	10/6 *Duelfer Report* released
Nov-04	48	—	137	1431	2638	11/2 Bush re-elected, 11/8 Fallujah assault
Dec-04	49	50	72	544	1333	
Jan-05	51	51	107	497	1448	1/25 End of WMD search declared
Feb-05	47	47	58	414	1599	
Mar-05	—	—	35	371	1333	
Apr-05	—	—	52	598	1200	
May-05	—	—	80	571	1777	5/25 UK Downing Street memo revealed to be faulty
Jun-05	47	50	78	512	1517	
Jul-05	49	52	54	477	1658	7/7 London bombing; Cindy Sheehan camps in front of Bush's ranch,
Aug-05	—	—	85	540	3303	8/29 Hurricane Katrina hits
Sep-05	49	53	49	545	1964	9/24 Major anti-war protests around the world.
Oct-05	48	48	96	607	1376	10/15 Iraqi referendum on the constitution
Nov-05	—	—	84	399	1640	
Dec-05	47	51	68	414	1348	
Jan-06	45	51	62	289	1778	

(cont.)

Table A3.1. (*Continued*)

	War right decision (%)	War going well (%)	US fatalities	US injuries	Iraqi civilians killed	Timeline
Feb-06	51	51	55	343	2165	
Mar-06	45	43	31	497	2378	
Apr-06	47	47	76	433	2284	
May-06	—	—	69	443	2669	
Jun-06	49	53	61	459	3149	6/6 Abu Musbab al-Zarqawi killed
Jul-06	44	53	43	525	3590	
Aug-06	45	41	65	592	3009	
Sep-06	49	47	72	790	3345	
Oct-06	45	37	106	781	3709	
Nov-06	41	32	70	548	3462	US Mid-term election
Dec-06	42	32	112	702	2914	
Jan-07	40	32	83	645	3500	1/10 Bush announces surge
Feb-07	40	35	81	519	2700	
Mar-07	43	40	81	613	2400	Mistreatment of US soldiers at Walter Reed uncovered
Apr-07	45	38	104	618	2500	
May-07	—	—	126	753	2600	5/25 Congress passes H.R. 2206
Jun-07	40	34	101	658	1950	6/11 US turns to arming Sunnis, 6/15 Surge begins, 6/25 Senator Lugar says surge not working
Jul-07	41	36	78	616	2350	Bush pardons Scooter Libby, Glasgow Airport scare

Aug-07	—	—	84	565	2000	Interim report card bad, bi-partisan Warner Lugar Amendment to force Bush to present a revised Iraq strategy by 10/16, Karl Rove resigns
Sep-07	42	41	65	361	1100	9/11 *Petraeus Report*, 9/16 Blackwater employees kill 17 Iraqi civilians, CBS airs major exposé on Blackwater
Oct-07	39	44	38	297	950	
Nov-07	39	48	37	204	750	11/24 Surge declared over, interest in news about returning war veterans peaks
Dec-07	36	41	23	211	750	
Jan-08	—	—	40	234	600	
Feb-08	38	48	29	215	700	2/21 Turkey launches offensive on PKK
Mar-08	—	—	38	282	750	Mahdi Army revolt
Apr-08	37	44	52	275	—	
May-08[a]	—	—	13	40	—	

[a] Through May 4, 2008.

Source: Pew (May 1, 2008); Brookings Iraq Index (May 1, 2008).

Table A4.1. Selected political scandals involving the Bush administration and the Republican Party, 2002–2007

January 2002	**Enron Scandal** The Bush administration was found to have close ties with, and insider information about the company.
March 2004	**Memo Leak Scandal** Senate Judiciary Committee, Republican staffers secretly accessed almost 5,000 computer files containing confidential Democratic strategy memos about President Bush's judicial nominees. Some of these memos were then leaked to the media.
April 28, 2004	**Abu Ghraib Scandal** CBS program *60 Minutes* aired the first public story about the torture of prisoners by US military personnel at the US prison at Abu Ghraib in Iraq.
June 2004	The Iraq Coalition Provisional Authority reported that a significant percentage of its assets were missing.
January 2005	It was revealed that the Bush administration paid a series of reporters for positive coverage of the Iraq War.
July 2005	**The Plame Affair** Key members of the Bush administration were accused of leaking the identity of a CIA agent, Valerie Plame, to members of the press in 2003 in order to undercut claims by her husband, Ambassador Joseph Wilson, who discounted the administration, that Iraq tried to purchase uranium from Niger in the run-up to the Iraq War. On July 1, 2005, an MSNBC reporter testified that Karl Rove was the source of the leak. Karl Rove, the chief architect of the Bush 2000 and 2004 election campaigns, resigned.
August 12, 2005	**Abramoff Scandal** A lobbyist with close associations with the Bush administration, Jack Abramoff, was indicted on charges of conspiracy and wire fraud. A Washington task force was formed to investigate charges of bribery of, and collusion with, key Republican members of Congress.

Table A4.1. *(Continued)*

September 28, 2005	US Congress Majority Leader Tom Delay was indicted for campaign finance violations.
December 2005	*The New York Times* publishes an article giving details of the National Security Agency conduct of warrantless wire-tappings of US civilians.
January 2006	Abramoff pleaded guilty. Tom Delay relinquished his post as Speaker of the House of Representatives.
February 2006	The Abramoff scandal widened as more Republican senators, including Harry Reid, were implicated for taking illegal or improper bribes from lobbyists.
September 2006	**The Foley Scandal** Conservative Congressman Mark Foley resigned after being accused of inappropriate advances toward teenage boys who had served as congressional pages in Washington, DC.
March 2007	**US Attorney Scandal** Attorney General Alberto Gonzales eventually resigned in the wake of the scandal. It included charges of corruption for his alleged role in firing eight US attorneys because they were investigating high-ranking GOP officials or because they refused to carry out indictments against Democratic office-holders whom the Bush administration wished to defeat in the November 2006 elections. He formally resigned in August 2007.
March 6, 2007	Scooter Libby, Vice President Dick Cheney's Chief of Staff, was indicted for perjury and obstruction of justice for his role in the Plame Affair.
August 2007	Conservative Senator Larry Craig was arrested for lewd and lascivious conduct in a Minneapolis, MN airport bathroom.
September 2007	**Blackwater Scandal** Public attention turned to the corrupt practices of paid contractors working in Iraq on behalf of the US government when Blackwater employees were implicated in the murder of 17 Iraqi civilians.

Table A4.2. Political scandals around the world, 1988–2008[a]

Year	Country	Scandal	Origination point[b]	Outcome
2008	USA	**Spitzer Scandal** New York governor Elliot Spitzer resigned after it became clear that he used state funds to purchase a prostitute.	Criminal investigation	Resignation
2008	Malaysia	**Sex Tape Scandal** Sodomy, murder, corruption, disappearing witnesses, and numerous other allegations rocked the Malaysian Prime Minister's office and brought massed protesters out into the streets.	Criminal investigation	Resignations and ongoing investigations
2007	South Korea	**The Grand National Party Bribery Scandal** Several members of now former president Roh Moo-hyun's administration, including his top anti-corruption agent, were accused of accepting bribes from a number of sources including Samsung Electronics. Accusations of corruption continued to surface implicating local GNP politicians as well as national ones.	Whistleblower	Indictments and criminal investigations (ongoing at time of writing)

2007	Nigeria	**The Etteh Contract Scandal** Patricia O. Etteh, the speaker of the Nigerian House of Representatives and the first female speaker in history, resigned amidst a highly mediated scandal involving accusations of corruption and misappropriation of funds. Etteh called the scandal a political witch-hunt stirred up by her enemies.	Journalist investigation	Resignation
2007–8	Japan	**J-Green Scandal** Japan's agricultural minister, Toshikatsu Matsuoka and Shinichi Yamazaki, a former executive director of a government environmental agency, committed suicide in two separate incidents after a widening scandal regarding suspicious book-keeping practices in the Abe administration.	Criminal investigation	Investigation
2007	USA	Conservative Senator **Larry Craig** was arrested for lewd and lascivious conduct in a Minneapolis, MN airport bathroom. Although he resisted calls for his immediate resignation, Craig conceded not to run for re-election in 2008.	Criminal investigation	Investigation

(cont.)

453

Table A4.2. (Continued)

Year	Country	Scandal	Origination point[b]	Outcome
2007	USA	**Attorney General Alberto Gonzales** was forced to resign under charges of corruption for his alleged role in firing eight US attorneys because they were investigating high-ranking GOP officials or because they refused to carry out indictments against Democratic office-holders who the Bush administration wished to defeat in the November 2006 elections. He formally resigned in August 2007.	Legislative investigation	Resignation
2007	Saudi Arabia/ UK/US	**Bandar–BAE Scandal** The *Guardian* and the BBC published reports that the British arms firm BAE had paid Prince Bandar of Saudi Arabia (former ambassador to the US) $2 billion in "marketing fees" as part of the 1985 al-Yamamah arms deal. Tony Blair ordered the corruption probe to be closed due to "national security" reasons, elevating the revelations into a scandal that rocked the Labour Party.	Journalist investigation	Resignations
2007	USA	**US Rep. William Jefferson,** a Democrat from Louisiana, was indicted for graft involving Nigerian business schemes that netted him over $500,000 in bribes.	Criminal investigation	Indictment

2006–8	Columbia	**Parapolitics Scandal** An array of congressmen, senators, and political insiders were implicated in collusion with paramilitary groups all but bringing Columbian political life to a standstill.	Criminal investigation	Criminal trial pending
2006	USA	**DC Madam** A US Postal Inspection investigation of Jeane Palfrey revealed her involvement in money laundering and prostitution. It soon became clear that many of her clients were high-profile DC insiders. In July 2007, Palfrey released her phone records to the public and several media outlets used the records to track down the identities of some of her more important clients.	Criminal investigation followed by journalist investigation	Resignations of numerous politicians and government bureaucrats
2006	USA	**Foley Scandal** Congressman Mark Foley was outed by ABC news for sending sexual instant messages to congressional pages. Foley resigned in shame and calls resounded for the Speaker of the House, Dennis Hastert's resignation and prompted inquiries into a number of other congressmen's behavior.	Journalist investigation	Resignation

(cont.)

Table A4.2. (Continued)

Year	Country	Scandal	Origination point[b]	Outcome
2006	Israel	**President Moshe Katsav** was charged with rape and molestation after ten different women filed claims against him. A widely reported media scandal, the investigation also uncovered infractions regarding the granting of pardons and suspicion of illegal wire-tapping. An unknown source leaked a tape of the President and his primary accuser (known as A) trying to blackmail him.	Journalist investigation	Katsav was suspended from office in March 2007 and formally resigned in August 2007.
2005–6	Brazil	**Lula Scandal** A widespread corruption and bribery investigation centering on claims of bribes for votes almost ended President Lula's political career. The scandal broke in June 2005 when Brazilian TV showed a video of a high-ranking postal official accepting a large amount of cash.	Journalist investigation	Secretary General Silvio Pereira stepped down as Workers Party head and three other major ministers resigned.
2005–6	Canada	**Sponsorship Scandal** Prime Minister Paul Martin was removed from power after a vote of no confidence in the wake of a high-profile scandal involving the misuse of government funds earmarked for a patriotism-building campaign in Quebec.	Government audit	Prime minister resigned as head of his party.

2005–6	USA	**Valerie Plame Affair** Key members of the Bush administration were accused of leaking the identity of a CIA agent, Valerie Plame, to members of the press in 2003 in order to undercut claims by her husband, Ambassador Joseph Wilson, who discounted the administration's account that Iraq tried to purchase uranium from Niger in the run-up to the Iraq War. On July 1, 2005, an MSNBC reporter testified that Karl Rove was the source of the leak. Karl Rove, the chief architect of the Bush 2000 and 2004 election campaigns, resigned.	Journalist investigation	Criminal prosecution and resignations
2005–7	Sweden/Czech Republic	**Gripen Affair** A long-running scandal involving the sale of fighter planes and numerous corporations such as Saab.	Journalist investigation	Numerous resignations
2005–8	USA	**Abramoff Scandal** A lobbyist with close associations with the Bush administration, Jack Abramoff was indicted on charges of conspiracy and wire fraud. A Washington task force was formed to investigate charges of bribery of, and collusion with, key Republican members of Congress as well as involvement with the Gambino crime family. US Congress Majority Leader Tom Delay was indicted for campaign finance violations. He relinquished his post as speaker of the House in January 2006.	Journalist investigation	Indictments and resignations of members of Congress

(cont.)

457

Table A4.2. (*Continued*)

Year	Country	Scandal	Origination point[b]	Outcome
2004	Costa Rica	Two scandals involving ex-presidents came to light in the summer of 2004. **Rafael Ángel Calderón**, President from 1990 to 1994, was charged with distributing, and taking an illegal commission of approximately $9 million on the sale of medical equipment by a Finnish company to the state health-care system, the CCSS. **Miguel Ángel Rodríguez**, President from 1998 to 2002, was charged with accepting a share of a $2.4 million payment made by Alcatel, a French company, for a contract with the Costa Rican state-owned telecoms and electricity firm, the ICE.	Journalist investigation	Calderón was incarcerated and then placed under house arrest.
2004	France	**City Hall Scandal** Former PM Alain Juppé, the head of the UMP party, and Chirac's right-hand man, was found guilty of using Paris city funds to pay party workers in the late 1980s and early 1990s when he was treasurer and Chirac was mayor. His trial was the highlight of a broader corruption scandal involving dozens of city and national employees including Chirac.	Journalist investigation	Criminal conviction

(*cont.*)

2003–4	France	**Toulouse Sex Ring** Major police and political officials, including Dominique Baudis, who was mayor of Toulouse from 1983 to 2001, were implicated in aiding serial killer Patrice Alègre's murder spree of prostitutes between 1992 and 1997 in one of the biggest media stories of the year.	Police investigation	Charges dropped
2003	Finland	**Iraqgate** Anneli Jäätteenmäki was appointed Prime Minister of Finland in April 2003. However, the lack of trust in Jäätteenmäki caused by the leak of secret documents about Finnish involvement in the Iraq War forced her to resign as Prime Minister just two months later.	Criminal investigation after secret documents were leaked to the press.	Martti Manninen, an advisor to the President of Finland, was convicted.
2003–5	United Nations	**Oil-for-Food Scandal** Approximately 2,000 firms that participated in the UN oil-for-food program in Iraq were found to be involved in bribes and surcharges to the Iraqi government.	Criminal investigation	Program discontinued
2002	Japan	**Suzuki Scandal** A high-level LDP member, Suzuki, was charged with accepting bribes from a lumber company in his constituency of Hokkaido. He resigned in February 2002 and was convicted in June. The scandal rocked the Foreign Ministry. Prime Minister Kuzami's political decline is also credited to his indifferent attitude toward the scandals.	Criminal investigation	Resignation

Table A4.2. (*Continued*)

Year	Country	Scandal	Origination point[b]	Outcome
2001–6	South Africa	**Arms Scandal** Numerous ANC officials were accused of taking cash and gifts from European arms dealers beginning in 2001. Deputy President and Thabo Mbeki's expected successor, Jacob Zuma, resigned amid accusations that he had accepted large cash payouts from his financial adviser Schabir Shaik on behalf of a French arms dealer to support their interests in a multi-billion dollar arms contract.	Unattributed rumors led to investigation.	Resignation
2001	Ukraine	**Cassette Scandal** Mykola Melnychenko, a former member of the presidential security service, released a tape containing a conversation between President Kuchma and other key officials about how to solve a number of issues illegally, including the murder of a journalist Gondadze. In 2005, a parliamentary commission formally implicated Kuchma and an ex-Interior Minister (who shot himself in the head) in the abduction. This affair is credited as a key impetus for the Orange Revolution of 2004.	Public accusation	Resignations and mass protests
2000	Peru	**Fujimori Scandal** President Fujimori resigned after the opposition party released a tape showing his security chief engaged in vote buying.	Public accusation	Fujimori fled the country.

1999	Canada	**Casinogate** The sitting Premier of British Columbia resigned over a scandal involving the fact that he granted a provincial government casino-gambling license to a company that was co-owned by his neighbor and friend, Dimitrios Pilarinos	The scandal entered the public sphere when the media filmed police searching the Premier's private home.	Resignation
1999	France	Finance Minister **Dominique Strauss-Kahn** resigned after being accused of receiving £60,000 for work he never did.	The press	Resignation
1999–2003	France	**Elf Affair** A long-running scandal involving bribes paid out by the state-run oil company. At the height of the scandal in 2001, President of the Constitutional Council, Roland Dumas was forced to resign and then sentenced to 30 months in jail for taking bribes from his mistress Christine Deviers-Joncour on behalf of the Elf Oil company during the 1980s and 1990s. The investigation began in 1993 and culminated in a series of high-profile trials in 2000–3. Dumas was the only politician convicted, but he eventually won an appeal.	Criminal investigation	Convictions

(cont.)

Table A4.2. (*Continued*)

Year	Country	Scandal	Origination point[b]	Outcome
1999	Germany	**Elf Oil Affair (aka: Kohlgate)** Helmut Kohl was accused of taking $10 million in kickbacks from Elf Oil for his 1994 election campaign. Many alleged that this was an effort by Mitterrand to ensure Kohl's re-election. In the wake of this scandal, the CDU Party largely dissolved.	Criminal investigation	Convictions
1998	USA	**Monica Lewinsky Scandal** President Clinton was impeached after allegations surfaced that he lied under oath about an affair with his White House intern. News of Clinton's infidelity first broke on the Internet news site, the Drudge Report.	Media leak (Drudge Report scooping *Newsweek*)	Presidential impeachment
1998	UK	**First Mandelson Scandal** Peter Mandelson resigns as Secretary of State for Trade and Industry after a massive press scandal, which uncovered the fact that he had received undisclosed loans from Geoffrey Robinson, the Treasury minister prior to taking office.	Department of Trade and Industry investigation	Resignation
1997	Czech Republic	**ODS Scandal** Prime Minister Václav Klaus resigned as a result of a party funding scandal.	Journalist investigation	Resignation

1997	South Korea	**Hanbo Affair or Hanbogate** Ten law-makers, including the Home Minister and Kim Hyun Chol, second son of Kim Yong Sam, were arrested in a scandal involving the bankruptcy of Hanbo, Korea's second largest steelmaker. The politicians were accused of accepting vast political contributions in exchange for preferential loans and laws.	Criminal investigation	Credited with the failure of President Kim's re-election bid
1997–8	USA	**Gingrich Scandal** Newt Gingrich resigned after an investigation into 80 accusations of corruption, including improper use of government resources and a $4.5 million book deal advance, which he eventually returned. While nearly all the charges were dropped, he paid $300,000 to the House Ethics Committee for the cost of the probe. The GOP suffered unexpected losses in the 1998 elections, which many attribute to this scandal.	Legislative investigation	Resignation and censure
1995–6	Argentina	**Peru–Ecuador Arms Scandal** The Defense Minister, Oscar Camilion, resigned after *La Nación* published an article reporting suspicions that Peru and Ecuador had received arms from Argentina. Air Force Commander Janu Paulik resigned in 1996 and many others involved in the scandal died under suspicious circumstances.	Press reports	Resignations

(cont.)

Table A4.2. (Continued)

Year	Country	Scandal	Origination point[b]	Outcome
1993–5	Belgium/ NATO	**The Agusta Scandal Willi Claes** NATO Secretary General, and several other Belgian politicians resigned amidst a bribery scandal that the police uncovered in the process of investigating a four-year-old murder of a former fellow leader of the Belgian Socialists, André Cools. Cools was shot to death outside his home because of his involvement in a scheme in which French and Italian arms manufacturers made political contributions to the Belgian Socialists in return for military contracts.	Police investigation	Resignation
1992–6	India	**The Hawala Scandal** lasted from 1992 to 1996, and involved a complex web of connections between the Rao government and money-laundering groups. Many politicians resigned.	Police investigation	Resignations and arrests. The Congress Party was again defeated in the 1996 elections.

1992	Denmark	**Immigration Visa Scandal** One of the largest scandals in Denmark's post-war history erupted when it became clear that the Schlüter government was actively trying to inhibit Sri Lankan refugees from joining their families who were already in Denmark.	Criminal investigation	Prime Minister Schlüter resigned in January 1993 leading to the first majority coalition government since 1971.
1992	Brazil	An influence-peddling scheme during the 1990 election campaign triggered a scandal that ended with the impeachment and resignation of Brazil's President **Fernando Collor de Mello** in 1992.	Public accusations	The President resigned in order to avoid being impeached.
1991	USA	**Bouncing House Scandal** This involved the revelation that dozens of congressmen had regularly overdrawn their accounts, a process that basically meant that they were receiving interest-free loans.	The press (*Roll Call*)	Resignation
1991	France	**Contaminated Blood Scandal** The public health body gave hemophiliacs blood contaminated with the HIV virus with full knowledge of the consequences.	The press (*L'Événement du Jeudi*)	Public trial of three cabinet ministers
1991–6	Spain	**Filesa Scandal** This contributed to the electoral defeat of Spain's Prime Minister Felipe González		Electoral defeat

(*cont.*)

Table A4.2. (*Continued*)

Year	Country	Scandal	Origination point[b]	Outcome
1990	Spain	**Juan Guerra Scandal** Jimenez (2004) and Heywood (2007) note that this scandal involving influence peddling transformed corruption into the most salient political issue in Spanish politics in the early 1990s.	Public accusations	Deputy Prime Minister Alfonso Guerra resigned.
1987–9	India	**Bofors Scandal** Corruption scandal involving Rajiv Gandhi which led to the defeat of Congress and Ghandhi's resignation.	Investigations by *The Hindu* and the *Indian Express*	Resignation and change of ruling party after 42 years in power

[a] This account includes major national political scandals that resulted in tangible political consequences, such as the resignation, impeachment, and/or indictment of political figures.

[b] By origination point, we mean the mechanism by which the alleged wrongdoing was brought into the public arena.

Source: Compiled from news reports by Amelia Arsenault, 2008.

Table A4.3. Selected political scandals in G-8 countries, 1988–2008[a]

Canada

2008　　**Couillard Affair**　Several Conservative MPs stepped down after allegations surfaced that they had had improper relations with Julie Couillard, a women with connections to a criminal biker gang, who was attempting to win a government contract.

2005–6　**Sponsorship Scandal**　Prime Minister Paul Martin was removed from power after a vote of no confidence in the wake of a high-profile scandal involving the misuse of government funds earmarked for a patriotism-building campaign in Quebec.

1998　　**APEC**　Pepper-spraying of political protesters resulted in a four-year inquiry into police procedures and the government's supervisory role. Solicitor General Andy Scott resigned after being overheard talking on an airplane about how a police officer would "take the fall" for the scandal.

1995–2003　**Airbus**　Long-running scandal involving charges that former Progressive Conservative Prime Minister Brian Mulroney took illegal kickbacks. Mulroney countersued for defamation.

1993　　**Shawinigate**　Allegations that Prime Minister Jean Chrétien participated in illegal real-estate transactions repeatedly resurfaced throughout his presidency.

France

2001–6　**Clearstream Affair**　Numerous politicians and members of the French Secret Service were accused of money-laundering. In 2006, anonymous allegations surfaced in the press that Nicolas Sarkozy, the Russian Mafia, and many others were also involved in the scandal. Public calls for Prime Minister Dominique de Villepin's resignation were made among claims that he instituted an investigation of Sarkozy (his chief rival for party leader) in order to damage his reputation.

(*cont.*)

Table A4.3. (*Continued*)

| 1996–2003 | **Elf Oil Affair** Forty executives of the former state-owned oil giant, politicians, and bureaucrats were brought to trial. The French Foreign Minister and his mistress were sentenced to prison terms (he was later acquitted). |
| 1991 | **Mitterrand–Pasqua Affair** This involved the secret sale and shipment of arms from Eastern Europe to the government of Angola by the French government, which led to 42 indictments. |

Germany

| 1999/2000 | **Kohlgate** Helmut Kohl was accused of taking $10 million in kickbacks from Elf Oil for his 1994 election campaign. It also became public that the CDU had accepted numerous illegal donations during Kohl's tenure and funneled the funds through secret bank accounts. In the wake of this scandal the CDU party largely dissolved.[b] |
| 1987–93 | **Barschel/Desk Drawer** (i.e. Waterkandgate) A vote-manipulation scandal broken by *Der Spiegel* involving murder and extensive cover-ups, which culminated in the resignation of two party minister presidents.[c] |

Italy

| 2007 | **Wire-tapping Scandal** *La Repubblica* published wire-taps between MediaSet (owned by Berlusconi) and RAI (state-owned) officials in which they conspired to present favorable coverage of Berlusconi while he was Prime Minister. |
| 2005–8 | **Bancopoli** Finance and banking scandal that resulted in the resignation of Banca d'Italia Governor Antonio Fazio and several high-ranking businessmen.[d] |

1992–6 **Tangentopoli** (i.e. Kickback City) A widespread corruption investigation involving politicians, the Vatican, and the Mafia. Over 6,000 defendants, including former Socialist Prime Minister Bettino Craxi, were charged in public investigations that culminated in the all but disintegration of Italy's two dominant post-World War II political parties.

Japan

2002 **Suzuki Scandal** A high-level LDP member, muneo Suzuki, was charged with accepting ¥5m ($40,000) in bribes from a lumber company in his constituency of Hokkaido. He resigned in February 2002 and was convicted in June. The scandal rocked the Foreign Ministry. Prime Minister Kuzami's political decline is also credited to his indifferent attitude toward the scandals.

1992 **Sagawa Kyūbin** A political bribery scandal involving links to the Mafia that led to the indictment of the Liberal Democratic Party's (LDP) Vice President Shin Kanemaru. It was credited with contributing to the party's first electoral defeat in 34 years in 1993.

1988 **Recruit Cosmos Scandal** An extensive and highly publicized political corruption scandal, in which 17 members of the Diet were convicted of insider trading and Prime Minister Noboru Takeshita's entire cabinet resigned.

Russia

2006 **Spy Rock** The Russian Federal Security Service held a press conference implicating 12 Russian NGOs as spies on behalf of the British Embassy in Moscow and claiming that the UK had embedded spy equipment within fake rocks in several public areas the same month that Putin authorized a bill banning foreign funding of NGOs.

(cont.)

Table A4.3. (*Continued*)

2001   **Three Whales**   Major corruption investigation involving furniture companies and federal officers. Key witnesses were murdered during the investigation, which ultimately led to the resignation and/or indictment of numerous high-ranking officials.

1997   **Sauna Scandal**   Russian Justice Minister Valentin Kovalev forced out of office after a video surfaced in the press (allegedly leaked by the Interior Ministry) of him engaging in group sex in a sauna.

1997   **Young Reformers Scandals**   In a series of "sleaze wars," strategic evidence was released that different high-ranking Kremlin officials were taking kickbacks appeared in the press throughout the year. Many believe that the information was released by Boris Berezovsky, Russia's richest man, who was a target of investigation by the subjects of the scandal.

UK

1998   **Peter Mandelson Scandal**   Blair's Trade and Industry Secretary resigned after a massive press scandal that uncovered the fact that he had received undisclosed loans from Geoffrey Robinson, the Treasury minister, prior to taking office.

1994–7   **Cash for Questions**   A scandal initiated by articles in the *Sunday Times* and the *Guardian* claiming that Tory MPs took cash from lobbyists in exchange for asking questions in the House of Commons on behalf of Harrods department store owner, Mohamed Al-Fayed. The affair is credited with helping lead to Labour's landslide victory in 1997.

USA

2006–8   **Jack Abramoff**   Congressman Bob Ney, two White House officials, and nine lobbyists and congressional aids were convicted of corruption.

2006   **Foley Scandal**   US Congressman Mark Foley was accused of sending explicit e-mails to current and former under-aged congressional pages. Foley resigned and the House Ethics Committee launched an investigation into the failure of the Republican leadership's reaction to the allegations.

2006   **DC Madam**   Numerous high-profile US politicians resigned after being implicated as clients of an upscale prostitution ring in Washington, DC. The madam under investigation also released full copies of her phone records to journalists and to public view on the Internet.

2006   **Abu Ghraib**   Pictures depicting US soldiers torturing prisoners at the Abu Ghraib prison in Iraq became public.

2003   **Valerie Plame**   Chief White House officials leaked Plame's identity as a CIA agent to the press in order to discredit her husband's claims that the White House presented false evidence for the Iraq War.

1998   **Monica Lewinsky Scandal**   President Clinton was impeached for lying under oath about his sexual relations with a White House intern.

1992   **House Banking Scandal**   The House Bank was forced to close in 1991 after it was found that several congressmen were abusing their accounts. The investigation led to a number of convictions, including those of five congressmen and one delegate after they left the House.

1992   **Whitewater**   Political controversy involving improper real-estate dealings of President Clinton and his wife. The scandal expanded after Deputy White House Council Vince Foster committed suicide which resulted in multiple investigations by Congress and the appointment of Kenneth Starr to conduct an independent investigation into the Clinton dealings.

(cont.)

Table A4.3. (*Continued*)

1989	**The Keating Five** US Senators Alan Cranston (D-CA), Dennis DeConcini (D-AZ), John Glenn (D-OH), John McCain (R-AZ), and Donald W. Riegle (D-MI) were accused of improperly aiding Charles H. Keating, Jr., chairman of the failed Lincoln Savings and Loan Association, which was the target of an investigation by the Federal Home Loan Bank Board (FHLBB). Only McCain and Glenn ran for re-election.

[a] This table is not an exhaustive account of political scandals. It includes heavily publicized, major political scandals with significant national political consequences.

[b] Wolfgang Hullen, the head of the Christian Democratic Union parliamentary delegation's finance and budget department, hanged himself at the height of the investigation. Kohlgate was a major turning point for post-reunification German media and politics. According to Esser and Hartung (2004), the scandal, as the first major scandal to occur after the government and national media had moved from Bonn to the new capital of Berlin in 1999, marked the end of the partisan press and Cold-War political culture that placed party survival over democratic norms of behavior.

[c] CDU Premier Minister Uwe Barschel resigned in 1987 under allegations of vote manipulation. It was revealed that he employed a tabloid journalist as an aide and through him initiated a series of schemes targeting his liberal left-wing opponent Björn Engholm. These activities included having him followed by private detectives, coercing someone to sue Engholm for tax evasion, releasing rumors that he was HIV positive, and casting him as a womanizer, a homosexual, and an endorser of pedophilia. Shortly afterward, two journalists found him murdered in a bathtub. Five years later, in 1993, minister president of SPD, Björn Engholm, was forced to resign when evidence surfaced that he was more involved in the scandal than previously known.

[d] The scandal exploded when *Il Giornale*, owned by Berlusconi's brother Paolo, published the transcripts of private phone exchanges between a number of defendants named in the scandal, many of whom were high-ranking officials in the center-left government coalition. The transcripts had no official bearing on the case and were not even officially entered as evidence. The source of the leaked transcripts remains unknown. However, the transcripts provided a major campaign issue for the April 2006 election.

Source: Media reports collected and elaborated by Amelia Arsenault, 2008.

Table A4.4. Non-voting measures of US political participation, 1980–2004 (percentages)

Year	Tried to influence others' votes	Attended political meeting	Worked for a party or candidate	Displayed button or bumper sticker	Gave $ to a campaign
1980	36	8	4	6	8
1984	32	8	4	9	8
1988	29	7	3	9	9
1992	37	8	3	11	7
1996	28	5	2	10	9
2000	34	5	3	10	9
2004	48	7	3	21	13

Data Source: US NES data compiled by Hetherington (2008: 10).

Table A4.5. Mobilization efforts by US political parties or other organizations, 1980–2004 (percentage reporting yes)

Year	Contacted by a party?	Contacted by something other than a party?
1980	24	10
1984	24	8
1988	24	8
1992	20	10
1996	26	10
2000	35	11
2004	43	18

Data Source: US NES data compiled by Hetherington (2008: 14).

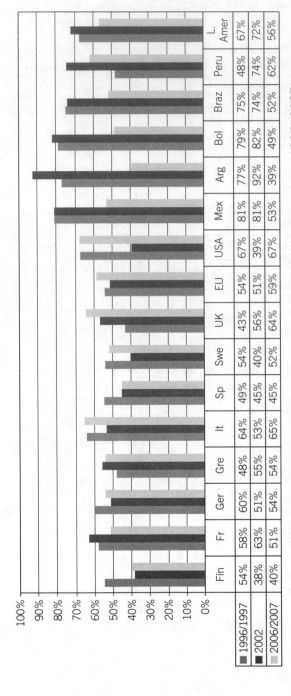

Fig. A4.1. Percentage of citizens expressing little or no trust in their national governments, 1996–2007

Notes: The numbers for Gallup and Eurobarometer are for 1997, 2002, and 2007; due to availability, Latinobarometer figures are for 1996, 2002, and 2006.

Questions: Eurobarometer: Do you tend to trust or tend not to trust your national government?

Gallup: How much of the time do you think you can trust government in Washington to do what is right? Figure reflects those reporting "Only some of the time," "Never."

Latinobarometer: *Por favor, mire esta tarjeta y dígame, para cada uno de los grupos/instituciones o personas mencionadas en la lista. ¿Cuánta confianza tiene usted en ellas: mucha, algo, poca o ninguna confianza en . . . ? Aquí solo "Mucha" y "Algo."*

Source: Eurobarometer (1997, 2002, 2007); Gallup Polls (1997, 2002, 2007); Latinobarometer (1996, 2002, 2006).

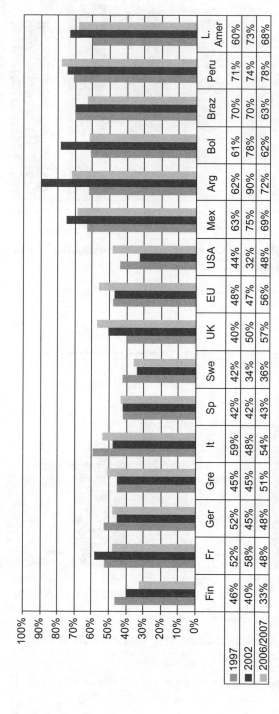

Fig. A4.2. Percentage of citizens expressing little or no trust in their national legislature or parliament, 1997–2007

Questions: Eurobarometer: Do you tend to trust or tend not to trust your national parliament?

Gallup: How much trust and confidence do you have at this time in the legislative branch, consisting of the US Senate and the House of Representatives?

Latinobarometer: *Por favor, mire esta tarjeta y dígame, para cada uno de los grupos/instituciones o personas mencionadas en la lista. ¿Cuánta confianza tiene usted en ellas: mucha, algo, poca o ninguna confianza en . . . ? Aquí solo "Mucha" y "Algo."*

Source: Eurobarometer (Europe), Gallup (USA), and Latinobarometer (Latin America) polls.

	Fin	Fr	Ger	Gre	It	Sp	Swe	UK	EU	USA	Mex	Arg	Bol	Braz	Peru	L. Amer
1997	46%	52%	52%	45%	59%	42%	42%	40%	48%	44%	63%	62%	61%	70%	71%	60%
2002	40%	58%	45%	45%	48%	42%	34%	50%	47%	32%	75%	90%	78%	70%	74%	73%
2006/2007	33%	48%	48%	51%	54%	43%	36%	57%	56%	48%	69%	72%	62%	63%	78%	68%

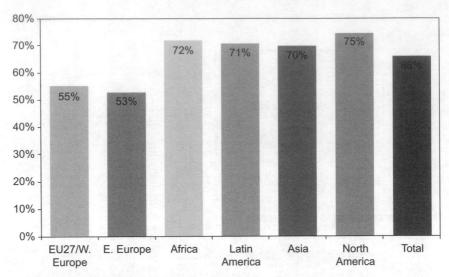

Fig. A4.3. Percentage of citizens who believe that national political parties are corrupt or extremely corrupt

Source: Global Corruption Barometer from data collected by Gallup International's Voice of the People Survey of 60 countries (2007).

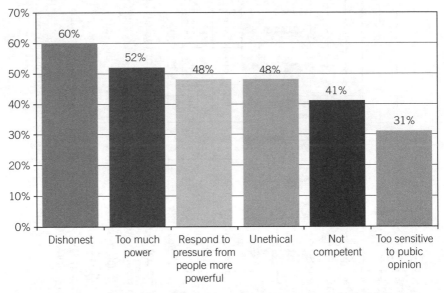

Fig. A4.4. Percentage of respondents expressing various views of their political leaders in 60 countries, 2007

Source: Gallup International's Voice of the People Survey of 60 countries (2007).

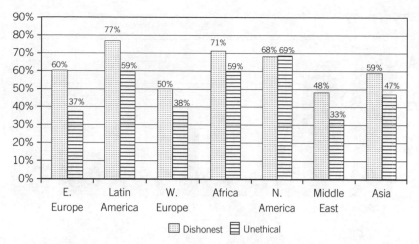

Fig. A4.5. Percentage of respondents by region who believe that their political leaders are dishonest and unethical, 2007

Source: Gallup International's Voice of the People Survey of 60 countries (2007).

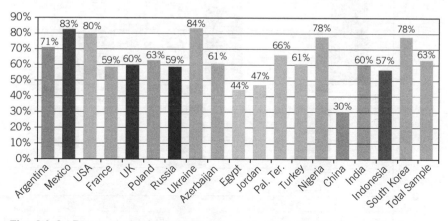

Fig. A4.6. Percentage of respondents who believe that their country is run by a few big interests, 2008

Source: WorldPublicOpinion.org survey of 19 countries (2008).

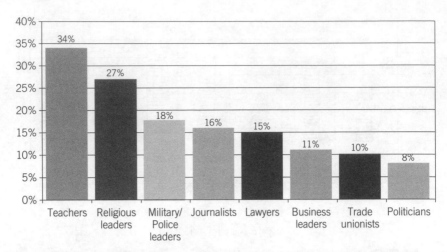

Fig. A4.7. Percentage of respondents in 60 countries expressing trust in various types of people, 2007

Source: Gallup International's Voice of the People Survey of 60 countries (2007).

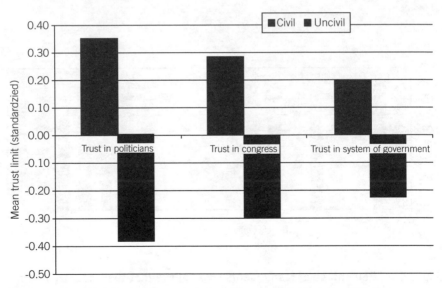

Fig. A4.8. Effects of incivility on trust in government and politicians, 2005

Note: Differences between civil and uncivil conditions were consistently significantly different in the expected direction ($F - 10.36$, $p < 0.01$; $F - 6.00$, $p < 0.01$; and $F - 3.12$, $p < 0.05$). Corresponding partial eta-squared values were 0.14, 0.06, 0.05.

Source: Mutz and Reeves (2005, source: experiment 1).

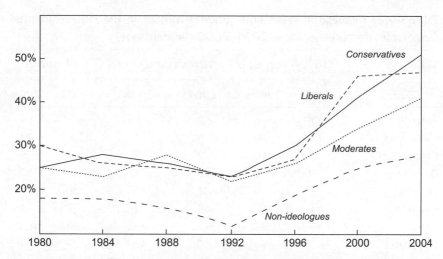

Fig. A4.9. US voters reporting contact from a political party, 1980–2004

Source: United States NES data compiled by Hetherington (2008: 15).

Table A5.1. Percentage of respondents who have heard about global warming by country, 2006

Britain	100
Japan	99
France	97
Germany	95
Spain	93
US	91
Russia	80
China	78
Turkey	75
India	57
Jordan	48
Egypt	47
Pakistan	12

Source: Pew (2006).

Table A5.2. Increase in youth and minority turnout in the US presidential Democratic primary elections, 2004–2008 (percentages)

State	18–29-year-olds		African Americans		Latinos	
	2004	2008	2004	2008	2004	2008
Arizona	7	8	2	8	17	18
California	11	16	8	7	16	30
Connecticut	5	10	7	9	2	6
Delaware	9	10	16	28	2	6
Florida	6	9	21	19	9	12
Georgia	11	18	47	51	3	3
Iowa	17	22	n.a.	n.a.	n.a.	n.a.
Louisiana	7	10	46	48	5	4
Maryland	8	14	35	37	3	4
Massachusetts	9	14	5	6	3	5
Mississippi	7	14	56	50	3	0
Missouri	9	14	15	17	1	4
New Hampshire	14	18	1	1	1	2
New York	8	15	20	16	11	10
Ohio	9	16	14	18	3	4
Oklahoma	6	9	8	6	2	4
Rhode Island	8	13	4	7	4	7
South Carolina	9	14	47	55	1	1
Tennessee	7	13	23	29	1	3
Texas	10	16	21	19	24	32
Vermont	10	11	1	1	1	3
Virginia	8	14	33	30	2	5
Wisconsin	11	16	6	8	3	4
Average	**9.0**	**13.7**	**6**	**8**	**3**	**4**
Increase		**+52.4**		**+7.8**		**+41.9**

Source: *Five Thirty Eight* (May 2008).

Table A5.3. Demographic voting patters for Obama and Clinton in the US 2008 presidential primary election[a] (percentages)

	Clinton	Obama
All	48	46
Men	43	50
Women	52	43
Whites	55	39
Blacks	15	82
Hispanics	61	35
White men	48	45
White women	60	34
Age 18–29 years	38	58
Age 65+ years	59	34
No college	52	42
College graduate	44	52
Whites no college	62	31
Whites college grad	48	47
Urban	44	52
Suburban	50	44
Rural	52	40
Income < $50K	51	44
$50K–100K	47	47
$100K +	45	51
Whites <$50K	51	44
Whites $50K–100K	54	39
Whites $100K +	48	47

[a] This table includes data from the 39 US states in which the National Election Pool conducts election day exit polls. The NEP is a consortium of American news organizations comprised of ABC, CBS, CNN, FOX, NBC, and the Associated Press, launched after a series of controversies about conflicting exit poll data in the 2000 and 2002 elections as reported by different news agencies. The table does not include some of the states who decide their candidate according to a caucus system, and so it does not fully reflect Obama's lead over Clinton. However, a precise estimate of the percentage of the popular vote won by each candidate is not available. US Democratic primary elections are decided on a state-by-state basis according to either direct election, caucuses, or a combination of the two. Four of the states which select their candidate by caucus do not even report the number of citizens who supported each candidate. Moreover, in the 2008 election, the DNC declared the Michigan (Obama removed his name from the ballot) and Florida elections invalid due to disputes over scheduling; therefore estimates differ depending on how and if the totals from these two states were included in the tabulation. Excluding the problem states (MI, FL, IA, NV, ME, WA), it is estimated that Obama won 48.1% (17,535,458 votes) of the popular vote compared to 48% won by Hillary Clinton (17,493,836 votes).

Source: ABC News citing National Election Pool results from the 39 states that had exit polls.

Table A5.4. Most important attribute of candidate when voting in 2008 Democratic primaries (percentages)

	Clinton	Obama
Brings change	29	68
Cares	48	42
Right experience	91	6
Best chance to win	50	47

Data Source: ABC News citing National Election Pool results from the 39 states that had exit polls.

Table A5.5. Most important issue when voting in 2008 Democratic primaries (percentages)

	Clinton	Obama
Economy	51	44
Iraq War	42	53
Health care	52	43

Data Source: ABC News citing National Election Pool results from the 39 states that had exit polls.

Table A5.6. Online political engagement during the 2008 US Democratic primary race: Percentage in each group of all adults surveyed (Internet and non-Internet users) who use the Internet, e-mail, or SMS to get news about politics or to exchange their views about the race.

Gender	
Male	50
Female	43
Age (years)	
18–29	58
30–49	56
50–64	41
65+	20

Table A5.6. (*Continued*)

Annual household income	
<$30,000	28
$30,000–$49,999	47
$50,000–$74,999	56
$75,000+	70
Race/ethnicity	
White (non-Hispanic)	47
Black (non-Hispanic)	43
Hispanic (English-speaking)	50
Education	
Less than high school	19
High-school graduate	32
Some college	56
College graduate	69

n = 2,251; margin of error ±2%.

Source: Pew Internet and American Life Spring Survey (2008).

Table A5.7. Internet politics: rumors and campaigns against 2008 US Democratic election candidates, June 2007– February 2008

Date	Candidate	Description
May 2008	Clinton	A doctored video that depicted Clinton advisor Mickey Kantor using slurs and obscenities to describe Indiana people in a documentary about the 1992 election circulated just days before the Indiana primary. The video was also sent to reporters along with the note, "You must report this. It will change the election."
	Obama	A chain e-mail circulates claiming that Michelle Obama had dedicated herself to putting the African American community "first and foremost" to the exclusion of all other American demographics.

Table A5.7. *(Continued)*

Date	Candidate	Description
	Obama	A chain e-mail circulates containing fake excerpts of Michelle Obama's Princeton senior thesis. The excerpts claim that the US was founded on "crime and hatred" and that whites in America are "ineradicably racist."
	Obama	A chain e-mail takes passages out of context from Obama's *Audacity of Hope* (2006) to claim that Obama will stand with the Muslim population if "the political winds shift in an ugly direction."
April 2008	Clinton	Clinton's pastor is allegedly a child molester.
	Obama	A chain letter started by Kenyan missionaries makes numerous claims about Obama's religion, including, "By the way. His true name is Barak Hussein Muhammed Obama. Won't that sound sweet to our enemies as they swear him in on the Koran! God bless you."
	Obama	Obama's comments at a San Francisco fund-raiser on April 11, when he said that small-town voters had become "bitter" over job losses and that they "cl[ung] to guns or religion or antipathy," were first recorded as an MP3 and then published by a blogger Mayhill Fowler. The event became a central narrative of the campaign heading into the Pennsylvania primary.[a]
March 2008	Obama & Clinton	E-mails circulate claiming that both Obama and Clinton want to raise interest rates and capital gains taxes on individuals from all income brackets, playing on the fears of voters troubled by the recent economic downturn.
	Obama	A chain e-mail warns readers that "According to The Book of Revelations the anti-christ is: The anti-christ will be a man, in his 40s, of MUSLIM descent, who will deceive the nations with persuasive language, and have a MASSIVE Christ-like appeal . . . the prophecy says that people will flock to him and he will promise false hope and world peace, and when he is in

Table A5.7. *(Continued)*

Date	Candidate	Description
		power, will destroy everything is it OBAMA??" According to PoliticalFact.com, following the e-mail's release Google counted over 625,000 searchers for Obama + Anti-christ
Feb 2008	Obama	Unattributed rumor circulates on the internet that the Ku Klux Klan, an organization endorsing white supremacy, had endorsed Obama.
	Obama	Unattributed rumor surfaces that Hugo Chávez was funding Obama's campaign.
	Obama	The Clinton campaign releases a photo of Obama dressed as a Somali elder.
Jan 2008	Obama	Limo driver Larry Sinclair posts a video on his web site alleging that Obama did drugs and engaged in oral sex with him.
	Clinton	A chain e-mail is widely circulated based on comments made by former Bill Clinton advisor, Dick Morris, attacking Hillary Clinton for flunking the Washington, DC bar exam (which she did).
	Clinton	A chain e-mail circulated claiming that Clinton interned with the head of the California Communist Party while a student. The e-mail was based on an article written by Dick Morris and published in *FrontMag* in August 2007. The claims made in the article by Morris have been proved false by multiple sources.[b]
	Clinton	A chain e-mail claims that Hillary's main extracurricular activity while at Yale Law School was helping the members of the Black Panthers who were on trial in Connecticut for torturing and murdering a federal agent.
	Obama	A rumor circulates claiming that Obama took his oath of office for the US Senate on the Qur'ān instead of the Bible.
Dec 2007	Obama	Separate claims appear that Obama's church is covertly Muslim and that it only admits African Americans.

Table A5.7. (*Continued*)

Date	Candidate	Description
Oct 2007	Obama	Obama accused of being unpatriotic for not wearing a flag pin in support of the troops.
	Obama	Obama accused of being unpatriotic for not having his hand over his heart during the National Anthem.[c]
	Obama	Gospel singer and "reformed homosexual" Donny McClurkin appears at an Obama fundraiser.
Aug 2007	Clinton	Clinton makes allegedly Marxist comments.
April 2007	Obama	Obama criticized over Selma speech anachronisms.
March 2007	Clinton	Anonymous anti-Clinton/pro-Obama video, a mashup of Apple's "Think Different" ad, is posted on YouTube.[d]
Feb 2007	Obama	On January 17, the day after Obama announced the creation of his presidential exploratory committee, the conservative *InsightMag.com* reported that "sources close to [a] background check," which was supposedly "conducted by researchers connected to" Hillary Clinton, discovered that Obama "spent at least four years in a so-called Madrassa, or Muslim seminary, in Indonesia." The article further reported that the "sources" said "[t]he idea is to show Obama as deceptive." These "sources" also speculated that the "the specific Madrassa Obama attended" might have taught "a Wahhabi doctrine that denies the rights of non-Muslims."[e]

[a] Caren Bohan, "Obama defends 'bitter' remarks; McCain attacks," Reuters, April 14, 2008.

[b] Julie Millican, "Dick Morris makes numerous false claims in purported attempt to "correct" Bill Clinton's "syrupy five minute ad for Hillary," *Media Matters*, August 15, 2007.

[c] Torie Bosch, "How Barack Obama broke the law," Slate.com, November 13, 2007.

[d] You can see the video here: http://www.youtube.com/watch?v=6h3G-lMZxjo.

[e] John W. Delicath, "Myths and falsehoods about Barack Obama," *Media Matters*, March 20, 2007.

Source: Collected by Sharon Fain and Amelia Arsenault, 2008. Documentation on chain e-mails found on Politicalfact.com, a service of the *St. Petersburg Times* and *Congressional Quarterly*.

Table A5.8. Major media frenzies and political scandals during the 2008 US Democratic primary election, May–January 2008

Date	Candidate	Description
4/28–5/3	Obama	Reverend Wright delivers inflammatory speeches before the National Press Club and the NAACP. Obama responds by condemning Wright. The story accounts for 70% of campaign coverage.
4/11	Obama	Obama calls some voters in Pennsylvania bitter.
3/24	Clinton	Clinton claims to have landed in Bosnia under sniper fire. An image quickly surfaced proving her claims false.[a] The story accounted for 63% of the week's campaign coverage.
3/18	Obama	Obama addresses connection to Wright and gives speech on race and America.[b]
3/14	Obama	Reverend Wright scandal at peak press coverage.
3/11	Obama	Clinton supporter Geraldine Ferraro calls Obama "very lucky to be who he is."[c]
3/07	Clinton	Obama advisor Samantha Power calls Clinton a "monster."[d]
2/25	Clinton	Clinton cites a *Saturday Night Live* comedy skit suggesting that the media had gone soft on Obama.
2/23	Clinton	Clinton claims Obama is using Karl Rove tactics and says "Shame on you."[e]
2/19	Obama	Clinton campaign alleges Obama plagiarized speeches.[f]
1/18	Clinton	Chris Matthews say Clinton is where she is because of sympathy over husband's infidelity.[g]
1/11	Obama	Bill Clinton calls Obama's bid for the White House a "fairy tale" and Hillary Clinton makes comments about political talkers versus doers, drawing parallels between Lyndon Johnson and Martin Luther King's respective roles in the Civil Rights Movement and the differences between the Clinton and Obama candidacies.[h]

Table A5.8. *(Continued)*

Date	Candidate	Description
1/07	Clinton	Clinton "chokes up" while campaigning in New Hampshire.[i]

[a] "Clinton says she 'misspoke' about sniper fire," CNN.com, March 25, 2008.

[b] "Obama urges Americans to help heal racial divide," CNN.com, March 19, 2008.

[c] Brian Montopoli, "Ferraro: Obama 'Very lucky to be who he is'," CBSnews.com, March 11, 2008.

[d] "Obama advisor resigns; called Clinton 'monster'," Associated Press, March 7, 2008.

[e] "Clinton tells Obama 'Shame on you'; Obama fires back," CNN.com, February 23, 2008.

[f] Beth Fouhy, "Clinton camp seeks to undermine Obama," Associated Press, February 19, 2008.

[g] David Bauder, "Matthews: I wronged Clinton with remark," Associated Press, January 18, 2008.

[h] "Bill Clinton defends 'fairy tale' remark on Obama," *Reuters*, January 11, 2008.

[i] Timothy Noah, "The politics of weeping," *Slate.com*, January 7, 2008.

Source: Collected from press and Internet sources by Sharon Fain and Amelia Arsenault, 2008. News coverage percentages obtained from the Project for Excellence in Journalism News Coverage Index.

Bibliography

Aarts, Kees and Semetko, Holli A. (2003) "The divided electorate: media use and political involvement," *Journal of Politics*, 65 (3), 759–84.

Abbate, Janet (1999) *Inventing the Internet*. Cambridge, MA: MIT Press.

ABC News (2008) "Government to 'lead by example' during Earth Hour" (March 29; retrieved May 25, 2008 from http://www.abc.net.au/news/).

Abcarian, Robin (2008) "Clinton consultant 'Ace' Smith feared and admired," *Los Angeles Times*, February 20, A14.

Abrahamson, Mark (2004) *Global Cities*. New York: Oxford University Press.

Accenture (2006) *Leadership in Customer Service: Building the Trust*. Minneapolis, MN: Accenture.

Adam, Barbara (1990) *Time and Social Theory*. Cambridge: Polity Press.

Aday, Sean, Cluverius, John, and Livingston, Steven (2005) "As goes the statue, so goes the war: the emergence of the victory frame in television coverage of the Iraq War," *Journal of Broadcasting and Electronic Media*, 49 (3), 314–31.

Adut, Ari (2004) "Scandal as norm entrepreneurship strategy: corruption and the French investigating magistrates," *Theory and Society*, 33, 529–78.

Advertising Age (2007) *2007 Marketer Profiles Yearbook*. New York: AdAge Group.

AFP (2008) "Earth Hour blackout highlights global warming" March 29 (retrieved May 25, 2008 from http://www.straitstimes.com).

Alinsky, Saul (1946) *Reveille for Radicals*. Chicago, IL: University of Chicago Press.

Allen, Louis (1991) *Political Scandals and Causes Célèbres since 1945*. London: Longman.

Alonso-Zaldívar, Carlos and Castells, Manuel (1992) *España: Fin de Siglo*. Madrid: Alianza Editorial.

Al-Sayyad, Nezar and Castells, Manuel (eds.) (2002) *Muslim Europe or Euro-Islam: Politics, Culture, and Citizenship in the Age of Globalization*. Lanham, MD: Lexington Books.

Amedo, José F. (2006) *La Conspiración: El Último Atentado de los GAL*. Madrid: Espejo de Tinta.

Anderson, Christopher J. and Tverdova, Yuliya V. (2003) "Corruption, political allegiances, and attitudes toward government in contemporary democracies," *American Journal of Political Science*, 47 (1), 91–109.

Bibliography

Andrade-Jimenez, Helen S. (2001) "Technology changing political dynamics," *IT Matters*, January 29 (retrieved June 3, 2004 from http://itmatters.com.ph/news/news_01292001a.html).

Anheier, Helmut, Glasius, Marlies, and Kaldor, Mary (eds.) (2004) *Global Civil Society 2004/5*. London: Sage.

—————— (2005) *Global Civil Society 2005/6*. London: Sage.

—————— (2006) *Global Civil Society 2006/7*. London: Sage.

Ansolabehere, Stephen and Iyengar, Shanto (1995) *Going Negative: How Attack Ads Shrink and Polarize the Electorate*. New York: Free Press.

——Behr, Roy L., and Iyengar, Shanto (1993) *The Media Game: American Politics in the Television Age*. New York: Macmillan.

——Gerber, Allen, and Snyder, James M., Jr. (2001) "Corruption and the growth of campaign spending," in Gerald Lubenow (ed.), *A User's Guide to Campaign Finance Reform*. Lanham, MD: Rowman and Littlefield.

Anson, Luis María (1996) *Contra el Poder*. Madrid: Temas de Hoy.

Antich, José (2004) "Responsabilidades ajenas y propias," *La Vanguardia*, March 21.

Antilla, Liisa (2005) "Climate of skepticism: US newspaper coverage of the science of climate change," *Global Environmental Change*, 15, 338–52.

Appadurai, Arjun (1996) *Modernity at Large: Cultural Dimensions of Globalization*. Minneapolis, MN: University of Minnesota Press.

—— (2002) "Deep democracy," *Public Culture*, 14 (1), 1–47.

Arendt, Hannah (1958) *The Human Condition*. Chicago, IL: University of Chicago Press.

Arillo, Cecilio T. (2003) *Power Grab*. Manila: Charles Morgan.

Arlachi, Pino (1995) "The Mafia, *Cosa Nostra*, and Italian institutions," in Salvatore Sechi (ed.), *Deconstructing Italy: Italy in the Nineties*, pp. 153–63. Berkeley, CA: University of California, International and Area Studies, Research Series.

Arquilla, John and Rondfeldt, David (2001) *Networks and Netwars: The Future of Terror, Crime, and Militancy*. Santa Monica, CA: Rand Corporation.

Arsenault, Amelia and Castells, Manuel (2006) "Conquering the minds, Conquering Iraq: the Social production of misinformation in the United States: a case study," *Information, Communication and Society*, 9 (3), 284–308.

—————— (2008a) "The structure and dynamics of global multi-media business networks," *International Journal of Communication*, 2, 707–48.

—————— (2008b) "Switching power: Rupert Murdoch and the global business of media politics: a sociological analysis," *International Sociology*, 23, 488–513.

Artz, Lee (2007) "The corporate model from national to transnational," in Lee Artz and Yahya R. Kamalipour (eds.), *The Media Globe: Trends in International Mass Media*, pp. 141–62. Plymouth: Rowman and Littlefield.

Asian Barometer (2008) "Survey results" (available online at http://www.asianbarometer.org/newenglish/surveys/SurveyResults.htm).

Au, Wagner James (2008) *The Making of Second Life: Notes from the New World*. New York: Collins.

Ayres, Jeffrey (1999) "From the streets to Internet," *Annals of the American Academy of Political and Social Sciences*, 566, 132–43.

Bacon, Perry, Jr. (2005) "Barack Obama: the future of the Democratic Party? The 2005 Time 100: leaders and revolutionaries," *Time Magazine* (available online at www.time.com/time/subscriber/2005/time100/leaders/100obama.html).

Bagalawis, Jennifer E. (2001) "How IT helped topple a president," *Computer World*, January 30, (retrieved June 3, 2004 from http://wireless.itworld.com/4273/CW_1-31-01_it/pfindex.html).

Bagdikian, Ben H. (1983) *The Media Monopoly*. Boston: Beacon Press.

——(2000) *The Media Monopoly*, 6th edn. Boston: Beacon Press.

——(2004) *The New Media Monopoly*. Boston: Beacon Press.

Baker, C. Edwin (2006) *Media Concentration and Democracy: Why Ownership Matters*. Cambridge: Cambridge University Press.

Baker, Stephen (2008) "Updated blog numbers from David Sifry," *Business Week*, January 18 (available online at www.businessweek.com/the_thread/blogspotting/archives/2008/01/updated_blog_nu.html?campaign_id=rss_blog_blogspotting).

Baker, Wayne E. (2005) *America's Crisis of Values: Reality and Perception*. Princeton, NJ: Princeton University Press.

Bamzai, Kaveree (2007) *Bollywood Today*. New Delhi: Lustre Press.

Banet-Weiser, Sarah (2007) *Kids Rule!: Nickelodeon and Consumer Citizenship*. Durham, NC: Duke University Press.

——Chris, Cynthia, and Freitas, Anthony (eds.) (2007) *Cable Visions: Television beyond Broadcasting*. New York: New York University Press.

Barber, Benjamin R. (2007) *Consumed: How Markets Corrupt Children, Infantilize Adults, and Swallow Citizens Whole*. New York: W. W. Norton.

Barisione, Mauro (1996) *L' immagine del Leader: Quanto Conta per Gli Elettori?* Bologna: Il Mulino.

Barker, Anthony (1992) *The Upturned Stone: Political Scandals in Twenty Democracies and their Investigation Process*. Colchester: University of Essex, Essex Papers in Politics and Government.

Barnard, Ann (2008) "Raucous Russian tabloids thrive," *The New York Times*, online edition, July 23.

Barreiro, Belen (2001) "Los determinantes de la participación en las elecciones Españolas de Marzo de 2000: el problema de la abstención en la izquierda," Working paper 2001/171. Madrid: CEACS-Instituto Juan March de Estudios e Investigaciones.

——and Sanchez-Cuenca, Ignacio (1998) "Análisis del cambio de voto hacia El PSOE en las elecciones de 1993," *Revista Española de Investigaciones Sociológicas*, 82, 191–211.

Bibliography

Barreiro, Belen and Sanchez-Cuenca, Ignacio (2000) "Las consecuencias electorales de la corrupción," *Historia y Política: Ideas, Procesos y Movimientos Sociales*, 4, 69–92.

Barringer, Felicity (2007) "Renewing a call to act against climate change," *The New York Times*, March 14 (retrieved May 24, 2008 from www.nyt.com).

Barstow, David (2008) "Behind TV analysts, Pentagon's hidden hand," *The New York Times*, April 20, A1.

Barzilai-Nahon, Karine (2008) "Toward a theory of network gatekeeping: A framework for exploring information control," *Journal of the American Society for Information Science and Technology*, 59 (9): 1493–512.

Baum, Matthew A. (2007) "Soft news and foreign policy: how expanding the audience changes the policies," *Japanese Journal of Political Science*, 8 (1), 115–45.

——and Groeling, Tim (2007) "Iraq and the 'Fox effect': An examination of polarizing media and public support for international conflict," unpublished paper presented at the American Political Science Association Annual Conference, Chicago, IL, August 30–September 2.

——— (2008) "New media and the polarization of American political discourse," *Political Communication*, 25 (4), 345–65.

Bauman, Zygmunt (1999) *In Search of Politics*. Stanford, CA: Stanford University Press.

BBC (2006) "UK planning law on climate change," *BBC News*, October 12 (retrieved May 26, 2008 from www.news.bbc.co.uk).

—— (2007a) "All countries need to take major steps on climate change: global poll," BBC World Service poll.

—— (2007b) "France 'dims' for climate protest," *BBC News*, February 1 (retrieved May 1, 2008, from www.news.bbc.co.uk).

Beck, Ulrich (2000) *What is Globalization?* Malden, MA: Blackwell.

—— (2005) *Power in the Global Age: A New Political Economy*. Cambridge: Polity Press.

Becker, Ernest (1973) *The Denial of Death*. New York: Free Press.

Beckett, Charlie and Mansell, Robin (2008) "Crossing boundaries: new media and networked journalism," *Communication, Culture and Critique*, 1 (1), 92–104.

Belloch, Santiago (1998) "Para terminar con Felipe González se rozó la estabilidad del estado: entrevista a Luis Maria Anson," *Tiempo*, February 23, 24–30.

Beniger, James R. (1986) *The Control Revolution: Technological and Economic Origins of the Information Society*. Cambridge, MA: Harvard University Press.

Benkler, Yochai (2006) *The Wealth of Networks: How Social Production Transforms Markets and Freedom*. New Haven, CT: Yale University Press.

Benner, Chris (2002) *Work in the New Economy: Flexible Labor Markets in Silicon Valley*. Malden, MA: Blackwell.

Bennett, Stephen Earl, Rhine, Staci L., and Flickinger, Richard (2004) "The things they cared about: change and continuity in Americans' attention to different news stories, 1989–2002," *Harvard International Journal of Press/Politics*, 9 (1), 75–99.

————————and Bennett, Linda L. M. (1999) " 'Video malaise' revisited: public trust in the media and government," *Harvard International Journal of Press/Politics*, 4 (4), 8–23.

Bennett, W. Lance (1990) "Toward a theory of press–state relations in the United States," *Journal of Communication*, 40 (2), 103–27.

—— (2003a) "The burglar alarm that just keeps ringing: a response to Zaller," *Political Communication*, 20 (April/June), 131–38.

—— (2003b) "Communicating global activism," *Information, Communication, and Society*, 6 (2), 143–68.

—— (2004) "Global media and politics: transnational communication regimes and civic cultures," *Annual Review of Political Science*, 7 (1), 125–48.

—— (2007) *News: The Politics of Illusion*, 7th edn. New York: Longman.

—— (2009) *News: The Politics of Illusion*, 8th edn. New York: Longman.

——Lawrence, Regina G., and Livingston, Steven (2006) "None dare call it torture: Indexing and the limits of press independence in the Abu Ghraib scandal," *Journal of Communication*, 56 (3), 467–85.

————————(2007) *When the Press Fails: Political Power and the News Media From Iraq to Katrina*. Chicago, IL: University of Chicago Press.

Bergan, Daniel, Gerber, Alan, Green, Donald, and Costas, Panagopoulos (2005) "Grassroots mobilization and voter turnout in 2004," *Public Opinion Quarterly*, 69 (5), 760–77.

Bergo, Sandy (2006) *A Wealth of Advice: Nearly $2 Billion Flowed through Consultants in the 2003–2004 Federal Elections*. Washington, DC: Center for Public Integrity.

Berrocal, Salome and Fernandez, Clara (2006) "Las elecciones legislativas de 2004: un analisis de las encuestas y de la gestión comunicativa en la campaña electoral: su proyeccion en la decisión de voto," *Doxa comunicación: revista interdisciplinar de estudios de comunicación y ciencias sociales*, 4, 189–208.

Best, Samuel, Brian, Chmielewski, and Krueger, Brian (2005) "Selective exposure to online foreign news during the conflict with Iraq," *Harvard International Journal of Press/Politics*, 10 (4), 52–70.

Billette, Alexandre (2008) "The Russian cyberspace," Millenio.com (available at http://www.milenio.com/index.php/2008/3/2/202127/).

Bimber, Bruce A. (2003) *Information and American Democracy: Technology in the Evolution of Political Power*. Cambridge: Cambridge University Press.

Blanco, Maria del Mar (2006) "Prensa y terror: tratamiento informativo de la tragedia," in A. Vara (ed.), *Cobertura Informativa del 11-M*. Pamplona: EUNSA.

Blanning, T. C. W. (2002) *The Culture of Power and the Power of Culture: Old Regime Europe, 1660–1789*. Oxford: Oxford University Press.

Bless, Herbert and Schwarz, Norbert (1998) "Context effects in political judgments: assimilation and contrast as a function of categorization processes," *European Journal of Social Psychology*, 28, 159–72.

Bibliography

Bless, Herbert, Igou, Eric R., Schwarz, Norbert, and Wanke, Michaela (2000) "Reducing context effects by adding context information: the direction and size of context effects in political judgment," *Personality and Social Psychology Bulletin*, 26, 1036–45.

Bless, Herbert, Schwarz, Norbert, and Wanke, Michaela (2003) "The size of context effects in social judgment," in Joseph P. Forgas, Kippling D. Williams, and William von Hippel (eds.), *Social Judgments: Implicit and Explicit Processes*, pp. 180–97. Cambridge: Cambridge University Press.

Blizzard Entertainment (2008) "Press release: *World of Warcraft* reaches new milestone: 10 million subscribers" (available online at http://www.blizzard.com/press/080122.shtml).

Blumler, Jay G. and Kavanagh, Dennis (1999) "The third age of political communication: influences and features," *Political Communication*, 16, 209–30.

Bobbio, Norberto (1994) *Destra e Sinistra: Ragione e Significati di una Distinzione Política*. Rome: Donzelli Editore.

Boczkowski, Pablo (2005) *Digitizing the News: Innovation in Online Newspapers*. Cambridge, MA: MIT Press.

—— (2007) "Information transparency: materiality and mimicry in the journalistic field and beyond," paper presented at the Annenberg Seminar "The Changing Faces of Journalism: Tradition, Tabloidization, Technology, and Truthiness," Los Angeles, CA, November.

Boehlert, Eric and Foser, Jamieson (2007) "Tucker Carlson on Obama's church: '[I]t's hard to call that Christianity,'" *County Fair: A Media Blog*, Washington, DC: Media Matters (available online at http://mediamatters.org/items/200702090009).

Boix, Caries and Riba, Clara (2000) "Las bases sociales y políticas de la abstención en las elecciones generales Españolas: recursos individuales, movilización estrategica e instituciones electorales," *Revista Española de Investigaciones Sociológicas*, 90, 95–128.

Booth, William (2006) "Al Gore, Sundance's leading man," *Washington Post*, January 26 (retrieved May 1, 2008 from http://www.washingtonpost.com/).

Borja, Jordi and Castells, Manuel (eds.) (1997) *Local and Global: Management of Cities in the Information Age*. London: Earthscan.

Bosetti, Giancarlo (2007) *Spin: Trucchi e Tele-imbrogli Della Política*. Venice: Marsilio.

Bouissou, Jean-Marie (1991) "Corruption à la Japonaise," *L'Histoire*, 142 (March), 84–7.

Bowler, Shaun and Sharp, Jeffrey (2004) "Politicians, scandals, and trust in government," *Political Behavior*, 26 (3), 271–87.

Boyd, Danah (2006a) "Identity production in a networked culture: why youth heart MySpace," paper presented at the American Association for the Advancement of Science Conference, St. Louis, Missouri, February 19.

—— (2006b) "Horizontal communication and the media industries panel," paper presented at the Annenberg Research Network on International Communication (ARNIC) Conference, Annenberg Research Center, Los Angeles, CA, October 6–7.

Boykoff, Maxwell. (2008) "Lost in translation? United States' television news coverage of anthropogenic climate change, 1995–2004," *Climate Change*, 86, 1–11.

—— and Boykoff, Jules (2004) "Balance as bias: global warming and the US prestige press," *Global Environmental Change*, 14 (2), 125–36.

—— —— (2007) "Climate change and journalistic norms: a case study of US mass-media coverage," *Geoforum*, 38, 1190–204.

Brader, Ted (2006) *Campaigning for Hearts and Minds: How Emotional Appeals in Political Ads Work*. Chicago, IL: University of Chicago Press.

—— and Valentino, Nicholas A. (2007) "Identities, interests, and emotions: symbolic versus material wellspring of fear, anger, and enthusiasm," in W. Russell Neuman, George E. Marcus, Ann N. Crigler, and Michael MacKuen (eds.), *The Affect Effect: Dynamics of Emotion in Political Thinking and Behavior*, pp. 180–201. Chicago, IL: University of Chicago Press.

Braudel, Fernand (1949) *La Mediterranée et le Monde Mediterranéen à l'Époque de Philippe II*. Paris: Armand Colin.

Bravo, Gustavo (2008) "Cuanto cuesta un voto?," *AND*, February 19.

Brechin, S. R. (2003) "Comparative public opinion and knowledge on global climatic change and the Kyoto protocol: the US versus the world?," *International Journal of Sociology and Social Policy*, 23 (10), 106–35.

Brehm, John and Rahn, Wendy (1997) "Individual-level evidence for the causes and consequences of social capital," *American Journal of Political Science*, 41 (3), 999–1023.

Brewer, Paul, Aday, Sean, and Gross, Kimberly (2003) "Rallies all around: the dynamics of system support," in Pippa Norris, Montague Kern, and Marion Just (eds.), *Framing Terrorism: The News Media, the Government, and the Public*, pp. 229–54. New York: Routledge.

Brough, Melissa (2008) "The saffron revolution – televised? The politics of protest on YouTube," unpublished paper written for the research seminar, Comm620Y on Communication, Technology, and Power, Annenberg School for Communication, University of Southern California, Los Angeles, spring.

Bruno, Antony (2007) "Monetizing membership: social networking," *Billboard*, November 24.

Buchanan, Mark (2002) *Small World: Uncovering Nature's Hidden Networks*. New York: Weidenfeld and Nicolson.

Bucy, Erik P. and Grabe, Maria Elizabeth (2007) "Taking television seriously: a sound and image bite analysis of presidential campaign coverage, 1992–2004," *Journal of Communication*, 57 (4), 652–75.

Bibliography

Burden, Barry C. (2002) "When bad press is good news: the surprising benefits of negative campaign coverage," *Harvard International Journal of Press/Politics*, 7 (3), 76–89.

Burnett, Robert and Marshall, P. David (2003) *Web Theory: An Introduction*. London: Routledge.

Burt, Ronald S. (1980) "Models of network structure," *Annual Review of Sociology*, 6, 79–141.

Bush, George (2004) "President Bush salutes soldiers in Fort Lewis, Washington," remarks by the president to the military personnel, Fort Lewis, Washington, June 18.

Cainzos, Miguel (2000) "El impacto de los escándalos de corrupción sobre el voto en las elecciones generales de 1996," *Historia y Política: Ideas, Procesos y Movimientos Sociales*, 4, 93–131.

Calderon, Fernando (ed.) (2003) *Es Sostenible la Globalización en America Latina?*, 2 vols. Santiago de Chile: Fondo de Cultura Economica.

—— (2006) *Las Nuevas Identidades de America Latina*. Research Report, Buenos Aires: United Nations Development Program.

—— (2007) "Aportes para una agenda de la gobernabilidad democrática en América Latina," unpublished paper delivered at the PAPEP project meeting, United Nations Development Program for Latin America, Montevideo, November 30.

Callahan, David (1995) "Liberal policy's weak foundations," *The Nation*, November 13, 568–72.

—— (1999) *$1 Billion for Ideas: Conservative Think Tanks in the 1990s*. Washington, DC: National Committee for Responsive Philanthropy.

CalTech/MIT Voting Technology Project (2006) "Conference proceedings: VTP Conference on Voter Authentication and Registration," Cambridge, MA, October 5–6, 2006 (available online at vote.caltech.edu/events/2006/VoterID/rpt.pdf).

Campbell, Rook (2008) "Corruption and money laundering in the international scene," unpublished research paper, Los Angeles, University of Southern California, School of International Relations.

Campo Vidal, Manuel (2004) *11M–14M: La Revuelta de los Móviles*. Canal Sur – TVC – Lua Multimedia, DVD documentary.

—— (2008) *El Poder de los Medios en España*. Barcelona: Ediciones UOC.

Capdevila, Arantxa, Aubia, Laia, and Gomez, Lorena (2006) "La cobertura informativa de las noches electorales: estudio comparativo de los programas especial elecciones en TVE, Tele 5, Antena 3 y TV3," in A. Vara (ed.), *Cobertura Informativa del 11-M*. Pamplona: EUNSA.

CAPF (2007) *Campaign Finance and Corruption: A Monitoring Report on Campaign Finance in the 2007 General Election*. Nairobi: Coalition for Accountable Political Financing (available online at http://capf.or.ke).

Cappella, Joseph N. and Jamieson, Kathleen Hall (1997) *Spiral of Cynicism: The Press and the Public Good*. New York: Oxford University Press.

Capra, Fritjof (1996) *The Web of Life: A New Scientific Understanding of Living Systems*. New York: Random House.

—— (2002) *Hidden Connections: Integrating the Biological, Cognitive and Social Dimensions of Life into a Science of Sustainability*. New York: Random House.

Caputo, Dante (ed.) (2004) *La Democracia en America Latina*. New York: Pograma de Naciones Unidas para el Desarrollo.

Cardoso, Gustavo (2006) *The Media in the Network Society: Browsing, News, Filters and Citizenship*. Lisboa: Lulu.com and Center for Research and Studies in Sociology.

Carnoy, Martin (2000) *Sustaining the New Economy: Work, Family and Community in the Information Age*. Cambridge, MA: Harvard University Press.

Caron, André H. and Caronia, Letizia (2007) *Moving Cultures: Mobile Communication in Everyday Life*. Montreal: McGill–Queen's University Press.

Carter, Shan and Cox, Amanda (2008) "Interactive graphic: how different groups voted in the 2008 Democratic presidential primaries," *The New York Times*, June 4 (available online at http://www.nytimes.com/2008/06/04/us/politics/04margins_graphic.html).

Casero, Andreu (2004) "Cobertura periodística del 11-M: la teoría del 'caso excepcional,' " *Quaderns del CAC*, 9–14.

Castells, Irene (1970) "Els rebomboris del pa de 1789 a Barcelona," *Recerques*, 1, 51–81.

Castells, Manuel (1980) *The Economic Crisis and American Society*. Princeton, NJ: Princeton University Press.

—— (1983) *The City and the Grassroots: A Cross-cultural Theory of Urban Social Movements*. Berkeley, CA: University of California Press.

—— (1996) *The Rise of the Network Society*, 1st edn. Oxford: Blackwell.

—— (1999) "Grassrooting the space of flows," *Urban Geography*, January.

—— (2000a) *End of Millennium*, 2nd edn. Oxford: Blackwell (first edition 1998).

—— (2000b) "Materials for an exploratory theory of the network society," *British Journal of Sociology*, 51, 5–24.

—— (2000c) *The Rise of the Network Society*, 2nd edn. Oxford: Blackwell (first edition 1996).

—— (2001) *The Internet Galaxy: Reflections on the Internet, Business, and Society*. Oxford: Oxford University Press.

—— (2004a) "Existe una identidad Europea?," in Manuel Castells and Narcís Serra (eds.), *Europa en Construcción: Integración, Identidades y Seguridad*, pp. 3–20. Barcelona: Fundació CIDOB.

—— (ed.) (2004b) *The Network Society: A Cross-cultural Perspective*. Northampton, MA: Edward Elgar.

—— (2004c) *The Power of Identity*, 2nd edn. Oxford: Blackwell (first edition 1997).

Bibliography

Castells, Manuel (2005a) "The crisis of democracy in Latin America," unpublished paper delivered at the Workshop on Democracy in Latin America, United Nations Development Program for Latin America, Los Angeles, November.

—— (2005b) *Globalización, Democracia y Desarrollo: Chile en el Contexto Mundial*. Santiago de Chile: Fondo de Cultura Economica.

—— (2006) *De la Funcion de Produccion Agregada a la Frontera De Posibilidades de Produccion: Crecimiento Economico, Tecnologia y Productividad en la Era de la Informacion*. Discurso de Ingreso en la Real Academia Espanola de Ciencias Economicas y Financieras. Barcelona: Ediciones de la Real Academia Espanola.

Castells, Manuel (2007) "Communication, power and counter-power in the network society," *International Journal of Communication*, 1 (1), 238–66.

—— (2008a) "Globalization, urbanization, networking," in *Urban Studies*, June.

—— (2008b) "The new public sphere: global civil society, communication networks and global governance," *Annals of the American Academy of Political and Social Science*, March.

—— Fernández-Ardèvol, Mireia, Qiu, Jack Linchuan, and Sey, Araba (2006a) "Electronic communication and socio-political mobilization: a new form of civil society," in Helmut Anheier, Marlies Glasius, and Mary Kaldor (eds.), *Global Civil Society 2005/6*, ch. 8. London: Sage.

—— —— —— —— (2006b) *Mobile Communication and Society: A Global Perspective*. A Project of the Annenberg Research Network on International Communication. Cambridge, MA: MIT Press.

—— and Himanen, Pekka (2002) *The Information Society and the Welfare State: The Finnish Model*. Oxford: Oxford University Press.

—— and Kiselyova, Emma (1995) *The Collapse of Soviet Communism: A View from the Information Society*. Berkeley, CA: University of California at Berkeley, International and Area Studies.

—— and Subirats, Marina (2007) *Mujeres y hombres: un amor imposible?* Madrid: Alianza Editorial.

—— and Tubella, Imma (eds.) (2007) *Research Report of the Project Internet Catalonia*. Barcelona: Internet Interdisciplinary Institute, Universitat Oberta de Catalunya, July, 10 vols (available online at http://www.uoc.edu/in3/pic/esp/).

—— —— Sancho, Teresa, and Roca, Meritxell (2007) *La transicion a la sociedad red*. Barcelona: Ariel.

CBS/MTV News (2008) *State of the Youth Nation 2008*, April 21 (available online at http://www.cbsnews.com/htdocs/pdf/cbsmtv_springpoll.pdf).

Ceberio, Jesus (2004) "A proposito de mentiras," *El Pais*, March 27.

Center for the Digital Future (2005) *The 2005 Digital Future Report: Surveying the Digital Future, Year Five. Five Years of Exploring the Digital Domain*. Los Angeles: University of Southern California, Annenberg School Center for the Digital Future.

—— (2007) *The 2007 Digital Future Report: Surveying the Digital Future, Year Seven.* Los Angeles: University of Southern California, Annenberg School Center for the Digital Future.

—— (2008) *The 2008 Digital Future Report: Surveying the Digital Future, Year Eight.* Los Angeles: University of Southern California, Annenberg School Center for the Digital Future.

Center for Journalism in Extreme Situations (2007–8) "Russia: authorities vs. the media," weekly bulletin, issues 1–21, January 2007–May 2008 (available online at http://www.cjes.ru/bulletin/?CategoryID=4andyear=2007andlang=eng).

Center for Responsive Politics (2008a) "Barack Obama: expenditures breakdown" (last accessed July 10, 2008 from http://www.opensecrets.org/pres08/expend. php?cycle=2008andcid=N00009638).

—— (2008b) "Hedgefund managers invest in Obama," *The Capital Eye.*, April 22 (available online at http://www.opensecrets.org/news/2008/04/hedge-fund-managers-invest-in-1.html).

—— (2008c) "Politicians and elections: an ongoing project tracking money in American politics" (available online at http://www.opensecrets.org/elections/index.php).

Center for the Study of the American Electorate (2008) *African-Americans, Anger, Fear and Youth Propel Turnout to Highest Level since 1960.* Washington, DC: CSAE, American University, December 18.

Centro de Investigaciones Sociológicas (1998) "Survey 2312" (available online at http://www.cis.es).

—— (2003) "Barómetro de abril," study no. 2.508, April.

—— (2004a) "Preelectoral elecciones generales y autonómicas de Andalucia 2004," study no. 2555, January–February.

—— (2004b) "Postelectoral elecciones generales y autonómicas de Andalucía 2004," study no. 2559, March 23.

Chadwick, Andrew (2006) *Internet Politics: States, Citizens, and New Communication Technologies.* New York: Oxford University Press.

Chalaby, Jean K. (2004) "Scandal and the rise of investigative reporting in France," *American Behavioral Scientist*, 47 (9), 1194–207.

Chang, Eric C. and Chu, Yun-han (2006) "Corruption and trust: exceptionalism in Asian democracies?," *Journal of Politics*, 68, 259–71.

Chatterjee, Anshu (2004) "Globalization and communal identity in Indian television," unpublished PhD dissertation, Berkeley, CA: University of California, Asian Studies Program.

Chen, Xiyuan (2004) "The last order of the emperor: production of emperor's will, power, succession, and historical writing," *National Taiwan University History Annals*, Taipei, June, 161–213.

Chester, Jeff (2007) *Digital Destiny: New Media and the Future of Democracy.* New York: New Press.

Bibliography

China Internet Network Information Center (2007) *Statistical Survey Report on the Internet Development in China*, 20th Report (available online at http://cnnic.cn/en/index/0O/index.htm).

Chinese Academy of Social Sciences (2008) *Surveying Internet Usage and its Impact in Seven Chinese Cities*. CASS China Internet Survey Report. Beijing: Chinese Academy of Social Sciences, Research Center for Social Development.

CIRCLE (2008) "Youth turnout rate rises to at least 52%," Center for Information and Research on Civic Learning and Engagement, Boston, November 5 (retrieved November 9, 2008 from http://www.civicyouth.org/).

Clapp, Jennifer and Dauvergne, Peter (2005) *Paths to a Green World: The Political Economy of the Global Environment*. London: MIT Press.

Clark, David D. (2007) "Network neutrality: words of power and 800-pound gorillas," special issue on Net neutrality, *International Journal of Communication*, 1, 701–8.

Clegg, Stewart (2000) "Power and authority: resistance and legitimacy," in Henri Goverde, Philip G. Cerny, Mark Haugaard, et al. (eds.), *Power in Contemporary Politics: Theories, Practices, Globalizations*, pp. 77–92. London: Sage.

CNN (2008) "Global warming could increase terrorism, official says," *CNN Politics*, June 25 (retrieved June 29, 2008, from http://edition.cnn.com/2008/POLITICS/06/25/climate.change.security/).

Cogan, Marin (2008) "The new class," *The New Republic.*, April 21 (available online at http://www.tnr.com/politics/story.html?id=d67776d8-ab4e-4c12-9c1f-bfa041dcb314&k=97935).

Cohen, Bernard Cecil (1963) *The Press and Foreign Policy*. Princeton, NJ: Princeton University Press.

Cohen, Florette, Ogilvie, Daniel M., Solomon, Sheldon, Greenberg, Jeff, et al. (2005) "American roulette: the effect of reminders of death on support for George W. Bush in the 2004 presidential election," *Analyses of Social Issues and Public Policy*, 5 (1), 177–87.

Colas, Dominique (1992) *La Glaive et le Fleau: Genealogie du Fanatisme et de la Société Civile*. Paris: Grasset.

Comas, Eva (2004) "La SER ante el 11–M," *Tripodos* (extra 2004), pp. 59–67.

Comella, Rosemary and Mahoy, Scott (2008) "The passion of the moment: emotional frame changes before key Democratic primaries in 2008," unpublished paper written for the Research Seminar, Comm620Y on Communication, Technology, and Power, spring. Los Angeles: University of Southern California, Annenberg School for Communication.

Comrie, Maggie (1999) "Television news and broadcast deregulation in New Zealand," *Journal of Communication*, 49 (2), 42–54.

ComScore (2008) "Google sites' share of online video market expands to 31% in November 2007, according to Comscore Video Metrix," press release, January 17.

Conservation Foundation (1963) *Implications of Rising Carbon Dioxide Content of the Atmosphere.* New York: Conservation Foundation.

Cook, Wanda D. (1977) *Adult Literacy Education in the United States.* Newark, DE: International Reading Association.

Cooke, Miriam and Lawrence, Bruce R. (2005) *Muslim Networks: From Hajj to Hip Hop.* Chapel Hill, NC: University of North Carolina Press.

Corporación Latinobarometro (2007) *Informe Latinobarometro* 2007. Santiago: Corporación Latinobarometro.

Costanza-Chock, Sasha (2006) "Horizontal communication and social movements," unpublished manuscript. Los Angeles: University of Southern California.

—— (forthcoming a) "Networked counterpublics: social movement ICT use in Buenos Aires and Los Angeles," unpublished PhD dissertation (in progress). Los Angeles: University of Southern California, Annenberg School for Communication.

—— (forthcoming b) "Police riot on the Net: from 'citizen journalism' to comunicación popular," *American Quarterly.*

Couldry, Nick and Curran, James (2003) *Contesting Media Power: Alternative Media in a Networked World.* Lanham, MD: Rowman and Littlefield.

Covington, Sally (1997) *Moving a Public Policy Agenda: The Strategic Philanthropy of Conservative Foundations.* Washington, DC: National Committee for Responsive Philanthropy.

Cowhey, Peter and Aronson, Jonathan (2009) *Transforming Global Information and Communication Markets: The Political Economy of Innovation.* Cambridge, MA: MIT Press.

Coyer, Kate, Dowmunt, Tony, and Fountain, Alan (2007) *The Alternative Media Handbook.* London: Routledge.

Crawford, Leslie, Levitt, Joshua, and Burns, Jimmy (2004) "Spain suffers worst day of terror," *Financial Times*, March 11.

Croteau, David and Hoynes, William (2006) *The Business of Media: Corporate Media and the Public Interest.* Thousand Oaks, CA: Pine Forge.

Cue, C. E. (2004) *¡Pasalo! Los cuatro dias de marzo que cambiaron el pais.* Barcelona: Ediciones Península.

Cullity, Jocelyn (2002) "The global Desi: cultural nationalism on MTV India," *Journal of Communication Inquiry*, 26 (4), 408–25.

Curran, James (2002) *Media and Power.* London: Routledge.

Cushman, John H. (1998) "Industrial group plans to battle climate treaty," *The New York Times*, April 26.

Dalton, Russell J. (2005a) "The myth of the disengaged American," *Public Opinion Pros*, October (available online at http://www.umich.edu/~cses/resources/results/POP_Oct2005_1.htm).

—— (2005b) "The social transformation of trust in government," *International Review of Sociology*, 15 (1), 133–54.

Bibliography

Dalton, Russell J. and Kuechler, Manfred (1990) *Challenging the Political Order: New Social and Political Movements in Western Democracies*. Cambridge: Polity Press.

—— and Steven, Weldon (2007) "Partisanship and party system institutionalization," *Party Politics*, 13 (2), 179–96.

—— and Wattenberg, Martin P. (2000) *Parties without Partisans: Political Change in Advanced Industrial Democracies*. New York: Oxford University Press.

Damasio, Antonio R. (1994) *Descartes' Error: Emotion, Reason, and the Human Brain*. New York: Putnam.

—— (1999) *The Feeling of What Happens: Body and Emotion in the Making of Consciousness*. New York: Harcourt Brace.

—— (2003) *Looking for Spinoza: Joy, Sorrow, and the Feeling Brain*. Orlando, FL: Harcourt.

—— and Meyer, Kaspar (2008) "Behind the looking glass," *Nature*, 454 (10): 167–8.

Danielian, Lucig H. (1992) "Interest groups in the news," in J. David Kennamer (ed.), *Public Opinion, the Press, and Public Policy*, pp. 63–80. Westport, CT: Praeger.

Davidson, Richard J. (1995) "Cerebral asymmetry, emotion and affective style," in Richard J. Davidson and Kenneth Hugdahl (eds.), *Brain Asymmetry*, pp. 361–87. Cambridge, MA: MIT Press.

Dear, Michael (2000) *The Postmodern Urban Condition*. Oxford: Blackwell.

—— (ed.) (2002) *From Chicago to LA: Making Sense of Urban Theory*. Thousand Oaks, CA: Sage

Deibert, Ronald, Palfrey, John, Rohozinski, Rafal, and Zittrain, Jonathan (eds.) (2008) *Access Denied: The Practice and Policy of Global Internet Filtering*. Cambridge, MA: MIT Press.

della Porta, Donatella, et al. (2006) *Globalization from Below*. Minneapolis, MN: University of Minnesota Press.

Delli Carpini, Michael and Williams, Bruce A. (2001) "Let us infotain you: politics in the new media environment," in Lance W. Bennett and Robert M. Entman (eds.) *Mediated Politics*, pp. 160–181. New York: Cambridge.

Demick, Barbara (2003) "Netizens crusade buoys new South Korean leader," *Los Angeles Times*, 10 February, A3.

De Moraes, Denis (ed.) (2005) *Por Otra Comunicación: Los Media, Globalización Cultural y Poder*. Barcelona: Icaria.

Denemark, David, Ward, Ian, and Bean, Clive (2007) "Election campaigns and television news coverage: the case of the 2001 Australian election," *Australian Journal of Political Science*, 42 (1), 89–109.

de Sola Pool, Ithiel (1983) *Technologies of Freedom*. Cambridge, MA: Belknap Press.

Dessa, Philadelphia (2007) "Globalization of media, localization of culture: the rise of the Nigerian film industry," unpublished paper completed for the class: COMM559 "Globalization, Communication and Society," Los Angeles: University of Southern California, Annenberg School of Communication.

de Ugarte, D. (2004) *Redes para ganar una guerra*. Barcelona: Ed. Icaria.

De Zengotita, Thomas (2005) *Mediated: How the Media Shapes Your World and the Way You Live in it*. New York: Bloomsbury.

Dimitrova, Daniela V. and Strömbäck, Jesper (2005) "Mission accomplished? Framing of the Iraq War in the elite newspapers in Sweden and the United States," *Gazette*, 67 (5), 399–417.

Dimock, Michael (2006) *Poll Analysis. Independents Sour on Incumbents: Many Say their Member Has Taken Bribes*. Washington, DC: Pew Research Center.

Dispensa, Jaclyn M. and Brulle, Robert J. (2003) "Media's social construction of environmental issues: focus on global warming – a comparative study," *International Journal of Sociology and Social Policy*, 23 (10), 74–105.

Domke, David Scott and Coe, Kevin M. (2008) *The God Strategy: How Religion Became a Political Weapon in America*. New York: Oxford University Press.

Dong, Fan (2008a) "The blogosphere in China: between self-presentation and celebrity," paper submitted for inclusion in the 2008 National Communication Association Conference, San Diego, CA, November 21–24.

—— (2008b) "Everything in existence is reasonable? The actual effectiveness of Internet control in China," unpublished research paper for Seminar Communications 620, Spring Semester, Los Angeles: University of Southern California, Annenberg School of Communication.

Dooley, Brendan and Baron, Sabrina (eds.) (2001) *The Politics of Information in Early Modern Europe*. London: Routledge.

Dornschneider, Stephanie (2007) "Limits to the supervisory function of the press in democracies: the coverage of the 2003 Iraq War in *The New York Times* and *Frankfurter Allgemeine Zeitung*," *Global Media Journal: Mediterranean Edition*, 2 (1), 33–46.

Downing, John D. H. (2000) *Radical Media*. Thousand Oaks, CA: Sage.

—— (2003) "The independent media center movement," in Nick Couldry and James Curran (eds.), *Contesting Media Power: Alternative Media in a Networked World*, pp. 243–58. Lanham, MD: Rowman and Littlefield.

Downs, A. (1972) "Up and down with ecology: the issue attention cycle," *The Public Interest*, 28, 38–50.

Drake, William J. and Nicolaidis, Kalypso (1992) "Ideas, interests, and institutionalization: 'trade in services' and the Uruguay round," *International Organization*, 46 (1), 37–100.

Dreier, Peter (2008) "Will Obama inspire a new generation of organizers?," *Huffington Post*, July 1 (available online at http://www.huffingtonpost.com/peter-dreier/obamas-new-generation-of_b_110321.html).

Drezner, Daniel (2007) "Foreign policy goes glam," *National Interest*, November/December.

Druckman, James (2003) "The power of television images: the first Kennedy–Nixon debate revisited," *Journal of Politics*, 65 (2), 559–71.

Bibliography

DuBravac, Shawn (2007) "The US television set market," *Business Economics*, 42 (3), 52–9.

Duelfer, Charles (2004) *Comprehensive Report of the Special Advisor to the DCI on Iraq's WMDs*. Washington, DC: Iraq Survey Group.

Dunlap, R. E. (1989) "Public opinion and environmental policy," in J. P. Lester (ed.), *Environmental Politics and Policy*, pp. 87–134. Durham, NC: Duke University Press.

Dunlap, R. E., Gallup, G. H., Jr., and Gallup, A. M. (1993) *Health of the Planet*. Princeton, NJ: George H. Gallup International Institute.

Duran, Rafael (2006) "Del 11-M al 14-M: tratamiento informativo comparado de TVE," in A. Vara (ed.), *Cobertura informativa del 11-M*. Pamplona: EUNSA.

Dutton, William (1999) *Society on the Line: Information Politics in the Digital Age*. Oxford: Oxford University Press.

Eco, Umberto (1994) "Does the audience have bad effects on television?," in Umberto Eco and Robert Lumlely (eds.), *Apocalypse Postponed*, pp. 87–102. Bloomington, IN: Indiana University Press.

The Economist (2008) "The world in figures. Industries: the world in 2008" (available online at http://www.economist.com/theworldin/forecasts/INDUSTRY_PAGES_2008.pdf).

Edelman (2008) "Edelman trust barometer 2008: The 9th annual global opinion leadership survey" (available online at http://www.edelman.co.uk/trustbarometer/files/trust-barometer-2008.pdf).

Edwards, George C., III, and Wood, Dan B. (1999) "Who influences whom? The president, Congress, and the media," *The American Political Science Review*, 93 (2), 327–44.

Eilperin, Juliet (2008) "Gore launches ambitious advocacy campaign on climate," *Washington Post*, March 31 (retrieved May 1, 2008 from http://www.washingtonpost.com/).

Ekman, Paul (1973) *Darwin and Facial Expression: A Century of Research in Review*. New York: Academic Press.

El-Nawawy, Mohammed and Iskandar, Adel (2002) *Al-Jazeera: How the Free Arab News Network Scooped the World and Changed the Middle East*. Cambridge, MA: Westview Press

Entman, Robert M. (2004) *Projections of Power: Framing News, Public Opinion, and US Foreign Policy*. Chicago, IL: University of Chicago Press.

—— (2007) "Framing bias: media in the distribution of power," *Journal of Communication*, 57 (1), 163–73.

Erbring, Lutz, Goldenberg, Edie N., and Miller, Arthur H. (1980) "Front page news and real-world cues: a new look at agenda-setting by the media," *American Journal of Political Science*, 24 (1), 16–49.

Esser, Frank and Hartung, Uwe (2004) "Nazis, pollution, and no sex: political scandal as a reflection of political culture in Germany," *American Behavioral Scientist*, 47 (8), 1040–78.

EUMap (2005) *Television across Europe: Regulations, Policy, and Independence*. Budapest: Open Society Initiative/EU Monitoring Advocacy Program.

—— (2008) *Television across Europe Part II: Regulations, Policy, and Independence*. Budapest: Open Society Initiative/EU Monitoring Advocacy Program.

Eurobarometer (2007) *Eurobarometer 67: Public Opinion in the European Union*. Brussels: European Commission.

—— (2008) *Standard Eurobarometer 69* (accessed May 24, 2008 from http://ec. europa.eu/public_opinion/archives/).

Euromonitor (2007) "Global market information database," Statistics Service of Euromonitor International. European Commission (various years) Eurobarometer.

Fackler, Tim and Tse-min, Lin (1995) "Political corruption and presidential elections, 1929–1992," *Journal of Politics*, 57 (4), 971–93.

Fahmy, Shahira (2007) "They took it down: exploring determinants of visual reporting in the toppling of the Saddam statue in national and international newspapers," *Mass Communication and Society*, 10 (2), 143–70.

Fairclough, Gordon (2004) "Generation why? The 386ers of Korea question old rules," *Wall Street Journal*, April 14: A1.

Fallows, James (1996) *Breaking the News: How the Media Undermine American Democracy*. New York: Pantheon.

Fan, David P., Wyatt, Robert O., and Keltner, Kathy (2001) "The suicidal messenger: how press reporting affects public confidence in the press, the military, and organized religion," *Communication Research*, 28 (6), 826–52.

Ferguson, Yale H. (2006) "The crisis of the state in a globalizing world," *Globalizations*, 3 (1), 5–8.

Fernández-Armesto, Felipe (1995) *Millennium: A History of the Last Thousand Years*. New York: Touchstone.

—— (2000) *Civilizations: Culture, Ambition, and the Transformation of Nature*. New York: Touchstone.

Feulner, Edwin J. (1986) *Ideas, Think Tanks, and Governments*. The Heritage Lectures. Washington, DC: Heritage Foundation.

Fine, Jon (2007) "Those hulking media failures: why so many conglomerates are splitting up and slimming down," *Business Week*, 4065, December 31, 104.

Fineman, Howard and Isikoff, Michael (1997) "Fund raising: strange bedfellows," *Newsweek*, 129 (10), 22–26.

Flew, Terry (2007) *Understanding Global Media*. New York: Palgrave Macmillan.

—— and Gilmour, Callum (2003) "A tale of two synergies: an institutional analysis of the expansionary strategies of News Corporation and AOL-Time Warner," paper presented to Managing Communication for Diversity, Australia and New Zealand Communications Association Conference, Brisbane, July 9–11.

Bibliography

Foucault, Michel (1975) *Surveiller et Punir.* Paris: Gallimard.

—— (1976) *Histoire de la Sexualité,* vol. 1: *La Volonté de Savoir.* Paris: Gallimard

—— (1984a) *Histoire de la Sexualité,* vol. 2: *L' Usage des Plaisirs.* Paris: Gallimard.

—— (1984b) *Histoire de la Sexualité,* vol. 3: *Le Souci de Soi.* Paris: Gallimard.

Fox, Elizabeth and Waisbord, Silvio R. (eds.) (2002) *Latin Politics, Global Media.* Austin, TX: University of Texas Press.

Fox News (2006) "Report: Hundreds of WMDs found in Iraq" (available online at http://www.foxnews.com/politics/2006/06/22/report-hundreds-wmds-iraq/).

Frammolino, Ralph and Fritz, Sara (1997) "Clinton led move for donors to stay night in White House," *Los Angeles Times,* February 26, A-1.

Francescutty, P., Baer A., Garcia J. M., and Lopez, P. (2005) "La noche de los moviles: medios, redes de confianza y movilización juvenil," in V. F. Sampedro Blanco (ed.), *13-M: Multitudes on Line,* pp. 63–83. Madrid: Ed. Catarata.

Frank, Thomas (2004) *What's the Matter with Kansas? How Conservatives Won the Heart of America.* New York: Henry Holt.

Fraser, Nancy (2007) "Transnationalizing the public sphere: on the legitimacy and efficacy of public opinion in a post-Westphalian world," *Theory, Culture and Society,* 24 (4), 7–30.

Freeman, Christopher (1982) *The Economics of Industrial Innovation.* London: Frances Pinter.

Fried, Amy (2005) "Terrorism as a context of coverage before the Iraq War," *Harvard International Journal of Press/Politics,* 10 (3), 125–32.

Fulford, Benjamin (2003) "Korea's weird wired world," *Forbes,* July 21, 92.

Fundación Alternativas (2007) *Informe sobre la democracia en España.*

Future Exploration Network (2007) *Future of the Media Report 2007.* Sydney: Future Exploration Network.

Gale (2008). Advertising agencies. *Encyclopedia of global industries* (online edition). Reproduced in Business and Company Resource Center. Farmington Hills, MI: Gale Group.

Gallese, Vittorio and Goldman, Alvin (1998) "Mirror neurons and the simulation theory of mind-reading," *Trends in Cognitive Sciences,* 4 (7), 252–54.

—— Keysers, Christian, and Rizzolatti, Giacomo (2004) "A unifying view of the basis of social cognition," *Trends in Cognitive Sciences,* 8 (9), 396–403.

Gallup (2008a) "Among blacks, Hillary Clinton's image sinks over last year," press release, June 6.

—— (2008b) "Hispanic voters solidly behind Obama," press release, July 2 (available online at http://www.gallup.com/poll/108532/Hispanic-Voters-Solidly-Behind-Obama.aspx).

Galperin, Hernan (2004) "Beyond interests, ideas, and technology: an institutional approach to communication and information policy," *The Information Society,* 20 (3), 159–68.

—— and Mariscal, Judith (eds.) (2007) *Digital Poverty: Latin American and Caribbean Perspectives*. Ottawa: Practical Action Publishing.

Gans, Curtis (2008a) "Much-hyped turnout record fails to materialize, convenience voting fails to boost balloting," American University, Center for the Study of the American Electorate (CSAE) (retrieved November 8, 2008 from http://i2.cdn.turner.com/cnn/2008/images/11/06/pdf.gansre08turnout.au.pdf).

—— (2008b) "2008 Report: primary turnout falls just short of record nationally, breaks record in most states," Washington, DC: American University, Center for the Study of the American Electorate.

Garrett, Sam R. (2008) "Campaign finance: legislative developments and policy issues in the 110th Congress (report)," *Congressional Research Service (CRS) Reports and Issue Briefs*.

Gentzkow, Matthew and Shapiro, Jesse M. (2006) "Media bias and reputation," *Journal of Political Economy*, 114 (2), 280–316.

—— Glaeser, Edward L., and Goldin, Claudia (2004) "The rise of the fourth estate: how newspapers became informative and why it mattered," Working Paper 10791, National Economic Bureau.

Gershon, Robert (2005) "The transnationals: media corporations, international TV trade and entertainment flows," in Anne Cooper-Chen (ed.), *Global Entertainment Media: Content, Audiences, Issues*, pp. 17–38. Mahwah, NJ: Lawrence Erlbaum.

Giddens, Anthony (1979) *Central Problems in Social Theory: Action, Structure, and Contradiction in Social Analysis*. Berkeley, CA: University of California Press.

—— (1984) *The Constitution of Society*. Cambridge: Polity Press.

Giles, David C. (2002) "Parasocial interaction: a review of the literature and a model for future research," *Media Psychology*, 4 (3), 279–305.

Gillan, Kevin, Pickerill, Jenny, and Webster, Frank (2008) *Anti-War Activism: New Media and Protest in the Information Age*. London: Palgrave-Macmillan.

Gillespie, Tarleton (2007) *Wired Shut: Copyright and the Shape of Digital Culture*. Cambridge, MA: MIT Press.

Ginley, Caitlin (2008) "Obama's rainmakers: a report of the buying of the Presidency 2008 Project," Washington, DC: Center for Public Integrity, June 12.

Ginsberg, Benjamin and Shefter, Martin (1999) *Politics by Other Means: Politicians, Prosecutors, and the Press from Watergate to Whitewater*. New York: W. W. Norton.

Gitlin, Todd (1980) *The Whole World is Watching: Mass Media in the Making and Unmaking of the New Left*. Berkeley, CA: University of California Press.

Glenny, Misha (2008) *McMafia: A Journey through the Global Criminal Underworld*. New York: Alfred Knopf.

Globescan (2006) BBC/Reuters/Media Center Poll: *Trust in the Media: Media More Trusted than Governments*. London: BBC/Reuters/Media Center.

Bibliography

Globescan and PIPA (2006) "Twenty nation poll finds strong global consensus: support for free market system, but also more regulation of large companies," Washington, DC: WorldPublicOpinion.org, March 3 (retrieved from http://www.worldpublicopinion.org/pipa/articles/btglobalizationtradera/154.php?nid=andid=andpnt=154).

Gluck, Marissa and Roca-Sales, Meritxell (2008) "The future of television? Advertising, technology, and the pursuit of audience," research report, Los Angeles, University of Southern California, Annenberg School for Communication, Norman Lear Center.

Goehler, Gerhard (2000) "Constitution and use of power," in Henri Goverde, Philip G. Cerny, Mark Haugaard, et al. (eds.), *Power in Contemporary Politics: Theories, Practices, Globalizations*, pp. 41–58. London: Sage.

Goffman, Erving (1959) *The Presentation of Self in Everyday Life*. Garden City, NY: Doubleday.

Golan, Guy (2006) "Inter-media agenda setting and global news coverage," *Journalism Studies*, 7 (2), 323–33.

Goldenberg, Edie N. (1975) *Making the Papers: The Access of Resource-poor Groups to the Metropolitan Press*. Lexington: Lexington Books.

Goldfarb, Michael (2000) "Our president/their scandal: the role of the British press in keeping the Clinton scandals alive," Working Paper Series, Harvard University, The Joan Shorenstein Center on the Press, Politics and Public Policy.

Goldsmith, Jack L. and Wu, Tim (2006) *Who Controls the Internet? Illusions of a Borderless World*. New York: Oxford University Press.

Gopal, Sangita and Moorti, Sujata (eds.) (2008) *Global Bollywood: Travels of Hindi Song and Dance*. Minneapoli, MN: University of Minnesota Press.

Gore, Albert (1992) *Earth in the Balance: Ecology and the Human Spirit*. New York: Houghton-Mifflin.

—— (2007) "Moving beyond Kyoto," *The New York Times*, July 1 (retrieved May 20, 2008 from http://www.nytimes.com/).

Graber, Doris A. (2001) *Processing Politics: Learning from Television in the Internet Age*. Chicago, IL: University of Chicago Press.

—— (2007) "The road to public surveillance: breaching attention thresholds," in W. Russell Neuman, George E. Marcus, Ann N. Crigler, and Michael MacKuen (eds.), *The Affect Effect: Dynamics of Emotion in Political Thinking and Behavior*, pp. 265–290. Chicago, IL: University of Chicago Press.

Graham, Stephen and Simon, Marvin (2001) *Splintering Urbanism: Networked Infrastructures, Technological Mobilities and the Urban Condition*. London: Routledge.

Gramsci, Antonio (1975) *Quaderni del carcere*. Torino: Einaudi.

Greco, Albert N. (1996) "Shaping the future: mergers, acquisitions, and the US communications, and mass media industries, 1990–1995," *Publishing Review Quarterly*, 12 (3), 5–16.

Green, Jason (2008) "Voter information center" at MyBarackObama.com (available online at http://my.barackobama.com/page/community/post/gwenalexander/gG5dfy).

Greenwalt, Anthony (2008) "The race factor redux," *Pew Research Center Publications* (retrieved May 8, 2008 from http://pewresearch.org/pubs/832/the-race-factor-redux).

Grewal, David Singh (2008) *Network Power: The Social Dynamics of Globalization.* New Haven, CT: Yale University Press.

Groeling, Tim and Linneman, Jeffrey (2008) "Sins of the father: does scandalous news undermine social trust?," paper presented at the International Communication Association Conference, Montreal, Canada, May 23–26.

Gross, Kimberly and Aday, Sean (2003) "The scary world in your living room and neighborhood: using local broadcast news, neighborhood crime rates, and personal experience to test agenda setting and cultivation," *Journal of Communication,* 53 (3), 411–26.

Groves, Stephen (2007) "Advancing freedom in Russia," The Heritage Foundation, Backgrounder #2088 (available online at http://www.heritage.org/research/worldwidefreedom/bg2088.cfm).

Guber, Deborah L. (2003) *The Grassroots of a Green Revolution: Polling America on the Environment.* Cambridge, MA: MIT Press.

Guehenno, Jean Marie (1993) *La Fin de la Democratie.* Paris: Flammarion.

Guidry, John A., Kennedy, Michael D., and Zald, Mayer N. (2000) *Globalizations and Social Movements: Culture, Power, and the Transnational Public Sphere.* Ann Arbor, MI: University of Michigan Press.

Gulati, Girish J., Just, Marion, and Crigler, Ann (2004) "News coverage of political campaigns," in Lynda Lee Kaid (ed.), *Handbook of Political Communication Research,* pp. 237–52. Mahwah, NJ: Lawrence Erlbaum.

Gunaratna, Rohan (2002) *Inside Al Qaeda: Global Network of Terror.* New York: Columbia University Press.

Guo, Z. and Zhao, L. (2004) *Focus on "Focus Interview."* Beijing: Tsinghua University Press.

Haas, P. M. (1992) "Introduction: epistemic communities and international policy coordination," *International Organization,* 46 (1), 1–36.

Habermas, Jürgen (1976) *Legitimation Crisis.* London: Heinemann Educational.

—— (1989) *The Structural Transformation of the Public Sphere: An Inquiry into a Category of Bourgeois Society.* Cambridge: Polity Press.

—— (1996) *Between Facts and Norms: Contributions to a Discourse Theory of Law and Democracy.* Cambridge, MA: MIT Press.

—— (1998) *Die Postnationale Konstellation: Politische Essays.* Frankfurt am Main: Suhrkamp.

Bibliography

Hachigian, Nina and Wu, Lily (2003) *The Information Revolution in Asia*. Santa Monica, CA: Rand Corporation.

Hafez, Kai (2005) "Arab satellite broadcasting: democracy without political parties?" *Transnational Broadcasting Studies*, 15 (Fall) (available online at http://www. tbsjournal.com/Archives/Fall05/Hafez.html).

Hall, Jane (2003) "Coverage of George W. Bush," *Harvard International Journal of Press/Politics*, 8 (2), 115–20.

Hall, Peter and Pain, Kathryn (2006) *The Polycentric Metropolis: Learning from Mega-city Regions in Europe*. London: Earthscan.

Hallin, Daniel C. (1986) *The "Uncensored War": The Media and Vietnam*. New York: Oxford University Press.

—— (1992) "Soundbite news: television coverage of elections, 1968–1988," *Journal of Communication*, 42 (2), 5–24.

—— and Mancini, Paolo (2004a) "Americanization, globalization, and secularization," in Frank Esser and Barbara Pfetsch (eds.), *Comparing Political Communication: Theories, Cases, and Challenges*, pp. 25–43. Cambridge: Cambridge University Press.

—— —— (2004b) *Comparing Media Systems: Three Models of Media and Politics*. Cambridge: Cambridge University Press.

Halperin, Mark (2008) "The page: Obama release on adding college Democrat superdelegate," *Time Magazine* (available online at http://thepage.time.com/ obama-release-on-adding-college-democrat-superdelegate/#).

Hammond, Allen, et al. (2007) *The Next 4 Billion: Market Size and Business Strategy and the Base of the Pyramid*. Washington, DC: World Resources Institute.

Hampton, Keith N. (2004) "Networked sociability online, off-line," in Manuel Castells (ed.), *The Network Society: A Cross-cultural Perspective*, pp. 217–32. Northampton, MA: Edward Elgar.

—— (2007) "Neighborhoods in the network society," *Information, Communication and Society*, 10 (5), 714–48.

Hardt, Michael and Negri, Antonio (2004) *Multitude*. New York: Penguin.

Harris Poll (2004a) "In spite of media coverage, widespread belief in weapons of mass destruction and Iraqi links to Al Qaeda remain virtually unchanged," Harris Poll #27, April 21 (available online at http://www.harrisinteractive. com/harris_poll/index.asp?PID=456).

—— (2004b) "Iraq, 9/11, Al Qaeda and weapons of mass destruction: what the public believes now, according to the latest Harris Poll," Harris Poll #79, October 21 (available online at http://www.harrisinteractive.com/harris_poll/index. asp?PID=508).

—— (2005) "Iraq, 9/11, Al Qaeda and weapons of mass destruction: what the public believes now, according to latest Harris Poll," Harris Poll #14, February 18 (available online at http://www.harrisinteractive.com/harris_poll/index. asp?PID=544).

—— (2006) "Belief that Iraq had weapons of mass destruction has increased substantially," Harris Poll #57, July 21 (available online at http://www.harrisinteractive.com/harris_poll/index.asp?PID=684).

Hart, Roderick P. (1999) *Seducing America: How Television Charms the Modern Voter.* Thousand Oaks, CA: Sage.

Harvard University Institute of Politics (2008) *The 14th Biannual Youth Survey of Politics and Public Service Report.* Cambridge, MA: Harvard University Press.

Harvey, David (1990) *The Condition of Postmodernity.* Oxford: Blackwell.

Haugaard, Mark (1997) *The Constitution of Power: A Theoretical Analysis of Power, Knowledge and Structure.* Manchester: Manchester University Press.

Hayashi, Aiko (2008) "Matsushita's Panasonic, Google to launch Internet TVs," *Reuters*, January 7 (available online at http://www.reuters.com/article/rbssConsumerGoodsAndRetailNews/idUST20271420080108).

Held, David (1991) "Democracy, the nation-state and the global system," *Economy and Society*, 20 (2), 138–72.

—— (2004) *Global Covenant: The Social Democratic Alternative to the Washington Consensus.* Cambridge: Polity Press.

—— and Kaya, Ayse (2006) *Global Inequality: Patterns and Explanations.* Cambridge: Polity Press.

—— and McGrew, Anthony (eds.) (2000) *The Global Transformations Reader: An Introduction to the Globalization Debate.* Cambridge: Polity Press.

—— —— (eds.) (2007) *Globalization Theory: Approaches and Controversies.* London: Polity Press.

—— —— Goldblatt, David, and Perraton, Jonathan (eds.) (1999) *Global Transformations: Politics, Economics and Culture.* Cambridge: Polity Press.

Hencke, David (2007) "A short history of Labour party funding scandals," *Guardian*, November 27.

Herbst, Susan (1998) *Reading Public Opinion: How Political Actors View the Democratic Process.* Chicago, IL: University of Chicago Press.

Herndon, Ruth Wallis (1996) "Literacy among New England's transient poor, 1750–1800," *Journal of Social History*, 29 (4), 963.

Hersh, Seymour H. (2004) "Torture at Abu Ghraib." *The New Yorker.* Posted April 30, 2004. May 10, 2004 edition.

Hesmondhalgh, David (2007) *The Cultural Industries.* Thousand Oaks, CA: Sage.

Hess, D. K. (2007) *Alternative Pathways in Science and Industry: Activism, Innovation, and the Environment in an Era of Globalization.* London: MIT Press.

Hetherington, Marc J. (2005) *Why Trust Matters: Declining Political Trust and the Demise of American Liberalism.* Princeton, NJ: Princeton University Press.

—— (2008) "Turned off or turned on? How polarization affects political engagement," in Pietro S. Nivola and David W. Brady (eds.), *Red and Blue Nation?* vol. 2: *Consequences and Correction of America's Polarized Politics*, pp. 1–54. Washington, DC: Brookings Institution.

Bibliography

Hetherington, Marc J., and Nelson, Michael (2003) "Anatomy of a rally effect: George W. Bush and the war on terrorism," *PS: Political Science and Politics*, 36 (1), 37–44.

—— and Rudolph, Thomas J. (2008) "Priming, performance, and the dynamics of political trust," *Journal of Politics*, 70, 498–512.

Heywood, Paul (2007) "Corruption in contemporary Spain," *Political Science and Politics*, 40, 695–9.

Hibbing, John R. and Theiss-Morse, Elizabeth (1995) *Congress as Public Enemy: Public Attitudes toward American Political Institutions*. New York: Cambridge University Press.

—— —— (1998) "The media's role in public negativity toward Congress: distinguishing emotional reactions and cognitive evaluations," *American Journal of Political Science*, 42 (2), 475–98.

Himanen, Pekka (2002) *The Hacker Ethic and the Spirit of the Information Age*. New York: Random House.

Hindman, Elizabeth (2005) "Jason Blair, *The New York Times*, and paradigm repair," *Journal of Communication*, June, 225–41.

Hindman, Matthew, Tsioutsiouliklis, Kostas, and Johnson, Judy A. (2003) "'Googlearchy': how a few heavily-linked sites dominate politics on the web," *Midwest Political Science Association*.

Holder, Kelly (2006) "Voting and registration in the election of November 2004," March. Washington, DC: The US Census Bureau.

Hollihan, Thomas A. (2008) *Uncivil Wars: Political Campaigns in a Media Age*. New York: Bedford St. Martin's.

Horsley, Scott (2007) "Interest in climate change heats up in 2008 race," *National Public Radio*, morning edition, June 8, 2007.

Howard, Philip N. (2003) "Digitizing the social contract: producing American political culture in the age of new media," *Communication Review*, 6 (3), 213–36.

—— (2005) "Deep democracy, thin citizenship: the impact of digital media in political campaign strategy," *Annals of the American Academy of Political and Social Science*, 597 (1), 153–70.

Hsing, You-tien (forthcoming) *The Great Urban Transformation: Land Development and Territorial Politics in China*. Oxford: Oxford University Press.

Huang, Chengju (2007) "Trace the stones in crossing the river: media structural changes in post-WTO China," *International Communication Gazette*, 69 (5), 413–30.

Huddy, Leonie and Gunnthorsdottir, Anna H. (2000) "The persuasive effects of emotive visual imagery: superficial manipulation or the product of passionate reason," *Political Psychology*, 21 (4), 745–78.

—— Feldman, Stanley, Capelos, Theresa, and Provost, Colin (2002) "The consequences of terrorism: disentangling the effects of personal and national threat," *Political Psychology*, 23 (3), 485–509.

———— and Cassese, Erin (2007) "On the distinct effects of anxiety and anger," in W. Russell Neuman, George E. Marcus, Ann N. Crigler, and Michael MacKuen (eds.), *The Affect Effect: Dynamics of Emotion in Political Thinking and Behavior*, pp. 202–30. Chicago, IL: University of Chicago Press.

———— Taber, Charles, and Lahav, Galya (2005) "Threat, anxiety, and support of antiterrorism policies," *American Journal of Political Science*, 49 (3), 593–608.

Hughes, Chris (2008) "Moving forward on My.BarackObama" (retrieved November 8, 2008 from http://my.barackobama.com/page/community/post/chrishughesatthecampaign/gGxZvh).

Hughes, Thomas Parke (1983) *Networks of Power: Electrification in Western Society, 1880–1930*. Baltimore, MD: Johns Hopkins University Press.

Hui, Wang (2003) *Neoliberalism in China*. Cambridge, MA: Harvard University Press.

Hutchings, Vincent L., Valentino, Nicholas A., Philpot, Tasha S., and White, Ismail K. (2006) "Racial cues in campaign news: the effects of candidate issue distance on emotional responses, political attentiveness and vote choice," in David P. Redlawsk (ed.), *Feeling Politics: Emotion in Political Information Processing*. New York: Palgrave Macmillan.

Hutton, Will and Giddens, Anthony (eds.) (2000) *On the Edge: Living with Global Capitalism*. London: Jonathan Cape.

Ibahrine, Mohammad (ed.) (2008) "Mobile communication and socio-political change in the Arab world," in James Everett, Katz (ed.), *Handbook of Mobile Communication Studies*, pp. 257–72. Cambridge, MA: MIT Press.

IBIS (2007a) *Agents and Managers for Artists, Athletes, Entertainers and Other Public Figures in the US: Industry Report 71141*. IBIS World Market Research Report, October 24.

—— (2007b) *News Syndicates in the US: Industry Report: 51411*. IBIS World Market Research Report, December 18.

—— (2007c) *Radio and Television Broadcasting and Wireless Communications Equipment Manufacturing in the US: Industry Report. 33422*. IBIS World Market Research Report, December 24.

—— (2008) *Global Advertising: Global Industry Report: L6731*. IBIS World Market Research Report, February 5.

Inglehart, Ronald (1990) *Culture Shift in Advanced Industrial Society*. Princeton, NJ: Princeton University Press.

—— (ed.) (2003) *Human Values and Social Change: Findings from the Values Surveys*. Leiden: Brill Academic.

—— and Catterberg, Gabriela (2002) "Trends in political action: the developmental trend and the post-honeymoon decline," *International Journal of Comparative Sociology*, 43 (3–5), 300–16.

—— Basanez, Miguel, Deiz-Medrano, Jaime, Halman, Loek, et al. (eds.) (2004) *Human Beliefs and Values: A Cross-cultural Sourcebook Based on the 1999–2002 Values Surveys*. Mexico: Siglo XXI.

Bibliography

Ingram, Helen, Milward, Brinton, and Laird, Wendy (1992) "Scientists and agenda setting: advocacy and global warming," in M. Waterstone (ed.), *Risk and Society: The Interaction of Science, Technology and Public Policy*, pp. 33–53. Dordrecht: Kluwer.

Instituto Opina (2004) "Pulsómetro para la Cadena SER," March 22 (available online at http://www.pscm-psoe.com/psclm/pb/periodico3/archivos/223200418958.pdf).

International Foundation for Election Systems (IFES) (2002) "Matrix on political finance laws and regulations," *Program on Political Finance and Public Ethics*, pp. 185–223 (available online at https://www.ifes.org/money_site/researchpubs/main.html)

International Journal of Communication (2007) Special Section on Net Neutrality, 1 (available online at http://ijoc.org/ojs/index.php/ijoc/issue/view/1).

IPCC (1995) *IPCC Second Assessment Report: Climate Change 1995*. Geneva, Switzerland: IPCC.

—— (2001) *IPCC Third Assessment Report: Climate Change 2001*. Geneva, Switzerland: IPCC.

—— (2007a) *Brochure: The IPCC and the "Climate Change 2007"* (report available at http://www.ipcc.ch/press/index.htm).

—— (2007b) *IPCC Fourth Assessment Report: Climate Change 2007*. Geneva, Switzerland: IPCC.

Iskandar, Adel (2005) "'The great American bubble': Fox News channel, the 'mirage' of objectivity, and the isolation of American public opinion," in Lee Artz and Yahya R. Kamalipour (eds.), *Bring 'Em on: Media and Politics in the Iraq War*, pp. 155–74. Lanham, MD: Rowman and Littlefield.

Ito, Mizuko, Okabe, Daisuke, and Matsuda, Misa (2005) *Personal, Portable, Pedestrian: Mobile Phones in Japanese Life*. Cambridge, MA: MIT Press.

ITU (2007) *World Information Society Report 2007: Beyond WSIS*. Geneva: International Telecommunications Union/United Nations Conference on Trade and Development.

Iturriaga, Diego (2004) "Cuatro dias que acabaron con ocho años: aproximación al estudio del macroacontecimiento del 11-14M," *Historia actual online*, pp. 15–30.

Iwabuchi, Koichi (2008) "Cultures of empire: transnational media flows and cultural (dis)connections in East Asia," in Paula Chakravartty and Yeuzhi Zhao (eds.), *Global Communications: Toward a Transcultural Political Economy*, pp. 143–61. Lanham, MD: Rowman and Littlefield.

Iyengar, Shanto and Kinder, Donald R. (1987) *News that Matters: Television and American Opinion*. Chicago, IL: University of Chicago Press.

Jacobs, Lawrence R. and Burns, Melanie (2008) *The Big Mobilization: Increased Voter Registration in 2008*. Report prepared by the Center for the Study of Politics and Governance, Humphrey Institute of Public Affairs, University of Minnesota, May 5.

Jacobson, Gary C. (2007a) "The public, the president, and the war in Iraq," in *The Polarized Presidency of George W. Bush*, Oxford Scholarship Online Monographs, pp. 245–85.

—— (2007b) "The war, the president, and the 2006 midterm elections," paper prepared for delivery at the Annual Meeting of the Midwest Political Science Association, the Palmer House Hilton, Chicago, Illinois, April 12–15.

Jacquet, Pierre, Pisani-Ferry, Jean, and Tubiana, Laurence (eds.) (2002) *Gouvernance Mondiale*. Paris: Documentation Française.

Jamieson, Kathleen Hall (1992) *Dirty Politics: Deception, Distraction, and Democracy*. New York: Oxford University Press.

—— (2000) *Everything You Think You Know about Politics – and Why You're Wrong*. New York: Basic Books.

—— and Campbell, Karlyn Kohrs (2006) *The Interplay of Influence: News, Advertising, Politics, and the Internet*. Belmont, CA: Thomson Wadsworth.

—— and Waldman, Paul (2003) *The Press Effect: Politicians, Journalists, and the Stories that Shape the Political World*. Oxford: Oxford University Press.

Jardin, André and Tudesq, André Jean (1973) *La France des Notables*. Paris: Éditions du Seuil.

Jenkins, Henry (2006) *Convergence Culture: Where Old and New Media Collide*. New York: New York University Press.

Jimenez, Fernando (2004) "The politics of scandal in Spain: morality plays, social trust, and the battle for public opinion," *American Behavioral Scientist*, 47 (8), 1099–121.

—— and Cainzos, Miguel (2004) "La repercusión electoral de los escándalos políticos: alcance y condiciones," *Revista Española de Ciencia Política*, 10, 141–70.

Jones, Jeffrey M. (2007a) "Low trust in federal government rivals Watergate levels," *Gallup News Service*, September 26.

—— (2007b) "Some Americans reluctant to vote for Mormon, 72-year-old presidential candidates," *Gallup News Service*, February 20.

Juan, M. (2004) *11/M: La trama completa*. Barcelona: Ediciones de la Tempestad.

Juris, Jeffrey S. (2008) *Networking Futures: The Movements against Corporate Globalization*. Durham, NC: Duke University Press.

Just, Marion, Crigler, Ann, and Belt, Todd (2007) "'Don't give up hope': emotions, candidate appraisals and votes," in W. Russell Neuman, George E. Marcus, Ann N. Crigler, and Michael MacKuen (eds.), *The Affect Effect: Dynamics of Emotion in Political Thinking and Behavior*, pp. 231–60. Chicago, IL: University of Chicago Press.

Kahneman, Daniel and Tversky, Amos (1973) "On the psychology of prediction," *Psychology Review*, 80, 237–51.

—— —— (1979) "Prospect theory: an analysis of decision under risk," *Econometrica*, 47, 263–91.

Bibliography

Kaldor, Mary (2001) *New and Old Wars: Organized Violence in a Global Era* (Spanish edition). Barcelona: Tusquets.

—— (2003) *The Global Civil Society: An Answer to War*. Cambridge: Polity Press.

Kanter, James and Revkin, Andrew C. (2007) "Last-minute wrangling on global warming report," *International Herald Tribune*, February 1 (retrieved May 1, 2008, from http://www.iht.com).

Kaplan, Martin, Castells, Manuel, Gluck, Marrisa, and Roca, Meritxell (2008) "The transformation of the advertising industry and its impact on the media in a digital environment," unpublished research report, Los Angeles, Annenberg School for Communication, Norman Lear Center.

Katz, James Everett (ed.) (2008) *Handbook of Mobile Communication Studies*. Cambridge, MA: MIT Press.

Katz, James Everett and Aakhus, Mark A. (2002) *Perpetual Contact: Mobile Communication, Private Talk, Public Performance*. Cambridge: Cambridge University Press.

—— and Rice, Ronald E. (2002) *Social Consequences of Internet Use: Access, Involvement, and Interaction*. Cambridge, MA: MIT Press.

Keck, Margaret E. and Sikkink, Kathryn (1998) *Activists beyond Borders: Advocacy Networks in International Politics*. Ithaca, NY: Cornell University Press.

Keeter, Scott (1987) "The illusion of intimacy: television and the role of candidate personal qualities in voter choice," *Public Opinion Quarterly*, 51 (3), 344–58.

—— Horowitz, Juliana, and Tyson, Alec (2008) *Gen Dems: The Party's Advantage among Young Voters Widens*. Washington, DC: Pew Research Center for the People and the Press, April 28.

Kellner, Douglas (2005) *Media Spectacle and the Crisis of Democracy*. Boulder, CO: Paradigm.

Kelly, E. (2008) "Senate poised to take up sweeping global warming bill," *USA Today*, May 17 (retrieved May 24, 2008 from http://www.usatoday.com/).

Kendall, Kathleen E. and Paine, Scott C. (2005) "Political images and voting behavior," in Kenneth L. Hacker (ed.), *Candidate Images in Presidential Elections*, pp. 19–35. London: Praeger.

Keohane, Robert O. (2002) *Power and Governance in a Partially Globalized World*. London: Routledge.

Kern, Montague, Just, Marion, and Norris, Pippa (2003) "The lessons of framing terrorism," in Pippa Norris, Montague Kern, and Marion Just (eds.), *Framing Terrorism: The News Media, the Government, and the Public*, pp. 281–308. New York: Routledge.

Kinder, Donald (1998) "Opinion and action in the realm of politics," in Daniel Todd Gilbert, Susan T. Fiske, and Gardner Lindzey (eds.), *The Handbook of Social Psychology*, pp. 778–867. New York: McGraw-Hill.

King, Joseph P. (1989) "Socioeconomic development and corrupt campaign practices in England," in Arnold J. Heidenheimer, Michael Johnston, and Victor T.

Le Vine (eds.), *Political Corruption: A Handbook*, pp. 233–50. New Brunswick, NJ: Transaction.

King, Ryan S. (2006) *A Decade of Reform: Felony Disenfranchisement Policy in the United States*. Washington, DC: The Sentencing Project.

Kiriya, Ilya (2007) "Las industrias de información y cultura en Rusia: entre mercancia e instrumento," *Zer*, 22, 97–117.

Kirkpatrick, David (2005) "TV host says US paid him to back policy," *New York Times*, January 8.

Kiyoshi, Koboyashi, Lakhsmanan, T. R., and Anderson, William P. (2006) *Structural Changes in Transportation and Communication in the Knowledge Society*. Northampton, MA: Edward Elgar.

Klein, Naomi (2002) *Fences and Windows*. New York: Picador.

—— (2007) *Shock Therapy: The Rise of Disaster Capitalism*. New York: Doubleday.

Klinenberg, Eric (2005) "Convergence: news production in a digital age," *Annals of the American Academy of Political and Social Science*, 597, 48–64.

—— (2007) *Fighting for Air: Conglomerates, Citizens, and the Battle to Control America's Media*. New York: Henry Holt.

Koskinen, Ilpo Kalevi (2007) *Mobile Multimedia in Action*. New Brunswick, NJ: Transaction.

Kramer, Andrew (2007) "50% good news is the bad news in Russian radio," *The New York Times*, April 22.

Krosnick, Jon, Holbrook, Allyson, Lowe, Laura, and Visser, Penny (2006) "The origins and consequences of democratic citizens' policy agendas: a study of popular concern about global warming," *Climatic Change*, 77, 7–43.

—— —— and Visser, Penny S. (2000) "The impact of the Fall 1997 debate about global warming on American public opinion," *Public Understanding of Science*, 9, 239–60.

Kull, Steven, Ramsay, Clay, and Lewis, Evan (2003–4) "Misperceptions, the media, and the Iraq war," *Political Science Quarterly*, 118 (4), 569–98.

—— —— Weber, Stephen, Lewis, Evan, et al. (2008) *World Public Opinion on Governance and Democracy*. Washington, DC: WorldPublicOpinion.org.

Kunda, Ziva (1990) "The case for motivated reasoning," *Psychology Bulletin*, 108 (3), 480–98.

LaBianca, Oystein (ed.) (2006) *Connectivity in Antiquity: Globalization as a Long-term Historical Process*. London: Equinox.

Labrousse, Ernest (1943) *La Crise de l'Économie Française à la Fin de l'Ancien Régime et au Debut de la Révolution*. Paris: Presses Universitaires de France.

Lakoff, George (1991) "Metaphor and war: the metaphor system used to justify war in the Gulf," *Viet Nam Generation Journal and Newsletter*, 3 (3).

—— (2004) *Don't Think of an Elephant! Know your Values and Frame the Debate: The Essential Guide for Progressives*. White River Junction, VT: Chelsea Green.

Bibliography

Lakoff, George (2005) "War on terror: rest in peace," *Alternet*, August 1 (available online at http://www.alternet.org/story/23810/).

—— (2008) *The Political Mind: Why You Can't Understand 21st-century Politics with an 18th-century Brain*. New York: Viking.

—— and Johnson, Mark (1980) *Metaphors We Live By*. Chicago, IL: University of Chicago Press.

Landau, Mark, Solomon, Sheldon, Greenberg, Jeff, Cohen, Florette, et al. (2004) "Deliver us from evil: the effects of mortality salience and reminders of 9/11 on support for President George W. Bush," *Personality and Social Psychology Bulletin*, 30 (9), 1136–50.

La Pastina, Antonio C., Rego, Cacilda M., and Straubhaar, Joseph (2003) "The centrality of telenovelas in Latin America's everyday life: past tendencies, current knowledge, and future research," *Global Media Journal*, 2 (2).

La Raja, Raymond J., Orr, Susan E., and Smith, Daniel A. (2006) "Surviving BCRA: state party finance in 2004," in John Green Clifford and Daniel J. Coffey (eds.), *The State of the Parties: The Changing Role of Contemporary American Politics*, pp. 113–34. Lanham: Rowman and Littlefield.

Lash, Scott and Urry, John (1994) *Economies of Signs and Spaces*. London: Sage.

—— and Lury, Celia (2007) *Global Culture Industry: The Mediation of Things*. Cambridge: Polity Press.

Latour, Bruno (2005) *Reassembling the Social: An Introduction to Actor-Network Theory*. Oxford: Oxford University Press.

La Vanguardia (2008) "La desmovilización de la izquierda devora la ventaja electoral del PSOE," January 4, front page.

Lawrence, Regina G. and Bennett, W. Lance (2001) "Rethinking media and public opinion: reactions to the Clinton–Lewinsky scandal," *Political Science Quarterly*, 116 (3), 425–46.

Lazarsfeld, Paul Felix, Berelson, Bernard, and Gaudet, Hazel (1944) *The People's Choice: How the Voter Makes Up his Mind in a Presidential Campaign*. New York: Duell, Sloan, and Pearce.

Leege, D. and Wald, K. (2007) "Meaning, cultural symbols, and campaign strategies," in W. Russell Neuman, George E. Marcus, Ann N. Crigler, and Michael MacKuen (eds.), *The Affect Effect: Dynamics of Emotion in Political Thinking and Behavior*, pp. 291–315. Chicago, IL: University of Chicago Press.

Lehmann, Ingrid A. (2005) "Exploring the transatlantic media divide over Iraq: how and why US and German media differed in reporting on UN weapons inspections in Iraq, 2002–2003," *Harvard International Journal of Press/Politics*, 10 (1), 63–89.

Leiserowitz, Anthony (2007) "International public opinion, perception and understanding of global climate change," *UN Human Development Report*.

Lenard, Patti Tamara (2005) "The decline of trust, the decline of democracy?" *Critical Review of International Social and Political Philosophy*, 8 (3), 363–78.

Lenhart, Amanda and Fox, Susannah (2006) *Bloggers: A Portrait of the Internet's New Story Tellers*. Washington, DC: Pew Internet and American Life Project.

Lessig, Lawrence (2004) *Free Culture: How Big Media Uses Technology and the Law to Lock Down Culture and Control Creativity*. New York: Penguin.

—— (2006) *Creative Economies*. East Lansing, MI: Michigan State University College of Law.

Levada Center (2008) "Trends in Russian media" (accessible online in Russian).

Levy, Clifford J. (2007) "No joke: Russian remakes of sitcoms are a hit," *The New York Times News*, September 10.

—— (2008) "It isn't magic: Putin's opponents are made to vanish from TV," *The New York Times*, June 3 (available online at http://www.nytimes.com/2008/06/03/world/europe/03russia.html).

Levy, Pierre (2001) *Cyberculture*. Minneapolis, MN: University of Minnesota Press.

Lichter, S. Robert (2001) "A plague on both parties: substance and fairness in TV election news," *Harvard International Journal of Press/Politics*, 6 (3), 8–30.

Liebes, Tamar and Blum-Kulka, Shoshana (2004) "It takes two to blow the whistle: do journalists control the outbreak of scandal?," *American Behavioral Scientist*, 47 (9), 1153–70.

Ling, Richard Seyler (2004) *The Mobile Connection: The Cell Phone's Impact on Society*. San Francisco, CA: Morgan Kaufmann.

Lipman, Masha (2008) "Putin's puppet press," *Washington Post*, May 20.

Liu, Ch. (2004) "The unknown inside stories about the supervision of public opinion by 'focus interview'," *China Youth Daily*, March 29.

Livingston, Steven and Bennett, W. Lance (2003) "Gatekeeping, indexing, and live-event news: is technology altering the construction of news?" *Political Communication*, 20 (4), 363–80.

Lizza, Ryan (2007) "The agitator: Barack Obama's unlikely political education," *The New Republic*, March 19 (available online at http://www.tnr.com/politics/story.html?id=a74fca23-f6ac-4736-9c78-f4163d4f25c7andp=8.)

Lodge, Milton and Taber, Charles (2000) "Three steps toward a theory of motivated political reasoning," in Arthur Lupia, Mathew D. McCubbins, and Samual L. Popkin (eds.), *Elements of Reason: Cognition, Choice, and the Bounds of Rationality* (Cambridge Studies in Public Opinion and Political Psychology). Cambridge: Cambridge University Press.

Louw, P. Eric (2001) *The Media and Cultural Production*. London: Sage.

Lowe, Vincent T., Brown, Katrina, Dessai, Suraje, Doria, Miguel, Haynes, Kat, and Vincent, Katherine (2006) "Does tomorrow ever come? Disaster narrative and public perceptions of climate change," *Public Understanding of Science*, 15, 435–57.

Lucas, Henry C., Jr. (1999) *Information Technology and the Productivity Paradox: Assessing the Value of the Investment in IT.* Oxford: Oxford University Press.

Lukes, Steven (1974) *Power: A Radical View*. London: Macmillan.

Bibliography

Lull, James (2007) *Culture-on-demand: Communication in a Crisis World*. Malden, MA: Blackwell.

Luther, Catherine A. and Miller, M. Mark (2005) "Framing of the 2003 US-Iraq war demonstrations: an analysis of news and partisan texts," *Journalism and Mass Communication Quarterly*, 82 (1), 78–96.

McCarthy, Caroline (2008) "ComScore: Facebook is beating MySpace worldwide," *CNET News* (available online at http://news.cnet.com/8301-13577_3-9973826-36.html).

McChesney, Robert W. (1999) *Rich Media, Poor Democracy: Communication Politics in Dubious Times*. Urbana, IL: University of Illinois Press.

McChesney, Robert W. (2004) *The Problem of the Media: US Communication Politics in the Twenty-first Century*. New York: Monthly Review Press.

—— (2007) *Communication Revolution: Critical Junctures and the Future of Media*. New York: New Press.

—— (2008) *The Political Economy of Media: Enduring Issues, Emerging Dilemmas*. New York: Monthly Review Press.

McClean, Shilo T. (2007) *Digital Storytelling: The Narrative Power of Visual Effects in Film*. Cambridge, Mass: MIT Press.

McClellan, Scott (2008) *What Happened: Inside the Bush White House and Washington's Culture of Deception*. New York: Public Affairs.

McCombs, Maxwell E. (2004) *Setting the Agenda: The Mass Media and Public Opinion*. Cambridge: Polity Press.

—— and Ghanem, Salma I. (2001) "The convergence of agenda-setting and framing," in Stephen D. Reese, Oscar H. Gandy, and August E. Grant (eds.), *Framing Public Life: Perspectives on Media and our Understanding of the Social World*, pp. 67–82. Mahwah, NJ: Lawrence Erlbaum.

—— and Zhu, Jian-Hua (1995) "Capacity, diversity, and volatility of the public agenda: trends from 1954 to 1994," *Public Opinion Quarterly*, 59 (4), 495–525.

—— Shaw, Donald Lewis, and Weaver, David H. (1997) *Communication and Democracy: Exploring the Intellectual Frontiers in Agenda-Setting Theory*. Mahwah, NJ: Lawrence Erlbaum.

McDonald, Michael (2004) "Up, up and away! Voter participation in the 2004 presidential election," *The Forum* 2(4) (available online at www.bepress.com/forum/vol2/iss4/art4).

—— (2005) "Turnout data" (available online at http://elections.gmu.edu/voter_turnout.htm).

—— (2008) "Preliminary 2008 turnout rates," George Mason. United States Elections Project, November 7 (retrieved November 8, 2008 from http://elections.gmu.edu/Blog.html).

McNair, Brian (2006) *Cultural Chaos: Journalism, News, and Power in a Globalised World*. London: Routledge.

Bibliography

McNeill, John and McNeill, William H. (2003) *The Human Web: A Bird's Eye View of World History*. New York: W. W. Norton.

McPhail, Thomas L. (2006) *Global Communication: Theories, Stakeholders, and Trends*. Malden, MA: Blackwell.

Machado, Decio (2006) "Intereses politicos y concentración de medios en el Estado Español," *Pueblos*, 25, 18–20.

MacKuen, Michael, Marcus, George E., Neuman, W. Russell, and Keele, Luke (2007) "The third way: the theory of affective intelligence and American democracy," in W. Russell Neuman, George E. Marcus, Ann N. Crigler, and Michael MacKuen (eds.), *The Affect Effect: Dynamics of Emotion in Political Thinking and Behavior*, pp. 124–51. Chicago, IL: University of Chicago Press.

Madden, Mary (2007) *Online Video*. Washington, DC: Pew Internet and American Life Project.

Madsen, Arnie (1991) "Partisan commentary and the first 1988 presidential debate," *Argumentation and Advocacy*, 27, 100–13.

Malone, Michael (2007) "Stations seek private-fund buyers," *Broadcasting and Cable*, June 25 (available online at http://www.broadcastingcable.com/article/CA6454849.html).

Mandese, Jo (2007) "Online ad growth rate ebbs in Q3, but continues to outpace all major media," *Online Media Daily*, November 12 (available online at media-post.com).

Mann, Michael (1986) *The Sources of Social Power*, vol. 1: *A History of Power from the Beginning to AD 1760*. Cambridge: Cambridge University Press.

—— (1992) *The Sources of Social Power*, vol. 2: *The Rise of Classes and Nation-states, 1760–1914*. Cambridge: Cambridge University Press.

Mann, Thomas and Wolfinger, Raymond (1980) "Candidates and parties in congressional elections," *American Political Science Review*, 74 (3), 617–32.

Mansell, Robin (ed.) (2002) *Inside the Communication Revolution: Evolving Patterns of Social and Technical Interaction*. Oxford: Oxford University Press.

—— and Steinmueller, W. Edward (2000) *Mobilizing the Information Society: Strategies for Growth and Opportunity*. Oxford: Oxford University Press.

Marcelo, Karlo B. and Kirby, Emily H. (2008) *The Youth Vote in the 2008 Super Tuesday States*. College Park, MD: The Center for Information and Research on Civic Learning and Engagement.

Marcus, George E. (2000) "Emotion in politics," *Annual Review of Political Science*, 3, 221–50.

—— (2002) *The Sentimental Citizen: Emotion in Democratic Politics*. University Park, PA: Pennsylvania State University Press.

—— (2008) "The theory of affective intelligence and civic society," paper prepared for the World Congress of the International Institute of Sociology, Budapest, June 26–30.

Bibliography

Marcus, George E., Neuman, W. Russell, and MacKuen, Michael (2000) *Affective Intelligence and Political Judgment*. Chicago, IL: University of Chicago Press.

Markoff, John (2006) *What the Dormouse Said: How the Sixties Counterculture Shaped the Personal Computer Industry*. New York: Penguin.

Markovits, Andrei and Silverstein, Mark (1988) *The Politics of Scandal: Power and Process in Liberal Democracies*. London: Holmes and Meier.

Marks, Stephen (2007) *Confessions of a Political Hitman: My Secret Life of Scandal, Corruption, Hypocrisy and Dirty Attacks that Decide Who Gets Elected (and Who Doesn't)*. Naperville, IL: Sourcebooks.

Marston, Sallie A., Woodward, Keith, and Jones, John Paul (2007) "Flattening ontologies of globalization: the Nollywood case," *Globalizations*, 4 (1), 45–63.

Martinez, Ibsen (2005) "Romancing the globe," *Foreign Policy*, November/December, 48–55.

Mateos, Araceli and Moral, Felix (2006) *El comportamiento electoral de los jovenes españoles*. Madrid: Ministerio de Trabajo y Asuntos Sociales/Instituto de la Juventud.

Mattelart, Armand (1979) *Multinational Corporations and the Control of Culture: The Ideological Apparatuses of Imperialism*. Sussex Atlantic Highlands, NJ: Harvester Press.

—— and Mattelart, Michele (1992) *Rethinking Media Theory: Signposts and New Directions*. Minneapolis, MN: University of Minnesota Press.

Melnikov, Mikhail (2008) "Russia: authorities vs. media: a weekly bulletin," *Center for Journalism in Extreme Situations*, 9 (268), February 26–March 3.

Melucci, Alberto (1989) *Nomads of the Present*. London: Hutchinson Radius.

Mermin, Jonathan (1997) "Television news and American intervention in Somalia: the myth of a media-driven foreign policy," *Political Science Quarterly*, 112 (3), 385–403.

Meyer, David S., Whittier, Nancy, and Robnett, Belinda (eds.) (2002) *Social Movements: Identity, Culture, and the State*. Oxford: Oxford University Press.

Michavila, Narciso (2005) *Guerra, Terrorismo y Elecciones: Incidencia Electoral de los Atentados Islamistas en Madrid*. Madrid: Real Instituto Elcano de Estudios Internacionales y Estrategicos, working paper no. 13/2005.

Milan, Stefania (2008) "Transnational mobilisation(s) on communication and media justice. Challenges and preliminary reflections on movement formation: the case of community media," unpublished research paper, European University Institute.

Miles, Hugh (2005) *Al-Jazeera: The Inside Story of the Arab News Channel that is Challenging the West*. New York: Grove Press.

Miller, Jade (2007) "Ugly Betty goes global: global networks of localized content in the telenovela Industry," paper presented at the Emerging Scholars Network of the International Association for Media and Communication Researchers (IAMCR) Conference, Paris, France, July 23–25.

Miller, M., Boone, J., and Fowler, D. (1990) "The emergence of the greenhouse effect on the issue agenda: a news stream analysis," *News Computing Journal*, 7, 25–38.

Miller, Toby, Govil, Nitin, McMurria, John, Maxwell, Richard, and Wang, Ting (2004) *Global Hollywood: No. 2*. London: BFI.

Mitchell, Robert Cameron, Mertig, Angela G., and Dunlap, Riley E. (1992) "Twenty years of environmental mobilization: trends among national environmental organizations," in Riley E. Dunlap and Angela G. Mertig (eds.), *American Environmentalism: The US Environmental Movement, 1970–1990*, pp. 11–26. Washington, DC: Taylor and Francis.

Mitchell, William (1999) *E-topia: Urban Life – But Not as We Know It*. Cambridge, MA: MIT Press.

—— (2003) *Me++*. Cambridge, MA: MIT Press.

Moaddel, Mansoor (ed.) (2007) *Values and Perceptions of the Islamic and Middle Eastern Publics*. New York: Palgrave Macmillan.

Modood, Tariq (2005) *Multicultural Politics: Racism, Ethnicity, and Muslims in Britain*. Minneapolis, MN: University of Minnesota Press.

Mokyr, Joel (1990) *The Lever of Riches. Technological Creativity and Economic Progress*. New York: Oxford University Press.

Monge, Peter and Contractor, Noshir (2003) *Theories of Communication Networks*. Oxford: Oxford University Press.

Montero J. R., Gunther, R., and Torcal, M. (1998) "Actitudes hacia la democracia en España: legitimidad, descontento y desafección," *Revista Española de Investigaciones Sociológicas*, 83, 9–49.

Montgomery, Kathryn C. (2007) *Generation Digital: Politics, Commerce, and Childhood in the Age of the Internet*. Cambridge, MA: MIT Press.

Morin, Richard and Claudia Deane (2000) "Why the Fla. exit polls were wrong," *Washington Post*, November 8, A10.

Morris, Jonathan and Clawson, Rosalee (2005) "Media coverage of Congress in the 1990s: scandals, personalities, and the prevalence of policy and process," *Political Communication*, 22, 297–313.

Morstein-Marx, Robert (2004) *Mass Oratory and Political Power in the Late Roman Republic*. Cambridge: Cambridge University Press.

Movius, Lauren (forthcoming) "Freeing the technologies of freedom: global social movements and Internet governance," unpublished PhD dissertation (in progress), Los Angeles, University of Southern California, Annenberg School of Communication.

Mulgan, Geoff (1991) *Communication and Control: Networks and the New Economies of Communication*. Cambridge: Polity Press.

Bibliography

Mulgan, Geoff (1998) *Connexity: How to Live in a Connected World*. Boston, MA: Harvard Business School Press.

——(2007) *Good and Bad Power: The Ideals and Betrayals of Government*, 2nd edn. London: Penguin.

Murdock, Graham (2006) "Cosmopolitans and conquistadors: empires, nations and networks," in Oliver Boyd-Barrett (ed.), *Communications Media, Globalization and Empire*, pp. 17–32. Eastleigh: John Libbey.

Murillo, Pablo (2008) "De nuevo, la financiación de los partidos políticos," *Expansion*, April 11.

Murray, Craig, Parry, Katy, Robinson, Piers, and Goddard, Peter (2008) "Reporting dissent in wartime: British press, the anti-war movement and the 2003 Iraq War," *European Journal of Communication*, 23 (1), 7–27.

Murrin, John M., Johnson, Paul E., and McPherson, James M. (2005) *Liberty, Equality, Power: A History of the American People*, 4th edn. Belmont, CA: Thomson/ Wadsworth.

Mutz, Diana C. and Reeves, Byron (2005) "The new videomalaise: effects of televised incivility on political trust," *American Political Science Review*, 99 (1), 1–15.

Myrdal, Gunnar (1944) *An American Dilemma: The Negro Problem and Modern Democracy*. London: Harper.

Nacos, Brigitte Lebens (2007) *Mass-mediated Terrorism: The Central Role of the Media in Terrorism and Counterterrorism*. Lanham, MD: Rowman and Littlefield.

——Block-Elkon, Yaeli, and Shapiro, Robert Y. (2008) "Prevention of terrorism in post-9/11 America: news coverage, public perceptions, and the politics of homeland security," *Terrorism and Political Violence*, 20 (1), 1–25.

Nagel, Jack H. (1975) *The Descriptive Analysis of Power*. New Haven, CT: Yale University Press.

NASS (2008) "NASS survey: state voter registration figures for the 2008 general election," National Association of Secretaries of State, November 3 (retrieved November 8, 2008 from: http://www.nass.org/.).

National Aeronautics and Space Administration (NASA) (2007) "GISS surface temperature analysis: Global temperature trends – 2007 summation" (available online at http://data.giss.nasa.gov/gistemp/2007/).

National Oceanic and Atmospheric Administration (NOAA) (2008) "Climate of 2007 in historical perspective: annual report" (available online at http://www.ncdc. noaa.gov/oa/climate/research/2007/ann/ann07.html).

National Science Foundation (2007) "Cyber-enabled discovery and innovation," NSF Fact Sheet.

Nelson, Jack (2003) "US government secrecy and the current crackdown on leaks," working paper, Joan Shorenstein Center, Harvard University.

——and Boynton, G. Robert (1997) *Video Rhetorics: Televised Advertising in American Politics*. Urbana, IL: University of Illinois Press.

Neuman, W. Russell (1991) *The Future of the Mass Audience*. Cambridge: Cambridge University Press.

——Marcus, George E., Crigler, Ann N., and MacKuen, Michael (eds.) (2007) *The Affect Effect: Dynamics of Emotion in Political Thinking and Behavior*. Chicago, IL: University of Chicago Press.

Nevitte, Neil (2003) "Authority orientations and political support: a cross-national analysis of satisfaction with governments and democracy," in Ronald Inglehart (ed.), *Mass Values and Social Change: Findings from the Values Surveys*, pp. 387–412. Leiden: Brill Academic.

Newell, Peter (2000) *Climate for Change: Non-state Actors and the Global Politics of the Greenhouse*. New York: Cambridge University Press.

Newman, Russell (2008) "Financialization of traditional media: the FCC at a nexus," unpublished paper written for the Research Seminar, Comm620Y on Communication, Technology, and Power, Los Angeles, University of Southern California, Annenberg School for Communication.

NewsCorp (2007) "Annual report 2007" (available online at http://www.newscorp.com/Report2007/AnnualReport2007/HTML1/default.htm).

Newton, D. (1993) *Global Warming: A Reference Handbook*. Oxford: ABC-CLIO.

The New York Times (2008) "National Election Pool exit polls table," poll conducted by Edison Media Research/Mitofsky (retrieved November 8, 2008 from http://elections.nytimes.com/2008/ results/president/exit-polls.html).

Nielsen (2007) "Average US home now receives a record 104.2 TV channels, according to Nielsen," Nielsen Media press release, March 19.

Nielsen/NetRatings (2007) "From 131 million to 360 million tudou.com triples weekly clip view in just three months," Nielsen Media press release, August 31.

9/11 Commission (2004) *The 9/11 Commission Report: Final Report of the National Commission on Terrorist Attacks upon the United States*. New York: W. W. Norton.

Nisbet, Matthew C. and Myers, Teresa (2007) "The polls – trends: twenty years of public opinion about global warming," *Public Opinion Quarterly*, 71 (3), 444–70.

Nobel Foundation (2007) Web site accessed March 29 at http//:nobelprize.org.

Norris, Pippa (1996) "Does television erode social capital? A reply to Putnam," *PS: Political Science and Politics*, 29 (3), 474–80.

——(2000) *A Virtuous Circle: Political Communications in Postindustrial Societies*. Cambridge: Cambridge University Press.

——and Inglehart, Ronald (2004) *Sacred and Secular: Religion and Politics Worldwide*. Cambridge: Cambridge University Press.

Noveck, Jocelyn and Fouhy, Beth (2008) "Clinton's female fans wonder what, if and when: Clinton's female supporters saddened as chance to elect a woman president slips away," *Associated Press*, May 17.

Nye, Joseph S. and Donahue, John D. (eds.) (2000) *Governance in a Globalizing World*. Washington, DC: Brookings Institution.

Bibliography

Obama, Barack (1995) *Dreams From my Father: A Story of Race and Inheritance*. New York: Three Rivers Press (2nd edn 2004).
—— (2007) *The Audacity of Hope: Thoughts on Reclaiming the American Dream*. New York: Canongate.
Obstfeld, Maurice and Taylor, Alan M. (2004) *Global Capital Markets: Integration, Crisis, and Growth*. Cambridge: Cambridge University Press.
OECD (2007) *Information and Communications Technologies: OECD Communications Outlook 2007*. Paris: OECD.
O'Neil, Patrick H. (1998) *Communicating Democracy: The Media and Political Transitions*. London: Lynne Rienner.
Ornstein, Norman J. (2008) "Obama's fundraising success may herald a whole new model," Washington, DC: American Enterprise Institute, June 30 (available online at http://www.aei.org/publications/filter.all,pubID.28218/pub_detail.asp).
Pacheco, I. (2004) *11-M: la respuesta*. Madrid: Asociación Cultural de Amigos del Arte Popular.
Page, Scott E. (2007) *The Difference: How the Power of Diversity Creates Better Groups, Firms, Schools, and Societies*. Princeton, NJ: Princeton University Press.
Palmer, Shelley (2008) "Obama vs. McCain: the first networked campaign," *Huffington Post*, media news (available online at http://www.huffingtonpost.com/shelly-palmer/obama-vs-mccain—the-fir_b_105993.html).
Panagopoulos, Costas and Wielhouwer, Peter (2008) "Polls and elections: the ground war 2000–2004 – strategic targeting in grassroots campaigns," *Presidential Studies Quarterly*, 38 (2), 347–62.
Paniagua, Francisco Javier (2005) "Tendencias de la comunicación política electoral en España," *Fisec Estrategias*, 1 (available online at http://www.fisec-estrategias.com.ar/1/fec_01_com_paniagua.pdf).
—— (2006) "Agenda de medios. ¿Estrategia de partido equivocada?," *Hologramatica*, 3 (6), 53–72.
Parks, Gregory Scott and Rachlinski, Jeffrey J. (2008) "Unconscious bias and the 2008 presidential election," Cornell Legal Studies research paper no. 08-007, March 4 (available online at http://ssrn.com/ abstract=1102704.).
Parsons, Talcott (1963) "On the concept of political power," *Proceedings of the American Philosophical Society*, 107, 232–62.
Partal, V. and Otamendi, M. (2004) *11-M: el periodismo en crisis*. Barcelona: Edicions Ara Libres.
Patterson, M. (1996) *Global Warming and Global Politics*. London: Routledge.
Patterson, Thomas (1993) *Out of Order*. New York: A. Knopf.
—— (2004) *Young Voters and the 2004 Election*. Boston, MA: Joan Shorenstein Center on the Press, Politics, and Public Policy, John F. Kennedy School of Government, Harvard University.

Penn, Mark J. and Zalesne, E. Kinney (2007) *Microtrends: The Small Forces Behind Tomorrow's Big Changes*. New York: Twelve.

Perez, Carlota (1983) "Structural change and the assimilation of new technologies in the economic and social systems," *Futures*, 15, 357–75.

Perlmutter, David D. (2008) *Blogwars*. New York: Oxford University Press.

Perloff, Richard M. (1998) *Political Communication: Politics, Press, and Public in America*. Mahwah, NJ: Lawrence Erlbaum.

Peruzzotti, Enrique (2003) "Media scandals and societal accountability: assessing the role of the senate scandal in Argentina," working paper prepared for the Conference Estrategias de Accountability Social en América Latina, Acciones Legales, Medios de Comunicación y Movilización.

Pew (2000) "Voters unmoved by media characterizations of Gore and Bush," Washington, DC: Pew Research Center for the People and the Press, July 27.

—— (2004a) "News audiences increasingly politicized, online news audience larger, more diverse," Pew Research Center Biennial News Consumption Survey, Washington, DC: Pew Research Center for the People and the Press, June 8 (available online at http://people-press.org/reports/display.php3?PageID=833).

—— (2004b) "76% have seen prison pictures. Bush approval slips: prison scandal hits home but most reject troop pullout," Washington, DC: Pew Research Center for the People and the Press, May.

—— (2006) "Partisanship drives opinion: little consensus on global warming," Washington, DC: Pew Research Center for the People and the Press.

—— (2007a) "Republicans lag in engagement and enthusiasm for candidates," Washington, DC: Pew Research Center for the People and the Press.

—— (2007b) "Views of press values and performance 1985–2007," Washington, DC: Pew Research Center for the People and the Press, August 9.

—— (2008a) "Obama weathers the Wright storm, Clinton faces credibility problem," Washington, DC: Pew Research Center for the People and the Press, March 27.

—— (2008b) "Fewer voters identify as Republicans," Washington, DC: Pew Research Center for the People and the Press, March 20.

—— (2008c) "Social networking and online videos take off: Internet's broader role in campaign 2008," Washington, DC: Pew Research Center for the People and the Press.

—— (2008d) "Inside Obama's sweeping victory," Pew Research Center for the People and the Press, November 5 (retrieved November 8, 2008 from http://pewresearch.org/pubs/1023/exit-poll-analysis-2008).

—— (2008e) "Public not desperate about economy or personal finances, Obama clearer than McCain in addressing crisis," Washington, DC: Pew Research Center for the People and the Press, October 15 (retrieved on November 8, 2008 from http://people-press.org/report/458/economic-crisis).

Bibliography

—— (2008f) "Growing doubts about McCain's judgment, age and campaign conduct," Washington, DC: Pew Research Center for the People and the Press, October 15 (retrieved on November 8, 2008 from http://people-press.org/report/462/obamas-lead-widens).

—— (2008g) "A deeper partisan divide over global warming," Washington, DC: Pew Research Center.

—— (2008h) "Increasing optimism about Iraq," Washington, DC: Pew Research Center, February 2008.

Pew Center on Global Climate Change (2008) "Climate action in Congress" (retrieved May 24, 2008 from http://www.pewclimate.org/).

Pew Global Attitudes Project (2005) "China's Optimism," Washington, DC: Pew Research Center, November 16.

—— (2008) "Global economic gloom: China and India notable exceptions," Washington, DC: Pew Research Center, June 12.

Pew Internet and American Life Project (2008) "Spring 2008 survey: final topline results," Washington, DC: Pew Research Center.

Pickerill, Jenny (2003) *Cyberprotest: Environmental Activism Online.* New York: Manchester University Press.

PIPA (2004) "US public beliefs and attitudes about Iraq," PIPA/Knowledge Networks Poll. Washington, DC: Program on International Policy Attitudes and Knowledge Networks, August 20 (available online at http://www.pipa.org/online_reports.html).

—— (2006) "Americans on Iraq: three years on," World Public Opinion/Knowledge Networks Poll Report. Washington, DC: Program on International Policy Attitudes, March 15.

Pitney, Nico (2008) "Debate analysis: ABC asked most scandal questions, Obama was clear target," *Huffington Post*, April 20 (available online at http://www.huffingtonpost.com/2008/04/20/debate-analysis-abc-asked_n_97599.html).

Plasser, Fritz (2000) "American campaign techniques worldwide," *Harvard International Journal of Press/Politics*, 5 (4), 33–54.

—— (2005) "From hard to soft news standards? How political journalists in different media systems evaluate the shifting quality of news," *Harvard International Journal of Press/Politics*, 10 (2), 47–68.

Popkin, Samuel L. (1991) *The Reasoning Voter: Communication and Persuasion in Presidential Campaigns.* Chicago, IL: University of Chicago Press.

—— (1994) *The Reasoning Voter: Communication and Persuasion in Presidential Campaigns*, 2nd edn. Chicago, IL: University of Chicago Press.

Porto, Mauro (2007) "TV news and political change in Brazil: the impact of democratization on TV Globo's journalism," *Journalism*, 8 (4), 363–84.

Postman, Neil (1986) *Amusing Ourselves to Death: Public Discourse in the Age of Show Business.* New York: Penguin.

—— (2004) "The information age: a blessing or a curse?" *Harvard International Journal of Press/Politics*, 9 (2), 3–10.

Poulantzas, Nicos (1978) *L'État, le Pouvoir, le Socialisme*. Paris: Presses Universitaires de France.

Price, Monroe E. (2002) *Media and Sovereignty: The Global Information Revolution and its Challenge to State Power*. Cambridge, MA: MIT Press.

Project for Excellence in Journalism (2007) *The State of the News Media 2007: An Annual Report on American Journalism*. Washington, DC: Pew Research Center (available online at www.stateofthenewsmedia.com/2007/index.).

—— (2008a) "Media passes on Times' Pentagon piece," Washington, DC: Pew Research Center (available online at http://journalism.org/node/10849).

—— (2008b) "Why news of Iraq dropped," March 26 (available online at http://www.journalism.org/node/10365).

—— and the Pew Research Center for the People and the Press (2000) *A Question of Character 2000: How the Media Have Handled the Issue and How the Public Reacted*. Baltimore, MD: Pew Research Center.

Public Opinion Foundation (Russia) (2007) "Mass media: preferred sources of information" (online report, July 27–28).

Puig, Carmina (2004) "Programació televisiva de l'11 i el 12 de març," *Quaderns del CAC*, 19–26.

Purdum, Todd S. (2006) "Karl Rove's split personality," *Vanity Fair*, December (available online at http://www.vanityfair.com/politics/features/2006/12/rove200612).

Putnam, Robert D. (1995) "Tuning in, tuning out: the strange disappearance of social capital in America," *PS: Political Science and Politics*, 28 (4), 664–83.

—— (2000) *Bowling Alone: The Collapse and Revival of American Community*. New York: Simon and Schuster.

—— (2008) "The rebirth of American civic life," *Boston Globe*, Op-Ed, D-9.

Qinglian, He (2004) "Media control in China," a report by Human Rights in China (available online at www.hrichina.org/public/contents/8991).

Qiu, Jack Linchuan (2004) "The Internet in China: technologies of freedom in a statist society," in Manuel Castells (ed.), *The Network Society: A Cross-cultural Perspective*, pp. 99–124. Northampton, MA: Edward Elgar.

—— (2007) "The wireless leash: mobile messaging service as a means of control," *International Journal of Communication*, 174–91.

—— (forthcoming) *The Working Class Network Society*. Cambridge, MA: MIT Press.

Qvortrup, Lars (2003) *The Hypercomplex Society*. New York: P. Lang.

—— (2006) "Understanding new digital media: medium theory or complexity theory?" *European Journal of Communication*, 21 (3), 345–56.

Rafael, Vincente L. (2003) "The cell phone and the crowd: Messianic politics in the contemporary Philippines," *Popular Culture*, 15 (3), 399–425.

Bibliography

Rai, Mugdha and Cottle, Simon (2007) "Global mediations: on the changing ecology of satellite television news," *Global Media and Communication*, 3 (1), 51–78.

Raichle, Marcus E., MacLeod, Ann Mary, Snyder, Abraham Z., Powers, William J., et al. (eds.) (2001) "A default mode of brain function," *Proceedings of the National Academy of Sciences*, 28 (2), 676–82.

Rainie, Lee (2008) "Video sharing websites," Washington, DC: Pew Internet and American Life Project, January 9 (available online at http://www.pewinternet. org/pdfs/Pew_Videosharing_memo_Jan08.pdf).

Ramírez, Pedro J. (2000) *Amarga victoria: la crónica oculta del histórico triunfo de Aznar sobre Gonzalez*. Barcelona: Planeta.

Randall, Vicki (1993) "The media and democratization in the third world," *Third World Quarterly*, 14, 625–47.

Rantanen, Terhi (2005) *The Media and Globalization*. London: Sage.

—— (2006) "Foreign dependence and domestic monopoly: the European news cartel and US associated presses, 1861–1932," *Media History*, 12 (1), 19–35.

Ray, Raka (1999) *Fields of Protest: Women's Movements in India*. Minneapolis, MN: University of Minnesota Press.

Redlawsk, David P., Civettini, Andrew J. W., and Lau, Richard R. (2007) "Affective intelligence and voting: information processing and learning in campaign," in W. Russell Neuman, George E. Marcus, Ann N. Crigler, and Michael MacKuen (eds.), *The Affect Effect: Dynamics of Emotion in Political Thinking and Behavior*, pp. 152–79. Chicago, IL: University of Chicago Press.

Regner, Isabelle and Le Floch, Valerie (2005) "When political expertise moderates the impact of scandals on young adults' judgments of politicians," *European Journal of Social Psychology*, 35 (2), 255–61.

Renshon, Stanley A. (2002) "The polls: the public's response to the Clinton scandals, part 2: diverse explanations, clearer consequences," *Presidential Studies Quarterly*, 32 (2), 412–27.

Reporters without Borders (2002) *Freedom of the Press Worldwide in 2002. 2002 Annual Report*. Paris: Reporters without Borders.

—— (2003) *Freedom of the Press Worldwide in 2003. 2003 Annual Report*. Paris: Reporters without Borders.

—— (2004) *Freedom of the Press Worldwide in 2004. 2004 Annual Report*. Paris: Reporters without Borders.

—— (2005) *Freedom of the Press Worldwide in 2005. 2005 Annual Report*. Paris: Reporters without Borders.

—— (2006) *Freedom of the Press Worldwide in 2006. 2006 Annual Report*. Paris: Reporters without Borders.

—— (2007) *Freedom of the Press Worldwide in 2007. 2007 Annual Report*. Paris: Reporters without Borders.

—— (2008) *Freedom of the Press Worldwide in 2008. 2008 Annual Report.* Paris: Reporters without Borders.

Reuters (2008) "The world turns out for World Wildlife Fund's Earth Hour," March 30.

Reynolds, Gretchen (1993) "Vote of confidence," *Chicago Magazine,* January (available online at http://www.chicagomag.com/Chicago-Magazine/January-1993/Vote-of-Confidence/).

Rhee, In-Yong (2003) "The Korean election shows a shift in media power," *Nieman Reports,* 57 (1), 95–6.

Rheingold, Howard (2003) *Smart Mobs: The Next Social Revolution.* Cambridge, MA: Basic Books.

—— (2008) "Mobile media and collective political action," in James Everett Katz (ed.), *Handbook of Mobile Communication Studies,* pp. 225–40. Cambridge, MA: MIT Press.

Rice, Ronald E. (ed.) (2008) *Media Ownership: Research and Regulation.* Cresskill, NJ: Hampton Press.

—— and Associates (1984) *The New Media: Communication, Research, and Technology.* Beverly Hills, CA: Sage.

Rich, Andrew (2004) *Think Tanks, Public Policy, and the Politics of Expertise.* Cambridge: Cambridge University Press.

—— (2005a) "The war of ideas: why mainstream and liberal foundations and the think tanks they support are losing in the war of ideas in American politics," *Stanford Social Innovation Review,* 3, 18–25.

—— (2005b) "War of ideas: part 2," unpublished working paper (available online at www.inclusionist.org/files/War%20of%20Ideas-Part%20II-Nov%202005.pdf).

—— and Weaver, R. Kent (2000) "Think tanks in the US media," *Harvard International Journal of Press/Politics,* 5 (4), 81–103.

Richardson, Dick and Rootes, Chris (eds.) (1995) *The Green Challenge: The Development of Green Parties in Europe.* London: Routledge.

Richardson, Glenn W. (2003) *Pulp Politics: How Political Advertising Tells the Stories of American Politics.* Lanham, MD: Rowman and Littlefield.

Rico, G. (2005) "Los factores de la personalización del voto en las elecciones generales en España," VII Congreso Español de Ciencia Política y de la Administración, Madrid, September 2005.

Riera, Miguel (ed.) (2001) *La batalla de Genova.* Barcelona: El Viejo Topo.

Riley, Patricia and Hollihan, Thomas A. (1981) "The 1980 presidential debates: a content analysis of the issues and arguments," *Speaker and Gavel,* 18 (2), 47–59.

Rizzo, Sergio and Stella, Gian Antonio (2007) *La Casta.* Rome: Saggi Italiani.

Rizzolatti, Giacomo and Craighero, Laila (2004) "The mirror neuron system," *Annual Review of Neuroscience,* 27 (1), 169–92.

Bibliography

Robinson, Michael J. (1975) "American political legitimacy in an era of electronic journalism: reflections on the evening news," in Douglass Cater and Richard Adler (eds.), *Television as a Social Force: New Approaches to TV Criticism*, pp. 97–139. New York: Praeger.

Robinson, Piers (2002) *The CNN Effect: The Myth of News, Foreign Policy, and Intervention*. London: Routledge.

Robinson, Robert V. and Jackson, Elton F. (2001) "Is trust in others declining in America? An age-period-cohort analysis," *Social Science Research*, 30 (1), 117–45.

Rodas, Laura (2004) "La informació televisiva els dies 11 i 12 de març," *Quaderns del CAC*, 27–35.

Rodriguez, Alex (2008) "Trial in Russia sends message to bloggers," *Chicago Tribune.com*, March 31.

Rodriguez, P. (2004) *11-M mentira de Estado: los tres días que acabaron con Aznar*. Barcelona: Ediciones B.

Rose-Ackerman, Susan (1999) *Corruption and Government: Causes, Consequences and Reform*. Cambridge: Cambridge University Press.

Rosenthal, Elizabeth, and Revkin, Andrew C. (2007) "Global warming called 'unequivocal'," *International Herald Tribune*, February 2 (retrieved May 24, 2008, from http://www.iht.com).

Rospars, Joe (2007) "Our MySpace experiment: personal blog entry," May 2. (available online at http://my.barackobama.com/page/community/post_group/ObamaHQ/CvSl).

Rude, George (1959) *The Crowd in the French Revolution*. Oxford: Oxford University Press.

Rutherford, Jonathan (2004) *A Tale of Two Global Cities: Comparing the Territorialities of Telecommunications Developments in Paris and London*. London: Ashgate.

Sabato, Larry J., Stencel, Mark, and Lichter, S. Robert (2000) *Peepshow: Media and Politics in an Age of Scandal*. Lanham, MD: Rowman and Littlefield.

Sakr, Naomi (2001) *Satellite Realms: Transnational Television, Globalization, and the Middle East*. London: I. B. Tauris.

——— (2006) "Challenger or lackey? The politics of news on Al-Jazeera," in Daya Kishan Thussu (ed.), *Media on the Move: Global Flow and Contra-flow*, pp. 116–32. New York: Routledge.

Salido, Noelia (2006) "Del 11M al 14M: jornadas de movil-ización social," in A. Vara and J. R. Virgili (eds.), *La comunicación en tiempos de crisis: del 11M al 14M*. Pamplona: Eusuna.

Salmon, Andrew (2004) "Parties rallying behind Internet in race for votes," *Washington Times*, April 11.

Sampedro Blanco, V. F., and Martinez, Nicolas D. (2005) "Primer voto: castigo poltico y descredito de los medios," in V. F. Sampedro Blanco (ed.), *13-M: Multitudes on Line*, pp. 24–62. Madrid: Ed. Catarata.

Samuelson, Robert J. (1998) "The attack culture revisited," *Washington Post*, August 26, A19.

Sanchez, Isabel (2004) "La programació i la informació televisives del dia de reflexió," *Quaderns del CAC*, 37–45.

Sanchez, J. M. (2005) "Cronologia," in V. F. Sampedro Blanco (ed.), *13-M: Multitudes on Line*, pp. 307–9. Madrid: Ed. Catarata.

Santos, Eva (2008) *Los partidos tiran de chequera*. Madrid: EFE Reportajes.

Sanz, Alberto and Sanchez-Sierra, Ana (2005) "Las elecciones generales de 2004 en España: política exterior, estilo de gobierno y movilización," working papers online series 48/2005, Departamento de Ciencia Política y Relaciones Internacionales, Facultad de Derecho, Universidad Autónoma de Madrid.

Sarewitz, Daniel, and Pielke, Roger (2000) "Breaking the global-warming gridlock," *The Atlantic online*, July 2000 (retrieved July 1, 2008 from http://www.theatlantic.com/).

Sassen, Saskia (2006) *Territory, Authority, Rights: From Medieval to Global Assemblages*. Princeton, NJ: Princeton University Press.

Scammell, Margaret (1998) "The wisdom of the war room: US campaigning and Americanization," *Media, Culture, and Society*, 20 (2), 251–76.

SCEP (Study of Critical Environmental Problems) (1970) *Man's Impact on the Global Environment: Assessment and Recommendation for Action*. Cambridge, MA: MIT Press.

Schatz, Amy (2007) "Bo, ur so gr8: how a young tech entrepreneur translated Barack Obama into the idiom of facebook," *Wall Street Journal*, A1.

Scheufele, Dietram A., and Tewksbury, David (2007) "Framing, agenda setting, and priming: the evolution of three media effects models," *Journal of Communication*, 57 (1), 9–20.

Schiller, Dan (1999) *Digital Capitalism: Networking the Global Market System*. Cambridge, MA: MIT Press.

—— (2007) *How to Think about Information*. Urbana, IL: University of Illinois Press.

Schreiber, Darren (2007) "Political cognition as social cognition: are we all political sophisticates?," in W. Russell Neuman, George E. Marcus, Ann N. Crigler, and Michael MacKuen (eds.), *The Affect Effect: Dynamics of Emotion in Political Thinking and Behavior*, pp. 48–70. Chicago, IL: University of Chicago Press.

Schudson, Michael (2002) "The news media as political institutions," *Annual Review of Political Science*, 5, 249–69.

—— (2004) "Notes on scandal and the Watergate legacy," *American Behavioral Scientist*, 47 (9), 1231–8.

Schwarz, Norbert and Bless, Herbert (1992) "Scandals and the public's trust in politicians: assimilation and contrast effects," *Personal and Social Psychology Bulletin*, 18 (5), 574–79.

Sears, David O. and Henry, P. (2005) "Over thirty years later: a contemporary look at symbolic racism," in Mark P. Zanna (ed.), *Advances in Experimental Social Psychology, Volume 37*, pp. 95–150. San Diego, CA: Elsevier Academic.

Bibliography

Seib, Philip (2008) "The Al Qaeda media machine," *Military Review*, May–June: 74–80.

Semetko, Holli A. and Scammell, Margaret (2005) "Television news and elections: lessons from Britain and the US," paper presented at the Annual Meeting of the American Political Science Association, Washington, DC, September 1–4.

Semple, Robert B. (2004) "Editorial observer: a film that could warm up the debate on global warming," *The New York Times*, May 27 (retrieved July 1, 2008 from www.nyt.com).

Senate Select Committee on Intelligence (2004) *Report on the US Intelligence Community's Pre-War Intelligence on Iraq*. United States Senate, July 7.

Sennett, Richard (1978) *The Fall of Public Man*. New York: Vintage Books.

SER (2004) "Pulsometro instituto opina," March 22. According to the National Oceanic and Atmospheric Administration's (NOAA) 2007 State of the Climate Report and the National Aeronautics and Space Administration's (NASA) 2007 Surface Temperature Analysis and National Climatic Data Center.

Sey, Araba (2008) "Mobile communication and development: a study of mobile phone use and the mobile phone industry in Ghana," unpublished PhD dissertation, Los Angeles: University of Southern California, Annenberg School for Communication.

—— and Castells, Manuel (2004) "From media politics to networked politics: the Internet and the political process," in Manuel Castells (ed.), *The Network Society: A Cross-cultural Perspective*, pp. 363–81. Northampton, MA: Edward Elgar.

Shah, Dhavan V., Cho, Jaeho, Eveland, William P., et al. (2005) "Information and expression in a digital age: modeling Internet effects on civic participation," *Communication Research*, 32, 531–65.

Shahnaz, Mahmud and McClellan, Steve (2007) "Branded content breaks into web video," *AdWeek*, 48 (9), 12.

Shuman, Michael H. (1998) "Why progressive foundations give too little to too many," *The Nation*. 266 (2), 11–15.

Sifry, David (2007) "The state of the live web: April 2007," *Technorati* (available online at http://www.sifry.com/alerts/archives/000493.html).

Simpser, Alberto (2004) "Making votes not count: expectations and electoral corruption," paper presented at the 2004 American Political Science Association Meeting, Chicago, Illinois.

Sinclair, John (1999) *Latin American Television: A Global View*. Oxford: Oxford University Press.

Sirota, David (2008) *The Uprising*. New York: Crown.

Slevin, Peter (2007) "For Clinton and Obama, a common ideological touchstone," *Washington Post*, A1, March 27.

Smith, Aaron and Rainie, Lee (2008) *The Internet and the 2008 Election*. Washington, DC: Pew Internet and American Life Project.

Solomon, Sheldon, Greenberg, Jeff, and Pyszczynski, Tom (1991) "A terror management theory of social behavior: the psychological functions of self-esteem and cultural worldviews," *Advances in Experimental Social Psychology*, 24, 93–159.

Solove, Daniel J. (2004) *The Digital Person: Technology and Privacy in the Information Age.* New York: New York University Press.

Sorkin, Andrew Ross (2008) "Hedge fund investing and politics," *The New York Times*, April 22.

Soroka, Stuart N. (2003) "Media, public opinion, and foreign policy," *Harvard International Journal of Press/Politics*, 8 (1), 27–48.

Spanish Parliament (2004) *Comision de investigación sobre el 11 de Marzo* (available online at http://www.congreso.es).

Spence, Jonathan D. (1996) *God's Chinese Son: The Taiping Heavenly Kingdom of Hong Xiuquan.* New York: Norton.

Spezio, Michael L. and Adolphs, Ralph (2007) "Emotional processing and political judgment: toward integrating political psychology and decision neuroscience," in W. Russell Neuman, George E. Marcus, Ann N. Crigler, and Michael MacKuen (eds.), *The Affect Effect: Dynamics of Emotion in Political Thinking and Behavior*, pp. 71–96. Chicago, IL: University of Chicago Press.

Spielman, Fran (2007) "Obama endorses Daley," *Chicago Sun Times*, January 22 (available online at http://www.suntimes.com/news/politics/obama/223272, obama012207.stng).

Sreberny-Mohammadi, Annabelle and Mohammadi, Ali (1994) *Small Media, Big Revolution: Communication, Culture, and the Iranian Revolution.* Minneapolis, MN: University of Minnesota Press.

Stamm, K. R., Clark, F., and Eblacas, P. R. (2000) "Mass communication and public understanding of environmental problems: the case of global warming," *Public Understanding of Science* (9), 219–37.

Standard and Poor's (2007a) *Industry Surveys: Movies and Home Entertainment*, September 2007.

—— (2007b) *NewsCorp: Business Summary*, September 25.

Stelter, Brian (2008) "Finding political news online: the young pass it on," *The New York Times*, March 22 (available online at http://www.nytimes.com/2008/03/27/us/politics/27voters.html?_r=1andfta=yandoref=slogin).

Stewart, Angus (2001) *Theories of Power and Domination: The Politics of Empowerment in Late Modernity.* London: Sage.

Stiglitz, Joseph (2002) *Globalization and its Discontents.* New York: W. W. Norton.

—— and Bilmes, Linda J. (2008) *The Three Trillion Dollar War: The True Cost of the Iraq Conflict.* New York: W. W. Norton.

Stop Climate Chaos (2008) "Manifesto" (retrieved July 1, 2008 from http://www.stopclimatechaos.org/about_us/8.asp).

Bibliography

Straubhaar, Joseph D. (1991) "Beyond media imperialism: asymmetrical interdependence and cultural proximity," *Critical Studies in Mass Communication*, 8 (1), 39–59.

Suarez, Sandra L. (2005) "Mobile democracy: text messages, voter turnout, and the 2004 Spanish general election," paper prepared for delivery at the 2005 Annual Meeting of the American Political Science Association.

Sussman, Gerald (2005) *Global Electioneering: Campaign Consulting, Communications, and Corporate Financing*. Lanham, MD: Rowman and Littlefield.

Swanson, David L. and Mancini, Paolo (1996) *Politics, Media, and Modern Democracy: An International Study of Innovations in Electoral Campaigning and their Consequences*. Westport, CN: Praeger.

Tabboni, Simonetta (2006) *Les Temps sociaux*. Paris: Armand Colin.

Tannenbaum, Percy, Greenberg, Bradley S., and Silverman, Fred R. (1962) "Candidate images," in Sidney Kraus (ed.), *The Great Debates*, pp. 271–88. Bloomington, IN: Indiana University Press.

Teachout, Zephyr and Streeter, Thomas (2008) *Mousepads, Shoe Leather, and Hope: Lessons from the Howard Dean Campaign for the Future of Internet Politics*. Boulder, CO: Paradigm.

Teer-Tomaselli, Ruth, Wasserman, Herman, and de Beer, Arnold S. (2006) "South Africa as a regional media power," in Daya Kishan Thussu (ed.), *Media on the Move: Global Flow and Contra-flow*, pp. 153–64. London: Routledge.

Teruel, Laura (2005) "La cobertura del 11M–15M en la prensa noruega: una perspectiva mediática desde el norte de Europa," *Revista Latina de Comunicación Social*, 60 (retrieved June 10, 2008 from http://www.ull.es/publicaciones/latina/200521teruel.htm).

Terzis, Georgios (ed.) (2008) *European Media Governance: The Brussels Dimension*. Chicago: Intellect.

Thomas, Douglas (2002) *Hacker Culture*. Minneapolis, MN: University of Minnesota Press.

Thompson, Edward P. (1963) *The Making of the English Working Class*. London: Victor Gollancz (read in the Penguin edn, 1980).

Thompson, John B. (2000) *Political Scandal: Power and Visibility in the Media Age*. Cambridge: Polity Press.

Thrall, A. Trevor, Lollio-Fakhreddine, Jaime, Berent, Jon, Donnelly, Lana, et al. (2008) "Star power: celebrity advocacy and the evolution of the public sphere," *Harvard International Journal of Press/Politics*, 13 (4), 362–85.

Thussu, Daya Kishan (1998) *Electronic Empires: Global Media and Local Resistance*. London: Arnold.

—— (ed.) (2006) *Media on the Move: Global Flow and Contra-flow*. London: Routledge.

Tiffen, Rodney (2004) "Tip of the iceberg or moral panic? Police corruption issues in contemporary New South Wales," *American Behavioral Scientist*, 47 (9), 1171–93.

Tilly, Charles (ed.) (1974) *The Formation of National States in Western Europe*. Princeton, NJ: Princeton University Press.

—— (1990) *Coercion, Capital and European States: AD 990–1992*. Malden, MA: Blackwell.

—— (1993) *European Revolutions: 1942–1992*. Oxford: Blackwell.

—— (2005) *Identities, Boundaries and Social Ties*. Boulder, CO: Paradigm.

Tongia, Rahul and Wilson, Ernest J. (2007) "Turning Metcalfe on his head: the multiple costs of network exclusion," unpublished paper presented at Telecommunications Policy Research Conference.

Touraine, Alain (1973) *Production de la société*. Paris: Seuil.

—— (1997) *Pourrons-nous vivre ensemble?* Paris: Fayard.

Transparency International (2003) *Global Corruption Barometer 2003*.

—— (2007) *Global Corruption Barometer 2007*.

Treisman, Daniel (2000) "The causes of corruption: a cross-national study," *Journal of Public Economics*, 76, 399–457.

Trimble, Linda and Sampert, Shannon (2004) "Who's in the game? The framing of election 2000 by the Globe and Mail and the National Post," *Canadian Journal of Political Science*, 37, 51–71.

Trumbo, Craig (1995) "Longitudinal modeling of public issues: an application of the agenda-setting process to the issue of global warming," *Journalism and Mass Communication Monographs*, 152, 1–57.

—— and Shanahan, James (2000) "Social research on climate change: where we have been, where we are, and where we might go," *Public Understanding of Science*, 9, 199–204.

Tubella, Imma (2004) "Internet, television, and the construction of identity," in Manuel Castells (ed.), *The Network Society: A Cross-cultural Perspective*, pp. 385–401. Northampton, MA: Edgar Elgar.

—— Tabernero, Carlos, and Dwyer, Vincent (2008) *La Guerra de las Pantallas: Internet y Television*. Barcelona: Ariel.

Tumber, Howard (2004) "Scandal and the media in the United Kingdom," *American Behavioral Scientist*, 47 (8), 1122–37.

—— and Waisbord, Silvio R. (2004a) "Introduction: political scandals and the media across democracies: volume I," *American Behavioral Scientist*, 47 (8), 1031–9.

—— —— (2004b) "Introduction: political scandals and the media across democracies: volume II," *American Behavioral Scientist*, 47 (9), 1143–52.

—— and Webster, Frank (2006) *Journalists under Fire: Information War and Journalistic Practices*. London: Sage.

Tuomi, Ilkka (2002) *Networks of Innovation: Change and Meaning in the Age of the Internet*. Oxford: Oxford University Press.

Turow, Joseph (2005) "Audience construction and culture production: marketing surveillance in the digital age," *Annals of the American Academy of Political and Social Science*, 597 (1), 103–21.

Bibliography

Tversky, Amos and Kahneman, Daniel (1992) "Advances in prospect theory: cumulative representation of uncertainty," *Journal of Risk and Uncertainty*, 5 (4), 297–323.

Ubertaccio, Peter N. (2006a) "Machine politics for the twenty-first century: multi-level marketing and party organizations," in John Clifford Green and Daniel J. Coffey (eds.), *The State of the Parties: The Changing Role of Contemporary American Politics*, pp. 173–86. Lanham, MD: Rowman and Littlefield.

—— (2006b) "Marketing parties in a candidate-centered polity: the Republican Party and George W. Bush," in Philip Davies and Bruce Newman (eds.), *Winning Elections with Political Marketing*, pp. 81–104. New York: Routledge.

UNCTAD. (2008) *Creative Economy Report 2008*. New York: United Nations Conference on Trade and Development.

Ungar, S. (1992) "The rise and (relative) decline of global warming as a social problem," *Sociological Quarterly*, 33 (4), 483–501.

United Nations (1992) "Framework convention on climate change" (retrieved March 18, 2008 from http://unfccc.int/essential_background/convention/background/items/1350.php).

Uslaner, Eric M. (2004) "Trust and corruption," in Johann Graf Lambsdorf, Markus Taube, and Mathias Schramn (eds.), *Corruption and the New Institutional Economics*, pp. 76–92. London: Routledge.

Uy-Tioco, Cecilia S. (2003) "The cell phone and Edsa 2: the role of communication technology in ousting a president," paper presented to the Fourth Critical Themes in Media Studies Conference, October 11, 2003, New School University, New York.

Valentino, Nicholas A., Hutchings, Vincent L., Banks, Antoine, and Davis, Anne (2008) "Is a worried citizen a good citizen? Emotions, political information seeking, and learning via the Internet," *Political Psychology*, 29 (2), 247–73.

—— —— and White, Ismail K. (2002) "Cues that matter: how political ads prime racial attitudes during campaigns," *American Political Science Review*, 96, 75–90.

Van Beek, Ursula and Klingemann, Hans-Dieter (eds.) (2004) *Democracy under Construction: Patterns from Four Continents*. Leverkusen Obladen: Barbara Budrich.

Van Belle, Douglas A. (2003) "Bureaucratic responsiveness to the news media: comparing the influence of *The New York Times* and network television news coverage on US foreign aid allocations," *Political Communication*, 20 (3), 263–86.

Villoria Mendieta, Manuel (2007) *Informe Global 2007 Sobre la Corrupción en España*. Madrid: Transparencia Internacional España.

Volkmer, Ingrid (1999) *News in the Global Sphere: A Study of CNN and its Impact on Global Communication*. Luton: University of Luton Press.

—— (2003) "The global network society and the global public sphere," *Journal of Development*, 46, 9–16.

Von Drehle, David (2008) "The year of the youth vote," *Time Magazine*, January 31(available online at http://www.time.com/time/nation/article/0,8599, 1708570,00.html).

VVAA (2004) *¡Pasalo! Relatos y Análisis Sobre el 11-M y los dis que le Siguieron*. Madrid: Traficantes de Sueños (www.traficantes.net).

Waisbord, Silvio (2004a) "MCTV: understanding the global popularity of television formats," *Television New Media*, 5 (4), 359–83.

—— (2004b) "Scandals, media, and citizenship in contemporary Argentina," *American Behavioral Scientist*, 47 (8), 1072–98.

Wallis, Cara (2008) "Techno-mobility in the margins: mobile phones and rural-to-urban migrant women in Beijing," unpublished PhD dissertation, Los Angeles: University of Southern California, Annenberg School for Communication.

Wapner, Paul Kevin (1996) *Environmental Activism and World Civic Politics*. Albany, NY: State University of New York Press.

Warf, Barney (2007) "Oligopolization of global media and telecommunications and its implications for democracy," *Ethics, Place, and Environment*, 10 (1), 89–105.

Warkentin, Craig (2001) *Reshaping World Politics: NGOs, the Internet, and Global Civil Society*. Oxford: Rowman and Littlefield.

Warren, Mark E. (2006) "Democracy and deceit: regulating appearances of corruption," *American Journal of Political Science*, 50 (1), 160–74.

Wasko, Janet (2001) *Understanding Disney: The Manufacture of Fantasy*. Cambridge: Polity Press.

Waterman, Peter (1998) *Globalization, Social Movements and the New Internationalism*. Washington: Mansell.

Wattenberg, Martin P. (1991) *The Rise of Candidate-centered Politics: Presidential Elections of the 1980s*. Cambridge, MA: Harvard University Press.

—— (2004) "Elections: personal popularity in US presidential elections," *Presidential Studies Quarterly*, 34 (1), 143–55.

—— (2006) "Elections: reliability trumps competence – personal attributes in the 2004 presidential election," *Presidential Studies Quarterly*, 36 (4), 705–13.

Watts, Duncan J. and Strogatz, Steven H. (1998) "Collective dynamics of 'small-world' networks," *Nature*, 393, 440–2.

Watts, Mark, Domke, David, Shah, Daron, and Fan, David P. (1999) "Elite cues and media bias in presidential campaigns: explaining public perceptions of a liberal press," *Communication Research*, 26 (2), 144–75.

Weart, Spencer (2007) "Discovery of global warming" (available online at http://www.aip.org/history/climate/index.html) which supplements the book *Discovery of Global Warming* (2003). Cambridge, MA: Harvard University Press.

Weber, Matthew (2007) "Conceptualizing interactive news media organizations as provisional settlements of convergence," unpublished paper completed for the class Comm 647, "Research Seminar on the Network Society," Los Angeles, University of Southern California, Annenberg School for Communication.

Weber, Max ([1919] 1946) "Politics as a vocation," in H. H. Gerth and C. Wright Mills (eds.), *From Max Weber: Essays in Sociology*. New York: Oxford University Press.

—— ([1922] 1978) *Economy and Society*. Berkeley, CA: University of California Press.

Weber, Steve (2004) *The Success of Open Source*. Cambridge, MA: Harvard University Press.

Welch, Susan and Hibbing, John (1997) "The effects of charges of corruption on voting behavior in congressional elections, 1982–1990," *Journal of Politics*, 59 (1), 226–39.

Wellman, Barry (1999) "The network community," in Barry Wellman (ed.), *Networks in the Global Village: Life in Contemporary Communities*, pp. 1–47. Boulder, CO: Westview Press.

—— and Haythornthwaite, Caroline (eds.) (2002) *The Internet in Everyday Life*. Malden, MA: Blackwell.

Wenger, Etienne (1999) *Communities of Practice: Learning, Meaning and Identity*. Cambridge: Cambridge University Press.

—— and Synder, William (2008) "Communities of practice: the organizational frontier," *Harvard Business Review* (available online).

West, Darrell M. (2001) *Air Wars: Television Advertising in Election Campaigns 1952–2000*, 3rd edn. Washington, DC: CQ Press.

—— (2005) *Air Wars: Television Advertising in Election Campaigns 1952–2004*. Washington, DC: CQ Press.

Westen, Drew (2007) *The Political Brain: The Role of Emotion in Deciding the Fate of the Nation*. New York: Public Affairs.

Western, Jon W. (2005) *Selling Intervention and War: The Presidency, the Media, and the American Public*. Baltimore, MD: Johns Hopkins University Press.

Whitaker, Reginald (1999) *The End of Privacy: How Total Surveillance is Becoming a Reality*. New York: New Press.

Williams, Bruce A. and Delli Carpini, Michael X. (2004) "Monica and Bill all the time and everywhere: the collapse of gatekeeping and agenda setting in the new media environment," *American Behavioral Scientist*, 47 (9), 1208–30.

Williams, Dmitri (2007) "The impact of time online: social capital and cyberbalkanization," *CyberPsychology and Behavior*, 10 (3), 398–406.

Wilson, Carroll L. and Matthews, William H. (eds.) (1971) *Inadvertent Climate Modification: Report of Conference, Study of Man's Impact on Climate (SMIC), Stockholm*. Cambridge, MA: MIT Press.

Wilson, Ernest J. (2004) *The Information Revolution and Developing Countries*. Cambridge, MA: MIT Press.

Wilson, K. M. (2000) "Communicating climate change through the media: predictions, politics, and perceptions of risk," in S. Allan, B. Adam, and C. Carter (eds.), *Environmental Risks and the Media*, pp. 201–17. London: Routledge.

Win, Hanna I. (2008) "Blogging Burma: how a web of tech-savvy chroniclers conquered censorship, poverty and fear to tell their story," unpublished master's thesis in print journalism, Los Angeles, University of Southern California, Annenberg School for Communication.

Winneg, Kenneth and Jamieson, Kathleen Hall (2005) "Elections: party identification in the 2004 election," *Presidential Studies Quarterly*, 35 (3), 576–89.

Winock, Michel (2004) *Las Voces de la libertad*. Barcelona: Edhasa (French edition, Paris: Seuil, 2001).

Winseck, Dwayne (2008) "The state of media ownership and media markets: competition or concentration and why should we care?," *Sociology Compass*, 2 (1), 34–47.

Wintour, Patrick (2006) "Ministers bow to pressure for climate bill," *Guardian*, October 25 (retrieved May 24, 2008 from http://www.guardian.co.uk/).

Wisconsin Advertising Project (2008) "Facts about tone of presidential advertising campaign from the Wisconsin Advertising Project," October 16 (retrieved November 8, 2008 from http://wiscadproject.wisc.edu/wiscads_release_101608.pdf).

Woessner, Matthew (2005) "Scandal, elites, and presidential popularity: considering the importance of cues in public support of the president," *Presidential Studies Quarterly*, 35 (1), 94–115.

World Economic Forum (2008) *Global Survey Highlights Fear of Future and Lack of Faith in World Leaders*. Global Survey Conducted by Gallup International. Geneva: WEF.

World Public Opinion (2006) "30-country poll finds worldwide consensus that climate change is a serious problem," April 25 (available online at www.worldpublicopinion.org).

—— (2007a) "Developed and developing countries agree: action needed on global warming," September 24 (available online at www. worldpublicopinion.org).

—— (2007b) "International polls find robust global support for increased efforts to address climate change" (retrieved May 25, 2008 from www.worldpublicopinion.org).

—— (2008) "World publics say governments should be more responsive to the will of the people," May 13 (available online at www. worldpublicopinion. org).

World Screen (2007) "Ugly Betty licensed to 130 territories worldwide," May 21 (available online at http://www.worldscreen.com/newscurrent.php?filename=disney052107.htm).

Wu, H. Denis (2007a) "A brave new world for international news? *International Communication Gazette*, 69 (6), 539–51.

Wu, Irene S. (2008) "Information, identity, and institutions: How technology transforms power in the world," research paper, Washington, DC: Georgetown University, Institute for the Study of Diplomacy.

Wu, Tim (2007b) "Wireless carterfone: Net neutrality special issue," *International Journal of Communication*, 1, 389–426.

Bibliography

Wyatt, Robert O., Edy, Jill L., Blake, Ken, and Mastin, Teresa (2000) "How general confidence in institutions predicts media credibility: a case against journalistic exceptionalism," paper presented at the World Association for Public Opinion Research, Portland, Oregon.

Zaller, John (1992) *The Nature and Origins of Mass Opinion*. New York: Cambridge University Press.

—— (1998) "Monica Lewinsky's contribution to political science," *Political Science Quarterly*, 31, 182–8.

Zaloom, Caitlin (2006) *Out of the Pits: Traders and Technology from Chicago to London*. Chicago, IL: University of Chicago Press.

Zaplana, Eduardo (2004) "Carta dirigida a Jesus Ceberio, director de *El País*, por Eduardo Zaplana, ministro portavoz del gobierno," *El País*, March 27.

Zhang, Weiwu and Chia, Stella C. (2006) "The effects of mass media use and social capital on civic and political participation," *Communication Studies*, 57 (3), 277–97.

Zhao, Yuezhi (2003) "Falun Gong, identity, and the struggle over meaning inside and outside China," in Nick Couldry and James Curran (eds.), *Contesting Media Power: Alternative Media in a Networked World*, pp. 209–26. Lanham, MD: Rowman and Littlefield.

—— (2008) *Communication in China: Political Economy, Power, and Conflict*. Lanham, MD: Rowman and Littlefield.

Index

Index

Index

Index

Index

Index

Index

Index

Index

Index

Index

Index

Index

Index

Index

Index

values
  and political decision-making 153–4
  and public opinion 153
Van Andel, Jay 207
Van Belle, Douglas A. 91
Vanguardia, La 353, 361
VEP-based voter turnout 294
vertical integration
  TV, radio and print press 109
  and US deregulation 105
  wireless communication 99
vertical/hierarchical organizations 22
VGTRK, Russia 269
Viacom 73, 75, 89
  as advertising purchaser 95
  institutional investors and beneficial
    ownership 444
  leadership and network connections 437
  relationship with CBS 82–3
victory frame, and Iraq War 172
Video News Releases (VNRs) 266
video politics 395
video recording, digital 60
Vietnam War 160, 180, 190, 206, 207
  US public opinion as condition of
    power 267
Vilaweb (Barcelona) 70
violence 11
  complementarity with discourse 11–12,
    15–16
  state monopoly 51
Virginia, and 2008 presidential campaign 407
virtual sit-ins 344
Vivendi Universal SA 86
vkontakte.ru 275
Voice of the People Survey, Latin America
  286
Voline (Russian anarchist) 344–5
Volkmer, Ingrid 122–3
Volvo 81
Von Drehle, David 394
VoteBuilder database, Democratic Party 215
voter perceptions, Obama/Clinton
  campaign 382–3, 383 Tab 5.3
voter registration, US 366–70, 366 n.57,
  366–7 n.58, 407
Voter Vault project 212, 213–14
voting behaviour, role of fear and enthusiasm
  in political advertising 151–2
voting patterns (1980-2004), US 473, 479–83
Vox television, Germany 86, 89

Waisbord, Silvio 253, 291
Wald, K. 191
Wall Street 44
Wall Street Journal, The 82, 91, 266
  acquired by Murdoch 429
Wall, Kevin 332
Wal-Mart 86
"war on terror" 7, 41, 156, 170–90, 208
  as frame 164, 170–3, 177
  media networks and 164
  metaphor activating fear frame 171
Warkentin, C. 325
Warner, John 335
Warner Brothers 77
Warren, Mark E. 287, 289
"Washington consensus" 43, 339
Washington Post, The 213
  Abu Ghraib torture reports 179
  poll after Monica Lewinsky scandal 252–3
Watergate scandal 207, 213, 239, 242–3,
  256
Wattenberg, Martin P. 202
weapons of mass destruction, and Iraq 156,
  167
Weart, S. 307
Weather.com 196
Weaver, R. Kent 209
Web 2.0 35, 56, 65, 97, 103, 113, 421, 429
  profit-making opportunities 106
  regulatory policies 106
Web 3.0 65, 113, 421
Weber, Max 12, 15, 17
Welch, Susan 250
West, Kayne 397
Westen, Drew 7, 145, 153, 154, 155, 169–70
What's the Matter with Kansas? (Frank) 155
Who Wants to Be a Millionaire TV show 90–1
Wielhouwer, Peter 215
Wi-Fi 63
Wikipedia 67–8
Will & Grace TV show 211
will.i.am 396
Williams, Armstrong 266
Wilson, Carroll 307
Wilson, Ernest J. 42
Wilson, Kris 316
WiMax networks 63
Winfrey, Oprah 377
wireless communication 4, 62–3, 64, 69, 73,
  75
  and the poor 63